D0984648

Robot Vision

Robot Vision

Berthold Klaus Paul Horn

The MIT Press
Cambridge, Massachusetts   London, England

McGraw-Hill Book Company
New York   St. Louis   San Francisco   Montreal   Toronto

This book is one of a series of texts written by faculty of the Electrical Engineering and Computer Science Department at the Massachusetts Institute of Technology. It was edited and produced by The MIT Press under a joint production-distribution arrangement with the McGraw-Hill Book Company.

Ordering Information:

North America
Text orders should be addressed to the McGraw-Hill Book Company.
All other orders should be addressed to The MIT Press.

Outside North America
All orders should be addressed to The MIT Press or its local distributor.

Third printing, 1987

This book was set under the direction of the author using the TEX typesetting system and was printed and bound by Halliday Lithograph in the United States of America.

Library of Congress Cataloging in Publication Data

Horn, Berthold Klaus Paul.
    Robot vision.

    (MIT electrical engineering and computer science
    series)
    Bibliography: p.
    Includes index.
    1. Robot vision.   I. Title.   II. Series
TJ211.3.H67   1986   629.8′92   85-18137
ISBN 0-262-08159-8 (MIT Press)
ISBN 0-07-030349-5 (McGraw-Hill)

Contents

Preface

Machine vision is a young and rapidly changing field. It is exciting to write about it, but it is also hard to know when to stop, since new results appear at frequent intervals. This book grew out of notes for the undergraduate course 6.801, "Machine Vision," which I have taught at MIT for ten years. A draft version of the book has been in use for five years. The exercises are mostly from homework assignments and quizzes. The course is a "restricted elective," meaning that students can take it or choose instead some other course related to artificial intelligence. Most students who elect to take it do so in their junior year. Several chapters of the book have also been used in an intensive one-week summer course on robotics for people from industry and other universities.

Ten years ago, it was possible to introduce both robot manipulation and machine vision in one term. Knowledge in both areas advanced so quickly, however, that this is no longer feasible. (The other half of the original course has been expanded by Tomas Lozano-Pérez into 6.802, "Robot Manipulation.") In fact, a single term now seems too short even to talk about all of the interesting facets of machine vision.

Rapid progress in the field has made it possible to reduce the coverage of less significant areas. What is less significant is, to some extent, a matter of personal opinion, and this book reflects my preferences. It could not be otherwise, for an in-depth coverage of everything that has been done in machine vision would require much more space and would not lend itself to presentation under a coherent theme. Material that appears to lack solid theoretical foundations has been omitted.

Similarly, approaches that do not lead to useful methods for recovering information from images have been left out, even when they claim legitimacy by appeal to advanced mathematics. The book instead includes information that should be useful to engineers applying machine vision methods in the "real world." The chapters on binary image processing, for example, help explain and suggest how to improve the many commercial devices now available. The material on photometric stereo and the extended Gaussian image points the way to what may be the next thrust in commercialization of the results of research in this domain.

Implementation choices and specific algorithms are not always presented in full detail. Good implementations depend on particular features of available computing systems, and their presentation would tend to distract from the basic theme. Also, I believe that one should solve the basic machine vision problem before starting to worry about implementation. In most cases, implementation entails little more than straightforward application of the classic techniques of numerical analysis. Still, details relating to the efficient implementation in both software and hardware are included, for example, in the chapters on binary image processing.

Almost from the start, the course attracted graduate students who felt a need for exposure to the field, and some material has been included to exploit their greater mathematical sophistication. This material should be omitted in courses designed for a different audience, because it is hard to lay the mathematical foundations and simultaneously cover all the material in this book in a single term. This should present no difficulties, since several topics can be taught essentially independently from the rest. Also note that most of the necessary mathematical tools are developed in the book's appendix.

Aside from the obvious pairing of some of the chapters (3 and 4, 6 and 7, 10 and 11, 12 and 17, 16 and 18), there is in fact little interdependence among them. Students lacking background in linear systems theory may be better served if the chapters on image processing (6, 7, and perhaps 9) are omitted. Similarly, the chapters dealing with time-varying images (12 and 17) may also be left out without loss of continuity. A few chapters present material that is not as well developed as the rest, and if these are avoided also, one is left with a short, basic course consisting of chapters 1, 2, 3, 4, 10, 11, 16, and 18. There should be no problem covering that much in one term.

This book is intended to provide deep coverage of topics that I feel are reasonably well understood. This means that some topics are treated in less detail, and others, which I consider too ad hoc, not at all. In this regard the present book can be considered to be complementary to *Computer Vision* by Dana Ballard and Christopher Brown, a book which covers a larger number of topics, but in less depth. Also, many of the elementary concepts are dealt with in more detail in the second edition of *Digital Picture Processing* by Azriel Rosenfeld and Avinash Kak.

There is a strong connection between what is discussed here and the study of biological vision systems. I place less emphasis on this, using as an excuse the existence of an outstanding book on this topic, *Vision: A Computational Investigation into the Human Representation and Processing of Visual Information*, by the late David Marr. In a similar vein, I have given somewhat less prominence to work on edge detection, feature-based stereo, and some aspects of the interpretation of time-varying images, since the books *From Images to Surfaces: A Computational Study of the Human Early Visual System* by Eric Grimson, *The Measurement of Visual Motion* by Ellen Hildreth, and *The Interpretation of Visual Motion* by Shimon Ullman cover these subjects in greater detail than I can here. The same goes for pattern classification, given the existence of such classics as *Pattern Classification and Scene Analysis* by Richard Duda and Peter Hart.

I have not been totally consistent, however, since there are two substantial chapters on image processing, despite the fact that the encyclopedic *Image Processing* by William Pratt covers this topic admirably. The reason is that this material is important for understanding preprocessing steps used in subsequent chapters.

Many of my students are at first surprised by the need for nontrivial mathematical techniques in this domain. To some extent this is because they have seen simple heuristic methods produce apparently startling results. Many such methods were discovered in the early days of machine vision and led to a false optimism about the expected rate of progress in the field. Later, significant limitations of these ad hoc approaches became apparent. It is obvious now that the study of machine vision needs to be supported by an understanding of image formation, just as the study of natural language requires some knowledge of linguistics. Not so long ago this would have been a minority view.

More seriously, machine vision is often considered merely as a means of analyzing sensor information for a system with "artificial intelligence." In artificial intelligence, there has been relatively little use, so far, of sophisticated mathematical manipulations. It is wrong to consider machine vision and robot manipulator control merely as the "I/O" of AI. The problems encountered in vision, manipulation, and locomotion are of interest in themselves. They are quite hard, and the tools required to attack them are nontrivial.

A system that successfully interacts with the environment can be understood, in part, by analyzing the physics of this interaction. In the case of vision this means that one ought to understand image formation if one wishes to recover information about the world from images. Modeling the physical interactions naturally leads to equations describing that interaction. The equations, in turn, suggest algorithms for recovering information about the three-dimensional world from images. This is my basic theme. Perhaps surprisingly, quite a few students find pleasure in applying mathematical methods learned in an abstract context to real problems. The material in this book provides them with motivation to practice methods and perhaps learn new concepts they would not have bothered with otherwise.

The emphasis in the first part of the book is on *early vision*—how to develop simple symbolic descriptions from images. Techniques for using these descriptions in spatial reasoning and in planning actions are less well developed and tend to depend on methodologies different from the ones appropriate to early vision. The last five chapters deal with methods that exploit the simple symbolic descriptions derived directly from images. Details of how to integrate a vision system into an overall robotics system are given in the final chapter, where a system for picking parts out of a bin is constructed.

A good part of the effort of writing this book went into the design of the exercises. They serve several purposes: Some help the reader practice ideas presented in a chapter; some develop ideas in more depth, perhaps using more sophisticated tools; and some introduce new research topics. The exercises in a given chapter are typically presented in this order, and hints are given to warn the reader about particularly difficult ones.

There has been a trend recently toward the use of more compact notation. In several instances, for example, components of vectors, such as surface normals and optical flow velocities, were used in early work. The current tendency is to use the vectors directly; for example, the Gaussian sphere is now employed instead of gradient space in the specification of surface orientation. In the body of this text I have used the component notation, which is easier to grasp initially. In some of the exercises, however, I have tried to show how problems can be solved more efficiently using more compact notation.

Most of the material included in this book has been presented elsewhere, but here it is organized in a more coherent way, using a consistent notation. In a few instances, new methods are presented that have not been published before. Because the field is changing rapidly, some of what is presented here may become obsolete, or at least of less interest, in just a few years. Conversely, some things that I have not covered may eventually form the basis for exciting new results. This is not a serious shortcoming, however, since my concern is more with the development of a solid approach to research in machine vision than with specific techniques for tackling particular problems.

When will we have a "general-purpose" vision system? Not in the foreseeable future, is my answer. This is not to say that machine vision is merely an intellectual exercise of no practical import. On the contrary, tremendous progress has been made in two ways: (a) by concentrating on a particular aspect of vision, such as interpretation of stereo pairs, and (b) by concentrating on a particular application, such as the alignment of parts for automated assembly. A truly general-purpose vision system would have to deal with all aspects of vision and be applicable to all problems that can be solved using visual information. Among other things, it would have to be able to reason about the physical world.

B.K.P.H.

Acknowledgments

The students of the "Machine Vision" course at MIT deserve much credit for helping me to formulate and revise this material. My teaching assistants have contributed to the generation of many of the problems. Robert Sjoberg also prepared careful notes on several topics that I have unfortunately been unable to incorporate due to time pressure. Robert Sjoberg, Andy Moulton, Eric Bier, Michael Gennert, and Jazek Myczkowski provided numerous useful comments on earlier drafts.

A few of the chapters are based on papers that I wrote jointly with others. I would like to thank Michael Brooks for his contribution to the discussion of the shape-from-shading problem (chapter 11), Brian Schunck for his help in the development of methods for the analysis of optical flow (chapter 12), Anna Bruss for her contribution to the analysis of the passive navigation problem (chapter 17), and Katsushi Ikeuchi for his serious dedication to implementing the bin-picking system (chapter 18).

Christopher Brown, Herbert Freeman, Eric Grimson, Ramesh Jain, Alan Mackworth, and Lothar Rossol provided helpful comments on an early draft. Michael Brady, Michael Brooks, Michael Gennert, and Ellen Hildreth went over recent versions of the book and made many useful suggestions. Michael Gennert contributed the problems on pattern classification (chapter 14). Careful reading by Boris Katz and Larry Cohen helped eliminate the more blatant linguistic problems. Unfortunately, I could not resist the temptation to rewrite much of the material as time went on and so have, no doubt, in the process reintroduced many bugs and typos.

The Department of Electrical Engineering and Computer Science gave me a six-month sabbatical to write the first draft. Carol Roberts typed that draft. Blythe Heepe drew most of the figures. Phyllis Rogers helped me with the bibliography. Michael Gennert came to my rescue by taking over final preparation of the camera ready copy. The illustration on the dust cover is used with the kind permission of the artist, Hajime Sorayama.

Marvin Minsky got me started in machine vision by suggesting the recovery of shape from brightness gradations in an image as a thesis topic. Patrick Winston was supportive of my approach to machine vision from the start, when it was not a popular one. Marvin is responsible for the creation, and Patrick for the survival and expansion of the Artificial Intelligence Laboratory at the Massachusetts Institute of Technology, where work on machine vision has flourished for almost twenty years.

Many of the ideas reported here result from research supported by the Defense Advance Research Projects Agency (DARPA) and the Office for Naval Research (ONR).

1

Introduction

In this chapter we discuss what a machine vision system is, and what tasks it is suited for. We also explore the relationship of machine vision to other fields that provide techniques for processing images or symbolic descriptions of images. Finally, we introduce the particular view of machine vision exploited in this text and outline the contents of subsequent chapters.

1.1 Machine Vision

Vision is our most powerful sense. It provides us with a remarkable amount of information about our surroundings and enables us to interact intelligently with the environment, all without direct physical contact. Through it we learn the positions and identities of objects and the relationships between them, and we are at a considerable disadvantage if we are deprived of this sense. It is no wonder that attempts have been made to give machines a sense of vision almost since the time that digital computers first became generally available.

Vision is also our most complicated sense. The knowledge we have accumulated about how biological vision systems operate is still fragmentary and confined mostly to the processing stages directly concerned with signals from the sensors. What we do know is that biological vision systems are complex. It is not surprising, then, that many attempts to provide machines with a sense of vision have ended in failure. Significant progress

Figure 1-1. A machine vision system can make a robot manipulator much more versatile by allowing it to deal with variations in part position and orientation. In some cases simple binary image-processing systems are adequate for this purpose.

has been made nevertheless, and today one can find vision systems that successfully deal with a variable environment as parts of machines.

Most progress has been made in industrial applications, where the visual environment can be controlled and the task faced by the machine vision system is clear-cut. A typical example would be a vision system used to direct a robot arm to pick parts off a conveyor belt (figure 1-1).

Less progress has been made in those areas where computers have been called upon to extract ill-defined information from images that even people find hard to interpret. This applies particularly to images derived by other than the usual optical means in the visual spectrum. A typical example of such a task is the interpretation of X-rays of the human lung.

It is of the nature of research in a difficult area that some early ideas have to be abandoned and new concepts introduced as time passes. While frustrating at times, it is part of the excitement of the search for solutions. Some believed, for example, that understanding the image-formation process was not required. Others became too enamored of specific computing

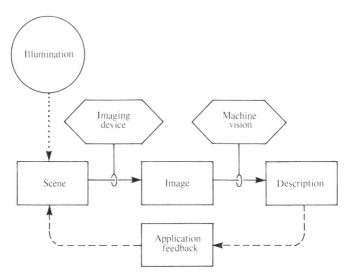

Figure 1-2. The purpose of a machine vision system is to produce a symbolic description of what is being imaged. This description may then be used to direct the interaction of a robotic system with its environment. In some sense, the vision system's task can be viewed as an inversion of the imaging process.

methods of rather narrow utility. No doubt some of the ideas presented here will also be revised or abandoned in due course. The field is evolving too rapidly for it to be otherwise.

We cannot at this stage build a "universal" vision system. Instead, we address ourselves either to systems that perform a particular task in a controlled environment or to modules that could eventually become part of a general-purpose system. Naturally, we must also be sensitive to practical considerations of speed and cost. Because of the enormous volume of data and the nature of the computations required, it is often difficult to reach a satisfactory compromise between these factors.

1.2 Tasks for a Machine Vision System

A machine vision system analyzes images and produces descriptions of what is imaged (figure 1-2). These descriptions must capture the aspects of the objects being imaged that are useful in carrying out some task. Thus we consider the machine vision system as part of a larger entity that interacts with the environment. The vision system can be considered an element of a feedback loop that is concerned with sensing, while other elements are dedicated to decision making and the implementation of these decisions.

The input to the machine vision system is an image, or several images, while its output is a description that must satisfy two criteria:

- It must bear some relationship to what is being imaged.
- It must contain all the information needed for the some given task.

The first criterion ensures that the description depends in some way on the visual input. The second ensures that the information provided is useful.

An object does not have a unique description; we can conceive of descriptions at many levels of detail and from many points of view. It is impossible to describe an object completely. Fortunately, we can avoid this potential philosophical snare by considering the task for which the description is intended. That is, we do not want just any description of what is imaged, but one that allows us to take appropriate action.

A simple example may help to clarify these ideas. Consider again the task of picking parts from a conveyor belt. The parts may be randomly oriented and positioned on the belt. There may be several different types of parts, with each to be loaded into a different fixture. The vision system is provided with images of the objects as they are transported past a camera mounted above the belt. The descriptions that the system has to produce in this case are simple. It need only give the position, orientation, and type of each object. The description could be just a few numbers. In other situations an elaborate symbolic description may be called for.

There are cases where the feedback loop is not closed through a machine, but the description is provided as output to be interpreted by a human. The two criteria introduced above must still be satisfied, but it is harder in this case to determine whether the system was successful in solving the vision problem presented.

1.3 Relation to Other Fields

Machine vision is closely allied with three fields (figure 1-3):

- Image processing.
- Pattern classification.
- Scene analysis.

Image processing is largely concerned with the generation of new images from existing images. Most of the techniques used come from linear systems theory. The new image may have noise suppressed, blurring removed, or edges accentuated. The result is, however, still an image, usually meant to be interpreted by a person. As we shall see, some of the techniques of image processing are useful for understanding the limitations of image-forming systems and for designing preprocessing modules for machine vision.

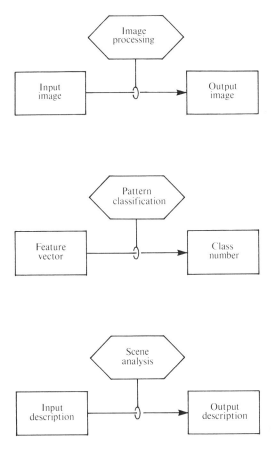

Figure 1-3. Three ancestor paradigms of machine vision are image processing, pattern classification, and scene analysis. Each contributes useful techniques, but none is central to the problem of developing symbolic descriptions from images.

Pattern classification has as its main thrust the classification of a "pattern," usually given as a set of numbers representing measurements of an object, such as height and weight. Although the input to a classifier is not an image, the techniques of pattern classification are at times useful for analyzing the results produced by a machine vision system. To recognize an object means to assign it to one of a number of known classes. Note, however, that recognition is only one of many tasks faced by the machine vision system. Researchers concerned with classification have created simple methods for obtaining measurements from images. These techniques, however, usually treat the images as a two-dimensional pattern of bright-

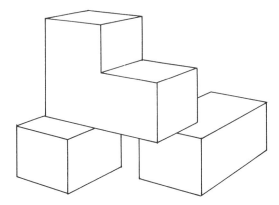

Figure 1-4. In scene analysis, a low-level symbolic description, such as a line drawing, is used to develop a high-level symbolic description. The result may contain information about the spatial relationships between objects, their shapes, and their identities.

ness and cannot deal with objects presented in an arbitrary attitude.

Scene analysis is concerned with the transformation of simple descriptions, obtained directly from images, into more elaborate ones, in a form more useful for a particular task. A classic illustration of this is the interpretation of line drawings (figure 1-4). Here a description of the image of a set of polyhedra is given in the form of a collection of line segments. Before these can be used, we must figure out which regions bounded by the lines belong together to form objects. We will also want to know how objects support one another. In this way a complex symbolic description of the image can be obtained from the simple one. Note that here we do not start with an image, and thus once again do not address the central issue of machine vision:

- Generating a symbolic description from one or more images.

1.4 Outline of What Is to Come

The generation of descriptions from images can often be conveniently broken down into two stages. The first stage produces a *sketch*, a detailed but undigested description. Later stages produce more parsimonious, structured descriptions suitable for decision making. Processing in the first stage will be referred to as *image analysis*, while subsequent processing of the results will be called *scene analysis*. The division is somewhat arbitrary, except insofar as image analysis starts with an image, while scene analysis begins with a sketch. The first thirteen chapters of the book are

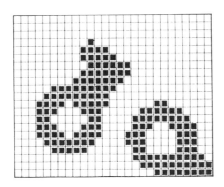

Figure 1-5. Binary images have only two brightness levels: black and white. While restricted in application, they are of interest because they are particularly easy to process.

concerned with image analysis, also referred to as *early vision*, while the remaining five chapters are devoted to scene analysis.

The development of methods for machine vision requires some understanding of how the data to be processed are generated. For this reason we start by discussing image formation and image sensing in chapter 2. There we also treat measurement noise and introduce the concept of convolution.

The easiest images to analyze are those that allow a simple separation of an "object" from a "background." These *binary images* will be treated first (figure 1-5). Some industrial problems can be tackled by methods that use such images, but this usually requires careful control of the lighting. There exists a fairly complete theory of what can and cannot be accomplished with binary images. This is in contrast to the more general case of *gray-level images*. It is known, for example, that binary image techniques are useful only when possible changes in the attitude of the object are confined to rotations in a plane parallel to the image plane. Binary image processing is covered in chapters 3 and 4.

Many image-analysis techniques are meant to be applied to regions of an image corresponding to single objects, rather than to the whole image. Because typically many surfaces in the environment are imaged together, the image must be divided up into regions corresponding to separate entities in the environment before such techniques can be applied. The required segmentation of images is discussed in chapter 5.

In chapters 6 and 7 we consider the transformation of gray-level images into new gray-level images by means of linear operations. The usual intent of such manipulations is to reduce noise, accentuate some aspect of the image, or reduce its dynamic range. Subsequent stages of the machine

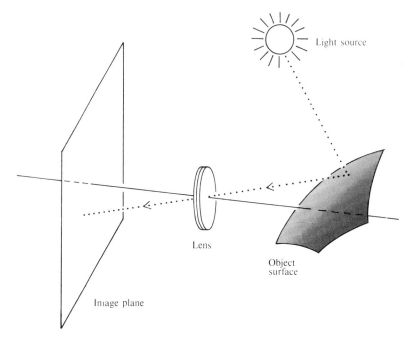

Figure 1-6. In order to use images to recover information about the world, we need to understand image formation. In some cases the image formation process can be inverted to extract estimates of the permanent properties of the surfaces of the objects being imaged.

vision system may find the processed images easier to analyze. Such filtering methods are often exploited in edge-detection systems as preprocessing steps.

Complementary to image segmentation is edge finding, discussed in chapter 8. Often the interesting events in a scene, such as a boundary where one object occludes another, lead to discontinuities in image brightness or in brightness gradient. Edge-finding techniques locate such features. At this point, we begin to emphasize the idea that an important aspect of machine vision is the estimation of properties of the surfaces being imaged. In chapter 9 the estimation of surface reflectance and color is addressed and found to be a surprisingly difficult task.

Finally, we confront the central issue of machine vision: the generation of a description of the world from one or more images. A point of view that one might espouse is that the purpose of the machine vision system is to invert the projection operation performed by image formation. This is not quite correct, since we want not to recover the world being imaged, but

 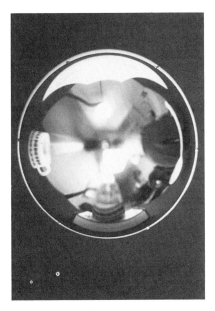

Figure 1-7. The appearance of the image of an object is greatly influenced by the reflectance properties of its surface. Perfectly matte and perfectly specular surfaces present two extreme cases.

to obtain a symbolic description. Still, this notion leads us to study image formation carefully (figure 1-6). The way light is reflected from a surface becomes a central issue. The apparent brightness of a surface depends on three factors:

- Microstructure of the surface.

- Distribution of the incident light.

- Orientation of the surface with respect to the viewer and the light sources.

In figure 1-7 we see images of two spherical surfaces, one covered with a paint that has a matte or diffuse reflectance, the other metallic, giving rise to specular reflections. In the second case we see a virtual image of the world around the spherical object. It is clear that the microstructure of the surface is important in determining image brightness.

Figure 1-8 shows three views of Place Ville-Marie in Montreal. The three pictures were taken from the same hotel window, but under different lighting conditions. Again, we easily recognize that the same objects are

Figure 1-8. The appearance of the image of a scene depends a lot on the lighting conditions. To recover information about the world from images we need to understand how the brightness patterns in the image are determined by the shapes of surfaces, their reflectance properties, and the distribution of light sources.

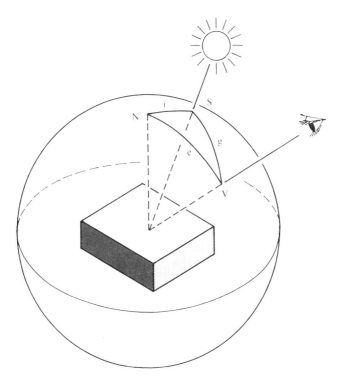

Figure 1-9. The reflection of light from a point source by a patch of an object's surface is governed by three angles: the incident angle i, the emittance angle e, and the phase angle g. Here N is the direction perpendicular, or normal, to the surface, S the direction to the light source, and V the direction toward the viewer.

depicted, but there is a tremendous difference in brightness patterns between the images taken with direct solar illumination and those obtained under a cloudy sky.

In chapters 10 and 11 we discuss these issues and apply the understanding developed to the recovery of surface shape from one or more images. Representations for the shape of a surface are also introduced there. In developing methods for recovering surface shape, we often consider the surface broken up into tiny patches, each of which can be treated as if it were planar. Light reflection from such a planar patch is governed by three angles if it is illuminated by a point source (figure 1-9).

The same systematic approach, based on an analysis of image brightness, is used in chapters 12 and 13 to recover information from time-varying images and images taken by cameras separated in space. Surface shape, object motion, and other information can be recovered from images using the methods developed in these two chapters. The relations between various coordinate systems, either viewer-centered or object-centered, are uncovered in the discussion of photogrammetry in chapter 13, along with an analysis of the binocular stereo problem. In using a machine vision system to guide a mechanical manipulator, measurements in the camera's coordinate system must be transformed into the coordinate system of the robot arm. This topic naturally fits into the discussion of this chapter also.

At this point, we turn from image analysis to scene analysis. Chapter 14 introduces methods for classifying objects based on feature measurements. Line drawings obtained from images of polyhedral objects are analyzed in chapter 15 in order to recover the spatial relationships between the objects.

The issue of how to represent visually acquired information is of great importance. In chapter 16 we develop in detail the extended Gaussian image, a representation for surface shape that is useful in recognition and allows us to determine the attitude of an object in space. Image sequences can be exploited to recover the motion of the camera. As a by-product, we obtain the shapes of the surfaces being imaged. This forms the topic of chapter 17. (The reader may wonder why this chapter does not directly follow the one on optical flow. The reason is that it does not deal with image analysis and so logically belongs in the part of the book dedicated to scene analysis.) Finally, in chapter 18 we bring together many of the concepts developed in this book to built a complete hand–eye system. A robot arm is guided to pick up one object after another out of a pile of objects. Visual input provides the system with information about the positions of the objects and their attitudes in space. In this chapter we introduce some new topics, such as methods for representing rotations in three-dimensional space, and discuss some of the difficulties encountered in building a real-world system.

Throughout the book we start by discussing elementary issues and well-established techniques, progress to more advanced topics, and close with less certain matters and subjects of current research. In the past, machine vision may have appeared to be a collection of assorted heuristics and ad hoc tricks. To give the material coherence we maintain a particular point of view here:

- Machine vision should be based on a thorough understanding of image formation.

This emphasis allows us to derive mathematical models of the image-analysis process. Algorithms for recovering a description of the imaged world can then be based on these mathematical models.

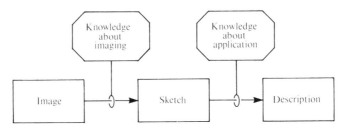

Figure 1-10. In many cases, the development of a symbolic description of a scene from one or more images can be broken down conveniently into two stages. The first stage is largely governed by our understanding of the image-formation process; the second depends more on the needs of the intended application.

An approach based on the analysis of image formation is, of course, not the only one possible for machine vision. One might start instead from existing biological vision systems. Artificial systems would then be based on detailed knowledge of natural systems, provided these can be adequately characterized. We shall occasionally discuss alternate approaches to given problems in machine vision, but to avoid confusion we will not dwell on them.

The transformation from image to sketch appears to be governed mostly by what is in the image and what information we can extract directly from it (figure 1-10). The transformation from a crude sketch to a full symbolic description, on the other hand, is mostly governed by the need to generate information in a form that will be of use in the intended application.

1.5 References

Each chapter will have a section providing pointers to background reading, further explanation of the concepts introduced in that chapters, and recent results in the area. Books will be listed first, complete with authors and titles. Papers in journals, conference proceedings, and internal reports of universities and research laboratories are listed after the books, but without title. Please note that the bibliography has two sections: the first for books, the second for papers.

There are now numerous books on the subject of machine vision. Of these, *Computer Vision* by Ballard & Brown [1982] is remarkable for its broad coverage. Also notable are *Digital Picture Processing* by Rosenfeld & Kak [1982], *Computer Image Processing and Recognition* by Hall [1979], and *Machine Perception* [1982], a short book by Nevatia. A recent addition is *Vision in Man and Machine* [1985] by Levine, a book that has a biological vision point of view and emphasizes applications to biomedical problems.

Many books concentrate on the image-processing side of things, such as *Computer Techniques in Image Processing* by Andrews [1970], *Digital Image Processing* by Gonzalez & Wintz [1977], and two books dealing with the processing of images obtained by cameras in space: *Digital Image Processing* by Castleman [1979] and *Digital Image Processing: A Systems Approach* by Green [1983]. The first few chapters of *Digital Picture Processing* by Rosenfeld & Kak [1982] also provide an excellent introduction to the subject. The classic reference on image processing is still Pratt's encyclopedic *Digital Image Processing* [1978].

One of the earliest significant books in this field, *Pattern Classification and Scene Analysis* by Duda & Hart [1973], contains more on the subject of pattern classification than one typically needs to know. *Artificial Intelligence* by Winston [1984] has an easy-to-read, broad-brush chapter on machine vision that makes the connection between that subject and artificial intelligence.

A number of edited books, containing contributions from several researchers in the field, have appeared in the last ten years. Early on there was *The Psychology of Computer Vision*, edited by Winston [1975], now out of print. Then came *Digital Picture Analysis*, edited by Rosenfeld [1976], and *Computer Vision Systems*, edited by Hanson & Riseman [1978]. Several papers on machine vision can be found in volume 2 of *Artificial Intelligence: An MIT Perspective*, edited by Winston & Brown [1979]. The collection *Structured Computer Vision: Machine Perception through Hierarchical Computation Structures*, edited by Tanimoto & Klinger, was published in 1980. Finally there appeared the fine assemblage of papers *Image Understanding 1984*, edited by Ullman & Richards [1984].

The papers presented at a number of conferences have also been collected in book form. Gardner was the editor of a book published in 1979 called *Machine-aided Image Analysis, 1978*. Applications of machine vision to robotics are explored in *Computer Vision and Sensor-Based Robots*, edited by Dodd & Rossol [1979], and in *Robot Vision*, edited by Pugh [1983]. Stucki edited *Advances in Digital Image Processing: Theory, Application, Implementation* [1979], a book containing papers presented at a meeting organized by IBM. The notes for a course organized by Faugeras appeared in *Fundamentals in Computer Vision* [1983].

Because many of the key papers in the field were not easily accessible, a number of collections have appeared, including three published by IEEE Press, namely *Computer Methods in Image Analysis*, edited by Aggarwal, Duda, & Rosenfeld [1977], *Digital Image Processing*, edited by Andrews [1978], and *Digital Image Processing for Remote Sensing*, edited by Bernstein [1978].

The IEEE Computer Society's publication *Computer* brought out a special issue on image processing in August 1977, the *Proceedings of the IEEE* devoted the May 1979 issue to pattern recognition and image processing, and *Computer* produced a special issue on machine perception for industrial applications in May 1980. A special issue (Volume 17) of the journal *Artificial Intelligence* was published in book form under the title *Computer Vision*, edited by Brady [1981]. The Institute of Electronics and Communication Engineers of Japan produced a special issue (Volume J68-D, Number 4) on machine vision work in Japan in April 1985 (in Japanese).

Not much is said in this book about biological vision systems. They provide us, on the one hand, with reassuring existence proofs and, on the other, with optical illusions. These startling effects may someday prove to be keys with which we can unlock the secrets of biological vision systems. A computational theory of their function is beginning to emerge, to a great extent due to the pioneering work of a single man, David Marr. His approach is documented in the classic book *Vision: A Computational Investigation into the Human Representation and Processing of Visual Information* [1982].

Human vision has, of course, always been a subject of intense curiosity, and there is a vast literature on the subject. Just a few books will be mentioned here. Gregory has provided popular accounts of the subject in *Eye and Brain* [1966] and *The Intelligent Eye* [1970]. Three books by Gibson—*The Perception of the Visual World* [1950], *The Senses Considered as Perceptual Systems* [1966], and *The Ecological Approach to Visual Perception* [1979]—are noteworthy for providing a fresh approach to the problem. Cornsweet's *Visual Perception* [1971] and *The Psychology of Visual Perception* by Haber & Hershenson [1973] are of interest also. The work of Julesz has been very influential, particularly in the area of binocular stereo, as documented in *Foundations of Cyclopean Perception* [1971]. More recently, in the wonderfully illustrated book *Seeing*, Frisby [1982] has been able to show the crosscurrents between work on machine vision and work on biological vision systems. For another point of view see *Perception* by Rock [1984].

Twenty years ago, papers on machine vision were few in number and scattered widely. Since then a number of journals have become preferred repositories for new research results. In fact, the journal *Computer Graphics and Image Processing*, published by Academic Press, had to change its name to *Computer Vision, Graphics and Image Processing* (CVGIP) when it became the standard place to send papers in this field for review. More recently, a new special-interest group of the Institute of Electrical and Electronic Engineers (IEEE) started publishing the *Transactions on Pattern Analysis and Machine Intelligence* (PAMI). Other journals, such as *Artificial Intelligence*, published by North-Holland, and *Robotics Research*, published by MIT Press, also contain articles on machine vision. There are several journals devoted to related topics, such as pattern classification.

Some research results first see the light of day at an "Image Understanding Workshop" sponsored by the Defense Advanced Research Projects Agency (DARPA). Proceedings of these workshops are published by Science Applications Incorporated, McLean, Virginia, and are available through the Defense Technical Information Center (DTIC) in Alexandria, Virginia. Many of these papers are later submitted, possibly after revision and extension, to be reviewed for publication in one of the journals mentioned above.

The Computer Society of the IEEE organizes annual conferences on Computer Vision and Pattern Recognition (CVPR) and publishes their proceedings. Also of interest are the proceedings of the biannual International Joint Conference on Artificial Intelligence (IJCAI) and the national conferences organized by the American Association for Artificial Intelligence (AAAI), usually in the years in between.

The thorough annual surveys by Rosenfeld [1972, 1974, 1975, 1976, 1977, 1978, 1979, 1980, 1981, 1982, 1983, 1984a, 1985] in *Computer Vision, Graphics and Image Processing* are extremely valuable and make it possible to be less than complete in providing references here. The most recent survey contained 1,252 entries! There have been many analyses of the state of the field or of particular views of the field. An early survey of image processing is that of Huang, Schreiber, & Tretiak [1971]. While not really a survey, the influential paper of Barrow & Tenenbaum [1978] presents the now prevailing view that machine vision is concerned with the process of recovering information about the surfaces being imaged. More recent surveys of machine vision by Marr [1980], Barrow & Tenenbaum [1981a], Poggio [1984], and Rosenfeld [1984b] are recommended particularly. Another paper that has been influential is that by Binford [1981].

Once past the hurdles of early vision, the representation of information and the modeling of objects and the physical interaction between them become important. We touch upon these issues in the later chapters of this book. For more information see, for example, Brooks [1981] and Binford [1982].

There are many papers on the application of machine vision to industrial problems (although some of the work with the highest payoff is likely not to have been published in the open literature). Several papers in *Robotics Research: The First International Symposium*, edited by Brady & Paul [1984], deal with this topic. Chin [1982] and Chin & Harlow [1982] have surveyed the automation of visual inspection.

The inspection of printed circuit boards, both naked and stuffed, is a topic of great interest, since there are many boards to be inspected and since it is not a very pleasant job for people, nor one that they are particularly good at. For examples of work in this area, see Ejiri et al. [1973], Danielsson & Kruse [1979], Danielsson [1980], and Hara, Akiyama, & Karasaki [1983]. There is a similar demand for such techniques in the manufacture of integrated circuits. Masks are simple black-and-white patterns, and their inspection has not been too difficult to automate. The inspection of integrated circuit wafers is another matter; see, for example, Hsieh & Fu [1980].

Machine vision has been used in automated alignment. See Horn [1975b], Kashioka, Ejiri, & Sakamoto [1976], and Baird [1978] for examples in semiconductor manufacturing. Industrial robots are regularly guided using visually obtained information about the position and orientation of parts. Many such systems use binary image-processing techniques, although some are more sophisticated. See, for example, Yachida & Tsuji [1977], Gonzalez & Safabakhsh [1982], and Horn & Ikeuchi [1984]. These techniques will not find widespread application if the user has to program each application in a standard programming language. Some attempts have been made to provide tools specifically suited to the vision applications; see, for example, Lavin & Lieberman [1982].

Papers on the application of machine vision methods to the vectorization of line drawings are mentioned at the end of chapter 4; references on character recognition may be found at the end of chapter 14.

1.6 Exercises

1-1 Explain in what sense one can consider pattern classification, image processing, and scene analysis as "ancestor paradigms" to machine vision. In what way do the methods from each of these disciplines contribute to machine vision? In what way are the problems addressed by machine vision different from those to which these methods apply?

2

Image Formation & Image Sensing

In this chapter we explore how images are formed and how they are sensed by a computer. Understanding image formation is a prerequisite for full understanding of the methods for recovering information from images. In analyzing the process by which a three-dimensional world is projected onto a two-dimensional image plane, we uncover the two key questions of image formation:

- What determines where the image of some point will appear?
- What determines how bright the image of some surface will be?

The answers to these two questions require knowledge of image projection and image radiometry, topics that will be discussed in the context of simple lens systems.

A crucial notion in the study of image formation is that we live in a very special visual world. It has particular features that make it possible to recover information about the three-dimensional world from one or more two-dimensional images. We discuss this issue and point out imaging situations where these special constraint do not apply, and where it is consequently much harder to extract information from images.

We also study the basic mechanism of typical image sensors, and how information in different spectral bands may be obtained and processed. Following a brief discussion of color, the chapter closes with a discussion of noise and reviews some concepts from the fields of probability and statistics. This is a convenient point to introduce convolution in one dimension, an idea that will be exploited later in its two-dimensional generalization. Readers familiar with these concepts may omit these sections without loss of continuity. The chapter concludes with a discussion of the need for quantization of brightness measurements and for tessellations of the image plane.

2.1 Two Aspects of Image Formation

Before we can analyze an image, we must know how it is formed. An image is a two-dimensional pattern of brightness. How this pattern is produced in an optical image-forming system is best studied in two parts: first, we need to find the geometric correspondence between points in the scene and points in the image; then we must figure out what determines the brightness at a particular point in the image.

2.1.1 Perspective Projection

Consider an ideal pinhole at a fixed distance in front of an image plane (figure 2-1). Assume that an enclosure is provided so that only light coming through the pinhole can reach the image plane. Since light travels along straight lines, each point in the image corresponds to a particular direction defined by a ray from that point through the pinhole. Thus we have the familiar *perspective projection.*

We define the *optical axis*, in this simple case, to be the perpendicular from the pinhole to the image plane. Now we can introduce a convenient Cartesian coordinate system with the origin at the pinhole and z-axis aligned with the optical axis and pointing toward the image. With this choice of orientation, the z components of the coordinates of points in front of the camera are negative. We use this convention, despite the drawback, because it gives us a convenient right-hand coordinate system (with the x-axis to the right and the y-axis upward).

We would like to compute where the image P' of the point P on some object in front of the camera will appear (figure 2-1). We assume that no other object lies on the ray from P to the pinhole O. Let $\mathbf{r} = (x, y, z)^T$ be the vector connecting O to P, and $\mathbf{r}' = (x', y', f')^T$ be the vector connecting O to P'. (As explained in the appendix, vectors will be denoted by boldface letters. We commonly deal with column vectors, and so must take the transpose, indicated by the superscript ^{T}, when we want to write them in terms of the equivalent row vectors.)

Here f' is the distance of the image plane from the pinhole, while x' and y' are the coordinates of the point P' in the image plane. The two

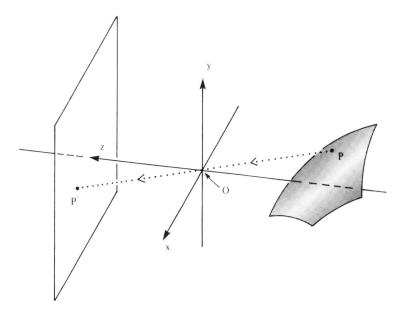

Figure 2-1. A pinhole camera produces an image that is a perspective projection of the world. It is convenient to use a coordinate system in which the xy-plane is parallel to the image plane, and the origin is at the pinhole O. The z-axis then lies along the optical axis.

---

vectors $\mathbf{r}$ and $\mathbf{r}'$ are collinear and differ only by a (negative) scale factor. If the ray connecting P to P' makes an angle α with the optical axis, then the length of $\mathbf{r}$ is just

$$r = -z \sec \alpha = -(\mathbf{r} \cdot \hat{\mathbf{z}}) \sec \alpha,$$

where $\hat{\mathbf{z}}$ is the unit vector along the optical axis. (Remember that z is negative for a point in front of the camera.)

The length of $\mathbf{r}'$ is

$$r' = f' \sec \alpha,$$

and so

$$\frac{1}{f'}\mathbf{r}' = \frac{1}{\mathbf{r} \cdot \hat{\mathbf{z}}}\mathbf{r}.$$

In component form this can be written as

$$\frac{x'}{f'} = \frac{x}{z} \qquad \text{and} \qquad \frac{y'}{f'} = \frac{y}{z}.$$

Sometimes image coordinates are normalized by dividing x' and y' by f' in order to simplify the projection equations.

2.1.2 Orthographic Projection

Suppose we form the image of a plane that lies parallel to the image at $z = z_0$. Then we can define m, the (lateral) *magnification*, as the ratio of the distance between two points measured in the image to the distance between the corresponding points on the plane. Consider a small interval $(\delta x, \delta y, 0)^T$ on the plane and the corresponding small interval $(\delta x', \delta y', 0)^T$ in the image. Then

$$m = \frac{\sqrt{(\delta x')^2 + (\delta y')^2}}{\sqrt{(\delta x)^2 + (\delta y)^2}} = \frac{f'}{-z_0},$$

where $-z_0$ is the distance of the plane from the pinhole. The magnification is the same for all points in the plane. (Note that $m < 1$, except in the case of microscopic imaging.)

A small object at an average distance $-z_0$ will give rise to an image that is magnified by m, provided that the variation in z over its visible surface is not significant compared to $-z_0$. The area occupied by the image of an object is proportional to m^2. Objects at different distances from the imaging system will, of course, be imaged with different magnifications. Let the *depth range* of a scene be the range of distances of surfaces from the camera. The magnification is approximately constant when the depth range of the scene being imaged is small relative to the average distance of the surfaces from the camera. In this case we can simplify the projection equations to read

$$x' = -mx \qquad \text{and} \qquad y' = -my,$$

where $m = f'/(-z_0)$ and $-z_0$ is the average value of $-z$. Often the scaling factor m is set to 1 or -1 for convenience. Then we can further simplify the equations to become

$$x' = x \qquad \text{and} \qquad y' = y.$$

This *orthographic projection* (figure 2-2), can be modeled by rays parallel to the optical axis (rather than ones passing through the origin). The difference between perspective and orthographic projection is small when the distance to the scene is much larger than the variation in distance among objects in the scene.

The *field of view* of an imaging system is the angle of the cone of directions encompassed by the scene that is being imaged. This cone of directions clearly has the same shape and size as the cone obtained by

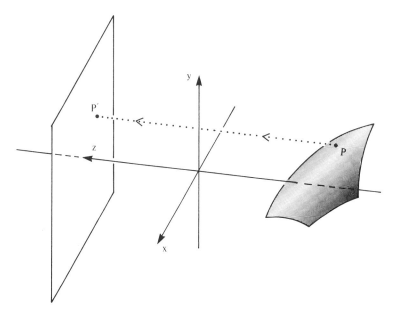

Figure 2-2. When the scene depth is small relative to the average distance from the camera, perspective projection can be approximated by orthographic projection. In orthographic projection, rays from a point in the scene are traced parallel to the projection direction until they intercept the image plane.

connecting the edge of the image plane to the center of projection. A "normal" lens has a field of view of perhaps 25° by 40°. A *telephoto lens* is one that has a long focal length relative to the image size and thus a narrow field of view. Conversely, a *wide-angle lens* has a short focal length relative to the image size and thus a wide field of view. A rough rule of thumb is that perspective effects are significant when a wide-angle lens is used, while images obtained using a telephoto lenses tend to approximate orthographic projection. We shall show in exercise 2-11 that this rule is not exact.

2.2 Brightness

The more difficult, and more interesting, question of image formation is what determines the brightness at a particular point in the image. *Brightness* is an informal term used to refer to at least two different concepts: image brightness and scene brightness. In the image, brightness is related to energy flux incident on the image plane and can be measured in a number of ways. Here we introduce the term *irradiance* to replace the informal

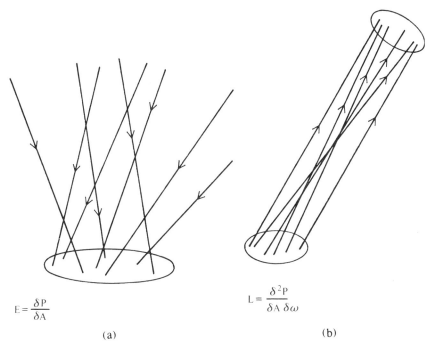

$$E = \frac{\delta P}{\delta A}$$

$$L = \frac{\delta^2 P}{\delta A \, \delta \omega}$$

(a)   (b)

Figure 2-3. (a) Irradiance is the power per unit area falling on a surface. (b) Radiance is the power emitted per unit area into a cone of directions having unit solid angle. The term *brightness* is used informally for both concepts.

term *image brightness*. Irradiance is the power per unit area $(\mathrm{W \cdot m^{-2}}$—watts per square meter) of radiant energy falling on a surface (figure 2-3a). In the figure, E denotes the irradiance, while δP is the power of the radiant energy falling on the infinitesimal surface patch of area δA. The blackening of a film in a camera, for example, is a function of the irradiance. (As we shall discuss a little later, the measurement of brightness in the image also depends on the spectral sensitivity of the sensor.) The irradiance at a particular point in the image will depend on how much light arrives from the corresponding object point (the point found by following the ray from the image point through the pinhole until it meets the surface of an object).

In the scene, brightness is related to the energy flux emitted from a surface. Different points on the objects in front of the imaging system will have different brightnesses, depending on how they are illuminated and how they reflect light. We now introduce the term *radiance* to substitute for the informal term *scene brightness*. Radiance is the power per unit foreshortened area emitted into a unit solid angle $(\mathrm{W \cdot m^{-2} \cdot sr^{-1}}$—watts per square meter per steradian) by a surface (figure 2-3b). In the figure, L is the radiance and $\delta^2 P$ is the power emitted by the infinitesimal surface patch of area δA into an infinitesimal solid angle $\delta\omega$. The apparent complexity of the definition of radiance stems from the fact that a surface emits light into a hemisphere of possible directions, and we obtain a finite amount only by considering a finite solid angle of these directions. In general the radiance will vary with the direction from which the object is viewed. We shall discuss radiometry in detail later, when we introduce the reflectance map.

We are interested in the radiance of surface patches on objects because what we measure, image irradiance, turns out to be proportional to scene radiance, as we show later. The constant of proportionality depends on the optical system. To gather a finite amount of light in the image plane we must have an aperture of finite size. The pinhole, introduced in the last section, must have a nonzero diameter. Our simple analysis of projection no longer applies, though, since a point in the environment is now imaged as a small circle. This can be seen by considering the cone of rays passing through the circular pinhole with its apex at the object point.

We cannot make the pinhole very small for another reason. Because of the wave nature of light, diffraction occurs at the edge of the pinhole and the light is spread over the image. As the pinhole is made smaller and smaller, a larger and larger fraction of the incoming light is deflected far from the direction of the incoming ray.

2.3 Lenses

In order to avoid the problems associated with pinhole cameras, we now consider the use of a lens in an image-forming system. An ideal lens produces the same projection as the pinhole, but also gathers a finite amount of light (figure 2-4). The larger the lens, the larger the solid angle it subtends when seen from the object. Correspondingly it intercepts more of the light reflected from (or emitted by) the object. The ray through the center of the lens is undeflected. In a well-focused system the other rays are deflected to reach the same image point as the central ray.

An ideal lens has the disadvantage that it only brings to focus light from points at a distance $-z$ given by the familiar lens equation

$$\frac{1}{z'} + \frac{1}{-z} = \frac{1}{f},$$

where z' is the distance of the image plane from the lens and f is the *focal length* (figure 2-4). Points at other distances are imaged as little circles. This can be seen by considering the cone of light rays passing through the lens with apex at the point where they are correctly focused. The size of

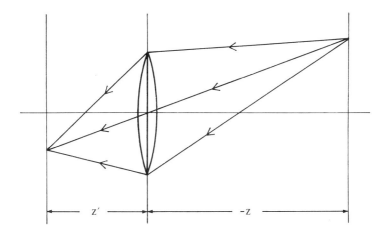

Figure 2-4. To obtain finite irradiance in the image plane, a lens is used instead of an ideal pinhole. A perfect lens generates an image that obeys the same projection equations as that generated by a pinhole, but gathers light from a finite area as well. A lens produces well-focused images of objects at a particular distance only.

the blur circle can be determined as follows: A point at distance $-\bar{z}$ is imaged at a point $\bar{z}'$ from the lens, where

$$\frac{1}{\bar{z}'} + \frac{1}{-\bar{z}} = \frac{1}{f},$$

and so

$$(\bar{z}' - z') = \frac{f}{(\bar{z} + f)} \frac{f}{(z + f)} (\bar{z} - z).$$

If the image plane is situated to receive correctly focused images of objects at distance $-z$, then points at distance $-\bar{z}$ will give rise to blur circles of diameter

$$\frac{d}{z'} |\bar{z}' - z'|,$$

where d is the diameter of the lens. The *depth of field* is the range of distances over which objects are focused "sufficiently well," in the sense that the diameter of the blur circle is less than the resolution of the imaging device. The depth of field depends, of course, on what sensor is used, but in any case it is clear that the larger the lens aperture, the less the depth of field. Clearly also, errors in focusing become more serious when a large aperture is employed.

Simple ray-tracing rules can help in understanding simple lens combinations. As already mentioned, the ray through the center of the lens is undeflected. Rays entering the lens parallel to the optical axis converge to a point on the optical axis at a distance equal to the focal length. This follows from the definition of focal length as the distance from the lens where the image of an object that is infinitely far away is focused. Conversely, rays emitted from a point on the optical axis at a distance equal to the focal length from the lens are deflected to emerge parallel to the optical axis on the other side of the lens. This follows from the reversibility of rays. At an interface between media of different refractive indices, the same reflection and refraction angles apply to light rays traveling in opposite directions.

A simple lens is made by grinding and polishing a glass blank so that its two surfaces have shapes that are spherical. The optical axis is the line through the centers of the two spheres. Any such simple lens will have a number of defects or aberrations. For this reason one usually combines several simple lenses, carefully lining up their individual optical axes, so as to make a compound lens with better properties.

A useful model of such a system of lenses is the *thick lens* (figure 2-5). One can define two *principal planes* perpendicular to the optical axis, and two *nodal points* where these planes intersect the optical axis. A ray arriving at the front nodal point leaves the rear nodal point without changing direction. This defines the projection performed by the lens. The distance between the two nodal points is the *thickness* of the lens. A *thin lens* is one in which the two nodal points can be considered coincident.

It is theoretically impossible to make a perfect lens. The projection will never be exactly like that of an ideal pinhole. More important, exact focusing of all rays cannot be achieved. A variety of aberrations occur. In a well-designed lens these defects are kept to a minimum, but this becomes more difficult as the aperture of the lens is increased. Thus there is a trade-off between light-gathering power and image quality.

A defect of particular interest to us here is called *vignetting*. Imagine several circular diaphragms of different diameter, stacked one behind the other, with their centers on a common line (figure 2-6). When you look along this common line, the smallest diaphragm will limit your view. As you move away from the line, some of the other diaphragms will begin to occlude more, until finally nothing can be seen. Similarly, in a simple lens, all the rays that enter the front surface of the lens end up being focused in the image. In a compound lens, some of the rays that pass through the first lens may be occluded by portions of the second lens, and so on. This will depend on the inclination of the entering ray with respect to the optical axis and its distance from the front nodal point. Thus points in the image away from the optical axis benefit less from the light-gathering power of the lens than does the point on the optical axis. There is a falloff

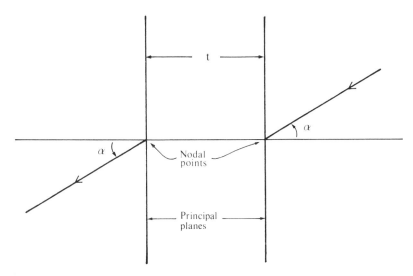

Figure 2-5. An ideal thick lens provides a reasonable model for most real lenses. It produces the same perspective projection that an ideal thin lens does, except for an additional offset, the lens thickness t, along the optical axis. It can be understood in terms of the principal planes and the nodal points at the intersections of the principal planes and the optical axis.

in sensitivity with distance from the center of the image.

Another important consideration is that the aberrations of a lens increase in magnitude as a power of the angle between the incident ray and the optical axis. Aberrations are classified by their *order*, that is, the power of the angle that occurs in this relationship. Points on the optical axis may be quite well focused, while those in a corner of the image are smeared out. For this reason, only a limited portion of the image plane is usable. The magnitude of an aberration defect also increases as a power of the distance from the optical axis at which a ray passes through the lens. Thus the image quality can be improved by using only the central portion of a lens.

One reason for introducing diaphragms into a lens system is to improve image quality in a situation where it is not necessary to utilize fully the light-gathering power of the system. As already mentioned, fixed diaphragms ensure that rays entering at a large angle to the optical axis do not pass through the outer regions of any of the lenses. This improves image quality in the outer regions of the image, but at the same time greatly increases vignetting. In most common uses of lenses this is not an important matter, since people are astonishingly insensitive to smooth spatial variations in image brightness. It does matter in machine vision,

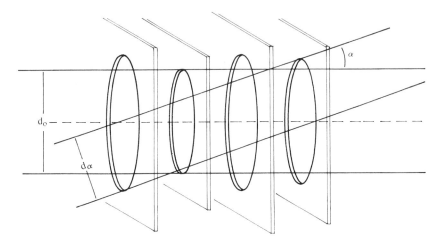

Figure 2-6. Vignetting is a reduction in light-gathering power with increasing inclination of light rays with respect to the optical axis. It is caused by apertures in the lens system occluding part of the beam of light as it passes through the lens system. Vignetting results in a smooth, but sometimes quite large, falloff in sensitivity toward the edges of the image region.

however, since we use the measurements of image brightness (irradiance) to determine the scene brightness (radiance).

2.4 Our Visual World

How can we hope to recover information about the three-dimensional world using a mere two-dimensional image? It may seem that the available information is not adequate, even if we take several images. Yet biological systems interact intelligently with the environment using visual information. The puzzle is solved when we consider the special nature of our usual visual world. We are immersed in a homogeneous transparent medium, and the objects we look at are typically opaque. Light rays are not refracted or absorbed in the environment, and we can follow a ray from an image point through the lens until it reaches some surface. The brightness at a point in the image depends only on the brightness of the corresponding surface patch. Surfaces are two-dimensional manifolds, and their shape can be represented by giving the distance $z(x', y')$ to the surface as a function of the image coordinates x' and y'.

This is to be contrasted with a situation in which we are looking into a volume occupied by a light-absorbing material of varying density. Here we may specify the density $\rho(x, y, z)$ of the material as a function of the coordinates x, y, and z. One or more images provide enough constraint to recover information about a surface, but not about a volume. In theory, an infinite number of images is needed to solve the problem of *tomography*, that is, to determine the density of the absorbing material.

Conditions of homogeneity and transparency may not always hold exactly. Distant mountains appear changed in color and contrast, while in deserts we may see mirages. Image analysis based on the assumption that conditions are as stated may go awry when the assumptions are violated, and so we can expect that both biological and machine vision systems will be misled in such situations. Indeed, some optical illusions can be explained in this way. This does not mean that we should abandon these additional constraints, for without them the solution of the problem of recovering information about the three-dimensional world from images would be ambiguous.

Our usual visual world is special indeed. Imagine being immersed instead in a world with varying concentrations of pigments dispersed within a gelatinous substance. It would not be possible to recover the distributions of these absorbing substances in three dimensions from one view. There just would not be enough information. Analogously, single X-ray images are not useful unless there happens to be sharp contrast between different materials, like bone and tissue. Otherwise a very large number of views must be taken and a tomographic reconstruction attempted. It is perhaps a good thing that we do not possess Superman's X-ray vision capabilities!

By and large, we shall confine our attention to images formed by conventional optical means. We shall avoid high-magnification microscopic images, for instance, where many substances are effectively transparent, or at least translucent. Similarly, images on a very large scale often show the effects of absorption and refraction in the atmosphere. Interestingly, other modalities do sometimes provide us with images much like the ones we are used to. Examples include scanning electron microscopes (SEM) and synthetic-aperture radar systems (SAR), both of which produce images that are easy to interpret. So there is some hope of analyzing them using the methods discussed here.

In view of the importance of surfaces, we might hope that a machine vision system could be designed to recover the shapes of surfaces given one or more images. Indeed, there has been some success in this endeavor, as we shall see in chapter 10, where we discuss the recovery of shape from shading. Detailed understanding of the imaging process allows us to recover quantitative information from images. The computed shape of a surface may be used in recognition, inspection, or in planning the path of a mechanical manipulator.

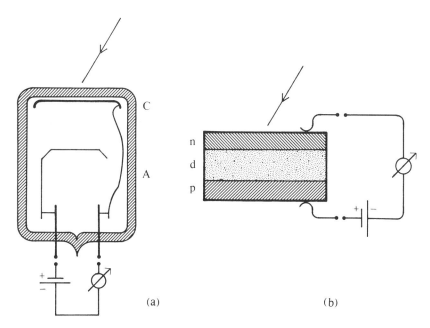

(a)   (b)

Figure 2-7. Photons striking a suitable surface generate charge carriers that are collected and measured to determine the irradiance. (a) In the case of a vacuum device, electrons are liberated from the photocathode and attracted to the positive anode. (b) In the case of a semiconductor device, electron–hole pairs are separated by the built-in field to be collected in an external circuit.

2.5 Image Sensing

Almost all image sensors depend on the generation of electron–hole pairs when photons strike a suitable material. This is the basic process in biological vision as well as photography. Image sensors differ in how they measure the flux of charged particles. Some devices use an electric field in a vacuum to separate the electrons from the surface where they are liberated (figure 2-7a). In other devices the electrons are swept through a depleted zone in a semiconductor (figure 2-7b).

Not all incident photons generate an electron–hole pair. Some pass right through the sensing layer, some are reflected, and others lose energy in different ways. Further, not all electrons find their way into the detecting circuit. The ratio of the electron flux to the incident photon flux is called the *quantum efficiency*, denoted $q(\lambda)$. The quantum efficiency depends on the energy of the incident photon and hence on its wavelength λ. It also depends on the material and the method used to collect the liberated electrons. Older vacuum devices tend to have coatings with relatively low quantum efficiency, while solid-state devices are near ideal for some wavelengths. Photographic film tends to have poor quantum efficiency.

2.5.1 Sensing Color

The sensitivity of a device varies with the wavelength of the incident light. Photons with little energy tend to go right through the material, while very energetic photons may be stopped before they reach the sensitive layer. Each material has its characteristic variation of quantum efficiency with wavelength.

For a small wavelength interval $\delta\lambda$, let the flux of photons with energy equal to or greater than λ, but less than $\lambda + \delta\lambda$, be $b(\lambda)\,\delta\lambda$. Then the number of electrons liberated is

$$\int_{-\infty}^{\infty} b(\lambda)q(\lambda)\,d\lambda.$$

If we use sensors with different photosensitive materials, we obtain different images because their spectral sensitivities are different. This can be helpful in distinguishing surfaces that have similar gray-levels when imaged with one sensor, yet give rise to different gray-levels when imaged with a different sensor. Another way to achieve this effect is to use the same sensing material but place filters in front of the camera that selectively absorb different parts of the spectrum. If the transmission of the ith filter is $f_i(\lambda)$, the effective quantum efficiency of the combination of that filter and the sensor is $f_i(\lambda)q(\lambda)$.

How many different filters should we use? The ability to distinguish among materials grows as more images are taken through more filters. The measurements are correlated, however, because most surfaces have a smooth variation of reflectance with wavelength. Typically, little is gained by using very many filters.

The human visual system uses three types of sensors, called *cones*, in daylight conditions. Each of these cone types has a particular spectral sensitivity, one of them peaking in the long wavelength range, one in the middle, and one in the short wavelength range of the visible spectrum, which extends from about 400 nm to about 700 nm. There is considerable overlap between the sensitivity curves. Machine vision systems often also use three images obtained through red, green, and blue filters. It should be pointed out, however, that the results have little to do with human color sensations unless the spectral response curves happen to be linear combinations of the human spectral response curves, as discussed below.

One property of a sensing system with a small number of sensor types having different spectral sensitivities is that many different spectral distributions will produce the same output. The reason is that we do not measure the spectral distributions themselves, but integrals of their product with the spectral sensitivity of particular sensor types. The same applies to biological systems, of course. Colors that appear indistinguishable to a human observer are said to be *metameric*. Useful information about the spectral sensitivities of the human visual system can be gained by systematically exploring metamers. The results of a large number of color-matching experiments performed by many observers have been averaged and used to calculate the so-called *tristimulus* or *standard observer curves*. These have been published by the *Commission Internationale de l'Eclairage* (CIE) and are shown in figure 2-8. A given spectral distribution is evaluated as follows: The spectral distribution is multiplied in turn by each of the three functions $x(\lambda)$, $y(\lambda)$, and $z(\lambda)$. The products are integrated over the visible wavelength range. The three results $\overline{X}$, $\overline{Y}$, and $\overline{Z}$ are called the tristimulus values. Two spectral distributions that result in the same values for these three quantities appear indistinguishable when placed side by side under controlled conditions. (By the way, the spectral distributions used here are expressed in terms of energy per unit wavelength interval, not photon flux.)

The actual spectral response curves of the three types of cones cannot be determined in this way, however. There is some remaining ambiguity. It is known that the tristimulus curves are fixed linear transforms of these spectral response curves. The coefficients of the transformation are not known accurately.

We show in exercise 2-14 that a machine vision system with the same color-matching properties as the human color vision system must have sensitivities that are linear transforms of the human cone response curves. This in turn implies that the sensitivities must be linear transforms of the known standard observer curves. Unfortunately, this rule has rarely been observed when color-sensing systems were designed in the past. (Note that we are not addressing the problem of color sensations; we are only interested in having the machine confuse the same colors as the standard observer.)

2.5.2 Randomness and Noise

It is difficult to make accurate measurements of image brightness. In this section we discuss the corrupting influence of noise on image sensing. In order to do this, we need to discuss random variables and the probability density distribution. We shall also take the opportunity to introduce the concept of convolution in the one-dimensional case. Later, we shall encounter convolution again, applied to two-dimensional images. The reader familiar with these concepts may want to skip this section.

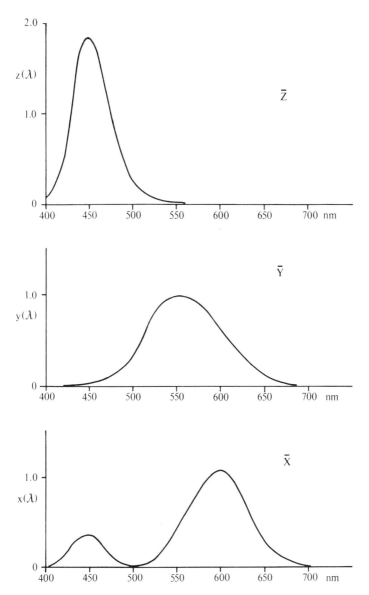

Figure 2-8. The tristimulus curves allow us to predict which spectral distributions will be indistinguishable. A given spectral distribution is multiplied by each of the functions $x(\lambda)$, $y(\lambda)$, and $z(\lambda)$, in turn, and the products integrated. In this way we obtain the tristimulus values, $\overline{X}$, $\overline{Y}$, and $\overline{Z}$, that can be used to characterize the spectral distribution. Spectral distributions that lead to the same tristimulus values appear the same when placed next to one another.

Measurements are affected by fluctuations in the signal being measured. If the measurement is repeated, somewhat differing results may be obtained. Typically, measurements will cluster around the "correct" value. We can talk of the probability that a measurement will fall within a certain interval. Roughly speaking, this is the limit of the ratio of the number of measurements that fall in that interval to the total number of trials, as the total number of trials tends to infinity. (This definition is not quite accurate, since any particular sequence of experiments may produce results that do not tend to the expected limit. It is unlikely that they are far off, however. Indeed, the probability of the limit tending to an answer that is not the desired one is zero.)

Now we can define the *probability density distribution*, denoted $p(x)$. The probability that a random variable will be equal to or greater than x, but less than $x + \delta x$, tends to $p(x)\delta x$ as δx tends to zero. (There is a subtle problem here, since for a given number of trials the number falling in the interval will tend to zero as the size of the interval tends to zero. This problem can be sidestepped by considering the cumulative probability distribution, introduced below.) A probability distribution can be estimated from a histogram obtained from a finite number of trials (figure 2-9). From our definition follow two important properties of any probability distribution $p(x)$:

$$p(x) \geq 0 \quad \text{for all } x, \qquad \text{and} \qquad \int_{-\infty}^{\infty} p(x)\, dx = 1.$$

Often the probability distribution has a strong peak near the "correct," or "expected," value. We may define the *mean* accordingly as the center of area, μ, of this peak, defined by the equation

$$\mu \int_{-\infty}^{\infty} p(x)\, dx = \int_{-\infty}^{\infty} x\, p(x)\, dx.$$

Since the integral of $p(x)$ from minus infinity to plus infinity is one,

$$\mu = \int_{-\infty}^{\infty} x\, p(x)\, dx.$$

The integral on the right is called the *first moment* of $p(x)$.

Next, to estimate the spread of the peak of $p(x)$, we can take the *second moment* about the mean, called the *variance*:

$$\sigma^2 = \int_{-\infty}^{\infty} (x - \mu)^2\, p(x)\, dx.$$

The square root of the variance, called the *standard deviation*, is a useful measure of the width of the distribution.

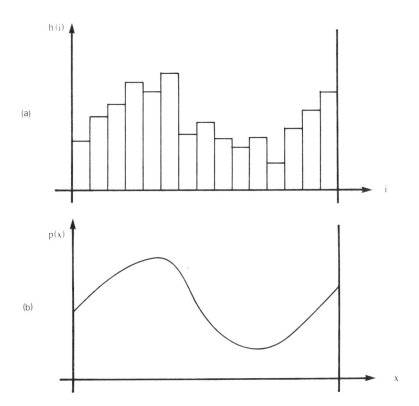

Figure 2-9. (a) A histogram indicates how many samples fall into each of a series of measurement intervals. If more and more samples are gathered, these intervals can be made smaller and smaller while maintaining the accuracy of the individual measurements. (b) In the limit the histogram becomes a continuous function, called the probability distribution.

Another useful concept is the *cumulative probability distribution*,

$$P(x) = \int_{-\infty}^{x} p(t)\, dt,$$

which tells us the probability that the random variable will be less than or equal to x. The probability density distribution is just the derivative of

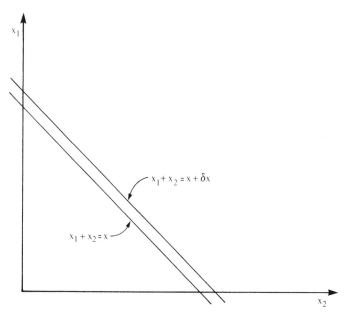

Figure 2-10. The probability distribution of the sum of two independent random variables is the convolution of the probability distributions of the two variables. This can be shown by integrating the product of the individual probability distributions over the narrow strip between $x_1 + x_2 = x$ and $x_1 + x_2 = x + \delta x$.

the cumulative probability distribution. Note that

$$\lim_{x \to \infty} P(x) = 1.$$

One way to improve accuracy is to average several measurements, assuming that the "noise" in them will be independent and tend to cancel out. To understand how this works, we need to be able to compute the probability distribution of a sum of several random variables.

Suppose that x is a sum of two independent random variables x_1 and x_2 and that $p_1(x_1)$ and $p_2(x_2)$ are their probability distributions. How do we find $p(x)$, the probability distribution of $x = x_1 + x_2$? Given x_2, we know that x_1 must lie between $x - x_2$ and $x + \delta x - x_2$ in order for x to lie between x and $x + \delta x$ (figure 2-10). The probability that this will happen is $p_1(x - x_2)\,\delta x$. Now x_2 can take on a range of values, and the probability that it lies in a particular interval x_2 to $x_2 + \delta x_2$ is just $p_2(x_2)\,\delta x_2$. To find the probability that x lies between x and $x + \delta x$ we must integrate the product over all x_2. Thus

$$p(x)\,\delta x = \int_{-\infty}^{\infty} p_1(x - x_2)\,\delta x\, p_2(x_2)\,dx_2,$$

or

$$p(x) = \int_{-\infty}^{\infty} p_1(x - t)\,p_2(t)\,dt.$$

By a similar argument one can show that

$$p(x) = \int_{-\infty}^{\infty} p_2(x - t)\,p_1(t)\,dt,$$

in which the roles of x_1 and x_2 are reversed. These correspond to two ways of integrating the product of the probabilities over the narrow diagonal strip (figure 2-10). In either case, we talk of a *convolution* of the distributions p_1 and p_2, written as

$$p = p_1 \otimes p_2.$$

We have just shown that convolution is commutative.

We show in exercise 2-16 that the mean of the sum of several random variables is equal to the sum of the means, and that the variance of the sum equals the sum of the variances. Thus if we compute the average of N independent measurements,

$$\overline{x} = \frac{1}{N}\sum_{i=1}^{N} x_i,$$

each of which has mean μ and standard deviation σ, the mean of the result is also μ, while the standard deviation is $\sigma/\sqrt{N}$ since the variance of the sum is $N\sigma^2$. Thus we obtain a more accurate result, that is, one less affected by "noise." The relative accuracy only improves with the square root of the number of measurements, however.

A probability distribution that is of great practical interest is the *normal* or *Gaussian* distribution

$$p(x) = \frac{1}{\sqrt{2\pi}\sigma} e^{-\frac{1}{2}\left(\frac{x-\mu}{\sigma}\right)^2}$$

with mean μ and standard deviation σ. The noise in many measurement processes can be modeled well using this distribution.

So far we have been dealing with random variables that can take on values in a continuous range. Analogous methods apply when the possible values are in a discrete set. Consider the electrons liberated during a fixed interval by photons falling on a suitable material. Each such event is independent of the others. It can be shown that the probability that exactly n are liberated in a time interval T is

$$P_n = e^{-m} \frac{m^n}{n!}$$

for some m. This is the *Poisson* distribution. We can calculate the average number liberated in time T as follows:

$$\sum_{n=1}^{\infty} n e^{-m} \frac{m^n}{n!} = m e^{-m} \sum_{n=1}^{\infty} \frac{m^{n-1}}{(n-1)!}.$$

But

$$\sum_{n=1}^{\infty} \frac{m^{n-1}}{(n-1)!} = \sum_{n=0}^{\infty} \frac{m^n}{n!} = e^m,$$

so the average is just m. We show in exercise 2-18 that the variance is also m. The standard deviation is thus $\sqrt{m}$, so that the ratio of the standard deviation to the mean is $1/\sqrt{m}$. The measurement becomes more accurate the longer we wait, since more electrons are gathered. Again, the ratio of the "signal" to the "noise" only improves as the square root of the average number of electrons collected, however.

To obtain reasonable results, many electrons must be measured. It can be shown that a Poisson distribution with mean m is almost the same as a Gaussian distribution with mean m and variance m, provided that m is large. The Gaussian distribution is often easier to work with. In any case, to obtain a standard deviation that is one-thousandth of the mean, one must wait long enough to collect a million electrons. This is a small charge still, since one electron carries only

$$e = 1.602192\ldots \times 10^{-19} \text{ Coulomb.}$$

Even a million electrons have a charge of only about 160 fC (femto-Coulomb). (The prefix *femto-* denotes a multiplier of 10^{-15}.) It is not easy to measure such a small charge, since noise is introduced in the measurement process.

The number of electrons liberated from an area δA in time δt is

$$N = \delta A \, \delta t \int_{-\infty}^{\infty} b(\lambda) \, q(\lambda) \, d\lambda,$$

where $q(\lambda)$ is the quantum efficiency and $b(\lambda)$ is the image irradiance in photons per unit area. To obtain a usable result, then, electrons must be collected from a finite image area over a finite amount of time. There is thus a trade-off between (spatial and temporal) resolution and accuracy.

A measurement of the number of electrons liberated in a small area during a fixed time interval produces a result that is proportional to the irradiance (for fixed spectral distribution of incident photons). These measurements are quantized in order to read them into a digital computer. This is done by analog-to-digital (A/D) conversion. The result is called a *gray-level*. Since it is difficult to measure irradiance with great accuracy, it is reasonable to use a small set of numbers to represent the irradiance levels. The range 0 to 255 is often employed—requiring just 8 bits per gray-level.

2.5.3 Quantization of the Image

Because we can only transmit a finite number of measurements to a computer, spatial quantization is also required. It is common to make measurements at the nodes of a square raster or grid of points. The image is then represented as a rectangular array of integers. To obtain a reasonable amount of detail we need many measurements. Television frames, for example, might be quantized into 450 lines of 560 *picture cells*, sometimes referred to as *pixels*.

Each number represents the average irradiance over a small area. We cannot obtain a measurement at a point, as discussed above, because the flux of light is proportional to the sensing area. At first this might appear as a shortcoming, but it turns out to be an advantage. The reason is that we are trying to use a discrete set of numbers to represent a continuous distribution of brightness, and the sampling theorem tells us that this can be done successfully only if the continuous distribution is smooth, that is, if it does not contain high-frequency components. One way to make a smooth distribution of brightness is to look at the image through a filter that averages over small areas.

What is the optimal size of the sampling areas? It turns out that reasonable results are obtained if the dimensions of the sampling areas are approximately equal to their spacing. This is fortunate because it allows us to pack the image plane efficiently with sensing elements. Thus no photons need be wasted, nor must adjacent sampling areas overlap.

We have some latitude in dividing up the image plane into sensing areas. So far we have been discussing square areas on a square grid. The picture cells could equally well be rectangular, resulting in a different resolution in the horizontal and vertical directions. Other arrangements are also possible. Suppose we want to tile the plane with regular polygons. The tiles should not overlap, yet together they should cover the whole plane. We shall show in exercise 2-21 that there are exactly three tessellations, based on triangles, squares, and hexagons (figure 2-11).

It is easy to see how a square sampling pattern is obtained simply by taking measurements at equal intervals along equally spaced lines in the image. Hexagonal sampling is almost as easy, if odd-numbered lines are

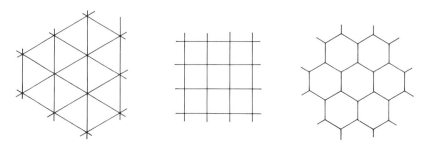

Figure 2-11. The plane can be tiled with three regular polygons: the triangle, the square, and the hexagon. Image tessellations can be based on these tilings. The gray-level of a picture cell is the quantized value of the measured power falling on the corresponding area in the image.

offset by half a sampling interval from even-numbered lines. In television scanning, the odd-numbered lines are read out after all the even-numbered lines because of field interlace, and so this scheme is particularly easy to implement. Hexagons on a triangular grid have certain advantages, which we shall come to later.

2.6 References

There are many standard references on basic optics, including *Principles of Optics: Electromagnetic Theory of Propagation, Interference and Diffraction of Light* by Born & Wolf [1975], *Handbook of Optics*, edited by Driscoll & Vaughan [1978], *Applied Optics: A Guide to Optical System Design* by Levi [volume 1, 1968; volume 2, 1980], and the classic *Optics* by Sears [1949]. Lens design and aberrations are covered by Kingslake in *Lens Design Fundamentals* [1978]. Norton discusses the basic workings of a large variety of sensors in *Sensor and Analyzer Handbook* [1982]. Barbe edited *Charge-Coupled Devices* [1980], a book that includes some information on the use of CCDs in image sensors.

There is no shortage of books on probability and statistics. One such is Drake's *Fundamentals of Applied Probability Theory* [1967].

Color vision is not treated in detail here, but is mentioned again in chapter 9 where we discuss the recovery of lightness. For a general discussion of color matching and tristimulus values see the first few chapters of *Color in Business, Science, and Industry* by Judd & Wyszeck [1975].

Some issues of color reproduction, including what constitutes an appropriate sensor system, are discussed by Horn [1984a]. Further references on color vision may be found at the end of chapter 9.

Straight lines in the three-dimensional world are projected as straight lines into the two-dimensional image. The projections of parallel lines intersect in a *vanishing point*. This is the point where a line parallel to the given lines passing through the center of projection intersects the image plane. In the case of rectangular objects, a great deal of information can be recovered from lines in the images and their intersections. See, for example, Barnard [1983].

When the medium between us and the scene being imaged is not perfectly transparent, the interpretation of images becomes more complicated. See, for example, Sjoberg & Horn [1983]. The reconstruction of absorbing density in a volume from measured ray attenuation is the subject of tomography; a book on this subject has been edited by Herman [1979].

2.7 Exercises

2-1 What is the shape of the image of a sphere? What is the shape of the image of a circular disk? Assume perspective projection and allow the disk to lie in a plane that can be tilted with respect to the image plane.

2-2 Show that the image of an ellipse in a plane, not necessarily one parallel to the image plane, is also an ellipse. Show that the image of a line in space is a line in the image. Assume perspective projection. Describe the brightness patterns in the image of a polyhedral object with uniform surface properties.

2-3 Suppose that an image is created by a camera in a certain world. Now imagine the same camera placed in a similar world in which everything is twice as large and all distances between objects have also doubled. Compare the new image with the one formed in the original world. Assume perspective projection.

2-4 Suppose that an image is created by a camera in a certain world. Now imagine the same camera placed in a similar world in which everything has half the reflectance and the incident light has been doubled. Compare the new image with the one formed in the original world. Hint: Ignore interflections, that is, illumination of one part of the scene by light reflected from another.

2-5 Show that in a properly focused imaging system the distance f' from the lens to the image plane equals $(1 + m)f$, where f is the focal length and m is the magnification. This distance is called the *effective focal length*. Show that the distance between the image plane and an object must be

$$\left(m + 2 + \frac{1}{m}\right) f.$$

How far must the object be from the lens for unit magnification?

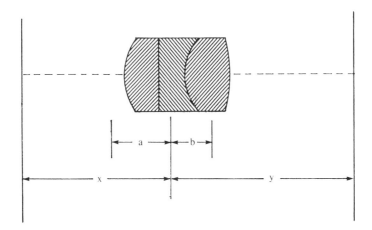

Figure 2-12. To determine the focal length and the positions of the principal planes, a number of measurements are made. Here, an object lying in a plane a distance x from an arbitrary reference point on one side of the lens is properly in focus in a plane on the other side at a distance y from the reference point. The two principal planes lie at distances a and b on either side of the reference point.

2-6   What is the focal length of a compound lens obtained by placing two thin lenses of focal length f_1 and f_2 against one another? Hint: Explain why an object at a distance f_1 on one side of the compound lens will be focused at a distance f_2 on the other side.

2-7   The *f-number* of a lens is the ratio of the focal length to the diameter of the lens. The f-number of a given lens (of fixed focal length) can be increased by introducing an aperture that intercepts some of the light and thus in effect reduces the diameter of the lens. Show that image brightness will be inversely proportional to the square of the f-number. Hint: Consider how much light is intercepted by the aperture.

2-8   When a camera is used to obtain metric information about the world, it is important to have accurate knowledge of the parameters of the lens, including the focal length and the positions of the principal planes. Suppose that a pattern in a plane at distance x on one side of the lens is found to be focused best on a plane at a distance y on the other side of the lens (figure 2-12). The distances x and y are measured from an arbitrary but fixed point in the lens. How many paired measurements like this are required to determine the focal length and the position of the two principal planes? (In practice, of course, more than the minimum required number of measurements would be taken, and a least-squares procedure would be adopted. Least-squares methods are discussed in the appendix.)

Suppose that the arbitrary reference point happens to lie between the two principal planes and that a and b are the distances of the principal planes from the reference point (figure 2-12). Note that $a + b$ is the thickness of the lens, as defined earlier. Show that

$$(ab + bf + fa) - \big(x_i(f + b) + y_i(f + a)\big) + x_i y_i = 0,$$

where x_i and y_i are the measurements obtained in the ith experiment. Suggest a way to find the unknowns from a set of nonlinear equations like this. Can a closed-form solution be obtained for f, a, b?

2-9 Here we explore a restricted case of the problem tackled in the previous exercise. Describe a method for determining the focal length and positions of the principal planes of a lens from the following three measurements: (a) the position of a plane on which a scene at infinity on one side of the lens appears in sharp focus; (b) the position of a plane on which a scene at infinity on the other side of the lens appears in sharp focus; (c) the positions of two planes, one on each side of the lens, such that one plane is imaged at unit magnification on the other.

2-10 Here we explore what happens when the image plane is tilted slightly. Show that in a pinhole camera, tilting the image plane amounts to nothing more than changing the place where the optical axis pierces the image plane and changing the perpendicular distance of the projection center from the image plane. What happens in a camera that uses a lens? Hint: Is a camera with an (ideal) lens different from a camera with a pinhole as far as image projection is concerned?

How would you determine experimentally where the optical axis pierces the image plane? Hint: It is difficult to find this point accurately.

2-11 It has been stated that perspective effects are significant when a wide-angle lens is used, while images obtained using a telephoto lenses tend to approximate orthographic projection. Explain why these are only rough rules of thumb.

2-12 Straight lines in the three-dimensional world are projected as straight lines into the two-dimensional image. The projections of parallel lines intersect in a *vanishing point*. Where in the image will the vanishing point of a particular family of parallel lines lie? When does the vanishing point of a family of parallel lines lie at infinity?

In the case of a rectangular object, a great deal of information can be recovered from lines in the images and their intersections. The edges of a rectangular solid fall into three sets of parallel lines, and so give rise to three vanishing points. In technical drawing one speaks of one-point, two-point, and three-point perspective. These terms apply to the cases in which two, one, or none of three vanishing points lie at infinity. What alignment between the edges of the rectangular object and the image plane applies in each case?

2-13   Typically, imaging systems are almost exactly rotationally symmetric about the optical axis. Thus distortions in the image plane are primarily radial. When very high precision is required, a lens can be calibrated to determine its radial distortion. Commonly, a polynomial of the form

$$\Delta r' = k_1(r') + k_3(r')^3 + k_5(r')^5 + \cdots$$

is fitted to the experimental data. Here $r' = \sqrt{x'^2 + y'^2}$ is the distance of a point in the image from the place where the optical axis pierces the image plane. Explain why no even powers of r' appear in the polynomial.

2-14   Suppose that a color-sensing system has three types of sensors and that the spectral sensitivity of each type is a sum of scaled versions of the human cone sensitivities. Show that two metameric colors will produce identical signals in the sensors.

Now show that a color-sensing system will have this property for all metamers only if the spectral sensitivity of each of its three sensor types is a sum of scaled versions of the human cone sensitivities. Warning: The second part of this problem is much harder than the first.

2-15   Show that the variance can be calculated as

$$\sigma^2 = \int_{-\infty}^{\infty} x^2 p(x)\, dx \; - \mu^2.$$

2-16   Here we consider the mean and standard deviation of the sum of two random variables.

(a) Show that the mean of $x = x_1 + x_2$ is the sum $\mu_1 + \mu_2$ of the means of the independent random variables x_1 and x_2.

(b) Show that the variance of $x = x_1 + x_2$ is the sum $\sigma_1^2 + \sigma_2^2$ of the variances of the independent random variables x_1 and x_2.

2-17   Suppose that the probability distribution of a random variable is

$$p(x) = \begin{cases} (1/2w), & \text{if } |x| \leq w; \\ 0, & \text{if } |x| > w. \end{cases}$$

What is the probability distribution of the average of two independent values from this distribution?

2-18   Here we consider some properties of the Gaussian and the Poisson distributions.

(a) Show that the mean and variance of the Gaussian distribution

$$p(x) = \frac{1}{\sqrt{2\pi}\sigma} e^{-\frac{1}{2}\left(\frac{x-\mu}{\sigma}\right)^2}$$

are μ and σ^2 respectively.

(b) Show that the mean and the variance of the Poisson distribution

$$p_n = e^{-m} \frac{m^n}{n!}$$

are both equal to m.

2-19   Consider the weighted sum of independent random variables

$$\sum_{i=1}^{N} w_i x_i,$$

where x_i has mean m and standard deviation σ. Assume that the weights w_i add up to one. What are the mean and standard deviation of the weighted sum? For fixed N, what choice of weights minimizes the variance?

2-20   A television frame is scanned in $1/30$ second. All the even-numbered lines in one field are followed by all the odd-numbered lines in the other field. Assume that there are about 450 lines of interest, each to be divided into 560 picture cells. At what rate must the conversion from analog to digital form occur? (Ignore time intervals between lines and between successive frames.)

2-21   Show that there are only three regular polygons with which the plane can be tiled, namely (a) the equilateral triangle, (b) the square, and (c) the hexagon. (By *tiling* we mean covering without gaps or overlap.)

3

Binary Images:
Geometric Properties

In this chapter we explore black-and-white (two-valued) images. These are easier to acquire, store, and process than images in which many brightness levels are represented. However, since binary images encode only information about the silhouette of an object, they are useful only in restricted situations. We discuss the conditions that must be satisfied for the successful application of binary image-processing techniques. In this chapter we concentrate on simple geometric properties such as image area, position, and orientation. These quantities are useful in directing the interaction of a mechanical manipulator with a part, for example. Other aspects of binary images, such as methods for iterative modification, are explored in the next chapter.

Since images contain a great deal of information, issues of representation become important. We show that the geometric properties of interest can be computed from projections of binary images. These projections are a great deal easier to store and to process. In much of this chapter we deal with continuous binary images, where a characteristic function is either zero or one at every point in the image plane. This makes the presentation simpler; but when we use a digital computer, the image must be divided into picture cells. The chapter concludes with a discussion of discrete binary images and ways of exploiting their spatial coherence to reduce transmission and storage costs, as well as processing time.

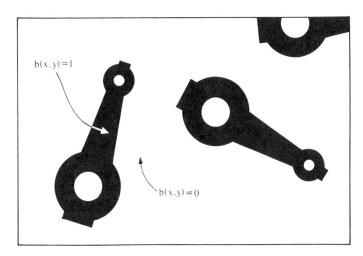

Figure 3-1. A binary image is defined by a characteristic function $b(x, y)$ that takes on the values zero or one. Often a binary image is obtained by thresholding an ordinary image. It can also result from thresholding distance in an "image" obtained by a distance-measuring technique.

3.1 Binary Images

Let us start by considering a single object in the field of view, with everything else taken as "background." If the object appears consistently darker (or brighter) than the background, it is easy to define a *characteristic function* $b(x, y)$ that is zero for all image points corresponding to the background and one for points on the object (figure 3-1). Such a two-valued function, called a *binary image*, can be obtained by *thresholding* the gray-level image. The thresholding operation simply defines the characteristic function to be zero where the brightness is greater than some threshold value and one where it is not (or vice versa).

Sometimes it is convenient to think of the image components, as well as the holes in them, as sets. This will allow us to combine images using set operations such as union and intersection. At other times it is convenient to use point-by-point Boolean operations, such as logical *and* ($\wedge$) and logical *or* ($\vee$). These are just two different ways of looking at the same basic operations.

For a given image size, a binary image is easier to digitize, store, and transmit than a full gray-level image, since it contains about an order of magnitude fewer bits. Naturally, some information is lost and fewer options are open to us in processing such an image. In fact, we can present a fairly complete theory of what can and cannot be done with binary images, something that still eludes us in the case of gray-level images.

First of all, we can compute various geometric properties, such as the size and position of the object in the image. If there is more than one object in the field of view, we can determine some topological properties of the assembly, such as the difference between the number of objects and the number of holes. It is also possible to label the individual objects and to perform the geometrical computations for each one separately. Finally, we can simplify binary images for further processing by modifying them in an iterative fashion.

Binary image processing is well understood and lends itself to high-speed hardware implementation, but one must keep in mind its limitations. We have already mentioned the need for high object-to-background contrast. Moreover, the pattern obtained must be essentially two-dimensional. Remember that all we have is the outline or silhouette of the object. This gives little information about the object's overall shape or its attitude in space.

The characteristic function $b(x, y)$ has a value for each point in the image. We call this a *continuous* binary image. Later, we shall consider discrete binary images, obtained by tessellating the image plane suitably.

3.2 Simple Geometrical Properties

Assume for now that we have a single object in the field of view. The area of the object, given the characteristic function $b(x, y)$, can be found as follows:

$$A = \iint_I b(x, y)\, dx\, dy,$$

where the integration is over the whole image I. If there is more than one object, this formula will give the total area.

3.2.1 Area and Position

How do we determine the position of the object in the image? Since the object is usually not just a single point, we must give a precise meaning to the term "position." The usual practice is to choose the center of area as the representative point (figure 3-2). The center of area is the center of mass of a figure of the same shape with constant mass per unit area. The center of mass, in turn, is that point where all the mass of the object could be concentrated without changing the first moment of the object about any axis. In the two-dimensional case the moment about the x-axis is

$$\overline{x} \iint_I b(x, y)\, dx\, dy = \iint_I x\, b(x, y)\, dx\, dy,$$

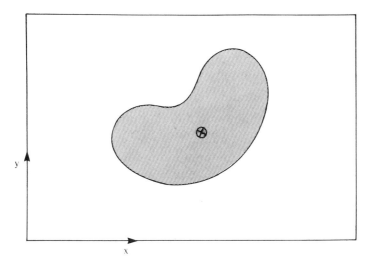

Figure 3-2. The position of a region in a binary image can be defined by the center of area of the region. This is the center of mass of a thin sheet of material of the same shape.

and the moment about the y-axis is

$$\overline{y} \iint_I b(x,y)\,dx\,dy = \iint_I y\,b(x,y)\,dx\,dy,$$

where $(\overline{x}, \overline{y})$ is the position of the center of area. The integrals appearing on the left of these equations are, of course, just the area A, as noted above. To find $\overline{x}$ and $\overline{y}$ we must assume that A is not equal to zero. Note, by the way, that A is the zeroth moment of $b(x,y)$.

3.2.2 Orientation

We also want to determine how the object lies in the field of view, that is, its *orientation*. This is a little harder. Let us assume that the object is somewhat elongated; then the orientation of the axis of elongation can be used to define the orientation of the object (figure 3-3). (There is a remaining two-way ambiguity, however, as discussed in exercise 3-7.) How precisely do we define the direction in which the object is elongated? The usual practice is to choose the axis of least second moment. This is the two-dimensional equivalent of the axis of least inertia. We find the line for which the integral of the square of the distance to points in the object is a

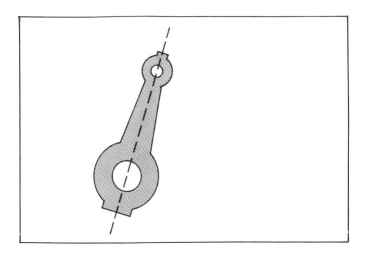

Figure 3-3. The orientation of a region in the image can be defined by the direction of the axis of least inertia. This is the axis about which the second moment of a thin sheet of material of the same shape is smallest.

minimum; that integral is

$$E = \iint_I r^2 b(x, y)\, dx\, dy,$$

where r is the perpendicular distance from the point (x, y) to the line sought after.

To choose a particular line in the plane, we need to specify two parameters. A convenient pair consists of the distance ρ from the origin to the closest point on the line, and the angle θ between the x-axis and the line, measured counterclockwise (figure 3-4). We prefer these parameters because they change continuously when the coordinate system is translated or rotated. There are no problems when the line is parallel, or nearly parallel, to either of the coordinate axes.

Using these parameters, we can write the equation of the line in the form

$$x \sin \theta - y \cos \theta + \rho = 0$$

by noting that the line intersects the x-axis at $-\rho/\sin\theta$ and the y-axis at $+\rho/\cos\theta$. The closest point on the line to the origin is at $(-\rho\sin\theta, +\rho\cos\theta)$. We can write parametric equations for points on the line as follows:

$$x_0 = -\rho\sin\theta + s\cos\theta \qquad \text{and} \qquad y_0 = +\rho\cos\theta + s\sin\theta,$$

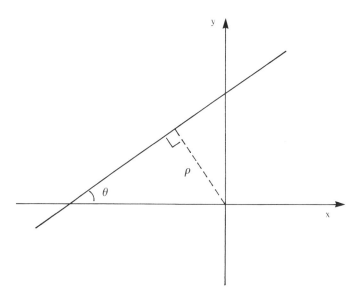

Figure 3-4. Two parameters useful for identifying a particular line in the plane are its inclination θ relative to the x-axis, and its perpendicular distance ρ from the origin.

where s is the distance along the line from the point closest to the origin.

Given a point (x, y) on the object, we need to find the closest point (x_0, y_0) on the line, so that we can compute the distance r between the point and the line (figure 3-5). Clearly

$$r^2 = (x - x_0)^2 + (y - y_0)^2.$$

Substituting the parametric equations for x_0 and y_0 we obtain

$$r^2 = (x^2 + y^2) + \rho^2 + 2\rho(x \sin \theta - y \cos \theta) - 2s(x \cos \theta + y \sin \theta) + s^2.$$

Differentiating with respect to s and setting the result equal to zero lead to

$$s = x \cos \theta + y \sin \theta.$$

This result can now be substituted back into the parametric equations for x_0 and y_0. From these we can compute the differences

$$x - x_0 = + \sin \theta \left(x \sin \theta - y \cos \theta + \rho \right),$$

$$y - y_0 = - \cos \theta \left(x \sin \theta - y \cos \theta + \rho \right),$$

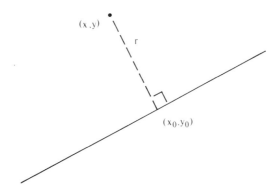

Figure 3-5. The perpendicular distance from a point (x, y) to a line can be found easily, once the closest point on the line, (x_0, y_0), is identified.

and thus

$$r^2 = (x \sin \theta - y \cos \theta + \rho)^2.$$

Comparing this result with the equation for the line, we see that the line is the locus of points for which $r = 0$! Conversely, it becomes apparent that the way we chose to parameterize the line has the advantage of giving us the distance from the line directly.

Finally, we can now address the minimization of

$$E = \iint_I (x \sin \theta - y \cos \theta + \rho)^2 \, b(x, y) \, dx \, dy.$$

Differentiating with respect to ρ and setting the result to zero lead to

$$A(\bar{x} \sin \theta - \bar{y} \cos \theta + \rho) = 0,$$

where $(\bar{x}, \bar{y})$ is the center of area defined above. Thus the axis of least second moment passes through the center of area. This suggests a change of coordinates to $x' = x - \bar{x}$ and $y' = y - \bar{y}$, for

$$x \sin \theta - y \cos \theta + \rho = x' \sin \theta - y' \cos \theta,$$

and so

$$E = a \sin^2 \theta - b \sin \theta \cos \theta + c \cos^2 \theta,$$

where a, b, and c are the second moments given by

$$a = \iint_{I'} (x')^2 \, b(x,y) \, dx' \, dy',$$

$$b = 2 \iint_{I'} (x'y') \, b(x,y) \, dx' \, dy',$$

$$c = \iint_{I'} (y')^2 \, b(x,y) \, dx' \, dy'.$$

Now we can write the formula for E in the form

$$E = \frac{1}{2}(a+c) - \frac{1}{2}(a-c)\cos 2\theta - \frac{1}{2}b\sin 2\theta.$$

Differentiating with respect to θ and setting the result to zero, we have

$$\tan 2\theta = \frac{b}{a-c},$$

unless $b = 0$ and $a = c$. Consequently

$$\sin 2\theta = \pm \frac{b}{\sqrt{b^2 + (a-c)^2}} \quad \text{and} \quad \cos 2\theta = \pm \frac{a-c}{\sqrt{b^2 + (a-c)^2}}.$$

Of the two solutions, the one with the plus signs in the expressions for $\sin 2\theta$ and $\cos 2\theta$ leads to the desired minimum for E. Conversely, the solution with minus signs in the two expressions corresponds to the maximum value for E. (This can be shown by considering the second derivative of E with respect to θ.) If $b = 0$ and $a = c$, we find that E is independent of θ. In this case, the object is too symmetric to allow us to define an axis in this way. The ratio of the smallest value for E to the largest tells us something about how "rounded" the object is. This ratio is zero for a straight line and one for a circle.

Another way to look at the problem is to seek the rotation θ that makes the 2×2 matrix of second moments diagonal. We show in exercise 3-5 that the calculation above essentially amounts to finding the eigenvalues and eigenvectors of the 2×2 matrix of second moments given by

$$\begin{pmatrix} a & b/2 \\ b/2 & c \end{pmatrix}.$$

3.3 Projections

The position and orientation of an object can be calculated using first and second moments only. (There is a remaining two-way ambiguity, however, as discussed in exercise 3-7.) We do not need the original image to obtain

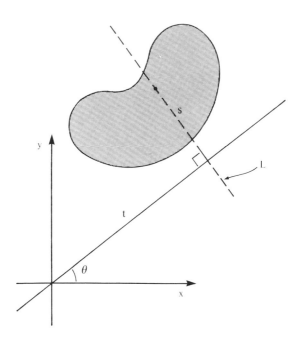

Figure 3-6. The projection of a region in the image onto a line that makes an angle θ with respect to the x-axis can be found by integrating along lines such as the one shown at L.

the first and second moments; projections of the image are sufficient. This is of interest since the projections are more compact and suggest much faster algorithms.

Consider a line through the origin inclined at an angle θ with respect to the x-axis (figure 3-6). Now construct a new line, intersecting the original line at right angles, at a point that is a distance t from the origin. Let distance along the new line be designated s. The integral of $b(x, y)$ along the new line gives one value of the *projection*. That is,

$$p_\theta(t) = \int_L b(t \cos \theta - s \sin \theta, t \sin \theta + s \cos \theta) \, ds.$$

The integration is carried out over the portion of the line L that lies within the image. The vertical projection ($\theta = 0$), for example, is simply

$$v(x) = \int_L b(x, y) \, dy,$$

while the horizontal projection ($\theta = \pi/2$) is

$$h(y) = \int_L b(x, y)\, dx.$$

Now, since

$$A = \iint_I b(x, y)\, dx\, dy,$$

we have

$$A = \int v(x)\, dx = \int h(y)\, dy.$$

More important,

$$\bar{x}A = \iint_I x\, b(x, y)\, dx\, dy = \int x\, v(x)\, dx$$

and

$$\bar{y}A = \iint_I y\, b(x, y)\, dx\, dy = \int y\, h(y)\, dy.$$

Thus the first moments of the projections are equal to the first moments of the original image.

To compute orientation we need the second moments, too. Two of these are easy to compute from the projections:

$$\iint_I x^2\, dx\, dy = \int x^2 v(x)\, dx \qquad \text{and} \qquad \iint_I y^2\, dx\, dy = \int y^2 h(y)\, dy.$$

We cannot, however, compute the integral of the product xy from the two projections introduced so far. We can add the diagonal projection ($\theta = \pi/4$),

$$d(t) = \int b\left(\frac{1}{\sqrt{2}}(t - s), \frac{1}{\sqrt{2}}(t + s) \right) ds.$$

Now consider that

$$\iint_I \frac{1}{2}(x + y)^2\, b(x, y)\, dx\, dy = \iint_I t^2\, b(x, y)\, ds\, dt = \int t^2\, d(t)\, dt,$$

and that

$$\iint_I \frac{1}{2}(x + y)^2\, b(x, y)\, dx\, dy = \iint_I \left(\frac{1}{2}x^2 + xy + \frac{1}{2}y^2 \right) b(x, y)\, dx\, dy.$$

So

$$\iint_I xy\, b(x, y)\, dx\, dy = \int t^2 d(t)\, dt - \frac{1}{2}\int x^2 v(x)\, dx - \frac{1}{2}\int y^2 h(y)\, dy.$$

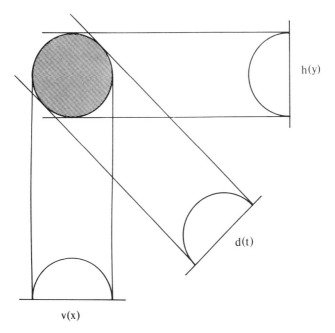

Figure 3-7. The horizontal, vertical, and diagonal projections contain all the information needed to compute the zeroth, first, and second moments of a region in the image. These moments, in turn, provide all of the information that we need to obtain the position and orientation of the region.

Thus all the integrals needed for the computation of the position and orientation of a region in the binary image can be found from the horizontal, diagonal, and vertical projections (figure 3-7).

It is interesting to compare tomographic reconstruction with what we are doing here. In *tomography* one obtains integrals of the absorbing density of the material in some body. The problem is to reconstruct the distribution of the material. In the case of X-ray tomography, the body is commonly treated as a stack of slices, and each slice is considered a separate two-dimensional problem. The projections obtained are analogous to the projections discussed above. It can be shown that the distribution of absorbing material can be determined if we have the projections for all directions, provided that the density is zero outside some bounded region.

How does tomographic reconstruction relate to what we are doing here? The main difference is that in our case the function over which the line integrals are taken can only have values zero and one. The other difference is that we are not capturing sufficient information to reconstruct the original

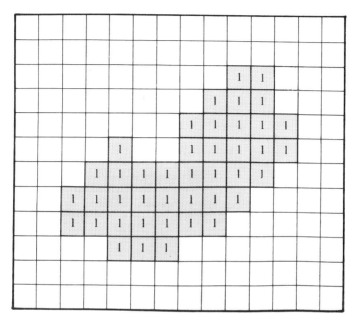

Figure 3-8. A discrete binary image consists of individual picture cells, each of which may be either a zero or a one.

binary image, but only enough to determine the center of area and axis of least inertia. There are some interesting unsolved problems in the reconstruction of binary images from projections. Suppose, for example, that there is only one region that is nonzero and that this region is convex. How many projections are required to determine fully the outline of the region? Further, are there any noncircular shapes that have the same horizontal and vertical projections as a circle?

3.4 Discrete Binary Images

So far we have dealt with continuous binary images, defined at all points in the image plane. It should be obvious that the integrals become sums when we turn to discrete binary images (figure 3-8). The area, for example, can be computed (in units of the area of a picture cell) using the sum

$$A = \sum_{i=1}^{n} \sum_{j=1}^{m} b_{ij},$$

where b_{ij} is the value of the binary image at the point in the ith row and the jth column. Here we have assumed that the image has been digitized on a square grid with n rows and m columns.

Usually the image is scanned out row by row, in the same sequence as the beam on a television set explores the screen (except for interlace). As each picture cell is read, we check whether $b_{ij} = 1$. If so, we add 1, i, j, i^2, ij, and j^2 to the accumulated totals for the area, first moments, and second moments, as appropriate. At the end of the scan, the area, position, and orientation can be easily calculated from these totals.

3.5 Run-Length Coding

For binary images there are several coding techniques that can compress the data even further. A popular one is *run-length coding*. This method exploits the fact that along any particular scan line there will usually be long *runs* of zeros or ones. Instead of transmitting the individual bits, then, we can send numbers indicating the lengths of such runs. The run-length code for the image line

0	1	1	1	1	0	0	0	1	1	0	0	0	0

is just $[1, 4, 3, 2, 4]$. Some special code may be used to indicate the beginning of each line. Further, a convention is followed as to whether the line starts with a zero or a one. If the line starts the other way, an initial run-length code of zero is sent.

Let us use the convention that r_{ik} is the kth run of the ith line and that the first run in each row is a run of zeros. (Thus all the even runs will correspond to ones in the image.) Suppose further that there are m_i runs on the ith line. (This number will be odd if the last run contains zeros.) How do we use run-length codes to rapidly compute the desired geometric properties? Clearly the area is just the sum of the run lengths corresponding to ones in the image:

$$A = \sum_{i=1}^{n} \sum_{k=1}^{m_i/2} r_{i,2k}.$$

Note that the sum is over the even runs only. The center of area is a little harder to calculate. First of all, we obtain the horizontal projection (figure 3-9) as follows:

$$h_i = \sum_{k=1}^{m_i/2} r_{i,2k}.$$

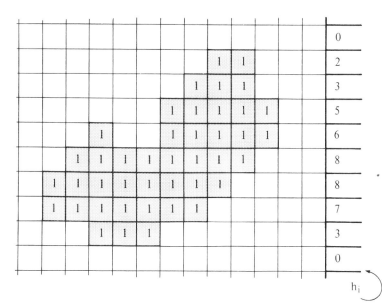

Figure 3-9. The horizontal projection gives for each row the number of picture cells in the row that have the value one. This projection is easy to obtain from the run-length-coded image. We simply take the sum of the even runs in each row.

From this we can easily compute the vertical position $\bar{i}$ of the center of area using

$$A\bar{i} = \sum_{i=1}^{n} i\,h_i.$$

But what about the vertical projection v_j? Remember that a particular entry in this projection is obtained by adding up all picture cell values in one column of the image. It is therefore hard to compute the vertical projection directly from the run lengths.

Now consider instead the first difference of the vertical projection,

$$\bar{v}_j = v_j - v_{j-1}, \quad \text{with } \bar{v}_1 = v_1.$$

Clearly it can be obtained by projecting not the image data, but the first horizontal differences of the image data:

$$\bar{b}_{i,j} = b_{i,j} - b_{i,j-1}.$$

The first difference $\bar{b}_{ij}$ has the advantage over b_{ij} itself that it is nonzero only at the beginning of each run. It equals $+1$ where the data change from

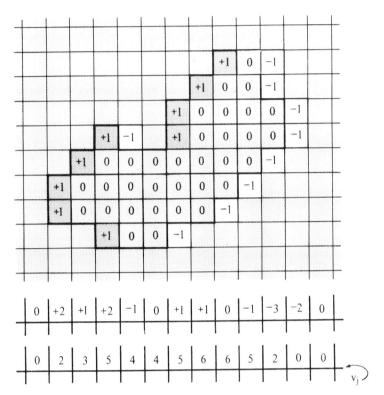

Figure 3-10. The first difference of the vertical projection can be computed from the projection of the first differences of the rows of the image. The vertical projection itself can then be found by summing the result from left to right.

a 0 to a 1, and -1 where the data change from a 1 to a 0 (figure 3-10). We can locate these places by computing the summed run-length code $\widetilde{r}_{ik}$:

$$\widetilde{r}_{ik} = 1 + \sum_{l=1}^{k} r_{il}$$

or, recursively, $\widetilde{r}_{i,0} = 1$ and $\widetilde{r}_{i,j+1} = \widetilde{r}_{i,j} + r_{i,j}$. Then, for a transition at $j = \widetilde{r}_{ik}$ we add $(-1)^{k+1}$ to the accumulated total for the first difference of the vertical projection $\overline{v}_j$.

From this first difference we can compute the vertical projection itself using the simple summation

$$v_j = \sum_{l=1}^{j} \overline{v}_l,$$

or, recursively, $v_0 = 0$ and $v_{j+1} = v_j + \overline{v}_{j+1}$. The computation is illustrated figure 3-10. Given the vertical projection, we can easily compute the horizontal position $\overline{j}$ of the center of area using

$$A\overline{j} = \sum_{j=1}^{m} j\, v_j.$$

We shall show in exercise 3-8 that the diagonal projection can be obtained in a way similar to that used to obtain the vertical projection.

3.6 References

Another discussion of binary image processing can be found in *Digital Picture Processing* by Rosenfeld & Kak [1982]. The book edited by Stoffel, *Graphical and Binary Image Processing and Applications* [1982], contains some interesting recent work in binary image processing. To see implementations of some of the algorithms discussed here, look in the chapter on binary image processing in *Lisp*, by Winston & Horn [1984]. Many interesting binary images produced by artists can be found in *Silhouettes—A Pictorial Archive of Varied Illustrations*, edited by Grafton [1979].

Run-length coding only exploits redundancy along one dimension. There have been several attempts to make use of spatial coherence in two dimensions in order to reduce transmission and storage costs. Perhaps the most successful scheme of this nature so far is that developed by IBM and described by Mitchell & Goertzel [1979]. Further references relating to binary image processing may be found at the end of the next chapter.

Simon Kahan of Bell Labs has solved one of the problems at the end of section 3.3. He has proven that no noncircular shape has the same horizontal and vertical projections as a circle.

3.7 Exercises

3-1   The extreme values of the moment of inertia can be written as

$$E = \frac{1}{2}(a + c) \pm \frac{1}{2}\sqrt{b^2 + (a - c)^2},$$

where a, b, and c are as defined in this chapter. Show that $E \geq 0$. When is $E = 0$?

3-2 Rewrite the expression for the second moment about an axis inclined by an angle θ,

$$E = \frac{1}{2}(a+c) - \frac{1}{2}(a-c)\cos 2\theta - \frac{1}{2}b\sin 2\theta,$$

in the form

$$E = \frac{1}{2}(a+c) + \sqrt{b^2 - (a-c)^2}\cos 2(\theta - \phi).$$

What is the angle ϕ?

3-3 Let a, b, and c be the integrals defined in this chapter.

(a) Write a, b, and c in terms of integrals over x and y, instead of x' and y'.

(b) Find expressions for $\sin\theta$ and $\cos\theta$ from the expressions given for $\sin 2\theta$ and $\cos 2\theta$.

3-4 It is useful, at times, to replace a shape with one that is simpler but has the same zeroth, first, and second moments. Consider a region whose boundary is an ellipse with semimajor axis α along the x-axis and semiminor axis β along the y-axis. The equation of this ellipse is

$$\left(\frac{x}{\alpha}\right)^2 + \left(\frac{y}{\beta}\right)^2 = 1.$$

Show that the minimum and maximum second moments of the region about an axis through the origin are

$$\frac{\pi}{4}\alpha\beta^3 \quad\text{and}\quad \frac{\pi}{4}\beta\alpha^3,$$

respectively. Now the second moment of any region about an axis inclined at an angle θ can be written in the form

$$E = a\sin^2\theta - b\sin\theta\cos\theta + c\cos^2\theta.$$

Compute the major and minor axes of an equivalent ellipse, that is, one that has the same second moment about any axis through the origin.

3-5 A vector $\mathbf{v}$ with the property that $\mathbf{Mv} = \lambda\mathbf{v}$ for some λ is called an *eigenvector* of the matrix $\mathbf{M}$. The constant multiplier λ is the corresponding *eigenvalue*.

(a) Show that the symmetric 2×2 matrix

$$\begin{pmatrix} a & b/2 \\ b/2 & c \end{pmatrix}$$

has two real eigenvalues given by

$$\frac{1}{2}(a+c) \pm \frac{1}{2}\sqrt{b^2 + (a-c)^2}.$$

Hint: A homogeneous set of linear equations has a solution only when the determinant of the coefficient matrix equals zero.

(b) Show that the corresponding eigenvectors are given by

$$\left(\sqrt{\sqrt{(a-c)^2 + b^2} - (c-a)}, +\sqrt{\sqrt{(a-c)^2 + b^2} - (a-c)} \right)^T,$$

and

$$\left(\sqrt{\sqrt{(a-c)^2 + b^2} - (a-c)}, -\sqrt{\sqrt{(a-c)^2 + b^2} - (c-a)} \right)^T.$$

(c) Show that the two eigenvectors are orthogonal and have magnitude

$$\sqrt{2\sqrt{(a-c)^2 + b^2}}.$$

(d) Relate these results to the problem of finding the axis of least inertia.

3-6 Show how the integral

$$\iint_I xy\, b(x,y)\, dx\, dy$$

can be computed from the horizontal and vertical projections and a projection $p_\theta(t)$ at angle θ, where

$$p_\theta(t) = \int b(t\cos\theta - s\sin\theta, t\sin\theta + s\cos\theta)\, ds.$$

What restriction must be placed on θ ?

3-7 The axis of least inertia uniquely defines a line through an object. The methods introduced so far do not, however, assign an orientation to this line. This two-way ambiguity in determining orientation may be significant in some applications. One can use auxiliary measurements to provide the needed extra bit of information. For example, it may be helpful to know where the point on the silhouette is that is furthest from the center of area.

Alternatively, we can consider computing higher-order moments. How many projections are required to find all moments up to the third? Which projections are most conveniently added to the ones we already have, that is, the horizontal ($\rightarrow$), the vertical ($\downarrow$), and the diagonal from NW to SE ($\seardiagonal$)?

3-8   Show exactly how diagonal projections in the NW-to-SE ($\searrow$) and NE-to-SW ($\swarrow$) directions can be computed from the run lengths.

3-9   If the scan line is very long, many bits must be reserved for each run-length number (for 4,096 picture cells, 12-bit numbers are needed). This is wasteful if most runs are short. Devise a scheme in which shorter numbers are sent.

3-10   Can the run-length code ever be less compact than the original image? If so, suggest preprocessing methods that might alleviate the problem.

3-11   Assuming a fixed picture, estimate how the number of bits increases when the number of rows and the number of columns are doubled. Consider both straightforward binary encoding as well as run-length coding of the image.

3-12   Suppose we have the following runs, r_{ik}:

1	4	2	5	2
1	8	1	3	1
2	6	2	2	2

Find the summed run-length codes $\bar{r}_{ik}$. From these find $\bar{v}_j$, the first difference of the vertical projection. Show that the vertical projection v_j is

0	2	3	3	3	2	2	3	2	1	3	3	1	0

3-13   In this chapter we have assumed that a binary image is represented by a matrix of zeros and ones. We might equally well use a list of the boundary curves of the regions in the image. Each boundary could be approximated by a polygon, for example. Show that the area of a region R can be computed as follows:

$$A = + \oint_{\partial R} x\,dy = - \oint_{\partial R} y\,dx,$$

where the integrals are taken in a counterclockwise fashion around the boundary ∂R of the region R. Develop similar integrals for the first and second moments needed in the computation of the center of area and the axis of least inertia. Hint: Use Gauss's integral theorem for converting area integrals into loop integrals.

4

Binary Images: Topological Properties

In this chapter we deal with cases in which more than one object appears in the field of view, and develop some more sophisticated methods for recovering information from binary images. In order to do this, we need to define carefully what it means for two picture cells to be connected. We study this question for different image tessellations and develop means for labeling distinct image components in a sequential pass over the image.

Images contain a lot of information. One hope for processing such data in a reasonable amount of time lies in massively parallel architectures. There are two elegant classes of methods for processing binary images in parallel: local counting methods and iterative modification methods. Both are explored in this chapter. To understand just what quantities can be computed in this way, we introduce the additive set property.

The methods developed here can be applied to problems in visual inspection, object detection, and recognition.

4.1 Multiple Objects

At times more than one object is in the field of view (figure 4-1). The calculations of area, center of area, and orientation will produce an "average" value for all the components of the binary image. This is usually not what is desired. Somehow the separate components of the image must be

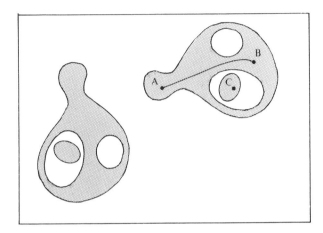

Figure 4-1. When several regions occur in an image, the computations of position and orientation have to be carried out separately for each. Picture cells must be labeled so that those belonging to a particular region can be distinguished from the rest. To do this we need to decide which points belong to the same region. Here A is considered to be connected to B because we can find a continuous curve connecting the two that lies entirely in the black region. Clearly A is not connected to C, because no such curve can be found.

labeled, and totals for the area and the first and second moments accumulated separately for each component.

4.1.1 Labeling Components

We consider two points in a binary image to be connected if a path can be found along which the characteristic function is constant. Thus in figure 4-1, A is connected to B but not connected to C. A *connected component* of a binary image is a maximal set of connected points, that is, a set such that a path can be found between any two of its points and all connected points are included. In the figure, there are four connected components and four holes (in addition to the background).

One way to label the objects in a discrete binary image is to choose a point where $b_{ij} = 1$ and assign a label to this point and its neighbors. Next, label all the neighbors of these neighbors (except those that have already been labeled), and so on. When this recursive procedure terminates, one component will have been labeled completely, and we can continue by choosing another point. To find new places to start from, we can simply scan through the image in any systematic way, starting a labeling operation whenever an unlabeled point is found where $b_{ij} = 1$. When we have tried every cell in this scan, all the objects in the binary image will have been assigned a label.

It should be clear that the "background" may be broken up into connected components, too—the objects can have holes. We can label these with a similar scheme, taking note of zeros instead of ones.

4.1.2 Connectedness

We have yet to consider carefully the meaning of the term *neighbor*. If we are dealing with a square tessellation, we should presumably regard the four picture cells touching a given cell on the edges as neighbors. But what about the four cells touching on the corner? There are two possibilities:

- Four-connectedness: only edge-adjacent cells are considered neighbors.

- Eight-connectedness: corner-adjacent cells are considered neighbors, too.

These alternatives are shown in the following diagrams:

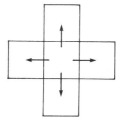 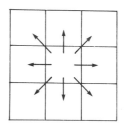

It turns out that neither of these choices is entirely satisfactory. We can see this by recalling that the background can be divided into connected components also. We would like our intuitions about connected components in continuous binary images to apply here. Thus, for example, a simple closed curve should separate the image into two simply connected regions (figure 4-2). This is called the *Jordan curve theorem*.

Now consider a simple image containing four picture cells with values one, each touching a central cell, which is zero:

0	1	0
1	0	1
0	1	0

This is a cross with the center missing. If we adopt the convention of four-connectedness, we see that there are four separate object components (O_1, O_2, O_3, and O_4):

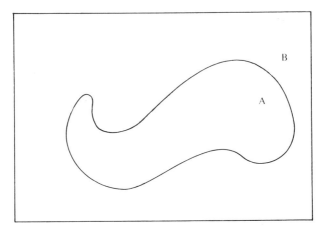

Figure 4-2. A simple closed curve divides the plane into two simply connected regions.

B_1	O_1	B_1
O_2	B_2	O_3
B_1	O_4	B_1

The four objects certainly do not form a closed curve, yet the background cell in the middle is not connected to the rest of the background. We have two background regions without a closed curve! Conversely, if we adopt the convention of eight-connectedness, the four picture cells do form a closed curve, yet the background cell in the middle is connected to the rest of the background:

B	O	B
O	B	O
B	O	B

We have a closed curve and only one background region!

One solution to this dilemma is to use four-connectedness for the object and eight-connectedness for the background (or vice versa). This asymmetry in the treatment of object and background may be undesirable, and it can be avoided by introducing a different kind of asymmetry. We regard as neighbors the four picture cells touching a given one on an edge as well as two of the four picture cells touching on the corners:

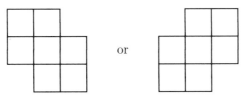

or

The two corner cells must be on the same diagonal to ensure symmetry in the relationship; that is, if picture cell A is a neighbor of picture cell B, then picture cell B should be a neighbor of picture cell A. From now on we shall use the first of the two options shown above, regarding the cells in the directions N, E, SE, S, W, and NW ($\uparrow,\rightarrow,\searrow,\downarrow,\leftarrow,\nwarrow$) as neighbors. Both object and background can be treated using six-connectedness without further inconsistencies. We shall use this convention for images with square tessellations.

On a hexagonal tessellation life is easier. All six picture cells touching a particular central cell are neighbors, so there is no ambiguity. What we have done above can be viewed as a simple skewing of the square grid into a hexagonal grid. To see this, consider shifting the row above a particular picture cell a half cell width to the right while shifting the row below to the left by the same amount:

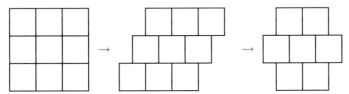

The chosen picture cell now touches six others, and they are exactly the ones we used in the definition of six-connectedness.

4.1.3 A Sequential Labeling Algorithm

We are now ready to describe a labeling algorithm that is better suited to sequential scanning of the image and does not require recursive calls. Suppose we are scanning row by row, top to bottom, and left to right (figure 4-3). Then, when we examine a particular cell, A, we know that the cell to its left, B, has been labeled, as has the cell directly above it, C. Further, D, the cell above B, is considered connected to A and must also be taken into account.

To simplify matters, assume that we are only labeling object components at the moment. Then if A is zero, there is nothing to do. If A is one, and if D has been labeled, we simply copy that label and move on. Similarly if one of B or C is labeled, we again copy that label. If neither B nor C is labeled, we must choose a new label for A. As far as we can tell, this is the first time we have run into a new component. The remaining

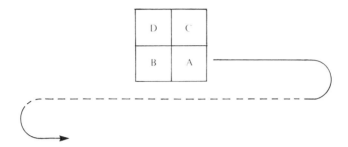

Figure 4-3. Labeling decisions are based on the labels already assigned to the four picture cells in a pattern window that is moved across the image in a regular raster scan.

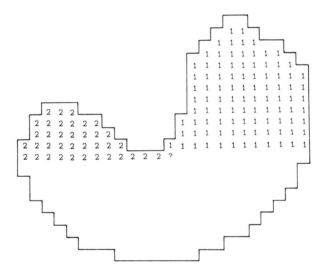

Figure 4-4. In the sequential labeling process we might discover that two regions previously thought to be separate are in fact connected. We must make a note of the equivalence of the two labels. (Reproduced by permission from *Lisp* by P.H. Winston & B.K.P. Horn, Addison-Wesley, Reading, Massachusetts, 1984.)

possibility is that both *B* and *C* carry labels. There is no problem if *B* and *C* have the same label; but since they are not neighbors in our scheme, they may have different labels. In this case we have just discovered that two different labels have both been used for parts of one component (figure 4-4). The parts are connected through *A*. We must make a note at this point that the two labels are equivalent, and use one of them for *A*.

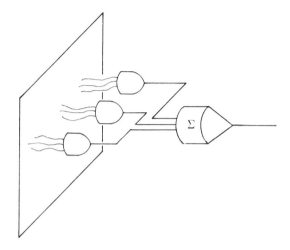

Figure 4-5. Local counting methods combine outputs from individual computing cells each connected to a few picture cells in a small neighborhood.

This is the price we pay for the sequential algorithm.

At the end of the scan, data for all parts with equivalent labels have to be merged. If all we are doing is accumulating totals for computing zeroth, first, and second moments, we can avoid even this step. We simply add the totals accumulated so far for the two components and add future increments to the combined totals.

If we wish to show the regions with unique labels, we need to do a second scan over the image, assigning to each region a representative label from the equivalence class to which its original label belongs.

4.2 Local Counting and Iterative Modification

So far we have concentrated on sequential processing of the information in a binary image. To increase speed and utilize the power of large-scale integrated circuits, we should also consider what can be computed by applying *local operations* in parallel to a binary image. By *local* we mean that each of the operations receives inputs only from a small area of the image.

There are two types of computations that can be done this way: We can combine, perhaps just by adding them up, the results of all the local operations to obtain a result in one step (figure 4-5) or we can create a new image from outputs of the local operations. The latter technique will be discussed in the next section.

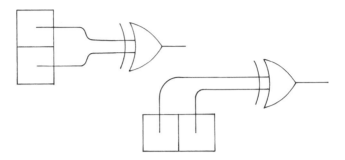

Figure 4-6. Places on the edge of an image region can be detected by taking the logical exclusive-or of values in neighboring cells.

4.2.1 Local Counting

Consider a very simple case first. Each of the local operators looks at a single picture cell and reports its value. When the outputs of the local operators are summed, the result is the total area of the objects in the field of view. Thus the area can be computed in parallel in one step (we ignore the problem of adding up all of those ones and zeros).

What other properties might be computed as a sum of local measurements? Perimeter is one: We simply count the places where zeros are next to ones. The local operators are of two kinds (figure 4-6): One type looks at two adjacent picture cells in a row, the other at two adjacent cells in a column. In each case the output is the exclusive-or $(a \otimes b)$ of the two values. The sum of all these outputs is an estimate of the perimeter.

Each of the two operators responds to two patterns. Here is one pattern that triggers the horizontal detector and one that triggers the vertical detector:

The computed perimeter is only an estimate, in the sense that the discrete binary image is usually based on an underlying continuous binary image, and the discrete version will tend to have more ragged object borders. In the case of a diagonal line, for example, the estimate is $\sqrt{2}$ times the "correct" value:

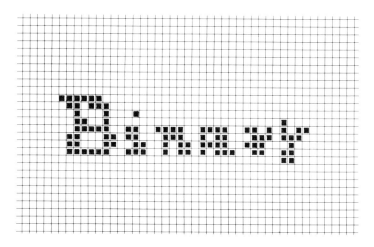

Figure 4-7. The Euler number is the difference between the number of objects and the number of holes. The Euler number of this binary image is 4 since there are 7 objects and 3 holes.

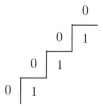

Averaging over all angles of inclination yields an average factor by which the perimeter is overestimated. It is $4/\pi = 1.273\ldots$. The estimate of the perimeter can be improved by dividing by this number.

Besides area and perimeter, we can also use a local counting method to compute the *Euler number*, which is defined as the difference between the number of bodies and the number of holes. The capital letter "B," for example, has Euler number -1 since it is an object with two holes (figure 4-7). The letter "i" has Euler number 2, the letter "n" has Euler number 1, and so on. It may seem strange that the Euler number can be computed by adding up local results. It turns out, for example, that neither the number of bodies nor the number of holes can be computed this way. Yet their difference, namely the Euler number, can!

4.2.2 The Additive Set Property

We can combine binary images in a number of ways. We can "or" them

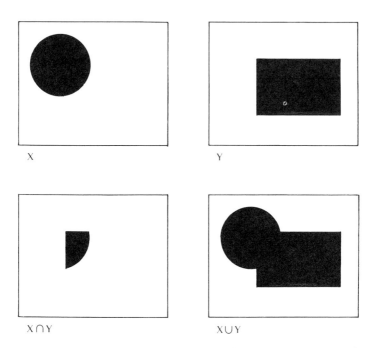

X

Y

X∩Y

X∪Y

Figure 4-8. Binary images can be thought of as sets. We can combine two binary images by taking the union or intersection of these sets. The area of the union, $X \cup Y$, of two binary images plus the area of the intersection, $X \cap Y$, equals the sum of the areas of the original images X and Y.

together. The result is the union of the objects in the two images. We can "and" them together. In this case the result is the intersection of the objects. An interesting question is how various properties of these derived images relate to corresponding properties of the original images. One reason we are interested in such questions is that we hope to break up the image into many parts, process the parts in parallel, and then combine the results.

If we call the original images X and Y (figure 4-8), the logical *or* ($\vee$) and the logical *and* ($\wedge$) of X and Y can be denoted $X \cup Y$ and $X \cap Y$, respectively. The areas are related by

$$A(X) + A(Y) = A(X \cup Y) + A(X \cap Y),$$

since the sum of the areas of X and Y is equal to the area of their union plus the area of the parts where they overlap. Any measurement on a binary image that satisfies this condition is said to have the *additive set property*. Perimeter also satisfies this condition, since the sum of the perimeters of

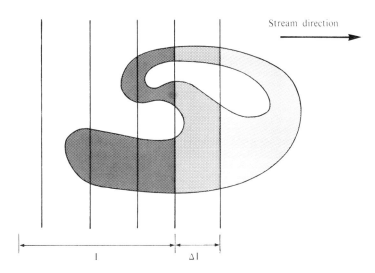

Figure 4-9. An image can be cut up into slices, each of which is simple to analyze. For quantities satisfying the additive set property, the value for the whole image can be computed from the values obtained for each of the slices. The computation can proceed incrementally, adding one new slice at a time.

X and Y is equal to the perimeters of their union plus the perimeter of the part where they overlap. It so happens that the Euler number also satisfies this condition. This is why all three of these properties can be computed by adding the outputs of local operators. The condition permits us to split an image up into smaller pieces and obtain an overall answer by combining the results of operations performed on these pieces. We can illustrate this for the Euler number.

Consider a continuous binary image. Choose a direction in the image and call it the *stream direction* (figure 4-9). Now slice the image into subimages using lines at right angles to the stream direction. Any measurement satisfying the additive set property can be computed incrementally by considering one of these strips at a time. If we call the added strip ΔI, and the part of the image considered so far I, then from the additive set property for the Euler number we obtain

$$E(I \cup \Delta I) - E(I) = E(\Delta I) - E(I \cap \Delta I).$$

Now we can address a problem glossed over so far: how wide to make the strips. Strips for which $E(\Delta I) = E(I \cap \Delta I)$ are of little interest. We concentrate on "interesting" places, where $E(\Delta I) \neq E(I \cap \Delta I)$. In the

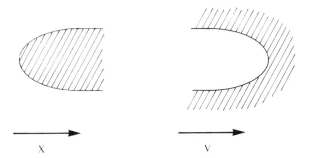

Figure 4-10. The interesting parts of image regions, as far as computation of the Euler number is concerned, are the convexities (X) and concavities (V) facing upstream.

case of the Euler number this happens when the strip ΔI contains a piece of a new object or the end of a hole. We call these pieces *upstream-facing convexities* and *upstream-facing concavities*, respectively (figure 4-10). In the first case the Euler number changes by

$$\Delta E = E(\Delta I) - E(I \cap \Delta I) = 1 - 0 = +1,$$

in the second by

$$\Delta E = E(\Delta I) - E(I \cap \Delta I) = 1 - 2 = -1.$$

(Note that I and ΔI just touch, so their intersection will be line segments.) The Euler number is just the difference between the number of upstream-facing convexities, X, and the number of upstream-facing concavities, V.

It is tempting to note the similarity of the above difference with that occurring in the definition of the Euler number. But B is not necessarily equal to X, nor is H necessarily equal to V. One can easily see this by considering a single object with many wiggles facing upstream (figure 4-11). Then both X and V are large (and $X = V + 1$), while $B = 1$ and $H = 0$. It could not be otherwise, since B and H do not satisfy the additive set property and thus cannot be computed by adding up the results of local operations.

Finally, we need to find an analogous method that applies to discrete binary images. Suppose we choose the stream direction to be from NW to SE ($\searrow$). Then we need to count the number of times we see each of the following patterns:

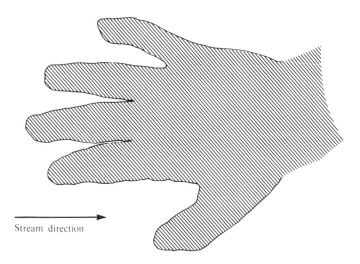

Figure 4-11. The Euler number is the difference between the number of upstream-facing convexities and the number of upstream-facing concavities. This does not mean that these should be identified with the number of objects and the number of holes, as this example illustrates.

0	0
0	1

and

0	1
1	1

For example, if the binary image contains a square with a square hole, then $X = 1$ and $V = 1$, so that $E = X - V = 0$, as it should (figure 4-12). Other patterns are obtained if we choose another stream direction, but of course the Euler number is not changed (even though X and V may be different).

4.2.3 Iterative Modification

Instead of adding up the outputs of the local operators, we can make a new binary image out of them (figure 4-13). The value for each new picture cell is determined by the result of the local computation at the corresponding picture cell in the original image. The new binary image can then be used as input to another cycle of computation. This process, called *iterative modification*, is useful because it allows us to incrementally change an image that is difficult to process into one that might succumb to the methods already discussed.

Useful changes only occur at the boundaries between the objects and the background. This is because all picture cells inside an object are treated

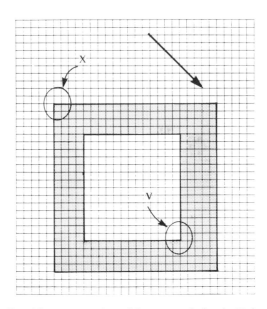

Figure 4-12. For this square region with a square hole, the Euler number is zero, since there is one upstream-facing convexity and one upstream-facing concavity.

uniformly, as are all those inside a component of the background. Thus the new image will usually differ from the original only at the boundaries. This in turn suggests that a single computational step has limited utility. More interesting things happen if we iterate, using the new image as input for the next step. Computations can be repeated either a fixed number of times or until no further changes are noted.

It is possible in this fashion to etch away the boundary of an object, for example, until only a skeleton is left. The *skeleton* is what remains of the figure after thinning has eroded so many cells that none of those left can be etched away without changing the connectivity. It is important not to etch away the last remnants of the skeleton. To deal with this issue we must consider how the Euler number changes when we change a particular picture cell. Those operations that do not change the Euler number are called *conservative*.

Fortunately, because the Euler number satisfies the additive set property, the change in Euler number depends only on the neighbors of a particular cell. If we turn a zero cell whose neighbors are all zero into a one (figure 4-14), we increase the Euler number by one, independently of the values of picture cells further away. Similarly, if all but one neighbor are zero, or all but one neighbor are one, then the Euler number is unchanged

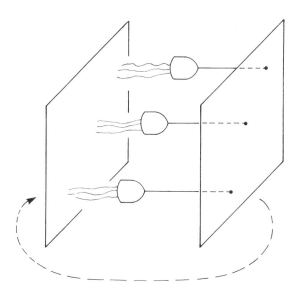

Figure 4-13. A new binary image is developed by means of many computing cells, each connected to a small number of neighboring picture cells.

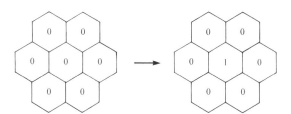

Figure 4-14. If we turn a zero into a one, in a sea of zeros, we create a new object and thus increase the Euler number by one.

when the cell is changed; we are simply extending a body or shrinking a hole.

Each picture cell has six neighbors in our scheme. Each neighbor can have a value of either zero or one. There are thus $2^6 = 64$ possible neighborhoods. For each neighborhood we can compute the Euler differential E^*, the change in Euler number when the picture cell in the center is changed from a zero to a one. (The change in Euler number when the center cell is changed from a one to a zero is just $-E^*$.) We are particularly interested in those neighborhoods for which $E^* = 0$, since we can freely alter picture

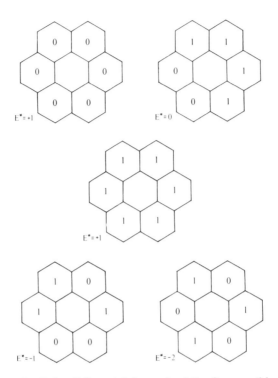

Figure 4-15. The Euler differential for each of the five possible classes of surround can be found by considering how the Euler number changes when the center cell is changed from a zero into a one.

cells in such neighborhoods without changing the Euler number. There are five cases (figure 4-15):

(1) $E^* = +1$ for a neighborhood that is all zeros: A new body is created.

(2) $E^* = +1$ for a neighborhood that is all ones: A hole is filled in.

(3) $E^* = 0$ when the six neighbors considered as a circular sequence can be divided into exactly one sequential group of zeros and one sequential group of ones.

(4) $E^* = -1$ when there are two groups of ones interlaced with two groups of zeros: Here two bodies are connected or a hole is split in two.

(5) $E^* = -2$ when three ones are interlaced with three zeros.

This covers all possibilities, since there are only six cells in the neighborhood. We can denote the specified sets of neighborhoods N_{+1}, N_0, N_{-1}, and N_{-2}, depending on their Euler differential.

There is one remaining difficulty. If we operate on all picture cells in parallel, we may inadvertently change the Euler number after all. The reason is that picture cells in the neighborhood of a particular cell can be changed, invalidating the calculation of the Euler differential for that cell. Two cells with value one, for example, touching on an edge, on a background of zeros, both have Euler differential zero:

0	0	0	0
0	1	1	0
0	0	0	0

$\rightarrow$

0	0	0	0
0	0	0	0
0	0	0	0

Thus it appears safe to remove them both!

If these operations were done sequentially, there would not be a problem, since the Euler differential for the second cell after removal of the first would be one; it would not be removed. We certainly do not want to resort to sequential operations, however. An alternative is to divide the image into interlaced subfields. Then neighboring cells are in different subfields, and these are operated upon sequentially. The smallest number of subfields that makes this possible is three. On a square picture cell tessellation, we can number the cells in a given row using the repeating sequence 1, 2, 3, 1, 2, 3, ... The row below it is labeled similarly, except that it starts at 2, and the row below that starts with 3:

1	2	3	1	2	3
2	3	1	2	3	1
3	1	2	3	1	2
1	2	3	1	2	3
2	3	1	2	3	1
3	1	2	3	1	2

According to the definition of neighborhood that we have been using, no two neighbors have the same label. This scheme is derived from an obvious way of coloring the hexagonal tessellation with three colors.

This takes care of the problem of interaction between changes to neighboring cells in a parallel scheme. We still need a concise notation to describe an iterative image-modification algorithm. First, we must specify a set S of neighborhoods. We define a_{ij} to have value one when the neighborhood of the picture cell at (i, j) is in this set. We use b_{ij} to denote the value of the picture cell itself. At each point in the tessellated image we compute a new binary value that is the result for that point of the iterative modification algorithm. It remains for us to specify how the new value, c_{ij}, is to be computed from a_{ij} and b_{ij}.

Here a, b, and c are *Boolean variables*, in that they can only take on the values zero and one. The computation of c from a and b can thus be specified by a *Boolean function* of two variables. There are $2^4 = 16$ possible Boolean functions of two variables, as follows:

ab	0	1	2	3	4	5	6	7	8	9	10	11	12	13	14	15
00	0	0	0	0	0	0	0	0	1	1	1	1	1	1	1	1
01	0	0	0	0	1	1	1	1	0	0	0	0	1	1	1	1
10	0	0	1	1	0	0	1	1	0	0	1	1	0	0	1	1
11	0	1	0	1	0	1	0	1	0	1	0	1	0	1	0	1

Here each column represents a Boolean functions while each row represents one of the possible combinations of values for the two inputs a and b. The value at the intersection of a particular row and a particular column is the output produced by the Boolean function when given the input shown on the left. The functions can be conveniently numbered, as shown on the top line.

Some of these functions are not very interesting. Number 0, for example, always produces zeros as output, while Number 15 always produces ones. Four more (Numbers 3, 5, 10, and 12) reproduce a, b and their complements $\bar{b}$, $\bar{a}$. More interesting are the logical *and* ($\wedge$—Number 1) and the logical *or* ($\vee$—Number 7). These are also written $a \cdot b$ and $a + b$, respectively. An important property of these particular operations is that they are monotonic. The first one can only remove ones from the image, since

$$a \cdot b \leq b,$$

while the second can only remove zeros, since

$$a + b \geq b.$$

Thus iterative operations using these functions are guaranteed to terminate, since they either eventually stop changing the image or end up filling it completely with ones or zeros, respectively. Some of the remaining Boolean operations, such as $\bar{a} \cdot b$ and $\bar{a} + b$, are of little interest since the same effect can be achieved by using the complement of the set S and employing $a \cdot b$ and $a + b$ instead. Finally, we are left with the exclusive-or (Number 6), denoted $a \otimes b$. This operation is not monotonic. Of the sixteen operations, then, four stand out as potentially useful:

1. $c_{ij} = a_{ij}$ This marks the places with the specified surround.
2. $c_{ij} = a_{ij} \cdot b_{ij}$ This tends to etch away the edges of objects.
3. $c_{ij} = a_{ij} + b_{ij}$ This tends to grow objects.
4. $c_{ij} = a_{ij} \otimes b_{ij}$ This generates waves propagating over the image.

The first of these is not very interesting since it makes sense only for a single step and thus cannot form the basis for an iterative scheme. Furthermore, the patterns one can detect in a small neighborhood are not very interesting. The fourth operation, called *custering*, has found no application. Finally, note that the third operation can be thought of as the second operation applied to the background. This is equivalent to complementing the image and the set S, since, by de Morgan's theorem,

$$\overline{a+b} = \overline{a} \cdot \overline{b}.$$

Consequently, we can focus our attention on a single kind of operation, called *thinning* or *shrinking*. If $S = N_0$, we have a skeletonizing operation that does not change the Euler number, since N_0 is the set of surrounds with Euler differential zero. A simply connected component will be reduced to a point, an object with a hole to a ring, and so on. By modifying the set S we can stop the computation before it reduces a simple object to a single point. In this way we retain more of the object's original shape.

Thickening or swelling of the objects can be accomplished by thinning or shrinking the background. Skeletonization reduces the components of the object to a thin *skeleton*, one picture cell wide in almost all places. The result is like a stick figure, with each picture cell connected to two neighbors, except for the ones at the end of a "stick" and the branch points where sticks are connected together. A simple sequential algorithm can be used to trace along the sticks. As a result, a binary image can be converted to a more manageable description in terms of its components, once it is reduced to a skeleton.

It should be noted that during any particular step of the computation nothing happens at most of the cells. Thus the massive parallelism is not really exploited. In fact one might wonder whether a sequential process applied to the boundaries could be just as efficient for typical binary images.

4.3 References

Many of the basic references on binary image processing were given at the end of the previous chapter. Efforts to extend the ideas presented here to three dimensions might benefit from a study of one of the space-filling tessellations found in the book *Polyhedra Primer* by Pearce & Pearce [1978] or in *Regular Figures* by Fejes Toth [1964]. For an attempt to apply the iterative modification ideas to gray-level images, see *Image Analysis and Mathematical Morphology* by Serra [1982].

Nagy [1969] wrote one of the earliest papers on binary image processing. Much of what is said in this chapter can be traced to an influential paper by Gray [1971]. The advantages of hexagonal tessellations have been exploited by Golay [1969], whose work was explained by Preston [1971]. The problem of connectivity was discussed by Rosenfeld [1970]. There has been a lot of interest in parallel operations, particularly those involving iterative modification. Some representative papers are those by Stefanelli [1971], Arcelli & Levialdi [1972], Levialdi [1972], Dyer & Rosenfeld [1979], Klette [1980], Pavlidis [1980, 1982], and Arcelli [1981]. Also of note is the paper by Deutsch [1972] on thinning algorithms on various tessellations.

Much graphical information now exists on paper in the form of maps, charts, and engineering drawings. To make this information available for use with modern tools such as computer-aided design (CAD) systems, we must convert it into a compatible symbolic representation. To start off with, the drawing must be transformed into a collection of line segments. This process is called *vectorization*. Thinning algorithms often are part and parcel of such a process. Tafoya [1978] describes a vectorization system developed by Broomal Industries. For other work on this problem see Gibson & Lucas [1982].

Industrial inspection methods for simple patterns such as the ones found on printed circuit boards have inspired methods for local parallel checking of widths of patterns and gaps between patterns. Some of these methods are described by Danielsson & Kruse [1979] and Danielsson [1980].

In tomography, when there is enough contrast in absorbing density between different materials in the object being scanned, it is possible to produce three-dimensional binary pictures. Extensions of the methods discussed here to the processing of three-dimensional binary pictures have been examined by Lobregt, Verbeek, & Groen [1980], Tsao & Fu [1981], Herman & Webster [1983], and Hafford & Preston [1984].

4.4 Exercises

4-1 Assume that none of the objects touch the image edge. Show that it is possible to compute perimeter using only operators that detect the condition $a\bar{b}$, where a and b are the values of two adjacent cells. Hint: Show that you do not need operators that detect the condition $\bar{a}b$.

4-2 Show that the perimeter of a circle is overestimated by a factor of $4/\pi$ using the simple method for computing perimeter. Hint: Find the length of the computed perimeter for a monotonic curve from (x_s, y_s) to (x_f, y_f) in terms of the starting and finishing values of x and y.

4-3 Suppose that the smallest rectangular region enclosing a convex curve has width W and height H. What estimate of the perimeter of the convex curve is obtained using the methods discussed in this chapter? What convex curve fitting into the same rectangle has the smallest perimeter? For this worst case, determine the ratio of the estimated perimeter to the true perimeter.

4-4 Estimates of area and perimeter can be obtained from gray-level images, provided that a threshold level is given that defines the region boundaries. These estimates of area and perimeter will be substantially better than those obtained from binary images after thresholding. For simplicity, consider a tessellation into hexagonal picture cells. A *cell-group polygon* is a set of cells that meet at a vertex. In the case of the hexagonal tessellation a cell-group polygon consists of three neighboring picture cells.

We can approximate the underlying image brightness function with a piece-wise linear function. This approximation can be thought of as a surface composed of triangular facets, one per cell group. Each corner of a triangular facet lies directly above the center of a particular picture cell, and the "height" of this corner is the gray-level of that picture cell.

Suppose that the given threshold is t and that the gray-levels at the corners A, B, and C of a particular facet are a, b, and c, respectively. Under what conditions does a portion of the boundary of a region pass through this facet?

If a portion of the boundary passes through a facet, it is possible, by reordering A, B, and C, to arrange for the threshold t to lie between a and b and also between a and c. Thus the portion of the boundary passing through the facet is a straight line connecting a point on the edge from A to B with a point on the edge from A to C. Find these two points.

Now calculate the length of the straight line connecting the two points. This is the contribution to the overall measure of perimeter from one picture cell group. Also calculate the area of the portion of the region that is above threshold inside the facet. Be careful to distinguish between the case in which two of the three gray-levels a, b, and c are below threshold and the case in which two of them are above threshold.

4-5 Show that slices containing both downstream-facing convexities and downstream-facing concavities do not change the Euler number in the incremental scheme of computing the Euler number. That is, in both cases, $\Delta E = 1 - 1 = 0$.

4-6 The stencils used for computing X and V in this chapter were designed for a stream direction from NW to SE ($\searrow$). Suppose we instead choose a stream direction from SW to NE ($\nearrow$). Show that the stencils

0	1
0	0

and

1	1
0	1

will not work for six-connectedness as we have defined it. Design correct stencils for a stream direction from SW to NE ($\nearrow$).

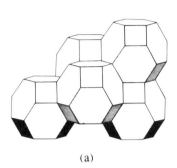
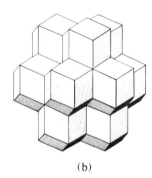

(a)   (b)

Figure 4-16. (a) The truncated octahedron is the only semiregular polyhedron that will fill space by itself. (b) The rhombic dodecahedron is the only
Archimedean dual that will fill space alone. (Figures reproduced by permission
from *Polyhedra Primer* by P. Pearce & S. Pearce, Van Nostrand Reinhold, New
York, 1978.)

4-7 How large a lookup table is needed to compute a result based on a cell and
its neighbors in a 3×3 image region?

4-8 There are obvious extensions of what we have done in this chapter to
three dimensions. This is especially useful in dealing with data obtained by a
tomographic machine, for example. In this case, each cell is zero or one, according
to whether that part of space is occupied by the object of interest or not. A
difficult issue, as is to be expected, is the choice of neighbors to which a particular
cell is considered connected. In the case of a tessellation into cubical cells, for
example, we might consider as neighbors:

- The 6 face-adjacent cells.
- The 6 face-adjacent and the 12 edge-adjacent cells.
- The 6 face-adjacent, the 12 edge-adjacent, and the 8 corner-adjacent cells.

Each of these choices leads to difficulties similar to the ones described for the
tessellation of the plane into squares. Unfortunately, the cube is the only regular
polyhedron that provides a space-filling tessellation.

There is only one semiregular polyhedron that can be used for this purpose:
the truncated octahedron. It has 14 faces and touches other cells only on its faces
(figure 4-16a).

(a) Devise a scheme for labeling all cells that are connected to a particular one
using this tessellation.

(b) Devise a local counting scheme that will determine the volume, surface area,
and Euler number of three-dimensional volumes. Warning: This takes a bit
of work.

(c) How can a tessellation composed of cubical cells be skewed so as to have the connectivity of the tessellation using the truncated octahedron? Hint: Use a method analogous to the one employed to skew a tessellation composed of square picture cells so that it has the connectivity of a tessellation of the plane into hexagonal cells.

We now have exhausted the possibilities using regular and semiregular polyhedra. The next most interesting cells to try are the duals of the Archimedean objects. The only one that provides us with a space-filling tessellation is the rhombic dodecahedron (figure 4-16b).

(d) Is there any difficulty in deciding which cells a particular one is connected to when we use this tessellation?

(e) Repeat parts (a) through (c) for the rhombic dodecahedron.

(f) What are the relative merits of the three space-filling tessellations we have explored?

4-9   We have demonstrated the division of a discrete image into the smallest possible number of subfields such that neighbors always belong to different subfields. For processing methods that depend on larger numbers of nearby cells, we need to use a larger number of subfields.

(a) Divide the image into four regular subfields.

(b) Divide the image into seven regular subfields.

4-10   Show that custering is reversible. In what order must the subfields be operated on? Can custering operations ever terminate?

4-11   Can a single thinning step be undone by a single thickening step? Can a single thickening step be undone by a single thinning step?

4-12   If we ignore rotations, then there are 14 possible surrounds of a cell on a hexagonal lattice, as follows:

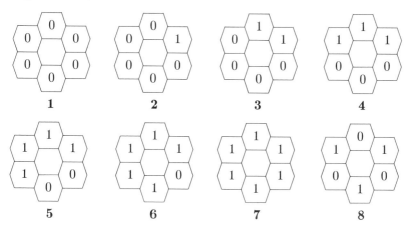

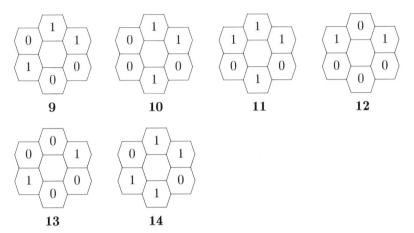

Show that the Euler differentials for the sets of surrounds are as follows:

- For $N_{-2} = \{8\}$, it is -2.
- For $N_{-1} = \{9, 10, 11, 12, 13, 14\}$, it is -1.
- For $N_0 = \{2, 3, 4, 5, 6\}$, it is 0.
- For $N_{+1} = \{1, 7\}$, it is $+1$.

For each surround, determine the number of ways in which it can be rotated to produce a different surround. Hint: The total should come to 64.

4-13 We can uniquely define the operation of an iterative modification scheme by specifying four things:

- The set S of surrounds (for which $a_{ij} = 1$).
- The Boolean function $L(a, b)$ (where $c_{ij} = L(a_{ij}, b_{ij})$).
- The number of iterations, n.
- The number of subfields, f, into which the image tessellation is divided.

Consider the following iterative modification schemes:

(1) $S = \{\}$, $L(a, b) = 0$, $n = 1$, $f = 1$
(2) $S = \{\}$, $L(a, b) = \bar{b}$, $n = 1$, $f = 1$
(3) $S = \{7\}$, $L(a, b) = ab$, $n = 1$, $f = 1$
(4) $S = \{1, 7\}$, $L(a, b) = \bar{a}b$, $n = 1$, $f = 1$
(5) $S = \{1\}$, $L(a, b) = ab$, $n = 1$, $f = 1$
(6) $S = \{1\}$, $L(a, b) = \bar{a}b$, $n = 1$, $f = 1$
(7) $S = \{2, 3, 4, 5, 6, 7, 8, 9, 10, 11, 12, 13, 14\}$, $L(a, b) = ab$, $n = 1$, $f = 1$
(8) $S = \{4\}$, $L(a, b) = ab$, $n = 1$, $f = 1$
(9) $S = \{2\}$, $L(a, b) = ab$, $n = 1$, $f = 1$
(10) $S = \{3, 4\}$, $L(a, b) = \bar{a}b$, $n = \infty$, $f = 3$
(11) $S = \{1, 2, 3\}$, $L(a, b) = \bar{a}b$, $n = \infty$, $f = 1$
(12) $S = \{5, 6, 7\}$, $L(a, b) = a + \bar{a}b$, $n = \infty$, $f = 3$

(13) $S = \{2, 3, 4, 5, 6\}$, $L(a, b) = \bar{a}b$, $n = \infty$, $f = 3$
(14) $S = \{1, 7, 8, 9, 10, 11, 12, 13, 14\}$, $L(a, b) = ab$, $n = \infty$, $f = 3$
(15) $S = \{4, 5, 6, 7\}$, $L(a, b) = a + \bar{a}b$, $n = \infty$, $f = 3$

For each of these schemes, find the description in words below that best fits the action it performs:

(a) Complements all picture cells in the image.
(b) Shrinks each blob to a single picture cell.
(c) Fills all simple holes, swells blobs until convex.
(d) Resets all cells to zero.
(e) Keeps only isolated cells that are one.
(f) Cuts off all appendages (that is, thin lines).
(g) Removes edges of blobs, keeping the interior.
(h) Cleans up isolated cells that are one.
(i) Marks all corners, flushes the rest.
(j) Fills in small cavities.
(k) Skeletonizes until lines are only one picture cell wide.
(l) Removes interiors of blobs, keeping only edges.
(m) Marks ends of lines only.
(n) Recognizes the capital letter "B."

5

Regions & Image Segmentation

Many machine vision algorithms are meant to be applied to the image of a single surface. If the image of a surface does not fill the field of view, attention should be confined to the region that corresponds to the surface. In this chapter we explore methods for segmenting images into regions that appear to be images of different surfaces. To do this, we first appeal to histograms of gray-levels and try to exploit the spatial coherence apparent in images. Distinguishing different image regions is simpler when registered images taken with different spectral sensitivities are available. In other words, color information is helpful.

We contrast methods that progress by subdividing existing regions with those that combine existing regions. In many cases, reliable segmentation is only possible after significant information has been extracted about the objects portrayed. Unfortunately, methods for extracting this information often require an image that has already been segmented. We briefly discuss this chicken-and-egg problem.

5.1 Thresholding Methods

To make a binary image from a gray-level image we have to set a threshold (figure 5-1). Picture cells in which the gray-level is above the threshold give rise to ones in the corresponding position of the binary image, and those below it give rise to zeros (or vice versa). How do we choose this threshold?

Figure 5-1. If the background is bright, with little light falling on the subject of interest, a binary image can be obtained easily by thresholding the brightness values. This particular picture may lead us to believe that mere silhouettes can convey a great deal of information about three-dimensional objects. The artist's carefully chosen viewpoint and our familiarity with the subject matter conspire to give this impression. Silhouettes of unfamiliar objects, taken from randomly chosen points of view, are typically quite difficult to interpret. (Reproduced from *Silhouettes*, edited by C. B. Grafton, Dover, New York, 1979.)

We would presumably like to find an automatic method that can handle variations in illumination and surface properties. One way to proceed is to analyze the occurrence of gray-levels in the image, independent of the positions of the picture cells.

For a continuous image, we can define the *brightness distribution function*, denoted $p(x)$. For small δx, $p(x)\delta x$ is the fraction of the image that has brightness equal to or greater than x, but less than $x + \delta x$. Integration yields the cumulative brightness distribution $P(x)$. For a given value of x, $P(x)$ is the fraction of the image that has brightness equal to or less than x:

$$P(x) = \int_0^x p(t)\,dt.$$

In a digitized image we can create a *gray-level histogram* that gives the number of picture cells having a particular gray-level. The *cumulative gray-level histogram* is obtained by summation. These tools will be useful here.

5.2 Histogramming

Consider the ideal situation of an object of uniform brightness lying on a background of uniform brightness. It is easy to choose a threshold as long as the two image regions do not have the same brightness. We can use any value between the gray-levels of the regions, such as an average of the two.

In practice, the picture cells corresponding to the object will not all have exactly the same gray-level (figure 5-2). This is due to a number of factors, including measurement noise. The determination of gray-levels involves measurement of relatively small numbers of electrons liberated by incident photons, and this gives rise some variability in the charges to be measured. More noise is introduced by the device used to amplify the charge. The effect of this noise is to smear out the probability distribution. To be precise, the probability distribution that we would have obtained in the absence of noise is convolved with the probability distribution of the additive noise. In addition, sensors do not usually give exactly the same response at each picture cell, nor are objects perfectly uniformly reflective or uniformly illuminated. For these and other reasons we must expect a spread in gray-level, for both the object and the background.

If we are lucky, the spread is small enough so that there will still exist a threshold value that separates the two groups of gray-levels. Such a threshold can be found by making a histogram of the gray-levels. We expect to see two peaks corresponding roughly to the object and the background, with a valley in between (figure 5-2). Ideally there will be a gap between the two peaks in the histogram, but even when the two clusters overlap a bit, we can choose a threshold where the histogram has a minimum. This will allow us to turn the gray-level image into a binary image with only a few errors in classification.

If the "signal" (the difference between the gray-levels of the object and the background) is not much larger than the "noise" (the spread in the distribution of gray-levels), we cannot hope to succeed by these means, of course. It is helpful in this case to average neighboring picture cells. This will reduce the noise by a factor proportional to the square root of the number of cells averaged. The signal level will not be affected, but spatial resolution will suffer.

So far we have assumed that each entry in the histogram corresponds to a single gray-level. It is possible to make a coarser histogram by pooling adjacent gray-levels. In constructing a histogram we always have a difficult

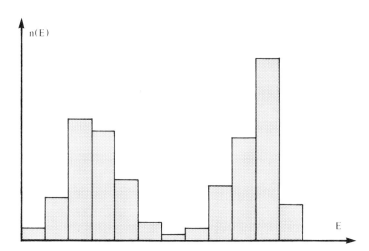

Figure 5-2. A histogram of gray-levels is sometimes useful in determining a threshold that can be used to segment the image into regions. Here $n(E)$ is the number of picture cells that have gray-level E.

choice to make: How wide should the bins of the histogram be? Each bin contains the number of picture cells with gray-levels between the lower and upper limit for that bin. If the bins are too wide, the resolution in gray-level is low (in the extreme case, there is only one bin and no resolution). If the bins are too narrow, each will contain only a few entries and the histogram will be very ragged (in the extreme case, almost all bins contain zero, with a few ones). It is hard to locate the minima in this latter case. Naturally, this effect is less pronounced when the object covers a large area. Often the histogram must be smoothed by combining neighboring bins, but in this case we sacrifice resolution.

Yet another difficulty is presented by picture cells overlapping the edge of the object (figure 5-3). These picture cells will have intermediate gray-levels, smearing out and merging the skirts of the two peaks. The magnitude of this effect depends on the fraction of picture cells that fall on the edge. This fraction in turn is inversely proportional to the square root of the ratio of the area of the object to the area of a picture cell. The problem is thus less pronounced if the object is imaged at high resolution. Conversely, the problem is aggravated by the averaging method proposed earlier for increasing the signal-to-noise ratio.

Another problem occurs when the image area occupied by the object is much larger or much smaller than that occupied by the background. In this case the smaller peak in the histogram may become submerged in the

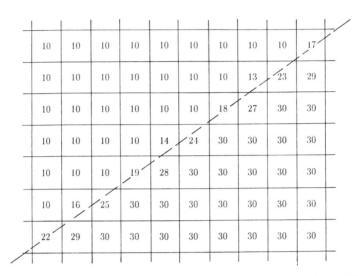

Figure 5-3. Picture cells overlapping the edge between two regions will have gray-levels intermediate in value to those of the two regions.

skirt of the larger peak. There may be no minimum at which to place a threshold. Keep in mind also that the histogram will be "noisy" because of the finite number of samples taken. So even if the underlying brightness distribution is smooth and has well-defined peaks, we cannot expect this to be true of the histogram of gray-levels.

If the fraction of the area occupied by the object is known, then a simple modification of our method will work. First, construct the cumulative histogram by summing the histogram itself. As mentioned before, the cumulative histogram gives for each gray-level the number of picture cells with that gray-level or a smaller one. Set the threshold at the level that has the requisite fraction of the total number of picture cells with lower gray-level. Note that we cannot now make use of the computed area of the binary image, since we have fixed it already in order to choose a threshold!

Some of the cleanest binary images are not made from the usual kind of optical image at all. For example, we can measure the distance above a reference plane of every point on the surface of an object. A binary image can then be derived by thresholding this "depth image." In this way the outline of an object lying on a table or conveyor belt can be ascertained.

The distance-measuring scheme itself can be optical (figure 5-4). In the figure, two light sources with cylindrical lenses produce sheets of light that intersect in a line lying on the surface of a conveyor belt. A camera above the belt is aimed so that this line is imaged on a linear array of

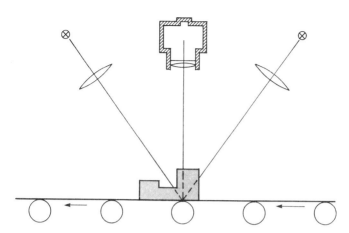

Figure 5-4. A binary image can be obtained by thresholding a depth image, which can in turn be derived by means of a particular kind of *structured lighting*. In this figure, for example, a surface is being illuminated by a sheet of light. A linear sensor is mounted vertically above the line where the sheet of light intersects the surface. When there is an object on the surface, it will intercept the sheet of light before it reaches the surface. The linear sensor will see light only where it strikes the surface. To obtain a full image, we have to scan the object past the sensitive area of the sensing system.

photosensors. When there is no object present, all the sensor cells are brightly illuminated. When part of an object interrupts the incident light, the corresponding region on the linear array is darkened. The motion of the belt scans the object past the sensor, generating the second image dimension. The width of the sheet of light and the optical arrangement are designed so that the inevitable small vertical displacements of the belt do not cause the sensor cells to receive significantly less illumination. As a consequence the device is able to determine whether the height of an object is within a given interval.

Two light sources are used to reduce "ghosts" due to shadowing of the belt by a part that has not yet reached the line on which the sensor is focused (deep holes, however, still present a problem and will not be seen by the device).

5.3 Spatial Coherence

In typical images, the gray-levels of neighboring picture cells are not independent. One can expect the image of a polyhedral object, for example, to contain regions in which brightness is essentially constant. Similarly,

0	0	0	0	0	0	0	0	1	1
0	0	1	0	0	0	1	1	1	1
0	0	0	0	0	1	1	1	1	1
0	1	0	0	0	1	1	0	1	1
0	0	0	1	1	1	1	1	1	1
0	0	1	1	1	0	1	1	1	1
1	1	1	1	1	1	1	1	1	1

Figure 5-5. Salt-and-pepper noise comes from the interaction of inaccuracy in brightness measurements and the fixed threshold used in developing a binary image. It is particularly prevalent near the edges of regions.

images of smoothly curved objects have brightness that varies slowly with position. We shall exploit this spatial coherence in a number of ways.

In image segmentation, there are, inevitably, a few cells that are misclassified, often due to the effects of noise. Unless the signal-to-noise ratio is poor, almost all of these errors will be isolated, except near the boundary of the object. This is called *salt-and-pepper noise* (figure 5-5). These errors can be removed easily, after thresholding, by noting that a particular cell is in a complementary neighborhood.

One can perhaps avoid making this kind of error in the first place by considering the gray-levels at neighboring points before thresholding. If a particular picture cell has a gray-level that is higher than the highest of the gray-levels of its neighbors, it may have been unduly affected by noise. It is an "outlier." It should then be replaced by the highest of the gray-levels of the neighbors. A similar "filtering" operation can be applied if the gray-level is lower than the lowest gray-level of the neighbors. Note that the gray-levels of picture cells on the boundary between the object and the background will not be altered by this operation.

Other filtering operations can be used to reduce noise. We have already mentioned averaging of neighboring cells. This operation tends to smear things out and thus reduces spatial resolution. As a result, it exacerbates the problems encountered at boundaries. Another possibility is to replace each gray-level not by the average of its neighbors but by the median value. (There are as many members of a set below the *median* as there are above it.) Like the first scheme, this does not affect picture cells on the boundary. The median is, however, more difficult to compute than the maximum or the minimum (or even the average).

Each of these methods allows us to reduce the number of picture cells that will later be misclassified by the simple thresholding method. It is, however, not possible to guarantee the results. Just as random noise can occasionally produce a gray-level far from the expected one for a particular picture cell, so it can affect several neighboring cells. The small probability of a large error at one picture cell is then multiplied by the small probabilities of large errors for the neighbors. The probability of the average or median being affected as much as an individual gray-level is relatively small.

We are making use here of spatial coherence. In the simple situations addressed so far, the object is assumed to have roughly uniform brightness, so that neighboring picture cells will tend to have similar gray-levels. In this situation we introduce constraints based on assumptions about what is in the image. This is an approach we shall exploit again later on.

5.4 Image Segmentation

It is desirable to break up an image into regions, each of which might correspond to the surface of an object in the environment being imaged. Further processing can then be separately applied to each of these image regions. So far we have considered a very simple case in which the objects and the background are uniform in brightness. We extend these methods now to cases in which each object has a different gray-level.

If we know the average gray-level of each of the regions, we may be able to select thresholds lying between these levels that will allow us to classify each of the picture cells. New problems crop up immediately, however. Suppose region A abuts region C. At their common boundary, gray-levels will be found that lie between the representative values for the two regions, as explained earlier. If a third region B, in another part of the picture, has a gray-level between those of regions A and C, then some of the boundary points will be misclassified as belonging to B. This can be avoided by using properties other than the gray-level. For example, the picture cells in question form a ragged, torn strip rather than a large, bloblike area. If we assume all regions to have at least a certain minimum width, we can remove the erroneously labeled points. We can also make use of the fact that these misclassified points are close to both region A and region C.

The required thresholds can sometimes be found using histogram analysis. Often, however, the histogram is quite ragged because fewer points correspond to a particular peak and because peaks tend to overlap more than in the case of a single object lying on a uniform background.

The noise problems alluded to earlier are also more severe here. If there are several regions, the smallest difference in gray-levels between two regions cannot be very large. It must be a small fraction of the overall range of gray-levels. If the overall range is N and there are R regions, the smallest difference must be less than or equal to $N/(R-1)$. The probability of misclassification is thus considerably increased. This problem can be alleviated somewhat by making use of spatial coherence.

5.5 Using Color

Another way to improve classification is to use information about color. Even when surfaces have similar gray-levels, as determined by using a single image sensor, they may still differ in color. One way to make use of this possibility is to digitize several images using sensors with different spectral responses. This can be done by placing colored filters in front of the lens. These filters selectively absorb some parts of the spectrum more than others and so alter the inherent response of the sensor to different wavelengths of light, as discussed in chapter 2. Typically three images are taken through red, green, and blue filters. For the discussion here, the detailed response curves of the filters are not important.

It is convenient to combine the gray-levels in these registered images into a vector at each picture cell. Each component of the vector is a gray-level obtained at that picture cell using one of the filters. Each region corresponds to a point or a cluster of points in the corresponding vector space. We show in exercise 5-7 that the distances between these clusters in n-dimensional color space will be at least as large the corresponding differences in the gray-levels of a black-and-white image.

Dividing up this space into volumes corresponding to different regions is not easy. We shall look at some methods for doing this in our discussion of pattern classification. One way to classify vectors is to measure the distance from representative or average vectors for each of the regions. We can assign the unknown to the class corresponding to the closest representative vector. This corresponds to dividing the space up using planes that are perpendicular to and that bisect the lines joining representative vectors.

5.6 Merging and Splitting

Suppose that by some method we have arrived at a detailed but crude segmentation of the image. We can, for example, simply group together neighboring cells that have the same gray-level. A better segmentation can then be constructed by combining neighboring regions that are similar. "Similar" may mean having gray-levels that differ by less than some threshold value. A test for similarity can also take into account geometric factors, such as the ratio of the length of the common boundary to the total length of boundary of two regions.

A more sophisticated test employs estimates of the average gray-level and the variance of the gray-level of each region. Using standard methods borrowed from statistics, we can find the probability that two regions have similar gray-levels only because of chance. If this probability is low, we merge the two regions. Merging is a monotonic operation that will eventually stop. Of course, by then the whole image may have been merged into one region!

At times, such a process may merge regions with similar gray-levels that should not be merged. Such errors can be detected using geometric considerations. If, for example, the boundary has two deep incisions into the shape from more or less opposite sides, then it is likely that a dividing line should be drawn between the tips of the two incisions (figure 5-6). Testing the mean and variance of the gray-levels of the resulting regions may confirm this suspicion. This leads to methods that split rather than merge regions. In a way these methods are looking for edges between regions with different gray-levels. Edge finding will be discussed in more detail later.

One of the problems with these methods for image segmentation is that the premise on which they are based often does not apply to real situations. While it is true that many surfaces have uniform reflectance, it is not true that they will be imaged with uniform brightness. As we shall see later, many factors influence brightness. Conversely, picture cells corresponding to points on surfaces of different objects may have similar gray-levels. Only in unusual situations can the image be usefully thought of as a collage of regions of uniform brightness.

It is often more fruitful to postpone segmentation until other information, such as an estimate of surface shape, has been found. One of the difficulties in evaluating schemes for image segmentation is the lack of a clear definition of the task. What is the "correct" segmentation? The answer to this question depends on what one wants to do with the result.

5.7 References

One of the earliest papers on region analysis is that of Brice and Fennema [1970]. Bajcsy [1973] was interested in segmentation based on texture measures. Also of note are papers by Gupta & Wintz [1975], Tenenbaum &

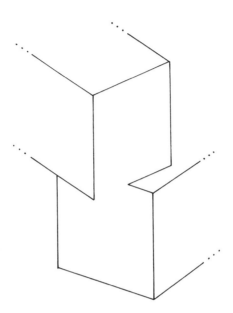

Figure 5-6. Sometimes the edges between regions can be inferred from the context.

Barrow [1976], and Haralick [1980]. Surveys of the problems of image segmentation have been provided by Rosenfeld & Davis [1979], Kanade [1980], and Gurari & Wechsler [1982]. A region-segmentation method based on multidimensional histograms was developed by Ohlander, Price, & Reddy [1978]. More recently, Pong et al. [1984] devised a new region grower using Haralick's facet model of the brightness surface.

The distance-measuring scheme described in this chapter using two planes of light was developed at General Motors Research Laboratory as part of a system called CONSIGHT that picks up parts from a conveyor belt. The CONSIGHT system has been described by Holland, Rossol, & Ward [1979]; some of its applications on the factory floor are listed in a paper by Ward et al. [1982].

A very different approach to problems of image segmentation and line finding can be found in the use of stochastic models of image generation. This may have been hinted at in the paper by Habibi [1972]. Recent work relevant to this topic may be found in Hansen & Elliott [1982], Blake [1983], Geman & Geman [1983], Cohen and Cooper [1984], and Marroquin [1985]. We discuss image models further in the next chapter.

5.8 Exercises

5-1 How is the area of a binary image affected by the choice of threshold? How does the error in area vary with the ratio of the area of the object to the area of a picture cell? Are elongated objects affected more by threshold variations than more rounded ones?

5-2 Show how to use swelling and thinning operations to remove salt-and-pepper noise.

5-3 A particular image is known to contain two classes of picture cells. Suppose that there are N_b picture cells corresponding to the background with gray-level distribution $p_b(x)$. Correspondingly, there are N_o picture cells corresponding to the object with gray-level distribution $p_o(x)$. We want to segment this image using a threshold that minimizes the "cost" of misclassification. Suppose that the cost of misclassifying a background cell as object is C_b, while the converse error costs C_o. What threshold T minimizes the total cost? Is there always a unique solution?

5-4 This is a continuation of the previous exercise. Suppose that the gray-level distributions are normal. Let the N_b background picture cells have a brightness that is a Gaussian random variable with mean μ_1 and variance σ_1^2. Similarly, the N_o object picture cells have mean μ_2 and variance σ_2^2. What value of T minimizes the total number of cells misclassified when, by chance,

$$\frac{N_b}{\sigma_b} = \frac{N_o}{\sigma_o}.$$

What is the value of T when $N_b = N_o$ and $\sigma_b = \sigma_o$?

5-5 Consider the following iterative scheme for finding a good threshold. Starting with an arbitrary value somewhere in the distribution, compute the average of the portion below threshold and the average of the portion above threshold. Now set a new threshold at the average of these two numbers. Comment on the convergence of this method. Is the solution unique? What if we use the weighted average of the two means, with the weights proportional to the integrals of the corresponding parts of the distribution?

5-6 Suppose that $P(x)$ is the probability of a gray-level at any picture cell being less than x. What is the probability that the maximum of the eight gray-levels in a 3×3 neighborhood surrounding a particular picture cell is less than x? What is the probability that the picture cell in the middle has a larger gray-level than the other eight?

5-7 Consider two color vectors $x = (x_1, \ldots, x_n)^T$ and $y = (y_1, \ldots, y_n)^T$. The corresponding gray-levels are formed from weighted sums of the color components

$$\sum_{i=1}^{n} w_i x_i \quad \text{and} \quad \sum_{i=1}^{n} w_i y_i, \quad \text{where} \sum_{i=1}^{n} w_i = 1.$$

Show that the distance between the color vectors is at least as large as the difference in gray-levels.

5-8 Consider median filtering using a 3×3 neighborhood. The new value is obtained by choosing the median of the nine gray-levels. If the probability of one gray-level being larger than x is $P = 0.1$, what is the probability that the median will be larger than x?

5-9 Consider average filtering using a 3×3 neighborhood. The new value is obtained by taking the average of the nine gray-levels. Assume additive noise with a normal distribution. If the probability of one gray-level being larger than x is 0.15, what is the probability of the average being larger than x?

5-10 Segmentation can be performed using "texture" rather than brightness. To do this, we have to compute some measure of the texture for each picture cell. Typically, this calculation involves the neighborhood of the picture cell at which the texture measure is to be computed. For example, we can use the standard deviation of the brightness of the picture cells in a neighborhood as a simple kind of measurement:

$$\sigma = \sqrt{\frac{\sum_{i=1}^{N} x_i^2 - \frac{1}{N}\left(\sum_{i=1}^{N} x_i\right)^2}{N-1}}$$

where N is the number of picture cells in the neighborhood and $\{x_i\}$ is the set of brightness values of those cells. Another common measurement is the range, defined as the difference between the maximum and minimum intensities in a neighborhood. Briefly discuss the relative merits and drawbacks of these two schemes. You may want to consider resolution, sensitivity to noise, neighborhood size, and computational complexity.

6

Image Processing: Continuous Images

It is often useful to transform an image in some way, producing a new one that is more amenable to further manipulation. Image processing involves the search for methods to accomplish such transformations. Most of the methods examined so far are linear and shift-invariant. Methods with these properties allow us to apply powerful analytic tools. We show in this chapter that linear, shift-invariant systems can be characterized by convolution, an operation introduced in its one-dimensional form when we discussed the probability distribution of the sum of two random variables.

We also demonstrate the utility of the concept of spatial frequency and of transformations between the spatial and the frequency domains. Image-processing systems, whether optical or digital, can be characterized either in the spatial domain, by their point-spread function, or in the frequency domain, by their modulation-transfer function. The tools discussed in this chapter will be applied to the analysis of partial differential operators used in edge detection, and to the analysis of optimal filtering methods for the suppression of noise.

Most of the methods discussed here are simple extensions to two dimensions of linear systems techniques for one-dimensional signals, but we shall not assume that the reader is familiar with these techniques. We treat the continuous case in this chapter and the discrete case in the next.

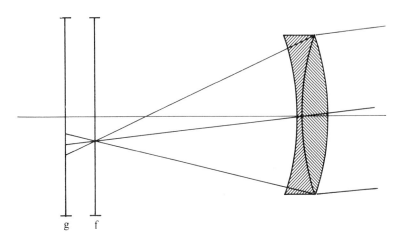

g   f

Figure 6-1. An out-of-focus image $g(x,y)$ can be thought of as a processed version of the ideal image $f(x,y)$.

6.1 Linear, Shift-Invariant Systems

An image can be thought of as a two-dimensional signal. We can develop an approach to image processing based on this observation. Consider an out-of-focus imaging system (figure 6-1). We can think of the image $g(x,y)$ produced by the defocused system as a processed version of the ideal image, $f(x,y)$, that one would obtain in a correctly focused imaging system. Now, if the lighting is changed so as to double the brightness of the ideal image, the brightness of the out-of-focus image is also doubled. Further, if the imaging system is moved slightly, so that the ideal image is shifted in the image plane, the out-of-focus image is similarly shifted. The transformation from the ideal image to that in the out-of-focus system is said to be a linear, shift-invariant operation. In fact, incoherent optical image-processing systems that are more complicated are typically also linear and shift-invariant. These terms will now be defined more precisely.

Consider a two-dimensional system that produces outputs $g_1(x,y)$ and $g_2(x,y)$ when given inputs $f_1(x,y)$ and $f_2(x,y)$, respectively:

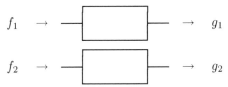

The system is called *linear* if the output $\alpha g_1(x,y) + \beta g_2(x,y)$ is produced when the input is $\alpha f_1(x,y) + \beta f_2(x,y)$, for arbitrary α and β:

$$\alpha f_1 + \beta f_2 \quad \rightarrow \quad \boxed{} \quad \rightarrow \quad \alpha g_1 + \beta g_2$$

Most real systems are limited in their maximum response and thus cannot be strictly linear. Moreover, brightness, which is power per unit area, cannot be negative. The original input, an image, is thus restricted to nonnegative values. Intermediate results of our computations can, however, have arbitrary values.

Now consider a system that produces output $g(x, y)$ when given input $f(x, y)$:

$$f(x, y) \quad \rightarrow \quad \boxed{} \quad \rightarrow \quad g(x, y)$$

The system is called *shift-invariant* if it produces the shifted output $g(x - a, y - b)$ when given the shifted input $f(x - a, y - b)$, for arbitrary a and b:

$$f(x - a, y - b) \quad \rightarrow \quad \boxed{} \quad \rightarrow \quad g(x - a, y - b)$$

In practice, images are limited in area, so that shift invariance only holds for limited displacements. Moreover, aberrations in optical imaging systems vary with the distance from the optical axis; such systems are therefore only approximately shift-invariant.

Methods for analyzing linear, shift-invariant systems are important for understanding the properties of image-forming systems. System shortcomings can often be discussed in terms of the linear, shift-invariant system that would transform the ideal image into the one actually observed. More importantly for us, a study of linear, shift-invariant systems leads to useful algorithms for processing images using either optical or digital methods.

A simple example of a linear, shift-invariant system is one that produces the derivative of its input with respect to x or y. Linearity follows from the rules for differentiating the product of a constant and some function and the rule for differentiating the sum of two functions. Shift invariance is equally easy to prove. Systems taking derivatives will prove useful as preprocessing stages in edge-detection systems.

We start by considering continuous images in order to lay the groundwork for the discrete operations. Linear, shift-invariant systems for processing images are extensions to two dimensions of one-dimensional linear, shift-invariant systems, such as simple passive electrical circuits. Not surprisingly, most of the results presented here can be derived using simple extensions of methods used to prove similar results applying to the one-dimensional case. To simplify matters, we shall factor functions of two variables into products of two functions of one variable whenever possible. This will allow us to split the two-dimensional integrals that arise into products of one-dimensional integrals.

In the analysis of one-dimensional systems, functions of time are typically used as both inputs and outputs. No system can anticipate its input. This places a severe restriction on systems for processing one-dimensional signals: They have to be causal. Only those that obey this restriction can be physically realized. There is no such problem in the synthesis of two-dimensional systems.

While we inherit the powerful methods of signal processing from one-dimensional systems, we must also point out the shortcomings. The constraints of linearity and shift invariance are severe and greatly limit the kinds of things we can do with an image. Still, it is hard to make progress without some guiding theory.

6.2 Convolution and the Point-Spread Function

Consider a system that, given an input $f(x, y)$, produces as its output

$$g(x, y) = \int_{-\infty}^{\infty} \int_{-\infty}^{\infty} f(x - \xi, y - \eta) h(\xi, \eta) \, d\xi \, d\eta.$$

Here g is said to be the convolution of f and h. It is easy to show that such a system is linear by applying it to $\alpha f_1(x, y) + \beta f_2(x, y)$ and noting that the output is $\alpha g_1(x, y) + \beta g_2(x, y)$. Here again $g_1(x, y)$ is the output produced when $f_1(x, y)$ is the input and $g_2(x, y)$ is the output produced when $f_2(x, y)$ is the input. The result follows from the rule for integrating the product of a constant and a function and from the rule for integrating the sum of two functions. It is also easy to show that the system is shift-invariant by applying it to $f(x - a, y - b)$ and noting that the output is $g(x - a, y - b)$. Thus a system whose response can be described by a convolution is linear and shift-invariant. We shall soon show the converse:

- Any linear, shift-invariant system performs a convolution.

Convolution is usually denoted by the symbol $\otimes$. So the above formula can be abbreviated

$$g = f \otimes h.$$

It would be useful to relate the function $h(x, y)$ to some observable property of the system. Given an arbitrary function $h(x, y)$, can we always find an input $f(x, y)$ that causes the system to produce $h(x, y)$ as output? That is, can we find an $f(x, y)$ such that

$$h(x, y) = \int_{-\infty}^{\infty} \int_{-\infty}^{\infty} f(x - \xi, y - \eta) h(\xi, \eta) \, d\xi \, d\eta \, ?$$

Cursory inspection suggests that if this is to be true for arbitrary $h(x, y)$, then $f(x, y)$ needs to be zero at all points away from the origin and "infinite" at the origin. The "function" we are looking for is called the *unit impulse*, denoted $\delta(x, y)$. It is also sometimes referred to as the *Dirac delta function*.

Loosely speaking, $\delta(x, y)$ is zero everywhere except at the origin, where it is "infinite." The integral of $\delta(x, y)$ over any region including the origin is one. (If we think of a function of x and y as a surface, then this integral is the volume under that surface.) The impulse $\delta(x, y)$ is not a function in the classical sense (that is, it is not defined by giving its value for all arguments). It is a *generalized function* that can be thought of as the "limit" as $\epsilon \to 0$ of a series of square pulses of width 2ϵ in x and y and of height $1/(4\epsilon^2)$. We shall have more to say about this later, but for now we simply note the *sifting property*,

$$\int_{-\infty}^{\infty} \int_{-\infty}^{\infty} \delta(x, y) h(x, y) \, dx \, dy = h(0, 0),$$

by which the impulse can be defined. It follows that

$$\int_{-\infty}^{\infty} \int_{-\infty}^{\infty} \delta(x - \xi, y - \eta) h(\xi, \eta) \, d\xi \, d\eta = h(x, y),$$

as can be seen by a simple change of variables. By comparing this with our original equation for the output of the system, we see that $h(x, y)$ is the response of the system when presented with the unit impulse as input.

Considered as an image, $\delta(x, y)$ is black everywhere except at the origin, where there is a point of bright light. Thus $h(x, y)$ tells us how the system blurs or spreads out a point of light. In the case of a two-dimensional system it is called the *point-spread function*. It is the response of the two-dimensional system to an impulse and is thus analogous to the familiar impulse response of a one-dimensional system.

We now want to show that the output of any linear, shift-invariant system is related to its input by convolution. The point-spread function of the system, $h(x, y)$, can be determined by applying the test input $\delta(x, y)$. Given that the response to an impulse is now known, it is convenient to think of the input, $f(x, y)$, as made up of an infinite collection of shifted, scaled impulses,

$$k(\xi, \eta) \delta(x - \xi, y - \eta).$$

A simple geometric construction will help show how this can be done. Divide the xy-plane into squares of width ϵ. On each such elementary square erect a pulse of height equal to the average of $f(x, y)$ in the square. Figure 6-2 shows a cross section through such a two-dimensional array of square pulses. The function $f(x, y)$ is approximated by the piecewise-constant function that is the sum of all these pulses.

We can go one step further and replace each rectangular pulse by an impulse at the center of its square base. The volume under the impulse can

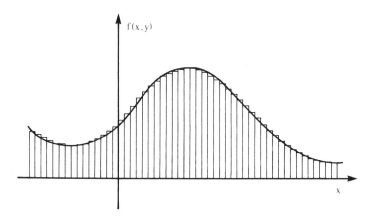

Figure 6-2. A continuous function can be thought of as the limit of a piecewise-constant function. In turn, each of the constant pieces can be replaced by an impulse whose area is proportional to the height of that piece. This leads to a decomposition of a function into impulses.

be made equal to the volume of the rectangular pulse, that is, the integral of the function $f(x, y)$ over the elementary square. If the function $f(x, y)$ is continuous, and ϵ is small enough, one can approximate this integral by the product of the value of $f(x, y)$ at the center of the square and the area of the square. The desired result is obtained in the limit as we let $\epsilon \to 0$.

The same decomposition of $f(x, y)$ in terms of impulses can be obtained by appealing to the sifting property of the unit impulse function. Either way, we find that

$$f(x, y) = \int_{-\infty}^{\infty} \int_{-\infty}^{\infty} f(\xi, \eta)\, \delta(x - \xi, y - \eta)\, d\xi\, d\eta.$$

Having decomposed the function in terms of impulses, we can determine the overall output, $g(x, y)$, when $f(x, y)$ is the input, by adding the responses of the system to the shifted, scaled impulses. This is so because the system is linear.

The response to $k\, \delta(x - \xi, y - \eta)$ is $k\, h(x - \xi, y - \eta)$, since the system is shift-invariant. Thus, since k is just $f(\xi, \eta)$,

$$g(x, y) = \int_{-\infty}^{\infty} \int_{-\infty}^{\infty} f(\xi, \eta)\, h(x - \xi, y - \eta)\, d\xi\, d\eta.$$

This can be written in the form $h \otimes f$. We show below that convolution is commutative, so that $h \otimes f = f \otimes h$, and so

$$g(x,y) = \int_{-\infty}^{\infty} \int_{-\infty}^{\infty} f(x - \xi, y - \eta) \, h(\xi, \eta) \, d\xi \, d\eta.$$

Linear, shift-invariant systems can always be described by a suitable point-spread function $h(x, y)$. Using this function we can compute the output $g(x, y)$, given an arbitrary input $f(x, y)$. The point-spread function is a complete characterization of a linear, shift-invariant system. We have thus shown that a linear, shift-invariant system performs a convolution.

We now show that convolution is commutative, that is, that

$$b \otimes a = a \otimes b.$$

Let $c = a \otimes b$, or

$$c(x,y) = \int_{-\infty}^{\infty} \int_{-\infty}^{\infty} a(x - \xi, y - \eta) \, b(\xi, \eta) \, d\xi \, d\eta.$$

Now let $x - \xi = \alpha$ and $y - \eta = \beta$, so that

$$c(x,y) = \int_{-\infty}^{\infty} \int_{-\infty}^{\infty} a(\alpha, \beta) \, b(x - \alpha, y - \beta) \, d\alpha \, d\beta.$$

Since α and β are arbitrary dummy variables, we can substitute ξ and η for them without changing the value of the integral. We obtain

$$c(x,y) = \int_{-\infty}^{\infty} \int_{-\infty}^{\infty} b(x - \xi, y - \eta) \, a(\xi, \eta) \, d\xi \, d\eta,$$

which is $b \otimes a$. Convolution is also associative; that is,

$$(a \otimes b) \otimes c = a \otimes (b \otimes c).$$

This allows us to consider the cascade of two systems with point-spread functions $h_1(x, y)$ and $h_2(x, y)$:

$$f \quad \rightarrow \quad \boxed{h_1} \quad\quad \boxed{h_2} \quad \rightarrow \quad g$$

If the input is $f(x, y)$, then the output of the first system is $f \otimes h_1$. This new signal is the input of the second system, and so the output of the second system is $(f \otimes h_1) \otimes h_2$. This can be written in the form $f \otimes (h_1 \otimes h_2)$, that is, the output produced when the input f is applied to a system with point-spread function $h_1 \otimes h_2$:

$$f \quad \rightarrow \quad \boxed{h_1 \otimes h_2} \quad \rightarrow \quad g$$

6.3 The Modulation-Transfer Function

It is harder to visualize the effect of convolution than it is the multiplication of two functions. Because convolution in the spatial domain becomes multiplication in the frequency domain, a transformation to the frequency domain is attractive in the case of linear, shift-invariant systems. Before we can explore these ideas, however, we must understand what frequency means for two-dimensional systems.

In the case of one-dimensional linear, shift-invariant systems we find that $e^{i\omega t}$ is an *eigenfunction* of convolution. An eigenfunction of a system is a function that is reproduced with at most a change in amplitude:

$$e^{i\omega t} \quad \rightarrow \quad \boxed{} \quad \rightarrow \quad A(\omega)\, e^{i\omega t}$$

Here $A(\omega)$ is the (possibly complex) factor by which the input signal is multiplied. That is, if we apply a complex exponential to a linear, shift-invariant system, we obtain a similar complex exponential waveform at the output, just scaled and shifted in phase. We call ω the frequency of the eigenfunction. In practice, we use real waveforms like $\cos \omega t$ and $\sin \omega t$, corresponding to the real and imaginary parts of $e^{i\omega t}$. The relationship between the two forms is, of course, just

$$e^{iwt} = \cos \omega t + i \sin \omega t.$$

The complex exponential form is used in deriving results because it makes the expressions more compact and helps avoid the need to treat cosines and sines separately.

In a two-dimensional linear, shift-invariant system, the input $f(x, y) = e^{+i(ux+vy)}$ gives rise to the output

$$g(x,y) = \int_{-\infty}^{\infty} \int_{-\infty}^{\infty} e^{i(u(x-\xi)+v(y-\eta))} h(\xi, \eta)\, d\xi\, d\eta,$$

or

$$g(x,y) = e^{+i(ux+vy)} \int_{-\infty}^{\infty} \int_{-\infty}^{\infty} e^{-i(u\xi+v\eta)} h(\xi, \eta)\, d\xi\, d\eta.$$

The double integral on the right is a function of u and v only, and the output $g(x, y)$ is therefore just a scaled, possibly shifted, version of the input $f(x, y)$. Thus $e^{+i(ux+vy)}$ is an eigenfunction of convolution in two dimensions:

$$e^{i(ux+vy)} \quad \rightarrow \quad \boxed{} \quad \rightarrow \quad A(u,v)\, e^{i(ux+vy)}$$

Note that frequency now has two components, u and v. We refer to the uv-plane as the *frequency domain*, in contrast to the xy-plane, which is referred to as the *spatial domain*.

The real waveforms $\cos(ux + vy)$ and $\sin(ux + vy)$ correspond to waves in two dimensions. The maxima and minima of $\cos(ux + vy)$ lie on parallel equidistant ridges along the lines

$$ux + vy = k\pi$$

for integer k (figure 6-3). Taking a cut through the surface at right angles to these lines, that is, in the direction (u, v), gives us sinusoidal waves with wavelength

$$\lambda = \frac{2\pi}{\sqrt{u^2 + v^2}}.$$

Such waves cannot occur on their own in an imaging system since brightness cannot be negative. There must be an added constant offset.

If we let

$$H(u, v) = \int_{-\infty}^{\infty} \int_{-\infty}^{\infty} e^{-i(u\xi + v\eta)} h(\xi, \eta) \, d\xi \, d\eta,$$

then, in the special case treated so far,

$$g(x, y) = H(u, v) f(x, y),$$

as can be seen from the integral given previously. Thus $H(u, v)$ characterizes the system for sinusoidal waveforms, just as $h(x, y)$ does for impulsive waveforms. For each frequency, it tells us the response of the system in amplitude and phase. In the case of a two-dimensional system it is called the *modulation-transfer function*. It is the frequency response of the two-dimensional system and so is analogous to the familiar frequency response of a one-dimensional system. (Note that $H(u, v)$ need not be real-valued.)

Just as we can learn much about the quality of an audio amplifier from its frequency response curve, so we can compare camera lenses, for example, by looking at their modulation-transfer function plots.

6.4 Fourier Transform and Filtering

An input $f(x, y)$ can be considered to be the sum of an infinite number of sinusoidal waves, just as earlier we thought of it as the sum of an infinite number of impulses. This is another convenient way to decompose the input, since we once again already know the system's response to each component, provided we are given the modulation-transfer function $H(u, v)$. If

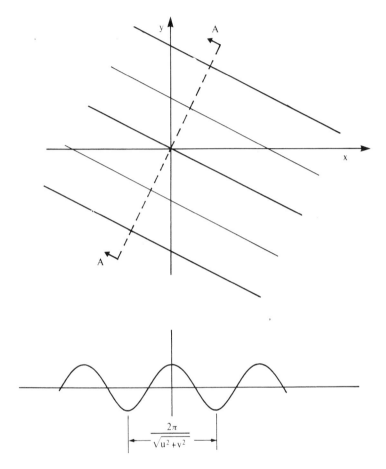

Figure 6-3. The eigenfunctions of two-dimensional linear, shift-invariant systems are complex exponentials. Their real parts are gratings, constant in one direction. Cross sections, such as the one taken along the line A–A, are sinusoidal.

we decompose $f(x, y)$ as

$$f(x, y) = \frac{1}{4\pi^2} \int_{-\infty}^{\infty} \int_{-\infty}^{\infty} F(u, v) e^{+i(ux+vy)} \, du \, dv,$$

then

$$g(x, y) = \frac{1}{4\pi^2} \int_{-\infty}^{\infty} \int_{-\infty}^{\infty} H(u, v) \, F(u, v) e^{+i(ux+vy)} \, du \, dv.$$

(The $1/4\pi^2$ occurs here for consistency with formulae introduced later on.) The only problem is that the decomposition into sinusoidal waves is not quite as trivial as the decomposition into impulses. How do we find $F(u, v)$ given $f(x, y)$? As we shall demonstrate in a moment, the answer turns out to be

$$F(u, v) = \int_{-\infty}^{\infty} \int_{-\infty}^{\infty} f(x, y) e^{-i(ux+vy)} \, dx \, dy$$

provided that this integral exists. We can see that this might be so by changing variables,

$$F(u, v) = \int_{-\infty}^{\infty} \int_{-\infty}^{\infty} f(\alpha, \beta) e^{-i(u\alpha+v\beta)} \, d\alpha \, d\beta,$$

and substituting into the expression for $f(x, y)$ to obtain

$$\frac{1}{4\pi^2} \int_{-\infty}^{\infty} \int_{-\infty}^{\infty} f(\alpha, \beta) \left[\int_{-\infty}^{\infty} \int_{-\infty}^{\infty} e^{i\left(u(x-\alpha)+v(y-\beta)\right)} \, du \, dv \right] d\alpha \, d\beta.$$

The inner integral does not converge. We show later, using so-called convergence factors, that it can be considered to equal $4\pi^2 \delta(x - \alpha, y - \beta)$. We therefore have

$$\int_{-\infty}^{\infty} \int_{-\infty}^{\infty} f(\alpha, \beta) \delta(x - \alpha, y - \beta) \, d\alpha \, d\beta = f(x, y),$$

so that

$$\frac{1}{4\pi^2} \int_{-\infty}^{\infty} \int_{-\infty}^{\infty} F(u, v) e^{+i(ux+vy)} \, du \, dv = f(x, y).$$

$F(u, v)$ is called the *Fourier transform* of $f(x, y)$. Similarly, we can define the Fourier transform $G(u, v)$ of the output $g(x, y)$. Finally,

$$G(u, v) = H(u, v) \, F(u, v),$$

which is simpler than

$$g(x, y) = \int_{-\infty}^{\infty} \int_{-\infty}^{\infty} f(x - \xi, y - \eta) h(\xi, \eta) \, d\xi \, d\eta.$$

Thus convolution has been transformed into multiplication!

We also see once again that the modulation-transfer function $H(u, v)$ specifies how the system attenuates or amplifies each component $F(u, v)$ of the input. A linear, shift-invariant system thus acts as a filter that selectively attenuates or amplifies various parts of the spectrum of possible frequencies. It can also shift their phase, but this is all it does. We might conclude that restricting ourselves to linear, shift-invariant systems seriously limits what we can accomplish, but at the same time it allows us to derive a lot of useful results, because the mathematics is manageable.

Note the minor asymmetry in the expressions for the forward Fourier transform

$$F(u,v) = \int_{-\infty}^{\infty} \int_{-\infty}^{\infty} f(x,y) e^{-i(ux+vy)}\, dx\, dy$$

and the inverse transform

$$f(x,y) = \frac{1}{4\pi^2} \int_{-\infty}^{\infty} \int_{-\infty}^{\infty} F(u,v) e^{+i(ux+vy)}\, du\, dv.$$

The constant multipliers are split up in this way to be consistent with other textbooks. The fact that the transforms are almost symmetric makes it possible to deduce properties that apply to the inverse transform, given properties that apply to the forward transform. Observe, however, that $F(u,v)$ is generally complex, whereas $f(x,y)$ is always real. Note also that $H(u,v)$ is the Fourier transform of $h(x,y)$.

Not all functions have a Fourier transform. Functions in certain simple classes are equal to the Fourier integrals of their Fourier transforms. But it is hard to characterize exactly which functions do, and which do not, have a transform.

A different kind of difficulty is that the integrals are taken over the whole xy-plane, whereas imaging devices only produce usable images over a finite part of the image plane. Moreover, computers only use discrete samples of these images. These two issues will be discussed in more detail in the next chapter.

6.5 The Fourier Transform of Convolution

Let $c = a \otimes b$; then the Fourier transform $C(u,v)$ of $c(x,y)$ is

$$\int_{-\infty}^{\infty} \int_{-\infty}^{\infty} \left[\int_{-\infty}^{\infty} \int_{-\infty}^{\infty} a(x - \xi, y - \eta) b(\xi, \eta)\, d\xi\, d\eta \right] e^{-i(ux+vy)}\, dx\, dy$$

or

$$\int_{-\infty}^{\infty} \int_{-\infty}^{\infty} \left[\int_{-\infty}^{\infty} \int_{-\infty}^{\infty} a(x - \xi, y - \eta) e^{-i(ux+vy)}\, dx\, dy \right] b(\xi, \eta)\, d\xi\, d\eta.$$

That is,

$$C(u,v) = \int_{-\infty}^{\infty} \int_{-\infty}^{\infty} A(u,v) e^{-i(u\xi+v\eta)} b(\xi, \eta)\, d\xi\, d\eta = A(u,v)B(u,v).$$

Convolution in the spatial domain becomes multiplication in the frequency domain. This it is the ultimate justification for the introduction of the complex machinery of the frequency domain. The commutativity and associativity of convolution follow directly from the corresponding properties of multiplication.

Noting the near-symmetry between forward and inverse transforms, we can show that the transform of the product $d = ab$ is

$$D(u,v) = \frac{1}{4\pi^2} A(u,v) \otimes B(u,v).$$

The argument is similar to the one used above.

Next, consider the convolution $c = a \otimes b$ at $(x,y) = (0,0)$:

$$c(0,0) = \int_{-\infty}^{\infty} \int_{-\infty}^{\infty} a(-\xi,-\eta)b(\xi,\eta)\,d\xi\,d\eta.$$

We also have

$$c(0,0) = \frac{1}{4\pi^2} \int_{-\infty}^{\infty} \int_{-\infty}^{\infty} C(u,v)\,du\,dv,$$

by taking the inverse transform of $C(u,v)$. Since

$$C(u,v) = A(u,v)B(u,v),$$

we have

$$\int_{-\infty}^{\infty} \int_{-\infty}^{\infty} a(-\xi,-\eta)b(\xi,\eta)\,d\xi\,d\eta = \frac{1}{4\pi^2} \int_{-\infty}^{\infty} \int_{-\infty}^{\infty} A(u,v)B(u,v)\,du\,dv.$$

If we reflect $a(x,y)$ and repeat the above argument for $a(-x,-y)$, we obtain instead

$$\int_{-\infty}^{\infty} \int_{-\infty}^{\infty} a(\xi,\eta)b(\xi,\eta)\,d\xi\,d\eta = \frac{1}{4\pi^2} \int_{-\infty}^{\infty} \int_{-\infty}^{\infty} A^*(u,v)B(u,v)\,du\,dv,$$

since the transform of $a(-x,-y)$ is $A^*(u,v)$, the complex conjugate of $A(u,v)$. In particular, we see that

$$\int_{-\infty}^{\infty} \int_{-\infty}^{\infty} a^2(\xi,\eta)\,d\xi\,d\eta = \frac{1}{4\pi^2} \int_{-\infty}^{\infty} \int_{-\infty}^{\infty} |A(u,v)|^2\,du\,dv,$$

assuming that $a(x,y)$ is real. Here $|A(u,v)|^2 = A^*(u,v)A(u,v)$. This result, equating power in the spatial domain with power in the frequency domain, is known as *Raleigh's theorem*. The discrete equivalent is *Parseval's theorem*.

6.6 Generalized Functions and Unit Impulses

The unit impulse $\delta(x, y)$ is not a function in the traditional sense, because we cannot define its value for all x and y. A consistent interpretation is possible, though, if we think of $\delta(x, y)$ as the limit of a sequence of functions. We need a function that depends on a parameter in such a way that its properties approach those defined for the unit impulse as the parameter tends to a specified limit. This sequence is said to define a *generalized function*. An example will help clarify this idea.

Consider the sequence of square pulses of unit volume:

$$\delta_\epsilon(x, y) = \begin{cases} 1/(4\epsilon^2), & \text{for } |x| \le \epsilon \text{ and } |y| \le \epsilon; \\ 0, & \text{for } |x| > \epsilon \text{ or } |y| > \epsilon. \end{cases}$$

Cross sections through three functions in this sequence look like this:

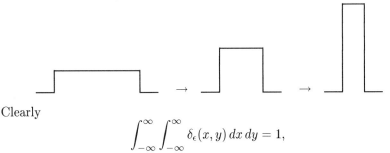

Clearly

$$\int_{-\infty}^{\infty} \int_{-\infty}^{\infty} \delta_\epsilon(x, y)\, dx\, dy = 1,$$

and further, if $f(x, y)$ is sufficiently well behaved,

$$\lim_{\epsilon \to 0} \int_{-\infty}^{\infty} \int_{-\infty}^{\infty} \delta_\epsilon(x, y) f(x, y)\, dx\, dy = \lim_{\epsilon \to 0} \frac{1}{4\epsilon^2} \int_{-\epsilon}^{\epsilon} \int_{-\epsilon}^{\epsilon} f(x, y)\, dx\, dy.$$

This is just $f(0, 0)$, as can be seen by expanding $f(x, y)$ in a Taylor series about the point $(0, 0)$. Also

$$\lim_{\epsilon \to 0} \delta_\epsilon(x, y) = 0 \qquad \text{for any } (x, y) \ne (0, 0).$$

Thus the sequence of functions $\{\delta_\epsilon(x, y)\}$ can be thought of as defining the unit impulse. When evaluating an integral involving $\delta(x, y)$, we can use $\delta_\epsilon(x, y)$ instead and then take the limit of the result as $\epsilon \to 0$.

From the form given for $\delta_\epsilon(x, y)$ we see that $\delta(x, y)$ can be thought of as the product of two one-dimensional unit impulses,

$$\delta(x, y) = \delta(x)\delta(y),$$

where the one-dimensional impulse is defined by the *sifting property*,

$$\int_{-\infty}^{\infty} f(x)\, \delta(x)\, dx = f(0) \quad \text{for arbitrary } f(x).$$

The integral of the one-dimensional unit impulse is the *unit step function*,

$$\int_{-\infty}^{x} \delta(t)\, dt = u(x),$$

where

$$u(x) = \begin{cases} 1, & \text{for } x > 0; \\ 1/2, & \text{for } x = 0; \\ 0, & \text{for } x < 0. \end{cases}$$

Conversely, we can think of the unit impulse as the derivative of the unit step function. This can be seen by considering the step function as the limit of a sequence $\{u_\epsilon(x)\}$, where

$$u_\epsilon(x) = \begin{cases} 1, & \text{for } x > +\epsilon. \\ (1/2)\big(1 + (x/\epsilon)\big), & \text{for } |x| \le \epsilon; \\ 0, & \text{for } x < -\epsilon. \end{cases}$$

Then clearly

$$\frac{d}{dx} u_\epsilon(x) = \begin{cases} 1/(2\epsilon), & \text{for } |x| \le \epsilon; \\ 0, & \text{for } |x| > \epsilon. \end{cases}$$

It must be pointed out that different sequences may define the same generalized function. We can, for example, consider the sequence of Gaussians,

$$\delta_\sigma(x, y) = \frac{1}{2\pi\sigma^2} e^{-\frac{1}{2}\frac{x^2+y^2}{\sigma^2}},$$

as $\sigma \to 0$. Functions in this sequence have unit volume, and $\delta_\sigma(x, y)$ tends to zero for all points $(x, y) \ne (0,0)$ as $\sigma \to 0$. The sequence $\delta_\sigma(x, y)$ has the advantage over $\delta_\epsilon(x, y)$ of being infinitely differentiable.

What is the Fourier transform of the unit impulse? We have

$$\int_{-\infty}^{\infty} \int_{-\infty}^{\infty} \delta(x, y) e^{-i(ux+vy)} \, dx \, dy = 1,$$

as can be seen by substituting $x = 0$ and $y = 0$ into $e^{-i(ux+vy)}$, using the sifting property of the unit impulse. Alternatively, we can use

$$\lim_{\epsilon \to 0} \int_{-\infty}^{\infty} \int_{-\infty}^{\infty} \delta_\epsilon(x, y) e^{-i(ux+vy)} \, dx \, dy,$$

or

$$\lim_{\epsilon \to 0} \frac{1}{2\epsilon} \int_{-\epsilon}^{\epsilon} e^{-iux} \, dx \, \frac{1}{2\epsilon} \int_{-\epsilon}^{\epsilon} e^{-ivy} \, dy,$$

that is,

$$\lim_{\epsilon \to 0} \frac{\sin u\epsilon}{u\epsilon} \frac{\sin v\epsilon}{v\epsilon} = 1.$$

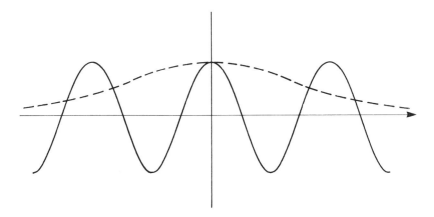

Figure 6-4. The integral of a sinusoid (shown solid) does not converge. If the integrand is multiplied by a Gaussian (shown dotted), however, we obtain a function that can be integrated. The original integral can be thought of as the limit of the integral with the convergence factor as the convergence factor is made flatter and flatter.

We conclude that a system whose point-spread function is the unit impulse is the identity system, since it does not modify anything in the signal. All frequencies are passed through with unit gain and no phase shift, since the modulation-transfer function $H(u, v)$ is unity: The output is equal to the input.

6.7 Convergence Factors and the Unit Impulse

The integral

$$\int_{-\infty}^{\infty} \int_{-\infty}^{\infty} e^{i(ua+vb)} \, du \, dv$$

does not converge. The problem is that the oscillations in the integrand do not die away as u and v become large. One way to assign a meaning to the integral, despite this problem, is to multiply the integrand by a *convergence factor* that forces it to be small when u and v are large (figure 6-4). The convergence factor has to depend on a parameter in such a way that the modified integral approaches the original one when the parameter approaches a specified limit. The value assigned to the integral is the limit of the modified integral as the parameter approaches this limit. The method will become clear as we apply the notion of convergence factor to the integral given above.

A convenient convergence factor, in this case, is the Gaussian,

$$c_\sigma(u, v) = e^{-\frac{1}{2}\frac{u^2+v^2}{\sigma^2}},$$

where σ is the parameter that will be varied. Note that

$$\lim_{\sigma \to \infty} c_\sigma(u, v) \to 1, \qquad \text{for any finite } (u, v).$$

The integral we have to evaluate is

$$\int_{-\infty}^{\infty} \int_{-\infty}^{\infty} e^{-\frac{1}{2}\frac{u^2+v^2}{\sigma^2}} e^{i(ua+vb)} \, du \, dv,$$

or

$$\int_{-\infty}^{\infty} e^{-\frac{1}{2}\left(\frac{u}{\sigma}\right)^2+iua} \, du \int_{-\infty}^{\infty} e^{-\frac{1}{2}\left(\frac{v}{\sigma}\right)^2+ivb} \, dv.$$

Now

$$\int_{-\infty}^{\infty} e^{-\frac{1}{2}\left(\frac{u}{\sigma}\right)^2} \cos(ua) \, du = \sqrt{2\pi}\sigma e^{-\frac{1}{2}a^2\sigma^2},$$

while

$$\int_{-\infty}^{\infty} e^{-\frac{1}{2}\left(\frac{u}{\sigma}\right)^2} \sin(ua) \, du = 0,$$

since $\sin(ua)$ is an odd function of u. The overall integral is thus

$$2\pi\sigma^2 e^{-\frac{1}{2}(a^2+b^2)\sigma^2},$$

which tends to zero as $\sigma \to \infty$ as long as $a^2 + b^2 \neq 0$. When $a = b = 0$, however, the result does not tend to a finite limit as $\sigma \to \infty$. The integral

$$\int_{-\infty}^{\infty} \int_{-\infty}^{\infty} e^{i(ua+vb)} \, du \, dv$$

must therefore be a scaled version of the impulse function $\delta(a, b)$. But what is the scale factor? Since

$$\int_{-\infty}^{\infty} \int_{-\infty}^{\infty} \delta(a, b) \, da \, db = 1,$$

we can determine the scale factor by considering

$$\lim_{\sigma \to \infty} \int_{-\infty}^{\infty} \int_{-\infty}^{\infty} 2\pi\sigma^2 e^{-\frac{1}{2}(a^2+b^2)\sigma^2} \, da \, db.$$

The double integral can be split into the product of two single integrals as follows:

$$2\pi\sigma^2 \int_{-\infty}^{\infty} e^{-\frac{1}{2}a^2\sigma^2} \, da \int_{-\infty}^{\infty} e^{-\frac{1}{2}b^2\sigma^2} \, db = 4\pi^2.$$

The product is independent of σ, and we finally have

$$\int_{-\infty}^{\infty} \int_{-\infty}^{\infty} e^{i(ua+vb)} \, du \, dv = 4\pi^2 \delta(a,b).$$

This result was used earlier in our discussion of the Fourier transform.

6.8 Partial Derivatives and Convolution

We shall use differentiation to accentuate edges in images, and it will be useful to know how the Fourier transform of the derived image is related to the Fourier transform of the original image. That is, if $F(u,v)$ is the Fourier transform of $f(x,y)$, what are the Fourier transforms of $\partial f/\partial x$ and $\partial f/\partial y$? Consider the transform

$$\int_{-\infty}^{\infty} \int_{-\infty}^{\infty} \frac{\partial f}{\partial x} e^{-i(ux+vy)} \, dx \, dy,$$

or

$$\int_{-\infty}^{\infty} \left[\int_{-\infty}^{\infty} \frac{\partial f}{\partial x} e^{-iux} \, dx \right] e^{-ivy} \, dy.$$

We can attack the inner integral using integration by parts:

$$\int_{-\infty}^{\infty} \frac{\partial f}{\partial x} e^{-iux} \, dx = \left[f(x,y)e^{-iux} \right]_{-\infty}^{\infty} + (iu) \int_{-\infty}^{\infty} f(x,y)e^{-iux} \, dx.$$

We cannot proceed, however, unless $f(x,y) \to 0$ as $x \to \pm\infty$. In that case the Fourier transform is just

$$\int_{-\infty}^{\infty} (iu) \int_{-\infty}^{\infty} f(x,y)e^{-i(ux+vy)} \, dx \, dy = iuF(u,v).$$

The integral does not converge if $f(x,y)$ does not tend to zero at infinity, but we can resort to convergence factors if this happens and obtain basically the same result. It is easy to show in a similar fashion that the Fourier transform of $\partial f/\partial y$ is just $ivF(u,v)$. We conclude that differentiation accentuates the high-frequency components and suppresses the low-frequency components. In fact, any constant offset or zero-frequency term is lost completely.

The Laplacian of the function $f(x,y)$ is defined as

$$\nabla^2 f = \frac{\partial^2 f}{\partial x^2} + \frac{\partial^2 f}{\partial y^2}.$$

So the Fourier transform of the Laplacian is just

$$-(u^2 + v^2) F(u,v).$$

We can think of $-(u^2 + v^2)$ as the modulation-transfer function of the operator ∇^2, in a sense to be made precise later. Note that this modulation-transfer function is rotationally symmetric, that is, it depends only on $(u^2 + v^2)$, not on u and v independently. This suggests that the Laplacian operator itself is rotationally symmetric.

It may seem a strange coincidence that taking derivatives in the spatial domain corresponds to multiplication in the frequency domain, since we saw earlier that convolution in the spatial domain corresponds to multiplication in the frequency domain. This becomes less surprising when we consider that differentiation is linear and shift-invariant! Is it possible that taking a derivative is just like convolution with some peculiar function? (It has to be a peculiar function, because it must be zero except at the origin, since the derivative operates locally.) Let us study this question in more detail.

The modulation-transfer function $H(u, v)$ corresponding to the first partial derivative with respect to x is iu. We can find the point-spread function corresponding to the first partial derivative by finding the inverse Fourier transform of iu:

$$\frac{1}{4\pi^2} \int_{-\infty}^{\infty} \int_{-\infty}^{\infty} iu e^{+i(ux+vy)} \, du \, dv.$$

This integral does not converge. We could attack it using a convergence factor, but it is easier to note that

$$\int_{-\infty}^{\infty} \int_{-\infty}^{\infty} e^{+i(ux+vy)} \, du \, dv = 4\pi^2 \delta(x, y).$$

The integral is thus

$$\frac{\partial}{\partial x} \delta(x, y),$$

since multiplication of the transform with iu corresponds to differentiation with respect to x. Now $\delta(x, y)$ is already somewhat pathological, so we cannot expect its derivative to be a function in the classic sense. It can, however, be defined as the limit of a sequence of functions, for example, by

$$\frac{\partial}{\partial x} \delta_\sigma(x, y) = -\frac{x}{2\pi\sigma^4} e^{-\frac{1}{2} \frac{x^2+y^2}{\sigma^2}}.$$

Alternatively, it can be thought of as the limit of the sequence

$$\delta_{x;\epsilon}(x, y) = \frac{1}{2\epsilon} \big(\delta(x + \epsilon, y) - \delta(x - \epsilon, y) \big),$$

where we have two closely spaced impulses of opposite polarity. The result, called a *doublet*, will be denoted $\delta_x(x, y)$. This definition corresponds to

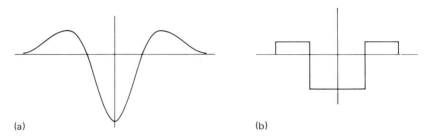

(a)   (b)

Figure 6-5. Application of the Laplacian operator can be thought of as a limit of convolutions with rotationally symmetric functions with a center–surround organization. (a) The Laplacian of the Gaussian provides an example of such a function with continuous derivatives. (b) We can instead use a piecewise-constant function.

the usual way of defining a partial derivative as the limit of a difference, for

$$f(x,y) \otimes \delta_{x;\epsilon}(x,y) = \frac{f(x+\epsilon,y) - f(x-\epsilon,y)}{2\epsilon},$$

so that

$$\lim_{\epsilon \to 0} f(x,y) \otimes \delta_{x;\epsilon}(x,y) = f(x,y) \otimes \delta_x(x,y) = \frac{\partial f}{\partial x}.$$

The generalized function corresponding to the Laplacian can be considered as the limit of the sequence

$$L_\sigma(x,y) = \left(\frac{x^2 + y^2 - \sigma^2}{2\pi\sigma^6} \right) e^{-\frac{1}{2}\frac{x^2+y^2}{\sigma^2}},$$

obtained by differentiating $\delta_\sigma(x,y)$, for example (figure 6-5a). This function is circularly symmetric. It has a central depression of magnitude $1/(2\pi\sigma^4)$ and radius σ surrounded by a circular wall of maximum height $e^{-3/2}/(\pi\sigma^4)$ and radius $\sqrt{3}\sigma$. The form of this function suggests another sequence (figure 6-5b):

$$L_\epsilon(x,y) = \begin{cases} -2/(\pi\epsilon^4), & \text{for } 0 \le x^2 + y^2 \le \epsilon^2; \\ +2/(3\pi\epsilon^4), & \text{for } \epsilon^2 < x^2 + y^2 \le 4\epsilon^2; \\ 0, & \text{for } 4\epsilon^2 < x^2 + y^2. \end{cases}$$

We shall find this form useful later when we look for discrete analogs of these continuous operators.

6.9 Rotational Symmetry and Isotropic Operators

The Laplacian is the lowest-order linear combination of partial derivatives that is rotationally symmetric. That is, the Laplacian of a rotated image is the same as the rotated Laplacian of an image. Conversely, if we rotate an image, take the Laplacian, and rotate it back, we obtain the same result as if we had just applied the Laplacian.

Another second-order operator that is rotationally symmetric is the quadratic variation,

$$\left(\frac{\partial^2}{\partial x^2}\right)^2 + 2\left(\frac{\partial^2}{\partial x \partial y}\right)\left(\frac{\partial^2}{\partial y \partial x}\right) + \left(\frac{\partial^2}{\partial y^2}\right)^2.$$

It is, however, not linear. If we allow nonlinearity, then the lowest-order rotationally symmetric differential operator is the squared gradient,

$$\left(\frac{\partial}{\partial x}\right)^2 + \left(\frac{\partial}{\partial y}\right)^2.$$

The Laplacian, the squared gradient, and the quadratic variation are useful in detecting edges in images, as we shall see in chapter 8.

Rotationally symmetric operators are particularly attractive because they treat image features in the same way, no matter what their orientation is. Also, a rotationally symmetric function can be described by a simple profile rather than a surface. Finally, the Fourier transform of a rotationally symmetric function can be computed using a single integral instead of a double integral, as we show next.

Let us introduce polar coordinates in both the spatial and the frequency domains (figure 6-6):

$$x = r\cos\phi \quad \text{and} \quad y = r\sin\phi,$$
$$u = \rho\cos\alpha \quad \text{and} \quad v = \rho\sin\alpha,$$

so that $ux + vy = r\rho\cos(\phi - \alpha)$. Now, if $f(x, y) = \overline{f}(r)$, then the transform

$$F(u, v) = \int_{-\infty}^{\infty} \int_{-\infty}^{\infty} f(x, y)e^{-i(ux+vy)} \, dx \, dy,$$

becomes just

$$\overline{F}(\rho) = \int_{-\pi}^{\pi} \int_{0}^{\infty} r\overline{f}(r)e^{-ir\rho\cos(\phi-\alpha)} \, dr \, d\phi.$$

(The r in the integrand is of course just the determinant of the Jacobian of the transformation from Cartesian to polar coordinates.) If we change

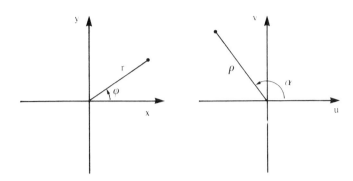

Figure 6-6. To deal with rotationally symmetric functions it is convenient to introduce polar coordinates for both the spatial and the frequency domains.

the order of integration, then a simple change of variables turns the inner integral into

$$\int_{-\pi}^{\pi} e^{-ir\rho\cos\phi}\, d\phi = 2\int_0^\pi \cos(r\rho\cos\phi)\, d\phi = 2\pi J_0(r\rho),$$

where $J_0(x)$ is the zeroth-order Bessel function. Thus if $F(u,v) = \overline{F}(\rho)$, then

$$\overline{F}(\rho) = 2\pi \int_0^\infty r\overline{f}(r)J_0(r\rho)\, dr.$$

Similarly, one can show that

$$\overline{f}(r) = \frac{1}{2\pi} \int_0^\infty \rho\overline{F}(\rho)J_0(r\rho)\, d\rho.$$

These two formulae define the *Hankel transforms*. (The asymmetry can be traced to our asymmetric definition of the Fourier transform.)

We conclude that the Fourier transform of a rotationally symmetric function is also rotationally symmetric. It is also real, which means that the phase shift is zero. We shall use these results in analyzing some simple imaging system defects. As an example, consider the point-spread function of a system that acts as a *lowpass filter* with cutoff frequency B, that is,

$$\overline{H}(\rho) = \begin{cases} 1, & \text{for } \rho \le B; \\ 0, & \text{for } \rho > B. \end{cases}$$

Taking the inverse transform, we obtain

$$\overline{h}(r) = \frac{1}{2\pi} \int_0^\infty \rho H(\rho)J_0(r\rho)\, d\rho = \frac{1}{2\pi} \int_0^B \rho J_0(r\rho)\, d\rho.$$

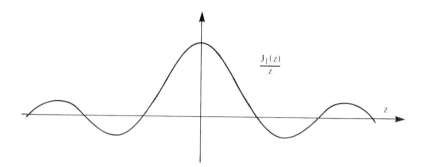

Figure 6-7. The function $J_1(z)/z$ plays the same role in two-dimensional systems as $\sin(z)/z$ does in one-dimensional systems. Convolution with this function removes all frequencies above a certain cutoff; that is, a system that has a point-spread function of this form acts as a lowpass filter.

Let $z = r\rho$; then

$$\bar{h}(r) = \frac{1}{2\pi}\frac{1}{r^2}\int_0^{rB} z J_0(z)\, dz.$$

Now

$$\frac{d}{dz} z J_1(z) = z J_0(z),$$

where $J_1(z)$ is the first-order Bessel function. Therefore

$$\bar{h}(r) = \frac{1}{2\pi}\frac{1}{r^2}(rB)J_1(rB) = \frac{1}{2\pi}B^2\frac{J_1(rB)}{(rB)}.$$

It can be shown that

$$\lim_{z\to 0}\frac{J_1(z)}{z} = \frac{1}{2},$$

so $\bar{h}(r)$ has a maximum at the origin and then drops smoothly to zero at $r = 3.83171\ldots$ (figure 6-7). It is negative for a while and then oscillates about zero with decreasing amplitude. The amplitude decreases asymptotically as $z^{-3/2}$. The function $J_1(z)/z$ plays a role for two-dimensional systems that is similar to that played by $\sin(z)/z$ in the case of one-dimensional systems.

It should be apparent, by the way, that a filter with a sharp cutoff will produce oscillatory responses, or "ringing" effects in the spatial domain (sometimes referred to as *Gibbs's phenomena*). In many cases a filter with a more gradual rolloff is better, since it suffers less from these overshoot phenomena. A Gaussian filter, for example, has a very smooth rolloff that extends over a considerable frequency band. It does not introduce any spurious inflections into the filtered image.

6.10 Blurring, Defocusing, and Motion Smear

In a typical imaging system we find that the rays that would be focused at a single point in an ideal system are, in fact, slightly spread out. This blurring of the image can take various forms, but it can sometimes be modeled by a Gaussian point-spread function,

$$h(x, y) = \frac{1}{2\pi\sigma^2} e^{-\frac{1}{2}\frac{x^2+y^2}{\sigma^2}},$$

with unit volume. This is a rotationally symmetric point-spread function, since it depends only on $x^2 + y^2$, not on x or y separately. We can compute its Fourier transform using the Hankel transform formula.

Note, however, that the Gaussian happens to be separable into the product of a function of x and a function of y. So another approach may be easier:

$$H(u, v) = \int_{-\infty}^{\infty} \int_{-\infty}^{\infty} \frac{1}{2\pi\sigma^2} e^{-\frac{1}{2}\frac{x^2+y^2}{\sigma^2}} e^{-i(ux+vy)} \, dx \, dy$$

$$= \frac{1}{\sqrt{2\pi}\sigma} \int_{-\infty}^{\infty} e^{-\frac{1}{2}\left(\frac{x}{\sigma}\right)^2} e^{-iux} \, dx \, \frac{1}{\sqrt{2\pi}\sigma} \int_{-\infty}^{\infty} e^{-\frac{1}{2}\left(\frac{y}{\sigma}\right)^2} e^{-ivy} \, dy.$$

The first integral on the right-hand side equals

$$\frac{1}{\sqrt{2\pi}\sigma} \int_{-\infty}^{\infty} e^{-\frac{1}{2}\left(\frac{x}{\sigma}\right)^2} \cos(ux) \, dx = \sigma e^{-\frac{1}{2}u^2\sigma^2}.$$

So finally,

$$H(u, v) = e^{-\frac{1}{2}(u^2+v^2)\sigma^2},$$

which is rotationally symmetric, as expected.

We note that low frequencies are passed unattenuated, while higher frequencies are reduced in amplitude, significantly so for frequencies above about $1/\sigma$. Now σ is a measure of the size of the original point-spread function; therefore, the larger the blur, the lower the frequencies that are attenuated. This is an example of the inverse relationship between scale changes in the spatial domain and corresponding scale changes in the frequency domain. In fact, if $\bar{r}$ is a measure of the radius of a blur in the spatial domain, and $\bar{\rho}$ is a measure of the radius of its transform, then $\bar{r}\bar{\rho}$ is constant.

One way to blur an image is to defocus it (figure 6-1). In this case the point-spread function is a little *pillbox*, as can be seen by considering the

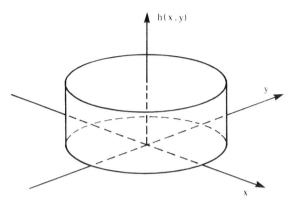

Figure 6-8. Defocusing an image amounts to convolving it with a pillbox, a circularly symmetric function of unit volume.

cone of light emanating from the lens with its vertex at the focal point. (This point does not lie on the image plane, but slightly in front of or behind it.) The image plane cuts this cone in a circle. Within the circle, brightness is uniform (figure 6-8), so we have

$$h(x, y) = \begin{cases} 1/(\pi R^2), & \text{for } x^2 + y^2 \leq R^2; \\ 0, & \text{for } x^2 + y^2 > R^2. \end{cases}$$

Here

$$R = \frac{1}{2} \frac{d}{f'} e,$$

where d is the diameter of the lens, f' the distance from the lens to the correctly focused spot, and e the displacement of the image plane. We can apply the Hankel transform formula to obtain

$$\overline{H}(\rho) = \frac{2}{R^2} \int_0^R r J_0(r\rho) \, dr = 2 \frac{J_1(R\rho)}{(R\rho)},$$

using the fact that

$$\frac{d}{dz} z J_1(z) = z J_0(z),$$

as noted before. Again, low frequencies are passed unattenuated, while higher frequencies are reduced in amplitude, and some are not passed at all. Some are even inverted, since $J_1(z)$ oscillates about zero. For frequencies for which $J_1(R\rho) < 0$ we find that the brightest parts of the defocused image coincide with the darkest parts of the ideal image, and vice versa. Components of the waveform with frequencies for which $J_1(R\rho) = 0$ are removed completely. Such components cannot be recovered from the defocused image. As mentioned before, the first zero of the function $J_1(z)$ occurs at $z = 3.83171\ldots$ .We observe again the inverse scaling in the spatial and frequency domains, since in our case $z = R\rho$. That is, the larger the defocus radius R, the lower the frequency ρ for which $J_1(R\rho) = 0$.

Another form of image degradation is due to image motion. This can result from motion of either the imaging system or the objects being imaged. In either case an image point is smeared into a line. For convenience, suppose the motion is along the x-axis and the length of the line is $2l$. Then the point-spread function can be described by the product

$$h_x(x, y) = \frac{1}{2l}\big(u(x + l) - u(x - l)\big)\,\delta(y),$$

where $u(z)$ is the unit step function, as before. In this case the point-spread function is not rotationally symmetric. Its Fourier transform can be found as follows:

$$H(u, v) = \int_{-\infty}^{\infty} \frac{1}{2l}\big(u(x - l) - u(l - x)\big)e^{-iux}\,dx \int_{-\infty}^{\infty} \delta(y)e^{-ivy}\,dy,$$

or

$$H(u, v) = \frac{1}{2l}\int_{-l}^{l} e^{-iux}\,dx,$$

so that

$$H(u, v) = \frac{\sin(ul)}{ul}.$$

The argument can easily be extended to motion in any direction. Once again, low frequencies are hardly affected, while higher ones are attenuated. Waves at some frequencies are inverted, and those for which $ul = \pi k$, where k is an integer, are completely suppressed. Waves with crests parallel to the direction of motion are not affected at all, of course.

6.11 Restoration and Enhancement

To undo the effects of image blur we can pass the image through a system with a modulation-transfer function $H'(u, v)$ that is the algebraic inverse of the modulation-transfer function $H(u, v)$ of the system that introduced the blur. That is,

$$H(u, v)H'(u, v) = 1.$$

Equivalently, we need a system with point-spread function $h'(x, y)$ such that the convolution of $h'(x, y)$ with $h(x, y)$ is the unit impulse. That is, $h'(x, y) \otimes h(x, y) = \delta(x, y)$:

$$f(x, y) \quad \rightarrow \quad \boxed{h(x, y)} \quad \longrightarrow \quad \boxed{h'(x, y)} \quad \longrightarrow \quad f(x, y)$$

The cascade of the two systems is the identity system.

An immediate problem is that we cannot recover frequencies that have been totally suppressed, for which $H(u, v) = 0$. A second problem occurs when we try to compute the inverse Fourier transform of $H'(u, v)$ in order to obtain $h'(x, y)$. It is likely that the needed integral will not converge, although we might be able to obtain a result by introducing a convergence factor. Such a result will not be a function in the classical sense, however.

The most serious problem is noise. Real image measurements are inexact, and we can usually model this defect as additive noise. The noise at one image point is typically independent of, and thus uncorrelated with, the noise at all other image points. It can be shown that this implies that the noise has a flat spectrum: The noise power in any given region of the frequency domain is as large as that in any other region with same area.

Unfortunately, the noise we are concerned with here is introduced after the blurring. The effect is that strongly attenuated frequencies tend to become submerged in the noise, and when we try to recover them by amplification, we also amplify the noise. This is the basic limitation of image restoration, and it is due to the fact that, at any given frequency, we cannot distinguish between signal and noise.

One approach to restoration is heuristic. We can design a system that has a modulation-transfer function approximately equal to the inverse of the modulation-transfer function of the blurring system. We place an upper limit, however, on the amplification. For example,

$$|H'(u, v)| = \min \left(\frac{1}{|H(u, v)|}, A \right),$$

where A is the maximum gain. Or more elegantly, we can use something like

$$H'(u, v) = \frac{H(u, v)}{H(u, v)^2 + B^2},$$

where $1/(2B)$ is the maximum gain, if $H(u, v)$ is real (figure 6-9).

6.12 Correlation and the Power Spectrum

When images are processed, it is at times useful to correlate them. In this way we can tell, for example, how similar two brightness patterns are (figure 6-10). The *crosscorrelation* of $a(x, y)$ and $b(x, y)$ is defined by

$$a \star b = \int_{-\infty}^{\infty} \int_{-\infty}^{\infty} a(\xi - x, \eta - y) \, b(\xi, \eta) \, d\xi \, d\eta.$$

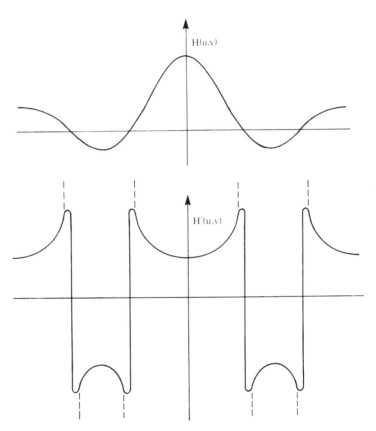

Figure 6-9. The inverse system that undoes the filtering performed by a given system has modulation-transfer function $H'(u, v)$ inversely proportional to the modulation-transfer function $H(u, v)$ of the given system. In practice, a limit is placed on the amplification of the inverse system in order to limit the amplification of noise.

We shall use the notation $\phi_{ab}(x, y)$ for this integral. Note the similarity to the definition of convolution. The only difference lies in the arguments of the first function in the integrand. Here $a(\xi, \eta)$ is simply shifted by (x, y) before being multiplied by $b(\xi, \eta)$. In convolution the first function is also "flipped over" in x and y:

$$a \otimes b = \int_{-\infty}^{\infty} \int_{-\infty}^{\infty} a(x - \xi, y - \eta) \, b(\xi, \eta) \, d\xi \, d\eta.$$

If $b(x, y) = a(x, y)$, the result is called the *autocorrelation*. The autocorrelation of a function is symmetric, that is, $\phi_{aa}(-x, -y) = \phi_{aa}(x, y)$. It

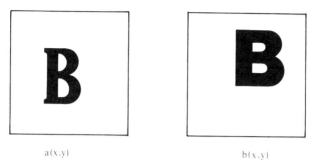

a(x,y)   b(x,y)

Figure 6-10. Correlation can be useful in comparing two similar images, $a(x, y)$ and $b(x, y)$. It can also be useful in determining the position of an image fragment consisting of a known pattern.

can be shown that the autocorrelation of any function has a maximum at $(x, y) = (0, 0)$, so that

$$\phi_{aa}(0, 0) \geq \phi_{aa}(x, y) \qquad \text{for all } (x, y).$$

If $b(x, y)$ is a shifted version of $a(x, y)$,

$$b(x, y) = a(x - x_0, y - y_0),$$

then a similar maximum will occur for the appropriate value of shift. That is,

$$\phi_{ab}(x_0, y_0) \geq \phi_{ab}(x, y) \qquad \text{for all } (x, y).$$

Note that there can be other maxima, particularly if $a(x, y)$ is periodic. Nevertheless, when $b(x, y)$ is approximately equal to a shifted version of $a(x, y)$, then the shift can be estimated by looking for maxima in ϕ_{ab}.

The Fourier transforms of the crosscorrelations and autocorrelations are often informative. They are called *power spectra* for reasons that will become apparent, and they are denoted $\Phi_{ab}(u, v)$ and $\Phi_{aa}(u, v)$, respectively. If the Fourier transform of $a(x, y)$ is $A(u, v)$, then

$$\Phi_{aa}(u, v) = |A(u, v)|^2 = A^*(u, v)A(u, v),$$

where $A^*(u, v)$ is the complex conjugate of $A(u, v)$. Thus Φ_{aa} is always real, a property that can also be deduced from the symmetry of ϕ_{aa} and the fact that the transform of $a(-x, -y)$ is $A^*(u, v)$. In any case, for small δu and δv,

$$\Phi_{aa}(u, v)\, \delta u\, \delta v$$

is the power in the rectangular region of the frequency domain lying between u and $u + \delta u$ and v and $v + \delta v$. This explains the origin of the term
power spectrum.

Even when the Fourier transform of $a(x, y)$ does not converge, its power
spectrum may still exist. It should also be noted that $A(u, v)$ uniquely
specifies $a(x, y)$ via the inverse Fourier transform, but there is no unique
function corresponding to a given $\Phi_{aa}(u, v)$. Infinitely many functions have
the same autocorrelation and thus the same power spectrum. The power
spectrum does not change, for example, when an image is translated, since
only the phase of the Fourier transform is changed. If an object can be
recognized from the power spectrum of an image, then it can be recognized
independently of its position. Great hope was held out at one time, for
this reason, that Fourier transform methods would be important in solving
recognition problems. Unfortunately, such methods only work when the
object is alone in the image and does not rotate or change size. Moreover,
as we have seen, the power spectra of different objects may be the same.

Random noise provides another interesting illustration. The Fourier
transform of an image in which each point has independent random noise
with mean zero and standard deviation σ is a similar random image with
mean zero and standard deviation $2\pi\sigma$. The average of the power spectra
of an infinite number of such random images tends to the constant $(2\pi\sigma)^2$
at all frequencies.

6.13 Optimal Filtering and Noise Suppression

The next section, dealing with optimal filtering, requires some patience
with nontrivial mathematical manipulations. The hasty reader may choose
to skip it on first reading without serious loss of continuity. It may be
worthwhile returning to this section later, however, since it is the first place
in this book where we introduce the tools of the calculus of variations.

Suppose that we are given the sum of the signal $b(x, y)$ and the noise
$n(x, y)$. Our task is to recover, as best we can, the signal $b(x, y)$. The measure of how well we succeed will be the integral of the square of the difference between the output $o(x, y)$ and the desired signal $d(x, y)$ (figure 6-11).
Usually $d(x, y)$ is just $b(x, y)$. We choose to minimize the integral of the
square of the error because it leads to tractable mathematics. (This, of
course, is the real reason for the popularity of least-squares methods in
general.)

We have to minimize the squared error

$$E = \int_{-\infty}^{\infty} \int_{-\infty}^{\infty} \big(o(x, y) - d(x, y)\big)^2 \, dx \, dy.$$

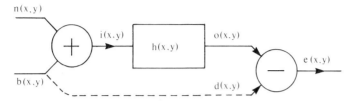

Figure 6-11. An optimal filter is one that minimizes the difference between the output $o(x, y)$ and the desired signal $d(x, y)$ when noise $n(x, y)$ is added to the input $b(x, y)$ of a linear, shift-invariant system with impulse response $h(x, y)$.

If we are going to use a linear system for the filtering operation, we can characterize the system by means of its point-spread function $h(x, y)$. The input to the system is

$$i(x, y) = b(x, y) + n(x, y),$$

and the output is

$$o(x, y) = i(x, y) \otimes h(x, y).$$

So

$$E = \int_{-\infty}^{\infty} \int_{-\infty}^{\infty} \left(o^2(x, y) - 2o(x, y)d(x, y) + d^2(x, y) \right) \, dx \, dy.$$

Since $o^2 = (i \otimes h)^2$,

$$o^2(x, y) = \int_{-\infty}^{\infty} \int_{-\infty}^{\infty} i(x - \xi, y - \eta)h(\xi, \eta) \, d\xi \, d\eta$$

$$\times \int_{-\infty}^{\infty} \int_{-\infty}^{\infty} i(x - \alpha, y - \beta)h(\alpha, \beta) \, d\alpha \, d\beta,$$

and so

$$\int_{-\infty}^{\infty} \int_{-\infty}^{\infty} o^2(x, y) \, dx \, dy$$

$$= \int_{-\infty}^{\infty} \int_{-\infty}^{\infty} \int_{-\infty}^{\infty} \int_{-\infty}^{\infty} \phi_{ii}(\xi - \alpha, \eta - \beta)h(\xi, \eta)h(\alpha, \beta) \, d\xi \, d\eta \, d\alpha \, d\beta,$$

where $\phi_{ii}(x, y)$ is the autocorrelation of $i(x, y)$. Moreover,

$$o(x, y)d(x, y) = \int_{-\infty}^{\infty} \int_{-\infty}^{\infty} i(x - \xi, y - \eta)h(\xi, \eta)d(x, y) \, d\xi \, d\eta,$$

and so

$$\int_{-\infty}^{\infty} \int_{-\infty}^{\infty} o(x,y)d(x,y)\, dx\, dy = \int_{-\infty}^{\infty} \int_{-\infty}^{\infty} \phi_{id}(\xi,\eta)h(\xi,\eta))\, d\xi\, d\eta,$$

where $\phi_{id}(x,y)$ is the crosscorrelation of $i(x,y)$ and $d(x,y)$. Finally we need

$$\int_{-\infty}^{\infty} \int_{-\infty}^{\infty} d^2(x,y) = \phi_{dd}(0,0),$$

where $\phi_{dd}(x,y)$ is the autocorrelation of $d(x,y)$. We can now rewrite the expression for the error term to be minimized in the form

$$E = \int_{-\infty}^{\infty} \int_{-\infty}^{\infty} \int_{-\infty}^{\infty} \int_{-\infty}^{\infty} \phi_{ii}(\xi - \alpha, \eta - \beta)h(\xi,\eta)h(\alpha,\beta)\, d\xi\, d\eta\, d\alpha\, d\beta$$

$$- 2 \int_{-\infty}^{\infty} \int_{-\infty}^{\infty} \phi_{id}(\xi,\eta)h(\xi,\eta)\, d\xi\, d\eta + \phi_{dd}(0,0).$$

This expression is to be minimized by finding the point-spread function $h(x,y)$. This is a problem in the *calculus of variations*. (The calculus of variations is covered in more detail in the appendix.) We shall attack the problem using the basic method of that speciality. In the typical calculus problem we look for a parameter value that results in a stationary value of a given function. In the problem here, we are looking instead for a function that leads to a stationary value of a given functional. A *functional* is an expression that depends on a function, as, for example, E above depends on $h(\xi,\eta)$.

Suppose that $h(x,y)$ gives the minimum value of E, and let $\delta h(x,y)$ be an arbitrary function used to modify $h(x,y)$. Then $h(x,y) + \epsilon\,\delta h(x,y)$ will give a value that cannot be less than E, no matter what $\delta h(x,y)$ is. Let the value be $E + \delta E$. If we are truly at a minimum, then

$$\lim_{\epsilon \to 0} \frac{\partial}{\partial \epsilon}(E + \delta E) = 0 \qquad \text{for all } \delta h(x,y).$$

If this were not the case, we could reduce E by adding a small multiple of $\delta h(x,y)$ to $h(x,y)$, thus contradicting the assumption that $h(x,y)$ is optimal. Now

$$\lim_{\epsilon \to 0} \frac{\partial}{\partial \epsilon}(E + \delta E)$$

$$= 2 \int_{-\infty}^{\infty} \int_{-\infty}^{\infty} \int_{-\infty}^{\infty} \int_{-\infty}^{\infty} \phi_{ii}(\xi - \alpha, \eta - \beta)h(\xi,\eta)\delta h(\alpha,\beta)\, d\xi\, d\eta\, d\alpha\, d\beta$$

$$- 2 \int_{-\infty}^{\infty} \int_{-\infty}^{\infty} \phi_{id}(\xi,\eta)\delta h(\xi,\eta)\, d\xi\, d\eta,$$

or

$$\lim_{\epsilon \to 0} \frac{\partial}{\partial \epsilon}(E + \delta E)$$

$$= -2 \int_{-\infty}^{\infty} \int_{-\infty}^{\infty} \left[\phi_{id}(\xi, \eta) - \int_{-\infty}^{\infty} \int_{-\infty}^{\infty} \phi_{ii}(\xi - \alpha, \eta - \beta) h(\alpha, \beta) \, d\alpha \, d\beta \right]$$
$$\times \, \delta h(\xi, \eta) \, d\xi \, d\eta.$$

If this is to be zero for all $\delta h(x, y)$, then the bracketed expression must be zero, or

$$\phi_{id}(\xi, \eta) = \int_{-\infty}^{\infty} \int_{-\infty}^{\infty} \phi_{ii}(\xi - \alpha, \eta - \beta) h(\alpha, \beta) \, d\alpha \, d\beta,$$

that is, perhaps surprisingly,

$$\phi_{id} = \phi_{ii} \otimes h \,.$$

This simple equation for $h(x, y)$ can be solved by taking the Fourier transform,

$$\Phi_{id} = H \Phi_{ii},$$

where Φ_{ii} and Φ_{id} are the power spectra. The power spectra are thus all we need to know to design the image-restoring system under the given assumptions. The same system will be optimal for a large class of images, not just a single one. (It would, of course, not be of much interest otherwise.)

As an example, consider a system designed to suppress noise, that is, a system that takes the sum of the image $b(x, y)$ and the noise $n(x, y)$ and produces an output $o(x, y)$ that is as close as possible, in the least-squares sense, to the original image $b(x, y)$. Here $d(x, y) = b(x, y)$ and

$$i(x, y) = b(x, y) + n(x, y).$$

So

$$\Phi_{id} = \Phi_{bb} + \Phi_{nb},$$

and

$$\Phi_{ii} = \Phi_{bb} + \Phi_{bn} + \Phi_{nb} + \Phi_{nn},$$

as can be seen by noting the definitions of Φ_{ii} and Φ_{id}. We now assume that the noise is not correlated to the signal, so that $\Phi_{bn} = \Phi_{nb} = 0$. Then

$$H = \frac{\Phi_{id}}{\Phi_{ii}} = \frac{\Phi_{bb}}{\Phi_{bb} + \Phi_{nn}} = \frac{1}{1 + \Phi_{nn}/\Phi_{bb}}.$$

It is clear what the optimal system is doing. In parts of the spectrum where the signal-to-noise ratio, Φ_{bb}/Φ_{nn}, is high, the gain is almost unity;

in parts where the noise dominates, the gain is very low, approximately Φ_{bb}/Φ_{nn}, which is just the signal-to-noise ratio.

Now consider the case where the signal $b(x, y)$ is passed through a system with point-spread function $h(x, y)$ before the noise $n(x, y)$ is added. The result,

$$i = b \otimes h + n,$$

is to be passed through a system with point-spread function $h'(x, y)$. The output

$$o = i \otimes h'$$

should be as close as possible to the original image $b(x, y)$, in the least-squares sense. Here $d(x, y) = b(x, y)$, so that

$$\Phi_{id} = H\Phi_{bb} + \Phi_{nb}$$

and

$$\Phi_{ii} = H^2\Phi_{bb} + H(\Phi_{nb} + \Phi_{bn}) + \Phi_{nn}.$$

Assuming that the noise is not correlated with the signal, we have

$$H' = \frac{\Phi_{id}}{\Phi_{ii}} = \frac{H\Phi_{bb}}{H^2\Phi_{bb} + \Phi_{nn}}.$$

If the signal-to-noise ratio is high in a particular part of the spectrum, then

$$H' \approx \frac{1}{H}$$

there, while gain is limited to about $H(\Phi_{bb}/\Phi_{nn})$ in parts where $\Phi_{nn} > |H|^2 \Phi_{bb}$. Note the similarity of this result to that derived heuristically earlier.

Finally, it may be instructive to consider the optimal filter for estimating a processed version of the image rather than the image itself. Suppose we want the least-squares estimate of

$$d(x, y) = b(x, y) \otimes p(x, y),$$

where $p(x, y)$ is the point-spread function of a processing filter. Then

$$\phi_{id} = i \star d = i \star (b \otimes p) = (i \star b) \otimes p = \phi_{ib} \otimes p,$$

so that

$$\Phi_{id} = \Phi_{ib} P,$$

where $P(u, v)$ is the Fourier transform of $p(x, y)$. Thus

$$H' = \frac{\Phi_{id}}{\Phi_{ii}} = \frac{\Phi_{ib}}{\Phi_{ii}} P.$$

The optimal filter is just the cascade of the optimal filter for recovering the image $b(x, y)$ and the processing filter $P(u, v)$. We do not need anything else.

We should note at this point that the design of the optimal filter here is much simpler than in the one-dimensional situation. This is because the impulse response in the one-dimensional case must be one-sided, since a system cannot anticipate its input. Limitations in the time domain do not translate easily into understandable limitations in the frequency domain. For example, it is hard to express the constraint that $f(t) = 0$ for $t < 0$ in terms of $F(\omega)$, the Fourier transform of $f(t)$. Fortunately, there is no such problem in the case of images, since the support of a point-spread function can extend in all directions from the origin. The *support* of a function is the region over which it is nonzero.

6.14 Image Models

In order to apply the optimal filtering methods, we must estimate the power spectra of the images to be processed. Looking at the spectra of a few "typical" images will quickly persuade you that most of the energy is concentrated at the lower frequencies. It is useful to know about this falloff with frequency since it helps separate the desired signal from the noise, which has a flat spectrum. The observed falloff in power with frequency is, in part, due to the fact that many objects or parts of objects are opaque and have nearly uniform brightness. The corresponding image patches are separated by discontinuities along edges where objects occlude one another.

A full discussion of image models lies beyond the scope of this book, but we can get a rough idea by considering a simple rectangular patch

$$f(x, y) = \begin{cases} 1, & \text{for } |x| \leq W \text{ and } |y| \leq H; \\ 0, & \text{for } |x| > W \text{ or } |y| > H. \end{cases}$$

The Fourier transform is

$$F(u, v) = WH \, \frac{\sin(uW)}{uW} \, \frac{\sin(vH)}{vH}.$$

Shifting the patch just changes the phase, not the magnitude, of the transform. Ignoring the oscillations, we see that the transform falls off as $1/(uv)$. Thus, depending on the direction we choose in the frequency domain, it falls off as $1/\rho$ or $1/\rho^2$ with distance ρ from the origin.

Another useful component of an image model might be the "pillbox" patch,

$$\overline{f}(r) = \begin{cases} 1, & \text{for } r \leq R; \\ 0, & \text{for } r > R. \end{cases}$$

The transform in this case is

$$\overline{F}(\rho) = 2R^2 \frac{J_1(\rho R)}{(\rho R)}.$$

For large arguments, $J_1(z)$ behaves like

$$\sqrt{\frac{2}{\pi z}} \sin(z - \pi/4),$$

so that, if we ignore the oscillations, $\overline{F}(\rho)$ falls off as $1/\rho^{3/2}$ for large ρ.

Image models containing polygonal or circular patches tend to have power spectra falling off as some power of frequency. At higher frequencies real images fall off even more rapidly, due to the resolution limits of the optical system. In telescopes, for example, there is an absolute cutoff frequency, determined by the ratio of the aperture diameter to the wavelength of light, above which there is no transmission at all. Microscopes have a similar absolute limitation determined by the numerical aperture of the objective and the wavelength of light.

A different application of the observation that most power in images is concentrated at low frequencies can be found in image reproduction. Methods for displaying images, such as the printing of halftones, photographic reproduction, and television, have limited *dynamic range*; that is, they can only show a certain range of gray-level values. In terms of the quality of reproduction, what we are interested in is the ratio of the brightest to the darkest reproducible gray-level. One important consideration in displaying images is that small brightness differences be perceptible. Even large differences in brightness between adjacent regions may not be noticeable if the regions are themselves very bright. What is important is the relative size of the brightness difference, that is, the ratio of the difference to the smaller of the two. It is for this reason that dynamic range is measured by the ratio of the brightest to the darkest level that can be reproduced, rather than the difference.

The dynamic range of color transparencies can be over a hundred to one, while that of newsprint is often not much more than ten to one. Natural images tend to have large dynamic ranges. Usually a compromise has to be struck when they are to be reproduced. If we try to impose the variation in image brightness unchanged onto the medium, the brightest and the darkest areas will not be reproduced properly. To avoid losing detail in the highlights and shadows due to saturation, we have to compress the dynamic range.

A power function can do this compression. If the brightness of the reproduction is $b'(x, y)$ and that of the original is $b(x, y)$, then

$$b'(x, y) = \big(b(x, y)\big)^\gamma,$$

where $0 < \gamma < 1$. Such reproductions are generally acceptable, although barely perceptible brightness differences in the original will be imperceptible in the reproduction.

Another approach is to take advantage of the fact that images usually contain large low-frequency components. A filter that attenuates low frequencies can be devised by subtracting from the image a smoothed version of the image. Such a filter will tend to reduce the dynamic range. An example is provided by a filter with a point-spread function

$$h(x, y) = \delta(x, y) - \frac{k}{2\pi\sigma^2} e^{-\frac{1}{2}\frac{x^2 + y^2}{\sigma^2}}$$

for $0 < k < 1$. The modulation-transfer function of this filter is

$$H(u, v) = 1 - k e^{-\frac{1}{2}(u^2 + v^2)\sigma^2}.$$

Other smoothing functions can be used. A photographic technique for achieving a similar effect is called *unsharp masking*. Here an out-of-focus image is "subtracted," in part, from the original. Note that, in this case, sharp edges are reproduced with their full contrast. We have to be careful in applying this process, however, since the brightness values in the image are shifted around and spurious changes in the appearance of the objects may result. As we shall see later, the brightness values are used in recovering surface shape, for example.

6.15 References

The classic reference on image processing is *Digital Image Processing* by Pratt [1978]. The first few chapters of *Digital Picture Processing* by Rosenfeld & Kak [1982] also provide an excellent introduction to the subject. Much of the two-dimensional analysis is a straightforward extension of the one-dimensional case aptly described in *Signals and Systems* by Oppenheim & Willsky [1983] and *Circuits, Signals, and Systems* by Siebert [1986]. The underlying theory of the Fourier transform is given in the standard reference *The Fourier Transform and Its Applications* by Bracewell [1965, 1978]. An enjoyable discussion of generalized functions appears in Lighthill's *Introduction to Fourier Analysis and Generalised Functions* [1978]. Even more detail can be found in *Generalized Functions: Properties and Operations* by Gel'fand & Shilov [1964]. Few texts explicitly discuss convergence factors; one that does is *Summable Series and Convergence Factors* by Moore [1966].

The basic work on optimal filtering is due to Wiener. He uses a delightfully symmetric definition of the Fourier transform in *Extrapolation, Interpolation, and Smoothing of Stationary Time Series with Engineering Applications* [1966]. The optimal filter is derived using the methods of the calculus of variations, for which volume I of *Methods of Mathematical Physics* by Courant & Hilbert [1953] may be the best reference. Image models are discussed in *Pattern Models* by Ahuja & Schachter [1983].

Image processing is a relatively old field that matured more than ten years ago. A survey of early work on image processing is provided by Huang, Schreiber, & Tretiak [1971]. The classic application of image processing method has been in improving image quality, as discussed by Schreiber [1978].

Detailed structure in an image that is too fine to be resolved, yet coarse enough to produce a noticeable fluctuation in the gray-levels of neighboring picture cells, constitutes *texture*. (Note that there are other notions of what is meant by the term texture.) Texture may be periodic, nearly periodic, or random. There has been work devoted to the derivation of texture measures that allow classification. Other efforts are directed at the segmentation of images into regions of differing texture, as in the work of Bajcsy [1973] and Ehrich [1977]. Methods for the analysis of gray-level co-occurrence histograms have found application in this domain. Another approach depends on the appearance of peaks in the frequency domain. Ahuja & Rosenfeld [1981] study the relationship of mosaic image models to the notion of texture. Further references relating to image processing will be given at the end of the next chapter.

6.16 Exercises

6-1   Find $k(\sigma)$ such that the family of functions

$$\delta_\sigma(x, y) = k(\sigma) e^{-\frac{1}{2}\frac{x^2 + y^2}{\sigma^2}}$$

defines the unit impulse $\delta(x, y)$ as $\sigma \to 0$.

6-2   Consider the family of functions

$$L_\delta(x, y) = \begin{cases} a, & \text{for } r \leq \delta; \\ b, & \text{for } \delta < r \leq 2\delta; \\ 0, & \text{for } 2\delta < r; \end{cases}$$

where $r = \sqrt{x^2 + y^2}$. For what values of a and b does this family define the generalized function that corresponds to the Laplacian? That is, when is the limit of the convolution of $L_\delta(x, y)$ with some given function $f(x, y)$ equal to $\nabla^2 f(x, y)$? Hint: It may help to apply the operator to the test function

$$\frac{1}{4}(x^2 + y^2),$$

whose Laplacian is known to be equal to one.

6-3 Show that if $f(x, y)$ is separable into a product of a function of x and a function of y, its Fourier transform $F(u, v)$ is also separable into a function of u and a function of v.

6-4 Show that if $f(x, y) \geq 0$ for all x and y, then $F(0, 0) \geq |F(u, v)|$ for all u and v. When is $F(0, 0) = F(u, v)$?

6-5 Usually the point-spread function $h(x, y)$ of an operator used for smoothing operations is largest at the origin, $(x, y) = (0, 0)$, positive everywhere, and dies away as x and y tend to infinity. It can be conveniently thought of as a mass distribution. Without loss of generality we shall assume that the center of mass of this distribution lies at the origin. We need to be able to say how "spread out" such a distribution is. The *radius of gyration* of a mass distribution is the distance from its center of mass at which a point of equal mass would have to be placed in order for it to have the same inertia as the given distribution. (The inertia of a point mass is the product of the square of the distance from the origin times the mass.)

The total mass M of a distribution $h(x, y)$ is just

$$M = \int_{-\infty}^{\infty} \int_{-\infty}^{\infty} h(x, y) \, dx \, dy,$$

while the radius of gyration R is defined by

$$\int_{-\infty}^{\infty} \int_{-\infty}^{\infty} r^2 h(x, y) \, dx \, dy = R^2 \int_{-\infty}^{\infty} \int_{-\infty}^{\infty} h(x, y) \, dx \, dy = M\,R^2,$$

where $r^2 = x^2 + y^2$.

(a) Find the radius of gyration of a pillbox defined by

$$b_V(x, y) = \begin{cases} 1/(\pi V^2), & \text{for } r \leq V; \\ 0, & \text{for } r > V. \end{cases}$$

(b) Find the radius of gyration of the Gaussian

$$G_\sigma(x, y) = \frac{1}{2\pi\sigma^2} e^{-\frac{1}{2}\frac{x^2 + y^2}{\sigma^2}}.$$

Note that the distributions in (a) and (b) both have "unit mass" and that it may help to convert the required integrals to polar coordinates.

(c) Show that the mass of the convolution of two smoothing functions is the product of the masses of the two functions. Also show that, when smoothing functions are convolved, their gyration radii squared add. That is, if $f = g \otimes h$, then $R_f^2 = R_g^2 + R_h^2$, where R_f, R_g, and R_h are the radii of gyration of f, g, and h, respectively.

(d) When a rotationally symmetric smoothing function is convolved with itself many times, it becomes indistinguishable from the Gaussian. Suppose that the pillbox is convolved with itself n times. What is the value of σ of the approximating Gaussian?

6-6 Show that $a \star (b \otimes c) = (a \star b) \otimes c$, where $\star$ denotes correlation and $\otimes$ denotes convolution.

6-7 The modulation-transfer function of an optical telescope is $A(u, v) = P(u, v) \otimes P(u, v)$, where $P(u, v)$ is the rotationally symmetric lowpass filter

$$P(u, v) = \begin{cases} 1, & \text{for } u^2 + v^2 \leq \omega^2; \\ 0, & \text{for } u^2 + v^2 > \omega^2, \end{cases}$$

for some ω, where ω is a function of the wavelength of light and the size of the collecting optics.

(a) Find $A(u, v)$. Hint: What is the overlap between two disks of equal diameter when their centers are not aligned?

(b) What is the corresponding point-spread function? Hint: What does multiplication in the frequency domain correspond to in the spatial domain?

6-8 Consider a system that blurs images according to a Gaussian point-spread function with standard deviation σ. Suppose that the noise power spectrum is flat with power N^2, the signal power spectrum is also flat with power S^2, and that $S^2 > N^2$. (Noise is added to the image after blurring.)

(a) Sketch the modulation-transfer function of the optimal filter for deblurring the image.

(b) What is the low-frequency response?

(c) What frequency is maximally amplified?

(d) What is the maximal gain?

6-9 It is difficult to measure the point-spread function of an optical system directly. Instead, we usually image a sharp edge between two regions with different brightnesses. In this fashion we obtain the *edge-spread function*.

(a) How would you obtain the *line-spread function* $l(x)$ from the response $e(x)$ to a unit step edge? The line-spread function is the response of the system to an impulsive line.

(b) Show that $l(x)$ is related to the point-spread function $h(r)$ by

$$l(x) = 2 \int_x^\infty \frac{r}{\sqrt{r^2 - x^2}} h(r)\, dr.$$

This is the definition of the *Abel transform*. Here $l(x)$ is the Abel transform of $h(r)$. Assume that the point-spread function is rotationally symmetric.

(c) Show that the Abel transform obeys the relationships

$$\int_{-\infty}^\infty l(x)\, dx = 2\pi \int_0^\infty h(r)\, r\, dr \qquad \text{and} \qquad l(0) = 2 \int_0^\infty h(r)\, dr.$$

(d) How would you recover the point-spread function from the measured line-spread function? Show that

$$h(r) = -\frac{1}{\pi} \int_r^\infty \frac{l'(x)}{\sqrt{x^2 - r^2}}\, dx = -\frac{1}{\pi} \int_r^\infty \sqrt{x^2 - r^2}\, \frac{d}{dx}\left(\frac{l'(x)}{x}\right) dx,$$

where $l'(x)$ is the derivative of $l(x)$ with respect to x. This is the inverse Abel transform.

6-10 A rotationally symmetric function $f(x,y)$ depends only on the radius r and does not depend on the polar angle θ, where

$$r = \sqrt{x^2 + y^2} \qquad \text{and} \qquad \theta = \tan^{-1}(y/x).$$

Show that the Gaussian is the only rotationally symmetric function that can be decomposed into the product of a function of x and a function of y; that is, $f(x,y) = g(x)h(y)$. Hint: First prove that $f(x,y)$ is rotationally symmetric if and only if

$$\frac{1}{x}\frac{\partial f}{\partial x} = \frac{1}{y}\frac{\partial f}{\partial y}.$$

You can then easily prove that, for some constant c,

$$\frac{dg}{dx} = c\, x\, g(x) \qquad \text{and} \qquad \frac{dh}{dy} = c\, y\, h(y).$$

7

Image Processing:
Discrete Images

In the previous chapter we explored linear, shift-invariant systems in the continuous two-dimensional domain. In practice, we deal with images that are both limited in extent and sampled at discrete points. The results developed so far have to be specialized, extended, and modified to be useful in this domain. Also, a few new aspects appear that must be treated carefully.

The sampling theorem tells us under what circumstances a discrete set of samples can accurately represent a continuous image. We also learn what happens when the conditions for the application of this result are not met. This has significant implications for the design of imaging systems.

Methods requiring transformation to the frequency domain have become popular, in part because of algorithms that permit the rapid computation of the discrete Fourier transform. Care has to be taken, however, since these methods assume that the signal is periodic. We discuss how this requirement can be met and what happens when the assumption does not apply.

7.1 Finite Image Size

In practice, images are always of finite size. Consider a rectangular image of width W and height H. Then the integrals in the Fourier transform no longer need to be taken to infinity:

$$F(u, v) = \int_{-H/2}^{H/2} \int_{-W/2}^{W/2} f(x, y) e^{-i(ux+vy)} \, dx \, dy.$$

Curiously, we do not need to know $F(u, v)$ for all frequencies in order to reconstruct $f(x, y)$. Knowing that $f(x, y) = 0$ for $|x| > W/2$ and $|y| > H/2$ provides a strong constraint. Put another way, there is a lot less information in a function that is nonzero only over a finite part of the image plane than in one that is not.

To see this, consider the image plane tiled with copies of the image. That is, extend the image in a doubly periodic fashion into a function

$$\tilde{f}(x, y) = \begin{cases} f(x, y), & \text{for } |x| \le W/2 \text{ and } |y| \le H/2; \\ f(x - kW, y - lH), & \text{for } |x| > W/2 \text{ or } |y| > H/2, \end{cases}$$

where

$$k = \left\lfloor \frac{x + W/2}{W} \right\rfloor \qquad \text{and} \qquad l = \left\lfloor \frac{y + H/2}{H} \right\rfloor.$$

Here $\lfloor x \rfloor$ is the largest integer that is not larger than x. The Fourier transform of the repeated image is

$$\tilde{F}(u, v) = \int_{-\infty}^{\infty} \int_{-\infty}^{\infty} \tilde{f}(x, y) e^{-i(ux+vy)} \, dx \, dy$$

$$= \sum_{k=-\infty}^{\infty} \sum_{l=-\infty}^{\infty} \int_{-H/2}^{H/2} \int_{-W/2}^{W/2} f(x, y) \, e^{-i(u(x-kW)+v(y-lH))} \, dx \, dy$$

$$= \sum_{k=-\infty}^{\infty} \sum_{l=-\infty}^{\infty} e^{iukW} e^{ivlH} F(u, v).$$

It is shown in exercise 7-1, using suitable convergence factors, that

$$\sum_{k=-\infty}^{\infty} e^{ikx} = 2\pi \sum_{k=-\infty}^{\infty} \delta(x - 2\pi k).$$

Thus

$$\tilde{F}(u, v) = 4\pi^2 \sum_{k=-\infty}^{\infty} \sum_{l=-\infty}^{\infty} \delta(uW - 2\pi k)\, \delta(vH - 2\pi l)\, F(u, v)$$

$$= 4\pi^2 \frac{1}{WH} \sum_{k=-\infty}^{\infty} \sum_{l=-\infty}^{\infty} \delta\left(u - \frac{2\pi}{W}k\right) \delta\left(v - \frac{2\pi}{H}l\right) F(u, v),$$

from which we see that $\widetilde{F}(u, v)$ is zero except at a discrete set of frequencies,

$$(u, v) = \left(\frac{2\pi}{W} k, \frac{2\pi}{H} l \right).$$

Thus, to find $\widetilde{f}(x, y)$ we only need to know $F(u, v)$ at these frequencies. But $f(x, y)$ can be obtained from $\widetilde{f}(x, y)$ by just "cutting out" the piece for which $|x| < W/2$ and $|y| < H/2$. So we only need to know

$$F_{kl} = F \left(\frac{2\pi}{W} k, \frac{2\pi}{H} l \right)$$

for all k and l to recover $f(x, y)$. This is a countable set of numbers.

Note that the transform of a periodic function is discrete. The inverse transform can be expressed in the form of a series, since

$$\widetilde{f}(x, y) = \frac{1}{4\pi^2} \int_{-\infty}^{\infty} \int_{-\infty}^{\infty} F(u, v) e^{+i(ux+vy)} \, dx \, dy$$

$$= \frac{1}{WH} \sum_{k=-\infty}^{\infty} \sum_{l=-\infty}^{\infty} \int_{-\infty}^{\infty} \int_{-\infty}^{\infty} \delta \left(u - \frac{2\pi}{W} k \right) \delta \left(v - \frac{2\pi}{H} l \right)$$

$$\times F(u, v) e^{+i(ux+vy)} dx dy$$

$$= \frac{1}{WH} \sum_{k=-\infty}^{\infty} \sum_{l=-\infty}^{\infty} F_{kl} \, e^{2\pi i (\frac{k}{W} x + \frac{l}{H} y)}.$$

Another way to look at this is to consider $f(x, y)$ a windowed version of some $\widetilde{f}(x, y)$, where $\widetilde{f}(x, y) = f(x, y)$ within the window. That is,

$$f(x, y) = \widetilde{f}(x, y) \, w(x, y),$$

where the window function $w(x, y)$ is defined as

$$w(x, y) = \begin{cases} 1, & \text{for } |x| \leq W/2 \text{ and } |y| \leq H/2; \\ 0, & \text{for } |x| > W/2 \text{ or } |y| > H/2. \end{cases}$$

The transform of $f(x, y)$ is then just the convolution of the transform of $\widetilde{f}(x, y)$ with the transform of $w(x, y)$. The latter is

$$WH \frac{\sin(uW/2)}{uW/2} \frac{\sin(vH/2)}{vH/2}.$$

The Fourier transform of $f(x, y)$ is thus a highly smoothed version of the transform of $\widetilde{f}(x, y)$. We shall see later that such a filtered function can be fully specified by suitably chosen samples. The function at points other than the given sample points can easily be found by interpolation from the given samples.

7.2 Discrete Image Sampling

When the image is digitized, the brightness is known only at a discrete set of locations. We can think of the result as defined by a discrete grid of impulses,

$$f(x,y) = wh \sum_{k=-\infty}^{\infty} \sum_{l=-\infty}^{\infty} f_{kl}\, \delta(x - kw, y - lh),$$

where w and h are the horizontal and vertical sampling intervals, respectively. The Fourier transform now becomes

$$F(u,v) = wh \int_{-\infty}^{\infty} \int_{-\infty}^{\infty} \sum_{k=-\infty}^{\infty} \sum_{l=-\infty}^{\infty} f_{kl}\, \delta(x - kw, y - lh) e^{-i(ux+vy)}\, dx\, dy$$

$$= wh \sum_{k=-\infty}^{\infty} \sum_{l=-\infty}^{\infty} f_{kl}\, e^{-i(ukw+vlh)}.$$

This is a periodic function. The period in u is $2\pi/w$ and that in v is $2\pi/h$. Thus a discrete function transforms into a periodic one. This means that we can forget the part of $F(u,v)$ for $|u| > \pi/w$ and $|v| > \pi/h$. We do not need it to recover $f(x,y)$.

It is of interest to recover the inverse transform of a function that is equal to $F(u,v)$ in this region and zero outside:

$$\tilde{F}(u,v) = \begin{cases} F(u,v), & \text{for } |u| \leq \pi/w \text{ and } |v| \leq \pi/h; \\ 0, & \text{for } |u| > \pi/w \text{ or } |v| > \pi/h. \end{cases}$$

The inverse transform is

$$\tilde{f}(x,y) = \frac{1}{4\pi^2} \int_{-\pi/h}^{\pi/h} \int_{-\pi/w}^{\pi/w} F(u,v) e^{+i(ux+vy)}\, dx\, dy.$$

This function is defined for all x and y, but we are particularly interested in its values at the grid points $(x,y) = (kw, lh)$. We can write the function as

$$\widetilde{f}(x,y) = \frac{wh}{4\pi^2} \int_{-\pi/h}^{\pi/h} \int_{-\pi/w}^{\pi/w} \sum_{k=-\infty}^{\infty} \sum_{l=-\infty}^{\infty} f_{kl}\, e^{-i(ukw+vlh)} e^{+i(ux+vy)}\, du\, dv$$

$$= \frac{wh}{4\pi^2} \sum_{k=-\infty}^{\infty} \sum_{l=-\infty}^{\infty} f_{kl} \int_{-\pi/h}^{\pi/h} \int_{-\pi/w}^{\pi/w} e^{i(u(x-kw)+v(y-lh))}\, du\, dv$$

$$= \sum_{k=-\infty}^{\infty} \sum_{l=-\infty}^{\infty} f_{kl}\, \frac{\sin\big(\pi(x/w-k)\big)}{\pi(x/w-k)}\, \frac{\sin\big(\pi(y/h-l)\big)}{\pi(y/h-l)}.$$

At $(x,y) = (kw, lh)$ the above reduces to f_{kl}. Between grid points, $\widetilde{f}(x,y)$ is interpolated using a kernel that is the product of a $\sin(x)/x$ term and a $\sin(y)/y$ term.

Another way to look at this is to consider the function created by multiplying $f(x,y)$ by the sampling grid:

$$g(x,y) = wh \sum_{k=-\infty}^{\infty} \sum_{l=-\infty}^{\infty} \delta(x - kw, y - lh).$$

The Fourier transform of the result is $1/(4\pi^2)$ times the convolution of the transform of $f(x,y)$ with the transform of the sampling grid. The latter is

$$4\pi^2 \sum_{k=-\infty}^{\infty} \sum_{l=-\infty}^{\infty} \delta\left(u - \frac{2\pi k}{w}, v - \frac{2\pi l}{h}\right),$$

so that the Fourier transform of $f(x,y)$ times $g(x,y)$ is a sampled version of the transform $F(u,v)$ of $f(x,y)$, namely

$$\sum_{k=-\infty}^{\infty} \sum_{l=-\infty}^{\infty} F\left(\frac{2\pi}{w}k, \frac{2\pi}{h}l\right) \delta\left(u - \frac{2\pi k}{w}, v - \frac{2\pi l}{h}\right).$$

7.3 The Sampling Theorem

From the foregoing discussion we see that a function that is bandlimited is fully specified by samples on a regular grid. This result is known as the *sampling theorem*. If $F(u,v) = 0$ for $|u| > \pi/w$ or $|v| > \pi/h$, then $f(x,y)$ can be recovered from the set $f(kw, lh)$ for all integers k and l. In fact, we have an explicit interpolation formula,

$$f(x,y) = \sum_{k=-\infty}^{\infty} \sum_{l=-\infty}^{\infty} f_{kl}\, \frac{\sin\big(\pi(x/w-k)\big)}{\pi(x/w-k)}\, \frac{\sin\big(\pi(y/h-l)\big)}{\pi(y/h-l)},$$

that does not involve the Fourier transform.

This is an important result because it justifies sampling the image. No information is lost, provided that the function sampled is "smooth" enough, that is, provided that it is bandlimited. The required sampling interval is also specified. If only frequencies less than B occur, the sampling interval can be as large as $\delta = \pi/B$. Stated in a different way, the sampling interval should be less than $\lambda/2$ when λ is the wavelength of the highest frequency present. If δ is the sampling interval, the result can be expressed in terms of the *Nyquist frequency*, π/δ. The signal can contain frequencies only up to the Nyquist frequency if it is to be faithfully reconstructed from samples.

The sampling theorem makes clear the dangers of applying this method to functions that are not limited in this way. Information is lost, and the original function cannot be recovered. What happens specifically is that higher frequencies, when sampled, look no different than frequencies within the acceptable interval. It is as if their frequencies were "folded back" at the frequency π/B. This is also called *aliasing*, since a wave of frequency $\omega > B$ produces the same samples as one of frequency $2B - \omega$.

One of the advantages of sampling an image with a sensor that has a finite area also becomes clear now. If each sensor element has a response function $r(x, y)$, the image is effectively convolved with $r(x, y)$ before sampling. This amounts to multiplication of the transform by the Fourier transform of $r(x, y)$. This smoothing operation will have the effect of attenuating the higher frequencies.

Suppose, for example, that rectangular sensors of width w and height h are tightly packed on the rectangular grid

$$r(x,y) = \begin{cases} 1, & \text{for } |x| \leq w/2 \text{ and } |y| \leq h/2; \\ 0, & \text{for } |x| > w/2 \text{ or } |y| > h/2. \end{cases}$$

Then

$$R(u,v) = wh \, \frac{\sin(uw/2)}{uw/2} \, \frac{\sin(vh/2)}{vh/2}.$$

This transfer function becomes zero for $u = \pm(2\pi/w)$ and $v = \pm(2\pi/h)$. This is twice the maximum frequency allowed by the sampling theorem. While this filter does pass some of the higher frequencies, it at least attenuates them significantly. To do better, adjacent sensing areas would have to overlap, and each sensing element would have to have sensitivity falling off toward its edge. Another way to achieve the desired effect is to have the imaging system itself introduce blurring of the right magnitude in order to lowpass filter the image sufficiently. The overall point-spread function is then equal to the convolution of the optical system point-spread function with the sensing element response function $r(x, y)$.

Ideally the sensor spacing should match the resolution of the optical elements. If they are too far apart, the conditions of the sampling theorem are violated. It is wasteful, on the other hand, to pack them too closely, since no new information is picked up by the extra sensing elements. The human visual system, for example, appears to have a reasonable match between resolution and sensor spacing, at least for intermediate opening of the pupil.

Filtering after sampling, of course, does no good. The damage has already been done. It is certainly possible to suppress higher frequencies within the acceptable band, but even higher frequencies in the original image have already been aliased down to lower frequencies in the sampled image. One cannot recover from such errors.

Bandlimited functions are "smooth" because their higher derivatives are limited in amplitude. For example, the transform of

$$f''(x, y) = \frac{\partial^2 f}{\partial x^2} + \frac{\partial^2 f}{\partial y^2}$$

is

$$F''(u, v) = -(u^2 + v^2)F(u, v).$$

So if $F(u, v) = 0$ for $|u| > B$ or $|v| > B$, then

$$|F''(u, v)| \leq B^2 |F(u, v)|.$$

Now the power in the signals $f(x, y)$ and $f''(x, y)$ is given by

$$P = \int_{-\infty}^{\infty} \int_{-\infty}^{\infty} f^2(x, y) \, dx \, dy = \frac{1}{4\pi^2} \int_{-\infty}^{\infty} \int_{-\infty}^{\infty} |F(u, v)|^2 \, du \, dv$$

and

$$P'' = \int_{-\infty}^{\infty} \int_{-\infty}^{\infty} (f''(x, y))^2 \, dx \, dy = \frac{1}{4\pi^2} \int_{-\infty}^{\infty} \int_{-\infty}^{\infty} |F''(u, v)|^2 \, du \, dv.$$

Therefore $P'' \leq B^4 P$. This places a constraint on how rapidly $f(x, y)$ can fluctuate.

So far we have assumed that the image is sampled at points lying on a rectangular grid. It turns out that there are some advantages to other sampling schemes. We can use hexagonal picture cells lying on a triangular grid, for example. Fewer samples are required using this tessellation when the image is limited to frequencies $\rho < B$, say. Such a circularly symmetric cutoff in the frequency domain is more natural than the rectangular one, for which the rectangular tessellation is well suited. The difference between the two tessellations comes from the different regions in the transform space that can be recovered without aliasing. For a square tessellation this region is square. To fit all of the disk $\rho < R$ into the square, its side must be of length 2ρ. For the hexagonal tessellation this region is hexagonal. To fit all of the disk $\rho < R$ into the hexagon, however, the maximum cross section need only be $\sqrt{3}\rho$.

7.4 The Discrete Fourier Transform

A discrete image has a periodic transform. If we think of the image as part of a periodic infinite image, then the transform is also discrete. Thus both the image and its transform are periodic and discrete. Both are fully defined by a finite number of values. If the image is specified by the values f_{kl} of $f(x, y)$ at points (kw, lh) for $k = 0, 1, \ldots, M - 1$ and $l = 0, 1, \ldots, N - 1$, the transform can be written as

$$F_{mn} = \sum_{k=0}^{M-1} \sum_{l=0}^{N-1} f_{kl}\, e^{-\pi i\left(\frac{km}{M} + \frac{ln}{N}\right)},$$

and the inverse transform as

$$f_{kl} = \frac{1}{MN} \sum_{k=0}^{M-1} \sum_{l=0}^{N-1} F_{mn}\, e^{+\pi i\left(\frac{km}{M} + \frac{ln}{N}\right)},$$

where again we have near symmetry in the definitions of the forward and inverse transforms. There is never any question about the existence of the transforms, since they consist of finite sums of finite values.

Note that this transform is based on an image that is doubly periodic. Unless the brightness of the left edge of the image happens to match that of the right edge, there will be a step discontinuity in brightness where adjacent copies of the image touch. Even if the image itself is very smooth, this discontinuity will introduce some high-frequency components into the transform. There are a number of ways to suppress this undesirable effect. One is to flip copies of the image over sideways before attaching them on the left and on the right. Similarly, copies of the image can be flipped over top to bottom before being attached at the top and the bottom. The brightness of the resulting doubly periodic function is continuous across the image border, but the odd derivatives of brightness are still discontinuous. Spurious spectral components will result, but at least these are typically smaller than those due to discontinuities in brightness itself.

The resulting function is periodic, though the period is twice as long as it was earlier when we simply replicated the image unchanged. On the other hand, the function is even in both x and y, so that only cosinusoidal components can occur. The discrete transform obtained, called the *cosine transform*, is explored further in exercise 7-6.

Another way to ameliorate effects of potential discontinuities at the image borders is to modulate the image by multiplying it by a function that drops to zero on the border. Adjacent copies will then automatically match. The modulation function itself should vary smoothly, so that it will not introduce spurious effects. Such a function is often called a *window function* since it provides us with a look through a weighted window into the potentially infinite image.

An example of a simple window function is

$$\frac{1}{2}\left(1 + \cos\left(2\pi\frac{x}{W}\right)\right)\frac{1}{2}\left(1 + \cos\left(2\pi\frac{y}{H}\right)\right) = \cos^2\left(\pi\frac{x}{W}\right)\cos^2\left(\pi\frac{y}{H}\right).$$

We saw earlier that, just as convolution in the image domain is equivalent to multiplication in the frequency domain, so multiplication in the image domain is equivalent to convolution in the frequency domain. Thus the transform of the windowed image is $4\pi^2$ times the transform of the original image convolved with the transform of the window function. Thus the transform is smeared out somewhat by windowing. The transform of the above window function is

$$\frac{1}{2}\left(\frac{1}{2}\delta\left(\frac{2\pi}{W} - u\right) + \delta(u) + \frac{1}{2}\delta\left(\frac{2\pi}{W} + u\right)\right)$$
$$\times \frac{1}{2}\left(\frac{1}{2}\delta\left(\frac{2\pi}{H} - v\right) + \delta(v) + \frac{1}{2}\delta\left(\frac{2\pi}{H} + v\right)\right);$$

each value in the transform is a local weighted average over a 3×3 neighborhood. The center is multiplied by the weight $1/4$, the four edge-adjacent neighbors by $1/8$, and the four neighbors on the corners by $1/16$. This convolutional weighting scheme can be represented by the following stencil:

$$\frac{1}{16}\begin{array}{|c|c|c|}\hline 1 & 2 & 1 \\ \hline 2 & 4 & 2 \\ \hline 1 & 2 & 1 \\ \hline\end{array}$$

A *stencil* is a pattern of weights used in computing a convolution, arranged in such a way as to suggest the spatial relationships between the places where the weights are applied.

One of the reasons for the attention given the discrete Fourier transform is that an algorithm has been discovered for computing it efficiently. The obvious implementation, in which each term f_{kl} is computed separately, requires MN multiplications for each of MN results, that is, M^2N^2 multiplications overall. The Fast Fourier Transform (FFT) takes only $4MN\log_2 MN$ multiplications to compute all results by clever sharing of intermediate terms. This makes it reasonable to compute convolutions by Fourier transformation, multiplication, and inverse transformation. Modern developments in parallel hardware, however, often favor direct convolution methods.

We now turn to a consideration of noise in images. The discrete Fourier transform of an image that is just noise will of course depend on the particular values at each picture cell. Can we say something in general about the transform? We are interested in the expected values of each of the transformed numbers. We have

$$F_{mn} = \sum_{k=0}^{M-1} \sum_{l=0}^{N-1} f_{kl}\, e^{-\pi i (\frac{km}{M} + \frac{ln}{N})}.$$

Here, each f_{kl} is a random value independent of the others. For the moment, allow f_{kl} to take on complex values. Note that

$$f_{kl}\, e^{-\pi i (\frac{km}{M} + \frac{ln}{N})}$$

is also a random value, with random phase, provided that f_{kl} has random phase. Thus each value F_{mn} is obtained by adding MN independent random complex numbers.

Now, if we further assume that f_{kl} has a normal distribution with zero mean and standard deviation σ, we can conclude that F_{mn} also has zero mean. The standard deviation will be $\sqrt{MN}\,\sigma$ since the standard deviation of the sum of the MN values is $\sqrt{MN}$ times their individual standard deviation. It can further be shown that the resulting values are independent. Thus the transform has properties identical to those of the original image (except for a scale factor); that is, the transform is a set of independent random numbers of mean zero and standard deviation $\sqrt{MN}\,\sigma$.

7.5 Circular Convolution

The interest in the discrete Fourier transform stems in large part from the fact that convolutions can be computed by multiplying Fourier transforms. Note, however, that there are problems at the edges of the window and the filter function. It is assumed that both are periodic. Thus near the left edge of the image the output will be affected somewhat by what appears near the right edge of the image.

This may be undesirable. An alternative is to extend the image with a border of zeros. The border should be as wide as the *support* of the filter, that is, the region over which the point-spread function of the filter is nonzero. Many filters do not have finite support and have to be artificially truncated. This includes the Gaussian blob, one of our favorites.

Adding a border of zeros has its own drawbacks since the output near the border will be affected by the image extension. This is not surprising if we consider the available image to be part of an unknown larger image. We have to guess at how the image can be extended. The part of the image affected this way is a border of width equal to the support of the filter. Only the part inside this border is trustworthy. If this is all that will be used, there is no point, of course, in adding a border of zeros outside the original image.

In summary, we have seen how imaging systems can be characterized by their point spread function or their modulation-transfer function. Shortcomings in such systems can be analyzed by studying the resulting point-spread function. The sampling theorem allows us to rationally match image sensors to image-forming systems. The optimal filtering methods allow us to design systems for extracting signals of interest in the presence of noise. Convolutional methods will also be useful in edge detection.

7.6 Some Useful Rules

Some of the results we have developed can be summarized in a short table:

Spatial domain	Frequency domain
Periodic	Discrete
Symmetric	Real
Sum of two functions	Sum of two transforms
Convolution of two functions	Product of two transforms
Periodic sampling	Periodic copies

The implications go both ways in this table. Thus, for example, the transform of a periodic function is discrete, and a function with a discrete transform is periodic. Furthermore, the columns can be relabeled in inverted order. That is, the transform of a discrete function is periodic, and a function with a periodic transform is discrete. There are many more such helpful relationships.

When the scale is compressed in one domain, it is expanded proportionally in the other, so that the product of corresponding measures of size is constant. For example, the product of the width of a Gaussian in the spatial domain and the width of its transform in the frequency domain is a constant.

A function has *finite support* when it is nonzero only over a bounded region. It can be shown that the transform of a function with finite support cannot also have finite support.

7.7 References

Many of the basic references on image processing were given at the end of the previous chapter. Hamming first presented fast methods for computing the discrete Fourier transform in *Numerical Methods for Scientists and Engineers* [1962]. Somehow his method was overlooked, to be rediscovered much later, as he observes dryly in another excellent book, *Digital Filters* [1977, 1983]. He treated relatively short vectors since he was interested in calculations that could be done by hand. It may not have been obvious to others how his technique generalized to input vectors of arbitrary lengths. *Fast Algorithms for Digital Signal Processing* by Blahut [1985] summarizes what is known about fast algorithms for the discrete Fourier transform and related problems.

The sampling theorem gives the conditions under which discrete samples contain enough information to fully describe a continuous image. Mersereau [1979] shows the advantage of hexagonal image tessellations for representing two-dimensional signals. Recovering the continuous image requires interpolation and convolution methods. A discrete image can be enlarged or reduced by sampling an interpolated version of the original. Hou & Andrews [1978] discuss one approach to this. Ahmed, Natarjan, & Rao [1974] discuss the discrete cosine transform, while Chen, Smith, & Fralick [1977] describe fast ways of computing it.

Image restoration has been one of the main applications of the results of the field of image processing. This is still an active area, as shown by the recent paper by Ramakrishna, Mullick, & Rathore [1985].

7.8 Exercises

7-1   Show that
$$\sum_{k=-\infty}^{\infty} e^{ikx} = 2\pi \sum_{k=-\infty}^{\infty} \delta(x - 2\pi k).$$

Hint: A Gaussian makes a suitable convergence factor for use in evaluating this sum.

7-2   A discrete two-dimensional system is characterized by the point-spread function $\{h_{ij}\}$. The output $\{g_{ij}\}$ is computed from the input $\{f_{ij}\}$ according to the rule
$$f_{i,j} = \sum_{k=-\infty}^{\infty} \sum_{l=-\infty}^{\infty} f_{i-k,j-l}\, h_{k,l}.$$

Compute the modulation-transfer function. Hint: Is the modulation-transfer function discrete? Is it periodic?

7-3   A discrete two-dimensional system performs a convolution, as in the previous exercise. Now suppose that the input $\{f_{ij}\}$ is just noise. That is, each of the f_{ij} is an independent random variable with zero mean and with variance σ^2.

(a)   What are the mean and variance of the output g_{ij}?

(b)   What point-spread function satisfying the constraint

$$\sum_{k=-\infty}^{\infty} \sum_{l=-\infty}^{\infty} h_{kl} = 1$$

minimizes the noise in the output? Hint: You may want to use a Lagrange multiplier to enforce the constraint in the minimization (see the appendix).

(c)   What point-spread function satisfying the constraint

$$\sum_{k=-\infty}^{\infty} \sum_{l=-\infty}^{\infty} (k^2 + l^2) h_{kl} = 1$$

minimizes the noise in the output? Warning: This part is harder than the rest of the problem.

7-4   Consider the discrete approximation of the Laplacian given by convolution with the following pattern of weights:

$$\frac{1}{6\epsilon^2}$$

1	4	1
4	−20	4
1	4	1

where ϵ is the spacing between picture cells. Write this weighting scheme as the sum of nine impulse functions. Find the Fourier transform and show that near the origin it tends to $-(u^2 + v^2)$ as $\epsilon \to 0$.

7-5   Consider the discrete approximation of the Laplacian used in the previous exercise. Apply this convolutional weighting scheme to a Taylor series expansion of the image brightness about the central point. Show that the result is independent of the constant and the linear terms. Show that it computes the expected combination of the second-order terms. Also work out the lowest-order error terms.

7-6   Suppose that an image $f(x, y)$ lies in the region $0 \le x \le W, 0 \le y \le H$. To avoid discontinuities in brightness at the borders, extend this by mirror imaging. For example, let $\widetilde{f}(x, y) = f(2W - x, y)$ for $W \le x \le 2W$, while $\widetilde{f}(x, y) = f(x, 2H - y)$ for $H \le y \le 2H$.

(a) Show that the extended image has period $2W$ in the x-direction and period $2H$ in the y-direction. Also show that the extended image is an even function of both x and y.

(b) Show that the extended image can be represented by the cosine series

$$\widetilde{f}(x, y) = \sum_{k=0}^{\infty} \sum_{l=0}^{\infty} C_{kl} \cos\left(\frac{x}{W} \pi k\right) \cos\left(\frac{y}{H} \pi l\right).$$

(c) Show that the coefficients of the cosine series can be found using

$$C_{ij} = \frac{4}{WH} \int_0^{+H} \int_0^{+W} f(x, y) \cos\left(\frac{x}{W} \pi i\right) \cos\left(\frac{y}{H} \pi j\right) dx\, dy,$$

for $i \neq 0$ and $j \neq 0$. Find the corresponding result for the cases where $i = 0$ or $j = 0$.

(d) How can the above method be modified to deal with an image that lies in the region $-W/2 \leq x \leq W/2$, $-H/2 \leq y \leq H/2$?

(e) Is it possible to replicate a hexagonal image region in a way that will ensure continuity in brightness across the image borders?

7-7   Show that, at least formally,

$$1 + \left(\frac{\sigma^2}{2} \nabla^2\right) + \frac{1}{2!} \left(\frac{\sigma^2}{2} \nabla^2\right)^2 + \frac{1}{3!} \left(\frac{\sigma^2}{2} \nabla^2\right)^3 + \cdots$$

is the inverse of convolution with the Gaussian

$$\frac{1}{2\pi\sigma^2} e^{-\frac{1}{2} \frac{x^2 + y^2}{\sigma^2}}.$$

Hint: Expand $e^{\frac{1}{2}\sigma^2 \omega^2}$ in a Taylor series.

Suppose that the first n terms of the series above are to be used to partially undo the blurring introduced by convolution with a Gaussian. Let the blurred image be $f(x, y)$, while the partially deblurred version is $g(x, y)$. Show that $g(x, y)$ can be found using the iterative scheme

$$g^0 = f,$$

$$g^{k+1} = f + \frac{1}{n-k} \left(\frac{\sigma^2}{2} \nabla^2\right) g^k \qquad \text{for } k = 0, 1, \ldots, n-1.$$

7-8   An image can be smoothed by means of a simple 2×2 averaging filter. The point-spread function of this filter can be written

$$h_{ij} = \begin{cases} 1/4, & \text{for } i = 0,\, 1,\, j = 0, 1; \\ 0, & \text{otherwise.} \end{cases}$$

Consider the function

$$h'_{ij} = \begin{cases} 1, & \text{for } i = -1, 0,\, j = -1, 0; \\ \text{even}\big(|x + 1/2| - 1/2\big)\,\text{even}\big(|y + 1/2| - 1/2\big), & \text{otherwise,} \end{cases}$$

where

$$\text{even}(z) = \begin{cases} +1, & \text{when } z \text{ is even;} \\ -1, & \text{when } z \text{ is odd.} \end{cases}$$

Show that h'_{ij} is a convolutional inverse to h_{ij}. (Note that, except near the axes, h'_{ij} is just a checkerboard of +1s and −1s.)

Discuss the difficulties we would encounter if we attempted to use this result in practice. Suggest a suitable window function that can be employed to attenuate the convolutional inverse for large arguments i and j. How would convolution of a filtered image with the product of this window function and h'_{ij} differ from convolution with the "exact" inverse?

7-9   Here we establish a useful correspondence between power series and discrete point-spread functions. We also show a way to approximate continuous Gaussian filters using a discrete filter. Consider two polynomials $f(x)$ and $g(x)$.

(a)   Show how the set coefficients of the product polynomial $f(x)g(x)$ can be obtained by discrete convolution of the sets of coefficients of the individual polynomials $f(x)$ and $g(x)$. Extend this to power series that include negative powers of x.

This result can be extended to two dimensions. That is, the coefficients of the power series $f(x, y)g(x, y)$ can be obtained by two-dimensional discrete convolution of the coefficients of the power series $f(x, y)$ and $g(x, y)$. Note that associativity and commutativity of multiplication of power series follows from the corresponding properties of discrete convolution. We now consider a particular example.

(b)   Show how convolution with a filter whose weights are given by the pattern

$$\frac{1}{16}\quad \begin{array}{|c|c|c|} \hline 1 & 2 & 1 \\ \hline 2 & 4 & 2 \\ \hline 1 & 2 & 1 \\ \hline \end{array}$$

can be accomplished by repeated convolution with a filter that has the pattern

$$\frac{1}{4} \begin{array}{|c|c|} \hline 1 & 1 \\ \hline 1 & 1 \\ \hline \end{array}$$

Show the weighting scheme that results when we convolve one more time with the 2×2 pattern shown.

(c) Show that the modulation-transfer function of a discrete convolutional filter can be obtained by substituting e^{-iuw} for x and e^{-ivh} for y in the corresponding power series, where w and h are the horizontal and vertical sampling intervals, respectively.

(d) What is the Fourier transform of the convolutional filter corresponding to the polynomial $1 + x + y + xy$?

A polynomial of particular interest is obtained by expanding $(1 + x)^n$:

$$(1+x)^n = \binom{n}{0} + \binom{n}{1} x + \binom{n}{2} x^2 + \cdots + \binom{n}{n-1} x^{n-1} + \binom{n}{n} x^n,$$

where the *binomial coefficients* are

$$\binom{n}{r} = \frac{n!}{(n-r)!\, r!}.$$

(e) Suppose that we convolve the filter in part (d) with itself n times to obtain the two-dimensional binomial distribution whose general term is

$$\binom{n}{k}\binom{n}{l} x^k y^l \qquad \text{for } 0 \leq x \leq n,\ 0 \leq y \leq n.$$

Show that the magnitude of the modulation-transfer function is

$$4^n \cos^n\left(\tfrac{1}{2} uw\right) \cos^n\left(\tfrac{1}{2} vh\right).$$

How can you remove the scale factor 4^n? How can you arrange for the modulation-transfer function to be real, at least when n is odd?

(f) The binomial distribution of order n approximates a Gaussian with mean $(n-1)/2$ and variance 2^{n-1}. The amplitude of this Gaussian is about 2^{n-1}. The modulation-transfer function also approximates a Gaussian. Find the amplitude, mean, and variance of the Gaussian approximated by

$$4^n \cos^n\left(\tfrac{1}{2} uw\right) \cos^n\left(\tfrac{1}{2} vh\right).$$

Hint: Find the first few terms in the Taylor series expansion of the two functions being compared and match coefficients.

The above analysis is useful when we wish to approximate a Gaussian with a finite, discrete filter. This is a better approach than simply truncating the continuous Gaussian after it becomes "small" enough. The latter approach introduces spurious high-frequency components due to the arbitrary cutoff.

7-10 Suppose that samples are taken not only of image brightness but also of the first partial derivatives of brightness. Show that fewer samples are required to capture all the information about a bandlimited image than are necessary when only brightness is sampled. Show how to recover the bandlimited image from its samples. Warning: This is not an easy problem.

7-11 How would you interpolate a bandlimited function from its samples on a hexagonal grid? Hint: What is the inverse Fourier transform of a function that is one inside a hexagonal region in the frequency domain and zero elsewhere?

8

Edges & Edge Finding

In this chapter we discuss edge detection and localization. Edges are curves in the image where rapid changes occur in brightness or in the spatial derivatives of brightness. The changes in brightness that we are particularly interested in are the ones that mirror significant events on the surface being imaged. These might be places where surface orientation changes discontinuously, where one object occludes another, where a cast shadow line appears, or where there is a discontinuity in surface reflectance properties. In each case, we hope to locate the discontinuity in image brightness, or its derivatives, in order to learn something about the corresponding feature on the object being imaged. We show in this chapter how differential operators can be used to accentuate those image features that help us locate places in the image where a fragment of an edge can be found. This is done first in the continuous domain, and then the results are applied to the discrete case.

Naturally, noise in the brightness measurements limits our ability to uncover edge information. We find trade-offs between sensitivity and accuracy and discover that to be detectable, short edges must have higher contrast than long edges. Edge detection can be considered complementary to image segmentation, since edges can be used to break up images into regions that correspond to different surfaces.

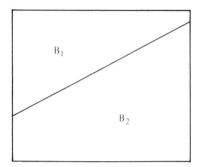

Figure 8-1. An idealized edge is a line separating two image regions of constant brightness.

8.1 Edges in Images

Intuitively, a simple edge is a border between two regions, each of which has approximately uniform brightness. Edges in images often result from *occluding contours* of objects. In this case the two regions are images of two different surfaces. Edges also arise from discontinuities in surface orientation and from discontinuities in surface reflectance properties. If we take a cross section of the image brightness along a line at right angles to an edge, we might hope to see a step discontinuity. In practice, the transition will not be abrupt because of blurring and limitations of the imaging device. Also, some edge transitions are better modeled as step transitions in the first derivative of brightness, rather than in the brightness itself.

For now, we shall use the simple model to gain some insight into operators that might enhance edges in images by producing high values near them. The edge-enhanced images must be processed further to extract lines or curves. Most effort has so far been concentrated on the edge-enhancement step, less on detection and localization of edge fragments, but this has changed recently. Least work has been done on the organization of the edge fragments into larger entities, that is, lines and curves in the image.

8.2 Differential Operators

A simple model for an edge in an image is a straight line separating two regions of contrast brightness (figure 8-1). We use the unit step function $u(t)$ defined by

$$u(z) = \begin{cases} 1, & \text{for } z > 0; \\ 1/2, & \text{for } z = 0; \\ 0, & \text{for } z < 0, \end{cases}$$

noting that it is the integral of the one-dimensional unit impulse

$$u(z) = \int_{-\infty}^{z} \delta(t)\, dt.$$

Suppose that the edge lies along the line

$$x \sin\theta - y \cos\theta + \rho = 0.$$

Then we can write the image brightness in the form

$$E(x, y) = B_1 + (B_2 - B_1)\, u(x \sin\theta - y \cos\theta + \rho).$$

The partial derivatives are

$$\frac{\partial E}{\partial x} = + \sin\theta\, (B_2 - B_1)\, \delta(x \sin\theta - y \cos\theta + \rho),$$

$$\frac{\partial E}{\partial y} = - \cos\theta\, (B_2 - B_1)\, \delta(x \sin\theta - y \cos\theta + \rho).$$

These differential operators are directional, producing results that depend on the orientation of the edge. The vector $(\partial E/\partial x, \partial E/\partial y)^T$ is called the *brightness gradient*. The brightness gradient is *coordinate-system-independent* in the sense that it maintains its magnitude and orientation relative to the underlying pattern when the pattern is rotated or translated.

Consider now the squared gradient,

$$\left(\frac{\partial E}{\partial x}\right)^2 + \left(\frac{\partial E}{\partial y}\right)^2 = \left((B_2 - B_1)\, \delta(x \sin\theta - y \cos\theta + \rho)\right)^2.$$

This operator, while nonlinear, is rotationally symmetric, treating edges at all angles equally.

The derivative of the unit impulse is called the unit *doublet*, denoted δ'. Using this notation, we have

$$\frac{\partial^2 E}{\partial x^2} = \sin^2\theta\, (B_2 - B_1)\, \delta'(x \sin\theta - y \cos\theta + \rho),$$

$$\frac{\partial^2 E}{\partial x \partial y} = - \sin\theta \cos\theta\, (B_2 - B_1)\, \delta'(x \sin\theta - y \cos\theta + \rho),$$

$$\frac{\partial^2 E}{\partial y^2} = \cos^2\theta\, (B_2 - B_1)\, \delta'(x \sin\theta - y \cos\theta + \rho).$$

The Laplacian of the image $E(x, y)$ is

$$\frac{\partial^2 E}{\partial x^2} + \frac{\partial^2 E}{\partial y^2} = (B_2 - B_1)\, \delta'(x \sin\theta - y \cos\theta + \rho),$$

a quantity that is also rotationally symmetric. Finally, the *quadratic variation*,

$$\left(\frac{\partial^2 E}{\partial x^2}\right)^2 + 2\left(\frac{\partial^2 E}{\partial x \partial y}\right)\left(\frac{\partial^2 E}{\partial y \partial x}\right) + \left(\frac{\partial^2 E}{\partial y^2}\right)^2$$
$$= \left((B_2 - B_1)\,\delta'(x\sin\theta - y\cos\theta + \rho)\right)^2,$$

is rotationally symmetric, too, as expected. In the case of our idealized edge image, the quadratic variation happens to be equal to the square of the Laplacian. Note that of the three rotationally symmetric operators considered, only the Laplacian retains the sign of the brightness difference across the edge, $B_2 - B_1$. This allows us to determine which side of the edge is brighter from the edge-enhanced image. Thus the Laplacian is the only one of the three operators that might permit reconstruction of the original image from the edge image. It is also the only one of the three that is linear.

8.3 Discrete Approximations

Consider a 2×2 group of picture cells:

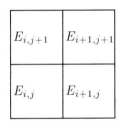

The derivatives at the center of this group can be estimated as follows:

$$\frac{\partial E}{\partial x} \approx \frac{1}{2\epsilon}\left((E_{i+1,j+1} - E_{i,j+1}) + (E_{i+1,j} - E_{i,j})\right),$$
$$\frac{\partial E}{\partial y} \approx \frac{1}{2\epsilon}\left((E_{i+1,j+1} - E_{i+1,j}) + (E_{i,j+1} - E_{i,j})\right),$$

where ϵ is the spacing between picture cell centers. Each estimate is the average of two finite-difference approximations.

A finite-difference approximation of a derivative always applies to a particular point. For example, the familiar first-difference formula gives an estimate that is unbiased for a point midway between the two places where the function is evaluated. The formulae shown above for estimating the partial derivatives are used because they are unbiased at the same point, namely the corner in the middle of the four picture cells. The squared gradient can now be approximated by

$$\left(\frac{\partial E}{\partial x}\right)^2 + \left(\frac{\partial E}{\partial y}\right)^2 \approx \left((E_{i+1,j+1} - E_{i,j})^2 + (E_{i,j+1} - E_{i+1,j})^2\right).$$

If we perform this simple computation all over the image, we obtain high values at places where the brightness changes rapidly. In regions of constant brightness the output is zero. (If noise is present, the output is nonzero, but fairly small.) The results can be written into a new image array, in which the edges will be strongly highlighted.

The squared gradient does not tell us anything about the direction of the edge. This information is in the gradient itself, which points in the direction of most rapid increase in brightness. The edge is at right angles to the gradient since

$$\left(\frac{\partial E}{\partial x}, \frac{\partial E}{\partial y}\right)^T = (\sin\theta, -\cos\theta)^T (B_2 - B_1)\delta(x\sin\theta - y\cos\theta + \rho),$$

so that $\partial E/\partial x$ is proportional to $\sin\theta$ and $\partial E/\partial y$ is proportional to $-\cos\theta$. The gradient will point in a direction at right angles to the edge even if the edge transition is more gradual, perhaps due to blurring. Naturally, a discrete approximation of the gradient may not produce very accurate estimates of edge direction, since the picture cells through which the edges pass have intermediate values of brightness.

Now consider a 3×3 group of picture cells:

$E_{i-1,j+1}$	$E_{i,j+1}$	$E_{i+1,j+1}$
$E_{i-1,j}$	$E_{i,j}$	$E_{i+1,j}$
$E_{i-1,j-1}$	$E_{i,j-1}$	$E_{i+1,j-1}$

To estimate the Laplacian at the center cell we use the approximations

$$\frac{\partial^2 E}{\partial x^2} \approx \frac{1}{\epsilon^2}\left(E_{i-1,j} - 2E_{i,j} + E_{i+1,j}\right),$$

$$\frac{\partial^2 E}{\partial y^2} \approx \frac{1}{\epsilon^2}\left(E_{i,j-1} - 2E_{i,j} + E_{i,j+1}\right),$$

so that

$$\frac{\partial^2 E}{\partial x^2} + \frac{\partial^2 E}{\partial y^2} \approx \frac{4}{\epsilon^2}\left(\frac{1}{4}(E_{i-1,j} + E_{i,j-1} + E_{i+1,j} + E_{i,j+1}) - E_{i,j}\right).$$

Here we subtract the value of the central picture cell from the average of the neighbors. The result is clearly zero in regions of constant brightness. This is true even in areas where brightness varies linearly.

Such approximations to differential operators are used in the finite-difference solution of partial difference equations. Recall what was said earlier about stencils. The coefficient by which a value is multiplied is called a *weight*. The pattern of weights, arranged spatially to indicate which picture cells they apply to, is called a *stencil* or *computational molecule*. The stencil in our case is

$$\frac{1}{\epsilon^2}\quad\begin{array}{|c|c|c|}\hline & 1 & \\ \hline 1 & -4 & 1 \\ \hline & 1 & \\ \hline\end{array}$$

where the term on the left is a multiplier to be applied to all weights. Remember that the application of the Laplacian is equivalent to convolution with a generalized function defined by a sequence of functions that feature a central depression surrounded by a positive wall. The above discrete approximation should remind you of the functions in that sequence.

On a squared grid it is hard to come up with a stencil that approximates the Laplacian and is symmetric. Earlier, when we tried to find a consistent definition of connectivity for binary images, we had to make a decision about which of the neighbors of a picture cell were to be considered connected to that picture cell. Here we are again faced with the issue of whether we should include only the edge-adjacent picture cells, or the corners as well. On a hexagonal grid this problem does not occur; all six neighbors are weighted equally (figure 8-2).

One way to proceed is to consider a coordinate system rotated 45° with respect to the xy-coordinate system. If we label the axes in the new coordinate system x' and y', we can use the approximation

$$\frac{\partial^2 E}{\partial x'^2} \approx \frac{1}{2\epsilon^2}\left(E_{i+1,j+1} - 2E_{i,j} + E_{i-1,j-1}\right),$$

$$\frac{\partial^2 E}{\partial y'^2} \approx \frac{1}{2\epsilon^2}\left(E_{i-1,j+1} - 2E_{i,j} + E_{i+1,j-1}\right),$$

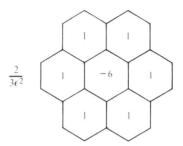

Figure 8-2. An excellent approximation of the Laplacian operator on a hexagonal grid is obtained by subtracting the value in the center from the average of the six neighboring cells. The result is multiplied by a constant that depends on the grid spacing ϵ.

so that

$$\frac{\partial^2 E}{\partial x^2} + \frac{\partial^2 E}{\partial y^2}$$

$$\approx \frac{2}{\epsilon^2}\left(\frac{1}{4}(E_{i+1,j+1} + E_{i-1,j+1} + E_{i+1,j-1} + E_{i-1,j-1}) - E_{i,j}\right).$$

The corresponding stencil is

$$\frac{1}{2\epsilon^2}\quad
\begin{array}{|c|c|c|}
\hline
1 & & 1 \\
\hline
 & -4 & \\
\hline
1 & & 1 \\
\hline
\end{array}$$

Clearly, linear combinations of the two stencils shown also produce estimates of multiples of the Laplacian. A popular combination that, as we show in exercise 8-8 provides a particularly accurate estimate of the Laplacian, is

$$\frac{1}{6\epsilon^2}\quad
\begin{array}{|c|c|c|}
\hline
1 & 4 & 1 \\
\hline
4 & -20 & 4 \\
\hline
1 & 4 & 1 \\
\hline
\end{array}$$

This is produced by adding two-thirds of the first to one-third of the second estimate introduced above. We show in the exercise that this operator can be written in the form

$$\nabla^2 + \frac{\epsilon^2}{12}\nabla^2(\nabla^2) + e,$$

where ∇^2 is the Laplacian and e contains terms of sixth and higher order multiplied by ϵ^4 and higher powers of ϵ.

Finally, to obtain a discrete approximation of the quadratic variation we need the cross derivative $\partial^2 E/\partial x \partial y$. A suitable stencil for computing it is

$$\frac{1}{4\epsilon^2}$$

-1		1
1		-1

It should be clear how to compute the quadratic variation now:

$$\left(\frac{\partial^2 E}{\partial x^2}\right)^2 + 2\left(\frac{\partial^2 E}{\partial x \partial y}\right)\left(\frac{\partial^2 E}{\partial y \partial x}\right) + \left(\frac{\partial^2 E}{\partial y^2}\right)^2$$

$$\approx \frac{1}{\epsilon^4}\Big((E_{i-1,j} - 2E_{i,j} + E_{i+1,j})^2 + (E_{i,j-1} - 2E_{i,j} + E_{i,j+1})^2$$

$$+ \frac{1}{8}(E_{i+1,j+1} - E_{i+1,j-1} + E_{i-1,j-1} - E_{i-1,j+1})^2\Big).$$

8.4 Local Operators and Noise

In practice, the local operators for accentuating edges introduced so far are not directly useful, mainly because their output is seriously degraded by noise in the image. Noise, being independent at different picture cells, has a flat spectrum. The high-frequency components of noise are greatly amplified by the simple differential operators, as we saw when we discussed image processing. Edges of low contrast are simply lost in the noise.

We can apply the optimal filtering methods explored in chapter 6. From our discussion there it should be apparent that the optimal filter for recovering the Laplacian, for example, is

$$H' = -\rho^2 \frac{1}{1 + \Phi_{nn}/\Phi_{bb}}.$$

We need to make some assumptions about the images in order to estimate the power spectrum Φ_{bb}. If an image has a flat power spectrum, little can be done. However, images tend to have spectra that fall off with frequency, as we discussed in chapter 6. The transform of a single step function, for example, falls off as the inverse of frequency. Images in which regions of uniform brightness are separated by sharp edges can be expected to have similar properties.

Suppose that $\Phi_{bb} = S^2/\rho^2$ and $\Phi_{nn} = N^2$. Then

$$H' = -\frac{\rho^2 S^2}{S^2 + \rho^2 N^2},$$

so that the optimal filter behaves like the Laplacian at low frequencies, but does not amplify high frequencies as much. The maximum gain is $-S^2/N^2$, equal to (minus) the signal-to-noise ratio.

The optimal filter can be decomposed into two filters. The first recovers the image as well as possible in a least-squares sense. This is done by multiplying the transform by $S^2/(S^2 + \rho^2 N^2)$. The second filter computes the desired output from the result produced by the first. In the case discussed here, this is accomplished by applying the Laplacian, that is, by multiplying by $-\rho^2$. It is clear that an image with little information content above a certain frequency is first lowpass filtered by the optimal filter. If the power spectrum rolls off at some known frequency, the optimal filter will tend to roll off near that frequency. Alternatively, we can apply this filter to the differential operator, since convolution is associative. The optimal estimator of the Laplacian of an image is an operator with nonzero spatial support, since it is obtained by applying the Laplacian to the optimal filter for estimating the image. This means that it is not local. In practice, the region over which the operator has substantial weight can be quite large.

If our objective is to obtain the best estimate of the image gradient, then we find the gradient of the estimate of the original image produced by the optimal filter. Alternatively we can take the x and y derivatives of the point-spread function of the optimal filter and use these directly in convolution with the computed image.

If, for example, the optimal filter for estimating the original image $E(x, y)$ is a Gaussian,

$$h(x, y) = \frac{1}{2\pi\sigma^2} e^{-\frac{1}{2}\frac{x^2+y^2}{\sigma^2}},$$

then the point-spread function of the optimal filters for recovering E_x and E_y are

$$h_x(x, y) = -\frac{x}{2\pi\sigma^4} e^{-\frac{1}{2}\frac{x^2+y^2}{\sigma^2}} \quad \text{and} \quad h_y(x, y) = -\frac{y}{2\pi\sigma^4} e^{-\frac{1}{2}\frac{x^2+y^2}{\sigma^2}},$$

respectively. The support of these operators is large, quite unlike the local operators considered earlier. Thus they compute weighted averages over large areas. As a result, noise contributions are reduced, while the

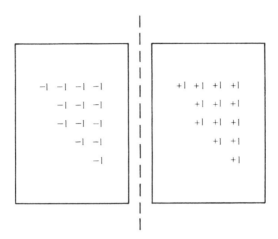

Figure 8-3. A simple edge operator subtracts the sum of the gray-levels obtained over one large area from the sum over an adjacent large area.

signal—the difference between the brightnesses of neighboring regions—is maintained.

We can proceed from this intuition by considering a simple method for estimating the difference in brightness across an edge (figure 8-3). Suppose we take the difference between the average of N picture cells on one side and the average of N picture cells on the other. The mean of the result is the brightness difference. The standard deviation of the noise in the result, on the other hand, is $\sigma/\sqrt{N/2}$, if the standard deviation in each measurement is σ. Thus the larger we make the patches on each side of the edge, the less will the result be affected by noise.

If the patches become very large, however, other image regions may be included (figure 8-4). The measurement will then be incorrect, unless the image contains just one edge.

8.5 Edge Detection and Localization

If the edge-enhanced signal is substantially above the noise, we might conclude that there is an edge at a certain point in the image. Such a decision is not perfectly reliable since the noise may just happen to add up sufficiently at that point. All we can do is try to reduce the probability of this happening by choosing the threshold applied to the edge-enhanced image so that the number of false edge points is acceptable.

If the threshold is too high, weak edges will be missed. So there is a trade-off between two kinds of errors. By increasing the size of the patches

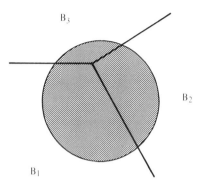

Figure 8-4. A limit to the size of the support region of an edge operator is set by the spacing between image features. If it is too large, other image detail will be included. In some places—for example, near joints in an image of a polyhedral scene—any finite support area will lead to inclusion of unwanted areas.

over which averages are taken, or equivalently by lowering the rolloff frequency above which image components are suppressed, we can reduce the effect of noise and make weak edges easier to detect. We face another trade-off immediately, however, since other edges in the image might be included in the larger patches. We note that short edges must have higher contrast in order to be detectable.

The enhanced image will have high values not just for the picture cells right on the edge, but also for a few neighboring ones. This effect is particularly pronounced if the image has been smoothed to reduce the effects of noise. Thus the problem of locating the edge arises. If it were not for noise, we would expect to find the largest values right on the edge. These large values could then be used to suppress neighboring large values.

In the case of the squared gradient, the edge-enhanced images will have a ridge for each edge with height proportional to the square of the brightness difference. In the case of the Laplacian and the quadratic variation, there will be two parallel ridges, one on each side of the edge. For the Laplacian the two ridges will have opposite polarity, and the edge can be located where the sign changes.

8.6 Conclusion and Examples

Eventually it will be necessary to identify the physical cause of the edge. What aspect of the three-dimensional scene created the changes in image brightness picked up by the edge detector? Little is understood about this

Figure 8-5. A photograph of a simple structure built out of children's toy blocks.

so far.

Much recent progress in edge detection can be attributed to attempts to build optimal edge operators and to understand in more detail the trade-offs between detection and localization. Much depends, of course, on the definition of optimality and the basic image model chosen. The limitations of the simple model of an edge as an ideal step function plus noise have been acknowledged, and more realistic models are emerging.

One of the problems with many edge-detection methods is that the premise on which they are based often does not apply to realistic situations. While it is true that many surfaces have uniform reflectance, it is not true that they will be imaged with uniform brightness. As we shall see later, many factors influence brightness. Conversely, picture cells corresponding to points on surfaces of different objects may very well have similar gray-levels. Only in unusual situations can the image be usefully thought of as a collage of regions of uniform brightness.

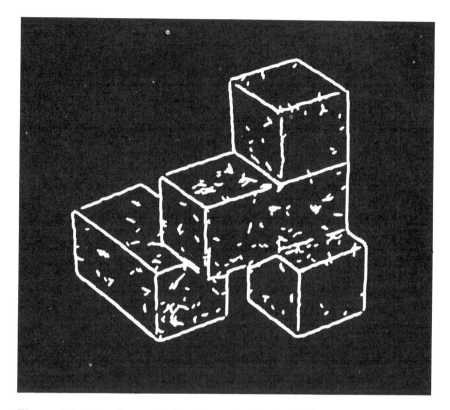

Figure 8-6. Edge fragments found by a simple edge finder.

One of the difficulties in evaluating schemes for edge detection is the lack of a clear definition of the task. How can we tell when an edge has been "missed," or where a "spurious" edge appears? The answer to this question depends on what we want to do with the result.

We now consider the results produced by an early edge-detection program to illustrate some of the ideas introduced above. Figure 8-5 shows a simple structure built using a few children's toy blocks. Figure 8-6 shows the output of an edge finder applied to the image of this scene. Even in this simple situation the edge fragments found are not perfect and will have to be carefully processed if they are to be integrated into a clean line drawing representing the edges of the objects.

8.7 References

Marr has had a strong influence on the prevalent view of the problem of early vision. His ideas can be found in the book *Vision: A Computational Investigation into the Human Representation and Processing of Visual Information* [1982]. Other books that discuss approaches to edge detection based on similar ideas are *From Images to Surfaces: A Computational Study of the Human Early Visual System* by Grimson [1981] and *The Measurement of Visual Motion* by Hildreth [1983].

Edge detection has been one of the most active fields in machine vision. The classic paper by Roberts [1965] showed how to extract edges from photographs of polyhedral objects digitized on a converted drum plotter. Because of the high quality of the input signal, and the clever postprocessing he employed, Roberts was able to obtain useful results with an operator that had very small support. This may have misled others into seeking operators featuring small support. Binford realized that a large image area was needed to provide sufficient evidence for an edge in a noisy image; see Horn [1971] and Binford [1981]. It was a while before this idea took hold, but when it did, the search was on for the "optimal" convolutional edge-enhancement operator with large support.

Not all methods for detecting and locating edges are based on the convolutional approach presented in this chapter. Duda & Hart [1972] considered use of the *Hough transform*, a mapping into the parameter space of the line sought after. (A discussion of shortcomings of the Hough transform is provided by Brown [1983].) The results produced by simple edge-finding schemes left a lot to be desired. This suggested that other knowledge should be brought to bear. Griffith [1973a,b], for example, introduced assumptions about the statistics of image features, while Shirai [1973] exploited expectations about the scene to focus attention on areas where lines were likely to be found. Hueckel [1971, 1973] developed a least-squares fitting scheme based on expansion of the brightness function in a region in terms of orthogonal functions. One advantage of his approach was that it forced the use of a reasonably large support region. Nevatia [1977a] simplified this method. More recently Haralick [1980] proposed the use of a piecewise-linear approximation of the brightness surface.

Application of a first-derivative operator must be followed by a search for peak values. A means of suppressing large values near the local maxima is also required. Partly for this reason, second-derivative operators became more popular, since the edge is located where their output is zero. Now linear first-derivative operators are directional. So a second advantage of second-derivative operators is that they can be made rotationally symmetric. The Laplacian and various discrete approximations had been proposed for edge detection. Horn [1972], for example, showed that it was the lowest-order linear operator that preserved information required to reconstruct the image. He later used the Laplacian in the computation of lightness [1974]. Modestino & Fries [1977] obtained an optimal estimate of the Laplacian over a large support area.

The Gaussian had been popular for smoothing operations for several reasons, one being that it is the only rotationally symmetric operator that is the product of two one-dimensional operators, as noted by Horn [1972]. Another reason was the well-known property that it has the smallest product of width in the spatial and frequency domains. The Gaussian, or rather the difference between two spatially displaced Gaussians, had been used in edge detection by MacLeod [1970a,b]. Some aspects of rotationally symmetric operators were discussed by Brady & Horn [1983]. Blake [1985] uses the concept of coordinate-system-independent vectors in his discussion of the lightness problem.

Marr [1976] at first proposed a directional operator for edge detection. He later claimed that a rotationally symmetric operator was optimal. The contours where the output of the operator passes through zero are called *zero-crossings*. A new theory of edge detection based on finding the zero-crossings of the output of an even-derivative operator applied to the image is described by Marr & Hildreth [1980] and Hildreth [1980]. They took the Laplacian operator and combined it with the Gaussian smoothing filter to produce a rotationally symmetric edge operator. Ideally, the zero-crossings of the filtered output are closed contours. This elegant new edge-finding method thus appears to answer the wish for a marriage of region segmentation and edge detection. Unfortunately, a good part of the zero-crossing contour length consists of segments not related to significant image detail.

Rosenfeld & Thurston [1971] may have been the first to propose working on an image simultaneously at several levels of resolution. Further results are reported in Rosenfeld, Thurston, & Lee [1972]. Marr & Hildreth [1980] and Hildreth [1980, 1983] developed the early vision processing module using the zero-crossings of the output of the Laplacian of Gaussians of four different widths. This is still an active area, as indicated by the recent paper by Hartley [1985]. Witkin [1983, 1984] has derived some interesting properties of a diagram tracking the zero-crossings over a continuum of scales. These have been applied mostly to one-dimensional problems so far. Yuille & Poggio [1983] have shown that the Gaussian is the only smoothing filter that will not introduce spurious zero-crossings into a signal.

Recently there has been more concern about the accuracy and sensitivity to noise of these edge-enhancement operators, expressed for example in a paper by Berzins [1984]. Directional operators might have advantages in this regard, as indicated in the exercises in this chapter. Haralick [1984] studied the use of the second derivative in the direction of the brightness gradient. This nonlinear operator had been used earlier for edge marking (see *Digital Picture Processing* by Rosenfeld & Kak [1976, 1982]), but not analyzed as carefully.

Canny [1983] has developed a one-dimensional operator that provides an optimal trade-off between localization and detection. He designed his operator to minimize the sum of two error criteria, namely the probability of failing to mark an edge or announcing an edge where there is none, and the distance between the detected edge and the true edge. His first error criterion also implicitly forces the probability of obtaining more than one response to a single edge to be low. Canny restricted his search for a solution to the space of linear, shift-invariant operators. He confirmed the trade-off between signal-to-noise ratio and localization and showed that the optimal operator can be written as a sum of four complex exponentials. The result contains an arbitrary spatial scale factor, so that operators of different sizes can be designed.

Since an edge has significant spatial extent, it can be located to a precision considerably finer than the width of one picture cell. Subpixel resolution has been of interest in both machine vision and biological vision, as shown, for example, in the papers by Fahle & Poggio [1980], Fang & Huang [1984b], and Tabatabai & Mitchell [1984]. Accuracy in edge detection can also be increased by tracking edges in time-varying imagery, as discussed by Haynes & Jain [1982].

Other aspects of edge detection are discussed in papers by Fram & Deutsch [1975], Gupta & Wintz [1975], Ramer [1975], O'Gorman & Clowes [1976], Nevatia [1977a,b], O'Gorman [1978], Nevatia & Babu [1980], Jacobus & Chien [1981], and Wojcik [1984]. Surveys of edge-detection techniques and of new ways to rationalize them include those by Davis [1975], Brooks [1978], Haralick [1980], and Peli & Malah [1982].

A very different approach to edge detection is based on stochastic models of the image. An example may be found in the paper by Cooper, Sung, & Schencker [1980] on adaptive boundary finding. Earlier related work is that of Habibi [1972] and Yakimovsky [1975]. A problem related to edge detection is that of line detection. Tafoya [1978] describes a system for *vectorization*, that is, production of a symbolic description from a line drawing.

8.8 Exercises

Two of the topics explored in the exercises are the properties of the Gaussian and the Laplacian, and the use of these operators in edge enhancement. To solve some of the problems, you may need the following integrals:

$$\int_0^\infty e^{-pz^2}\, dz = \frac{1}{2}\sqrt{\frac{\pi}{p}} \qquad \text{for } p > 0,$$

$$\int_0^\infty z^{2n} e^{-pz^2}\, dz = \frac{(2n-1)!!}{2(2p)^n}\sqrt{\frac{\pi}{p}} \qquad \text{for } p > 0 \text{ and } n \geq 0,$$

$$\int_0^\infty z^{2n+1} e^{-pz^2}\, dz = \frac{n!}{2p^{n+1}} \qquad \text{for } p > 0 \text{ and } n \geq 0,$$

where

$$(2n)!! = 2 \cdot 4 \cdot 6 \cdots (2n) \qquad (2n+1)!! = 1 \cdot 3 \cdot 5 \cdots (2n+1).$$

8-1 Why did we not show a stencil for the discrete approximation of the quadratic variation?

8-2 Show that the constant multiplier in the simple approximation for the Laplacian operator on a hexagonal grid must be $2/(3\epsilon^2)$ (figure 8-2).

8-3 One way to detect edges in an image is to look for extrema in the edge-enhanced image, produced by applying a first-derivative operator to a smoothed image. A different strategy involves finding the zeros in the output produced by a second-derivative operator. The *zero-crossings* are places where the output changes sign. (To be more precise, at a zero-crossing the function is zero, and in any small circular neighborhood of the crossing a point can be found where the function is positive and another where it is negative.)

The Laplacian is a second-derivative operator that is rotationally symmetric. It suffers, however, from relatively poor signal-to-noise performance. It has been suggested that one might instead use the second derivative of brightness in the direction of the brightness gradient.

(a) Give a unit vector in the direction of the brightness gradient. Find the sine and cosine of the angle θ between this vector and the x-axis. Hint: You might need the identities

$$1 + \tan^2 \theta = \sec^2 \theta \qquad \text{and} \qquad \sin^2 \theta + \cos^2 \theta = 1,$$

depending on your approach to this problem.

(b) What is E', the first directional derivative of brightness in the direction of the brightness gradient? How is this related to the magnitude of the brightness gradient?

(c) Express E'', the second directional derivative of brightness, in terms of the first and second partial derivatives with respect to x and y.

(d) Is this directional second-derivative operator linear?

(e) Is it rotationally symmetric?

(f) What is E'' where the brightness gradient is zero?

8-4   The concept of noise in a continuous image is not a trivial one. Yet it is useful in the analysis of continuous versions of the operators used to extract edges, for example. It is convenient to deal with noise waveforms $n(x, y)$ that have zero mean, that is, waveforms for which, on average,

$$\iint_R n(x, y) \, dx \, dy = 0$$

over any image region R. We also assume that the values of the noise waveform at different points in the image can be considered to be independent random variables, and that the noise has the same "power" in one area of the image as it does in any other. Suppose, then, that the autocorrelation of a noise waveform $n(x, y)$ over a region R is given, on average, by

$$\phi_R(x, y) = \iint_R n(\xi - x, \eta - y) \, n(\xi, \eta) \, d\xi \, d\eta = A N^2 \delta(x, y),$$

where A is the area of the image region R. Note the linear dependence of the integral on the area of the region. This is reasonable, since we expect the result computed over one half of the region to be independent of the result computed over the other half, and so when we add these two random variables we expect the variances to add.

The quantity N^2 characterizes the "power" of the noise per unit area. Note that the actual power per unit area is infinite, since we are dealing with a "signal" with a perfectly flat spectrum, that is, noise of infinite bandwidth. Only by limiting the frequency range do we obtain a finite power per unit area. Passing the noise through a smoothing filter is one way to do this.

(a) We are interested in the power per unit area of the noise after it is passed through a filter with a given point-spread function $h(x, y)$. The integral of the square of the filtered noise is, on average,

$$\iint_R o^2(x, y) \, dx \, dy,$$

where $o(x, y) = n(x, y) \otimes h(x, y)$. Show that the integral of the square of the output is

$$A N^2 \int_{-\infty}^{\infty} \int_{-\infty}^{\infty} h^2(x, y) \, dx \, dy.$$

Note that the output noise is no longer uncorrelated, but that this does not affect our integral of the square of the noise waveform.

(b) Consider passing an image through a Gaussian smoothing filter with point-spread function

$$g(x, y) = \frac{1}{2\pi\sigma^2} e^{-\frac{1}{2}\frac{x^2 + y^2}{\sigma^2}}.$$

What is the noise power per unit area in the output? How does this vary with σ? Consider the limit as $\sigma \to 0$.

8-5   In this problem we compare the performance of three edge-enhancement operators. In each case we first convolve the image with a Gaussian to smooth it and thus reduce the effects of noise. Then we apply a differential operator to increase the high-frequency components. One of the operators is a directional first derivative. Another is a directional second derivative. The third is the Laplacian, which is rotationally symmetric. We explore the response of each operator to a step edge (the signal) and to random noise. The performance index in each case will be the ratio of the peak signal to the root-mean-square noise.

Let

$$G_x = \frac{1}{\sqrt{2\pi}\sigma}e^{-\frac{1}{2}\frac{x^2}{\sigma^2}} \quad \text{and} \quad G_y = \frac{1}{\sqrt{2\pi}\sigma}e^{-\frac{1}{2}\frac{y^2}{\sigma^2}}.$$

The rotationally symmetric Gaussian G is just the product $G_x\,G_y$, or, if we let

$$G'_x = \frac{1}{\sqrt{2\pi}\sigma}e^{-\frac{1}{2}\frac{x^2}{\sigma^2}}\delta(y) \quad \text{and} \quad G'_y = \frac{1}{\sqrt{2\pi}\sigma}e^{-\frac{1}{2}\frac{y^2}{\sigma^2}}\delta(x),$$

G is just the convolution $G'_x \otimes G'_y$. Also note that differentiating the convolution of the image with a Gaussian leads to the same result as does convolution of the image with the derivative of the Gaussian. This is because differentiation is a linear, shift-invariant operation and so commutes with convolution.

The three operators can be written in terms of their point-spread functions as

$$O_1 = \frac{\partial}{\partial x}G, \qquad O_2 = \frac{\partial^2}{\partial x^2}G, \qquad O_3 = \nabla^2 G.$$

Our test image will be a vertical unit step edge passing through the origin,

$$E(x,y) = u(x),$$

which we can also think of as

$$E(x,y) = \int_{-\infty}^{x} \delta(s)\,ds,$$

where δ is the unit impulse function.

(a) Determine the response of each operator to this edge. Plan your attack carefully. Hint: Remember that differentiation and integration can be thought of as convolution with a suitable generalized function. Some work can be saved by noting that several of the operations commute. You may not want to determine the point-spread functions of the three operators explicitly at this stage, for example.

(b) Determine the maxima and minima of the enhanced image in each case. Two of the enhanced images should have the same extrema.

If the image noise is characterized as in the previous exercise by the integral

$$\iint_R n(\xi - x, \eta - y)\,n(\xi, \eta)\,d\xi\,d\eta = AN^2\delta(x,y),$$

then the noise power per unit area in the edge-enhanced result can be shown to be

$$N^2 \int_{-\infty}^{\infty} \int_{-\infty}^{\infty} O^2(x, y) \, dx \, dy,$$

where $O(x, y)$ is the point-spread function of the operator.

(c) Compute the variance of the noise for each of the three operators. Compute the ratio of peak signal to root-mean-square noise in each case. Here the root mean square is just the square root of the variance. For fixed "size" σ of the operator, which one has the best performance? Which one performs worst?

(d) The signal-to-noise ratio depends on the "size" σ of the operator. How much larger must the support of the third operator be than that of the first for them to have equal signal-to-noise performance?

8-6   The zero-crossing of the Laplacian of the Gaussian applied to an image of an ideal straight step edge lies right on top of the edge. Here we explore what happens when the edge is curved. Consider an image of an ideal disk-shaped object,

$$L(x, y) = \begin{cases} 1, & \text{for } x^2 + y^2 \leq R^2; \\ 0, & \text{for } x^2 + y^2 > R^2. \end{cases}$$

Zero-crossings, if any, of the convolution of this image with the Laplacian of the Gaussian form circles, because of the rotational symmetry of the image and the operators involved. Determine whether there is such a zero-crossing contour with radius R. If not, is there a zero-crossing nearby? Are there any spurious zero-crossing contours at other radii? Hint: It is difficult to find the convolution of the Gaussian with the disk, so make use of the fact that linear operations can be applied in any order.

8-7   Edge-enhancement operators are designed to operate well when there is a single straight edge in their support region. Such operators are affected by other image detail in the region over which their convolution weights are nonzero. In particular, they do not respond as expected near a gray-level corner. Consider a semi-infinite corner defined as follows:

$$E(x, y) = \begin{cases} 1, & \text{for } 0 \leq \theta \leq \alpha; \\ 0, & \text{otherwise}, \end{cases}$$

where θ is defined by

$$x = r \cos \theta \qquad \text{and} \qquad y = r \sin \theta$$

for some r. Find the convolution of the corner with the Gaussian for $\alpha = \pi/2$. Find the zero-crossing of the Laplacian applied to the result. (It is difficult to find the convolution for arbitrary values of α, so work it out only for the special case $\pi/2$.)

8-8   Show, using Taylor series expansion, that the operators represented by the three stencils

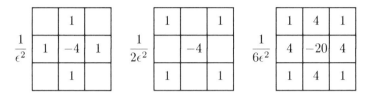

produce

$$\nabla^2 + \frac{\epsilon^2}{12}\left(\frac{\partial^4}{\partial x^4} + \frac{\partial^4}{\partial y^4}\right) + O(\epsilon^4),$$

$$\nabla^2 + \frac{\epsilon^2}{12}\left(\frac{\partial^4}{\partial x^4} + 6\frac{\partial^4}{\partial x^2\partial y^2} + \frac{\partial^4}{\partial y^4}\right) + O(\epsilon^4),$$

$$\nabla^2 + \frac{\epsilon^2}{12}\nabla^2(\nabla^2) + O(\epsilon^4),$$

respectively, where ∇^2 is the Laplacian.

8-9   Show that the image of an edge produced by an out-of-focus imaging system has brightness transition

$$\frac{1}{2} + \frac{1}{\pi}\left(\sin^{-1}\left(\frac{x}{R}\right) + \frac{x}{R}\sqrt{1 - \left(\frac{x}{R}\right)^2}\right)$$

for $|x| < R$. Use a vertically oriented unit step edge at $x = 0$ as input, and assume that the blur circle has radius R. Remember that the integral of the blur function has to be equal to one, since energy is merely redistributed, not absorbed or created. Hint: The edge-spread function is the integral of the line-spread function.

Show that the maximum slope of the edge-spread function is $4/\pi$ times as large as the ratio of the height of the transition to its width.

8-10   Rotationally symmetric operators are useful in that they produce scalar outputs that are independent of the particular choice of coordinate system. We have seen several rotationally symmetric operators, including the squared gradient, the quadratic variation, and the Laplacian. Also useful is the concept of a *coordinate-system-independent vector*. The magnitude of such a vector is independent of the choice of coordinate system, and the vector points in a direction that is fixed with respect to the surface. The brightness gradient is an example of a coordinate-system-independent vector.

(a) Suppose that the transformation from (x, y) to (x', y') is given by

$$\begin{pmatrix} x' \\ y' \end{pmatrix} = \mathbf{R} \begin{pmatrix} x \\ y \end{pmatrix},$$

where

$$\mathbf{R} = \begin{pmatrix} c & +s \\ -s & c \end{pmatrix}$$

is an orthonormal rotation matrix; that is, $c^2 + s^2 = 1$. Show that

$$\begin{pmatrix} E_{x'} \\ E_{y'} \end{pmatrix} = \mathbf{R} \begin{pmatrix} E_x \\ E_y \end{pmatrix}.$$

(b) Show that $(E_x, E_y)^T$ is a coordinate-system-independent vector. Derive a rotationally symmetric scalar from it.

(c) Now show that

$$\begin{pmatrix} E_{x'x'} \\ E_{x'y'} \\ E_{y'x'} \\ E_{y'y'} \end{pmatrix} = \mathbf{R} \otimes \mathbf{R} \begin{pmatrix} E_{xx} \\ E_{xy} \\ E_{yx} \\ E_{yy} \end{pmatrix},$$

where

$$\mathbf{R} \otimes \mathbf{R} = \begin{pmatrix} c^2 & sc & sc & s^2 \\ -sc & c^2 & -s^2 & sc \\ -sc & -s^2 & c^2 & sc \\ s^2 & -sc & -sc & c^2 \end{pmatrix}$$

is the *Kronecker product* of the rotation matrix $\mathbf{R}$ with itself.

(d) Conclude that

$$\left(\sqrt{\sqrt{(E_{xx} - E_{yy})^2 + 4E_{xy}^2} + (E_{xx} - E_{yy})} \, , \right.$$

$$\left. \sqrt{\sqrt{(E_{xx} - E_{yy})^2 + 4E_{xy}^2} - (E_{xx} - E_{yy})} \right)^T$$

is a coordinate-system-independent vector. Derive a rotationally symmetric scalar from it.

(e) Derive two rotationally symmetric scalars by combining first- and second-order coordinate-system-independent vectors. Hint: Use dot-products, and rotate one of the vectors by $90°$ to obtain the second scalar.

(f) Show that $(a^2 - b^2)(c^2 - d^2) + 4abcd$ and $(a^2 + c^2)(b^2 + d^2)$ are rotationally symmetric scalars when $(a, b)^T$ and $(c, d)^T$ are coordinate-system-independent vectors.

(g) Conclude that

$$(E_x^2 - E_y^2)(E_{xx} - E_{yy}) - 4E_x E_y E_{xy} \quad \text{and} \quad (E_x^2 - E_y^2)E_{xy} + E_x E_y (E_{xx} - E_{yy})$$

are rotationally symmetric scalars.

8-11 In some cases we want to detect lines in images rather than edges. For example, there is a lot of interest in turning engineering drawings into symbolic form for further processing in computer-aided design (CAD) systems. The "lines" in this case are one-dimensional curves of low brightness. So instead of looking for extrema in the first derivative, or zero-crossings in the second derivative, we ought to look for extrema in brightness, or zero-crossings of the first derivatives.

(a) Explain why a detector that checks whether $E_x = 0$ and $E_y = 0$ will not perform well. Hint: Consider what happens when the minimum brightness along the line is not constant.

(b) Consider $E(x, y)$ as a three-dimensional surface. Show that the direction of steepest ascent is given by the unit vector

$$\frac{1}{\sqrt{E_x^2 + E_y^2}} (E_x, E_y)^T$$

and that the slope in that direction is $\sqrt{E_x^2 + E_y^2}$.

(c) Find unit vectors in the two directions in which the second directional derivative has its extrema. Show that the two directions are at right angles to one another and that the second directional derivative attains the extreme values

$$\frac{1}{2} \left((E_{xx} + E_{yy}) \pm \sqrt{(E_{xx} - E_{yy})^2 + 4E_{xy}^2} \right).$$

Hint: In exercise 3-5 in chapter 3 we found the eigenvalues and eigenvectors of a symmetric 2×2 matrix.

(d) Explain why the center of the sought-after line can be defined to lie where the direction of steepest ascent is parallel to the direction in which the second derivative is smallest.

(e) Develop a nonlinear operator that will detect this condition.

(f) What difficulties does your operator have with areas where brightness is constant or varies linearly with x and y? Suggest ways to deal with these problems.

8-12 Some methods for detecting edge fragments rely on a surface-fitting approach rather than convolution. Suppose we want to find the ideal step edge that best fits the image brightness in a region R. Let the ideal step edge be a transition between a region A of brightness a and a region B of brightness b. We use the average, $m = (a + b)/2$, and the difference, $c = b - a$, in the following discussion. The brightness of the ideal image can be written

$$P(x, y) = m + c\big(u(t) - 1/2\big),$$

where $t = -x \sin \theta + y \cos \theta - \rho$ is the perpendicular distance of a point from the edge and

$$u(t) = \begin{cases} 0, & \text{for } t < 0; \\ 1/2, & \text{for } t = 0; \\ 1, & \text{for } t > 0, \end{cases}$$

is the unit step function. It is useful also to introduce a measure of distance along the edge, $s = x \cos \theta + y \sin \theta$.

The error term we are trying to minimize by suitable choice of m, c, and the location of the edge is

$$J = \iint_R \big(E(x,y) - P(x,y) \big)^2 \, dx \, dy,$$

where $E(x,y)$ is the observed image brightness.

(a) Show that the average brightness along the edge has to be m. That is,

$$\int_L E(x,y) ds = m \, l,$$

where l is the length of the portion L of the edge falling within the region R.

(b) Show that the first moment of brightness calculated along the edge has to be zero, if it is measured relative to the center of L. That is,

$$\int_L E(x,y)(s - s_0) ds = 0,$$

where s_0 is the value of s at the center of L.

(c) Suppose that the areas of the regions A and B are A_a and A_b, respectively, while the average brightnesses observed in the two regions are E_a and E_b. Show that

$$A_a E_a + A_b E_b = (A_a + A_b)m + (A_a - A_b)(c/2),$$
$$A_a E_a - A_b E_b = (A_a - A_b)m + (A_a + A_b)(c/2).$$

(d) Finally, show that $m = (E_a + E_b)/2$ and $c = E_a - E_b$.

9

Lightness & Color

In order to recognize an object or measure some of its properties, we need to recover information about its shape and reflectance from an image. In this chapter we discover that it is not trivial to obtain surface reflectance information from image brightness measurements. This is because image brightness depends on many factors, such as the illumination of the object, not just on surface reflectance. If we can estimate surface reflectance from images taken through several carefully chosen filters, we can estimate the color of the surface.

We solve the problem here for the special case of a Mondrian picture. This task provides us with an opportunity to apply several of the tools developed in earlier chapters, particularly methods for analyzing linear, shift-invariant systems and some of the operators suggested for edge detection. The iterative scheme we derive here bears a strong resemblance to those we shall discuss in chapters 11 and 12 for recovering shape from shading and for analyzing time-varying imagery. We also explore some physical models that will help us understand these computations and discuss how a parallel computer might be structured for carrying them out at high speed.

9.1 Surface Reflectance and Land's Experiments

One of the properties that is particularly useful in recognition is the reflectance of an object's surface. The brightness of a point in the image is proportional to the reflectance of the corresponding object point. It is, however, also proportional to the amount of light falling on the object. In general, image brightness can depend on yet other factors, such as the orientation of the surface patch under consideration. Thus image brightness cannot be used directly in estimating the reflectance of the surface.

Edwin Land drew attention to these problems in a series of ingenious experiments. In one, he placed sheets of gray paper in a variety of places around a room. Each sheet was carefully selected to have a reflectance appropriate for the position it was to occupy. Relatively dark grays were used in parts of the room that were brightly lit, while relatively light grays occupied the areas that were shaded from direct light. Land used a photometer to ensure that the amount of light received by the viewer from each sheet was the same. Thus a sheet of almost black paper in one part of the room reflected as much light as a sheet of white paper in another position. Despite this, the viewer had no difficulty determining the reflectances of the different sheets of paper.

Multiple values of reflectance, measured in several spectral bands, are very useful for recognition. We can attempt to estimate the "color" of a surface using images obtained through several filters. We face the problem discussed above again, since the spectral distribution of energy in the incident light affects brightness in the image. If we can come up with a way to extricate reflectance from irradiance in one image, then we can do this for multiple images taken with different spectral sensitivities. The problem of estimating color is thus basically solved if we can estimate reflectance from a single image.

In another of Land's experiments, a scene composed of colored objects was illuminated by colored light sources with strong spatial gradients. (A strong spatial variation in illumination can be produced, for example, by placing the light source close to the objects, but off to the side; those objects nearer the source are more strongly illuminated than those farther away.) Using two sources, one emitting more strongly in the long wavelength end of the spectrum, the other more strongly in the middle, Land set up a situation in which the incident light varied dramatically in brightness and color from one part of the scene to another. Using a photometer, he balanced the brightnesses of spatially separated areas in the scene in the different spectral bands. These areas did not look the same, however. Observers were able to identify the colors of the areas almost as well as if they were viewing the scene under more natural lighting conditions.

This shows that it is possible to recover surface reflectance information from image brightness measurements. Land developed a scheme for doing this in the one-dimensional case. The scheme, which he called the *retinex*, works well for certain simple scenes that we shall now explore.

Figure 9-1. A Mondrian is a figure consisting of patches of constant color. Uneven illumination will lead to an image in which the patches are not of constant brightness.

9.2 Mondrian Pictures

Consider a simple situation in which the surface orientation does not play a role—a scene composed of a group of patches of constant reflectivity (figure 9-1). Such an arrangement was dubbed a *Mondrian* by Land. (Piet Cornelis Mondrian was a turn-of-the-century Dutch artist who produced numerous paintings consisting of overlapping patches of more or less uniform color.)

In the simple situation here, scene radiance is proportional to the product of the irradiance falling on the object and the reflectance of the surface. The image irradiance, in turn, is proportional to the scene radiance. We can write

$$b'(x, y) = r'(x, y)\, e'(x, y),$$

where $b'(x, y)$ is the image irradiance at the image point (x, y), while $r'(x, y)$ is the reflectance and $e'(x, y)$ the irradiance at the point on the Mondrian corresponding to the image point (x, y). (We use primes here so that we can later use the same variables without the primes to denote the logarithms of these quantities. The logarithms will be more frequently referred to.) Our task is to separate the two contributions to the spatial variation in image irradiance.

9.3 Recovering Lightness

How can we recover $r'(x, y)$ and $e'(x, y)$, given only their product? This is obviously impossible without further assumptions. For a Mondrian, $r'(x, y)$ is constant within a patch and has sharp discontinuities at edges between patches. Conversely, we can assume that $e'(x, y)$ varies smoothly, for while the brightness of the incident light may vary from place to place, it will not do so abruptly. An exception would be a sharp shadow cast by an object illuminated by a point source.

If we were to take the Fourier transform of $e'(x, y)$, the energy would be concentrated mostly in the low frequencies, whereas the sharp edges in $r'(x, y)$ ensure that its Fourier transform has high-frequency components also. This suggests filtering the image to bring out the high-frequency components. A related way to approach this problem is to try to accentuate the edges. Partial derivatives will do that, as we have seen.

Our plan is to produce an intermediate result in which the contribution of one of the two components of image irradiance is increased relative to the other, so that we can remove the weaker one. Of course, we shall need to recover the remaining component from the result. This means that we must be able to undo the first, edge-accentuating, operation. Linear, shift-invariant operations suggest themselves, since we know how to find their inverses.

Edges at all orientations ought to be treated equally. Rotationally symmetric operators are therefore called for. The lowest-order linear combination of partial derivatives that is rotationally symmetric is the Laplacian,

$$\nabla^2 = \frac{\partial^2}{\partial x^2} + \frac{\partial^2}{\partial y^2}.$$

To make it easier to separate the contributions of irradiance from those of reflectance, we first take the logarithm of image brightness, so that the product is turned into a sum,

$$b(x, y) = r(x, y) + e(x, y),$$

where $b = \log b'$, $e = \log e'$, and $r = \log r'$. (Fortunately both r' and e' are positive.) Then we have,

$$d = \nabla^2 b = \nabla^2 r + \nabla^2 e.$$

Now, $\nabla^2 e$ will have finite values, since e varies smoothly. In fact, if e varies linearly with x and y, then $\nabla^2 e = 0$ (the same is true of any harmonic function, since it is a solution of Laplace's equation).

On the other hand, $\nabla^2 r$, while zero almost everywhere, is "infinite" on the edges between patches. Each step edge gives rise to a doublet edge that can be thought of as two closely spaced impulse edges of opposite

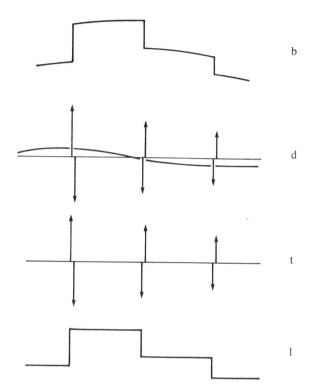

Figure 9-2. The sequence of processing steps in recovering lightness is illustrated here in one dimension. The process starts with differentiation to accentuate the edge signal. Thresholding then removes the slow fluctuations due to uneven lighting. The inverse operation, in this case, is simply integration. The recovered lightness l is an estimate of the surface reflectance r.

polarity. There is a large positive impulse on the darker side of the edge, and a large negative impulse on the brighter side. The amplitude of this doublet is proportional to the difference in the logarithm of reflectance, $r(x, y)$, across the edge.

Now we can apply a nonlinear "threshold" operator that discards all finite values, retaining only the doublets. If T is the operator, then

$$t = T(\nabla^2 r + \nabla^2 e) = \nabla^2 r.$$

Having eliminated the effect of e, we must now recover r.

In figure 9-2 we see the sequence of signals in the one-dimensional case, where differentiation replaces application of the Laplacian, and where r can be recovered simply by integrating the thresholded signal t. This is Land's retinex scheme.

We cannot recover r completely, however, as we shall see. As a consequence, it makes sense not to call the final result of this computation "reflectance," but to choose the term "lightness" instead. Lightness is the estimate of reflectance obtained from the image. (Under extreme circumstances to be described, it can be quite different from the reflectance.) The logarithm of lightness will be denoted $l(x, y)$.

9.4 Solving the Inverse Problem

We have to solve the partial differential equation

$$\left(\frac{\partial^2}{\partial x^2} + \frac{\partial^2}{\partial y^2} \right) l(x, y) = t(x, y),$$

which is called *Poisson's equation*. This form arises often in the analysis of problems in physics.

We can obtain some insight into this problem by introducing a physical model. Consider a planar resistive sheet into which current is injected. The potential on the resistive sheet satisfies Poisson's equation if the current density is $t(x, y)$ at the point (x, y). Usually such a problem is given with suitable boundary conditions. Such boundary conditions are not available to us here; we have to consider the resistive sheet as extending to infinity.

One way to solve an elliptic partial differential equation is to find the *Green's function* $g(x, y; \xi, \eta)$ for it. The solution is then given in integral form by

$$l(x, y) = \iint_R t(\xi, \eta) \, g(x, y; \xi, \eta) \, d\xi \, d\eta.$$

The Green's function for a particular problem depends on the boundary of the region R. If the boundary is at infinity, all points are treated the same and the integration conveniently simplifies to a convolution,

$$l(x, y) = \int_{-\infty}^{\infty} \int_{-\infty}^{\infty} t(\xi, \eta) \, g(x - \xi, y - \eta) \, d\xi \, d\eta.$$

We must now find the Green's function for Poisson's equation.

Note that $l = t \otimes g$. Taking the Fourier transform, we have

$$L = TG,$$

where L, T, and G are the Fourier transforms of l, t, and g, respectively. Recall that taking the Laplacian of a function can be thought of as convolving the function with a peculiar generalized function whose transform is

$-\rho^2$. Thus $t = \nabla^2 l$ becomes $T = -\rho^2 L$, upon taking the Fourier transform. Clearly, then,

$$G = -1/\rho^2,$$

and to find the point-spread function $g(x, y)$, we have to find the inverse transform of $G(u, v)$,

$$g(r) = -\frac{1}{2\pi} \int_0^\infty \frac{1}{\rho} J_0(r\rho) \, d\rho,$$

where J_0 is the Bessel function of order zero, as before. The integral for $g(r)$ does not converge. In particular, it is infinite for $r = 0$. Using suitable convergence factors, it can be shown to be equal to

$$g(r) = \frac{1}{2\pi} \log(r) + c,$$

except at $r = 0$. Here c is an arbitrary offset. We show in exercise 9-1 that

$$\left(\frac{\partial^2}{\partial x^2} + \frac{\partial^2}{\partial y^2} \right) \log(x^2 + y^2) = 4\pi \, \delta(x, y),$$

a result that can be established using methods developed in our discussion of generalized functions.

9.5 Normalization of Lightness

We recover the logarithm of the lightness, $l(x, y)$, by convolving the "thresholded" result with $g(x, y)$. Reflectance cannot be recovered completely, however. We know, for example, that the Laplacian removes the zero-frequency component, since it corresponds to multiplication by $-\rho^2$ in the frequency domain. Thus a constant offset cannot be recovered. Now a constant offset in $l(x, y)$ corresponds to a constant multiplier in $l'(x, y)$, so we can recover reflectance only up to a scale factor. This is illustrated by noting that we would obtain the same image if we halved all the reflectances and doubled the irradiance.

Often we are only concerned with *matte* surfaces, which do not exhibit specular or glossy reflections. In this case there is an upper limit to reflectance, represented by a surface that reflects all incident light, absorbing none. We shall assign the value one to the reflectance of this ideal matte surface. All reflectance values for matte surfaces must be less than or equal to one, or equivalently, $r(x, y) \le 0$. If there is such a "white" object, then the constant multiplier can be recovered. The computed values of $l(x, y)$ are adjusted by adding a constant so that the brightest value is zero, corresponding to a reflectance of one. If, by chance, there is no white patch, all other values will be erroneously scaled up.

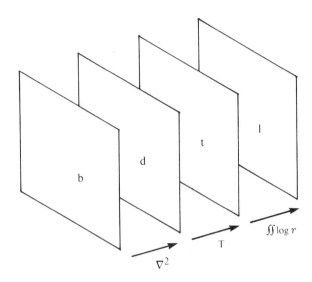

Figure 9-3. The computation of lightness in two dimensions involves several stages. The intermediate results are imagelike two-dimensional functions. The Laplacian operator is first applied to the logarithm of image irradiance in order to accentuate edges. The result is thresholded to remove smooth fluctuations due to spatial variations in the incident light distribution. Finally, the logarithm of lightness is estimated by convolving the result with the appropriate Green's function.

To summarize the process: We take the Laplacian of the logarithm of the image and threshold the result before taking the inverse transform by convolution with the appropriate Green's function (figure 9-3). Normalization is accomplished by adding a constant so that the maximum equals zero. Finally, we compute lightness by taking the antilogarithm.

Note that once we have an estimate of the reflectance, the irradiance can also be computed, since

$$e(x, y) = b(x, y) - r(x, y).$$

9.6 Selecting a Threshold

We might well feel a bit uncomfortable with a thresholding operation that separates infinite from finite components. In practice, all images have finite resolution, so that edges correspond to rapid, but not steplike, transitions in brightness. Application of the Laplacian thus produces large, but finite, values on either side of the edge. We use a finite threshold that is a compromise between insensitivity to weak edges and sensitivity to background variations. The calculation of reflectance is no longer exact in this case; it will be slightly corrupted by fluctuations in irradiance across the patches.

Why carry out this sequence of complicated forward and inverse transformations? Couldn't we perhaps just apply the one-dimensional method to image irradiance along curves in the image? That is, couldn't we trace along a curve, ignore smooth changes, and note the ratio of brightness across each edge as it is encountered? Normalized reflectance could then be computed by setting the largest value found to one and determining the remaining values by multiplying out all the ratios between the corresponding patches. This is not the best way to make use of all the information in the image, however, if there is any noise. The effects of noise are minimized by a process that takes into account information all along an edge, not just the brightness ratio at one point. Still, estimation of reflectance will be affected by the noise to some extent. As we saw earlier, not much can be done unless the noise has spectral characteristics that differ from those of the signal.

9.7 Computing Lightness in the Discrete Case

In order to implement this idea for estimating reflectance from image brightness, we have to consider discrete images. The Laplacian can be estimated using the stencil

$$\frac{1}{6\epsilon^2} \begin{array}{|c|c|c|} \hline 1 & 4 & 1 \\ \hline 4 & -20 & 4 \\ \hline 1 & 4 & 1 \\ \hline \end{array}$$

or something similar. Applying it to a sampled image will produce results similar to those described earlier, except that the values near the edges will be finite.

One remaining problem is to decide how finely the image should be sampled. Let ϵ be the spacing between picture cells. Smooth background fluctuations produce results that are more or less independent of ϵ. Near an edge, however, the result will vary as $1/\epsilon^2$, since the sharp discontinuity has a fixed brightness difference and the weights in the stencil vary as $1/\epsilon^2$. This suggests that as the image is sampled more finely, better results are obtained, that is, the signal-to-noise ratio is improved.

Real images have finite resolution, however, and a point will be reached at which the stencil covers the blurred, smooth transition of an edge. Further decreases in ϵ will not increase the result near the edge (figure 9-4).

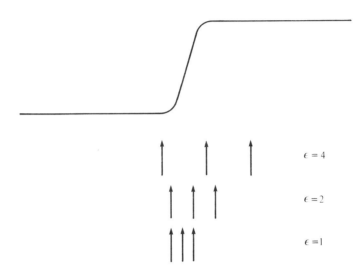

Figure 9-4. Separation of the slow lighting fluctuations from the rapid surface reflectance changes is improved when the picture cell spacing is small. There is no advantage, however, to making the spacing smaller than is warranted by the resolution inherent in the imaging system. As shown here, a spacing of $\epsilon = 2$ produces twice the separation between the image components as does a spacing of $\epsilon = 4$. On the other hand, little is gained by reducing the spacing to $\epsilon = 1$.

Thus the best results are obtained when the sampling matches the resolution of the image. This is in agreement with our earlier discussion of image sampling. Another way to look at this is to note that our operator does a good job of estimating the Laplacian of smooth image variations, but underestimates the value near an edge, unless sampling is fine enough to resolve the edge.

The next task is to construct an operator that will undo the edge enhancement introduced by application of the stencil given above. We could convolve the intermediate result with a discrete approximation of

$$\frac{1}{2\pi} \log \sqrt{x^2 + y^2}.$$

It should be clear, however, that a discrete approximation to the inverse of the Laplacian will not be an exact inverse for the discrete approximation to the Laplacian. We need to find a discrete function that produces the unit impulse when convolved with the given stencil, that is, a function f such that $g \otimes f = \delta$. This convolution can be expanded into

$$-20f_{i,j} + 4\left(f_{i+1,j} + f_{i,j+1} + f_{i-1,j} + f_{i,j-1}\right)$$
$$+ \left(f_{i+1,j+1} + f_{i-1,j+1} + f_{i-1,j-1} + f_{i+1,j-1}\right) = 0$$

for $(i,j) \neq (0,0)$ and

$$-20f_{0,0} + 4\left(f_{1,0} + f_{0,1} + f_{-1,0} + f_{0,-1}\right)$$
$$+ \left(f_{1,1} + f_{-1,1} + f_{-1,-1} + f_{1,-1}\right) = 6\epsilon^2.$$

This is a set of linear equations in the unknowns $\{f_{ij}\}$. There is one equation for each unknown. Unfortunately, because there are an infinite number of unknowns, the usual techniques are not directly applicable.

We can approximate the answer by taking a finite image size and hence a finite support for the discrete inverse. For reasonable accuracy we ought to use a large image size, in which case iterative techniques such as the Gauss–Seidel method are useful. This amounts to solving each of the equations above for the dominant term

$$f_{i,j}^{n+1} = \frac{1}{5}\left(f_{i+1,j}^n + f_{i,j+1}^n + f_{i-1,j}^n + f_{i,j-1}^n\right)$$
$$+ \frac{1}{20}\left(f_{i+1,j+1}^n + f_{i-1,j+1}^n + f_{i-1,j-1}^n + f_{i+1,j-1}^n\right)$$

for $(i,j) \neq (0,0)$, where the superscripts denote the iteration number. For $(i,j) = (0,0)$, a constant equal to $(3/10)\epsilon^2$ is subtracted from the right-hand side of the iterative formula. Starting values can be found by using the continuous solution as an approximation.

The result of thresholding the edge-enhanced image is convolved with this discrete approximation to obtain the result. The intermediate result has to be extended with zeros. Note that extending the original image with zeros is not appropriate, since spurious edges would be introduced at the image border.

An alternative to finding the inverse of the discrete approximation to the Laplacian is to solve directly the equations

$$-20r_{i,j} + 4\left(r_{i+1,j} + r_{i,j+1} + r_{i-1,j} + r_{i,j-1}\right)$$
$$+ \left(r_{i+1,j+1} + r_{i-1,j+1} + r_{i-1,j-1} + r_{i+1,j-1}\right) = 6\epsilon^2 t_{i,j},$$

where $\{t_{ij}\}$ is the thresholded intermediate result. Iterative methods are again suggested:

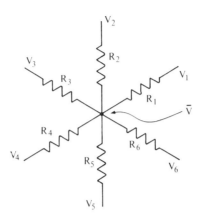

Figure 9-5. A network of resistors computes a weighted average $\overline{V}$ of the applied potentials $V_1, V_2, \ldots, V_6$.

$$r_{i,j}^{n+1} = \frac{1}{5}\left(r_{i+1,j}^n + r_{i,j+1}^n + r_{i-1,j}^n + r_{i,j-1}^n\right)$$

$$+ \frac{1}{20}\left(r_{i+1,j+1}^n + r_{i-1,j+1}^n + r_{i-1,j-1}^n + r_{i+1,j-1}^n\right) - \frac{3}{10}\epsilon^2 t_{i,j}.$$

Care has to be taken at the image boundary, as before.

9.8 A Physical Model

A physical implementation is suggested by the form of the equations. We note that the equations we are trying to solve require that the difference between the value at a point and a weighted average of the neighboring values be equal to some specified input.

A weighted average is easily computed by a network of resistors (figure 9-5). Consider n resistors of resistance R_i, each connected on one end to a source of voltage V_i. If the resistors are connected together at their other end, we obtain a voltage

$$\overline{V} = \frac{\sum_{i=1}^n V_i/R_i}{\sum_{i=1}^n 1/R_i}.$$

This is easily shown by noting that the current in the ith resistor is $(V_i - \overline{V})/R_i$ and that by Kirchhoff's law the currents must cancel each other out at the common node. Now imagine injecting a current I into this common

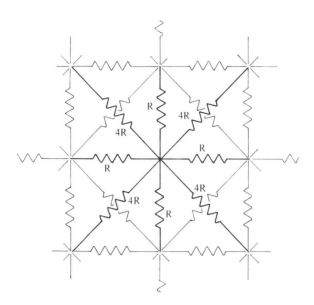

Figure 9-6. A simple network of resistors computes the inverse operation in the recovery of lightness.

node. The voltage there will rise by

$$\frac{I}{\sum_{i=1}^{n} 1/R_i},$$

as can be seen by redoing the above calculation for the case in which the currents into the node add up to $-I$.

Now consider a rectangular network of resistors (figure 9-6), where each node is connected to its immediate neighbors in the same row or column by a resistor of resistance R and to its four neighbors in the diagonal directions by resistors of resistance $4R$. Current is injected proportional to the thresholded value at each node. That is, the current at node (i, j) is $(5/R)t_{ij}$. The potentials at the nodes satisfy the equations given above and thus form the desired output. Once again, care has to be taken at the boundaries.

Note that this method for solving the implicit equation applies equally well if we change the weight factors. There are many other methods for solving these equations in parallel. One method employs operational amplifiers, devices that sum constant multiples of their inputs, in a feedback circuit reminiscent of the Gauss–Seidel iteration (figure 9-7). In each case we have to determine whether the iteration will converge or not.

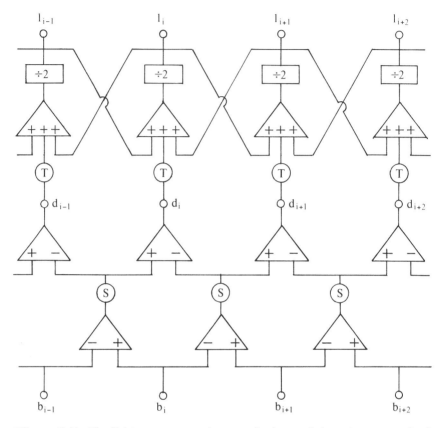

Figure 9-7. The lightness computation can also be carried out by a network of operational amplifiers arranged in layers. Shown here is a circuit for the solution of the one-dimensional problem. This circuit is used in exercise 9-4 to construct a network suitable for the two-dimensional case.

We have now developed a method for estimating the reflectance of a set of partially overlapping patches. By repeating this calculation for images taken through several filters, we can assign a "color" to each of the patches. In this case we do not even need to have a white patch for normalization. For each filter we simply require that at least one of the surfaces reflect all of the incident light within the spectral band of that filter. The maximally reflecting surfaces can be different for different filters.

The method presented here will not work when the surface reflectance of an object varies smoothly from place to place, because such smooth variations are suppressed by the thresholding. We face a related problem with curved objects, since they give rise to shaded images, as we note in the next chapter. Such images are not dealt with here. Also, the normalization method will fail if one of the patches is a light source, since it could be brighter than a white patch. For similar reasons, a specularly reflecting surface can throw off the normalization.

What we have shown is that in extracting useful information from the image we do not use the raw image brightness measurements directly. They are used only to estimate properties, such as reflectance, of the objects portrayed. One difficulty we face is that too many factors are confounded in the image. Often additional assumptions must be made if we are to make progress in deciphering the puzzle.

9.9 References

Humans have been speculating about color vision for a long time. Some of the results of this speculation over the last few centuries are brought together by MacAdam in *Sources of Color Science* [1970]. *Color Vision* by Wasserman [1978] is also useful for reviewing the history of the problem. Other books of great interest are *The Perception of Color* by Evans [1974] and *Seeing* by Frisby [1979].

There are numerous books that discuss partial differential equations, among them *Partial Differential Equations: Theory and Technique* by Carrier & Pearson [1976], volume 2 of *Methods of Mathematical Physics* by Courant & Hilbert [1962], *Partial Differential Equations* by John [1971], and a book with the same title by Moon & Spencer [1969].

Land first startled the world with his experiments on color vision in 1959. His retinex theory was published in 1964. Land & McCann [1971] developed it into the lightness theory. McCann, Land, & Tatnall [1970] compared human visual responses to an early version of their theory of lightness computation. Land [1983] still maintains an interest in the problem.

Horn [1974] extended Land's retinex to two dimensions and presented several analog models and parallel architectures for implementing the computation. The idea was based in part on an earlier use of the Laplacian in an edge-marking scheme by Horn [1972]. Marr [1974] related one of the architectures proposed to the structure of the interconnections in the layers of the primate retina. (There now seems to be some evidence that lightness is computed in the visual cortex, however.) Blake [1985] improved upon Horn's method in a significant way, by changing the place where the thresholding operation occurs.

There is much interest in the kind of massively parallel computation that was first proposed for the computation of lightness. (For another view of parallel computation in vision see Ballard, Hinton, & Sejnowshi

[1983]. For ideas on programming a modern parallel machine see Chrisman [1984].) Poggio & Koch [1984] have related some of these ideas to regularization and proposed analog models for the computations. Traditional methods for iteratively solving elliptic partial differential equations on a grid have suffered from slow convergence. Recently, multiresolution methods have been explored that appear to reduce this problem greatly. Terzopoulos [1983, 1984a,b] has applied these methods to several machine-vision algorithms, including the computation of lightness.

It would be a hopeless task to try to survey the literature on color vision. Here we just mention a few random samples. The reader of Lettvin's [1967] fascinating analysis of the problem may come away believing that it is impossible to see colors! Livingstone & Hubel [1984] provide up-to-date information on the anatomy and physiology of the color system in the primate visual cortex.

9.10 Exercises

9-1   Let $r^2 = x^2 + y^2$ and

$$\nabla^2 = \frac{\partial^2}{\partial x^2} + \frac{\partial^2}{\partial y^2}.$$

(a) Show that, except at $r = 0$, $\nabla^2 \log r^2 = 0$.

(b) Consider instead $\nabla^2 \log(r^2 + \sigma^2)$. What generalized function does this family of functions define as σ tends to zero? Hint: It might help to convert the integral of the result to polar coordinates.

9-2   Given the integral

$$\int_0^\infty r \left(\log \frac{r}{a + \sqrt{a^2 + r^2}} \right) J_0(rz)\, dr = -\frac{1}{z^2} \left(1 - e^{az} \right) \qquad \text{for } z \neq 0,$$

explain why it is reasonable to think of $-2\pi/\rho^2$ as the Fourier transform of $\log r$, where $\rho^2 = u^2 + v^2$ and $r^2 = x^2 + y^2$.

9-3   Shown in figure 9-8 are outlines of regions in which brightness varies smoothly in an image, together with some spot measurements taken in each case on both sides of an edge where there is a rapid transition in brightness. Assuming that the maximum reflectance is one, determine the reflectances of the patches that gave rise to each of the image regions. What is the minimum reflectance? Are the given data consistent?

9-4   Show how to extend the network in figure 9-7 to two dimensions so that it can be applied to the computation of lightness from an image. Hint: First build a series of parallel layers each containing such a network. Then add a second set of parallel layers rotated $60°$, and a third set rotated $120°$.

The final summing amplifiers receive inputs from six surrounding cells. Show that their outputs have to be divided by 6, not 2 as in the one-dimensional case.

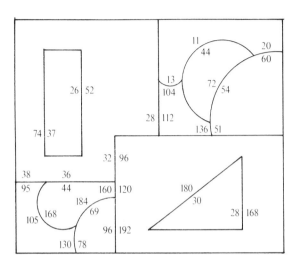

Figure 9-8. A sample Mondrian with pairs of brightness measurements, each pair giving the brightnesses on opposite sides of an edge.

10

Reflectance Map: Photometric Stereo

We are now ready to look more carefully at how the brightness pattern in an image depends on the shape of the object being imaged. In this chapter we develop the photometric stereo method for recovering the orientation of surface patches from a number of images taken under different lighting conditions. In the next chapter we consider the more difficult problem of recovering surface shape from a single image. The photometric stereo method is simple to implement, but requires control of the lighting. The orientation of a patch of the surface corresponding to a given picture cell is determined by means of a simple lookup table, which is built using a calibration object of known shape. The orientations of the surface patches are conveniently represented as a needle diagram.

In order to understand how these methods work, we need to know something about radiometry. We have to make more precise the term "brightness" and learn how image irradiance depends on scene radiance. The detailed dependence of surface reflection on the geometry of incident and emitted rays is given by the bidirectional reflectance distribution function. The reflectance map can be derived from that function and the distribution of light sources. The reflectance map is useful because it makes explicit the relationship between surface orientation and brightness. It is of critical importance in recovering surface orientation from measurements of brightness. In practice, one can determine the reflectance map experimentally, using a calibration object of known shape, rather than computing it from the bidirectional reflectance distribution function. The reader with less interest in radiometry may want to skip the first few sections and proceed directly to the discussion of the reflectance map.

Finally, we introduce the image irradiance equation, which will play an important role in the next chapter.

10.1 Image Brightness

The image of a three-dimensional object depends on its shape, its reflectance properties, and the distribution of light sources. Three views of a portion of the surface of Mars are shown in figure 10-1. The three images were obtained using a camera in a fixed position. The differences between them are due to differences in lighting conditions. While clearly the same underlying surface is being portrayed, the detailed patterns of brightness are quite different. Some edges that show up in strong contrast in one of the pictures, for example, are not visible in another. This example demonstrates the importance of the position and distribution of the sources of illumination in determining the brightness pattern.

The image of a three-dimensional object also depends on the position of the object relative to the imaging system and on the object's attitude in space. In the case of a solid of revolution, attitude has only two degrees of freedom, so that the attitude can be specified by giving the direction of the axis of revolution. Figure 10-2 shows how the silhouette of a push-pin changes with its attitude. More important, note how the brightness pattern within the silhouette changes, particularly where the glossy surface reflects light from the source directly toward the viewer. These variations in the image of an object become even more complicated when we consider general shapes, for then attitude has three degrees of freedom. It is clear that the binary image-processing methods discussed earlier will be of no avail in that situation.

We have to understand how the image is formed in order to turn the process around and recover information about the permanent properties of the object, such as its shape and surface reflectance. However, to understand how the brightness at a particular point in the image is determined, we must first discuss radiometry.

10.2 Radiometry

The amount of light falling on a surface is called the *irradiance*. It is the power per unit area ($W \cdot m^{-2}$—watts per square meter) incident on the surface. The amount of light radiated from a surface is called the *radiance*. It is the power per unit area per unit solid angle ($W \cdot m^{-2} \cdot sr^{-1}$—watts per

Figure 10-1. The appearance of a surface depends greatly on the lighting conditions. We have to understand how images are formed if we are to recover information about the surface from one or more images. Shown here are three views of the surface of Mars taken by Viking Lander I. (Pictures IPL PIC ID 77/03/06/134059, 77/02/09/172643, and 77/02/05/042935, courtesy of the National Space Science Data Center, Greenbelt, Maryland.)

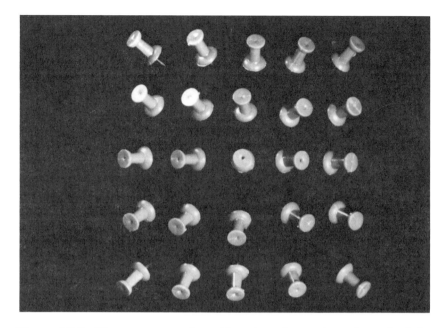

Figure 10-2. The appearance of an object depends greatly on its attitude in space relative to the viewer. Not only does the outline vary, but the brightness pattern within the silhouette changes.

square meter per steradian) emitted from the surface. The complexity of the latter concept stems from the fact that a surface can radiate into a whole hemisphere of possible directions and can radiate different amounts of energy in different directions.

The solid angle of a cone of directions is defined as the area cut out by the cone on the unit sphere. A hemisphere of directions, for example, has a solid angle of 2π. A small planar patch of area A at distance R from the origin (figure 10-3) subtends a solid angle

$$\Omega = \frac{A \cos \theta}{R^2},$$

where θ is the angle between a surface normal and a line connecting the patch to the origin.

Brightness is determined by the amount of energy an imaging system receives per unit apparent area. The unit area mentioned in the definition of radiance is the foreshortened area, the surface area multiplied by the cosine of the angle between a perpendicular to the surface and the specified direction.

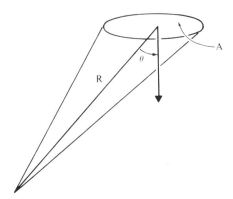

Figure 10-3. The solid angle subtended by a small patch is proportional to its area A and the cosine of the angle of inclination θ; it is inversely proportional to the square of its distance R from the origin.

10.3 Image Formation

We next find the relationship between the radiance at a point on an object (scene radiance) and the irradiance at the corresponding point in the image (image irradiance). Consider a lens of diameter d at a distance f from the image plane (figure 10-4). Let a patch on the surface of the object have area δO, while the corresponding image patch has area δI. Suppose that the ray from the object patch to the center of the lens makes an angle α with the optical axis and that there is an angle θ between this ray and a surface normal. The object patch is at a distance $-z$ from the lens, measured along the optical axis. (The minus sign arises from our convention for the coordinate system, with the z-axis pointing toward the image plane.)

The ratio of the area of the object patch to that of the image patch is determined by the distances of these patches from the lens and by foreshortening. Rays passing through the center of the lens are not deflected. As a result, the solid angle of the cone of rays leading to the patch on the object is equal to the solid angle of the cone of rays leading to the corresponding patch in the image. The apparent area of the image patch as seen from the center of the lens is $\delta I \cos \alpha$, while the distance of this patch from the center of the lens is $f / \cos \alpha$. Thus the solid angle subtended by this patch is just

$$\frac{\delta I \cos \alpha}{(f / \cos \alpha)^2}.$$

Similarly, the solid angle of the patch on the object as seen from the center

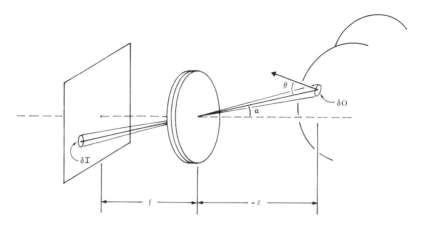

Figure 10-4. To see how image irradiance is related to the radiance of the surface, we must determine the size of the region in the image that corresponds to the patch on the surface.

of the lens is

$$\frac{\delta O \cos \theta}{(z/\cos \alpha)^2}.$$

If these two solid angles are to be equal, we must have

$$\frac{\delta O}{\delta I} = \frac{\cos \alpha}{\cos \theta} \left(\frac{z}{f}\right)^2.$$

Next, we need to determine how much of the light emitted by the surface makes its way through the lens (figure 10-5). The solid angle subtended by the lens, as seen from the object patch, is

$$\Omega = \frac{\pi}{4} \frac{d^2 \cos \alpha}{(z/\cos \alpha)^2} = \frac{\pi}{4} \left(\frac{d}{z}\right)^2 \cos^3 \alpha.$$

Thus the power of the light originating on the patch and passing through the lens is

$$\delta P = L \, \delta O \, \Omega \cos \theta = L \, \delta O \, \frac{\pi}{4} \left(\frac{d}{z}\right)^2 \cos^3 \alpha \cos \theta,$$

where L is the radiance of the surface in the direction toward the lens. This power is concentrated in the image (if we ignore losses in the lens). Since

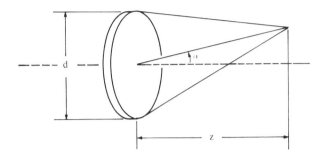

Figure 10-5. To see how image irradiance is related to the radiance of the surface, we must determine how much of the light emitted by the surface is gathered by the lens. This depends on the solid angle that the lens subtends when viewed from the light-emitting surface.

no light from other areas reaches this image patch, we have

$$E = \frac{\delta P}{\delta I} = L \frac{\delta O}{\delta I} \frac{\pi}{4} \left(\frac{d}{z}\right)^2 \cos^3 \alpha \cos \theta,$$

where E is the irradiance of the image at the patch under consideration. Substituting for $\delta O / \delta I$, we finally obtain

$$E = L \frac{\pi}{4} \left(\frac{d}{f}\right)^2 \cos^4 \alpha.$$

Thus image irradiance is proportional to scene radiance. This is the fundamental relationship we shall exploit in recovering information about objects from their images.

The factor of proportionality in the formula above contains the inverse of the square of the effective *f-number*, f/d. It also contains a term that falls off with the cosine to the fourth power of the angle that the ray from the image point to the center of the lens makes with the optical axis. This falloff in sensitivity is not very important when the image covers only a narrow angle, as in a telephoto lens. Moreover, in typical lens systems, multiple apertures, lined up for axial rays, cut off part of the light for ray directions that are inclined to the optical axis. This vignetting effect, discussed in chapter 2, often causes a much more serious falloff in brightness than the cosine term. Multiple apertures are usually introduced to minimize distortions that would otherwise increase in severity as some power of the off-axis angle α. In any case, the dependence of the sensitivity of a given imaging system on the off-axis angle is fixed and can be accounted for.

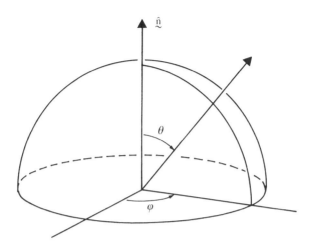

Figure 10-6. The direction of incident and emitted light rays can be specified in a local coordinate system using the polar angle θ and the azimuth ϕ.

To summarize: The important thing is that what we measure—the image irradiance E—is proportional to what we are interested in—the scene radiance L. Looked at another way, we have defined radiance so that it corresponds to our intuitive notion of "brightness," which is, after all, related to image irradiance.

10.4 Bidirectional Reflectance Distribution Function

What determines scene radiance? Scene radiance depends on the amount of light that falls on a surface and the fraction of the incident light that is reflected. It also depends, however, on the geometry of light reflection, as the example of a mirror clearly shows. That is, the radiance of a surface will generally depend on the direction from which it is viewed as well as on the direction from which it is illuminated.

We can describe these directions in terms of a local coordinate system erected on the surface (figure 10-6). Consider a perpendicular to the surface (the normal $\hat{n}$) and an arbitrary reference line drawn on the surface. Directions can be described by specifying the angle θ between a ray and the normal and the angle ϕ between a perpendicular projection of the ray onto the surface and the reference line on the surface.

These angles are called the *polar angle* and *azimuth*, respectively. They allow us to specify the direction (θ_i, ϕ_i) from which light is falling on the surface and the direction (θ_e, ϕ_e) into which it is emitted toward the viewer

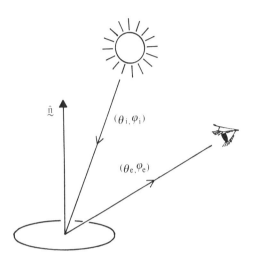

Figure 10-7. The bidirectional reflectance distribution function is the ratio of the radiance of the surface patch as viewed from the direction (θ_e, ϕ_e) to the irradiance resulting from illumination from the direction (θ_i, ϕ_i).

(figure 10-7).

We can now define the *bidirectional reflectance distribution function* (BRDF) $f(\theta_i, \phi_i; \theta_e, \phi_e)$, which tells us how bright a surface appears when viewed from one direction while light falls on it from another. Let the amount of light falling on the surface from the direction (θ_i, ϕ_i)—the irradiance—be $\delta E(\theta_i, \phi_i)$. Let the brightness of the surface as seen from the direction (θ_e, ϕ_e)—the radiance—be $\delta L(\theta_e, \phi_e)$. The BRDF is simply the ratio of radiance to irradiance,

$$f(\theta_i, \phi_i; \theta_e, \phi_e) = \frac{\delta L(\theta_e, \phi_e)}{\delta E(\theta_i, \phi_i)}.$$

We shall study specific examples of BRDFs for several idealized surfaces later in this chapter.

A function of four variables is a bit too cumbersome to use directly in exploring the relationship between image irradiance and surface shape. Fortunately, for many surfaces the radiance is not altered if the surface is rotated about the surface normal. In this case, the BRDF depends only on the difference $\phi_e - \phi_i$, not on ϕ_e and ϕ_i separately. This is certainly true of matte surfaces and specularly reflecting surfaces. It is not true of surfaces with oriented microstructure, as for example the mineral called tiger's eye or the iridescent feathers of some birds.

There is an interesting constraint on the form of the BRDF. If two

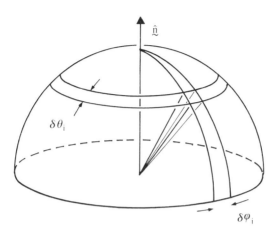

Figure 10-8. In the case of an extended light source, we must integrate the product of the bidirectional reflectance distribution function and the source radiance over all incident directions.

surfaces are in thermal equilibrium, radiation reaching one from the other must be balanced by radiation flowing in the opposite direction. If this were not the case, the surface receiving more radiation would heat up and the other would cool down, thus disturbing the equilibrium. This would violate the second law of thermodynamics. It is easy to show that this implies that the BRDF is constrained by the *Helmholtz reciprocity condition*:

$$f(\theta_i, \phi_i; \theta_e, \phi_e) = f(\theta_e, \phi_e; \theta_i, \phi_i).$$

10.5 Extended Light Sources

So far we have considered the case in which all of the light comes from one direction. In practice, there can be several light sources, or even extended sources, such as the sky. In the case of an extended source, we must consider a nonzero solid angle of directions to obtain a nonzero radiance. Consider an infinitesimal patch of the sky, of size $\delta\theta_i$ in polar angle and $\delta\phi_i$ in azimuth (figure 10-8). This patch subtends a solid angle

$$\delta\omega = \sin\theta_i \, \delta\theta_i \, \delta\phi_i.$$

If we let $E(\theta_i, \phi_i)$ be the radiance per unit solid angle coming from the direction (θ_i, ϕ_i), then the radiance from the patch under consideration is

$$E(\theta_i, \phi_i) \sin\theta_i \, \delta\theta_i \, \delta\phi_i,$$

and the total irradiance of the surface is

$$E_0 = \int_{-\pi}^{\pi} \int_{0}^{\pi/2} E(\theta_i, \phi_i) \sin \theta_i \cos \theta_i \, d\theta_i \, d\phi_i,$$

where the $\cos \theta_i$ term accounts for the foreshortening of the surface as seen from the direction (θ_i, ϕ_i).

To obtain the radiance of the surface we must integrate the product of the BRDF and the irradiance over the hemisphere of possible directions from which light can fall on a surface. Thus

$$L(\theta_e, \phi_e) = \int_{-\pi}^{\pi} \int_{0}^{\pi/2} f(\theta_i, \phi_i; \theta_e, \phi_e) E(\theta_i, \phi_i) \sin \theta_i \cos \theta_i \, d\theta_i \, d\phi_i.$$

Again, the $\cos \theta_i$ term in the integrand accounts for foreshortening. The result is a function of two variables only, θ_e and ϕ_e, which specify the direction of the ray emitted toward the viewer.

10.6 Surface Reflectance Properties

An *ideal Lambertian surface* is one that appears equally bright from all viewing directions and reflects all incident light, absorbing none. From this definition we can deduce that the BRDF $f(\theta_i, \phi_i; \theta_e, \phi_e)$ must be a constant for such a surface. What is this constant? To determine it, we integrate the radiance of the surface over all directions and equate the total radiance so obtained to the total irradiance:

$$\int_{-\pi}^{\pi} \int_{0}^{\pi/2} f \, E \, \cos \theta_i \sin \theta_e \cos \theta_e \, d\theta_e \, d\phi_e = E \cos \theta_i,$$

or

$$2\pi f \int_{0}^{\pi/2} \sin \theta_e \cos \theta_e \, d\theta_e = 1.$$

Using the identity $2 \sin \theta \cos \theta = \sin 2\theta$, we obtain $\pi f = 1$. Thus, for an ideal Lambertian surface,

$$f(\theta_i, \phi_i; \theta_e, \phi_e) = \frac{1}{\pi}.$$

Note that since the BRDF is constant for a Lambertian surface, we can compute the radiance L from the irradiance E_0 using

$$L = \frac{1}{\pi} E_0.$$

This simple method cannot, of course, be used for surfaces with other reflectance properties.

The other extreme of surface reflectance properties is illustrated by an ideal specular reflector, which reflects all of the light arriving from the direction (θ_i, ϕ_i) into the direction $(\theta_i, \phi_i + \pi)$ (figure 10-9). The BRDF in this case is proportional to the product of two impulses, $\delta(\theta_e - \theta_i)$ and $\delta(\phi_e - \phi_i - \pi)$. But what is the factor of proportionality k? Once again we integrate over all emittance directions to compute the total radiance of the surface and equate this to the irradiance:

$$\int_{-\pi}^{\pi} \int_{0}^{\pi/2} k\,\delta(\theta_e - \theta_i)\,\delta(\phi_e - \phi_i - \pi) \sin\theta_e \cos\theta_e\, d\theta_e\, d\phi_e = 1,$$

or

$$k \sin\theta_i \cos\theta_i = 1.$$

Thus, in this case,

$$f(\theta_i, \phi_i; \theta_e, \phi_e) = \frac{\delta(\theta_e - \theta_i)\delta(\phi_e - \phi_i - \pi)}{\sin\theta_i \cos\theta_i}.$$

We can use this result immediately to determine the radiance of a specularly reflecting surface under an extended source:

$$L(\theta_e, \phi_e) = \int_{-\pi}^{\pi} \int_{0}^{\pi/2} \frac{\delta(\theta_e - \theta_i)\delta(\phi_e - \phi_i - \pi)}{\sin\theta_i \cos\theta_i} E(\theta_i, \phi_i) \sin\theta_i \cos\theta_i\, d\theta_i\, d\phi_i$$

$$= E(\theta_e, \phi_e - \pi).$$

The radiance is just equal to the radiance of the reflected piece of the extended source. This makes eminent sense, since we are looking at the virtual image of the extended source. This simple relationship obviously does not hold for surfaces with other reflectance properties.

The BRDF can be determined experimentally by illuminating a flat sample of the material of interest with a lamp mounted on a goniometer and measuring its irradiance using a sensor mounted on another goniometer. (A *goniometer* has two axes of rotation, so that a device mounted on it can be aimed in an accurately known direction.) The experimental determination of the BRDF is quite tedious because of the four variables involved. Fortunately, only three—θ_i, θ_e, and $(\phi_e - \phi_i)$—are typically really significant.

Another way to obtain the BRDF is to model how light is reflected from a surface and to find the corresponding reflectance properties analytically or by numerical simulation. This has been done for some simple models of surface microstructure. Closed-form solutions are often possible if suitable approximations are introduced. We shall not pursue this topic further here.

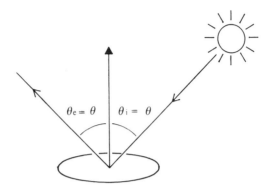

Figure 10-9. A specular surface reflects all incident light in a direction that lies in the same plane as the incident ray and the surface normal. The emittance angle θ_e between the reflected ray and the normal equals the incident angle θ_i between the incident ray and the normal.

10.7 Surface Brightness

How bright will a Lambertian surface be when it is illuminated by a point source of radiance E? A point source located in direction (θ_s, ϕ_s) has radiance

$$E(\theta_i, \phi_i) = E \frac{\delta(\theta_i - \theta_s)\, \delta(\phi_i - \phi_s)}{\sin \theta_s},$$

where the $\sin \theta_i$ term ensures that the integral of this expression is just E. That is, we must have

$$\int_{-\pi}^{\pi} \int_{0}^{\pi/2} E(\theta_i, \phi_i) \sin \theta_i \, d\theta_i \, d\phi_i = E.$$

Using the known BRDF for a Lambertian surface, it is easy to show that in this case

$$L = \frac{1}{\pi} E \cos \theta_i \qquad \text{for } \theta_i \geq 0$$

This is the familiar "cosine" or Lambert's law of reflection from matte surfaces. (Note that the dependence on the cosine of the incident angle comes directly from the dependence of the irradiance on that factor and so can be traced to the foreshortening of the surface as seen from the light source.) Surfaces covered with finely powdered transparent materials, such as barium sulfate or magnesium carbonate, come closest to obeying Lambert's law. It is a reasonable approximation for many other materials, such as paper, snow, and matte paint.

Next, consider the same surface under a "sky" of uniform radiance E. Here

$$L = \int_{-\pi}^{\pi} \int_{0}^{\pi/2} \frac{E}{\pi} \sin \theta_i \cos \theta_i \, d\theta_i \, d\phi_i = E.$$

The radiance of the patch is the same as the radiance of the source!

This leads to an interesting thought experiment. If we were to build a bottle of arbitrary shape, coated the interior with Lambertian material, and then introduced some light through a tiny hole, every surface patch would be equally bright. Peering through another tiny hole, we would not be able to discern the shape of the inner surface, since every portion of it would look equally bright. With an overcast sky, snow fields tend to have very low contrast and make vision difficult for the same reason. This is called a *white-out* condition. The fact that the surface is white is, of course, not the problem, since the shape of the surface is easy to discern under point-source illumination. Recall that a specular surface under a uniform extended source also appears to have the same radiance as the extended source. So Lambertian reflection is not required for this effect to occur.

A more complicated case, but more realistic perhaps, is a hemispherical sky above a tilted Lambertian surface patch. We show in exercise 10-3 that the total radiance in this case is

$$\frac{E}{2}(1 + \cos \alpha) = E \cos^2 \frac{\alpha}{2},$$

where α is the inclination of the surface normal with respect to the vertical direction. The variation in brightness due to surface orientation changes is less here than it would be if there were a single point source overhead.

10.8 Surface Orientation

The BRDF is of fundamental importance for understanding reflectance from a surface. It is not exactly what we need, however, to understand image formation. First of all, to factor in the distribution of light sources we need to integrate the BRDF over all possible directions of the incident light. This yields a function that depends on two parameters only. We can relate these two parameters to surface orientation, a very important aspect of the surfaces being imaged. To do this successfully, however, we have to abandon the local coordinate system used in the definition of the BRDF and use a viewer-centered coordinate system instead.

Let us start by developing a reasonable notation for surface orientation. A smooth surface has a tangent plane at every point. The orientation of this tangent plane will be taken to represent the orientation of the surface at that point. The surface normal, a unit vector perpendicular to the

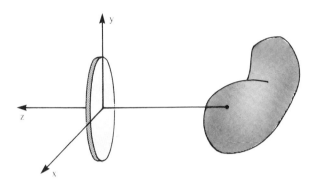

Figure 10-10. A surface can be conveniently described in terms of its perpendicular distance $-z(x, y)$ from some reference plane parallel to the image plane.

tangent plane, is appropriate for specifying the orientation of this plane. The normal vector has two degrees of freedom, since it is a vector with three components and one constraint—that the sum of squares of the components must equal one.

Alternatively, we can imagine placing this vector with its tail at the center of a unit sphere, called the *Gaussian sphere*. The head of the vector touches the sphere at a particular point, which we can use to denote surface orientation. The position of this point on the sphere can be specified by two variables, polar angle and azimuth, say, or latitude and longitude.

We must fix the coordinate system relative to which these measurements are to be made. It is convenient to choose this system so that one axis is lined up with the optical axis of the imaging system. We can place the origin of the system at the center of the lens, with two axes parallel to the image plane. Since we would like to have a right-handed coordinate system, we choose to have the z-axis point toward the image.

A portion of a surface can now be described by its perpendicular distance $-z$ from the lens plane (or any reference plane parallel to it). This distance will depend on the lateral displacement (x, y) (figure 10-10). What we would like to do next is to write the surface normal in terms of z and the partial derivatives of z with respect to x and y.

The surface normal is perpendicular to all lines in the tangent plane of the surface. As a result, it can be found by taking the cross-product of any two (nonparallel) lines in the tangent plane (figure 10-11). Consider taking a small step δx in the x-direction starting from a given point (x, y).

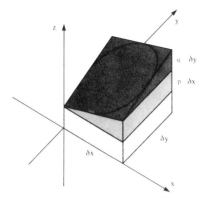

Figure 10-11. Surface orientation can be parameterized by the first partial derivatives p and q of the surface height z.

The change in z can be shown (using Taylor series expansion) to be

$$\delta z = \frac{\partial z}{\partial x}\delta x + e,$$

where e contains higher-order terms. We use the abbreviations p and q for the first partial derivatives of z with respect to x and y, respectively. Thus p is the slope of the surface measured in the x-direction, while q is the slope in the y-direction. The relationship of p and q to the orientation of the surface patch is shown in figure 10-12. If we take a small step of length δx in the x-direction, the height changes by $p\,\delta x$. Similarly, a small step of length δy in the y-direction leads to a change in height of $q\,\delta y$.

We can write the first small step in vector form as $(\delta x, 0, p\,\delta x)^T$. Thus a line parallel to the vector

$$\mathbf{r}_x = (1, 0, p)^T$$

lies in the tangent plane at (x, y). Similarly, a line parallel to

$$\mathbf{r}_y = (0, 1, q)^T$$

lies in the tangent plane also. A surface normal can be found by taking the cross-product of these two lines. It remains for us to decide whether we want the normal to point toward or away from the viewer. If we let it point toward the viewer, we obtain

$$\mathbf{n} = \mathbf{r}_x \times \mathbf{r}_y = (-p, -q, 1)^T.$$

Appropriately enough, (p, q) is called the *gradient* of the surface, since its components, p and q, are the slopes of the surface in the x- and y-directions,

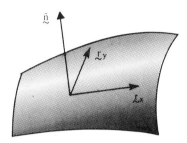

Figure 10-12. The normal is parallel to the cross-product of any two distinct tangents.

respectively.

The unit surface normal is just

$$\hat{\mathbf{n}} = \frac{\mathbf{n}}{|\mathbf{n}|} = \frac{(-p, -q, 1)^T}{\sqrt{1 + p^2 + q^2}}.$$

We can immediately calculate the angle θ_e between the surface normal and the direction to the lens, provided that the point considered is close to the optical axis relative to the distance from the reference plane. In this case the unit view vector $\hat{\mathbf{v}}$ from the object to the lens is $(0, 0, 1)^T$, so that

$$\cos \theta_e = \frac{1}{\sqrt{1 + p^2 + q^2}},$$

a result obtained by taking the dot-product of the two unit vectors.

How do we specify where the light sources are located? Assuming that they are far away from the object, relative to the size of the object, we can specify the direction to each one by a fixed vector. There exists a surface orientation that corresponds to this vector, that is, a surface oriented perpendicularly to the rays arriving from the source. If a normal to this surface is $(-p_s, -q_s, 1)^T$, then the gradient (p_s, q_s) can be used to specify the direction of the source (provided it lies on the same side of the object as the viewer).

From now on, we shall assume that the viewer and the light sources are far from the objects being imaged.

10.9 The Reflectance Map

The reflectance map makes explicit the relationship between surface orientation and brightness. It encodes information about surface reflectance properties and light-source distributions. It is a representational tool used in developing methods for recovering surface shape from images.

Consider a source of radiance E illuminating a Lambertian surface. The scene radiance is

$$L = \frac{1}{\pi} E \cos \theta_i \qquad \text{for } \theta_i \geq 0,$$

where θ_i is the angle between the surface normal and the direction toward the source. Taking dot-products of the corresponding unit vectors, we obtain

$$\cos \theta_i = \frac{1 + p_s p + q_s q}{\sqrt{1 + p^2 + q^2}\sqrt{1 + p_s^2 + q_s^2}}.$$

This gives us a good idea of how brightness depends on surface orientation. The result is called the *reflectance map*, denoted $R(p,q)$. The reflectance map depends on the properties of the surface material of the object and the distribution of light sources. (Note that radiance cannot be negative, so we should, strictly speaking, impose the restriction $0 \leq \theta_i \leq \pi/2$. The radiance will be zero for values of θ_i outside this range.)

Image irradiance is proportional to a number of constants, such as the inverse of the square of the f-number and the fixed brightness of the source. For this reason, the reflectance map is usually normalized in some way, for example, so that its maximum is one. For the Lambertian surface illuminated by a single distant point source we can use

$$R(p,q) = \frac{1 + p_s p + q_s q}{\sqrt{1 + p^2 + q^2}\sqrt{1 + p_s^2 + q_s^2}}.$$

Thus, aside from a fixed scale factor, the reflectance map gives the dependence of scene radiance on surface orientation.

It is often convenient to plot the surface $R(p,q)$ as a function of the gradient (p,q). The pq-plane is called *gradient space*, and every point in it corresponds to a particular surface orientation. The point at the origin, for example, respresents the orientation of all planes that are perpendicular to the viewing direction. A contour map in gradient space can be used to depict a reflectance map (figure 10-13). In the case of Lambertian surface material, contours of constant brightness are nested conic sections in the pq-plane, since $R(p,q) = c$ implies

$$(1 + p_s p + q_s q)^2 = c^2 (1 + p^2 + q^2)(1 + p_s^2 + q_s^2).$$

The maximum of $R(p,q)$ is at $(p,q) = (p_s, q_s)$, as we show in exercise 10-11.

As another example, consider a surface that emits radiation equally in all directions. (This is actually not physically plausible, but we shall describe a feasible modification later.) Such a surface appears brighter

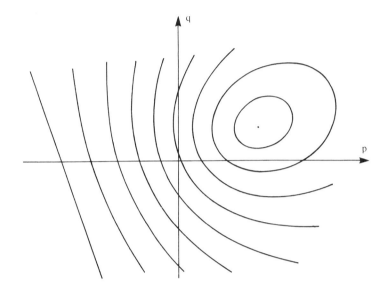

Figure 10-13. The reflectance map is a plot of brightness as a function of surface orientation. Here it is shown as a contour map in gradient space. In the case of a Lambertian surface under point-source illumination, the contours turn out to be nested conic sections. The maximum of $R(p, q)$ occurs at the point $(p, q) = (p_s, q_s)$, found inside the nested conic sections, while $R(p, q) = 0$ all along the line on the left side of the contour map.

when viewed obliquely, since the same power comes from a foreshortened area. This sort of behavior is clearly different from that of a Lambertian surface. Brightness in this case depends on the inverse of the cosine of the emittance angle. Taking into account the foreshortened area as seen from the source, we find that the radiance is proportional to $\cos\theta_i / \cos\theta_e$. Since $\cos\theta_e = 1/\sqrt{1 + p^2 + q^2}$, we have

$$R(p, q) = \frac{1 + p_s p + q_s q}{\sqrt{1 + p_s^2 + q_s^2}}.$$

The contours of constant brightness are parallel straight lines (figure 10-14), since $R(p, q) = c$ implies

$$1 + p_s p + q_s q = c\sqrt{1 + p_s^2 + q_s^2}.$$

These lines are orthogonal to the direction (p_s, q_s).

It turns out that no real surface can have radiance proportional to $\cos\theta_i / \cos\theta_e$, for this expression can be shown to violate the basic constraint

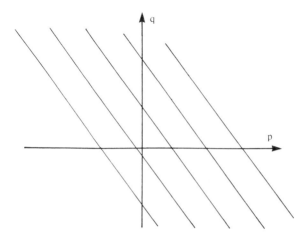

Figure 10-14. In the case of the material in the maria of the moon, the reflectance map can be closely approximated by a function of a linear combination of the components of the gradient. The contours of constant brightness are parallel straight lines in gradient space.

discovered by Helmholtz. The square root of this expression, however, does obey Helmholtz reciprocity, as shown by Minnaert. We are interested here in the shape of the contours in gradient space, and these are straight lines for any function of $\cos\theta_i / \cos\theta_e$, including, of course, its square root. Curiously, the material in the maria of the moon has reflectance properties that can be modeled reasonably well by a function of $\cos\theta_i / \cos\theta_e$.

As a final example, consider a glossy surface. The light reflected from many surfaces has two components, one due to reflection at the interface between air and the material of the surface, the other due to internal scattering of light that has penetrated into the surface layer. If the outer surface is perfectly smooth, the first component of reflection will be essentially mirrorlike or specular. The second component will be diffuse or matte. If the surface is not perfectly smooth, the specular component will tend to be smeared out, so that a point source will give rise to a high peak in the reflectance map, rather than an ideal impulse. This is called *glossy* reflection.

Absorption by the particles in the surface layer will change the brightness of the matte component, while the brightness of the glossy component depends primarily on the refractive index of the material in which these particles are embedded. As a result, the spectral composition of the glossy component is usually fairly close to that of the incident light, while the diffuse component is strongly affected by selective absorption in the surface

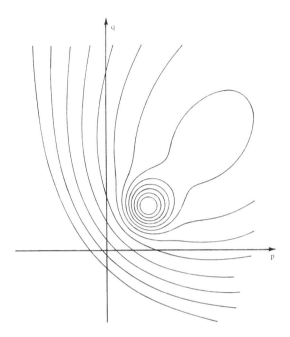

Figure 10-15. Many real surfaces combine diffuse and glossy components of reflection. The glossy component comes from reflection at the interface between air and the surface material, while the diffuse component can be traced to the component of light that has penetrated some distance into the surface, to be refracted and reflected until it reemerges from the surface layer. The reflectance map for such a material illuminated by a point source can have two peaks, corresponding to the surface orientations that maximize each of the two different types of reflection.

layer.

The surface orientation that maximizes the diffuse reflection component is typically one for which the surface normal points at the light source. The surface orientation that maximizes the glossy component, on the other hand, is usually one for which the surface normal points about halfway between the light source and the viewer. Correspondingly, the reflectance map can have two maxima (figure 10-15). Typically, the global maximum is at the glossy peak.

10.10 Shading in Images

How is the brightness pattern recorded in the image affected by the shape of an object? As an example, consider a polyhedron. Ideally, the image

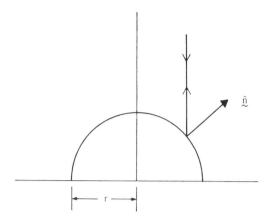

Figure 10-16. The reflectance map is circularly symmetric when the source lies in the same direction as the viewer. In the case of a Lambertian sphere, we obtain a smooth falloff in brightness toward the edge of the circular image of the sphere. This shading effect allows us to estimate the shape of the object.

of a polyhedron will consist of polygonal regions of uniform brightness, since all points on a face of a polyhedron have the same orientation. The brightness of a region in the image depends on the orientation of the corresponding face of the polyhedron. Now consider instead a smoothly curved object. The image of such an object will have spatial variations in brightness due to the fact that surface patches with different orientations appear with different brightness. This variation of brightness is called *shading*. Unfortunately, it depends on more than just the shape of an object. The reflectance properties of the surface and the distribution of light sources are also important.

The reflectance map captures the dependence of brightness on surface orientation. At a particular point in the image we measure the image irradiance $E(x, y)$. It is proportional to the radiance at the corresponding point on the surface imaged, as determined by the projection equation. If the surface gradient at that point is (p, q), then the radiance there is $R(p, q)$. If we normalize by setting the constant of proportionality to one, we obtain

$$E(x, y) = R(p, q).$$

This *image irradiance equation* is fundamental to the methods for recovering surface shape discussed in this and the next chapter.

As an illustration of the shading effect, consider a sphere with a Lambertian surface illuminated by a point source at essentially the same place as the viewer (figure 10-16). In this case $\theta_e = \theta_i$ and $(p_s, q_s) = (0, 0)$, so that

$$R(p, q) = \frac{1}{\sqrt{1 + p^2 + q^2}}.$$

If the sphere is on the optical axis, we can write the equation for its surface as

$$z = z_0 + \sqrt{r^2 - (x^2 + y^2)} \qquad \text{for } x^2 + y^2 \leq r^2,$$

where r is the radius and $-z_0$ is the distance of its center from the lens. Thus

$$p = -\frac{x}{z - z_0} \qquad \text{and} \qquad q = -\frac{y}{z - z_0},$$

so that

$$\frac{1}{\sqrt{1 + p^2 + q^2}} = \frac{z - z_0}{r}.$$

Finally, we have

$$E(x, y) = R(p, q) = \sqrt{1 - \frac{x^2 + y^2}{r^2}}.$$

The brightness falls off smoothly from its maximum at the center of the image of the sphere to zero at the edges. It is this variation in brightness that allows us to conclude that this is an image of a round, probably spherical, object.

If the sphere had a surface with different reflectance properties, it would give rise to a different image. For example, if

$$R(p, q) = \frac{1 + p_s p + q_s q}{\sqrt{1 + p_s^2 + q_s^2}}$$

and $(p_s, q_s) = (0, 0)$, we would obtain a uniformly bright disk in the image. We can see this also by noting that brightness is a function of $\cos \theta_i / \cos \theta_e$ in this case, and $\theta_e = \theta_i$. Thus such a sphere, illuminated from a position near that of the viewer, appears flat to someone used to objects with surface materials that have reflectance properties similar to those of a Lambertian surface. This is why the full moon looks like a flat disk marked with blotches. The blotches are brightness variations due to differences in the surface's reflecting efficiency. Often reflectance properties can be described in terms of the product of two factors: a geometric term expressing the dependence on the angles of light reflection, and another term that is the fraction of the incident light reemitted by the surface. The latter factor is called the *albedo*. We shall discuss methods later for recovering both shape and albedo from images.

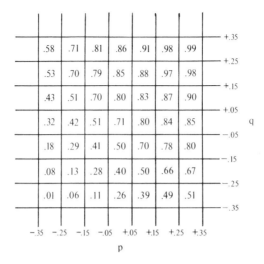

Figure 10-17. To produce shaded graphics, we can encode the reflectance map in a quantized lookup table.

10.11 Shaded Graphics

The reflectance map $R(p, q)$ comes in handy when we are portraying a shape graphically. To compute the gray-level at a point in the image of a given surface, $z(x, y)$, we find the point of intersection of the corresponding ray from the viewer with that surface. Then we find the gradient (p, q) at that point and use $R(p, q)$ to determine the appropriate brightness.

Reproduction media are limited in the number of gray-levels they can display, and humans can only resolve a relatively small number of brightness gradations. Consequently, we do not need to know $R(p, q)$ with extreme precision. This makes it possible to use a lookup table to estimate $R(p, q)$ based on quantized values of p and q (figure 10-17). A simple computation then allows us to determine the brightness for each point in the image. This information can be loaded into a hardware lookup memory between the frame buffer and the display. The *frame buffer* is a memory normally used to store image gray-levels. In the method discussed here, it stores encoded surface orientation instead. Changes in surface reflectance properties and light-source arrangements require nothing more complicated than changing the lookup table.

A *block diagram* obtained from a digital terrain model of the Dent de Morcles region in the southwestern part of Switzerland is shown in figure 10-18. A block diagram is the oblique projection of a set of profiles

Figure 10-18. A block diagram made from a depth map of the surface of a mountainous region of the earth. (Digital terrain model kindly provided by Kurt Brassel.)

obtained by cutting the surface with a series of parallel vertical planes running from west to east.

Figure 10-19 shows two orthographic shaded views of the same surface, obtained using the shading methods described above, under two different assumed lighting conditions.

10.12 Photometric Stereo

The reflectance map is extremely useful in computer graphics, where an image is created from a description of the shape of an object. But we would like to go in the other direction: Given an image, we would like to be able to recover the shape. There is a unique mapping from surface orientation, specified by p and q, to radiance, given by the reflectance map $R(p, q)$. The inverse mapping is not unique. An infinite number of surface orientations give rise to the same brightness. A contour of constant $R(p, q)$ connects such a set of orientations in the reflectance map.

Figure 10-19. Shaded views of the surface shown in the previous figure. Here we are looking down on the surface from above. In the figure on the left, the light is assumed to come from the lower right, as is appropriate for a point on the earth north of the equator in the morning. In the figure on the right, the light is assumed to come from the lower left, corresponding to lighting conditions in the afternoon.

Surface orientation can usually be determined uniquely for some special points, such as those where the brightness is a maximum or minimum of $R(p, q)$. For a Lambertian surface, for example, $R(p, q) = 1$ only when $(p, q) = (p_s, q_s)$. In general, however, the mapping from brightness to surface orientation cannot be unique, since brightness only has one degree of freedom, while orientation has two.

To recover surface orientation locally, we must introduce additional information. To determine two unknowns, p and q, we need two equations. Two images, taken with different lighting, will yield two equations for each image point (figure 10-20):

$$R_1(p, q) = E_1 \qquad \text{and} \qquad R_2(p, q) = E_2.$$

If these equations are linear and independent, there will be a unique solution for p and q.

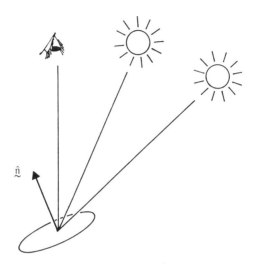

Figure 10-20. In photometric stereo, more than one image is taken from the same viewpoint with different lighting. The brightness of a patch of the surface will generally be different under the two lighting conditions.

Suppose, for example, that

$$R_1(p,q) = \sqrt{\frac{1+p_1p+q_1q}{r_1}} \quad \text{and} \quad R_2(p,q) = \sqrt{\frac{1+p_2p+q_2q}{r_2}},$$

where

$$r_1 = \sqrt{1+p_1^2+q_1^2} \quad \text{and} \quad r_2 = \sqrt{1+p_2^2+q_2^2}.$$

Then

$$p = \frac{(E_1^2r_1-1)q_2-(E_2^2r_2-1)q_1}{p_1q_2-q_1p_2}, \quad q = \frac{(E_2^2r_2-1)p_1-(E_1^2r_1-1)p_2}{p_1q_2-q_1p_2},$$

provided $p_1/q_1 \neq p_2/q_2$. Thus a unique solution can be obtained for surface orientation at each point, given two registered images taken with different lighting conditions. This is an illustration of the method of *photometric stereo*.

Incidentally, the condition $p_1/q_1 \neq p_2/q_2$ precludes the use of this approach on telescopic images of the maria of the moon obtained from earth, because the moon orbits the earth in a plane that is almost the same as the plane in which the earth orbits the sun. The light-source positions corresponding to various phases of the moon all lie along a straight line passing through the origin in gradient space. The form of the equation

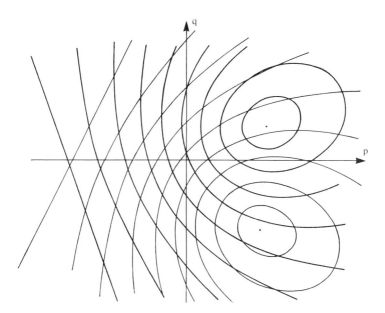

Figure 10-21. In the case of a Lambertian surface illuminated successively by two different point sources, there are at most two surface orientations that produce a particular pair of brightness values. These are found at the intersection of the corresponding contours in two superimposed reflectance maps.

above also suggests that the error in the gradient (p, q) due to the error in brightness (E_1, E_2) depends inversely on $p_1 q_2 - q_1 p_2$. For best results, the two light-source directions should be far apart in gradient space.

If the equations are nonlinear, we can have either no solutions or several solutions (figure 10-21). Suppose, for example, that

$$R_1(p, q) = \frac{1 + p_1 p + q_1 q}{\sqrt{1 + p^2 + q^2}\sqrt{1 + p_1^2 + q_1^2}}$$

and

$$R_2(p, q) = \frac{1 + p_2 p + q_2 q}{\sqrt{1 + p^2 + q^2}\sqrt{1 + p_2^2 + q_2^2}}.$$

We show in exercise 10-13 that there can be two solutions, one solution, or none, depending on the particular values of R_1 and R_2. (In pathological cases, such as when $(p_1, q_1) = (p_2, q_2)$, there can even be an infinite number of solutions.)

Often it is better to use three rather than two different illuminating conditions. In some cases this makes the equations linear. More important, it can improve accuracy and increase the range of surface orientations over which a solution can be obtained. Finally, the third image can allow us to recover another parameter, albedo, as shown in the next section.

10.13 Recovering Albedo

Often a surface is not uniform in its reflectance properties. The easiest situation to deal with is one in which radiance is the product of a reflectance factor, or *albedo*, and some function of orientation only. Here we take albedo to be a number between zero and one that indicates how much light the surface reflects relative to some ideal surface with the same geometric dependence in the BRDF. Suppose, for example, that a matte surface behaves like a Lambertian surface, except that it is "gray," that is, it does not reflect all of the incident light. Its brightness is $\rho \cos \theta_i$, where ρ is the albedo, which can vary from place to place. To recover the albedo and the gradient (p, q), we need three pieces of information, which we can obtain from three image measurements.

As before, we can work out the solution directly in terms of the components of the normal vector, or we can use a more compact notation. If we introduce unit vectors in the directions of three source positions,

$$\hat{\mathbf{s}}_i = \frac{(-p_i, -q_i, 1)^T}{\sqrt{1 + p_i^2 + q_i^2}} \qquad \text{for } i = 1, 2, 3,$$

then

$$E_i = \rho(\hat{\mathbf{s}}_i \cdot \hat{\mathbf{n}}) \qquad \text{for } i = 1, 2, 3,$$

where

$$\hat{\mathbf{n}} = \frac{(-p, -q, 1)^T}{\sqrt{1 + p^2 + q^2}}$$

is the unit surface normal. We thus have three equations

$$E_1 = \rho(\hat{\mathbf{s}}_1 \cdot \hat{\mathbf{n}}), \quad E_2 = \rho(\hat{\mathbf{s}}_2 \cdot \hat{\mathbf{n}}), \quad E_3 = \rho(\hat{\mathbf{s}}_3 \cdot \hat{\mathbf{n}})$$

for the unit vector $\hat{\mathbf{n}}$ and the albedo ρ. We can combine these equations to obtain $\mathbf{E} = \rho \mathbf{S} \hat{\mathbf{n}}$, where the rows of the matrix $\mathbf{S}$ are the source directions $\hat{\mathbf{s}}_1$, $\hat{\mathbf{s}}_2$, and $\hat{\mathbf{s}}_3$, and the components of the vector $\mathbf{E}$ are the three brightness measurements. Thus $\rho \hat{\mathbf{n}} = \mathbf{S}^{-1} \mathbf{E}$, provided that the matrix $\mathbf{S}$ is not singular. We show in exercise 10-16 that in fact

$$\rho \hat{\mathbf{n}} = \frac{1}{[\hat{\mathbf{s}}_1 \hat{\mathbf{s}}_2 \hat{\mathbf{s}}_3]} \big(E_1(\hat{\mathbf{s}}_2 \times \hat{\mathbf{s}}_3) + E_2(\hat{\mathbf{s}}_3 \times \hat{\mathbf{s}}_1) + E_3(\hat{\mathbf{s}}_1 \times \hat{\mathbf{s}}_2) \big),$$

where $[\hat{\mathbf{s}}_1 \hat{\mathbf{s}}_2 \hat{\mathbf{s}}_3]$ is the triple product $\hat{\mathbf{s}}_1 \cdot (\hat{\mathbf{s}}_2 \times \hat{\mathbf{s}}_3)$. The direction of the surface normal is therefore a constant times a linear combination of three

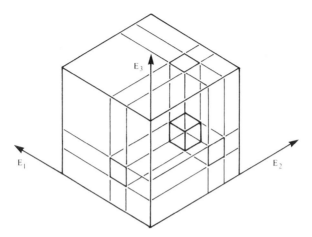

Figure 10-22. Photometric stereo is a fast and robust method for recovering surface shape. The calculation can be encoded in a lookup table based on quantized values of the brightness measurements.

vectors, each of which is perpendicular to two of the light-source directions. Each of these vectors is multiplied by the brightness observed when the third source is used. The albedo is recovered by finding the length of the resulting vector. The computation is straightforward in this case, and a unique result is assured.

10.14 Lookup Tables for Surface Orientation

The reflectance map is usually determined experimentally, in which case it will not be possible to find a closed-form solution to the photometric stereo problem. Moreover, even if a closed-form solution can be found, it usually involves a great deal of computation. Lookup tables indexed on the observed brightness measurements offer a solution to this impasse (figure 10-22). They provide rapid results and adequate accuracy, given that brightness can only be measured with limited accuracy anyway.

The lookup table can be constructed from a reflectance map given as an explicit formula, or it can be filled in experimentally. A calibration object of known shape, such as a sphere, is imaged. The gray-levels obtained at a particular point under various lighting conditions are used to determine an entry in the table. The surface orientation is computed using the known shape of the object and is entered in the appropriate place in the table. Gaps that occur in the table when the sampling of the calibration object does not touch a point with the corresponding orientation can be filled in by interpolation.

When the photometric stereo technique is applied to an image, a surface orientation estimate is obtained for every picture cell. The result is called a *needle diagram*. It can be displayed graphically by showing a top view of the surface covered with a regular grid of short normal vectors. Each "needle" is the projection of a surface normal vector erected on the patch of the surface corresponding to a particular picture cell. The direction of the needle in the picture is the direction of steepest descent on the surface, and the length is the foreshortened length, proportional to the sine of the angle between the normal and the viewing direction. A needle diagram encodes surface shape and can be used to recognize an object and recover its orientation in space. An example of a needle map is shown in chapter 18, where we discuss picking parts out of a bin. Needle diagrams are used there to provide information that will allow us to determine the attitude in space of an object of known shape.

There are, of course, other ways to encode surface shape, as, for example, in a depth map. A needle diagram can be obtained trivially from a depth map by taking first differences to estimate the gradient, but the reverse problem is overdetermined and requires a least-squares method. We postpone discussion of this problem to the last part of the next chapter, after we introduce the calculus of variations.

10.15 References

A book by Moon & Spencer, *The Photic Field* [1981], discusses radiometry and methods for calculating light flux. It is based in part on Moon's earlier book *The Scientific Basis of Illumination Engineering* [1961], which deals mostly with the flow of light flux in buildings.

The Gaussian sphere and the stereographic projection are described in the book *Geometry and the Imagination* by Hilbert & Cohn-Vossen [1952]. Do Carmo also discusses the Gauss map and Gaussian curvature in *Differential Geometry of Curves and Surfaces* [1976]. Shafer [1985] uses gradient space to analyze shadows and occluding contours in his book *Shadows and Silhouettes in Computer Vision*.

The terms used in radiometry have changed over the years, becoming standardized only relatively recently. This was a problem in particular in the case of the notion of "reflectance." Fortunately, Nicodemus et al. [1977] at the National Bureau of Standards have resolved these issues.

Horn [1977] introduced the reflectance map and showed several of its applications to machine vision. Later, Horn & Sjoberg [1979] related the reflectance map to the bidirectional reflectance distribution function of Nicodemus et al.. Attempts to automate hill shading have a long history; see, for example, Brassel [1974]. Horn [1981] explained these attempts in terms of the unifying notation provided by the reflectance map. Horn & Bachman [1978] registered satellite images with digital elevation models using similar techniques.

A large video lookup table to store the quantized reflectance map is described by Sloan & Brown [1979] and Bass [1981]. Methods developed in computer graphics for portraying shape made use of shading, often based on heuristic approaches. In a few cases, however, fairly realistic physical models of surface structure were employed. See, for example, Tuong-Phong [1975]. Better models for surface reflection are dealt with in the references mentioned at the end of the next chapter.

The photometric stereo method was developed by Woodham [1978b, 1980] and analyzed by Horn, Woodham, & Silver [1978]. Silver [1980] developed ways to apply the basic method to surfaces whose reflectance properties depend on several parameters, while Ikeuchi [1981b] used extended light sources to deal with surfaces that have specular or glossy reflectance properties. Since then, others have used and analyzed the method; see, for example, Coleman & Jain [1982], Ray, Birk, & Kelley [1983], and Horn & Ikeuchi [1984].

Use of the needle diagram for describing surface topography was reported by Horn in 1979. Application of photometric stereo to the bin picking problem is described in chapter 18.

10.16 Exercises

10-1   In this chapter we determined the cosines of the emittance angle θ_e and the incident angle θ_i in terms of the components of the gradient, p and q. In order to calculate an angle accurately we must know both its cosine and its sine. Show that

$$\sin \theta_e = \sqrt{\frac{p^2 + q^2}{1 + p^2 + q^2}}, \quad \sin \theta_i = \sqrt{\frac{(p - p_s)^2 + (q - q_s)^2 + (q_s p - p_s q)^2}{(1 + p^2 + q^2)(1 + p_s^2 + q_s^2)}}.$$

10-2   Here we consider some apparent paradoxes relating to image and scene brightness.

(a)   Why is the irradiance of the image of a surface independent of the distance from the surface? After all, when the lens is twice as far from the surface, it collects only one-quarter as much of the light emitted from a given surface patch.

(b)   Show that the radiance of the image of a surface in a perfectly specular mirror is equal to the radiance of the surface itself, independent of the shape of the mirror.

(c)   The term *intensity*, frequently misused, refers to the power emitted per unit solid angle by a light source (W·sr^{-1}—watts per steradian). Show that the intensity of the virtual image of a point source formed by a convex mirror is

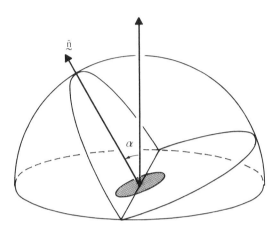

Figure 10-23. A surface patch inclined to the horizontal will receive radiation only from a portion of a hemispherical sky.

less than the intensity of the point source itself. How does the intensity of the virtual image vary with the curvature?

(d) Reconcile the apparently contradictory conclusions of parts (b) and (c).

10-3 Consider a hemispherical sky above a tilted Lambertian surface patch (figure 10-23). Suppose that the surface normal makes an angle $\alpha < \pi/2$ with respect to the zenith. The half of the hemisphere above the surface is unoccluded and thus gives rise to a component of radiance equal to $E/2$, using the result obtained previously for a Lambertian surface. The other half has a dark sector. Only a section from the zenith up to polar angle θ' is visible.

(a) Show that
$$\sin \theta' \sin \alpha \cos \phi = \cos \theta' \cos \alpha,$$

by considering the relevant spherical triangle. Conclude that
$$\tan \left(\frac{\pi}{2} - \theta' \right) = \tan \alpha \cos \phi.$$

Hint: See the appendix for useful formulae from spherical trigonometry.

(b) The contribution from the bright sector of this hemisphere is
$$\int_{-\pi/2}^{\pi/2} \int_0^{\theta'} \frac{E}{\pi} \sin \theta \, \cos \theta \, d\theta \, d\phi.$$

Show that
$$\frac{E}{2\pi} \int_{-\pi/2}^{\pi/2} \sin^2 \theta' \, d\phi = \frac{E}{2\pi} \int_{-\pi/2}^{\pi/2} \frac{1}{1 + \tan^2 \alpha \, \cos^2 \phi} \, d\phi.$$

Hint: $\int \sin \theta \, \cos \theta = (1/2) \sin^2 \theta$.

(c) Show that the contribution to the radiance from the portion of the sky considered is

$$\int \frac{1}{1 + a^2 \cos^2 \phi} \, d\phi = \frac{1}{\sqrt{1 + a^2}} \tan^{-1} \left(\frac{\tan \phi}{\sqrt{1 + a^2}} \right),$$

or $(E/2) \cos \alpha$. Conclude that the total radiance is

$$\frac{E}{2} (1 + \cos \alpha) = E \cos^2 \frac{\alpha}{2}.$$

10-4   Determine the reflectance map for a specular surface illuminated by a point light source. That is, find the radiance from the appropriate bidirectional reflectance distribution function and the light-source distribution. Hint: This may seem a bit tricky because the integrand contains the product of two impulse functions, but it can be dealt with easily using the sifting property of the unit impulse.

10-5   The bidirectional reflectance distribution function for a *Minnaert surface* is

$$f(\theta_i, \phi_i; \theta_e, \phi_e) = \frac{k + 1}{2\pi} \left(\cos \theta_i \ \cos \theta_e \right)^{k-1},$$

where $0 \leq k \leq 1$. A collimated point source from the direction (θ_s, ϕ_s) with irradiance E_0 is given by

$$E_i(\theta_i, \phi_i) = E_0 \frac{\delta(\theta_i - \theta_s) \, \delta(\phi_i - \phi_s)}{\sin \theta_s}.$$

Show that the radiance of the surface is

$$L_r = E_0 \frac{k + 1}{2\pi} \cos^{k-1} \theta_e \cos^k \theta_i,$$

provided that $-\pi/2 \leq \theta_i \leq \pi/2$. For what values of k is the radiance independent of viewing direction?

10-6   The *gnomonic projection* can be used to map the Gaussian sphere, centered at the origin, onto the plane tangent at the north pole. This is done by projecting lines from the origin through points on the sphere onto the plane $z = 1$. The point $\hat{\mathbf{n}}$ on the Gaussian sphere maps into the point

$$\frac{\hat{\mathbf{n}}}{\hat{\mathbf{n}} \cdot \hat{\mathbf{z}}}$$

in the plane. This plane is just the gradient space we have been using.

(a) The *stereographic projection* provides another way to map the Gaussian sphere onto a plane. Here, a line is constructed from the south pole of the sphere, through points on the sphere, onto the plane $z = 1$. What point in the $z = 1$ plane corresponds to the point $\hat{n}$ on the Gaussian sphere? Hint: Figure 11.9 might be helpful in visualizing the relationships.

(b) What contour on the sphere corresponds to points on the occluding boundary of an object? Where in the stereographic plane does this contour map to? Assume that the direction from the scene to the viewer is parallel to the north-south axis of the sphere. Hint: On the occluding contour the viewing direction is tangent to the surface.

10-7   The reflectance map can be parameterized in various ways. In this chapter we have concentrated on using the gradient (p, q) as a means of specifying surface orientation. In some cases, the Gaussian sphere is more suitable for this purpose. Each point on the Gaussian sphere corresponds to a particular direction, from the center of the sphere to that point. The orientation of a surface patch can be specified by giving the direction of its surface normal. Thus a given surface orientation can be identified with a particular point on the Gaussian sphere. The reflectance map is merely a means of associating brightness with orientation.

(a) What are the contours of constant brightness on the Gaussian sphere in the case of a Lambertian surface illuminated by a point source? Hint: See figure 10-24a.

(b) Show that there are at most two surface orientations that give rise to a given pair of brightness values when the photometric stereo method is applied to a Lambertian surface. Assume that two different light sources are used. Hint: See figure 10-24b.

10-8   A perfectly specular surface illuminated by a single point source gives rise to a simple reflectance map. It can be represented on the Gaussian sphere by an impulse lying halfway between the direction toward the source and the direction toward the viewer.

(a) Now consider a glossy surface whose microstructure can be modeled in terms of a random variation in surface orientation about a local average. Suppose that there is a limit to the angular deviation of the normal from the local average normal. Describe the reflectance map of this surface on the Gaussian sphere.

(b) Next, consider a perfectly specular surface illuminated by a circularly symmetric source. Suppose that the source has a limited diameter. What is the reflectance map in this case? Hint: It is not the same as the one derived above, although somewhat similar.

(c) Compare the two reflectance maps. How would you distinguish between the two cases in practice?

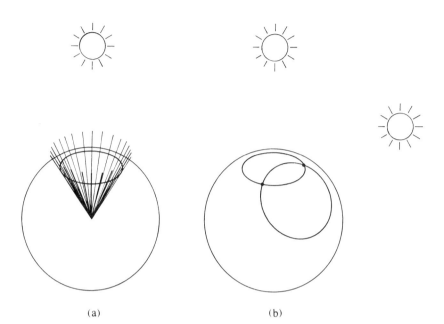

(a)   (b)

Figure 10-24. The reflectance map can be plotted on the Gaussian sphere. (a) The contours of constant brightness are particularly simple for a Lambertian surface illuminated by a point source. (b) This makes it easy to prove that there are at most two solutions to the two-source photometric stereo problem in this case.

10-9 Show that in the case of Lambertian reflectance, the average brightness of a region R of a surface is the dot-product of the average surface normal $\overline{\mathbf{n}}$ and the unit vector $\hat{\mathbf{s}}$ in the direction of the light source. Here

$$A\overline{\mathbf{n}} = \iint_R \hat{\mathbf{n}}\, dA,$$

where A is the area of the region in the image. What happens when part of the region is self-shadowed? What does this tell us about the problem of recovering shape from shading? Hint: Note that $\overline{\mathbf{n}}$ is usually not a unit vector.

Suppose we were to model the microstructure of a surface using undulations on a scale too small to resolve. Suppose also that, considered on this small scale, the undulating surface behaved like a Lambertian reflector. Would the surface, considered on a scale at which the undulations cannot be resolved, behave like a Lambertian reflector? Treat separately the two limiting cases in which the incident rays and the direction to the viewer become nearly tangent to the surface.

10-10 Show that in the case of Lambertian reflectance, an extended light source can be replaced by an equivalent point source whose brightness and position can be determined by integrating the brightness of the extended source over the unit sphere of incident directions,

$$\overline{E}\,\overline{\mathbf{s}} = \iint_S E(\hat{\mathbf{s}})\,\hat{\mathbf{s}}\,dS,$$

where $E(\hat{\mathbf{s}})$ is the radiance of the source in the direction $\hat{\mathbf{s}}$. What does this tell us about the problem of recovering shape from shading?

Apply this idea to the hemispherical sky example. Show that the equivalent light source is at an angle $\alpha/2$ from the nadir, and that its brightness is proportional to $\cos(\alpha/2)$. Hint: Some part of the extended light source cannot be seen from the surface patch.

10-11 A Lambertian surface illuminated by a point source has a reflectance map of the form

$$R(p,q) = \frac{1 + p_s p + q_s q}{\sqrt{1 + p^2 + q^2}\sqrt{1 + p_s^2 + q_s^2}},$$

where the light source lies in the direction $(-p_s, -q_s, 1)^T$.

(a) What value of the gradient (p, q) maximizes this expression? Is your maximum a global one? Is it unique?

(b) For what values of the gradient is $R(p, q) = 0$? What is the corresponding contour in gradient space?

10-12 Suppose that a surface has brightness $\sqrt{\cos\theta_i/\cos\theta_e}$, or

$$R(\hat{\mathbf{n}}) = \sqrt{\frac{\hat{\mathbf{n}} \cdot \hat{\mathbf{s}}}{\hat{\mathbf{n}} \cdot \hat{\mathbf{v}}}},$$

where $\hat{\mathbf{n}}$ is the unit surface normal, $\hat{\mathbf{s}}$ is the direction toward the light source, and $\hat{\mathbf{v}}$ is the direction toward the viewer. We measure the brightness at a particular point on the surface under two lighting conditions. We obtain brightness E_1 using light source $\hat{\mathbf{s}}_1$, and brightness E_2 using light source $\hat{\mathbf{s}}_2$. Show that

$$\hat{\mathbf{n}} \cdot \left(E_1^2\,\hat{\mathbf{v}} - \hat{\mathbf{s}}_1\right) = 0 \quad \text{and} \quad \hat{\mathbf{n}} \cdot \left(E_2^2\,\hat{\mathbf{v}} - \hat{\mathbf{s}}_2\right) = 0.$$

Conclude that $\hat{\mathbf{n}}$ is parallel to

$$\mathbf{n} = \pm\left(E_1^2(\hat{\mathbf{s}}_2 \times \hat{\mathbf{v}}) - E_2^2(\hat{\mathbf{s}}_1 \times \hat{\mathbf{v}}) + (\hat{\mathbf{s}}_1 \times \hat{\mathbf{s}}_2)\right).$$

The sign is to be chosen to make $\hat{\mathbf{n}} \cdot \hat{\mathbf{z}} > 0$. Hint: You can check the result by taking dot-products with $\hat{\mathbf{s}}_1$, $\hat{\mathbf{s}}_2$, and $\hat{\mathbf{n}}$.

10-13   An ideal Lambertian surface leads to image irradiance

$$E = \frac{1 + p_s p + q_s q}{\sqrt{1 + p^2 + q^2}\sqrt{1 + p_s^2 + q_s^2}}$$

when a point source is located at $(-p_s, -q_s, 1)^T$. A single measurement confines the surface gradient to a conic section (hyperbola, parabola, or ellipse) in pq-space. In photometric stereo, we move the light source to obtain two measurements, E_1 and E_2. This confines the surface gradient to the intersection of two conic sections in gradient space. In general, two conic sections can intersect in as many as four distinct places. Prove that there are at most two solutions for p and q when E has the form given above. Hint: Show that all solutions must lie on a straight line.

10-14   For an ideal Lambertian surface under point-source illumination, the image irradiance is $\cos \theta_i$, which can be written in the form of a dot-product of unit vectors,

$$E = \hat{\mathbf{n}} \cdot \hat{\mathbf{s}},$$

where $\hat{\mathbf{n}}$ is a unit vector normal to the surface and $\hat{\mathbf{s}}$ is a unit vector in the direction of the light source. Suppose, as in the previous exercise, that two measurements, E_1 and E_2, are taken with two light-source positions, $\hat{\mathbf{s}}_1$ and $\hat{\mathbf{s}}_2$. Determine the two possible solutions for the unit surface normal. When is there only one solution? Hint: Use the methods for solving vector equations described in the appendix. Alternatively, use the methods for solving spherical triangles found there.

10-15   Suppose that three light sources, which can be turned on and off, are placed far from a Lambertian surface patch. The angles between the directions to the sources, as viewed from the surface patch, are $90°$ (figure 10-25). Show that the three values of observed brightness are proportional to the direction cosines of the normal vector of the surface patch expressed in a coordinate system defined by the directions to the three light sources. Conclude that

$$\rho\,\hat{\mathbf{n}} = \mathbf{Re},$$

where ρ is the albedo, $\hat{\mathbf{n}}$ the unit surface normal, $\mathbf{e}$ the vector whose components are the three measurements, and $\mathbf{R}$ the rotation matrix corresponding to the transformation between the coordinate system defined by the three light source directions and the viewer coordinate system. Note: This is much simpler than the general case covered in this chapter.

10-16   We saw that in the case of a Lambertian surface and three light sources, the photometric stereo problem reduces to solving the three equations,

$$E_1 = \rho(\hat{\mathbf{s}}_1 \cdot \hat{\mathbf{n}}), \quad E_2 = \rho(\hat{\mathbf{s}}_2 \cdot \hat{\mathbf{n}}), \quad E_3 = \rho(\hat{\mathbf{s}}_3 \cdot \hat{\mathbf{n}}),$$

for the unit vector $\hat{\mathbf{n}}$ and the albedo ρ.

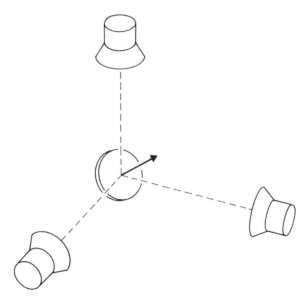

Figure 10-25. If three light sources in directions at right angles to one another are used to illuminate a Lambertian surface, the brightness measurements are proportional to the direction cosines of the surface normal, independent of the viewing direction.

(a) By subtracting equations pairwise, show that

$$\rho\,\hat{\mathbf{n}} \cdot (E_1\hat{\mathbf{s}}_2 - E_2\hat{\mathbf{s}}_1) = 0 \qquad \text{and} \qquad \rho\,\hat{\mathbf{n}} \cdot (E_2\hat{\mathbf{s}}_3 - E_3\hat{\mathbf{s}}_2) = 0.$$

(b) Now use the fact that $\hat{\mathbf{n}}$ is perpendicular to both $(E_1\hat{\mathbf{s}}_2 - E_2\hat{\mathbf{s}}_1)$ and $(E_2\hat{\mathbf{s}}_3 - E_3\hat{\mathbf{s}}_2)$ to show that it must be parallel to

$$(E_1\hat{\mathbf{s}}_2 - E_2\hat{\mathbf{s}}_1) \times (E_2\hat{\mathbf{s}}_3 - E_3\hat{\mathbf{s}}_2) = E_2\big(E_1(\hat{\mathbf{s}}_2 \times \hat{\mathbf{s}}_3) + E_2(\hat{\mathbf{s}}_3 \times \hat{\mathbf{s}}_1) + E_3(\hat{\mathbf{s}}_1 \times \hat{\mathbf{s}}_2)\big).$$

(c) Conclude that

$$\rho\,\hat{\mathbf{n}} = k\big(E_1(\hat{\mathbf{s}}_2 \times \hat{\mathbf{s}}_3) + E_2(\hat{\mathbf{s}}_3 \times \hat{\mathbf{s}}_1) + E_3(\hat{\mathbf{s}}_1 \times \hat{\mathbf{s}}_2)\big)$$

for some constant k.

(d) By taking the dot-product of this relationship with $\hat{\mathbf{s}}_1$, and remembering that $E_1 = \rho(\hat{\mathbf{n}} \cdot \hat{\mathbf{s}}_1)$, show that

$$\rho\,(\hat{\mathbf{n}} \cdot \hat{\mathbf{s}}_1) = k\,E_1[\hat{\mathbf{s}}_1\,\hat{\mathbf{s}}_2\,\hat{\mathbf{s}}_3],$$

where $[\hat{\mathbf{s}}_1\,\hat{\mathbf{s}}_2\,\hat{\mathbf{s}}_3]$ is the triple product $\hat{\mathbf{s}}_1 \cdot (\hat{\mathbf{s}}_2 \times \hat{\mathbf{s}}_3)$.

(e) Show that $k = 1/[\hat{\mathbf{s}}_1\,\hat{\mathbf{s}}_2\,\hat{\mathbf{s}}_3]$, so that

$$\rho\,\hat{\mathbf{n}} = \frac{\big(E_1(\hat{\mathbf{s}}_2 \times \hat{\mathbf{s}}_3) + E_2(\hat{\mathbf{s}}_3 \times \hat{\mathbf{s}}_1) + E_3(\hat{\mathbf{s}}_1 \times \hat{\mathbf{s}}_2)\big)}{[\hat{\mathbf{s}}_1\,\hat{\mathbf{s}}_2\,\hat{\mathbf{s}}_3]}.$$

10-17   In this chapter we discussed a method for recovering albedo and orientation of a Lambertian surface using three light sources. This method works only for surface patches oriented so that they receive light from all three sources.

(a) Here we study the range of orientations that can be recovered successfully. Show that this range can be thought of as a spherical triangle on the unit sphere. Demonstrate that the corners of this triangle lie at $\hat{s}_3 \times \hat{s}_1$, $\hat{s}_2 \times \hat{s}_3$, and $\hat{s}_1 \times \hat{s}_2$. Hint: A distant point source will illuminate surface patches with orientations lying in a hemisphere.

(b) What are the angles at the corners of this triangle? What is the solid angle of directions of the surface normal for which the photometric stereo method works? Hint: The area of a spherical triangle with angles α, β, and γ is equal to the radius squared times the *spherical excess*, the difference between the sum of the angles and π:

$$A = R^2(\alpha + \beta + \gamma - \pi).$$

(c) How can we maximize the range of orientations? Hint: The spherical triangle under consideration cannot be made larger then a hemisphere.

(d) There is an additional consideration. It is wasteful to have part of the spherical triangle lie in the hemisphere that corresponds to orientations of surface patches that are turned away from the viewer. Show that this will not happen if the view vector lies inside the spherical triangle formed by $\hat{s}_1$, $\hat{s}_2$, and $\hat{s}_3$, that is, if

$$\hat{v} = a\hat{s}_1 + b\hat{s}_2 + c\hat{s}_3 \qquad \text{for some } a \geq 0, \, b \geq 0, \text{ and } c \geq 0.$$

We are not entirely free to place the light sources anywhere we want. We know, for example, that if two of them are in the same place, no new information is obtained when the second image is taken. Also, when two of them lie in nearly the same direction, there will be only a very small difference in the measurements they provide. It is likely that noise will have a bad influence on the result in this case.

(e) Consider small variations in the brightness measurements. How do they affect the resulting estimates of the surface normal? Hint: Differentiate the equation for $\rho\hat{n}$ with respect to the vector $\mathbf{E} = (E_1, E_2, E_3)^T$.

(f) The standard deviation in the result equals the derivative so obtained times the standard deviation in the measurements. How can the sensitivity to noise be minimized? Hint: The triple product $[\hat{s}_1 \, \hat{s}_2 \, \hat{s}_3]$ is the volume of the parallelepiped that can be built by extending the corner formed by the three unit vectors.

(g) Discuss the conflict between the source placements suggested by the above considerations. Consider ways to overcome these limitations using extended light sources.

10-18   We might want to take more than two brightness measurements in order
to improve accuracy when using the photometric stereo method. Imagine that n
light sources are used in turn to obtain n images. Suppose that the surface under
consideration is Lambertian and that the direction to the ith source is given by
the unit vector $\hat{\mathbf{s}}_i$. This time we assume that the surface can have an albedo ρ
different from one. At each point in the image, we wish to find the unit surface
normal $\hat{\mathbf{n}}$ that minimizes

$$\sum_{i=1}^{n} (\rho\,\hat{\mathbf{n}} \cdot \hat{\mathbf{s}}_i - E_i)^2 \,,$$

where E_i is the ith measurement of brightness at that point.

(a) Show that the vector that minimizes the error sum is

$$\rho\,\hat{\mathbf{n}} = \left[\sum_{i=1}^{n} \hat{\mathbf{s}}_i \hat{\mathbf{s}}_i^T \right]^{-1} \sum_{i=1}^{n} E_i \hat{\mathbf{s}}_i,$$

where $\mathbf{a}\mathbf{b}^T$ is the *dyadic product* of the vectors $\mathbf{a}$ and $\mathbf{b}$,

$$\begin{pmatrix} a_x b_x & a_x b_y & a_x b_z \\ a_y b_x & a_y b_y & a_y b_z \\ a_z b_x & a_z b_y & a_z b_z \end{pmatrix},$$

and $[\ ]^{-1}$ indicates the inverse of the matrix.

(b) What is the smallest number n of measurements needed to guarantee that
the indicated matrix inverse exists? Warning: This part of the problem is
nontrivial.

(c) How does all this change if we assume that the albedo is one? Hint: You
may need to introduce a Lagrange multiplier to enforce this constraint, as
explained in the appendix.

11

Reflectance Map:
Shape from Shading

In the previous chapter we introduced the reflectance map and the image irradiance equation, and we used them to recover surface orientation from registered images taken under different lighting conditions. In this chapter we concentrate on the recovery of surface shape from a single image. This is a more difficult problem that will require the development of more advanced tools. We first examine the case of a linear reflectance map. It turns out that, under point-source illumination, the reflectance maps of the surface material in the maria of the moon and on rocky planets such as Mercury are functions of linear combinations of the components of the gradient. Next, we consider the shape-from-shading problem when the reflectance map is rotationally symmetric. This applies, for example, to images taken with the scanning electron microscope. We then solve the general case.

The image irradiance equation can be viewed as a nonlinear first-order partial differential equation. The traditional methods for solving such equations depend on growing characteristic strips. This is a sequential process. We are more interested in methods that ultimately lead to parallel algorithms. Consequently, we formulate a minimization problem that leads to a relaxation algorithm on a grid. We choose to minimize the integral of the difference between the observed brightness and that predicted for the estimated shape.

It is, of course, very important to know whether a solution to these problems exists and whether there is more than one solution. Unfortunately, these existence and uniqueness questions are difficult to decide without detailed assumptions about the reflectance map. We briefly explore what is known in this regard and then finish the chapter by showing how the ideas developed here can be applied to improve the results obtained by means of the photometric stereo method discussed in the previous chapter.

11.1 Recovering Shape from Shading

How can we recover the shape of a surface from a single image? Different parts of the surface are oriented differently and thus will appear with different brightnesses. We can take advantage of this spatial variation of brightness, referred to as *shading*, in estimating the orientation of surface patches. Measurement of brightness at a single point in the image, however, only provides one constraint, while surface orientation has two degrees of freedom. Without additional information, we cannot recover the orientation of a surface patch from the image irradiance equation

$$E(x, y) = R(p, q).$$

We have already discussed one method for introducing another constraint: the use of additional images taken under different lighting conditions.

11.1.1 Growing a Solution

But what if we have only one image? People can estimate the shapes of facial features using a single picture reproduced in a magazine. This suggests that there is enough information or that we implicitly introduce additional assumptions. Many surfaces are smooth, lacking discontinuities in depth. Also, there are often no discontinuities in the partial derivatives. An even wider class of objects have piecewise-smooth surfaces, with departures from smoothness concentrated along edges.

The assumption of smoothness provides a strong constraint. Neighboring patches of the surface cannot assume arbitrary orientations. They have to fit together to make a continuous, smooth surface. Thus a global method exploiting a smoothness constraint can be envisioned.

11.1.2 Linear Reflectance Maps

To begin with, we consider some special cases. Suppose that

$$R(p, q) = f(ap + bq),$$

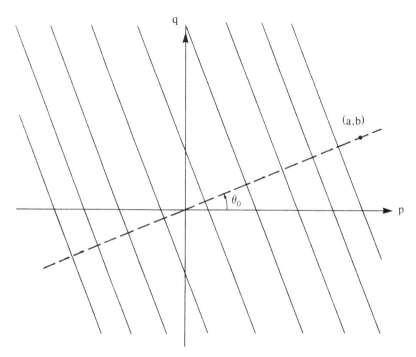

Figure 11-1. A reflectance map that is a function of a linear combination of the components of the gradient is particularly simple. The contours of constant brightness are parallel straight lines in gradient space.

where a and b are constants (figure 11-1).

Here f is a strictly monotonic function that has an inverse, f^{-1} (figure 11-2). From the image irradiance equation we then have

$$ap + bq = f^{-1}\big(E(x, y)\big).$$

We cannot determine the gradient (p, q) at a particular image point from a measurement of image brightness alone, but we do have one equation that constrains its possible values.

The slope of the surface, in a direction that makes an angle θ with the x-axis, is

$$m(\theta) = p \cos \theta + q \sin \theta.$$

This is the directional derivative. Now choose a particular direction θ_0 (figure 11-1), where $\tan \theta_0 = b/a$, that is,

$$\cos \theta_0 = a/\sqrt{a^2 + b^2} \qquad \text{and} \qquad \sin \theta_0 = b/\sqrt{a^2 + b^2}.$$

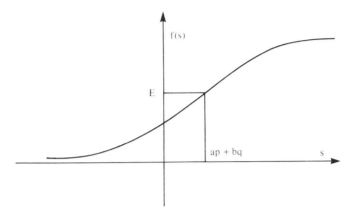

Figure 11-2. If the function f is continuous and monotonic, an inverse can be found and $s = ap + bq$ can be recovered from the brightness measurement $E(x, y)$.

The slope in this direction is

$$m(\theta_0) = \frac{ap + bq}{\sqrt{a^2 + b^2}} = \frac{1}{\sqrt{a^2 + b^2}} f^{-1}\big(E(x, y)\big).$$

Thus we can determine the slope in a particular direction. Note that we know nothing about the slope in the direction at right angles to this, however.

Starting at a particular image point we can take a small step of length $\delta\xi$, producing a change in z of $\delta z = m\,\delta\xi$. Thus

$$\frac{dz}{d\xi} = \frac{1}{\sqrt{a^2 + b^2}} f^{-1}\big(E(x, y)\big),$$

where

$$x(\xi) = x_0 + \xi\cos\theta \qquad \text{and} \qquad y(\xi) = y_0 + \xi\sin\theta.$$

Suppose that we start the solution at the point $(x_0, y_0, z_0)^T$ on the surface. Integrating the differential equation for z derived above, we obtain

$$z(\xi) = z_0 + \frac{1}{\sqrt{a^2 + b^2}} \int_0^\xi f^{-1}\big(E(x, y)\big)\, d\xi,$$

where x and y in the integrand are the linear functions of ξ given above. In this fashion we obtain a profile of the surface along a line in the special direction defined above (one of the straight lines in figure 11-3). The profile is called a *characteristic curve*. In practice, of course, the integrand will not be given as a formula, so that numerical integration is called for.

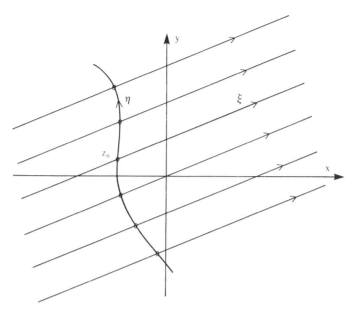

Figure 11-3. The base characteristics are parallel straight lines when the reflectance map is a function of a linear combination of the components of the gradient. The surface can be recovered by integration along these lines, provided the height $z_0(\eta)$ along some initial curve is given.

We cannot determine the absolute distance to the surface—the constant of integration—since the absolute distance does not influence the shading, only variations in depth do. If we require information about absolute distance, we shall need to know the value z_0 at one point. The shape can be recovered without this additional information, however.

Now suppose that we are given initial information not just at a point, but as a profile $z(\eta)$ along some curve that is nowhere parallel to the special direction (a, b) (figure 11-3). Then we can integrate along lines starting at points of this initial curve. The whole surface can be explored in this way if the initial curve extends far enough. The general case, to be explored later, is similar in that the surface is determined by integration along special curves in the image. The general case differs, however, in that these curves are not predetermined straight lines.

The special case discussed here is of practical importance because the material in the maria of the moon has reflectance properties that can be closely approximated by some function of $\cos \theta_i / \cos \theta_e$, as already mentioned. The reflectance map, in this case, is a function of a linear combination of p and q. This was the version of the shape-from-shading problem that first received attention. We use orthographic projection for simplicity here, but the method can be extended to the case of perspective projection.

11.1.3 Rotationally Symmetric Reflectance Maps

If the light source is distributed in a rotationally symmetric fashion about the viewer, then the reflectance map is rotationally symmetric, too. That is, we can write

$$R(p, q) = f(p^2 + q^2)$$

for some f. One situation leading to a rotationally symmetric reflectance map is provided by a hemispherical sky, if we assume that the viewer is looking straight down from above. Another example is that of a point source at essentially the same place as the viewer.

Now suppose that the function f is strictly monotonic and differentiable, with inverse f^{-1}. From the image irradiance equation we obtain

$$p^2 + q^2 = f^{-1}\big(E(x, y)\big).$$

The direction of steepest ascent makes an angle θ_s with the x-axis, where $\tan \theta_s = q/p$, so that

$$\cos \theta_s = p/\sqrt{p^2 + q^2} \qquad \text{and} \qquad \sin \theta_s = q/\sqrt{p^2 + q^2}.$$

The slope in the direction of steepest ascent is

$$m(\theta_s) = \sqrt{p^2 + q^2} = \sqrt{f^{-1}\big(E(x, y)\big)}.$$

Thus in this case we can find the slope of the surface, given its brightness, but we cannot find the direction of steepest ascent.

Suppose we did know the direction of steepest ascent, given by (p, q). Then we could take a small step of length $\delta \xi$ in the direction of steepest ascent. The changes in x and y would be given by

$$\delta x = \frac{p}{\sqrt{p^2 + q^2}} \delta \xi \qquad \text{and} \qquad \delta y = \frac{q}{\sqrt{p^2 + q^2}} \delta \xi.$$

The change in z would be

$$\delta z = m \, \delta \xi = \sqrt{p^2 + q^2} \, \delta \xi = \sqrt{f^{-1}\big(E(x, y)\big)} \, \delta \xi.$$

To simplify these equations, we could take a step of length $\sqrt{p^2 + q^2} \, \delta \xi$ rather than $\delta \xi$. Then

$$\delta x = p \, \delta \xi, \quad \delta y = q \, \delta \xi, \quad \delta z = (p^2 + q^2) \, \delta \xi = f^{-1}\big(E(x, y)\big) \, \delta \xi.$$

The problem with this approach is that we need to determine the values of p and q at the new point in order to continue the solution. We need to develop equations for the changes δp and δq in p and q, respectively.

Before we address this issue, let us look at the image brightness gradient $(E_x, E_y)^T$. We know that a planar surface patch gives rise to a region of uniform brightness in the image. Thus a nonzero brightness gradient can occur only where the surface is curved. To find the brightness gradient, we differentiate the image irradiance equation

$$E(x, y) = f(p^2 + q^2)$$

with respect to x and y. Let r, s, and t be the second partial derivatives of z with respect to x and y as defined by

$$r = \frac{\partial^2 z}{\partial x^2}, \quad \frac{\partial^2 z}{\partial x \partial y} = s = \frac{\partial^2 z}{\partial y \partial x}, \quad t = \frac{\partial^2 z}{\partial y^2}.$$

Then, using the chain rule for differentiation, we obtain

$$E_x = 2(p\,r + q\,s)f' \quad \text{and} \quad E_y = 2(p\,s + q\,t)f',$$

where $f'(s)$ is the derivative of $f(s)$ with respect to its single argument s.

Now we return to the problem of determining the changes δp and δq occasioned by the step $(\delta x, \delta y)$ in the image plane. We find

$$\delta p = r\,\delta x + s\,\delta y \quad \text{and} \quad \delta q = s\,\delta x + t\,\delta y$$

by simple differentiation. In our case $\delta x = p\,\delta \xi$ and $\delta y = q\,\delta \xi$, so that

$$\delta p = (p\,r + q\,s)\,\delta \xi \ \text{ and } \quad \delta q = (p\,s + q\,t)\,\delta \xi,$$

or

$$\delta p = \frac{E_x}{2f'}\delta \xi \quad \text{and} \quad \delta q = \frac{E_y}{2f'}\delta \xi.$$

In the limit as $\delta \xi \to 0$, we obtain the differential equations

$$\dot{x} = p, \quad \dot{y} = q, \quad \dot{z} = p^2 + q^2,$$

$$\dot{p} = \frac{E_x}{2f'}, \quad \dot{q} = \frac{E_y}{2f'},$$

where the dots denote differentiation with respect to ξ. Given starting values, this set of five ordinary differential equations can be solved numerically to produce a curve on the surface of the object. Curves generated in this fashion are called *characteristic curves*, and in this particular case they happen to be the curves of steepest ascent. These curves are everywhere perpendicular to the contours of constant height. In the case treated previously, in which the reflectance map was a linear function of p and q, the characteristic curves were parallel planar sections of the surface.

By differentiating $\dot{x} = p$ and $\dot{y} = q$ one more time with respect to ξ, we obtain the alternate formulation

$$\ddot{x} = \frac{E_x}{2f'}, \quad \ddot{y} = \frac{E_y}{2f'}, \quad \dot{z} = f^{-1}\big(E(x,y)\big).$$

Naturally, these equations can only be solved numerically, since E_x and E_y are image brightness measurements, not functions of x and y given in closed form.

The special case discussed above is of practical importance, since scanning electron microscopes produce images analogous to those produced in an optical system with a light source disposed around the viewer in a rotationally symmetric fashion. In such a device a focused beam of electrons strikes a surface in a position determined by two orthogonal deflection coils. Secondary electrons are generated as a result of collisions between the incident primary electrons and the atoms in the material. Some of these escape and are collected by an electrode. Secondary electrons generated deep inside the material have less of a chance to escape than those generated near the surface. The secondary electron flux is thus lowest when the beam strikes the surface at right angles and is highest at grazing incidence. The probing beam scans out a raster, while the brightness of a cathode ray tube scanned in the same fashion is modulated in proportion to the secondary electron current. The result is a (highly magnified) picture of the surface. People find such pictures easy to interpret, because they exhibit shading due to the dependence of brightness on surface orientation. The only strange thing about these images is that surface patches perpendicular to the viewer appear darkest, not brightest, in a scanning electron microscope picture.

11.1.4 The General Case

Suppose that we have the coordinates of a particular point on the surface and that we wish to extend the solution from this point. Taking a small step $(\delta x, \delta y)$, we note once more that the change in depth is given by

$$\delta z = p\,\delta x + q\,\delta y,$$

where p and q are the first partial derivatives of z with respect to x and y (figure 11-4). We cannot proceed unless p and q are also known. Unfortunately, the image irradiance equation provides only one constraint; this is not enough information to allow a solution for both p and q.

Suppose for the moment that we did know p and q at the given point. Then we could extend the solution from (x, y) to $(x + \delta x, y + \delta y)$. But to

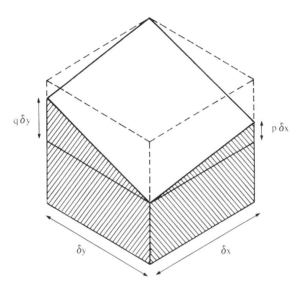

Figure 11-4. The change in height, δz, is the sum of $p\,\delta x$, the change in height due to a small step in the x-direction, and $q\,\delta y$, the change in height due to a small step in the y-direction.

continue from there we would need the new values of p and q at that point (figure 11-5). Now the changes in p and q can be computed using

$$\delta p = r\,\delta x + s\,\delta y \quad \text{and} \quad \delta q = s\,\delta x + t\,\delta y,$$

where r, s, and t are the second partial derivatives of z with respect to x and y. This can be written in a more compact form as

$$\begin{pmatrix} \delta p \\ \delta q \end{pmatrix} = \mathbf{H} \begin{pmatrix} \delta x \\ \delta y \end{pmatrix},$$

where $\mathbf{H}$ is the *Hessian matrix* of second partial derivatives:

$$\mathbf{H} = \begin{pmatrix} r & s \\ s & t \end{pmatrix}.$$

The Hessian provides information on the curvature of the surface. For small surface inclinations, its determinant is the Gaussian curvature, to be introduced later. Also, the *trace* of the Hessian (the sum of its diagonal elements) is the Laplacian of depth, which for small surface inclinations is twice the so-called *mean curvature*. We shall explore surface curvature in chapter 16, where we discuss extended Gaussian images.

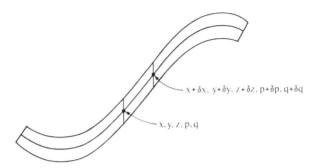

$x+\delta x, y+\delta y, z+\delta z, p+\delta p, q+\delta q$

x, y, z, p, q

Figure 11-5. The solution of the shape-from-shading problem is determined by solving five differential equations for x, y, z, p, and q. The result is a characteristic strip, a curve in space along which surface orientation is known.

To use the Hessian matrix for computing the changes in p and q, we need to know its components, the second partial derivatives of z. To keep track of them we would need still higher derivatives. We could go on differentiating ad infinitum. Note, however, that we have not yet used the image irradiance equation! Differentiating it with respect to x and y, and using the chain rule, we obtain

$$E_x = r\, R_p + s\, R_q \qquad \text{and} \qquad E_y = s\, R_p + t\, R_q,$$

or

$$\begin{pmatrix} E_x \\ E_y \end{pmatrix} = \mathbf{H} \begin{pmatrix} R_p \\ R_q \end{pmatrix},$$

where the Hessian $\mathbf{H}$ once again makes an appearance. This is a relationship between the gradient $(E_x, E_y)^T$ in the image and the gradient $(R_p, R_q)^T$ in the reflectance map. We cannot solve for $\mathbf{H}$, since we have only two equations and three unknowns r, s, and t, but fortunately we do not need the individual elements of $\mathbf{H}$. While we cannot continue the solution in an arbitrary direction, we can do so in a specially chosen direction. This is the key idea. Let

$$\begin{pmatrix} \delta x \\ \delta y \end{pmatrix} = \begin{pmatrix} R_p \\ R_q \end{pmatrix} \delta \xi,$$

where $\delta \xi$ is a small quantity. Then

$$\begin{pmatrix} \delta p \\ \delta q \end{pmatrix} = \mathbf{H} \begin{pmatrix} \delta x \\ \delta y \end{pmatrix} = \mathbf{H} \begin{pmatrix} R_p \\ R_q \end{pmatrix} \delta \xi,$$

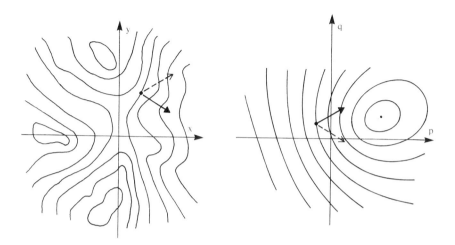

Figure 11-6. Curiously, the step taken in pq-space is parallel to the gradient of $E(x, y)$, while the step taken in xy-space is parallel to the gradient of $R(p, q)$.

or

$$\begin{pmatrix} \delta p \\ \delta q \end{pmatrix} = \begin{pmatrix} E_x \\ E_y \end{pmatrix} \delta \xi.$$

Thus, if the direction of the change in the image plane is parallel to the gradient of the reflectance map, then the change in (p, q) can be computed. The direction of the change in gradient space is parallel, in turn, to the gradient in the image (figure 11-6). We can summarize all this in five ordinary differential equations:

$$\dot{x} = R_p, \qquad \dot{y} = R_q, \qquad \dot{z} = p\,R_p + q\,R_q,$$

$$\dot{p} = E_x, \qquad \dot{q} = E_y,$$

where the dots denote differentiation with respect to ξ. A solution of these differential equations is a curve on the surface. The parameter ξ will vary along this curve. By rescaling the equations, we can easily arrange for ξ to be any function of length along the curve.

11.2 Characteristic Curves and Initial Curves

The curves traced out by the solutions of the five ordinary differential equations are called *characteristic curves*, and their projections in the image are called *base characteristics*. The solutions for x, y, z, p, and q actually form a *characteristic strip*, since they define not only a curve in space but surface orientation along this curve as well (figure 11-5).

To obtain the whole surface we must patch together characteristic strips. Each requires a point where initial values are given in order to start the solution. If we are given an initial curve on the surface, a solution for the surface can be obtained as long as this curve is nowhere parallel to any of the characteristics. On this curve, starting values of p and q can be obtained using the image irradiance equation,

$$E(x, y) = R(p, q),$$

and the known derivatives of z along the curve. Suppose, for example, that the initial curve is given in terms of a parameter η, as $x(\eta)$, $y(\eta)$, and $z(\eta)$. Then, along this curve,

$$\frac{\partial z}{\partial \eta} = p\frac{\partial x}{\partial \eta} + q\frac{\partial y}{\partial \eta}.$$

We have just derived the method of characteristic strip expansion for solving first-order partial differential equations. In our case the relevant equation is the image irradiance equation, a (possibly very nonlinear) first-order partial differential equation.

Figure 11-7 shows a digitized picture of a face, the face with base characteristics superimposed, and the face with a contour map of the recovered shape.

11.3 Singular Points

We are normally not given an initial curve along with the image of an object. How much can we tell about shape in the absence of such auxiliary information? Are there any points where surface orientation can be determined directly? Suppose that $R(p, q)$ has a unique isolated maximum at (p_0, q_0); that is,

$$R(p, q) < R(p_0, q_0) \qquad \text{for all } (p, q) \neq (p_0, q_0).$$

Also assume that at some point (x_0, y_0) in the image, $E(x_0, y_0) = R(p_0, q_0)$. Then it is clear that at this point the gradient (p, q) is uniquely determined to be (p_0, q_0). It would seem, then, that we could start the solution at such a singular point. Unfortunately, at a maximum of $R(p, q)$ the partial derivatives R_p and R_q are zero. Thus the solution will not move from such a point because $\dot{x}$ and $\dot{y}$ are zero. One way to bypass this apparent impasse is to construct a small "cap" at this point and start the solution at the edge of this cap, as we shall show in the next section.

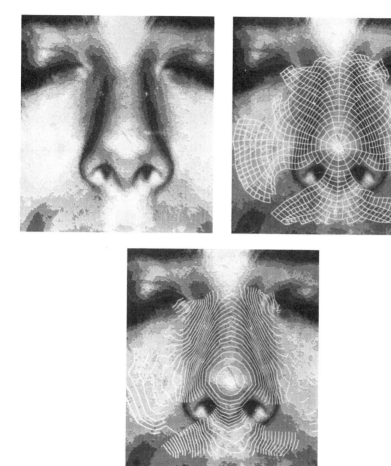

Figure 11-7. The shape-from-shading method is applied here to the recovery of the shape of a nose. The first picture shows the (crudely quantized) gray-level image available to the program. The second picture shows the base characteristics superimposed, while the third shows a contour map computed from the elevations found along the characteristic curves.

11.4 Power Series near a Singular Point

To observe what happens near a singular point, consider the reflectance map

$$R(p, q) = \frac{1}{2}(p^2 + q^2).$$

In this case we have a unique isolated minimum. Let there be a singular point at the origin such that $E(0,0) = 0$. We conclude that $(p, q) = (0, 0)$ at this point. If the surface is smooth enough, we can expand z as a power series in x and y with the first-order terms missing. If we also ignore higher-order terms near the origin, we can write

$$z = z_0 + \frac{1}{2}(ax^2 + 2bxy + cy^2).$$

Thus

$$p = ax + by \qquad \text{and} \qquad q = bx + cy.$$

Substituting these values in the formula for the reflectance map, we obtain

$$E(x, y) = \frac{1}{2}(a^2 + b^2)x^2 + (a + c)bxy + \frac{1}{2}(b^2 + c^2)y^2.$$

Our task is to determine the coefficients a, b, and c, given the image brightness and its derivatives near the origin. Before we go on, observe that the surface

$$z = z_0 - \frac{1}{2}\left(ax^2 + bxy + \frac{1}{2}cy^2\right)$$

gives rise to exactly the same shading pattern, so we already know that there will be at least two solutions.

The brightness gradient is given by

$$E_x = (a^2 + b^2)x + (a + c)b\,y,$$

$$E_y = (a + c)b\,x + (b^2 + c^2)y.$$

Thus $(E_x, E_y)^T = (0, 0)^T$ at $(x, y) = (0, 0)$, as it should. We cannot use the brightness gradient to recover the shape. Differentiating again, we obtain the three equations

$$E_{xx} = a^2 + b^2, \quad E_{xy} = (a + c)b, \quad E_{yy} = b^2 + c^2,$$

in the three unknowns a, b, and c. Three second-order polynomials in three unknowns can have up to eight solutions. The three equations found here have a rather special form, however, and there are only four solutions, as shown in exercise 11-10.

In any case, given one of these local solutions, we can construct a small cap. The edge of this region then constitutes an initial strip for the method of characteristic strip expansion, since p and q as well as z are known on the edge. Note also that the solution will move away from the edge, since R_p and R_q are nonzero there.

The above analysis can be generalized to singular points away from the origin and to other rotationally symmetric reflectance maps. It provides

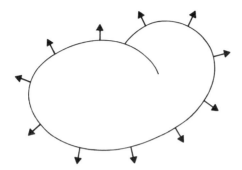

Figure 11-8. The occluding boundary provides an important constraint on the solutions of the shape-from-shading problem. The surface orientation of any solution has to match the known surface orientation along the silhouette.

a means for starting a solution a small distance away from the singular point. A possible problem is that more than one shape might give rise to the same shading, since the nonlinear equations containing the coefficients of the power series near the singular point can have more than one solution, as they did here.

11.5 Occluding Boundaries

At what other point is the surface orientation known? If the object has a smooth surface, then the silhouette also provides valuable information (figure 11-8). The occluding boundary is the curve on the surface that projects to the silhouette. The orientation there is known, since the tangent plane includes the direction to the observer and also the tangent at the corresponding point on the silhouette. In other words, the surface normal on the occluding boundary lies in a plane parallel to the image plane and is perpendicular to the silhouette.

The only problem with this kind of information is that the slope of the surface is infinite on the occluding boundary. It is thus difficult to incorporate this information as an "initial curve." Nevertheless, it is possible to show that if the reflectance map is a strictly monotonic function of a quadratic function of p and q, then there is a unique surface corresponding to a particular shaded image that exhibits a simple closed silhouette. Conversely, if the reflectance map is a linear function in p and q, then an infinite number of surfaces gives rise to the same shading. In many cases shading and auxiliary information determine a surface uniquely. In some cases they do not, unfortunately: The shading on a small patch of the

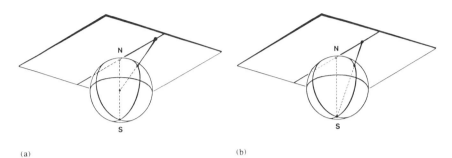

(a)   (b)

Figure 11-9. Because points on the Gaussian sphere specify directions in space, the reflectance map can be plotted on the Gaussian sphere. (a) More commonly, we project the upper hemisphere onto an infinite plane, called the gradient space. If we want to deal with the occluding boundary of an object, another projection is more useful. (b) Here, the whole sphere, except for one point, is projected onto a plane, called the stereographic plane. (Figures reproduced with permission from the chapter by Woodham in *Image Understanding 1984*, edited by S. Ullman & W. Richards, Ablex Publishing Corp., Norwood, New Jersey, 1984.)

surface of an object, for example, without any other information, does not determine the local shape of the surface.

11.6 Stereographic Projection

Orientation has two degrees of freedom. We can specify the orientation of a patch by giving its gradient (p, q). Alternatively we can erect a unit normal $\hat{n}$. As noted in the previous chapter, we can use the Gaussian sphere to represent the direction in which the surface normal is pointing. The Gaussian sphere itself is often inconvenient to use because of its curved surface. This is why we usually project it onto a plane to obtain the *gradient space* (figure 11-9a).

Consider an axis through the sphere parallel to the z-axis. We can project points on the "northern" hemisphere onto a plane tangent at the "north" pole, using the center of the sphere as the center of projection. This is called the *gnomonic* projection. It is easy to show that position in this plane equals $(-p, -q)$. One disadvantage of gradient space (the plane so defined) is that we can only project one hemisphere onto the plane if we want to avoid ambiguity.

Often we are only concerned with surface elements facing the viewer. These correspond to points on the northern hemisphere. But at times directions in the other hemisphere are needed also. In a scene lit from behind, for example, the direction to the light source can be specified by a point in the southern hemisphere. We just came across another difficulty with gradient space. Orientations of surface patches on the occluding boundary correspond to points on the equator of the Gaussian sphere, which project to infinity in gradient space.

One way out of these difficulties is provided by the *stereographic projection*. Here again we project onto a plane tangent at the north pole, but this time the center of projection is the south pole (figure 11-9b). All points on the sphere, except for the south pole, can be mapped. The equator projects to a circle of radius two. Let us call the coordinates in stereographic space f and g. We show in exercise 11-13 that

$$f = \frac{2p}{1 + \sqrt{1 + p^2 + q^2}} \quad \text{and} \quad g = \frac{2q}{1 + \sqrt{1 + p^2 + q^2}}.$$

Conversely,

$$p = \frac{4f}{4 - f^2 - g^2} \quad \text{and} \quad q = \frac{4g}{4 - f^2 - g^2}.$$

An added advantage of stereographic space is that it is a conformal projection of the Gaussian sphere. That is, angles on the surface of the sphere are projected faithfully into equal angles in the plane. One disadvantage, however, is that some formulae become more complicated when expressed in stereographic coordinates.

11.7 Relaxation Methods

The method of characteristic strip expansion suffers from a number of practical problems, including sensitivity to measurement noise. Special means must be employed to prevent adjacent characteristics from crossing over each other as a result of small errors accumulating in the numerical integration of the differential equations. This method also makes it hard to utilize the information on surface orientation available on the occluding boundary. Finally, it suggests neither biological nor parallel machine implementations.

More desirable would be an iterative scheme similar to one of the finite-difference methods used for solving elliptic second-order partial differential equations. This would immediately suggest ways to incorporate boundary and other auxiliary information.

11.7.1 Minimization in the Continuous Case

Our objective is to find two functions, $f(x, y)$ and $g(x, y)$, that ensure that the image irradiance equation,

$$E(x, y) = R_s(f, g),$$

is satisfied, where $R_s(f, g)$ is the reflectance map expressed in stereographic coordinates. We also want $f(x, y)$ and $g(x, y)$ to correspond to a smooth surface. Of the many ways to measure smoothness, we choose one that penalizes rapid changes in f and g. We try to minimize the integral

$$e_s = \iint_I \left((f_x^2 + f_y^2) + (g_x^2 + g_y^2) \right) dx\, dy,$$

where f_x, f_y, g_x, and g_y are the first partial derivatives of f and g with respect to x and y. Other measures of departure from "smoothness" could also be used. These would lead to somewhat different algorithms.

So far, the plan is to minimize e_s subject to the constraint that f and g must satisfy the image irradiance equation. In practice, there are errors in both the measurements of the irradiance and the determination of the reflectance map. Instead of insisting on equality of $E(x, y)$ and $R_s(f, g)$, we could try to minimize the error

$$e_i = \iint_I \left(E(x, y) - R_s(f, g) \right)^2 dx\, dy.$$

Overall, then, we are to minimize $e_s + \lambda e_i$, where λ is a parameter that weights the errors in the image irradiance equation relative to the departure from smoothness. This parameter should be made large if brightness measurements are very accurate, and small if they are very noisy.

The minimization of an integral of the form

$$\iint F(f, g, f_x, f_y, g_x, g_y)\, dx\, dy$$

is a problem in the calculus of variations (a topic covered in the appendix). The corresponding Euler equations are

$$F_f - \frac{\partial}{\partial x} F_{f_x} - \frac{\partial}{\partial y} F_{f_y} = 0,$$

$$F_g - \frac{\partial}{\partial x} F_{g_x} - \frac{\partial}{\partial y} F_{g_y} = 0,$$

where F_f is the partial derivative of F with respect to f. In the present case,

$$F = (f_x^2 + f_y^2) + (g_x^2 + g_y^2) + \lambda \left(E(x, y) - R_s(f, g) \right)^2.$$

The aim is to minimize the integral of F. The Euler equations for this problem yield

$$\nabla^2 f = -\lambda \left(E(x, y) - R_s(f, g) \right) \frac{\partial R_s}{\partial f},$$

$$\nabla^2 g = -\lambda \left(E(x, y) - R_s(f, g) \right) \frac{\partial R_s}{\partial g},$$

where

$$\nabla^2 = \frac{\partial^2}{\partial x^2} + \frac{\partial^2}{\partial y^2}$$

is the Laplacian operator. The result is a coupled pair of elliptic second-order partial differential equations. These can be solved by iterative methods once the values of f and g on the silhouette are introduced.

11.7.2 Minimization in the Discrete Case

We can develop a numerical method either by approximating the continuous solution found in the previous section or by directly minimizing a discrete version of the integral. Readers uncomfortable with the calculus of variations may be more satisfied with the latter approach. We can measure the departure from smoothness at the point (i,j) by

$$s_{i,j} = \frac{1}{4}\big((f_{i+1,j} - f_{i,j})^2 + (f_{i,j+1} - f_{i,j})^2$$
$$+ (g_{i+1,j} - g_{i,j})^2 + (g_{i,j+1} - g_{i,j})^2\big),$$

while the error in the image irradiance equation is given by

$$r_{ij} = \big(E_{ij} - R_s(f_{ij}, g_{ij})\big)^2,$$

where E_{ij} is the observed image irradiance at the grid point (i,j). We seek a set of values $\{f_{ij}\}$ and $\{g_{ij}\}$ that minimize

$$e = \sum_i \sum_j (s_{ij} + \lambda r_{ij}).$$

Differentiating e with respect to f_{kl} and g_{kl}, we obtain

$$\frac{\partial e}{\partial f_{kl}} = 2(f_{kl} - \overline{f}_{kl}) - 2\lambda\big(E_{kl} - R_s(f_{kl}, g_{kl})\big)\frac{\partial R_s}{\partial f},$$

$$\frac{\partial e}{\partial g_{kl}} = 2(g_{kl} - \overline{g}_{kl}) - 2\lambda\big(E_{kl} - R_s(f_{kl}, g_{kl})\big)\frac{\partial R_s}{\partial g},$$

where $\overline{f}$ and $\overline{g}$ are local averages of f and g:

$$\overline{f}_{i,j} = \frac{1}{4}\left(f_{i+1,j} + f_{i,j+1} + f_{i-1,j} + f_{i,j-1}\right),$$

$$\overline{g}_{i,j} = \frac{1}{4}\left(g_{i+1,j} + g_{i,j+1} + g_{i-1,j} + g_{i,j-1}\right).$$

We have to be careful when performing this differentiation, since f_{kl} and g_{kl} occur in four terms of the sum; the new subscripts k and l are introduced to avoid confusion with the subscripts i and j that occur in the sum.

The extremum is to be found where the above derivatives of e are equal to zero. If we rearrange the resulting equations by solving for f_{kl} and g_{kl}, an iterative solution method suggests itself:

$$f_{kl}^{n+1} = \overline{f}_{kl}^{\,n} + \lambda\big(E_{kl} - R_s(f_{kl}^n, g_{kl}^n)\big)\frac{\partial R_s}{\partial f},$$

$$g_{kl}^{n+1} = \overline{g}_{kl}^{\,n} + \lambda\big(E_{kl} - R_s(f_{kl}^n, g_{kl}^n)\big)\frac{\partial R_s}{\partial g},$$

where the new values for f and g at each grid point are obtained using the old values of f and g in evaluating $R_s(f,g)$, $\partial R_s/\partial f$, and $\partial R_s/\partial g$. It can be shown that a stable method is obtained if we use the local averages $\overline{f}$ and $\overline{g}$ in evaluating $R_s(f,g)$ and the two partial derivatives, provided suitable boundary conditions are introduced and λ is small enough.

The simple iterative scheme described above can be improved in various ways. The estimates of the Laplacians of f and g, proportional to $(\overline{f}_{kl} - f_{kl})$ and $(\overline{g}_{kl} - g_{kl})$, can be replaced by more accurate formulae, for example. Then the local average is computed as

$$\overline{f}_{i,j} = \frac{1}{5}\left(f_{i+1,j} + f_{i,j+1} + f_{i-1,j} + f_{i,j-1}\right)$$

$$+ \frac{1}{20}\left(f_{i+1,j+1} + f_{i+1,j-1} + f_{i-1,j-1} + f_{i-1,j+1}\right),$$

and similarly for $\overline{g}_{i,j}$. The computation of the average can be represented by the stencil

$$\frac{1}{20}\quad\begin{array}{|c|c|c|}\hline 1 & 4 & 1 \\\hline 4 & & 4 \\\hline 1 & 4 & 1 \\\hline\end{array}$$

which is derived directly from one we used earlier to approximate the Laplacian operator.

Figure 11-10 shows a picture made from the image of a small resin droplet obtained by means of a scanning electron microscope. To apply the iterative shape-from-shading scheme, we have to know the reflectance map. A commonly used model of secondary electron emission from a surface suggests that brightness should vary as the secant of the incident angle, $\sec\theta_i$. Using this model, we obtained the shape shown in figure 11-11.

11.7.3 Application to Photometric Stereo

The gradient values computed at adjacent image points using the photometric stereo method are not necessarily consistent. Even in the case of a

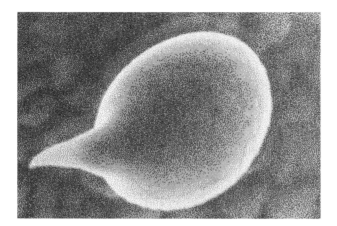

Figure 11-10. Display of the image of a small resin droplet on a flower of a *Cannabis sativa* plant. (Reproduced by permission from the book *Magnifications—Photography with the Scanning Electron Microscope* by David Scharf, Schocken Books, New York, 1977.)

planar surface, there can be fluctuations in estimated surface orientation due to measurement errors. If we know that the surface is smooth, we can use the method presented in this chapter to improve the results of the photometric stereo method.

If there are n images, we can formulate this problem in terms of the minimization of

$$e = \iint_I \left((f_x^2 + f_y^2) + (g_x^2 + g_y^2) \right) \, dx \, dy$$

$$+ \sum_{i=1}^{n} \lambda_i \iint_I \left(E_i(x,y) - R_i(f,g) \right)^2 \, dx \, dy,$$

where E_i is the brightness measured in the ith image and R_i is the corresponding reflectance map. The constant multipliers λ_i are parameters that weight the errors in the image irradiance equations relative to the departure from smoothness. They are unequal if the information provided by the cameras is not all equally reliable.

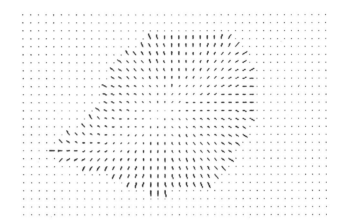

Figure 11-11. Needle diagram calculated by the iterative scheme under the assumption that the reflectance map is $\sec \theta_i$. (The surface orientation data are actually available on a finer grid; they are sampled coarsely here for display purposes.) The needle diagram is the estimate of the shape of the surface of the resin droplet shown in the previous figure. (Figure kindly provided by Katsushi Ikeuchi.)

The Euler equations in this case yield

$$\nabla^2 f = - \sum_{i=1}^{n} \lambda_i \big(E_i(x,y) - R_i(f,g) \big) \frac{\partial R_i}{\partial f},$$

$$\nabla^2 g = - \sum_{i=1}^{n} \lambda_i \big(E_i(x,y) - R_i(f,g) \big) \frac{\partial R_i}{\partial g}.$$

The corresponding discrete equations suggest an iterative scheme:

$$f_{kl}^{n+1} = \overline{f}_{kl}^{n} + \sum_{i=1}^{n} \lambda_i \big(E_{i;kl} - R_i(f_{kl}, g_{kl}) \big) \frac{\partial R_i}{\partial f},$$

$$g_{kl}^{n+1} = \overline{g}_{kl}^{n} + \sum_{i=1}^{n} \lambda_i \big(E_{i;kl} - R_i(f_{kl}, g_{kl}) \big) \frac{\partial R_i}{\partial g}.$$

The simple photometric stereo method discussed in the previous chapter can be used to obtain good initial values for $\{f_{kl}\}$ and $\{g_{kl}\}$. This will ensure rapid convergence to the solution.

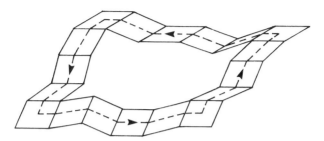

Figure 11-12. If surface orientation is known, elevation of the surface above some reference plane can be determined by integration along curves in the image. To be consistent, the integral of the surface gradient along a closed curve should be zero, since the overall change in elevation when one walks in a closed loop on a single-valued surface is zero.

11.8 Recovering Depth from a Needle Diagram

Several machine vision methods, including photometric stereo, produce surface shape information in the form of a *needle diagram*, in which surface orientation is given for every picture cell. In some cases we may want to represent surface shape in a different way. Often a *depth map*, giving height above some reference plane, is a desirable objective.

Given p and q, the partial derivatives of $z(x, y)$ with respect to x and y, we can recover $z(x, y)$ by integrating along arbitrary curves in the plane

$$z(x, y) = z(x_0, y_0) + \int_{(x_0, y_0)}^{(x,y)} (p \, dx + q \, dy).$$

In practice, p and q are recovered from noisy image data by imperfect methods. Thus the above integral might depend on the path chosen. Indeed, an integral along a closed path, as shown in figure 11-12, can be different from zero. Now since both p and q are available, we actually have more information than we really need. This suggests that we use a least-squares method to find the surface that best fits the imperfect estimate of the surface gradient.

We can, for example, choose $z(x, y)$ so as to minimize the error

$$\iint_I \left((z_x - p)^2 + (z_y - q)^2 \right) \, dx \, dy,$$

where p and q are the given estimates of the components of the gradient, while z_x and z_y are the partial derivatives of the best-fit surface. Again, this is a problem in the calculus of variations. We have to minimize an integral of the form

$$\iint F(z, z_x, z_y) \, dx \, dy.$$

The Euler equation is

$$F_z - \frac{\partial}{\partial x} F_{z_x} - \frac{\partial}{\partial y} F_{z_y} = 0,$$

so that from

$$F = (z_x - p)^2 + (z_y - q)^2$$

we obtain

$$\frac{\partial}{\partial x}(z_x - p) + \frac{\partial}{\partial y}(z_y - q) = 0,$$

or just

$$\nabla^2 z = p_x + q_y.$$

This equation accords with intuition, since it states that the Laplacian of the desired surface must equal $p_x + q_y$, which is an estimate of the Laplacian based on the given data.

As usual, we also need to know what to do about the boundary of the region over which this equation is to be solved. The *natural boundary condition* (see appendix) for an integral of the form

$$\iint F(z, z_x, z_y) \, dx \, dy$$

is

$$F_{z_x} \frac{dy}{ds} - F_{z_y} \frac{dx}{ds} = 0.$$

Here s is arclength along the boundary. We note at this point that $(dx/ds, dy/ds)^T$ is a tangent vector. In our case we obtain

$$(z_x - p)\frac{dy}{ds} = (z_y - q)\frac{dx}{ds},$$

or

$$(z_x, z_y)^T \cdot \left(\frac{dy}{ds}, -\frac{dx}{ds}\right)^T = (p, q)^T \cdot \left(\frac{dy}{ds}, -\frac{dx}{ds}\right)^T,$$

where the vector

$$\left(\frac{dy}{ds}, -\frac{dx}{ds}\right)^T$$

is a normal to the boundary curve at the point s. This result is eminently reasonable, since it states that the normal derivative of the desired surface must equal the estimate of the normal derivative obtained from the data.

An iterative method can be used to solve this equation. It can be based on a discrete approximation of the equation or a least-squares analysis applied directly to a discrete approximation of the original error integral, thus sidestepping the need for application of the calculus of variations.

Initial values can be generated by some simple scheme, such as integrating $p(x, 0)$ along the x-axis to obtain one profile, then integrating $q(x_0, y)$ along y starting at each point x_0 on the x-axis. (This crude method by itself, of course, does not produce a particularly good surface.)

11.9 References

The scanning electron microscope is described in *Scanning Electron Microscopy* by Wells [1974]. Many interesting pictures made using such instruments are shown in *Tissues and Organs: a Text-Atlas of Scanning Electron Microscopy* by Kessel & Kardon [1979] and in *Magnifications—Photography with the Scanning Electron Microscope* by Scharf [1977].

There are numerous books discussing partial differential equations, among them *Partial Differential Equations: Theory and Technique* by Carrier & Pearson [1976] and volume II of *Methods of Mathematical Physics* by Courant & Hilbert [1962]. But perhaps the most relevant for the first-order equations explored in this chapter is Garabedian's *Partial Differential Equations* [1964].

The calculus of variations is also the topic of many books, including *Calculus of Variations: With Applications to Physics & Engineering* by Weinstock [1974] and volume I of *Methods of Mathematical Physics* by Courant & Hilbert [1953]. In some of the exercises we relate the methods used in this chapter to *regularization* techniques for producing well-posed problems from ill-posed ones. Regularization is discussed by Tikhonov & Arsenin in *Solutions of Ill-Posed Problems* [1977].

There was a lot of interest in determining the shape of the surface features of the moon from telescopic images taken from the earth, at least until we could send probes, and finally people, to the vicinity of our rocky satellite. Since the libration of the moon, as well as the ratio of the radius of the earth to the distance between the two bodies, is small, we always see the moon from essentially the same direction. Thus binocular stereo can be ruled out as a viable method for recovering surface shape in this instance. Astronomers used shadows to estimate the relief of crater edges above the surrounding terrain. Van Digellen [1951] was the first to suggest the possibility of using shading, but he was only able to make some heuristic estimates of surface slope in the direction of the light source. Rindfleisch [1966] used photometric models developed in Russia by Fesenkov [1962] and others to derive a complex integration method for recovering the shape along profiles that we now know to be characteristic lines.

Horn [1970, 1975a] found the general solution of the shape-from-shading problem and later [1977] reworked the solution to make use of the reflectance map. Woodham [1979, 1981, 1984] provides excellent discussions of this topic, using the Hessian matrix as a tool.

The existence and uniqueness of solutions to the nonlinear first-order partial differential equation were explored by Bruss [1981, 1982, 1983], Brooks [1982], and Deift & Sylvester [1981].

Horn [1970] searched for a way to reformulate the problem so that the solution would take the form of a parallel iterative algorithm on a grid, much like the one he later used for the computation of lightness [1974]. Strat [1979] developed the first such algorithm. This algorithm was not, however, able to deal with the occluding boundary, since it used the gradient to parameterize surface orientation. Ikeuchi & Horn [1981] rectified this problem by introducing stereographic coordinates and a "lack-of-smoothness" term, now recognized as a regularization term. (For other ideas on parallel computation in vision, see Ballard, Hinton, & Sejnowshi [1983]. For a discussion of the use of regularization in dealing with ill-posed early vision problems, see Poggio & Torre [1984].)

Unfortunately the method of Ikeuchi and Horn, in turn, did not guarantee the integrability of the resulting needle diagram. Horn & Brooks [1985] have remedied this deficiency by using the surface normal to parameterize surface orientation. They avoid the use of a regularizing term in their work.

Shape can also be calculated from texture gradients or regular patterns; see Horn [1970], Bajcsy & Lieberman [1976], Witkin [1981], and Ikeuchi [1984]. These methods are inherently simpler, however, since more information is available at each image point than when shading is used.

Most shape-from-shading methods require that the reflectance map be given. There have been attempts to reduce dependence on such detailed knowledge. Pentland [1984], for example, tries to extract information locally. This inevitably requires strong assumptions, such as that the surface is spherical. Local methods cannot lead to unique results, since it is known from the work of Bruss [1981, 1982, 1983] and Brooks [1982] that singular points and occluding boundaries provide strong constraints, which are not available to a method that only considers shading in a small region of the image.

A compromise between exact knowledge of the reflectance map and not knowing anything at all is the use of a parameterized reflectance map. It is possible, for example, to recover the position of the light source from the image when certain assumptions are made. See Pentland [1982], Lee [1983], and Brooks & Horn [1985].

One can say something about the relationship between shading and surface shape without detailed solution of the image irradiance equation.

For an example, see Koenderink & van Doorn [1980]. The silhouette of
the image of an object provides a great deal of information. Marr [1977]
was concerned with the recovery of surface shape information from the
occluding contour alone. Stevens [1981] considered the recovery of surface
shape from special contours on the surface.

Much work has been devoted to understanding the interaction of light
with the surface layer of an object. Typically a surface layer model is either
so complex that only numerical results can be obtained or so simple as to
be unrealistic. The photometric model of the lunar surface was refined by
Minnaert [1961], whose reflectance function is used in exercise 11-1. Useful
models for glossy reflection were developed by Torrance & Sparrow [1967]
and Trowbridge & Reitz [1975].

11.10 Exercises

11-1   Consider a sphere of Lambertian material with center on the optical axis.
Assume that the light source is a point source of unit intensity in the direction
$(-p_s, -q_s, 1)^T$.

(a)   What is the irradiance $E(x, y)$? Assume that the radius of the sphere is R
and that the image is obtained using orthographic projection.

(b)   Show that contours of constant brightness in the image are nested ellipses
of equal eccentricity. Hint: What are the contours of constant brightness on
the sphere?

(c)   What do the contours of constant brightness in the image look like if we
assume instead that the surface has the reflectance properties of the material in the maria of the moon? Hint: What are the contours of constant
brightness on the sphere in this case?

11-2   Show that the slope of a surface in the direction that makes an angle θ
with the x-axis is

$$m(\theta) = p\cos\theta + q\sin\theta.$$

Find the direction of steepest ascent. Conclude that the slope in the direction of
steepest ascent is

$$m(\theta_s) = \sqrt{p^2 + q^2}.$$

11-3   Show that the two surfaces

$$z_1 = 2(x^2 + xy + y^2) \qquad \text{and} \qquad z_2 = (x^2 + 4xy + y^2)$$

give rise to the same shading near the origin if a rotationally symmetric reflectance
map applies.

11-4 When are the base characteristics parallel straight lines in the image plane? That is, what class of reflectance maps lead to solutions that have this property, independent of the shape of the surface? Hint: For the base characteristics to be straight lines there must be a proportionality between $\dot{x}$ and $\dot{y}$ in the equations for the characteristic strip.

11-5 Suppose that the reflectance map is linear in p and q, so that

$$R(p,q) = ap + bq + c.$$

We have an image, including the silhouette of a simple convex object of shape $z = f(x,y)$. Show that the surface

$$\bar{z} = f(x,y) + g(bx - ay),$$

for an arbitrary differentiable function $g(s)$, will give rise to the same image. Does the surface $\bar{z}$ have the same silhouette? Assume that the derivative of g is bounded.

11-6 Scanning electron microscope images are unusual in that surface patches inclined relative to the viewer are brighter than a patch that is orthogonal to the viewing direction. One might imagine that simply printing such images in negative form would improve their interpretability. This is not the case. Explain why. Hint: "Shadows" in scanning electron microscope images are dark.

11-7 Here we explore the importance of singular points in reducing the ambiguity in the shape-from-shading problem. Suppose that we have a paraboloid defined by the equation

$$z(x,y) = z_0 + \frac{1}{2}(x^2 + y^2)$$

and a reflectance map

$$R(p,q) = p^2 + q^2.$$

(a) Show that the image can be written

$$E(x,y) = x^2 + y^2$$

and that there is a singular point at the origin.

(b) Now demonstrate that the image irradiance equation that applies here can be expressed in polar coordinates as

$$z_r^2 + \frac{1}{r^2}z_\theta^2 = r^2,$$

where z_r and z_θ are the partial derivatives of z with respect to r and θ, respectively.

(c) Show that the solution of this equation is the paraboloid we started with, provided that $z_\theta = 0$. (We cannot, of course, distinguish a convex paraboloid from a concave paraboloid, or recover its absolute distance from the viewer.)

(d) Now suppose instead that $z_\theta = k$. Show that the solution in this case is

$$z(r) = z_0 \pm \int_{r_0}^{r} \sqrt{t^2 - \frac{k^2}{t^2}} \, dt.$$

Over what range of r is this expression valid?

(e) Perform the indicated integration and conclude that

$$z(r) = z_0 \pm \frac{1}{2} \left(\sqrt{r^4 - k^2} + k \sin^{-1} \frac{k}{r^2} \right).$$

(f) The solution is unique if the image includes the singular point. Is the solution unique if we are only given the part of the image in an annular ring around the singular point? What if we are given the image in a simply connected region that does not include the singular point?

11-8   For a surface of low inclination (that is, small z_x and z_y), the Gaussian curvature and the mean curvature are given by

$$\kappa_1 \kappa_2 \approx z_{xx} z_{yy} - z_{xy} z_{yx} \quad \text{and} \quad \frac{1}{2}(\kappa_1 + \kappa_2) \approx \frac{1}{2}(z_{xx} + z_{yy}).$$

Express these results in terms of the Hessian matrix $\mathbf{H}$.

11-9   The Gaussian curvature of a surface $z(x, y)$ can be written in the form

$$\kappa = \frac{z_{xx} z_{yy} - z_{xy} z_{yx}}{\left(1 + z_x^2 + z_y^2\right)^2}.$$

Rewrite this in terms of p and q as well as r, s, and t as defined in this chapter.

A *ruled surface* is one that can be generated by sweeping a straight line, called the *generator*, through space. At each point on a ruled surface, we can find a tangent that lies in the surface (the generator for that part of the surface). A hyperboloid is an example of a ruled surface. *Developable surfaces* constitute a subclass of ruled surfaces. Intuitively, a developable surface is one that can be cut open and flattened out. In the case of a developable surface, all points on a tangent that lies in the surface have a common normal direction. Cylindrical and conical surfaces are examples of developable surfaces (figure 11-13). The Gaussian curvature on a developable surface is everywhere zero.

Suppose we are told that a surface we are viewing happens to be developable. Show that we can perform a local shading analysis to recover the second partial derivatives of the surface. Specifically, show that

$$r = \frac{E_x^2}{R_p E_x + R_q E_y}, \quad s = \frac{E_x E_y}{R_p E_x + R_q E_y}, \quad t = \frac{E_y^2}{R_p E_x + R_q E_y}.$$

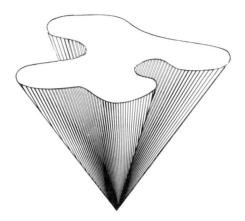

Figure 11-13. A developable surface, such as a cone, has zero Gaussian curvature everywhere.

11-10 Here we consider in detail what happens near a singular point in the case of a simple reflectance map. Suppose that the surface shape near the origin is given by

$$z = z_0 + \frac{1}{2} (x \quad y) \begin{pmatrix} a & b \\ b & c \end{pmatrix} \begin{pmatrix} x \\ y \end{pmatrix}.$$

Let the reflectance map be

$$R(p, q) = \frac{1}{2}(p^2 + q^2).$$

We wish to determine exactly how many solutions there are locally for surface shape, and how they are related to one another.

(a) Show that

$$E(x, y) = \frac{1}{2} (x \quad y) \begin{pmatrix} a & b \\ b & c \end{pmatrix}^2 \begin{pmatrix} x \\ y \end{pmatrix}.$$

(b) Show that

$$\begin{pmatrix} E_{xx} & E_{xy} \\ E_{yx} & E_{yy} \end{pmatrix} = \begin{pmatrix} a & b \\ b & c \end{pmatrix}^2 = \begin{pmatrix} a^2 + b^2 & (a+c)b \\ (a+c)b & b^2 + c^2 \end{pmatrix}.$$

Next, we evaluate the second partial derivatives in a rotated coordinate system. Suppose that

$$\begin{pmatrix} x' \\ y' \end{pmatrix} = \begin{pmatrix} \cos\theta & \sin\theta \\ -\sin\theta & \cos\theta \end{pmatrix} \begin{pmatrix} x \\ y \end{pmatrix}.$$

For convenience, we call the rotation matrix in this equation $\mathbf{R}(\theta)$. We shall also use the shorthand notation $c = \cos\theta$ and $s = \sin\theta$.

(c) Show that

$$\begin{pmatrix} E_{x'x'} & E_{x'y'} \\ E_{y'x'} & E_{y'y'} \end{pmatrix} = \mathbf{R}(\theta) \begin{pmatrix} E_{xx} & E_{xy} \\ E_{yx} & E_{yy} \end{pmatrix} \mathbf{R}^T(\theta)$$

$$= \begin{pmatrix} c^2 E_{xx} + 2sc\, E_{xy} + s^2 E_{yy} & (c^2 - s^2) E_{xy} - sc(E_{xx} - E_{yy}) \\ (c^2 - s^2) E_{xy} - sc(E_{xx} - E_{yy}) & s^2 E_{xx} - 2sc\, E_{xy} + c^2 E_{yy} \end{pmatrix}.$$

Hint: Use the chain rule for differentiation.

(d) Show that the off-diagonal elements, $E_{x'y'}$ and $E_{y'x'}$, are zero when

$$\tan 2\theta = \frac{2E_{xy}}{E_{xx} - E_{yy}}.$$

Find expressions for $\sin 2\theta$ and $\cos 2\theta$.

(e) Show that

$$\cos^2 \theta = \frac{1}{2} \frac{\sqrt{(E_{xx} - E_{yy})^2 + 4E_{xy}^2} + (E_{xx} - E_{yy})}{\sqrt{(E_{xx} - E_{yy})^2 + 4E_{xy}^2}},$$

$$\sin^2 \theta = \frac{1}{2} \frac{\sqrt{(E_{xx} - E_{yy})^2 + 4E_{xy}^2} - (E_{xx} - E_{yy})}{\sqrt{(E_{xx} - E_{yy})^2 + 4E_{xy}^2}}.$$

Conclude that

$$E_{x'x'} = \frac{1}{2} \left(1 + \sqrt{(E_{xx} - E_{yy})^2 + 4E_{xy}^2} \right),$$

$$E_{y'y'} = \frac{1}{2} \left(1 - \sqrt{(E_{xx} - E_{yy})^2 + 4E_{xy}^2} \right).$$

Hint: The eigenvalues and eigenvectors of a symmetric 2×2 matrix are developed in exercise 3-5.

(f) Show that the second-order polynomial for z does not contain a cross-term in the rotated coordinate system. That is, we can write

$$z = a'(x')^2 + c'(y')^2.$$

Find a' and c' in terms of a, b, and c.

(g) Show that there are exactly four surfaces that have the observed second-order partial derivatives of image brightness. How are they related? Hint: What are the Gaussian curvatures of the solutions?

11-11   A surface $z(x, y)$ with continuous second partial derivatives has to satisfy an *integrability constraint*, that is,

$$\frac{\partial^2 z}{\partial x \partial y} = \frac{\partial^2 z}{\partial y \partial x},$$

or $p_y = q_x$. The iterative shape-from-shading scheme presented in this chapter does not guarantee this. Suppose you wish to minimize the brightness error,

$$\iint_I \big(E(x, y) - R(p, q)\big)^2 \, dx \, dy,$$

by suitable choice of the two functions $p(x, y)$ and $q(x, y)$, subject to the integrability constraint $p_y = q_x$.

(a) Show that the appropriate Euler equations are

$$\big(E(x, y) - R(p, q)\big) R_q = -\lambda_x \quad \text{and} \quad \big(E(x, y) - R(p, q)\big) R_p = +\lambda_y,$$

where $\lambda(x, y)$ is a Lagrange function and

$$R_p = \frac{\partial R}{\partial p}, \qquad R_q = \frac{\partial R}{\partial q}, \qquad \lambda_x = \frac{\partial \lambda}{\partial x}, \qquad \lambda_y = \frac{\partial \lambda}{\partial y}.$$

(b) Conclude that the desired functions $p(x, y)$ and $q(x, y)$ must satisfy the equation

$$\big((E - R) R_{pp} - R_p^2\big) p_x + \big((E - R) R_{pq} - R_p R_q\big)(p_y + q_x) + \big((E - R) R_{qq} - R_q^2\big) q_y$$
$$= (E_x R_p + E_y R_q),$$

as well as the constraint $p_y = q_x$. Hint: Total derivatives with respect to x and y are required in order to eliminate the Lagrange multiplier.

(c) Show that you end up with the same Euler equation if you try to minimize

$$\iint_I \big(E(x, y) - R(z_x, z_y)\big)^2 \, dx \, dy$$

by suitable choice of $z(x, y)$.

11-12   Suppose instead that you wish to minimize the sum of the brightness error and the deviation from integrability,

$$\iint_I \Big(\big(E(x, y) - R(p, q)\big)^2 + \lambda(p_y - q_x)^2\Big) \, dx \, dy,$$

by suitable choice of the two functions $p(x, y)$ and $q(x, y)$.

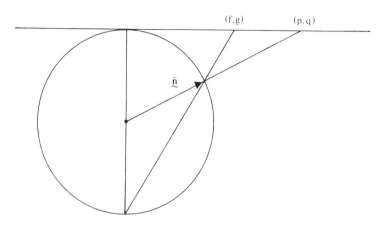

Figure 11-14. Cross section of the Gaussian sphere and a plane tangent at the north pole. The gnomonic projection is obtained by connecting points on the surface of the sphere to its center. The stereographic projection is obtained by connecting points on the surface of the sphere to its south pole.

(a) How does this approach differ from that of the previous problem? Hint: Note that λ here is a constant.

(b) Show that the appropriate Euler equations are

$$\big(E(x,y) - R(p,q)\big)R_p = \lambda(p_{yy} - q_{xy}),$$

$$\big(E(x,y) - R(p,q)\big)R_q = \lambda(q_{xx} - p_{xy}).$$

(c) Suggest an iterative scheme based on isolation of the central values in discrete approximations of the second-order derivatives p_{yy} and q_{xx}.

11-13 Here we explore the stereographic projection of the Gaussian sphere. A cross section through the Gaussian sphere useful for understanding the gnomonic and stereographic projections is shown in figure 11-14.

(a) Show that the relationship between the stereographic projection and the gnomonic projection can be expressed in the form

$$f = \frac{2p}{1 + \sqrt{1 + p^2 + q^2}}, \qquad g = \frac{2q}{1 + \sqrt{1 + p^2 + q^2}}.$$

(b) Show that

$$p = \frac{4f}{4 - f^2 - g^2} \qquad \text{and} \qquad q = \frac{4g}{4 - f^2 - g^2}.$$

(c) Further, show that the integrability condition $p_y = q_x$ can be expressed in terms of stereographic coordinates as

$$f_y(4 + f^2 - g^2) - g_x(4 - f^2 + g^2) + 2fg(g_y - f_x) = 0.$$

11-14 Show that
$$\nabla \times (-p, -q, 1)^T = 0,$$

where $\nabla \times \mathbf{n}$ is the *curl* of the vector $\mathbf{n}$. Hint: First show that

$$(-p, -q, 1)^T = \nabla \big(z_0 - z(x, y)\big),$$

where $\nabla f(x, y, z)$ is the gradient

$$\left(\frac{\partial f}{\partial x}, \frac{\partial f}{\partial y}, \frac{\partial f}{\partial z} \right)^T$$

of the function $f(x, y, z)$.

11-15 Suppose that we have calculated a discrete needle map $\{(p_{ij}, q_{ij})\}$ by means of some shape-from-shading method. We now wish to recover the surface $\{z_{ij}\}$. To do this, we minimize

$$\sum_{i=1}^{n} \sum_{j=1}^{m} (z_x - p_{ij})^2 + (z_y - q_{ij})^2$$

by suitable choice of $\{z_{ij}\}$. Use the estimates

$$z_x \approx \frac{1}{2h} \big(z_{i,j+1} - z_{i,j} + z_{i+1,j+1} - z_{i+1,j} \big),$$

$$z_y \approx \frac{1}{2h} \big(z_{i+1,j} - z_{i,j} + z_{i+1,j+1} - z_{i,j+1} \big),$$

for the derivatives. Note that these estimates are unbiased for the corners where four picture cells meet, not for picture-cell centers. Show that a necessary condition for a minimum is that

$$\frac{1}{h} \big(4z_{k,l} - (z_{k+1,l-1} + z_{k-1,l+1} + z_{k+1,l+1} + z_{k-1,l-1}) \big)$$

$$= \big(p_{k,l-1} - p_{k,l} + p_{k-1,l-1} - p_{k-1,l} \big) + \big(q_{k-1,l} - q_{k,l} + q_{k-1,l-1} - q_{k,l-1} \big).$$

Compare this result to that obtained in the continuous case in this chapter using the calculus of variations.

11-16 So far we have assumed that we know where the light sources are and that we do not know the shape of the object. At times we may in fact know the shape of some object in the scene, but not where the light is coming from. Assume that the surface is Lambertian and that it is illuminated by a distant point source. How can we recover the direction $\mathbf{s}$ to that source?

(a) Minimize the integral of the square of the difference between the observed and the predicted brightness,

$$\iint_I \left(E(x, y) - \mathbf{n}(x, y) \cdot \mathbf{s} \right)^2 dx\, dy.$$

(b) Show that

$$\iint_I E\mathbf{n}\, dx\, dy = \left[\iint_I \mathbf{n}\mathbf{n}^T\, dx\, dy \right] \mathbf{s},$$

where $\mathbf{n}\mathbf{n}^T$ is the dyadic product of $\mathbf{n}$ with itself, which is a 3×3 matrix.

(c) Conclude that the unknown source position can be computed as follows:

$$\mathbf{s} = \left[\iint_I \mathbf{n}\mathbf{n}^T\, dx\, dy \right]^{-1} \iint_I E\mathbf{n}\, dx\, dy.$$

(d) Develop a suitable discrete scheme based on this analysis. Replace the integrals by sums.

(e) How many points on the surface of the object must be measured to ensure that the sum of the dyadic products is a nonsingular matrix? Warning: This part is harder than the rest of the problem.

(f) Can the same sort of thing be done for a surface whose brightness is proportional to $\sqrt{\cos\theta_i / \cos\theta_e}$? Hint: In this case, it may be inconvenient to minimize the difference between the observed and the predicted brightness. Instead, minimize a related quantity in order to make sure that the resulting equations are tractable.

12

Motion Field & Optical Flow

A great deal of useful information can be extracted from time-varying images. At first, it might seem foolhardy to consider processing sequences of images, given the difficulty of interpreting even a single image. Curiously, though, some information is easier to obtain from a time sequence. The apparent motion of brightness patterns observed when a camera is moving relative to the objects being imaged is called the optical flow. In this chapter we discover how, given a sequence of images, we can calculate the optical flow. We start by contrasting the optical flow with the motion field, a purely geometric concept. A constraint equation is then uncovered that relates the gradient of brightness to the local flow velocity. We find that it is not possible to recover the optical flow locally. Additional information is required. One way to provide such information is to make assumptions about the shapes of the surfaces being imaged. We derive an iterative scheme for estimating the optical flow under the assumption that it varies smoothly.

The optical flow is a useful concept even when the surfaces being imaged deform, but in the special case of rigid body motion the optical flow is highly constrained. In chapter 17, where we explore passive navigation, we discuss how to recover both the motion of the camera relative to a fixed environment and the shapes of the surfaces being imaged. Some of methods we discuss there use the optical flow as an intermediate result.

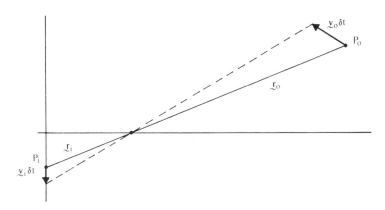

Figure 12-1. Displacement of a point in the environment causes a displacement of the corresponding image point. The relationship between the velocities can be found by differentiating the perspective projection equation.

12.1 Motion Field

When objects move in front of a camera, or when a camera moves through a fixed environment, there are corresponding changes in the image. These changes can be used to recover the relative motions as well as the shapes of the objects.

We first define the *motion field*, which assigns a velocity vector to each point in the image. At a particular instant in time, a point P_i in the image corresponds to some point P_o on the surface of an object. The two are connected by the projection equation. In the case of perspective projection, a ray from the image point through the center of the lens can be extended until it strikes an opaque surface (figure 12-1).

Let the object point P_o have velocity $\mathbf{v}_o$ relative to the camera. This induces a motion $\mathbf{v}_i$ in the corresponding image point P_i. The point P_o moves $\mathbf{v}_o\,\delta t$ in a time interval δt, and its image P_i moves $\mathbf{v}_i\,\delta t$. The velocities are given by

$$\mathbf{v}_o = \frac{d\mathbf{r}_o}{dt} \qquad \text{and} \qquad \mathbf{v}_i = \frac{d\mathbf{r}_i}{dt},$$

where r_o and r_i are related by

$$\frac{1}{f'}\mathbf{r}_i = \frac{1}{\mathbf{r}_o \cdot \hat{\mathbf{z}}}\mathbf{r}_o.$$

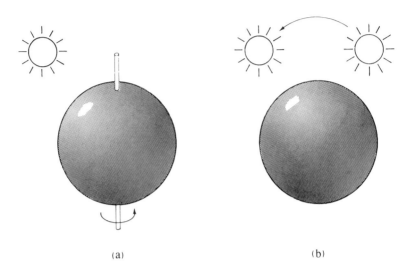

(a)   (b)

Figure 12-2. The optical flow is not always equal to the motion field. In (a) a smooth sphere is rotating under constant illumination—the image does not change, yet the motion field is nonzero. In (b) a fixed sphere is illuminated by a moving source—the shading in the image changes, yet the motion field is zero.

Differentiation of this perspective projection equation yields

$$\frac{1}{f'}\mathbf{v}_i = \frac{(\mathbf{r}_o \cdot \hat{\mathbf{z}})\mathbf{v}_o - (\mathbf{v}_o \cdot \hat{\mathbf{z}})\mathbf{r}_o}{(\mathbf{r}_o \cdot \hat{\mathbf{z}})^2} = \frac{(\mathbf{r}_o \times \mathbf{v}_o) \times \hat{\mathbf{z}}}{(\mathbf{r}_o \cdot \hat{\mathbf{z}})^2}.$$

We shall not pursue this any further in this chapter. What is important here is that a vector can be assigned in this way to every image point. These vectors constitute the motion field.

Neighboring points on an object have similar velocities. We expect, then, that the induced motion field in the image is also continuous in most places. Exceptions will occur on the silhouettes of the images of the objects, where discontinuities in the motion field can be expected.

12.2 Optical Flow

Brightness patterns in the image move as the objects that give rise to them move. *Optical flow* is the apparent motion of the brightness pattern. Ideally the optical flow will correspond to the motion field, but we show next that this need not always be so.

Consider first a perfectly uniform sphere rotating in front of an imaging system (figure 12-2a). There will be spatial variation of brightness, or

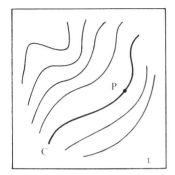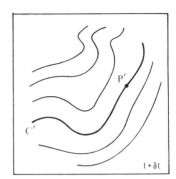

Figure 12-3. The apparent motion of brightness patterns is an awkward concept. It is not easy to decide which point P' on a contour C' of constant brightness in the second image corresponds to a particular point P on the corresponding contour C in the first image.

shading, in the image of the sphere, since the surface is curved. This shading, however, does not move with the surface, and so the image does not change with time. In this case the optical flow is zero everywhere, despite a nonzero motion field. Next, consider a fixed sphere illuminated by a moving light source (figure 12-2b). The shading in the image will change as the source moves. In this case the optical flow is clearly nonzero, while the motion field is zero everywhere. Virtual images and shadows lead us to other cases in which the optical flow is not equal to the motion field.

What is accessible to us is the optical flow, and we shall have to depend on the fact that, except for special situations such as the ones discussed above, the optical flow is not too different from the motion field. This will allow us to estimate relative motion by means of the changing image.

What do we mean by apparent motion of the brightness pattern? Consider a point P in the image with brightness E at time t (figure 12-3). To which point P' in the image at time $t + \delta t$ does it correspond—that is, how did the brightness pattern move in the intervening time? Typically there will be many points near P with the same brightness E. If brightness varies continuously in the part of the image of interest, then the point P will lie on an isobrightness contour C. At time $t + \delta t$ there will be some nearby isobrightness contour C' with the same brightness level. But what is the correspondence between points on C and points on C'? This question is hard to answer since the two contours will typically not even have exactly the same shape.

We thus note that the optical flow is not uniquely determined by local information in the changing image. Another example will make this clear.

Consider a patch of uniform brightness in the image that does not change with time. Perhaps the "most likely" optical flow is one that is zero everywhere. But in fact within the uniform patch we can assign any pattern of vector displacements we like. Presumably, though, we would prefer the simplest explanation of the observed changing (or in this case unchanging) image.

Let $E(x, y, t)$ be the irradiance at time t at the image point (x, y). Then, if $u(x, y)$ and $v(x, y)$ are the x and y components of the optical flow vector at that point, we expect that the irradiance will be the same at time $t + \delta t$ at the point $(x + \delta x, y + \delta y)$, where $\delta x = u \delta t$ and $\delta y = v \delta t$. That is,

$$E(x + u\, \delta t, y + v\, \delta t, t + \delta t) = E(x, y, t)$$

for a small time interval δt. This single constraint is not sufficient to determine both u and v uniquely. It is also clear that we can take advantage of the fact that the motion field is continuous almost everywhere.

If brightness varies smoothly with x, y, and t, we can expand the left-hand side of the equation above in a Taylor series and so obtain

$$E(x, y, t) + \delta x \frac{\partial E}{\partial x} + \delta y \frac{\partial E}{\partial y} + \delta t \frac{\partial E}{\partial t} + e = E(x, y, t),$$

where e contains second- and higher-order terms in δx, δy, and δt. Canceling $E(x, y, t)$, dividing through by δt, and taking the limit as $\delta t \to 0$, we obtain

$$\frac{\partial E}{\partial x} \frac{dx}{dt} + \frac{\partial E}{\partial y} \frac{dy}{dt} + \frac{\partial E}{\partial t} = 0,$$

which is actually just the expansion of the equation

$$\frac{dE}{dt} = 0$$

in the total derivative of E with respect to time. Using the abbreviations

$$u = \frac{dx}{dt}, \qquad v = \frac{dy}{dt},$$

$$E_x = \frac{\partial E}{\partial x}, \quad E_y = \frac{\partial E}{\partial y}, \quad E_t = \frac{\partial E}{\partial t},$$

we obtain

$$E_x u + E_y v + E_t = 0.$$

The derivatives E_x, E_y, and E_t are estimated from the image. The above equation is called the *optical flow constraint equation*, since it expresses a constraint on the components u and v of the optical flow.

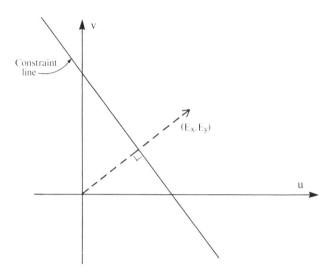

Figure 12-4. Local information on the brightness gradient and the rate of change of brightness with time provides only one constraint on the components of the optical flow vector. The flow velocity has to lie along a straight line perpendicular to the direction of the brightness gradient. We can only determine the component in the direction of the brightness gradient. Nothing is known about the flow component in the direction at right angles.

Consider a two-dimensional space with axes u and v, which we shall call *velocity space* (figure 12-4). Values of (u, v) satisfying the constraint equation lie on a straight line in velocity space. All that a local measurement can do is to identify this constraint line. We can rewrite the constraint equation in the form

$$(E_x, E_y) \cdot (u, v) = -E_t.$$

The component of optical flow in the direction of the brightness gradient $(E_x, E_y)^T$ is thus

$$\frac{E_t}{\sqrt{E_x^2 + E_y^2}}.$$

We cannot, however, determine the component of the optical flow at right angles to this direction, that is, along the isobrightness contour. This ambiguity is also known as the *aperture problem*.

12.3 Smoothness of the Optical Flow

Now it is time to introduce additional constraint. In chapter 17, where we

explore passive navigation, we shall make the assumption that we are dealing with rigid bodies. In that case, translation and rotation of the camera
relative to the object are the key parameters to recover. The assumption of
rigid body motion is very restrictive and provides a powerful constraint on
the solution. Here, however, we want to explore less limiting assumptions
so that we can deal with more general situations, such as deforming elastic
bodies.

Usually the motion field varies smoothly in most parts of the image.
We shall try to minimize a measure of departure from smoothness,

$$e_s = \iint \left((u_x^2 + u_y^2) + (v_x^2 + v_y^2) \right) \, dx \, dy,$$

the integral of the square of the magnitude of the gradient of the optical
flow. The error in the optical flow constraint equation,

$$e_c = \iint \left(E_x u + E_y v + E_t \right)^2 dx \, dy,$$

should also be small. Overall, then, we want to minimize $e_s + \lambda e_c$, where λ is
a parameter that weights the error in the image motion equation relative to
the departure from smoothness. This parameter will be large if brightness
measurements are accurate and small if they are noisy. Minimizing an
integral of the form

$$\iint F(u, v, u_x, u_y, v_x, v_y) \, dx \, dy$$

is a problem in the calculus of variations (see the appendix). The corresponding Euler equations are

$$F_u - \frac{\partial}{\partial x} F_{u_x} - \frac{\partial}{\partial y} F_{u_y} = 0,$$

$$F_v - \frac{\partial}{\partial x} F_{v_x} - \frac{\partial}{\partial y} F_{v_y} = 0.$$

In our case,

$$F = (u_x^2 + u_y^2) + (v_x^2 + v_y^2) + \lambda \left(E_x u + E_y v + E_t \right)^2,$$

so the Euler equations yield

$$\nabla^2 u = \lambda \left(E_x u + E_y v + E_t \right) E_x,$$

$$\nabla^2 v = \lambda \left(E_x u + E_y v + E_t \right) E_y,$$

where

$$\nabla^2 = \frac{\partial^2}{\partial x^2} + \frac{\partial^2}{\partial y^2}$$

is the Laplacian operator. This coupled pair of elliptic second-order partial differential equations can be solved using iterative methods.

12.4 Filling in Optical Flow Information

We can derive some information about the solution method by inspecting these equations. For example, where the brightness gradient is zero, the right-hand sides of the equations are also zero. In these regions, u and v each satisfy Laplace's equation. Thus, in regions of uniform brightness, where the optical flow velocity cannot be found locally, it is interpolated from the optical flow velocities in surrounding areas. Similarly, along an edge, the optical flow component in the direction of the edge itself cannot be found but must be interpolated from values further along the edge. In this case, however, the motion of the edge itself at least provides constraint in the direction of the brightness gradient.

At a corner, the direction of the brightness gradient changes rapidly as we go from one picture cell to another, so that constraint is available in a small neighborhood to determine the optical flow fully. Reliable information is available at *brightness corners*, less so at places where brightness is constant along some direction in the image, and least where brightness does not vary spatially at all. In the case of a rectangular region of uniform brightness moving against a background, information is filled in from the corners and the edges.

12.5 Boundary Conditions

A problem is said to be *well-posed* if a solution exists and if the solution is unique. A partial differential equation typically has an infinite number of solutions unless it is constrained by suitable boundary conditions. Hence, a problem leading to a partial differential equation is well-posed when boundary conditions are given that will ensure a unique solution. In the case of an elliptic linear second-order partial differential equation, such as Poisson's equation, giving the value of the function on a simply closed curve enclosing the region of interest is one way to guarantee a unique solution. Alternatively, we can give the *normal derivative*, that is, the derivative of the unknown function in a direction perpendicular to the boundary curve. Higher-order differential equations typically require additional constraint, such as both the value of the function and the normal derivative.

When we use the calculus of variations, we may have information about the behavior of the solution on the boundary, or we may instead allow the boundary to be free. The latter case leads to *natural boundary conditions* (see the appendix for more details). In minimizing an integral of the form

$$\iint F(u, v, u_x, u_y, v_x, v_y)\, dx\, dy$$

the natural boundary conditions can be shown to be

$$F_{u_x}\frac{dy}{ds} = F_{u_y}\frac{dx}{ds} \qquad \text{and} \qquad F_{v_x}\frac{dy}{ds} = F_{v_y}\frac{dx}{ds},$$

where s denotes arclength along the boundary curve. Now

$$\hat{\mathbf{n}} = \left(\frac{dy}{ds}, -\frac{dx}{ds}\right)^T$$

is a unit vector perpendicular to the boundary. We can thus rewrite the above conditions in the form

$$\left(F_{u_x}, F_{u_y}\right)^T \cdot \hat{\mathbf{n}} = \mathbf{0} \qquad \text{and} \qquad \left(F_{v_x}, F_{v_y}\right)^T \cdot \hat{\mathbf{n}} = \mathbf{0}.$$

In our case,

$$\left(u_x, u_y\right)^T \cdot \hat{\mathbf{n}} = \mathbf{0} \qquad \text{and} \qquad \left(v_x, v_y\right)^T \cdot \hat{\mathbf{n}} = \mathbf{0},$$

that is, the normal derivatives of u and v must be zero.

12.6 The Discrete Case

We could now approximate the continuous solution using a finite-difference scheme, but readers not yet comfortable with the calculus of variations might prefer the following direct method. Using the values of the optical flow at the grid point (i, j) and its neighbors (figure 12-5) allows us to measure the departure from smoothness as

$$s_{i,j} = \frac{1}{4}\big((u_{i+1,j} - u_{i,j})^2 + (u_{i,j+1} - u_{i,j})^2$$

$$+ (v_{i+1,j} - v_{i,j})^2 + (v_{i,j+1} - v_{i,j})^2\big),$$

while the error in the optical flow constraint equation is

$$c_{ij} = \left(E_x u_{ij} + E_y v_{ij} + E_t\right)^2,$$

where E_x, E_y, and E_t are estimates of the rates of change of brightness with respect to x, y, and t at the point (i, j). We seek a set of values $\{u_{ij}\}$ and $\{v_{ij}\}$ that minimize

$$e = \sum_i \sum_j (s_{ij} + \lambda\, c_{ij}).$$

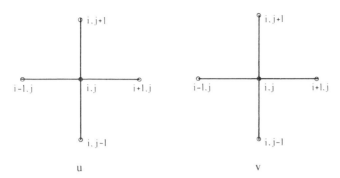

Figure 12-5. The sum of squares of the first partial derivatives of u and v can be estimated using the differences of the optical flow components at neighboring points.

Differentiating e with respect to u_{kl} and v_{kl} yields

$$\frac{\partial e}{\partial u_{kl}} = 2(u_{kl} - \bar{u}_{kl}) + 2\lambda \left(E_x u_{kl} + E_y v_{kl} + E_t\right) E_x,$$

$$\frac{\partial e}{\partial v_{kl}} = 2(v_{kl} - \bar{v}_{kl}) + 2\lambda \left(E_x u_{kl} + E_y v_{kl} + E_t\right) E_y,$$

where $\bar{u}$ and $\bar{v}$ are local averages of u and v. The extremum occurs where the above derivatives of e are zero. The resultant equations can be rewritten in the form

$$(1 + \lambda E_x^2)u_{kl} + \lambda E_x E_y v_{kl} = \bar{u}_{kl} - \lambda E_x E_t,$$

$$\lambda E_y E_x u_{kl} + (1 + \lambda E_y^2)v_{kl} = \bar{v}_{kl} - \lambda E_y E_t.$$

We can think of this as a pair of equations in u_{kl} and v_{kl}. The determinant of the 2×2 coefficient matrix is

$$1 + \lambda(E_x^2 + E_y^2),$$

so that

$$\left(1 + \lambda(E_x^2 + E_y^2)\right) u_{kl} = +(1 + \lambda E_y^2)\bar{u}_{kl} - \lambda E_x E_y \bar{v}_{kl} - \lambda E_x E_t,$$

$$\left(1 + \lambda(E_x^2 + E_y^2)\right) v_{kl} = -\lambda E_y E_x \bar{u}_{kl} + (1 + \lambda E_x^2)\bar{v}_{kl} - \lambda E_y E_t.$$

We can solve these equations now for u_{kl} and v_{kl}. The result immediately

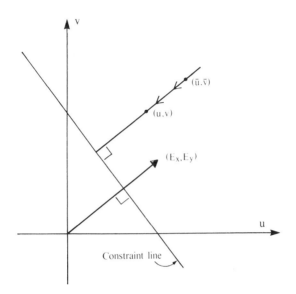

Figure 12-6. In the iterative scheme for estimating the optical flow, the new value (u, v) at a point is the average of the values of the neighbors, $(\bar{u}, \bar{v})$, minus an adjustment in the direction toward the constraint line.

suggests an iterative scheme such as

$$u_{kl}^{n+1} = \bar{u}_{kl}^n - \frac{E_x \bar{u}_{kl}^n + E_y \bar{v}_{kl}^n + E_t}{1 + \lambda(E_x^2 + E_y^2)} E_x,$$

$$v_{kl}^{n+1} = \bar{v}_{kl}^n - \frac{E_x \bar{u}_{kl}^n + E_y \bar{v}_{kl}^n + E_t}{1 + \lambda(E_x^2 + E_y^2)} E_y.$$

There is an interesting geometric interpretation of these equations (figure 12-6). The new value of (u, v) at a point is set equal to the average of the surrounding values, minus an adjustment, which in velocity space is in the direction of the brightness gradient.

To implement this scheme we need to estimate the spatial and time derivatives of brightness. This can be done easily using first differences of values on a grid (figure 12-7). If the indices i, j, and k correspond to x, y, and t, respectively, then consistent estimates of the three first partial derivatives can be obtained as follows:

$$E_x \approx \frac{1}{4\delta x} \left(E_{i+1,j,k} + E_{i+1,j,k+1} + E_{i+1,j+1,k} + E_{i+1,j+1,k+1} \right)$$

$$- \frac{1}{4\delta x} \left(E_{i,j,k} + E_{i,j,k+1} + E_{i,j+1,k} + E_{i,j+1,k+1} \right),$$

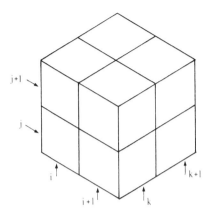

Figure 12-7. The first derivatives required in the iterative scheme can be estimated using first differences in a $2 \times 2 \times 2$ cube of brightness values. The estimates apply to the point where four picture cells meet, at a time halfway between two successive images.

$$E_y \approx \frac{1}{4\,\delta y}\left(E_{i,j+1,k} + E_{i,j+1,k+1} + E_{i+1,j+1,k} + E_{i+1,j+1,k+1}\right)$$

$$-\frac{1}{4\,\delta y}\left(E_{i,j,k} + E_{i,j,k+1} + E_{i+1,j,k} + E_{i+1,j,k+1}\right),$$

$$E_t \approx \frac{1}{4\,\delta t}\left(E_{i,j,k+1} + E_{i,j+1,k+1} + E_{i+1,j,k+1} + E_{i+1,j+1,k+1}\right)$$

$$-\frac{1}{4\,\delta t}\left(E_{i,j,k} + E_{i,j+1,k} + E_{i+1,j,k} + E_{i+1,j+1,k}\right).$$

This means that the optical flow velocities will be estimated at points lying between picture cells and between successive frames.

Figure 12-8 shows four successive synthetic images of a rotating sphere covered with a smoothly varying brightness pattern. Spatial and time derivatives of brightness estimated from these images provide the input to the iterative optical flow algorithm described above.

The estimated optical flow after 1, 4, 16, and 64 iterations is shown in figure 12-9. The first guess is influenced strongly by the brightness pattern on the sphere. After a few iterations, the estimated flow vectors converge to the correct solution, except on the silhouette.

The computed motion field is shown for comparison in figure 12-10b. The estimated optical flow shown in figure 12-10a differs only a little from the motion field, except on the silhouette.

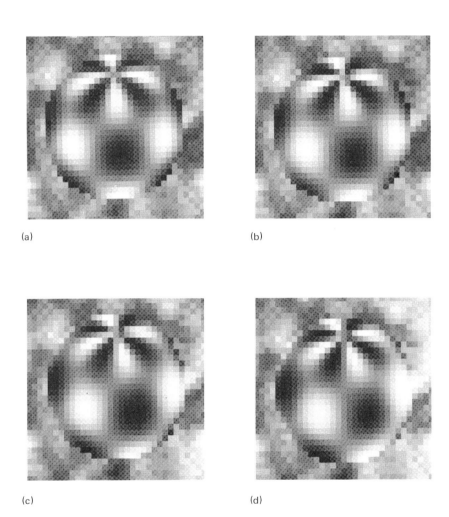

(a)   (b)

(c)   (d)

Figure 12-8. Four frames of a synthetic image sequence showing a sphere slowly rotating in front of a randomly patterned background.

12.7 Discontinuities in Optical Flow

There will be discontinuities in the optical flow on the silhouettes, where one object occludes another. We must detect these places if we are to prevent the method presented above from trying to continue the solution smoothly from one region to the other. This seems like a chicken-and-egg problem: If we have a good estimate of the optical flow, we can look for places where it changes very rapidly in order to segment the picture. On

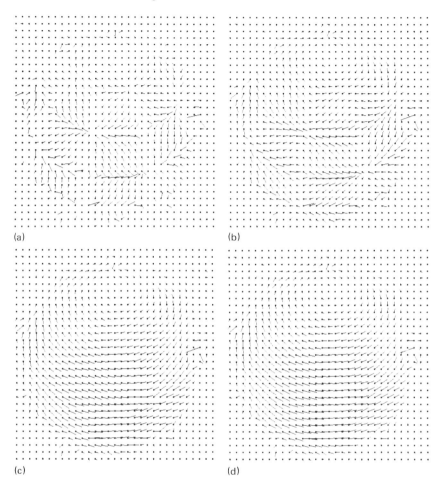

(a)

(b)

(c)

(d)

Figure 12-9. Estimates of the optical flow shown in the form of needle diagrams after 1, 4, 16, and 64 iterations of the algorithm.

the other hand, if we could segment the picture well, we would produce a better estimate of the optical flow. The solution to this dilemma is to incorporate the segmentation into the iterative solution for the optical flow. That is, after each iteration we look for places where the flow changes rapidly. At these places we set down marks that inhibit the next iteration from smoothly connecting the solution across the discontinuities. We first set the threshold for this decision very high in order to prevent premature carving up of the image. We reduce the threshold as better and better estimates of the optical flow become available.

We can get some feel for how well our assumption of smoothness holds

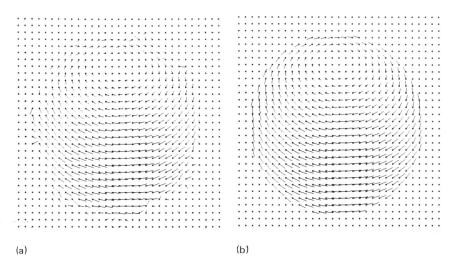

(a)   (b)

Figure 12-10. (a) The estimated optical flow after several more iterations. (b) The computed motion field.

up in situations of practical interest. A common case is that of an object performing a rigid body motion, a translation, and a rotation. For simplicity, we shall work here with orthographic projection. Translation leads to uniform optical flow in the image region corresponding to the moving object. The flow within that region is (exceptionally) smooth. As expected, there will be discontinuities at the boundaries of the region, where the object occludes the background.

Rotation is a little harder to understand. First of all, we are concerned here with instantaneous quantities only. That is, we are concerned only with derivatives of coordinates at a particular instant in time; we do not follow the motion over time. We show in exercise 12-6 that rotation about an arbitrary axis is equivalent to rotation about a parallel axis through the origin, combined with a translation. This compensating translation is equal to the cross-product of a vector from the origin to the axis and the rotation vector. In any case, we can, without loss of generality, restrict our attention to rotation about an axis through the origin.

Suppose that the rotation of the object is specified by the vector $\omega = (\alpha, \beta, \gamma)^T$, where the length of the vector gives the rate of rotation, while the axis of rotation lies along the vector. The velocity of a point on the object is equal to the cross-product of a vector $\mathbf{r} = (x, y, z)^T$, from the axis of rotation to the point, and the given rotation vector ω. Since we are dealing with orthographic projection, the image coordinates x' and y' are the same as the object coordinates x and y, respectively. The components

u and v of the optical flow are just the x and y components of the velocity of the point on the object:

$$u = \beta z - \gamma y \qquad \text{and} \qquad v = \gamma x - \alpha z.$$

It is now trivial to determine the departure from smoothness of the optical flow. We have

$$(u_x^2 + u_y^2) + (v_x^2 + v_y^2) = (\alpha^2 + \beta^2)(z_x^2 + z_y^2) - 2\gamma(\alpha z_x + \beta z_y) + 2\gamma^2.$$

The optical flow will not be smooth near silhouettes of smoothly curved objects, since the slope of the surface approaches infinity there. Moreover, rotation about the optical axis increases the measure that we used for the departure from smoothness.

An important application of the method for computing the optical flow is in passive navigation. Here we must determine the path and instantaneous attitude of a vehicle from information gleaned about the environment, but without emitting sampling radiation from the vehicle. This is a subject to which we shall return in chapter 17.

12.8 References

The books by Hildreth, *The Measurement of Visual Motion* [1983], and Ullman, *The Interpretation of Visual Motion* [1979], discuss the determination and interpretation of visual motion. Huang edited a collection of work presented at a NATO conference in *Image Sequence Processing and Dynamic Scene Analysis* [1983].

The calculus of variations is treated in many books, including volume I of *Methods of Mathematical Physics* by Courant & Hilbert [1953] and *Calculus of Variations: With Applications to Physics & Engineering* by Weinstock [1974].

There are numerous books discussing partial differential equations, among them *Partial Differential Equations: Theory and Technique* by Carrier & Pearson [1976], volume II of *Methods of Mathematical Physics* by Courant & Hilbert [1962], *Partial Differential Equations* by John [1971], and a book of the same title by Moon & Spencer [1969]. Regularization is discussed by Tikhonov & Arsenin in *Solutions of Ill-Posed Problems*, [1977].

Some of the earliest work on time-varying imagery had as its motive compression of the highly redundant video signal of a typical slow-changing scene. See, for example, Limb & Murphy [1975], Netravali & Robbins [1979], and Stuller, Netravali, & Robbins [1980]. Other early work was done by Fennema & Thompson [1979].

Gibson coined the term "optical flow." For some of his ideas, see Gibson et al. [1959]. This area has seen tremendous activity in the last five years. Horn & Schunck [1981] developed a simple iterative algorithm for estimating the optical flow. Schunck & Horn [1981] expanded on this and explored a slightly different approach. Edges at various scales contain most of the information in an image, and Hildreth [1983, 1984] has therefore approached the problem from the point of view of determining the motion of curves, such as zero-crossing contours, rather than the brightness pattern directly. Nagel [1982, 1983a] has developed methods for tracking brightness corners. One of his schemes [1983b] is a complex modification of the method developed by Horn & Schunck that allows smoothing effects to propagate only in certain directions.

Another approach to the problem involves tracking distinctive brightness patterns in the image. Edges in particular seem to be suitable targets for such an effort, as shown by Haynes & Jain [1982] and Hildreth [1983, 1984]. Other relevant papers include Thompson [1981], Marr & Ullman [1981], Ullman [1981], Schalkoff & McVey [1982], Paquin & Dubois [1983], Wohn, Davis, & Thrift [1983] and Longuet-Higgins & Prazdny [1980].

12.9 Exercises

12-1 Optical flow cannot be determined locally in image regions where brightness is constant and thus the brightness gradient is zero. The method presented in this chapter fills the flow in from the surround using Laplace's equation. Here we investigate circumstances in which the filling-in operation happens to produce exactly the desired result.

(a) Consider a brightness pattern translating with velocity (u_0, v_0) in the image. Suppose that the optical flow velocity has been determined accurately on the border ∂R of some region R where brightness is constant. Show that the solutions of the Laplace equations $\nabla^2 u = 0$ and $\nabla^2 v = 0$, given the boundary conditions, produce the correct optical flow in the region R. Hint: The expected flow will be the unique solution of the problem if and only if the Laplacian within the region is zero and the flow satisfies the boundary conditions.

(b) Does the filling-in method always produce the correct optical flow in the case of translation of the camera parallel to a planar surface that is perpendicular to the optical axis?

(c) Consider a brightness pattern rotating about the image point (x_0, y_0) with angular velocity ω. What is the optical flow? Suppose that the optical flow velocity has been determined accurately on the border ∂R of some region R in which brightness is constant. Do the solutions of the Laplace equations $\nabla^2 u = 0$ and $\nabla^2 v = 0$, given the boundary conditions, produce the correct optical flow in the region R?

(d) Does the filling-in method always produce the correct optical flow in the case of rotation of the camera about the optical axis?

12-2   Consider a camera moving along its optical axis toward a planar surface at right angles to the optical axis.

(a) Show that the optical flow is given by

$$u = \frac{W}{Z}x \qquad \text{and} \qquad v = \frac{W}{Z}y,$$

where W is the velocity and Z the distance to the plane. (Note the lack of dependence on the focal length of the lens.)

(b) Is the optical flow stationary (that is, independent of time)?

(c) Is the Laplacian of the optical flow zero?

(d) How could you predict the time to impact? (Note that this can be done despite the fact that we cannot recover the absolute value of either height or velocity.)

12-3   Here we consider some optical flow patterns that do not correspond to rigid body motions.

(a) Suppose you are looking down on the surface of a liquid in a container with a flat bottom. The liquid is running out of a hole in the center of the bottom of the container. If you assume that the depth of the liquid is constant (despite the flow), what is the optical flow? Assume that the optical axis is perpendicular to the surface of the liquid and that it passes through the hole. Hint: The flow of liquid through any one cylindrical surface with axis passing through the hole must equal the flow through any other cylindrical surface with axis passing through the hole.

(b) Find the Laplacian of the flow in the above case. Is there a singularity (that is, a place where the flow becomes infinite)?

(c) A cross section through a flow vortex, around a line in three dimensions, shows circular symmetry with no material moving inward or outward. Furthermore, the angular momentum of a layer of given thickness at one radial distance from the line is the same as that of another layer at a different radial distance. What is the optical flow?

(d) Find the Laplacian of the flow in the above case. Is there a singularity?

12-4   Show that the Laplacian of a second-order polynomial in x and y is zero if the coefficients of x^2 and y^2 are equal in magnitude and opposite in sign. Apply this result to the previous problems.

12-5   Suppose we use as the measure of departure from smoothness the integral

$$e_s = \iint \left(\nabla^2 u\right)^2 + \left(\nabla^2 v\right)^2 \, dx\,dy,$$

instead of

$$e_s = \iint \left((u_x^2 + u_y^2) + (v_x^2 + v_y^2)\right) \, dx\,dy.$$

What would be the appropriate Euler equations?

12-6   Show that rotation about an arbitrary axis is equivalent to rotation about an axis through the origin combined with a translation. Show that the compensating translation is equal to the cross-product of a vector from the origin to the axis and the rotation vector.

12-7   A rigid body rotates about an axis through the origin. The axis of rotation is parallel to the vector $\boldsymbol{\omega}$, while the angular velocity is given by the magnitude of this vector. The velocity of a point $\mathbf{r}$ on the body is the cross-product $\boldsymbol{\omega} \times \mathbf{r}$. Define $\mathbf{r} = (x, y, z)^T$ and $\boldsymbol{\omega} = (\alpha, \beta, \gamma)^T$. Show that the smoothness of the optical flow is related to the smoothness of the rotating body. What happens on the silhouette? Assume orthographic projection. Hint: Show that $\nabla^2 u$ and $\nabla^2 v$ are related to $\nabla^2 z$.

12-8   Here we study the interaction of shading and motion. When an object moves in front of a camera, the brightness at a given point in the image changes, because different patches of surface are imaged there at different times. These patches can have different reflectance properties and different orientations. We assume from now on that the reflectance map is the same for all points on the surface and consider only the effect of varying surface orientation. Now, when a new patch is brought into view, we must, first of all, consider how its orientation, before it was moved, differed from that of the old patch. This is not sufficient, however. We must also take into account how the orientation of the new patch was changed by rotation.

(a) Suppose a part of the surface of the object translates in such a way that the corresponding image patch has velocity (u, v) in the xy-plane. What is the rate of change of p and q due to this motion alone? Show that the resulting change in brightness is

$$\frac{dE}{dt} = \frac{dR}{dt} = - \begin{pmatrix} u & v \end{pmatrix} \begin{pmatrix} r & s \\ s & t \end{pmatrix} \begin{pmatrix} R_p \\ R_q \end{pmatrix},$$

where r, s, and t are the second partial derivatives of z. Rewrite this in terms of the image brightness gradient $(E_x, E_y)^T$. Hint: Note that the x-coordinate of the point on the surface that corresponds to a fixed place in the image decreases with time.

(b) A rigid body rotates about an axis through the origin. The axis of rotation is parallel to the vector $\boldsymbol{\omega}$, while the angular velocity is given by the magnitude of this vector. Consider a point with coordinates $\mathbf{r} = (x, y, z)^T$, and let the components of the rotation vector be given by $\boldsymbol{\omega} = (\alpha, \beta, \gamma)^T$. Show that

$$\frac{d\mathbf{r}}{dt} = \begin{pmatrix} \beta z - \gamma y \\ \gamma x - \alpha z \\ \alpha y - \beta x \end{pmatrix}.$$

Now assume orthographic projection, that is, $x' = x$ and $y' = y$. What is the induced motion field (u, v) in this case?

(c) As the object rotates, the orientation of a particular patch changes. Find $d\hat{\mathbf{n}}/dt$ in terms of $\boldsymbol{\omega}$ and $\hat{\mathbf{n}}$. Next, find an expression for $d\hat{\mathbf{n}}/dt$ in terms of dp/dt and dq/dt by differentiating the equation

$$\hat{\mathbf{n}} = \frac{\mathbf{n}}{\mathbf{n} \cdot \hat{\mathbf{v}}},$$

where

$$\mathbf{n} = (-p, -q, 1)^T \quad \text{and} \quad \mathbf{n} \cdot \hat{\mathbf{v}} = \sqrt{1 + p^2 + q^2}.$$

By identifying suitable terms, show that in this case

$$\frac{\partial p}{\partial t} = pq\,\alpha - (1 + p^2)\beta - q\,\gamma,$$

$$\frac{\partial q}{\partial t} = (1 + q^2)\alpha - pq\,\beta + p\,\gamma.$$

(d) An object rotates in front of an image-forming system. As already mentioned, the brightness changes at a point in the image can be thought of as resulting from two contributions:

- A portion of the surface with a different orientation is brought into view.

- The surface patch brought into view is rotated as it is moved, thus changing its orientation.

We computed the first contribution in part (a), assuming a motion field (u, v). In part (b) we computed the velocity of the image point corresponding to a particular point on the object. For simplicity we assume orthographic projection, so that x' and y' in the image are just the first two components of $\mathbf{r} = (x, y, z)^T$. The second contribution was computed in part (c). Now combine these two to find dp/dt and dq/dt as functions of the components of $\boldsymbol{\omega} = (\alpha, \beta, \gamma)^T$.

(e) As an application of these results, consider a sphere of radius R with center at the origin. Show that

$$p = -\frac{x}{z} \quad \text{and} \quad q = -\frac{y}{z}.$$

Also show that

$$r = -\frac{1}{z}\left(1 + \left(\frac{x}{z}\right)^2\right), \quad s = -\frac{xy}{z^3}, \quad \text{and} \quad t = -\frac{1}{z}\left(1 + \left(\frac{y}{z}\right)^2\right).$$

What is the determinant of the Hessian matrix?

(f) Substitute these results for the first and second partial derivatives of z into the formulae for dp/dt and dq/dt developed in part (d). Show that

$$\frac{dE}{dt} = 0$$

for any rotation $\boldsymbol{\omega}$, as expected for a rotating sphere with uniform surface properties.

12-9 In developing machine vision algorithms, it is often useful to start with a controlled situation in which the answer is known. This usually requires use of synthetic images based on models of surface shape, reflectance, and motion. Suppose you are asked to create synthetic image data for a proposed optical flow algorithm. Assume that the surface is given as a function of two parameters, ξ and η. The radiance of the surface is $L(\xi, \eta)$. The surface is translating with velocity $\mathbf{t}$ and rotating with angular velocity $\boldsymbol{\omega}$ relative to the viewer. Describe how you would create the synthetic image and determine its spatial and time derivatives.

12-10 Here we study the optical flow produced by a rotating sphere covered with a pattern of varying reflectance. Our aim is to determine whether the optical flow constraint equation holds.

Consider a sphere of radius R, with center at the origin, rotating about the y-axis with angular velocity ω. An image is obtained by orthographic projection along the z-axis. That is, $x' = x$ and $y' = y$, where (x', y') are the coordinates of a point in the image corresponding to the point $(x, y, z)^T$ on the surface of the sphere.

Points on the sphere can be referenced using longitude ξ and latitude η at time $t = 0$. This coordinate system rotates with the sphere, so that a particular surface marking is associated with fixed (ξ, η). We shall need transformations between image coordinates and coordinates on the surface of the sphere.

(a) Find formulae for x' and y' in terms of ξ, η, and t. Find formulae for ξ and η in terms of x', y', and t.

(b) Determine the components u and v of the motion field. Is the motion field stationary (that is, constant with respect to time)?

(c) Show that the Jacobian of the coordinate transformation from (x', y') to (ξ, η) is

$$J = \begin{pmatrix} \frac{\partial \xi}{\partial x'} & \frac{\partial \xi}{\partial y'} \\ \frac{\partial \eta}{\partial x'} & \frac{\partial \eta}{\partial y'} \end{pmatrix} = \begin{pmatrix} \frac{1}{\sqrt{R^2 - x^2 - y^2}} & \frac{xy}{(R^2 - y^2)\sqrt{R^2 - x^2 - y^2}} \\ 0 & \frac{1}{\sqrt{R^2 - y^2}} \end{pmatrix}.$$

Hint: If $\tan \theta = a/b$, then

$$\frac{d\theta}{dx} = \frac{1}{1 + (a/b)^2} \frac{d}{dx}\left(\frac{a}{b}\right) = \frac{b\frac{da}{dx} - a\frac{db}{dx}}{a^2 + b^2}.$$

Now suppose that a reflectance pattern $R(\xi, \eta)$ on the sphere is given in terms of longitude ξ and latitude η. Image brightness will be proportional to reflectance, provided that the sphere is illuminated evenly from all directions.

(d) Determine E_x, E_y, and E_t in terms of R_ξ and R_η, using the chain rule for differentiation and the partial derivatives in the Jacobian.

(e) Is the optical flow constraint equation,

$$uE_x + vE_y + E_t = 0,$$

satisfied everywhere, independent of the reflectance pattern on the sphere? If not, how should it be modified? Warning: This may be tricky.

13

Photogrammetry & Stereo

When one asks how it is that we can see objects in depth, that vision is "three-dimensional," the most common reply is that we use the difference between the images in our left and right eyes to judge depth. While binocular stereo provides only one of many depth cues, it is the one that, superficially at least, seems easiest to understand. Points on the surfaces of objects are imaged in different relative positions depending on their distances from the viewer.

We start this chapter by exploring photogrammetry, in order to understand how points in the environment are imaged by cameras in different positions and with different orientations. To interpret a stereo pair, we must start by recovering the transformation between the two camera coordinate systems. We begin with the simple situation in which both distances and directions are known. We then tackle the more difficult problem in which only directions are measured. We also apply these techniques to calibrate a machine vision coordinate system to a mechanical manipulator's coordinate system; this determines the *hand–eye* transform.

The key to an automated stereo system is a method for determining which point in one image corresponds to a given point in the other image. We leave this, the most challenging part of the problem, to the end. A number of different approaches are discussed, including correlation methods, gray-level matching, and edge-based methods. At this time, edge-based

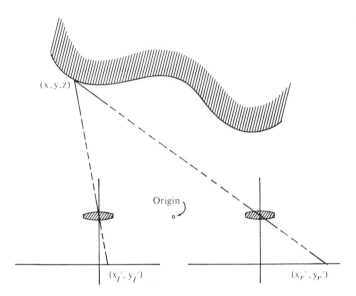

Figure 13-1. Simple camera geometry for stereo photography. The optical axes are parallel to one another and perpendicular to the baseline connecting the two cameras.

methods appear to be the most successful, but they provide only sparse depth information. Interpolation must be employed to fill in the rest. We end the chapter by discussing methods for smooth interpolation.

13.1 Disparity between the Two Images

A simple example will illustrate the basic geometry. Suppose that we rigidly attach two cameras to each other so that their optical axes are parallel and separated by a distance b (figure 13-1). The line connecting the lens centers is called the *baseline*. Assume that the baseline is perpendicular to the optical axes and orient the x-axis so that it is parallel to the baseline. The coordinates of a point $(x, y, z)^T$ in the environment are measured relative to an origin midway between the lens centers. Let the image coordinates in the left and right images be (x'_l, y'_l) and (x'_r, y'_r), respectively. Then

$$\frac{x'_l}{f} = \frac{x + b/2}{z} \qquad \text{and} \qquad \frac{x'_r}{f} = \frac{x - b/2}{z},$$

while

$$\frac{y'_l}{f} = \frac{y'_r}{f} = \frac{y}{z},$$

where f is the distance from the lens center to the image plane in both cameras. These three equations can be solved for the three unknowns x, y, and z. First, note that

$$\frac{x_l' - x_r'}{f} = \frac{b}{z}.$$

The difference in image coordinates, $x_l' - x_r'$, is called the *disparity*. We have

$$x = b\,\frac{(x_l' + x_r')/2}{x_l' - x_r'}, \quad y = b\,\frac{(y_l' + y_r')/2}{x_l' - x_r'}, \quad z = b\,\frac{f}{x_l' - x_r'}.$$

Distance is inversely proportional to disparity. The distance to near objects can therefore be measured accurately, while that to far objects cannot. Note also that the disparity is directly proportional to b, the distance between lens centers. Thus, given a fixed error in determining the disparity, the accuracy of the depth determination increases with increasing baseline. Unfortunately, as the separation of the cameras increases, the two images become less similar. Some objects imaged by one camera may not even be visible to the other, for example. Disparity is also proportional to the effective focal distance f, because the images are magnified as the focal length is increased.

A point in the environment visible from both camera stations gives rise to a pair of image points called a *conjugate pair*. Note that a point in the right image corresponding to a specified point in the left image must lie somewhere on a particular line, because the two have the same y-coordinate. This line is the *epipolar line*. A feature that appears in the left image may or may not have a counterpart in the right image; but if it does, it must appear on the corresponding epipolar line. It cannot appear elsewhere. Note that for this simple geometry all epipolar lines are parallel to the x-axis. This is not true in the general case, as we shall see.

Figure 13-2 shows a stereo pair taken by Viking Lander I on the surface of Mars. The spacing between the pictures is chosen so as to permit viewing with a pocket stereoscope. Here we are interested primarily in measuring the disparity, though. The change in disparity from the horizon to the nearest rocks is quite dramatic, since the baseline is large (0.8 meter) and the nearest rocks are only a couple of meters away. It is instructive to measure the distance between corresponding points in the foreground and compare this with the distance between corresponding points nearer to the horizon.

13.2 Photogrammetry

In practice, the two cameras used to obtain a stereo pair will not be aligned exactly, as we have assumed so far in our simplified analysis. It would be very difficult to arrange for the optical axes to be exactly parallel and for

Figure 13-2. Views of the surface of Mars taken by two cameras mounted on Viking Lander I. Disparity changes rapidly as we move from the horizon toward the images of nearby rocks. (Pictures IPL PIC ID 78/10/19/171012 and 78/10/19/175118, courtesy of the National Space Science Data Center, Greenbelt, Maryland.)

the baseline to be exactly perpendicular to the optical axes. In fact, if the two cameras are to be exposed to more or less the same collection of objects, they may have to be turned so that their optical axes come closest within the region where these objects lie.

One of the most important practical applications of stereo is in photogrammetry. In this field the shape of the surface of an object is determined from overlapping photographs taken by carefully calibrated cameras. The information needed to generate topographic maps of the surface of the earth, for example, is obtained from a series of images taken at fixed intervals by a camera carried in an airplane along a predetermined flight line. With high enough resolution, topographic maps can even be derived from satellite images. Adjacent pairs of photographs are presented to the left and right eye in a device called a *stereo comparator* that makes it possible for an observer to accurately measure the disparity of identifiable points on the surface. Contour maps are then traced using an artificial floating mark whose apparent height can be selected by the operator.

The pilot of the plane taking the photographs always attempts to expose the film at predetermined positions with the optical axes oriented vertically, but departures from the ideal are the rule. Before we can use the resulting photographs, then, we must determine the relation between the camera's positions and orientations when the exposures were made. This

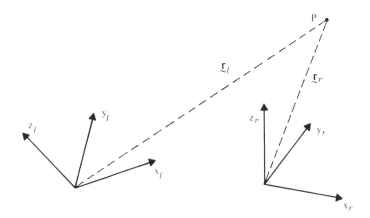

Figure 13-3. The transformation from one camera station to another can be represented by a rotation and a translation. The relation between the coordinates, $\mathbf{r}_l$ and $\mathbf{r}_r$, of a point P can be given by means of a rotation matrix and an offset vector.

process, called *relative orientation*, determines the transformation between coordinate systems fixed to the camera at the two exposure stations.

At times we also need to relate three-dimensional coordinates determined by a stereo system, or by some other system capable of measuring distances, such as a laser range finder, to coordinates measured in another system. This is the problem of *absolute orientation*, which we shall discuss first, since it is somewhat simpler to understand than the relative orientation problem.

The transformation between two camera stations can be treated as a rigid body motion and can thus be decomposed into a rotation and a translation (figure 13-3). If $\mathbf{r}_l = (x_l, y_l, z_l)^T$ is the position of point P measured in the left camera coordinate system and $\mathbf{r}_r = (x_r, y_r, z_r)^T$ is the position of the same point measured in the right camera coordinate system, then

$$\mathbf{r}_r = \mathbf{R}\,\mathbf{r}_l + \mathbf{r}_o,$$

where $\mathbf{R}$ is a 3×3 *orthonormal matrix* representing the rotation and $\mathbf{r}_o$ is an offset vector corresponding to the translation. An orthonormal matrix has columns that are mutually orthogonal unit vectors, so that

$$\mathbf{R}^T\mathbf{R} = \mathbf{I},$$

where $\mathbf{I}$ is the 3×3 identity matrix.

13.3 Absolute Orientation

In this section we assume that the actual three-dimensional coordinates $\mathbf{r}_l$ and $\mathbf{r}_r$ are known. The recovery of the relation between two coordinate systems is called *absolute orientation*. We use it, for example, when we have measured points using a stereo system in a coordinate system attached to the cameras and we know the coordinates of the same points in another system, perhaps that of a second stereo system or of a mechanical manipulator.

We can expand the equation $\mathbf{r}_r = \mathbf{R}\,\mathbf{r}_l + \mathbf{r}_o$ to

$$r_{11}x_l + r_{12}y_l + r_{13}z_l + r_{14} = x_r,$$

$$r_{21}x_l + r_{22}y_l + r_{23}z_l + r_{24} = y_r,$$

$$r_{31}x_l + r_{32}y_l + r_{33}z_l + r_{34} = z_r,$$

where the first three columns of coefficients, $r_{11} \ldots r_{31}$, $r_{12} \ldots r_{32}$, and $r_{13} \ldots r_{33}$, are the three columns of the rotation matrix $\mathbf{R}$, while the fourth column, $r_{14} \ldots r_{34}$, is the offset vector $\mathbf{r}_o$. Normally we might view this set of equations as a means of computing $\mathbf{r}_r = (x_r, y_r, z_r)^T$ given $\mathbf{r}_l = (x_l, y_l, z_l)^T$. Here we instead consider the coefficients $r_{11}, r_{12}, \ldots, r_{34}$ as unknowns to be determined given corresponding values of x_l, y_l, z_l, x_r, y_r, and z_r.

Clearly we cannot find twelve unknowns given only three equations. How can we impose more constraint? If we can identify several conjugate pairs, we can obtain several sets of equations. With four points, for example, we end up with twelve equations, enough to solve for the twelve unknowns. The equations are linear, so that in general there will be a unique solution, as shown in exercise 13-4.

13.3.1 Orthonormality of the Rotation Matrix

In the above approach we did not enforce the orthonormality of the rotation submatrix. Inaccuracies in the measurements will inevitably lead to a submatrix that is not quite orthonormal. One way out of this difficulty is to find the orthonormal matrix closest, in a least-squares sense, to the one computed by the simple method above.

A better approach is to incorporate the six constraints directly. They can be written

$$r_{11}^2 + r_{12}^2 + r_{13}^2 = 1,$$

$$r_{21}^2 + r_{22}^2 + r_{23}^2 = 1,$$

$$r_{31}^2 + r_{32}^2 + r_{33}^2 = 1,$$

and

$$r_{11}r_{21} + r_{12}r_{22} + r_{13}r_{23} = 0,$$

$$r_{21}r_{31} + r_{22}r_{32} + r_{23}r_{33} = 0,$$

$$r_{31}r_{11} + r_{32}r_{12} + r_{33}r_{13} = 0,$$

since $\mathbf{R}^T\mathbf{R} = \mathbf{I}$. It might seem that measurements of two points in the two coordinate systems should now provide enough information, since they lead to six equations, which, with the six constraints above, should allow us to solve for the twelve unknowns. However, this is not the case. We might expect more than one solution, since the set of equations is now nonlinear, but the situation is actually worse.

The indicated approach does not work because some of the information provided is redundant. The distance between the two points must be the same in the two coordinate systems:

$$(x_{l,2} - x_{l,1})^2 + (y_{l,2} - y_{l,1})^2 + (z_{l,2} - z_{l,1})^2$$
$$= (x_{r,2} - x_{r,1})^2 + (y_{r,2} - y_{r,1})^2 + (z_{r,2} - z_{r,1})^2.$$

This follows from the condition of orthonormality. Thus the second point provides only two pieces of new information, not three.

Moreover, because of measurement errors, the second point provides inconsistent information. Of the three new equations, then, one must be discarded to avoid conflict, and a third point is thus needed. It turns out that the third point provides only one independent additional constraint, since two of the three equations it provides must be discarded to avoid inconsistency. This is a nice illustration of how blind equation counting can lead us astray. We have to make sure that the equations that are counted are independent and consistent.

Iterative methods for solving the nonlinear equations need good starting values. These are easily found if approximate information on the relative orientation of the two coordinate systems is available. This is always the case in photogrammetry.

13.3.2 Geometrical Interpretation of Absolute Orientation

It is hard to develop a good intuitive feel for a problem through blind manipulation of sets of equations. Physical models that satisfy the same equations can be very useful in clarifying the basic issues. Here, for example, we can ascertain how much constraint is required to tie two coordinate systems together by reasoning about a simple model.

Consider two rigid solids, rotated and displaced relative to each other. Now choose a point in each of them and move one of the solids to bring the two points into coincidence (figure 13-4a). With this attachment, one

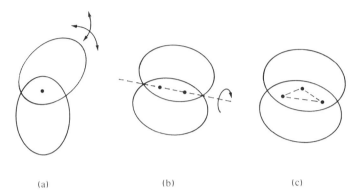

Figure 13-4. The relationship between two coordinate systems is easy to find if we can measure the coordinates of a number of points in both systems. It takes three measurements to tie two coordinate system together uniquely. (a) A single measurement leaves three degrees of freedom of motion. (b) A second measurement removes all but one degree of freedom. (c) A third measurement rigidly attaches the two coordinate systems to each other.

of the rigid solids can still rotate (in three different ways) relative to the other.

Now choose a second point in each object. If these points are at the same distance from the previously chosen points, they can also be brought into coincidence (figure 13-4b). One object can still rotate relative to the other, but only about the line connecting the two chosen points.

Finally, choose a third point in each object. If these new points have the same distances from each of the two points already chosen, then they, too, can be brought into coincidence (figure 13-4c). Now the two objects are rigidly connected, unless, of course, the three chosen points lie on a straight line.

13.3.3 Solving the Overdetermined Systems

As mentioned above, three points provide too much information. When we add the second point, for example, we really only need to know its direction (two unknowns). We thus have an overdetermined set of equations. The best way to deal with this situation is to use a least-squares method. We know that the equations will not be satisfied exactly because of measurement errors. We therefore try to minimize the sum of the squares of the errors. Let $\mathbf{e} = (e_x, e_y, e_z)^T$ be an error vector, where

$$\mathbf{e}_i = (\mathbf{R}\,\mathbf{r}_{l,i} + \mathbf{r}_o) - \mathbf{r}_{r,i}$$

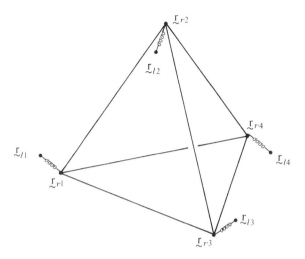

Figure 13-5. The least-squares problem can be modeled by a mechanical system in which corresponding points in the two coordinate systems are attached to each other by means of springs. The solution to the least-squares problem corresponds to the equilibrium position of the system, which minimizes the energy stored in the springs.

at the ith sample point. Using the notation $|\mathbf{e}|^2 = \mathbf{e} \cdot \mathbf{e}$, we can write the term we wish to minimize as

$$\sum_{i=1}^{3} |\mathbf{e}_i|^2 ,$$

subject to the six constraints due to the requirement that $\mathbf{R}$ be orthonormal.

The minimization is with respect to the parameters $r_{11}, r_{12}, \ldots, r_{34}$. This is a nontrivial task because of the nonlinearity of the equations. Lagrange multipliers can be introduced and a solution found (see the appendix for a discussion of constrained minimization). We can, of course, now take more than three measurements to increase accuracy further. The sum of error terms given above just has to be extended to include the new values.

Additional insight is gained by considering a mechanical analog of this solution method. Suppose that each point on one of the objects is attached to the corresponding point on the other by means of a spring (figure 13-5). This mechanical system will seek its least-energy state. Since the energy in a spring is proportional to the square of its length, the stable state is the one in which the sum of the squares of the lengths of the springs is minimized.

13.4 Relative Orientation

We want to relate the coordinate systems of two cameras to each other, but we do not know the points $\mathbf{r}_l = (x_l, y_l, z_l)^T$ and $\mathbf{r}_r = (x_r, y_r, z_r)^T$ themselves, only their projections in the image. Given the focal lengths of the cameras, we can determine the ratios of x and y to z using

$$\frac{x'_l}{f} = \frac{x_l}{z_l} \qquad \text{and} \qquad \frac{y'_l}{f} = \frac{y_l}{z_l},$$

and similarly for x'_r and y'_r. We can regard z_l and z_r as additional unknowns. Each pair of corresponding points now provides only one constraint, not three. It appears that twelve pairs would be needed to determine the twelve unknowns. Unfortunately, the equations are nonlinear. This makes them harder to solve and raises the specter of multiple solutions. We have, for a given point pair,

$$r_{11} x'_l + r_{12} y'_l + r_{13} f + r_{14} \frac{f}{z_l} = x'_r \frac{z_r}{z_l},$$

$$r_{21} x'_l + r_{22} y'_l + r_{23} f + r_{24} \frac{f}{z_l} = y'_r \frac{z_r}{z_l},$$

$$r_{31} x'_l + r_{32} y'_l + r_{33} f + r_{34} \frac{f}{z_l} = f \frac{z_r}{z_l}.$$

There are three equations in the fourteen unknowns $r_{11}, r_{12}, \ldots, r_{34}, z_l$, and z_r. Each additional point pair provides three more equations, but also introduces two more unknowns.

Note that the unknowns $r_{14}, r_{24}, r_{34}, z_l$, and z_r appear in ratios only. Thus uniform scaling will not affect the above equations. That is, if there is a solution with offset vector $\mathbf{r}_o = (r_{14}, r_{24}, r_{34})^T$ and distances $z_{l,i}$ and $z_{r,i}$ for the ith point in the left- and right-hand coordinate systems, respectively, then there is also a solution with offset vector $k \, \mathbf{r}_o$ and distances $k \, z_{l,i}$ and $k \, z_{r,i}$ (for $k \neq 0$).

We can show that this is reasonable by considering what happens when all distances are doubled—both the baseline separation between the two camera systems and the separation between the points. Directions and angles are not altered by this operation—the points project the same way into the images.

To force a unique solution, then, we need an additional constraint. A simple one might be

$$\mathbf{r}_o \cdot \mathbf{r}_o = 1.$$

13.4.1 Constraints Due to Orthonormality

We have not yet used the fact that the rotation matrix should be orthonormal. This introduces six additional constraints. Given n point pairs, we have $12 + 2n$ unknowns and $7 + 3n$ constraints. A solution is thus possible if we have five point pairs, provided that the equations are independent. This will be the case unless the points are badly chosen (for example, if they all lie in a plane).

While it is of theoretical interest to discover the minimum number of point pairs, in practice we always use more pairs. This is because individual measurements are not precise and we can improve the overall accuracy by using additional data. Moreover, choosing more than the minimum number of points allows us to check for gross errors. If the transformation computed using $n - 1$ of the points does not fit the remaining point reasonably well, we might well suspect the data for that point.

There is no closed-form solution to the problem of relative orientation, but various iterative methods can be used to find a solution that minimizes the sum of the squares of the errors.

13.4.2 A Geometrical Interpretation of Relative Orientation

It may, once again, be helpful to consider a simple physical model that gives us a feel for how much constraint is imposed between two coordinate systems when it is known that a given ray from the origin of one coordinate system intersects a particular ray from the origin of another system.

Consider two Cartesian coordinate systems rotated and translated relative to each other. Now choose a ray through the origin in each. Rotate one system until the two rays collide. Attach a movable collar at their intersection (figure 13-6a). The coordinate systems still have considerable freedom of movement.

Now repeat with a second ray for each coordinate system (figure 13-6b). Rotation about the line joining the two points of intersection is still possible. Moreover, the origin of one system can be moved along a sector of the circle that passes through the two points, since a sector of a circle subtends the same angle from all points on the circumference of the circle. In fact, if we fix the two points, the origin of each system can be moved anywhere on a toroidal surface generated by rotating the corresponding circle about the line joining the two points. (This surface, by the way, has two cusps, one at each end of the line.)

Even with three points, the transformation is not fully determined (figure 13-6c). Consider the three rays from a single camera position. Intersect them with an arbitrary plane. Now construct the three toroidal surfaces by considering the points pairwise. The origin of the second coordinate system is at an intersection of the three surfaces. We can, however, find an infinite

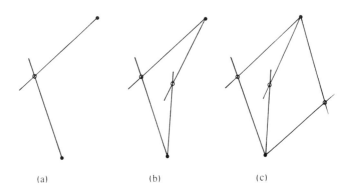

(a)   (b)   (c)

Figure 13-6. The situation is more complicated when we only know the directions to the points. Then even three measurements are not enough. Three degrees of freedom remain when we tie two sets of rays together using three moving collars.

number of solutions by choosing different planes of intersection. There are three degrees of freedom here. The orientation of the plane has two, and its distance from the origin has another. It becomes harder to see what happens as we add yet more points. In practice, we use a least-squares formulation with four or more points.

13.5 Using a Known Relative Orientation

From now on we shall assume that the relative orientations of the camera stations are known. An image point (x'_l, y'_l) in the left image corresponds to a ray through the origin of the coordinate system:

$$x_l = x'_l\, s, \qquad y_l = y'_l\, s, \qquad z_l = f\, s.$$

In the right coordinate system the coordinates of points on this ray are

$$x_r = (r_{11}x'_l + r_{12}y'_l + r_{13}f)s + r_{14},$$
$$y_r = (r_{21}x'_l + r_{22}y'_l + r_{23}f)s + r_{24},$$
$$z_r = (r_{31}x'_l + r_{32}y'_l + r_{33}f)s + r_{34},$$

and they project into

$$\frac{x'_r}{f} = \frac{x_r}{z_r} \qquad \text{and} \qquad \frac{y'_r}{f} = \frac{y_r}{z_r},$$

assuming that the two image planes are at the same distance f from the two lenses. If we use the abbreviations

$$x_r = as + u, \quad y_r = bs + v, \quad z_r = cs + w,$$

then

$$\frac{x'_r}{f} = \frac{a}{c} + \frac{cu - aw}{c} \frac{1}{cs + w},$$

$$\frac{y'_r}{f} = \frac{b}{c} + \frac{cv - bw}{c} \frac{1}{cs + w}.$$

This is a straight line connecting the point $(u/w, v/w)$, for $s = 0$, to $(a/c, b/c)$, as $s \to \infty$. (The first of these points is the image of the left camera station in the right-hand image; the second is the vanishing point for the ray.) It describes a ray from the right camera station parallel to the given ray from the left camera station.

This is all illustrated in figure 13-7. Consider the left camera for the moment. The center of the lens is at S_l, while the image of the point P is at P'_l. The right camera station is imaged at S'_l, and the vanishing point of the ray from the right camera station to the point P lies at D'_l. The points S'_l, P'_l, and D'_l lie on a straight line, which is obtained by cutting the image plane with a plane containing the point P and the camera stations S_l and S_r. A similar line is obtained in the right image. These are the *epipolar lines*. An object imaged on the epipolar line in the left image can only be imaged on the corresponding epipolar line in the right image (if it is imaged at all).

An epipolar line is the intersection of the image plane with an *epipolar plane*, which is a plane containing the two lens centers. The epipolar lines in one image all radiate from one point, namely the image of the other camera station. Of course, in practice, the image plane will be of limited extent and might not actually include the image of the other camera station.

13.6 Computing Depth

Once $\mathbf{R}$ and $\mathbf{r}_o$ are known, we can compute the position of a point with known left and right image coordinates. If (x'_l, y'_l) and (x'_r, y'_r) are these coordinates, then

$$\left(r_{11} \frac{x'_l}{f} + r_{12} \frac{y'_l}{f} + r_{13} \right) z_l + r_{14} = \frac{x'_r}{f} z_r,$$

$$\left(r_{21} \frac{x'_l}{f} + r_{22} \frac{y'_l}{f} + r_{23} \right) z_l + r_{24} = \frac{y'_r}{f} z_r,$$

$$\left(r_{31} \frac{x'_l}{f} + r_{32} \frac{y'_l}{f} + r_{33} \right) z_l + r_{34} = z_r.$$

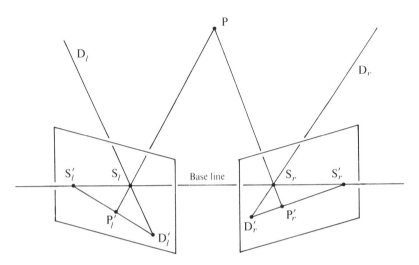

Figure 13-7. The images P'_l and P'_r of a point P in the environment must lie on corresponding epipolar lines. All epipolar lines in the right image pass through the image S'_r of the left camera's center of projection S_l, and vice versa.

We can use any two of these equations to solve for z_l and z_r and then compute

$$\mathbf{r}_l = (x_l, y_l, z_l)^T = \left(\frac{x'_l}{f}, \frac{y'_l}{f}, 1 \right)^T z_l,$$

$$\mathbf{r}_r = (x_r, y_r, z_r)^T = \left(\frac{x'_r}{f}, \frac{y'_r}{f}, 1 \right)^T z_r.$$

13.7 Exterior Orientation

So far we have been concerned with the problem of relating the coordinate systems of two cameras. This is done in order to determine where the epipolar lines lie, so that we can efficiently match features in the two images. This matching process, to be analyzed in more detail later, provides us with depth information in a *viewer-centered* coordinate system. Often this information has to be related to an external, *object-centered* coordinate system. This happens, for example, when the visual information is used to guide a mobile platform, or to command a mechanical manipulator to interact with the objects being viewed. In photogrammetry this is referred to as *exterior orientation*, while the term *hand–eye calibration* is commonly used in robotics.

The problem here is a mix of the two we have considered so far: In one system distances are known, while in the other we only have direction rays. Let us distinguish coordinates in the external system by the subscript a and coordinates in the camera system by the subscript c. We can write, just as we did when we related the coordinate systems of two cameras,

$$r_{11}x_a + r_{12}y_a + r_{13}z_a + r_{14} = x_c,$$

$$r_{21}x_a + r_{22}y_a + r_{23}z_a + r_{24} = y_c,$$

$$r_{31}x_a + r_{32}y_a + r_{33}z_a + r_{34} = z_c,$$

where the 3×3 submatrix is orthonormal. In the camera system only the ratios of x_c and y_c to z_c are accessible to us, since

$$\frac{x'}{f} = \frac{x_c}{z_c} \quad \text{and} \quad \frac{y'}{f} = \frac{y_c}{z_c}.$$

Overall we have

$$\frac{x'}{f} = \frac{r_{11}x_a + r_{12}y_a + r_{13}z_a + r_{14}}{r_{31}x_a + r_{32}y_a + r_{33}z_a + r_{34}},$$

$$\frac{y'}{f} = \frac{r_{21}x_a + r_{22}y_a + r_{23}z_a + r_{24}}{r_{31}x_a + r_{32}y_a + r_{33}z_a + r_{34}}.$$

Our problem is to determine the twelve coefficients of the transformation. Since the submatrix is orthonormal, there are, of course, only six degrees of freedom. One way to proceed is to use a number of calibration points whose coordinates are known in the external system. The transformation can be recovered if we measure the coordinates of the corresponding points in the image. Each such measurement provides two independent constraints. Three points should therefore provide enough information, as long as they are not collinear.

Each measurement of the image coordinates x' and y' leads to two constraint equations,

$$x' \left(r_{31}x_a + r_{32}y_a + r_{33}z_a + r_{34} \right) - f \left(r_{11}x_a + r_{12}y_a + r_{13}z_a + r_{14} \right) = 0,$$

$$y' \left(r_{31}x_a + r_{32}y_a + r_{33}z_a + r_{34} \right) - f \left(r_{21}x_a + r_{22}y_a + r_{23}z_a + r_{24} \right) = 0,$$

which are linear in the twelve unknowns $r_{11}, r_{12}, \ldots, r_{34}$. The system of equations to be solved is nonlinear, however, because the orthonormality constraint contributes six equations containing products of the unknown coefficients. Consequently, we might expect more than one solution. The argument made before, that the camera must lie on the intersection of three toroidal surfaces, applies here also, and we might therefore expect to see up to eight solutions. If we know roughly where the camera is, and how it is oriented, then we can discard all but one of these solutions and obtain a unique answer. In any case, a fourth point should settle the issue, unless it is chosen poorly. In practice, to increase accuracy and to have a check on measurement errors, we use more points and apply a least-squares method. The nonlinearity of the problem precludes a closed-form solution, and we must resort to iterative methods.

13.8 Interior Orientation

We have glossed over one detail: We have implicitly assumed that we know the effective focal length, that is, the exact distance from the lens to the image plane, as well as the exact place where the optical axis pierces this plane. We need this information to effect the transformation from the camera coordinates x_c, y_c, and z_c to the image coordinates x' and y'. We have implicitly assumed that the origin of the image coordinate system lies on the optical axis. Now, we can certainly choose the camera coordinate system axes to be parallel to the axes of the image coordinate system, so rotation is not an issue, but we do need to know f, and we also need to place the origin of the image coordinate system on the optical axis.

The information we need is obtained through the process of *internal orientation*. If the lens has radial distortions that are significant enough to influence the results, then the problem of internal orientation is taken to include the measurement of this distortion as a function of radial distance from the origin.

Curiously, we can get around the problem of discovering the exact distance from the lens to the image plane and the exact place where the optical axis pierces it by combining internal orientation with exterior orientation. The idea is to acknowledge that image measurements are not perfect and to relax the assumption of orthonormality. This simplifies the problem, since the remaining equations are linear.

So far we have also assumed perfect measurements of the image coordinates x' and y'. In an electron-optical system for image acquisition, however, it may be difficult to guarantee that the two axes of the measurement system are exactly orthogonal and that distances measured along the axes are scaled equally. We can take these effects into account by introducing a linear transformation from the ideal coordinates to those actually used. An *affine* transformation in the plane is linear and can account for uniform scaling, translation, rotation, skewing, and shearing. Such a transformation can absorb all of the departures from the ideal situation that we have discussed:

- Scaling error, due to inaccurate knowledge of f.
- Translation error, due to inaccurate knowledge of the origin.

- Rotation, due to inaccurate knowledge of image sensor rotation.

- Skewing error, due to departures from orthogonality in the sensor.

- Shearing error, due to unequal scaling in the image axes.

An affine transformation has six parameters and can be written in the form

$$x' = a_{11}(x_c/z_c) + a_{12}(y_c/z_c) + a_{13},$$

$$y' = a_{21}(x_c/z_c) + a_{22}(y_c/z_c) + a_{23},$$

so that

$$\frac{x'}{f} = \frac{s_{11}x_a + s_{12}y_a + s_{13}z_a + s_{14}}{s_{31}x_a + s_{32}y_a + s_{33}z_a + s_{34}},$$

$$\frac{y'}{f} = \frac{s_{21}x_a + s_{22}y_a + s_{23}z_a + s_{24}}{s_{31}x_a + s_{32}y_a + s_{33}z_a + s_{34}},$$

where the new coefficients $\{s_{ij}\}$ are sums of products of the old coefficients $\{r_{ij}\}$ with the coefficients $\{a_{ij}\}$ of the affine transformation. These equations have the same form as those we studied earlier. The difference is that the 3×3 submatrix of coefficients need no longer be orthonormal. As a result, we need not consider the nonlinear equations induced by the orthonormality constraint. We are left with one pair of linear equations of the form

$$x'\left(s_{31}x_a + s_{32}y_a + s_{33}z_a + s_{34}\right) - f\left(s_{11}x_a + s_{12}y_a + s_{13}z_a + s_{14}\right) = 0,$$

$$y'\left(s_{31}x_a + s_{32}y_a + s_{33}z_a + s_{34}\right) - f\left(s_{21}x_a + s_{22}y_a + s_{23}z_a + s_{24}\right) = 0,$$

for each image measurement. It appears, at first, that we need six such measurements to solve for the twelve unknowns. However, these equations are homogeneous, or, put another way, the transformation is not affected by uniform scaling of all coefficients, so that we actually only have eleven degrees of freedom. In any case, without further assumptions, five measurements are not enough, and six are more than enough. In practice, many more points are measured and a least-squares method is used to find the best-fitting transformation. This is simple now, since the equations are all linear, as we demonstrate in exercise 13-11.

A method similar to the one described above is needed to relate the coordinate system of an industrial robot to that of an image sensor. We explore some approximations that are even simpler to deal with in the exercises. We shall see an application of such methods in chapter 18, where we put together many of the ideas in this book in order to construct a system that picks parts out of a bin.

13.9 Finding Conjugate Points

Now we are ready to tackle the key problem in stereo: How can we locate corresponding points in two images? The *correspondence problem* is that of identifying features in two images that are projections of the same entity in the three-dimensional world. Once this is done, we can compute the distance to this entity. A point on the surface of an object might not be visible from either camera station; but if it does appear in both images, then, as we have shown, the two image points must lie on corresponding epipolar lines.

How can we identify conjugate points? One school of thought has it that we ought to analyze each image separately first and extract "features." These might be objects that have been identified or places where there are distinctive gray-level patterns that we have some confidence in matching. A convenient feature for this purpose is an edge. We might also look for gray-level "corners," where the brightness surface has nonzero Gaussian curvature.

We shall examine edge-based methods later, but for now we follow a different approach. We might hope that the brightness patterns are the same or at least similar in a small neighborhood of each image point. An extreme notion might be that the gray-levels at the two points should be equal. Usually, however, there will be several places on corresponding epipolar lines where the gray-levels match. How can we distinguish among them?

13.9.1 Gray-Level Matching

Consider a portion of a surface that is smooth and not tilted too much with respect to lines connecting it to each camera station. Then neighboring points on the surface will map into neighboring points in both images. Thus we might expect gray-levels of neighboring points in one image to match gray-levels of neighboring points in the other image. We can think of the problem, then, as one of matching gray-level waveforms on corresponding epipolar lines. These waveforms are not simply shifted versions of one another, but are compressed and expanded as a result of differences in the foreshortening of surface intervals as viewed from two camera stations.

Consider the simple geometry of camera positions we started with (figure 13-1), where

$$\frac{x'_l}{f} = \frac{x + b/2}{z} \quad \text{and} \quad \frac{x'_r}{f} = \frac{x - b/2}{z}.$$

We are to find a function $z(x, y)$ such that

$$E_l(x'_l, y'_l) = E_r(x'_r, y'_r),$$

or

$$E_l \left(f \frac{x + b/2}{z(x, y)}, y' \right) = E_r \left(f \frac{x - b/2}{z(x, y)}, y' \right).$$

It is convenient to change variables at this point, so that we can work in image coordinates $(x', y')^T$ rather than the world coordinates $(x, y, z)^T$. Let

$$\frac{x'}{f} = \frac{x}{z} \quad \text{and} \quad d(x', y') = \frac{b f}{z}.$$

We are looking for a disparity function $d(x', y')$ such that

$$E_l \left(x' + \frac{1}{2} d(x', y'), y' \right) = E_r \left(x' - \frac{1}{2} d(x', y'), y' \right).$$

We also want z, and hence d, to vary smoothly. Thus we might look for a solution that minimizes some measure of departure from smoothness, such as

$$e_s = \iint (\nabla^2 d)^2 \, dx' \, dy'.$$

(We chose the Laplacian squared here as the smoothness term, because a method based on the sum of the squares of first derivatives tends to flatten the solutions excessively.) Image brightness measurements are not exact, so we should not insist that the condition $E_l = E_r$ be obeyed exactly. Instead we minimize

$$e_i = \iint (E_l - E_r)^2 \, dx' \, dy'.$$

Overall, then, we are minimizing $e_s + \lambda e_i$, where λ is a weighting factor that is large if brightness measurements are accurate and small if they are not. The Euler equation here is

$$F_d - \frac{\partial}{\partial x'} F_{d'_x} - \frac{\partial}{\partial y'} F_{d'_y} = 0,$$

where

$$F = (\nabla^2 d)^2 + \lambda \left(E_l \left(x' + \frac{1}{2} d(x', y'), y' \right) - E_r \left(x' - \frac{1}{2} d(x', y'), y' \right) \right)^2,$$

so that

$$\nabla^2 (\nabla^2 d) = \lambda (E_l - E_r) \frac{1}{2} \left(\frac{\partial E_l}{\partial x'} + \frac{\partial E_r}{\partial x'} \right).$$

Here E_l and $\partial E_l / \partial x'$ are measured at the point $\left(x' + (1/2) d(x', y'), y' \right)$ in the left image and E_r and $\partial E_r / \partial x'$ are measured at the point $\left(x' - \right.$

$(1/2)d(x', y'), y')$ in the right image. The operator

$$\nabla^2(\nabla^2) = \frac{\partial^4}{\partial x'^4} + 2\frac{\partial^4}{\partial x'^2 y'^2} + \frac{\partial^4}{\partial y'^4}$$

is called the *biharmonic operator*.

In the discrete case we use $\kappa(d_{ij} - \overline{d}_{ij})$ instead of $\nabla^2(\nabla^2 d)$, where $\overline{d}$ is the result of convolving d with a computational molecule derived from a molecule that is appropriate for the biharmonic operator. This leads to an iterative scheme of the form

$$d_{ij}^{n+1} = \overline{d}_{ij}^n - \frac{\lambda}{\kappa}(E_l - E_r)\frac{1}{2}\left(\frac{\partial E_l}{\partial x'} + \frac{\partial E_r}{\partial x'}\right),$$

where the partial derivatives of E_l and E_r are estimated using first differences. If the left picture is brighter than the right picture at an estimated match point, then the disparity will be increased or decreased depending on whether the brightness gradients are positive or negative. It should be clear that this will tend to reduce the difference in brightness.

Note also that neighboring disparities will tend to be similar. This scheme, then, has some desirable properties. It has problems, however, when the gray-levels at corresponding points in the two images do not match. Disparity also changes rapidly where objects overlap. Most serious, though, is the need for good initial values. Without them, convergence is not likely. The problem is that individual disparity values can be pulled in the wrong direction by the effects of the brightness gradients. Alternatively, they can be locked into a spurious match. The problem occurs when the correct match is much more than one picture cell away from the correct estimate. If the gray-level surface fluctuates a great deal, the estimates of the brightness gradients can be quite wrong.

Smoothing or blurring the images helps to reduce these effects, since components with high spatial frequencies are removed. This suggests performing the match first on a pair of smoothed images and then using the results as initial values for a computation on a finer scale. To obtain good initial values for the match on the smoothed images, we could smooth them even more. The smoothed images do not have to be sampled as finely. In this way we can generate a sequence of images, each a smoothed and reduced version of the previous one. The matching results on the reduced version are used as initial values for the iterative process applied to the less smoothed image.

A similar iterative adjustment of disparity arrays is used in some automated stereo systems. The method works well if reasonable initial values are available. It does not work well where disparity changes rapidly, where the images lack detail at a particular scale, or where the gray-levels of conjugate points do not match.

The gray-levels of conjugate points are in general not exactly the same since the surface is being observed from two different directions. Specular surfaces present an extreme example. Such a surface can be oriented to reflect rays from the light source toward one eye of the viewer and none toward the other. More commonly, small but noticeable differences between gray-levels recorded in the two images will occur.

13.9.2 Correlation Methods

If conjugate patches of two images have similar brightness patterns, we can try to locate them by correlating patches of the two images. Given a patch from one image, we compute the correlation with all patches along the corresponding epipolar line. We then choose the point with the largest correlation value.

How large should the patches be? If they are too small, the brightness pattern will not be distinctive enough—many false matches may be found. If they are too large, resolution is lost, since neighboring image regions with different disparities will be combined in the measurement. Worse, the two patches will not match well, unless disparity is constant. Again a multiple resolution scheme suggests itself: First, find correlation matches on reduced images. Then use these to confine the search for matches in the next higher resolution pair of images.

While correlation methods are often the first ones to be suggested, they do not perform very well. Perhaps their most serious shortcoming is their sensitivity to differences in foreshortening (figure 13-8). If a surface is tilted relative to the baseline, it will appear shorter in one image than in the other. We cannot expect the two gray-level waveforms to be particularly well correlated in this case.

Correlation methods need not be applied directly to the raw images, though. They work better when the edges have been enhanced, for example, but it is not possible to overcome their basic shortcomings in this fashion. These shortcomings include the sensitivity of these methods to differences in foreshortening and their inability to determine disparity in regions that lack image detail.

A modification of the correlation approach that leads to usable results is the incorporation of warping in the images to undo the foreshortening effect. It is possible to compensate for foreshortening by referring both left and right images to some fictitious intermediate image, one we would obtain using a camera position between the two actual camera positions. Alternatively, one image can be referred to the other. In either case, the shape of the surface is needed to undo the foreshortening effects. This appears to pose a chicken-and-egg problem, since the whole point is to recover the shape using correlation matching! In practice, we use an iterative

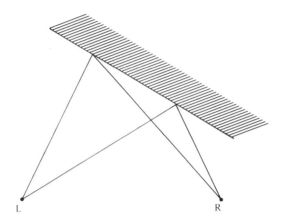

Figure 13-8. An inclined area will have different amounts of foreshortening in two images. This seriously affects the performance of straightforward correlation schemes.

scheme in which the current estimate of the disparity is employed to warp the images before they are subjected to the correlation method. The result produced by the correlation peak finder is then used to update the estimate of disparity.

Such an iterative scheme is not guaranteed to converge. Indeed, machines using approaches like this depend on operator assistance to help them in areas where the method fails.

13.9.3 Edge-Matching Methods

If the gray-level is more or less constant in a part of the image, it is hard to find conjugate points. Correlation methods using patches smaller than the size of the uniform region will produce no clear maximum. The gray-level matching methods discussed earlier will obtain disparities in such regions by filling in from neighboring areas that have suitable gray-level variations.

It might be more reasonable to estimate disparity only where there are rapid fluctuations, as on the edges between patches of more or less uniform brightness. Matching is now carried out between crude symbolic descriptions of the images rather than between the images themselves. Some of the same issues are relevant, however. First, there is the possibility of false matches. Since there may be many edges in either image along a given epipolar line, some additional information is needed to disambiguate the situation. We can, for example, associate auxiliary information with each edge, recording such things as the difference in gray-level value across the

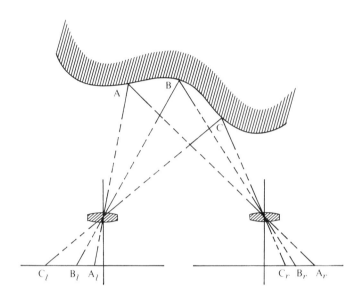

Figure 13-9. If we are looking at a continuous surface, images of points along a particular epipolar line will be ordered the same way as the images of these points along the corresponding epipolar line in the other image. This provides a powerful constraint on the matching of features.

edge. Matches between edges are only acceptable when the edge descriptions match reasonably well. Moreover, when we are looking at a continuous surface, the edges must be ordered the same way along corresponding epipolar lines (figure 13-9). Only if one object lies in front of another can the sequence of edges be different in two images.

In particularly simple cases, all edges visible in one image are also visible in the other. Most automated schemes will not work well if this condition is not satisfied. Aerial photography of urban areas violates this condition, since the vertical sides of some buildings will be visible in one image but not in the other.

Even with such helpful assumptions and the fact that matching can be confined to corresponding epipolar lines, there is still a great deal of ambiguity. It might help to note that matches on neighboring epipolar lines are usually not too different. The most useful method again involves multiple scales.

When we smooth the images, we lose detail, and edges corresponding to small image features disappear. Matching along epipolar lines is simplified by reducing the number of edges to match. We start by matching edges in images that have been smoothed a great deal. These matches are then used to limit and guide the search for matches at higher resolution. It is possible to estimate the distribution of intervals along epipolar lines between edges using our knowledge of the degree of smoothing. This, in turn, allows us to determine the probability of inadvertently matching edges that do not correspond. The interval over which a search for a matching edge is conducted can be limited appropriately to keep the probability of error acceptably low.

We recall that the brightness changes more rapidly at an edge than in other places. Thus the first derivative of brightness has a maximum and the second derivative has a zero there; that is, there is an inflection point in the brightness. We can thus search for potential edge locations in the smoothed images by looking for the zero-crossings of the second derivatives. In chapter 8, where we discussed edge detection, we explored the application of the Laplacian operator to a smoothed image. Smoothing can be accomplished by convolution with a Gaussian, and Gaussians of various widths can be used to achieve filtering at different scales.

In our previous discussion of edge detection, we were interested in rotationally symmetric operators, since lines of all orientations were to be found. Here we are primarily interested in edges that make a large angle with the epipolar lines, since edges parallel to an epipolar line provide no useful disparity information. It is therefore convenient to consider the second derivative along the direction of the epipolar image line. One advantage of this approach becomes apparent when we remember that a rotationally symmetric edge operator is somewhat more sensitive to noise than a directional one with the same size support.

13.9.4 Interpolation

One disadvantage of methods that match points of rapid brightness change is that disparity is only known at these points. If disparity is needed everywhere, we must use an interpolation scheme. How can we interpolate a smooth surface from known points? This is a problem that has been addressed in many contexts. Methods for interpolating from a regular grid are particularly well understood. Here, however, the data are given along contours that are not in predetermined positions.

A number of issues arise in selecting an interpolation method. Aside from producing a smooth surface, we would also hope for a unique solution, for example. Moreover, the result should not depend on the orientation of the coordinate axes. This suggests rotationally symmetric operators. One way to come up with a suitable method is to consider a physical analog. Assume, for example, that the known disparity values along edges are represented by "walls" of height proportional to the disparity. The walls are built along the curve that the edge takes in the image. Now let us stretch a rubber sheet over these walls, tacking it down to the tops of the walls. The height of the rubber sheet is taken to be the interpolated disparity value.

The resulting surface is continuous and does not depend on the orientation of the coordinate axes. It is also smooth, except on the walls, where discontinuities in the surface normal occur. The rubber sheet takes on the shape that minimizes the stored energy. For small deflections, this energy is proportional to

$$\iint (z_x^2 + z_y^2) \, dx \, dy.$$

Considering the Euler equation for this problem yields the Laplace equation

$$\nabla^2 z = 0,$$

except on the walls, as can be verified by applying the calculus of variations.

To avoid discontinuities in surface normal across a wall, we can use a thin sheet of metal instead of the rubber sheet. The thin sheet will also adopt a shape that minimizes the internal energy. For small deflections the internal energy is proportional to

$$\iint (\nabla^2 z)^2 \, dx \, dy.$$

The Euler equations for this problem yield the biharmonic equation

$$\nabla^2 (\nabla^2 z) = 0,$$

or

$$\frac{\partial^4 z}{\partial x^4} + 2 \frac{\partial^4 z}{\partial x^2 \partial y^2} + \frac{\partial^4 z}{\partial y^4} = 0,$$

except on the walls, as can be verified by applying the calculus of variations. These equations can be solved numerically using straightforward iterative schemes.

Such methods produce good results where the surface is continuous. Problems occur where one object occludes another, since disparity is not continuous there. It is therefore necessary to start by segmenting the image into regions where disparity is continuous. The interpolation process can then be applied to these regions separately.

13.10 References

Binocular stereo in biological vision systems is discussed at length by Julesz in *Foundations of Cyclopean Perception* [1971]. He demonstrated, using random-dot stereograms, that matching occurs before recognition. Grimson discusses edge-based automated stereo in detail in *From Images to Surfaces: A Computational Study of the Human Early Visual System* [1981]. Moravec [1981] describes work at Stanford on a motion stereo system for a mobile cart in *Robot Rover Visual Navigation*. One of many excellent texts on photogrammetry is *Elements of Photogrammetry* by Wolf [1974]. Least-squares methods often lead to problems that can be tackled using the pseudoinverse. Here one can recommend Albert's *Regression and the Moore–Penrose Pseudoinverse* [1972].

The photogrammetric aspects of the use of machine vision have usually been considered too trivial to report and were buried in internal reports. See, for example, Sobel [1970], Horn [1972], and Ganapathy [1984]. This is despite the fact that they form an important part of any hand–eye system or mobile robot system. Longuet-Higgins [1981] reported on the reconstruction of scenes from one or more views in an article in *Nature*. Fischler & Bolles [1981] showed that there are four solutions to the problem of determining the location of a camera from a minimum number of known points on the surface.

There were several large-scale efforts in the late sixties and early seventies to devise machines that would recover surface topography from pairs of aerial photographs. Most of these relied on correlation or some simple modification thereof, because the focus was on speed, whereas attention should have been concentrated first on solving the basic matching problem. Most projects ended after discovering the difficulties noted in this chapter, but a few machines eventually achieved reasonable performance on simple terrain. Significant operator interaction is still required, though. An early version of one such machine, the UNAMACE, is described by Bertram [1969], while Kelly, McConnell, & Mildenberger [1977] describe the Gestalt photomapper, apparently the most successful commercial effort so far. Konecny & Pape [1981] provide a useful review of the various machines built up to 1981. Five papers dealing with automated stereo matching can be found in the April 1983 issue of *Photogrammetric Engineering and Remote Sensing*.

Levine, O'Handley, & Yagi [1973] developed a stereo system for a proposed Mars Rover using an adaptive correlation window. Mori, Kidode, & Asada [1973] used an iterative method that would undo the warping introduced by variable foreshortening. Similar methods were later incorporated in many correlation-based schemes. See Gruen [1985] for a method involving iterative adjustment of the foreshortening correction. Keating, Wolf, & Scarpace [1975] pointed out the utility of exploiting the epipolar constraint to restrict the matching search.

Sutro & Lerman [1973] developed a simple gray-level matching method that used a disparity array and a scheme for eliminating false matches. Dev

[1975] used disparity arrays and proposed excitatory and inhibitory interactions, found again later in Marr & Poggio's [1976] first stereo system. See also Marr, Palm, & Poggio [1978]. These efforts were concerned with the random-dot stereograms popularized by Julesz. Marr & Poggio [1979] later came up with a different method based on matching zero-crossings, many details of which were fleshed out by Grimson. Grimson [1982, 1983b, 1984], for example, developed the methods needed to interpolate the surface from the sparse data provided by the matching of zero-crossings. Marroquin [1984] dealt with the depth discontinuities that the simple interpolation methods do not treat.

Grimson also showed [1983a] that, provided reasonable assumptions were made about the reflectance properties of the surface, inflection points would not go unnoticed in the search for zero-crossings. A popular account of the two stereo theories mentioned above was presented by Poggio [1984] in *Scientific American*.

The method of Barnard & Thompson [1980] matches points located by an interest operator. Mayhew & Frisby [1981] disputed the sufficiency of matching only zero-crossings and developed their own method for stereo matching. For more recent work along these lines, see Mayhew [1982] and Mayhew & Longuet-Higgins [1984]. Baker & Binford [1981, 1982] developed yet another stereo matching method at Stanford University. More recently, Ohta & Kanade [1983] at Carnegie-Mellon University pursued use of dynamic programming in the matching stage.

Nishihara [1983] developed a method that can determine disparity values on a coarse raster quickly, using a binary correlation method applied to the sign bit of the output of the edge-enhancement filter. He addressed himself to the need for speed in industrial applications, as for example in picking parts out of a bin. An experiment along these lines has been reported by Ikeuchi et al. [1984].

Brady & Horn [1983] studied rotationally symmetric operators such as the ones used in surface interpolation and edge-enhancement operations. The interpolation schemes developed by Grimson involve iterative solution of discrete versions of elliptic partial differential equations. As in the case of the computation of lightness, slow convergence can be a problem. Multiresolution methods have been developed that appear to reduce this problem greatly. Terzopoulos [1983, 1984a,b] has explored application of these methods to several machine vision algorithms, including interpolation.

There are representations for rotation other than orthonormal matrices. The book by Korn & Korn [1968], for example, lists seven such methods. In chapter 18, where we develop a system for picking parts out of a bin, we study unit quaternions and find that they have certain advantages. Some of the orientation problems do not have closed-form solutions using

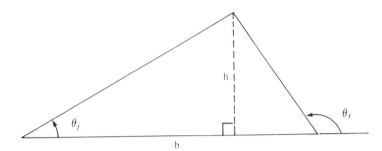

Figure 13-10. In the simple stereo camera geometry shown in figure 13-1, it is easy to relate distance h to disparity $\theta_r - \theta_l$ and other quantities shown in the figure.

the notation introduced here, yet can be solved using unit quaternions. For examples of this see Thompson [1959] and Schut [1960].

13.11 Exercises

13-1   Here we explore the relationship between distance and disparity. Let the length of the baseline, the line connecting two camera stations, be b. Suppose that an object can be seen from both station points and that the lines from the left and right cameras to the object make angles θ_l and θ_r, respectively, with the baseline (see figure 13-10).

(a) Show that the perpendicular distance to the object from the baseline (or its extension, if needed) is
$$h = b\frac{\sin\theta_r\,\sin\theta_l}{\sin(\theta_r - \theta_l)}.$$
Note the inverse dependence on the disparity $\theta_r - \theta_l$.

(b) What is the variance in the distance h if the variance in the measurements θ_r and θ_l is σ^2? Hint: Differentiate h with respect to θ_r and θ_l.

(c) How does the accuracy of this stereo method degrade with distance?

13-2   In this exercise we mount an analytic attack on the problem solved geometrically in the previous exercise. Let the image coordinates in the left and right images be (x'_l, y'_l) and (x'_r, y'_r), respectively, while the coordinates of a point $(x, y, z)^T$ in the environment are measured relative to a point midway between the lens centers. Assume that the line connecting the lens centers is perpendicular to the optical axes, that the x-axes are parallel to this line, and that the optical axes are parallel. Show that the relative error in distance measurement is proportional to the relative error in disparity measurement, that is,
$$\frac{\delta z}{z} = -\frac{\delta(x'_l - x'_r)}{(x'_l - x'_r)}.$$

13-3   This exercise exposes the redundancy encountered when the coordinates of many points are measured in two different coordinate systems. Let the transformation between two camera stations be given by

$$\mathbf{r}_r = \mathbf{R}\mathbf{r}_l + \mathbf{r}_o, \quad \text{where } \mathbf{R}^T\mathbf{R} = \mathbf{I}.$$

Show that the distance between two particular points is the same in the left and right coordinate systems; that is,

$$\left|\mathbf{r}_{l,2} - \mathbf{r}_{l,1}\right|^2 = \left|\mathbf{r}_{r,2} - \mathbf{r}_{r,1}\right|^2,$$

where we use the standard notational shorthand $|\mathbf{x}|^2 = \mathbf{x} \cdot \mathbf{x}$.

13-4   In this problem we develop a method for uncovering the transformation between two coordinate systems, that is, we solve the absolute orientation problem. Rewrite the equations

$$\mathbf{r}_{r,i} = \mathbf{M}\mathbf{r}_{l,i} + \mathbf{r}_o \qquad \text{for } r = 1, 2, 3, 4,$$

in a form that shows as unknowns the elements $r_{11}, r_{12}, \ldots, r_{34}$ of the matrix formed by adjoining the vector $\mathbf{r}_o$ to $\mathbf{M}$. The coefficient matrix should be square. Do not assume that $\mathbf{M}$ is orthonormal. Show that the system of equations is singular if all four points lie in a plane. Conclude that in general four points uniquely determine absolute orientation.

13-5   Here we explore a different method for solving the absolute orientation problem. Let $\mathbf{a}_{i,j} = \mathbf{r}_{l,i} - \mathbf{r}_{l,j}$ be the difference between the coordinates of the ith and j^{th} point in the left image coordinate system. Similarly, $\mathbf{b}_{i,j} = \mathbf{r}_{r,i} - \mathbf{r}_{r,j}$. Given four points, construct three sets of such differences by taking them in pairs. Now construct 3×3 matrices $\mathbf{A}$ and $\mathbf{B}$ by adjoining these difference vectors:

$$\mathbf{A} = (\mathbf{a}_{1,2} \quad \mathbf{a}_{2,3} \quad \mathbf{a}_{3,4}) \qquad \text{and} \qquad \mathbf{B} = (\mathbf{b}_{1,2} \quad \mathbf{b}_{2,3} \quad \mathbf{b}_{3,4}).$$

Show that the rotation matrix $\mathbf{M}$ is given by $\mathbf{M} = \mathbf{A}\mathbf{B}^{-1}$, provided that $\mathbf{B}$ is not singular. When is $\mathbf{B}$ singular? How can the offset $\mathbf{r}_o$ be computed? Under what circumstances will $\mathbf{M}$ be orthonormal?

13-6   We now consider situations in which more than the minimum required number of measurements are available and a least-squares approach is appropriate.

(a) Find the matrix $\mathbf{M}$ and the offset $\mathbf{r}_o$ that minimize the error sum

$$\sum_{i=1}^{n} \mathbf{e}_i^2,$$

where $\mathbf{e}_i = (\mathbf{M}\mathbf{r}_{l,i} + \mathbf{r}_o) - \mathbf{r}_{r,i}$. Note that $\mathbf{M}$ need not be orthonormal in this part.

(b) Find the orthonormal matrix $\mathbf{R}$ and the offset $\mathbf{r}_o$ that minimize the error sum

$$\sum_{i=1}^{n} \mathbf{e}_i^2,$$

where $\mathbf{e}_i = (\mathbf{R}\mathbf{r}_{l,i} + \mathbf{r}_o) - \mathbf{r}_{r,i}$. Note that $\mathbf{R}$ has to be orthonormal in this part. Warning: This part of the problem is much harder than the previous one.

13-7 Once again, suppose that we have two devices capable of measuring the positions of points in space. These devices are linear to high accuracy, but are not ideal in other ways. Specifically, the axes of their coordinate systems are not necessarily orthogonal, and the scales along the different coordinate axes are not necessarily equal.

To use these devices effectively, we must find the relationship between measurements made by one device and measurements made by the other. Let the transformation from one, $(a, b, c)^T$, to the other, $(d, e, f)^T$, be given by

$$\begin{pmatrix} d \\ e \\ f \end{pmatrix} = \mathbf{M} \begin{pmatrix} a \\ b \\ c \end{pmatrix} + \begin{pmatrix} x \\ y \\ z \end{pmatrix},$$

where

$$\mathbf{M} = \begin{pmatrix} m_{11} & m_{12} & m_{13} \\ m_{21} & m_{22} & m_{23} \\ m_{31} & m_{32} & m_{33} \end{pmatrix}$$

and x, y, and z are offsets.

To determine the spatial relationship between the two devices, we measure several sample points using both of them. Let the coordinates of the ith point be $(a_i, b_i, c_i)^T$ as measured by one of the devices and $(d_i, e_i, f_i)^T$ as measured by the other.

(a) What is the smallest number n of sample points that must be measured in both coordinate systems to determine the coefficients of the transformation? Hint: Determine how many unknowns there are, and how many independent constraints each measurement provides.

(b) Show that this transformation can also be written in the form

$$\begin{pmatrix} d \\ e \\ f \end{pmatrix} = \mathbf{N} \begin{pmatrix} a \\ b \\ c \\ 1 \end{pmatrix}.$$

What is the shape of the matrix $\mathbf{N}$, and how are its coefficients n_{ij} related to the coefficients m_{ij} of the matrix $\mathbf{M}$?

(c) Now form the matrix $\mathbf{A}$ by adjoining the column vectors $(a_i, b_i, c_i, 1)^T$, which are in turn built from the measurements by adjoining a "1." Also form the matrix $\mathbf{D}$ by adjoining the column vectors $(d_i, e_i, f_i)^T$. That is, the ith column of $\mathbf{D}$ is the ith measurement vector in the second system. Clearly, $\mathbf{N}\mathbf{A} = \mathbf{D}$. State conditions on the number of measurements n and on the matrix $\mathbf{A}$ or the matrix $\mathbf{D}$ that will guarantee a unique solution for the unknown matrix $\mathbf{N}$.

(d) Show that a point $\mathbf{x}$ lies in the plane defined by three points $\mathbf{u}$, $\mathbf{v}$, $\mathbf{w}$ if and only if $\mathbf{x} = \alpha\mathbf{u} + \beta\mathbf{v} + \gamma\mathbf{w}$ for some α, β, γ such that $\alpha + \beta + \gamma = 1$. Hint: You might want to use the fact that the volume of the parallelepiped defined by the edge vectors $\mathbf{k}$, $\mathbf{l}$, and $\mathbf{m}$ is given by the triple product $[\mathbf{k}\,\mathbf{l}\,\mathbf{m}] = (\mathbf{k}\times\mathbf{l})\cdot\mathbf{m}$.

(e) Give a necessary and sufficient condition for the existence of a unique solution for $\mathbf{N}$ in terms of the relative positions of the sample points $(a_i, b_i, c_i)^T$. Hints: When is the volume of the parallelepiped zero? Is the determinant of a matrix altered by subtracting one row from another? Is the determinant of a 3×3 matrix equal to the triple product of its rows considered as vectors?

13-8   Up to this point, we have made measurements in both coordinate systems of all three coordinates for each test point. Now we consider the problem of relative orientation, in which directions only are available. Consider the three equations

$$r_{11}x_l' + r_{12}y_l' + r_{13}f + r_{14}\frac{f}{z_l} = x_r'\frac{z_r}{z_l},$$

$$r_{21}x_l' + r_{22}y_l' + r_{23}f + r_{24}\frac{f}{z_l} = y_r'\frac{z_r}{z_l},$$

$$r_{31}x_l' + r_{32}y_l' + r_{33}f + r_{34}\frac{f}{z_l} = f_r'\frac{z_r}{z_l}.$$

Eliminate z_r and z_l to obtain one equation in the unknowns $r_{11}, r_{12}, \ldots, r_{34}$. Base a method for recovering the unknowns from several image measurements on this equation.

13-9   The three linear equations in z_l and z_r given above provide more than enough information. Due to measurement error, though, they may be inconsistent.

(a) Find the solution that minimizes the errors in the object. That is, find the point P^* that minimizes the sum of the squares of the distances between point P^* and the two rays defined by the image points (x_l', y_l') and (x_r', y_r').

(b) Find the solution that minimizes the errors in the image. That is, find the point P^* that minimizes the sum of the squares of the distances between the observed image points (x_l', y_l') and (x_r', y_r') and the projections of point P^* in the image planes. Warning: This may be harder than the previous part of this problem.

13-10 Suppose that you want to determine a *hand–eye transform*, that is, a transformation from the coordinate system of a mechanical manipulator to that of an electronic camera. This is a problem of exterior orientation. Assume that the camera system can determine the position of the image of a special mark on the gripper of the robot arm. You are free to command the arm to move to any position in its workspace. The transformation, as usual, can be broken down into a translation and a rotation. Show that you need at least four calibration points to determine the transformation.

13-11 In the calibration method we described for determining the exterior orientation, we obtained two linear equations in the unknown coefficients for every measurement made. Suppose that the point $(x, y, z)^T$ in the external coordinate system is imaged at (x', y'). The idea is to use several such measurements to provide enough information to pin down the unknown parameters of the coordinate transformation.

(a) Show that the two constraints induced by a single measurement can be written in the form $\mathbf{u} \cdot \mathbf{c} = \mathbf{0}$ and $\mathbf{v} \cdot \mathbf{c} = \mathbf{0}$, where

$$\mathbf{u} = (-fx, -fy, -fz, -f, 0, 0, 0, 0, x'x, x'y, x'z, x')^T,$$

$$\mathbf{v} = (0, 0, 0, 0, -fx, -fy, -fz, -f, y'x, y'y, y'z, y')^T,$$

$$\mathbf{c} = (s_{11}, s_{12}, s_{13}, s_{14}, s_{21}, s_{22}, s_{23}, s_{24}, s_{31}, s_{32}, s_{33}, s_{34})^T.$$

(b) Now consider accumulating a large enough number of measurement vectors, $\mathbf{u}_i$ and $\mathbf{v}_i$, to fully constrain the unknown vector $\mathbf{c}$. Show that five measurements are not enough and that six are too many.

(c) Find a vector $\mathbf{c}$ that is orthogonal to eleven vectors obtained from the six measurements by discarding one constraint. Hint: The so-called Gram–Schmidt orthogonalization procedure can be used to construct a set of orthonormal vectors that span the same space as the given vectors obtained directly from the measurements.

(d) Now, instead, set one of the coefficients, r_{34}, for example, equal to one. This is reasonable because we know that the transformation is not changed if all the coefficients are multiplied by the same positive constant. Write a set of eleven linear equations whose solution yields the unknown vector.

(e) Suppose that more than six measurements are taken to improve accuracy. It is no longer possible to find a set of coefficients that will make all of the constraint equations exactly equal to zero. Instead, minimize the sum of squares of the errors,

$$\sum_{i=1}^{n} (\mathbf{w}_i \cdot \mathbf{c})^2,$$

where the $\mathbf{w}_i$ are vectors obtained from the measurements. To avoid the trivial solution in which all coefficients are zero, you will need to impose some additional constraint, such as $|\mathbf{c}| = 1$. Hint: The constraint can be imposed using a Lagrange multiplier, as shown in the appendix.

(f) Finally, instead of imposing a nonlinear constraint as we did in the previous part, we can solve the minimization problem when one of the coefficients, s_{34}, for example, is fixed in value. Hint: Set up a matrix whose rows contain the first eleven components of the measurement vectors.

13-12 We can avoid the full complexity of the general transformation between an external coordinate system, such as that of a mechanical manipulator, and that of a camera by approximately lining up the axes of the two systems. Here we explore one such method. Let us distinguish coordinates in the external system with the subscript a and coordinates in the camera system with the subscript c. Then we can write, just as we did when we related the coordinate systems of two cameras,

$$r_{11}x_a + r_{12}y_a + r_{13}z_a + r_{14} = x_c,$$

$$r_{21}x_a + r_{22}y_a + r_{23}z_a + r_{24} = y_c,$$

$$r_{31}x_a + r_{32}y_a + r_{33}z_a + r_{34} = z_c,$$

where the 3×3 submatrix is orthonormal. We explore a particularly simple case first.

(a) Suppose that the xy-plane of the external coordinate system is exactly parallel to the xy-plane of the camera coordinate system. Which terms in the transformation are zero? Now consider a plane $z_a = z_0$ in the external coordinate system. Show that the image coordinates for the point $(x, y, z_0)^T$ in the external plane are given by

$$\frac{x'}{f} = \frac{1}{z_0 + r_{34}}\left(r_{11}x + r_{12}y + r_{14}\right),$$

$$\frac{y'}{f} = \frac{1}{z_0 + r_{34}}\left(r_{21}x + r_{22}y + r_{24}\right).$$

Conclude that the transformation from the external plane to the image plane is composed of a translation, a rotation, and a linear scaling operation. Hint: $x'/f = x_c/z_c$ and $y'/f = y_c/z_c$

In practice, it is not possible to make the image plane exactly parallel to the xy-plane of the external coordinate system. So we next treat a more general case.

(b) Suppose that the image plane is tilted relative to the xy-plane of the external coordinate system, but only a little bit. That is, r_{31} and r_{32} (as well as r_{13} and r_{23}) are small. Show that

$$\frac{x'}{f} \approx \frac{1}{r_{33}z_0 + r_{34}}\left(r_{11}x + r_{12}y + (r_{13}z_0 + r_{14})\right)\left(1 - \frac{r_{31}x + r_{32}y}{r_{33}z_0 + r_{34}}\right),$$

$$\frac{y'}{f} \approx \frac{1}{r_{33}z_0 + r_{34}}\left(r_{21}x + r_{22}y + (r_{23}z_0 + r_{24})\right)\left(1 - \frac{r_{31}x + r_{32}y}{r_{33}z_0 + r_{34}}\right).$$

Hint: $1/(1 + \epsilon) \approx (1 - \epsilon)$ for $|\epsilon| \ll 1$.

(c) Conclude that the transformation from the plane in the external coordinate system to the image plane can be adequately approximated by an affine transformation, that is, a linear transformation of the form

$$x' = a_{11}x + a_{12}y + a_{13},$$

$$y' = a_{21}x + a_{22}y + a_{23}.$$

Find the six coefficients a_{ij} in terms of the coefficients r_{ij} and the focal length f. To make this approximation, is it necessary to make any additional assumptions about the distance to the objects in the scene or about the size of the field of view? Hint: Ignore second-order terms.

(d) Note that there may now be some skewing between axes and differences in magnification measured in different directions. Show that the transformation is no longer just a composition of translation, rotation, and scaling. Hint: Show that the 2×2 submatrix need not be orthonormal.

(e) Devise a calibration procedure for estimating the six parameters of the affine transformation. How many test points must be measured? Hint: Each test point contributes two independent constraints.

(f) Invert the affine transformation to determine the point in the plane that corresponds to a particular point in the image. Hint: The inverse transformation is also affine.

(g) Explain how you could use two such affine transformations, determined for two parallel external planes, $z = z_1$ and $z = z_2$ say, to find the ray in the external coordinate system on which an object must lie in order to appear at a particular point $(x', y')^T$ in the image.

13-13 Suppose you wish to accurately determine the position and attitude of a large object that is constrained to be near some standard position and attitude. You have available a number of camera systems, each of which is capable of accurately locating the image of some notable feature on a portion of the surface of the object. Show that you need three cameras to determine the position and attitude of the object. How would you calibrate the system? That is, how would you determine the parameters needed in the algorithm for recovering the position and attitude?

13-14 Now we concentrate on the stereo matching problem. Show that if a single continuous surface is imaged, then conjugate points have to be in the same order in both images. That is, if A images to the left of B in one image, then A cannot be imaged to the right of B in the other. Under what circumstances can a reversal of order occur?

13-15 In edge-based stereo methods, edges in the left image are matched with edges in the right image to obtain disparity measurements. Here we limit ourselves to matching along a single epipolar line, thus reducing the problem to one of matching in one dimension.

(a) Suppose there are n edges in each image along an epipolar line. If each edge has a unique match in the other image, how many different mappings are there? Do not include the constraint that edges must be ordered the same way in both images.

(b) Now add the constraint that edges must be ordered the same way in both images. If every edge has a unique match, how many different mappings are there?

(c) Now let the right image have m edges $(m < n)$. Then $n - m$ of the left edges will be matched with the "null edge." How many different mappings are there if we do not require that order be preserved?

(d) Repeat part (c) for the case in which the edges are ordered the same way in both images.

(e) Now consider the case in which there are n edges in the left image and m edges in the right image, and any edge can either have a match in the other image or not. How many different mappings are there with and without the ordering constraint? Warning: We do not know the answer.

You should find that adding the ordering constraint greatly simplifies the problem. However, there are cases in which this constraint does not hold, as we saw in the previous exercise. These cases seem to be difficult even for humans to disambiguate.

13-16   Consider the following gray-level matching scheme for the stereo problem. The camera positions are such that

$$\frac{x_l'}{f} = \frac{x + b/2}{z} \quad \text{and} \quad \frac{x_r'}{f} = \frac{x - b/2}{z}.$$

We want to find a function $z(x, y)$ such that $E_l(x_l', y_l') = E_r(x_r', y_r')$. This can be approached by minimizing a function of the form $e_s + \lambda e_i$, where

$$e_s = \int\!\!\int (\nabla^2 z)^2 \, dx \, dy \quad \text{and} \quad e_i = \int\!\!\int (E_l - E_r)^2 \, dx \, dy.$$

What must $\nabla^2(\nabla^2 z)$ be equal to? How does this result differ from the one derived earlier in which the smoothness term applied to disparity instead of distance? Given the result developed in the last part of exercise 13-1, which of the two methods is to be preferred?

14

Pattern Classification

The methods discussed so far in this book belong to the realm of image analysis or early vision, that is, the processing of images themselves to extract useful data. The information so derived might go into a sketch, a detailed symbolic description of what is in the image. In the rest of the book we concern ourselves with scene analysis, that is, what can be done with this detailed information. This chapter deals with one of the simplest applications—the classification of objects based on measurements obtained from images.

One of the tasks a machine vision system must accomplish is recognition. After it has estimated various properties of an object, such as surface reflectance or color, the system needs some scheme to assign the object to one of a number of known classes. The field of pattern classification provides means for accomplishing this task. The basic idea is to extract features—measurements of quantities thought to be useful in distinguishing members of different classes. Measurements of different features are then adjoined to form a feature vector. In this way the information obtained from the image of an object is used to identify a point in some multidimensional space. In this chapter we discuss a number of methods for dividing this space into regions that correspond to different classes. An unknown is assigned to the class whose label adorns the region into which the feature vector falls. The assumption is that feature vectors of members of different classes tend to form separate clusters.

We also discuss how we might form these clusters based on models of probability distributions. We close by emphasizing that the performance of a classification method is limited by the quality of the feature measurements provided.

14.1 Introductory Example

The plan in pattern classification is to measure characteristic features of the entities we want to classify and use them to determine class membership. If, for example, all cats weighed less than 10 kg and all dogs weighed more, we could use this information to classify a set of animals. This example illustrates both the advantages and the disadvantages of the pattern classification approach. Because some cats weigh more than 10 kg and many dogs weigh less, our criterion does not lead to perfect discrimination. The method, while simple, is not foolproof. Various embellishments will lead to better, but also more complicated, methods.

Continuing with our simple example, we might first try to select a better weight threshold. To do this well we should obtain statistical information on the distribution of weights for both cats and dogs. Looking at the probability distributions of weight, we might hope to locate a value that provides better separation. It would also help us to know what fraction of the test cases are expected to be cats and what fraction dogs.

We can make two kinds of errors here: A cat could be misclassified as a dog, and vice versa. A good threshold might be one that minimized the number of expected errors. Commonly, though, the classification decision leads to some action, and we can use these actions to attach a cost to each error. We can then adjust the threshold to minimize this cost rather than simply minimizing the total number of expected errors.

14.2 Feature Vectors

Given that we cannot achieve perfect classification using one measurement, we might introduce others. We might find the age of the animals, for example, and choose a second threshold for discrimination on the basis of the fact that cats tend to live a little longer than dogs. The results of the two separate tests can be combined using such logical operations as *and* ($\wedge$) and *or* ($\vee$).

A more intelligent use of the data is suggested by the fact that age and weight are correlated. The two measurements can be combined, perhaps by dividing weight by age, or by dividing weight by the average of the expected weights for that age for both types of animals. Discrimination based on the derived factor is likely to be better than one based on either factor alone.

We can do better still by considering a labeled scattergram of weight versus age. A *scattergram* shows the points in a feature space corresponding to the known samples from the different classes. The density of points, for a particular class, tends to the two-dimensional probability distribution for that class as more and more samples are included. If we are lucky, we might find that a smooth curve can be drawn that separates all the points labeled "cat" from all the points labeled "dog." It is quite likely that we cannot do this, however. In that case we might at least be able to draw a curve that divides the plane in such a way that we make only a few errors.

To do better, we need more measurements. The space that we have to divide into compartments corresponding to different classes will then have more dimensions. Frequently this approach leads to rapidly diminishing returns. That is, new measurements are often correlated with measurements already available and thus provide little new information. Such measurements do not improve discrimination. Moreover, some measurements might be unrelated to the particular decision to be made.

To use statistical information as a guide to the selection of decision boundaries, we must derive multidimensional probability distributions. Complicated decision methods can be invented, but these are often hard to implement or require large amounts of computation.

Of course, if you know animals, you know that cats have retractable claws and dogs do not. Thus, in this case discrimination is possible using one binary feature. The lesson here is that pattern classification methods should not be adopted blindly; the results are only as good as the features selected for measurement. No amount of sophistication in the decision algorithm can make up for a poor selection of features.

14.3 The Basic Approach

Each measurement is called a *feature*. The basic paradigm is to make n measurements on the entity to be classified and then consider the result as a point in an n-dimensional *feature space*. A *feature vector* is formed by adjoining the feature measurements. Various algorithms have been explored for dividing the feature space into compartments that can be used in classification. The unknown entity is assigned to a class corresponding to the compartment into which its feature vector falls.

What does all this have to do with machine vision? Once an image has been segmented, measurements can be made on each of the image regions. An attempt can then be made to identify the object that gave rise to each region by classification based on these measurements. Examples of simple features are area, perimeter, and minimum and maximum inertia of a binary image region.

A significant problem with these methods is the acquisition of enough information to allow intelligent placement of the decision boundaries. If the underlying probability distributions are available, we can place the boundaries to minimize some error criterion. Usually, though, these distributions are estimated from a finite number of examples drawn from each of the classes, and we can often work directly with this information, rather than estimating probability densities.

The underlying assumption here is that points belonging to the same class tend to cluster and that points belonging to different classes tend to be separated. At times these assumptions are not warranted: Pattern classification methods are not good for distinguishing rational from irrational numbers or black from white squares on a checkerboard, for example.

A serious problem in the application of machine vision is that images are two-dimensional projections of a three-dimensional reality. It is difficult to come up with simple feature measurements, based directly on the image, that will be independent of the object's spatial attitude as well as of lighting and distance. Pattern classification methods will only perform well when they are based on features that are invariant to the particular imaging situation, that is, when we have extracted estimates of true properties of the object, such as reflectance and shape. But by then, of course, the problem has basically been solved!

14.4 Nearest-Neighbor Classification

Suppose that we have been given examples drawn from each of a number of classes. Let the feature vector of the jth sample in the ith class be $\mathbf{x}_{i,j}$. One way to classify an unknown vector $\mathbf{x}$ is to find the nearest example and note the class that it belongs to. That is, if for some k and l,

$$|\mathbf{x}_{k,l} - \mathbf{x}| < |\mathbf{x}_{i,j} - \mathbf{x}| \qquad \text{for all } i \text{ and } j,$$

then the unknown $\mathbf{x}$ is assigned to class k.

There are two problems with this simple idea. First, while the examples corresponding to individual classes often form *clusters*, these clusters can overlap. Unknowns that fall into a region of overlap will be considered to belong to the class that happens to have a representative nearby. Thus classification in such regions is essentially random. This may well be the best we can do, but a simple boundary is usually preferable.

One way to do better is to look at several neighbors. We might, for example, assign an unknown to the class that occurs most often among the k nearest neighbors. This makes for somewhat better performance in the overlap regions, since it provides an estimate of which class has the highest probability density there.

A second problem with nearest-neighbor classification is computational. A lot of storage is required if many examples are given. Moreover, distances between the unknown and all the examples must be computed, unless some scheme is used to divide up the space. Still, it is a straightforward method that does not require many assumptions about the distribution of the class representatives.

In some cases the clusters will form nonoverlapping blobs. If the convex hulls of the clusters do not intersect, the faces of the convex hull can be used instead of all the examples in the clusters. This results in a considerable savings in both storage and computational effort.

A big advantage of nearest-neighbor classification is that clusters can have complicated shapes; they need not be rotationally symmetric or even convex.

14.5 Nearest-Centroid Classification

Now suppose that the examples for each class form a nice round cluster and that clusters corresponding to different classes are similar in extent and do not overlap too much. It might seem wasteful to have to remember all the examples for each class in this case. Instead, the center of mass can be used to represent each one. An unknown is then considered to belong to the class whose center of mass is nearest to it.

Both storage and computation are greatly reduced by this process. Moreover, classes are now separated by smooth boundaries. In fact, the components are polytopes bounded by hyperplanes. (*Polytopes* are generalizations of convex polyhedra to other than three dimensions. They are formed by the intersection of halfspaces.) To show that the boundaries are hyperplanes, suppose that $\mathbf{x}$ is a point on the boundary between the compartment that contains the centroid $\overline{\mathbf{x}}_1$ and the one that contains the centroid $\overline{\mathbf{x}}_2$. Then

$$|\overline{\mathbf{x}}_1 - \mathbf{x}| = |\overline{\mathbf{x}}_2 - \mathbf{x}| .$$

Squaring both sides, we have

$$|\overline{\mathbf{x}}_1 - \mathbf{x}|^2 = |\overline{\mathbf{x}}_2 - \mathbf{x}|^2 ,$$

or

$$\overline{\mathbf{x}}_1^2 - 2\overline{\mathbf{x}}_1 \cdot \mathbf{x} + \mathbf{x}^2 = \overline{\mathbf{x}}_2^2 - 2\overline{\mathbf{x}}_2 \cdot \mathbf{x} + \mathbf{x}^2,$$

so that

$$(\overline{\mathbf{x}}_1 - \overline{\mathbf{x}}_2) \cdot \mathbf{x} = \frac{1}{2}(\overline{\mathbf{x}}_1 - \overline{\mathbf{x}}_2) \cdot (\overline{\mathbf{x}}_1 + \overline{\mathbf{x}}_2).$$

This equation is linear in $\mathbf{x}$. It describes a hyperplane with normal $\overline{\mathbf{x}}_1 - \overline{\mathbf{x}}_2$ passing though the point $(1/2)(\overline{\mathbf{x}}_1 + \overline{\mathbf{x}}_2)$. The boundary is thus the perpendicular bisector of the line connecting the two centroids.

This simple way of dividing up the feature space is appropriate if the clusters are rotationally symmetric and similar in extent—or if they are well separated.

14.6 Example: Classification of Leukocytes

Figure 14-1 is a scattergram of two feature measurements obtained from microscopic images. The data are derived from samples of the five common types of white blood cells. The centroids of the clusters are shown by underlining the letter corresponding to a particular class. The dashed lines show the best linear boundaries for separating the five classes.

It is clear that reliable classification using just these two features is not possible. Other measurements are needed. We might, for example, measure the brightness of various parts of the stained cell in different spectral bands. These measurements on their own would not provide reliable classification either (see figure 14-2). We can, however, construct a four-dimensional space using all four of the features introduced so far, and the samples shown here turn out to be separable by hyperplanes in this space.

14.7 Design Using Probability Density Models

If one of two neighboring clusters is much smaller than the other, it makes sense to move the boundary between them closer to the centroid of the smaller one. Similarly, if the clusters are elongated in a direction other than along the line connecting their centroids, the boundary should be tilted toward the direction of their elongation. The best way to approach these modifications of the simple scheme presented above is to use simple models of the probability distributions.

The Gaussian distribution in n dimensions,

$$\frac{1}{(2\pi)^{n/2}\sigma^n} e^{-\frac{1}{2}\frac{|\mathbf{x}-\overline{\mathbf{x}}|^2}{\sigma^2}},$$

with mean $\overline{\mathbf{x}}$ and standard deviation σ, is commonly employed. This is done not so much because it approximates probability distributions found in practice, but because it leads to tractable mathematics. We start with two distributions with the same spread σ and centroids at $\overline{\mathbf{x}}_1$ and $\overline{\mathbf{x}}_2$, respectively. We might decide to place the boundaries where the probability densities have decayed to the same value, that is, where

$$\frac{1}{(2\pi)^{n/2}\sigma^n} e^{-\frac{1}{2}\frac{|\mathbf{x}-\overline{\mathbf{x}}_1|^2}{\sigma^2}} = \frac{1}{(2\pi)^{n/2}\sigma^n} e^{-\frac{1}{2}\frac{|\mathbf{x}-\overline{\mathbf{x}}_2|^2}{\sigma^2}},$$

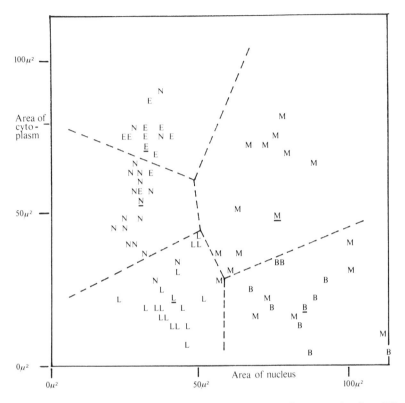

Figure 14-1. Scattergram of cytoplasm area versus nuclear area for five different common types of white blood cells. The letters denote the different classes, with the centroids underlined. The dashed lines show linear boundaries that best separate the classes. Several samples are misclassified. (Plotted from data in "Automated Leukocyte Recognition" by I.T. Young, Ph.D. thesis, MIT, Cambridge, Massachusetts, 1969.)

or simply

$$\left| \mathbf{x} - \overline{\mathbf{x}}_1 \right| = \left| \mathbf{x} - \overline{\mathbf{x}}_2 \right|.$$

This again is the equation of the perpendicular bisector of the line connecting $\overline{\mathbf{x}}_1$ to $\overline{\mathbf{x}}_2$. We have found a particular theoretical model that justifies the method earlier introduced using heuristic arguments. The boundary is placed so that equal numbers of the two different types of errors are made.

14.8 Clusters with Different Shapes

We now suppose that one class is much more common than the other.

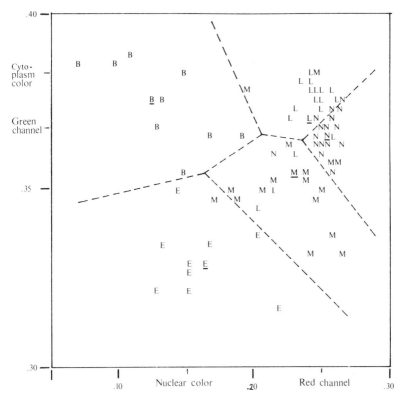

Figure 14-2. Scattergram of brightness of the cytoplasm and the nucleus measured through two different filters. The centroids are indicated by underlining, and the dashed lines are the linear boundaries that best separate the classes. It is clear that reliable classification using just these two features is not possible. (Plotted from data in "Automated Leukocyte Recognition" by I.T. Young, Ph.D. thesis, MIT, Cambridge, Massachusetts, 1969.)

Using the perpendicular bisector as the boundary leads to equal fractional errors. That is, the same fraction of unknowns from each class will be misclassified. This may or may not be what is desired. Certainly the total error in this case can be decreased by moving the boundary toward the centroid of the class that occurs less frequently. This change increases the occurrence of the rare errors and decreases the occurrence of the common errors. Let p_1 and p_2 be the probabilities of the unknown being in the first and second class, respectively. Then we want

$$\frac{p_1}{(2\pi)^{n/2}\sigma^n} e^{-\frac{1}{2}\frac{|x-\bar{x}_1|^2}{\sigma^2}} = \frac{p_2}{(2\pi)^{n/2}\sigma^n} e^{-\frac{1}{2}\frac{|x-\bar{x}_2|^2}{\sigma^2}},$$

or

$$\log p_1 - \frac{|\mathbf{x} - \overline{\mathbf{x}}_1|^2}{2\sigma^2} = \log p_2 - \frac{|\mathbf{x} - \overline{\mathbf{x}}_2|^2}{2\sigma^2}.$$

That is,

$$(\overline{\mathbf{x}}_1 - \overline{\mathbf{x}}_2) \cdot \mathbf{x} = \frac{1}{2}(\overline{\mathbf{x}}_1 - \overline{\mathbf{x}}_2) \cdot (\overline{\mathbf{x}}_1 + \overline{\mathbf{x}}_2) + \sigma^2(\log p_2 - \log p_1).$$

This, once again, is the equation of a hyperplane with normal $\overline{\mathbf{x}}_1 - \overline{\mathbf{x}}_2$. This time, however, it is displaced from the point midway between $\overline{\mathbf{x}}_1$ and $\overline{\mathbf{x}}_2$ by

$$\frac{1}{|\overline{\mathbf{x}}_1 - \overline{\mathbf{x}}_2|}\sigma^2 \log \frac{p_2}{p_1}$$

toward the centroid associated with the smaller of the probabilities p_1 and p_2. Note, by the way, that if σ and the ratio of p_2 to p_1 are large enough, the hyperplane may not even pass between the two centroids!

Next consider the case in which one cluster is more compact than the other. The boundary ought to be closer to the centroid of the more compact cluster. Let the two distributions have spreads σ_1 and σ_2, respectively. Then if we match probability densities on the boundary, we obtain

$$\frac{1}{(2\pi)^{n/2}\sigma_1^n}e^{-\frac{1}{2}\frac{|\mathbf{x} - \overline{\mathbf{x}}_1|^2}{\sigma^2}} = \frac{1}{(2\pi)^{n/2}\sigma_2^n}e^{-\frac{1}{2}\frac{|\mathbf{x} - \overline{\mathbf{x}}_2|^2}{\sigma^2}},$$

or

$$-n\log\sigma_1 - \frac{|\mathbf{x} - \overline{\mathbf{x}}_1|^2}{2\sigma_1^2} = -n\log\sigma_2 - \frac{|\mathbf{x} - \overline{\mathbf{x}}_2|^2}{2\sigma_2^2}.$$

This time the $\mathbf{x}^2$ terms do not cancel. The boundary surface is thus quadratic, not a hyperplane. While it may be harder to visualize, we can still use this equation to implement the decision method.

These results can be extended to the situation in which there are more than two classes. The boundary placement need not be guided by simple matching of probability densities. We can instead use maximum-likelihood methods or minimize some cost function. The mathematics can become intractable, however.

The simple model of the probability distributions used so far does not allow us to deal with clusters that have complex shapes. Clusters in the shape of a banana, a torus, or even a helix are hard to deal with. At times a class might even give rise to several separate clusters; in this case it is possible to treat each cluster separately in classification.

In general, if the feature measurements are suitable, any simple classification method will work. Conversely, if the measurements are not suitable, even sophisticated methods will not help.

14.9 Automatic Cluster Formation

Occasionally points will form such distinct clusters that we can contemplate automated means of discovering which points belong together. This is referred to as *unsupervised learning*. Some such methods work by successively merging existing clusters. At first, we consider each data point a separate embryonic cluster. At each step of the iterative process, we find two clusters containing two points that are closer together than any other two points in distinct clusters. These two clusters are merged. The iteration is stopped either when the expected number of clusters has been found or when the next point to be added to a cluster is more than some threshold distance away. Numerous heuristics have been developed to guide this process.

A contrasting strategy splits existing clusters along lines of weakness. Initially the whole collection of points is considered to be one huge cluster. At each stage a cluster is found that can be split in two. The iteration stops either when a desired number of divisions has been achieved or when splitting no longer appears attractive in terms of some predetermined criterion. In most cases of interest to us here, however, we know which points belong together in a class.

14.10 A Fairy Tale

Once upon a time there were two neighboring farmers, Jed and Ned. Each owned a horse, and the horses both liked to jump the fence between the two farms. Clearly the farmers needed some means to tell whose horse was whose.

So Jed and Ned got together and agreed on a scheme for discriminating between the horses. Jed would cut a small notch in one ear of his horse. Not a big, painful notch, but one just big enough to be seen. Well, wouldn't you know it, the day after Jed cut the notch in horse's ear, Ned's horse got caught on the barbed wire fence and tore his ear the exact same way!

Something else had to be devised, so Ned tied a big blue bow on the tail of his horse. But the next day, Jed's horse jumped the fence, ran into the field where Ned's horse was grazing, and chewed the bow right off the other horse's tail. Ate the whole bow!

Finally, Jed suggested, and Ned concurred, that they should pick a feature that was less apt to change. Height seemed like a good feature to use. But were the heights different? Well, each farmer went and measured his horse, and do you know what? The brown horse was a full two inches taller than the white one!

As from any fairy tale, a moral can be extracted from this one:

- When you have difficulty in classification, do not look for ever more esoteric mathematical tricks; instead, find better features.

14.11 References

There is a vast literature on pattern classification. The classic *Pattern Classification and Scene Analysis* by Duda & Hart [1973] covers that topic as well as early machine vision work. For a more recent effort see Kanal's *Pattern Recognition* [1980]. The automatic generation of classifiers is a problem of great interest in biology, as discussed by Sokal & Sneath in *Principles of Numerical Taxonomy* [1963]. Another book on this topic is *Cluster Analysis* by Everitt [1980]. Drake's *Fundamentals of Applied Probability Theory* [1967] is a representative text on probability and statistics.

The automatic generation of clusters and taxonomies has fascinated researchers for a long time. The hope is that automation will remove the inevitable bias of the person devising a taxonomy. A recent paper on this subject is that by Michalski & Stepp [1983].

The automatic classification of white blood cells was a burning issue in the late sixties and early seventies, since many leukocyte differentials were done manually each day, the cost was rapidly rising, and the results were not always reliable. Young [1969] described a system that was able to distinguish between the five major types of cells. Ingram & Preston [1970] discussed this problem in a popular article. The interest in the problem faded when it was found possible to stain the cells in such a way that a simple particle-counting method could reliably and cheaply yield accurate numbers. It turns out, however, that such chemical techniques cannot yet deal with the pathological cells, and machine vision techniques may yet play a role after all. See, for example, the article by Brenner et al. [1974].

On the whole, machine vision methods have not had a great deal of impact on the processing of images of biomedical interest. This is in part because they are very different from the images we are used to, being obtained by means of optical microscopes, electron microscopes, tomographic devices, and radioisotope scanners. People find many of these images hard to interpret and so often cannot form reliable judgments based on them. It is unrealistic to expect machine vision methods to uncover information that the marvelous human visual system has difficulty finding. For some examples of work on images of biomedical interest, see Preston [1976], Savol, Li, & Hoy [1980], Selfridge & Prewitt [1981], and De Souza [1983].

The classic application of pattern recognition methods is to character recognition. Printed characters can be read at high speed, provided they are in a known character font and without defects. Systems for reading characters in fixed fonts are now commercially available; their cost is related to speed and reliability. Only recently has it become possible to deal with degraded characters. Hand-printed characters are another matter. Isolated hand-printed characters can now be recognized under favorable circumstances. In Japan, numbers printed by hand in predetermined locations on envelopes are used to direct the delivery of the mail. See Mori et al. [1970] and Mori, Yamamoto, & Yasuda [1984]. Duerr et al. [1980] give an account of another system that deals with handwritten numerals. Cursive script still poses many tricky problems, some analogous to those in speech recognition.

The fairy tale was told to me by Michael Gennert, who attributed it to Kermit Klingbail of PAR Technology Corporation, New Hartford, New York.

14.12 Exercises

14-1 We observe a vector $\mathbf{x}$ and want to assign $\mathbf{x}$ to one of c classes. Let $\Pr\big(C_i \mid \mathbf{x}\big)$ be the probability that C_i is the class to which $\mathbf{x}$ belongs. It makes sense to assign it to the most likely class $C_m(\mathbf{x})$ such that

$$\Pr\big(C_m \mid \mathbf{x}\big) \geq \Pr\big(C_i \mid \mathbf{x}\big) \qquad \text{for } i = 1, 2, \ldots, c.$$

(a) Show that

$$\Pr\big(C_m \mid \mathbf{x}\big) \geq \frac{1}{c}.$$

(b) The average probability of error is

$$P_e = 1 - \int \Pr\big(C_m \mid \mathbf{x}\big) p\big(\mathbf{x}\big) \, d\mathbf{x}.$$

Show that $P_e \leq \frac{c-1}{c}$. When is $P_e = \frac{c-1}{c}$?

14-2 The general multivariate normal density for n variables is written

$$p(\mathbf{x}) = \frac{1}{(2\pi)^{n/2} \|\Sigma\|^{1/2}} e^{-\frac{1}{2}(\mathbf{x}-\overline{\mathbf{x}})^T \Sigma^{-1} (\mathbf{x}-\overline{\mathbf{x}})},$$

where $\overline{\mathbf{x}}$ is the *mean vector* and Σ is the *covariance matrix*. If the components of $\mathbf{x}$ are independent, then the components of the matrix Σ are

$$\sigma_{ij} = \begin{cases} \sigma_i^2, & \text{for } i = j; \\ 0, & \text{for } i \neq j. \end{cases}$$

Assuming that the components of $\mathbf{x}$ are independent, show that $p(\mathbf{x})$ can be written in the form

$$p(\mathbf{x}) = \prod_{i=1}^{n} p_i(x_i).$$

What is $p_i(x_i)$?

14-3   Here we examine the shape of the decision surface for the 2-class multi-dimensional classifier discussed in section 14.8. Let class i have mean vector $\bar{\mathbf{x}}_i$ and covariance matrix $\sigma_i^2 \mathbf{I}$, for $i = 1, 2$. Samples from each class obey a normal distribution,

$$p_i(\mathbf{x}) = \frac{1}{(2\pi)^{n/2}\sigma_i^n} e^{-\frac{1}{2}\frac{|\mathbf{x}-\bar{\mathbf{x}}_i|^2}{\sigma_i^2}}.$$

Show that the decision surface is rotationally symmetric. What is the axis of symmetry? Hint: Decompose the distance between a vector to be classified and each class mean into two orthogonal components.

14-4   The error rate for the nearest-neighbor classifier can be estimated in several ways. In this problem we examine a classifier under the assumption that there are very many known samples in each class. Let $p_{e,i}(\mathbf{x})$ be the probability of misclassifying a vector $\mathbf{x}$ from class i, and let $p_{c,i}(\mathbf{x})$ be the probability of correctly classifying a vector $\mathbf{x}$ from class i.

(a) If pr_i is the a priori probability for class i, show that the probability of correctly classifying a vector from class i is

$$p_{c,i}(\mathbf{x}) = \frac{\mathrm{pr}_i p_i(\mathbf{x})}{\sum\limits_{j} \mathrm{pr}_j p_j(\mathbf{x})},$$

where $p_i(\mathbf{x})$ is the probability distribution for class i. What is $p_{e,i}(\mathbf{x})$?

(b) Assume there are only two equally likely classes. Show that the average probability of correctly classifying a vector from class i is

$$P_{c,i} = \int \frac{p_i^2(\mathbf{x})}{p_1(\mathbf{x}) + p_2(\mathbf{x})} d\mathbf{x}.$$

Show that $P_{c,i}$ is independent of i. Show that the average probability of error $P_{e,i}$ is also independent of i and is given by

$$P_e = P_{e,i} = \int \frac{p_1(\mathbf{x})p_2(\mathbf{x})}{p_1(\mathbf{x}) + p_2(\mathbf{x})} d\mathbf{x}.$$

(c) Now let the vectors in class i be distributed by

$$p_i(\mathbf{x}) = \frac{1}{(2\pi)^{n/2}\sigma^n} e^{-\frac{1}{2}\frac{|\mathbf{x}-\bar{\mathbf{x}}_i|^2}{\sigma^2}}.$$

Show that the probability of error is

$$P_e = \frac{1}{2\sqrt{2\pi}} e^{-\frac{1}{8}d^2} \int e^{-\frac{1}{2}z^2} \left(\cosh\frac{zd}{2}\right)^{-1} dz,$$

where $d = |\bar{\mathbf{x}}_1 - \bar{\mathbf{x}}_2|/\sigma$. Conclude that $P_e \leq \frac{1}{2}e^{-\frac{1}{8}d^2}$. When does $P_e = \frac{1}{2}e^{-\frac{1}{8}d^2}$?

Note: It is best to use a nearest-centroid classifier when the data are known to be normally distributed. Nonetheless, even a nearest-neighbor classifier achieves a low error rate when the distance between class means is greater than σ.

14-5   Classifier parameters are often estimated from sample vectors whose class is initially known, a process known as *training* or *supervised learning.* Here we determine the absolute minimum number of samples needed to train various classifiers. Assume that there are c equally likely classes and that the dimensionality of the feature space is n. Furthermore, assume that we choose the sample vectors intelligently, so that we do not choose the same sample vector twice.

(a) What is the absolute minimum number of samples needed to build a nearest-neighbor classifier? Aside: Strictly speaking, nearest-neighbor classifiers are not trained.

Let each class be characterized by its mean vector $\bar{\mathbf{x}}_i$ and covariance matrix $\boldsymbol{\Sigma}_i$, where $\boldsymbol{\Sigma}_i$ is symmetric and positive-definite.

(b) If $\boldsymbol{\Sigma}_i = \sigma^2 \mathbf{I}$, independent of i, what is the minimum number of samples needed to train a nearest-centroid classifier?

The variance σ^2 of a scalar normal random variable x can be estimated from s samples x_i by the following unbiased estimator:

$$\sigma^2 = \frac{1}{s-1} \sum_{j=1}^{s} (x_j - \bar{x})^2,$$

where $\bar{x}$ is the estimated mean.

(c) If

$$\boldsymbol{\Sigma}_i = \begin{pmatrix} \sigma_1^2 & & 0 \\ & \ddots & \\ 0 & & \sigma_n^2 \end{pmatrix}$$

independent of i, what is the minimum number of samples needed to train the classifier?

(d) If $\boldsymbol{\Sigma}_i = \sigma_i^2 \mathbf{I}$, what is the minimum number of samples needed?

(e) If

$$\boldsymbol{\Sigma}_i = \begin{pmatrix} \sigma_{i,1}^2 & & 0 \\ & \ddots & \\ 0 & & \sigma_{i,n}^2 \end{pmatrix}$$

what is the minimum number of samples needed?

In the most general case, $\boldsymbol{\Sigma}_i$ need not be diagonal. It can be estimated from s samples by the following unbiased estimator:

$$\boldsymbol{\Sigma}_i = \frac{1}{s-1} \sum_{j=1}^{s} (\mathbf{x}_{i,j} - \bar{\mathbf{x}}_i)(\mathbf{x}_{i,j} - \bar{\mathbf{x}}_i)^T,$$

where $\mathbf{x}_{i,j}$ is the jth sample from class i. This is a straightforward generalization of the unbiased variance estimator for a scalar random variable.

(f) Show that there are $cn(n+3)/2$ different parameters that must be estimated.

(g) The above result might suggest that at least $c(n+3)/2$ samples are needed to train the classifier. This figure is too low, however, because $\mathbf{\Sigma}_i$ must be positive-definite. Prove that the minimum number of samples needed to train the classifier is $c(n+1)$ by showing that when the above estimator is used, $\mathbf{\Sigma}_i$ is singular (and thus not positive-definite) for $s \leq d$ and that $\mathbf{\Sigma}_i$ can be nonsingular for $s \geq n + 1$. Warning: This part is difficult.

Important note: In practice, a classifier designer will use training sets that are at least three or four times larger than the minimum to ensure robust estimation of the classifier parameters.

15

Polyhedral Objects

Ideally, the image of a polyhedral object will be composed of a number of regions of uniform brightness corresponding to the faces of the object. Such an image is highly redundant and can be conveniently described by a line drawing. Line drawings can be obtained using the edge-detection schemes described in chapter 8. In this chapter we discuss how to interpret line drawings of scenes that contain one or more polyhedral objects. There are two aspects to this problem. The first is to determine which regions in the image belong together, in the sense that they correspond to faces of the same polyhedral object. We develop labeling techniques that make use of precompiled tables of valid labelings for joins where lines come together.

The second part of the problem is the recovery of three-dimensional information about the vertices, edges, and faces of the objects. We use gradient space, introduced earlier in our discussion of shading, to help in this endeavor. We find that a line drawing alone does not provide enough constraint to allow full recovery of three-dimensional shape. The addition of brightness measurements for each of the regions removes the ambiguity. We end the chapter with a brief discussion of a simple closed-loop hand–eye system that uses a mechanical manipulator to build a copy of a structure composed of children's toy blocks.

15.1 Line Drawings of Polyhedral Scenes

Suppose we know that in a particular situation we will only see objects bounded by planar faces; smoothly curved surfaces will not occur. Numerous simplifications arise in this situation. Perhaps most important is the fact that polyhedra can be represented conveniently in the computer. We can, for example, give the coordinates of the vertices, then note which vertices are connected. Alternatively, the equations of the planar faces can be given, together with notes describing which of their intersections lie on the object. There are many ways to represent polyhedral objects in terms of vertices, edges, and faces. The important thing is that no inherent approximation is involved, as is usually the case with curved surfaces.

A planar face has the same surface orientation throughout. To a first approximation such a face gives rise to a region of constant brightness in the image. An edge on the object, corresponding to a discontinuity in surface orientation, will usually give rise to a discontinuity in brightness. This discontinuity will extend along the line in the image that is the projection of the edge. It seems, then, that the image should consist of a patchwork of polygonal regions, each of uniform brightness.

Edge-detection and line-finding methods might be expected to produce a perfect line drawing from the image. In practice, regions rarely have constant brightness, and the brightness discontinuities between regions can be submerged in noise. The line drawings produced will not be perfect for these reasons, but for now we assume that they are.

To change the topic slightly for a moment, consider an issue glossed over previously when we expressed concern about evaluating the performance of segmentation and edge-detection schemes. These misgivings came about because we lacked a clear idea of what the ideal output of either of these two types of systems ought to be when they are presented with an arbitrary image. In the case of a scene composed of polyhedral objects, the issue is clear: A scene segmenter ought to produce a set of regions corresponding to faces of the polyhedral objects, while an edge finder ought to recover a set of lines corresponding to the edges. It is not obvious what scene segmentation or edge finding should lead to when we are dealing with a scene that is not composed of polyhedral objects.

15.2 Recovering Three-Dimensional Structure

Given a line drawing of a polyhedron, we might be asked to determine its three-dimensional structure. Curiously, good methods for attacking this problem have been found, while we still struggle with the problem of making a good line drawing in the first place! Each vertex lies on a ray defined by the corresponding junction in the line drawing. We do not know how far along this ray the vertex lies, however. Determining the arrangement of vertices in three dimensions, then, implies finding the distances to each of the vertices.

If all the faces are triangular, we receive no help in this task, since we can freely move all of the vertices along the rays. If a face has four sides, and hence four vertices, a constraint on their distances is induced by their coplanarity. Suppose that the four vertices have coordinates $\mathbf{v}_1$, $\mathbf{v}_2$, $\mathbf{v}_3$, and $\mathbf{v}_4$. Then $\mathbf{v}_4$ must lie on the plane defined by $\mathbf{v}_1$, $\mathbf{v}_2$, and $\mathbf{v}_3$. Equivalently we want the volume of the parallelepiped with sides $\mathbf{v}_2 - \mathbf{v}_1$, $\mathbf{v}_3 - \mathbf{v}_1$, and $\mathbf{v}_4 - \mathbf{v}_1$ to be zero. That is,

$$\left[(\mathbf{v}_2 - \mathbf{v}_1)\, (\mathbf{v}_3 - \mathbf{v}_1)\, (\mathbf{v}_4 - \mathbf{v}_1) \right] = 0,$$

or

$$\left[\mathbf{v}_4\, \mathbf{v}_1\, \mathbf{v}_2 \right] + \left[\mathbf{v}_2\, \mathbf{v}_3\, \mathbf{v}_4 \right] = \left[\mathbf{v}_1\, \mathbf{v}_2\, \mathbf{v}_3 \right] + \left[\mathbf{v}_3\, \mathbf{v}_4\, \mathbf{v}_1 \right],$$

where the triple product $[\mathbf{a}\,\mathbf{b}\,\mathbf{c}]$ is $\mathbf{a} \cdot (\mathbf{b} \times \mathbf{c})$. If we assume that the image was formed by perspective projection, then

$$\mathbf{v}_1 = z_1\, \overline{\mathbf{v}}_1, \quad \mathbf{v}_2 = z_2\, \overline{\mathbf{v}}_2, \quad \mathbf{v}_3 = z_3\, \overline{\mathbf{v}}_3, \quad \mathbf{v}_4 = z_4\, \overline{\mathbf{v}}_4,$$

where z_1, z_2, z_3, and z_4 are the distances to the points and $\overline{\mathbf{v}}_1$, $\overline{\mathbf{v}}_2$, $\overline{\mathbf{v}}_3$, and $\overline{\mathbf{v}}_4$ are vectors to the known image points.

The above constraint can be written

$$\frac{\left[\overline{\mathbf{v}}_4\, \overline{\mathbf{v}}_1\, \overline{\mathbf{v}}_2 \right]}{z_3} + \frac{\left[\overline{\mathbf{v}}_2\, \overline{\mathbf{v}}_3\, \overline{\mathbf{v}}_4 \right]}{z_1} = \frac{\left[\overline{\mathbf{v}}_1\, \overline{\mathbf{v}}_2\, \overline{\mathbf{v}}_3 \right]}{z_4} + \frac{\left[\overline{\mathbf{v}}_3\, \overline{\mathbf{v}}_4\, \overline{\mathbf{v}}_1 \right]}{z_2}.$$

This equation is linear in the reciprocals of the distances. The coefficients are determined from the coordinates of the points in the image plane.

Thus a face with four sides provides one constraint on the four unknown distances. Similarly, a face with p_i sides provides $p_i - 3$ constraints. The total number of constraints is

$$\sum_{i=1}^{m} (p_i - 3),$$

where m is the number of faces and p_i is the number of vertices on the ith face. The number of unknowns is p, the total number of vertices. Note that this is not equal to

$$\sum_{i=1}^{m} p_i,$$

since some vertices will be found on more than one face.

As an example, look at a cube from a point somewhere along a line connecting its center to one of its corners. Three faces are visible, each with four vertices. Together, they provide three constraints. Unfortunately, there are seven vertices and thus seven unknowns. We know that we cannot determine the absolute distance to the cube from a single image, so we might as well set one of these distances to some fixed value. That still leaves us three constraints short. Are there situations in which the image information provides complete constraint?

The answer is no. We can show that

$$(p - 3) \geq \sum_{i=1}^{m} (p_i - 3).$$

This is certainly true for a single polygon with p sides. If we bring together two polygons with p_1 and p_2 sides along an edge of common length, then a new figure results that has a number of vertices two less than the sum of the number of vertices of the component figures. Since

$$(p_1 + p_2 - 2) - 3 > (p_1 - 3) + (p_2 - 3),$$

the inequality above is preserved.

Suppose that instead we draw a line across a polygon with p sides, splitting it into two polygons with p_1 and p_2 sides, respectively. The number of vertices remains the same. Now $p = p_1 + p_2 - 2$, and since

$$(p_1 + p_2 - 2) - 3 > (p_1 - 3) + (p_2 - 3),$$

the inequality is preserved once more.

We always have at least three more unknowns than constraints. A unique solution is not possible without additional information, such as the lengths of some of the sides, the angles between them, or the plane in which some of the vertices lie.

The fact that the system of equations is underdetermined is no guarantee that it is consistent, by the way. If two faces meet along two edges, for example, we obtain two pairs of equations that are not consistent, unless the two edges are collinear. The only other possibility is that the two faces are coplanar, in which case we would not expect to see a brightness discontinuity between them. Configurations of lines that do not correspond to objects composed of planar faces lead to more subtle inconsistencies.

15.3 Gradient Space

If we know the coordinates of the vertices, we can determine the equations of the planes in which the faces lie. Conversely, we can establish these first, then compute the coordinates of the vertices. We choose to consider the case of orthographic projection here. What we need to do is to determine the orientation of each face. If the equation of a plane is

$$ax + by + cz = d,$$

then

$$\frac{\partial z}{\partial x} = -\frac{a}{c} \quad \text{and} \quad \frac{\partial z}{\partial y} = -\frac{b}{c}.$$

The gradient $(-a/c, -b/c)$ can be used to define the orientation of a plane. Thus each face of the polyhedron corresponds to a point in gradient space. We need to determine the arrangement of these points.

What constraints are there on the positions of these points in gradient space? It turns out that the lines in the image are of great importance. Suppose we have two planes with normals $\mathbf{a}$ and $\mathbf{b}$. Their line of intersection will be parallel to the cross-product of the two normals,

$$\mathbf{v} = \mathbf{a} \times \mathbf{b}.$$

The orthographic projection of this vector into the image plane is

$$\mathbf{v} - (\mathbf{v} \cdot \hat{\mathbf{z}})\hat{\mathbf{z}},$$

where $\hat{\mathbf{z}}$ is the unit vector along the optical axis. This can be written

$$(\hat{\mathbf{z}} \cdot \hat{\mathbf{z}})\mathbf{v} - (\mathbf{v} \cdot \hat{\mathbf{z}})\hat{\mathbf{z}},$$

or

$$(\hat{\mathbf{z}} \times \mathbf{v}) \times \hat{\mathbf{z}},$$

since $(\mathbf{a} \times \mathbf{b}) \times \mathbf{c} = (\mathbf{a} \cdot \mathbf{c})\mathbf{b} - (\mathbf{b} \cdot \mathbf{c})\mathbf{a}$. Thus the line in the image that is the projection of the edge is parallel to

$$\big(\hat{\mathbf{z}} \times (\mathbf{a} \times \mathbf{b})\big) \times \hat{\mathbf{z}}.$$

The gradient-space points A and B corresponding to the two planes are

$$\left(-\frac{\mathbf{a}}{\mathbf{a} \cdot \hat{\mathbf{z}}} - \hat{\mathbf{z}}\right) \quad \text{and} \quad \left(-\frac{\mathbf{b}}{\mathbf{b} \cdot \hat{\mathbf{z}}} - \hat{\mathbf{z}}\right),$$

respectively. The line connecting these two points in gradient space is parallel to

$$\frac{(\mathbf{b} \cdot \hat{\mathbf{z}})\mathbf{a} - (\mathbf{a} \cdot \hat{\mathbf{z}})\mathbf{b}}{(\mathbf{a} \cdot \hat{\mathbf{z}})(\mathbf{b} \cdot \hat{\mathbf{z}})} = \frac{\hat{\mathbf{z}} \times (\mathbf{a} \times \mathbf{b})}{(\mathbf{a} \cdot \hat{\mathbf{z}})(\mathbf{b} \cdot \hat{\mathbf{z}})}.$$

We saw earlier that the line in the image is parallel to $(\hat{\mathbf{z}} \times (\mathbf{a} \times \mathbf{b})) \times \hat{\mathbf{z}}$. So the line in gradient space must be perpendicular to the image line!

Each image line separating regions gives rise to one constraint of this kind. In the case of the cube we obtain three constraints, one for each line radiating outward from the vertex facing the viewer. If the gradient-space points corresponding to the three visible regions are A, B, and C, then they form a triangle, the angles of which are determined by the angles between the three lines radiating from the central corner. The three constraints determine the shape and orientation of the gradient-space figure, but not its size and position.

Again, line drawings that do not correspond to any polyhedron do not have proper gradient-space figures. If two faces intersect in two edges, for example, these edges must be collinear unless the two planes have the same gradient.

15.4 Shading and the Gradient Space

Use of the gradient space here may have reminded you of the reflectance map that tells us how bright a surface patch with a given orientation should appear. This provides additional constraint that is normally lost in the line drawing. Suppose, however, that we do have a representation that allows us to retain the measured brightness of each region. Then the image irradiance equation gives us one constraint for each region. The corresponding point in gradient space must fall on a particular contour of the reflectance map.

Consider again the image of a cube. We obtain three constraints from the condition that the lines in gradient space must be orthogonal to the lines in the image. We obtain three more from the image irradiance equation. This is enough to solve for the six unknowns, that is, the three positions in gradient space. In fact, for more complex polyhedra the problem is now overdetermined, there being more constraints than unknowns. Any trihedral corner in isolation allows for a local solution. It is clear, then, that shading provides a powerful additional cue.

15.5 Segmentation and Multiple Objects

So far we have dealt with a single polyhedron. The lines in the image are the projections of edges lying between faces on the object. In some cases both faces are visible, in others only one. Edges in the latter case are called *occluding edges*. In the case of a single convex polyhedron, only the lines forming the silhouette of the line drawing correspond to occluding edges. The edges corresponding to all other lines lie between visible faces. Thus all interior lines generate a constraint on the gradients of adjacent faces.

If there are multiple objects, the situation is more complicated, since some interior lines of the line drawing correspond to edges where one object occludes another. The problem here is to figure out which regions in the image belong together, in the sense that the corresponding faces all belong to the same object. How do we segment the image into collections of regions corresponding to separate objects?

This problem cannot be solved if objects are allowed to touch each other, since we cannot tell from an image whether the objects are solidly connected where they touch or whether they can be separated. Suppose, for example, that we put a cube on the end of a brick-shaped object lying flat. We cannot tell from an image whether this is a single L-shaped object or two objects.

The two faces corresponding to the regions on either side of an occluding line do not intersect in an edge corresponding to that line. The edge is generated instead by the intersection of a hidden face and one of the two visible ones—the other visible face bears no relation to the edge. Clearly, then, the gradient-space constraint cannot be imposed on the two visible faces.

We could try to determine the three-dimensional structure of a scene assuming that all lines correspond to *connect* edges—those between visible faces. Typically we would quickly find the resulting equations to be inconsistent.

At this point we could remove one of the constraints and try again. If the equations are no longer inconsistent, then it is possible to interpret the line drawing in terms of an arrangement of polyhedra. This is not to say that no other interpretations are possible. For example, we could assume that all the edges are occluding edges. Then the faces would be portions of arbitrary planes arranged in any way we please along the rays through their vertices.

A line in an image corresponds either to an obscuring edge or to one that separates two connected faces of a polyhedral object. It is easy to systematically explore all possible combinations of interpretations for all of the lines in the image. Typically, the "most-connected" interpretation arrived at agrees with human judgment of what a line drawing is supposed to represent. Naturally, all of these considerations are moot if the brightness values of the region are known, since there is then no ambiguity.

Segmentation of an image into regions corresponding to distinguishable entities in the environment is a ubiquitous problem. Many techniques for analyzing images apply only if they are confined to one such region and fail if applied, without restriction, to the whole image. Methods for determining the translational and rotational components of motion from the optical flow, for example, do not work if the data are a mixture of information from two objects moving in different ways. As we saw, the computation of optical flow is definitely hampered by the lack of image segmentation.

15.6 Labeling Line Drawings

Often the available information does not permit a complete determination of the three-dimensional structure. Yet some information can be determined from what is available. It can be useful simply to distinguish lines that correspond to connected edges from those that do not.

If a line corresponds to an occluding edge, it is helpful to know which of the two regions on either side of the line corresponds to the occluding face. We shall use a convenient graphical notation, labeling occluded lines with arrows. The direction of the arrow indicates which region corresponds to the occluding face; the corresponding image region lies to our right when we look in the direction of the arrow.

If the line corresponds to an edge between two visible faces, we can also distinguish two qualitatively different cases. In one situation the edge is *convex*—that is, the relative positions of the two gradients in gradient space are the same as those of the two regions in the image. In the other, the edge is *concave*—that is, the relative positions of the gradients of the two faces are reversed in gradient space relative to their positions in the image. We denote a convex edge by a plus sign and a concave edge by a minus sign.

Altogether, then, each line in the line drawing must have one of four different labels, and our task is to discover this labeling. Certain combinations of labels are impossible, as we shall see.

We restrict ourselves to the situation in which three faces meet at a vertex. (Other types of vertices tend to complicate the analysis.) Furthermore, we assume that all lines meeting at a point in the image correspond to edges that meet at a vertex on some object. In this way we avoid an *accidental alignment* in which we happen to be viewing a vertex from a direction that makes it line up with a more distant edge. We also assume that the outer lines of the line drawing—its silhouette—correspond to edges that occlude the "background."

A vertex at which three faces meet can be viewed only from certain directions and can give rise to only a few possible configurations of labels at the corresponding join of lines in the image. First, consider the corner of a cube. The three planes meeting at the corner divide space up into octants. The corner can be viewed from each of the seven octants in which the material of the cube does not occlude the corner. Viewed from a point along a line from the center to the corner, three lines are seen meeting at a point, each line to be labeled *convex*. From anywhere within that octant, the arrangement of lines looks pretty much the same, with the angles between lines always less than $180°$.

Thus one possible labeling of a *Y-joint*—a joint at which three lines meet with angles less than $180°$—is to have all three lines convex.

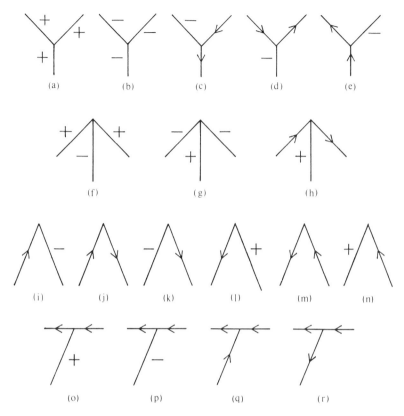

Figure 15-1. In a polyhedral world in which only trihedral vertices are allowed, it is easy to set up a dictionary of all allowed labelings, since there are only four joint types.

The remaining octants come in two groups of three. From one of these groups we can also see three lines, but now one of the angles is larger than 180°. The two lines forming this angle are obscuring edges. A possible labeling of this *arrow-joint* has the shaft labeled *convex*, while the other two lines are labeled *obscuring*, in the sense that the faces on the side containing the shaft of the arrow correspond to the obscuring faces.

From the other octants only two lines appear, both obscuring. Thus one possible labeling of an *L-joint* has both lines obscuring, in the sense that the obscuring face is on the side where the angle between the lines is less than 180°.

This exercise can now be repeated for the situation in which 3, 5, and 7 octants are occupied by the object, instead of just one. In the last case,

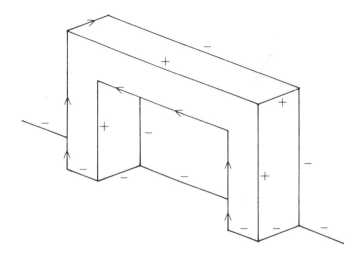

Figure 15-2. Each line in a line drawing can be assigned a label in such a way that the combination of labels at each vertex can be found in the dictionary. If no consistent labeling exists, then the scene is "impossible," that is, no collection of polyhedra with trihedral vertices could have given rise to it. There may, on the other hand, be several different valid labelings.

for example, we find only one more possible labeling for a Y-joint—one in which all the lines are concave. Altogether we find 5 possible labels for a Y-joint, 3 for an arrow-joint, and 6 for an L-joint (figure 15-1). Compare this to all possible ways of assigning four labels to three lines or two lines, respectively!

If one object occludes another, we might see a *T-joint*, at which an edge of one object partially occludes an edge of another. The point where the lines meet in the image does not correspond to a vertex, a particular point on an object, as it does in the other cases. Thus the upright portion of the "T" can be labeled in four different ways. The bar of the T, however, must be labeled *occluding*. Thus there are four possible ways to label a T-joint.

We have now developed a "dictionary" of possible joint labelings (figure 15-1). How do we apply this dictionary to label a line drawing? The labels we choose must be consistent with the dictionary. Each line can have only one label, and both of its ends must be labeled the same way. As an example, a valid labeling of a line drawing representing a fireplace with a mantel is shown in figure 15-2.

One way to proceed would be to try all possible ways of labeling a line drawing and check whether the result is consistent with the dictionary.

Because a drawing with n lines leads to 4^n possible assignments, though, this is not a good approach, except for very simple images.

A more reasonable approach is to organize the algorithm as a tree search. We choose a joint, label it in an acceptable way, move along one line to a second joint, choose a label from the dictionary consistent with what we already have, and so on. When a joint cannot be labeled, we back up and try another alternative for the last choice. Such a *depth-first* tree search can still be very slow for a complicated scene.

It might help to start by eliminating labels that are "obviously" wrong to avoid retrying them many times. One way to do this is to check for local consistency only. Start by tabulating at each joint the possible labels from the dictionary. Now systematically eliminate those that are not consistent. For example, if joints A and B are connected by a line and the possible labels at B allow only *convex* and *concave* as labels for the line joining them, then all labels at A that require the line to be obscuring can be removed.

This is an iterative process, since the reduced set of possibilities at joint A may further constrain the possibilities at joint B and others. This *constraint propagation* process is rapid, despite its iterative nature. While it is not guaranteed to eliminate all but the correct labelings, it often does just that. At times, though, a complicated situation requires that the results be further processed by the tree-search method.

These labeling methods can be further extended to deal with shadows, which actually reduce ambiguity. It is also possible to deal with planes instead of solid objects, in which case ambiguity is increased. In the case of objects with curved surfaces, the situation becomes much more complicated, since an edge can change type from one end to the other.

15.7 The Copy Demonstration

An early version of these labeling ideas was used in a system built in 1970 by Patrick Winston, Berthold Horn, and Eugene Freuder to perform the "copy-demo." An edge finder, devised in part by Thomas Binford, analyzed the image of a simple structure built by stacking toy blocks. This line drawing was then transformed into a symbolic description of the scene, in which the objects were identified and their spatial relationships made explicit. Based on this description, a plan was developed for taking the structure apart.

Separate calibration programs determined distortions in the camera as well as the *hand–eye transformation*—the transformation from the coordinate system of the mechanical manipulator to that of the camera. Least-squares techniques were employed, quite similar to the ones discussed in chapter 13. The mechanical manipulator carried out the reverse of the

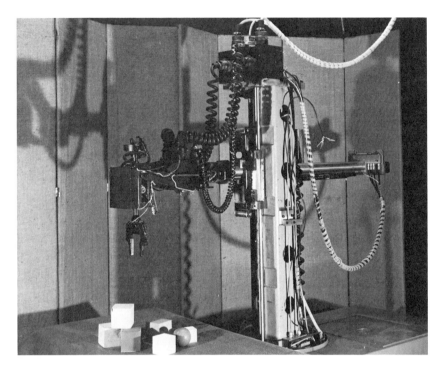

Figure 15-3. The mechanical manipulator used in the "copy-demo," one of the first projects in which visual information was used to plan the motions of an industrial robot. (Photo by Steve Slesinger.)

assembly plan in order to build a copy of the structure using spare parts found in a "warehouse" (figure 15-3).

15.8 References

Roberts [1965] not only developed a line finder, but also pioneered the interpretation of the resulting line drawings. His program found the best fit between what appeared in the line drawing and the stored models it had available. Guzmán-Arenas [1968a,b] developed a heuristic program that did not require explicit models of the objects. For a while its success encouraged the heuristic programming school of artificial intelligence. Soon, however, it was discovered that a potentially endless series of exceptions would have to be dealt with by means of various ad hoc fixes.

It turns out that line finders are not perfectly reliable and that missing lines and extra lines confuse the simple schemes. Freuder came up with a heuristic method that was used in 1970 in the M.I.T. "copy-demo" system; see Winston [1972] and Freuder [1976, 1980]. Falk [1972], facing the same kinds of problems in hand–eye work at Stanford, invented another way to deal with imperfect line drawings. For other early work see Barrow & Popplestone [1971].

The next step in the evolution of line interpretation schemes was taken independently by Clowes [1971] and Huffman [1971]. The new labeling schemes for lines appeared to provide a means of distinguishing impossible from possible scenes. There were two problems with these schemes; one was the possibility of many valid labelings applying to a simple scene, and the other was the lack of an efficient, systematic way to uncover all of the legal labelings. Waltz [1972] found that adding information from shadows, while making the labeling dictionary much larger, greatly reduced the ambiguity. He also invented the "constraint propagation" scheme, which quickly finds a set of potential labelings that then can be subjected to more thorough checking. Rosenfeld, Hummel, & Zucker [1976] applied relaxation algorithms to the scene-labeling problem. Ullman [1979] considered relaxation methods as iterative schemes for solving constrained optimization problems. Cooperative processes are surveyed by Davis & Rosenfeld [1980], while Hummel & Zucker [1980] study the foundations of relaxation labeling processes.

The work of Huffman and Clowes has been extended in several ways. First of all, there have been efforts to deal with worlds more complex than that of children's blocks. Kanade [1980b, 1981, 1983], for example, dealt with free-standing surfaces, his so-called Origami world. Many more papers have been published, since the analysis of line drawings was at one point the focus of vision work in the artificial intelligence community. Representative papers are those of Sankar [1977] and Barrow & Tenenbaum [1981b].

Quantitative analysis started early on, almost in parallel with the line-labeling work. Mackworth [1973] introduced the gradient space in order to deal with metric aspects of line drawings. He was motivated by the discovery that line drawings that could not be the projections of collections of polyhedral objects would be labeled and accepted by the schemes that did not take quantitative information into account. The gradient space was then adopted by Horn [1977] in the definition of the reflectance map. Mackworth [1977] provides a very readable critique of the efforts in scene analysis up to that point. Huffman [1975] used the Gaussian sphere and Gaussian curvature to reason about the folding of paper. Huffman [1977a,b] explored the dual space in his search for the ultimate method for distinguishing impossible from possible objects. Draper [1981] continued use of the gradient space and the dual space in line-drawing interpretation. Shafer, Kanade, & Kender [1983] extended the use of gradient space to the case of perspective projection, and Shafer & Kanade [1983] found shadows useful in discovering surface orientation.

The final breakthrough in the quantitative analysis came with Sugihara's [1982a,b, 1984a,b] systematic analytical attack. Shapira [1984] pointed out a problem with Sugihara's result that has, however, been resolved since then. Sugihara's work has not received the attention it deserves, since it does not fit into the mold of previous work and depends on mathematical techniques that may not be accessible to all.

Line drawings of smoothly curved objects have also been considered. Work in this area includes that of Turner [1974], Shapira & Freeman [1979], Jain & Aggarwal [1979], and Draper [1981]. Malik [1985] recently came up with a rigorous scheme for interpreting line drawings of opaque objects with piecewise-smooth surfaces.

15.9 Exercises

15-1   Are there other valid labelings of the line drawing of the fireplace with a mantel shown in figure 15-2? If so, which lines have labels that are the same in all possible labelings?

15-2   Imagine that you find yourself in a world of smooth, convex objects. By *smooth* we mean continuous in first derivatives; that is, there are no discontinuities in surface orientation and therefore no edges. Assume an image-processing system that provides flawless line drawings of the scene before the camera. Assume *general position*, meaning that you do not need to consider accidental alignments.

(a)   List all possible ways that a line may be labeled. Hint: Note that lines appear only where the line of sight is tangent to the surface.

(b)   List the joint types and all possible ways of labeling a joint of each type. Hint: There is only one joint type.

(c)   What extensions would be needed to deal with smooth objects that are not convex? Hint: Consider "joints" at which one line ends without meeting another.

15-3   Suppose that each line in a drawing can be labeled in one of four different ways and that there are n lines in a drawing. Compare the computational requirements of the following approaches to line labeling:

• Brute-force—systematically try all possibilities.

• Tree search—depth-first, for example.

• Constraint propagation—the iterative elimination of inconsistent labels.

How many steps do you expect each method to take? Assume that the average branching factor in the case of tree search is two, while constraints typically propagate to 2.5 neighboring vertices in the filtering approach. Make other suitable assumptions to render the problem manageable.

15-4 In reasoning about points, lines, and planes in space, it is often useful to use a construct called *dual space*. The point $\mathbf{a}$ in object space corresponds to the plane with equation $\mathbf{a} \cdot \mathbf{v} = 1$ in dual space. Symmetrically, the plane with equation $\mathbf{a} \cdot \mathbf{v} = 1$ in object space maps into the point $\mathbf{a}$ in dual space. Note that the dual of the dual of a point or a plane is the point or plane itself.

(a) Show that the unit normal of the plane $\mathbf{a} \cdot \mathbf{v} = 1$ is $\hat{\mathbf{a}} = \mathbf{a}/|a|$ and that the perpendicular distance of the plane from the origin is $1/|a|$, where $|a| = \sqrt{\mathbf{a} \cdot \mathbf{a}}$.

(b) A line can be defined either by two points it passes through or as the intersection of two planes that contain it. What is the dual of the line connecting the two points $\mathbf{a}_1$ and $\mathbf{a}_2$? What is the dual of the line formed by the intersection of the two planes $\mathbf{a}_1 \cdot \mathbf{v} = 1$ and $\mathbf{a}_2 \cdot \mathbf{v} = 1$? Hint: The line of intersection of two planes is perpendicular to the normals of both planes.

(c) Now superimpose dual space on object space. Show that a line is perpendicular to its dual. Hint: The lines need not intersect, so just show that the dot-product of vectors parallel to the directions of the two lines is zero.

We can project object space orthographically into image space. That is, a point $\mathbf{v}$ in object space is mapped into

$$\mathbf{v}' = \mathbf{v} - (\mathbf{v} \cdot \hat{\mathbf{z}})\hat{\mathbf{z}}$$

in image space. (We can drop the third component of this vector since it is zero.) We use perspective projection, on the other hand, to map dual space into gradient space. That is, a point $\mathbf{v}$ in dual space is mapped into

$$\mathbf{v}' = \frac{\mathbf{v}}{\mathbf{v} \cdot \hat{\mathbf{z}}} - \hat{\mathbf{z}}$$

in gradient space. (Once again, the third component of this vector can be dropped since it is zero.)

(d) Project a line into image space and project its dual into gradient space. Now superimpose image space and gradient space. Show that the two projected lines are perpendicular to each other. Hint: This does not follow directly from the fact that the lines in object space and dual space are perpendicular.

15-5 Suppose the polyhedral objects being imaged are known to be rectangular. The problem here is to determine the attitude in space of a rectangular polyhedron, or brick, from the angles between the three lines in the projection of one corner (figure 15-4). Let us call these three lines L_a, L_b, and L_c. They correspond to three edges E_a, E_b, and E_c on the object. We know that these three edges are mutually orthogonal.

Suppose that the angle between L_b and L_c (that is, the angle opposite the line L_a) is A, the angle opposite L_b is B, and the angle opposite L_c is C. Assume orthographic projection. Let a be the angle between the edge E_a and a plane parallel to the image plane, with b and c defined similarly. The attitude in space of the brick is fully determined once we know these three angles.

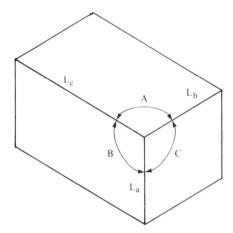

Figure 15-4. The orientation in space of a rectangular object can be recovered from an orthographic view. The angles A, B, and C measured in the image allow us to determine the angles between each of the three edges meeting at the corner and a plane parallel to the image plane.

Show that

$$\sin a = \sqrt{\frac{\cos B \cos C}{\sin B \sin C}} \qquad \text{and} \qquad \cos a = \sqrt{-\frac{\cos A}{\sin B \sin C}}.$$

Similar formulae for the other two angles can be obtained by simultaneous cyclical permutation of the variables. Hint: You might find useful the relationships between the sides and angles of spherical triangles given in the appendix.

16

Extended Gaussian Images

Representational issues are of great importance in machine vision. In this chapter we explore a particular way of representing the shape of an object. Extended Gaussian images are useful for such tasks as recognition and determining the attitude of an object in space. Extended Gaussian images can be computed easily from needle diagrams obtained using photometric stereo, or depth maps obtained using the binocular stereo method. To introduce this concept, we first describe the Gaussian image and define Gaussian curvature. When we use a computer to manipulate this kind of information, it must be discretized. The orientation histogram is a discrete version of the extended Gaussian image. We discuss various ways of tessellating the surface of the unit sphere used to generate the cells needed for the orientation histogram.

Several examples of extended Gaussian images are developed. Those of solids of revolution are particularly easy to derive. In the exercises we explore the extended circular image, the two-dimensional analog of the extended Gaussian image. The extended circular image is useful in the analysis and processing of curves in the plane. We also introduce the support function and the mixture of two objects, two new concepts that are important in a scheme for matching an experimentally obtained orientation histogram with a stored prototype. The matching problem and the problem of determining the attitude of an object using an orientation histogram are explored in more detail in chapter 18, where we discuss a system that picks parts out of a bin.

16.1 Convex Polyhedra

In order to recognize objects and determine their attitude in space, we must have a way to represent the shapes of their surfaces. One possibility is to give the distances to the surfaces along rays corresponding to each picture cell. This representation is called a *depth map*. A range finder produces surface descriptions in this form. Unfortunately, these distances do not transform in a simple way when an object rotates. Alternatively, the surface orientation might be given for points on the surface corresponding to each picture cell. Such a representation is called a *needle diagram*. Photometric stereo produces surface descriptions in this form. This, too, is not a particularly helpful representation when it comes to comparing surfaces of objects that may be rotated relative to one another.

The extended Gaussian image, on the other hand, does make it easy to deal with varying attitude of an object in space. Some information appears to be discarded in the formation of the extended Gaussian image, but curiously, at least in the case of convex objects, the representation is nevertheless unique. That is, no two convex objects have the same extended Gaussian image.

We start our discussion with objects having planar faces. Minkowski showed that a convex polyhedron is fully specified by the area and orientation of its faces. We then review the definition of the Gaussian sphere, introduced in chapters 10 and 11 in our discussion of the reflectance map. Imagine moving the unit surface normal of each face so that its "tail" is at the center of a unit sphere. The "head" of the unit normal then lies on the surface of the sphere. Each point on this *Gaussian sphere* corresponds to a particular surface orientation. The *extended Gaussian image* is obtained by placing a mass at each point on the sphere equal to the surface area of the corresponding face of the polyhedron (figure 16-1).

It seems at first as if some information is lost in this mapping, since the positions of the surface normals are discarded. Viewed another way, the information on which face is adjacent to which is lost. It can nevertheless be shown that (up to translation) the extended Gaussian image uniquely defines a convex polyhedron. Iterative algorithms have recently been invented for recovering a convex polyhedron from its extended Gaussian image.

Mass distributions on the sphere that lie entirely on a great circle correspond to infinitely long, infinitely narrow cylinders (figure 16-2). We shall exclude such pathological cases from our considerations.

Some properties of the extended Gaussian image are important. First, note that the total mass of the extended Gaussian image is just equal to

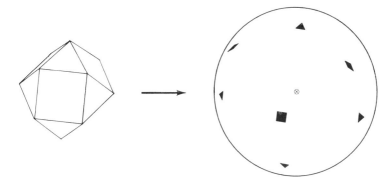

Figure 16-1. The extended Gaussian image of a polyhedron is a collection of impulses on the unit sphere. Each face corresponds to an impulse with weight equal to its area, at a place on the sphere where the tangent is parallel to the face. To make this figure easier to interpret, we give each spot on the sphere the shape of the corresponding face on the cuboctahedron. Impulses on the other side of the sphere are not shown.

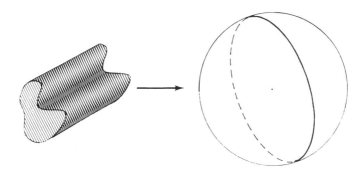

Figure 16-2. Mass distributions on the sphere that are entirely confined to a great circle do not correspond to bounded closed figures. They can be thought of as the limits of the extended Gaussian images of families of cylindrical objects as they are made longer and longer and, at the same time, narrower and narrower.

the total surface area of the polyhedron. Next, if the polyhedron is closed, it will have the same projected area when viewed from any pair of opposite directions. This can be shown to imply that the center of mass of the extended Gaussian image is at the origin. An equivalent representation, called a *spike model*, is a collection of vectors parallel to the surface normals, with lengths equal to the areas of the corresponding faces (figure 16-3). The

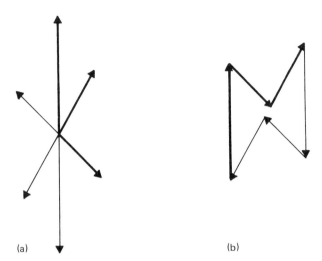

(a)   (b)

Figure 16-3. (a) The extended Gaussian image of a polyhedron can be turned into a spike model in which each vector has length proportional to the area of a face and direction parallel to the normal to that face. (b) If the polyhedron has a closed surface, these vectors must form a closed loop when placed end to end.

result regarding the center of mass is equivalent to the statement that the vectors in the spike model must add up to zero.

These ideas will now be extended to smoothly curved surfaces.

16.2 The Gaussian Image

We can map a given point on a surface onto a unit sphere by finding the point on the sphere that has the same surface normal as the point on the original surface (figure 16-4). In this way we can map information associated with points on the surface onto points on the Gaussian sphere. In the case of a convex object (with positive curvature everywhere), no two points have the same surface normal. The mapping from the object to the Gaussian sphere is then invertible; that is, there is a unique point on the surface corresponding to each point on the unit sphere. If the surface has patches with zero curvature, lines or areas may correspond to a single point on the Gaussian sphere, but the same mapping can be used.

One useful property of the Gaussian image is that it rotates with the object. A surface normal on the sphere that is parallel to a particular surface normal on the object will still be parallel to this surface normal when both are rotated. A rotation of the object thus corresponds to an equal rotation of the Gaussian sphere.

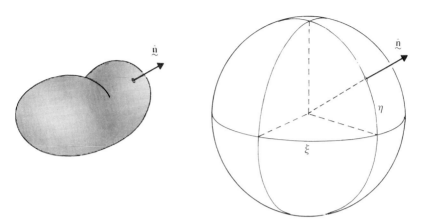

Figure 16-4. The image of a point on the surface under the Gaussian map is the point on the unit sphere that has the same surface orientation.

16.3 Gaussian Curvature

Consider a small patch of area δO on the object (figure 16-5). Each point in this patch corresponds to a particular point on the Gaussian sphere. The patch on the object therefore maps onto a patch on the Gaussian sphere whose area we can call δS. If the surface is strongly curved, the normals of points in the object patch will point in a wide fan of directions. The corresponding points on the Gaussian sphere will be spread out. Conversely, if the surface is planar, the surface normals on the object will be parallel and will map into a single point.

These considerations suggest a suitable definition of curvature. The *Gaussian curvature* K is defined as the limit of the ratio of the two areas as they tend to zero. That is,

$$K = \lim_{\delta O \to 0} \frac{\delta S}{\delta O} = \frac{dS}{dO}.$$

From this differential relationship we can obtain two useful integrals. Consider first integrating over a finite patch O on the object,

$$\iint_O K \, dO = \iint_S dS = S,$$

where S is the area of the corresponding patch on the Gaussian sphere. The expression on the left is called the *integral curvature*. This relationship allows us to deal with surfaces that have discontinuities in surface normal.

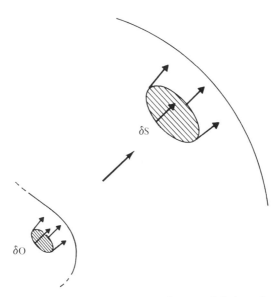

Figure 16-5. The Gaussian image of a surface patch is just the set of images of the points in the patch. The magnitude of the Gaussian curvature is equal to the ratio of the area δS of the patch on the unit sphere to the area δO of the patch on the surface of the object. It is positive if the boundaries of the two patches are traversed in the same sense, and negative otherwise.

Now consider instead integrating over a patch S on the Gaussian sphere:

$$\iint_S 1/K \, dS = \iint_O dO = O,$$

where O is the area of the corresponding patch on the object. This relationship suggests the use of the inverse of the Gaussian curvature in the definition of the extended Gaussian image. It also shows, by the way, that the integral of $1/K$ over the Gaussian sphere is just the total area of the object.

16.4 The Extended Gaussian Image

A mapping can be defined that associates the inverse of the Gaussian curvature at a point on the surface with the corresponding point on the unit sphere. Let u and v be parameters used to specify points on the original surface. Similarly, let ξ and η be parameters used to specify points on the Gaussian sphere (these could be longitude and latitude, for example). We

Figure 16-6. A patch inclined with respect to the viewing direction is foreshortened. The ratio of apparent to actual area equals the cosine of the angle between the surface normal $\hat{\mathbf{s}}$ and the direction toward the viewer, $\hat{\mathbf{v}}$.

define the *extended Gaussian image* as

$$G(\xi, \eta) = \frac{1}{K(u, v)},$$

where (ξ, η) is the point on the Gaussian sphere corresponding to the point (u, v) on the original surface. It can be shown that this mapping is unique (up to translation) for convex objects. That is, there is only one convex object corresponding to a particular extended Gaussian image. The proof is unfortunately not constructive, so that there is no direct method for recovering the object.

Consider viewing a convex object (at a great distance) from a direction given by the unit view vector $\hat{\mathbf{v}}$. A surface patch with unit normal $\hat{\mathbf{s}}$ will be visible only if $\hat{\mathbf{s}} \cdot \hat{\mathbf{v}} \geq 0$. Suppose its surface area is δO. Due to foreshortening, it will appear only as large as a patch of area $(\hat{\mathbf{s}} \cdot \hat{\mathbf{v}}) \delta O$ normal to $\hat{\mathbf{v}}$ (figure 16-6). Let $H(\hat{\mathbf{v}})$ be the unit hemisphere for which $\hat{\mathbf{s}} \cdot \hat{\mathbf{v}} \geq 0$. Then the apparent area of the surface is

$$\iint_{H(\hat{\mathbf{v}})} G(\hat{\mathbf{s}}) (\hat{\mathbf{s}} \cdot \hat{\mathbf{v}}) \, dS,$$

when viewed from the direction $\hat{\mathbf{v}}$. This clearly ought to be the same as the apparent area when the object is viewed from the opposite direction, that is,

$$\iint_{H(-\hat{\mathbf{v}})} G(\hat{\mathbf{s}}) (\hat{\mathbf{s}} \cdot -\hat{\mathbf{v}}) \, dS.$$

Consequently,

$$\iint_{S} G(\hat{\mathbf{s}}) (\hat{\mathbf{s}} \cdot \hat{\mathbf{v}}) \, dS = \hat{\mathbf{v}} \cdot \iint_{S} G(\hat{\mathbf{s}}) \hat{\mathbf{s}} \, dS = 0,$$

where the integral now is taken over the whole sphere. Since this result holds true for all view vectors $\hat{\mathbf{v}}$, we must have

$$\iint_{S} G(\hat{\mathbf{s}}) \hat{\mathbf{s}} \, dS = \mathbf{0}.$$

That is, the center of mass of the extended Gaussian image is at the origin. (This result, by the way, is often not helpful in practice, since we can usually see only one side of the object.)

Another property of the extended Gaussian image is also easily demonstrated. The total mass of the extended Gaussian image equals the total surface area of the object. If we wish to deal with objects of the same shape but differing size, we can normalize the extended Gaussian image by dividing it by the total mass.

We can think of the extended Gaussian image in terms of a mass density on the unit sphere. It is then possible to deal in a consistent way with places on the surface where the Gaussian curvature is zero, using the integral of $1/K$ shown earlier. A planar region, for example, corresponds to a point mass. This yields an impulse function on the Gaussian sphere with volume proportional to the area of the planar region. (The volume under a function defined on the sphere is just the integral of the function taken over the surface of the sphere.)

Three things happen when the surface is not convex:

- The Gaussian curvature for some points will be negative.

- More than one point on the object will contribute to a given point on the sphere.

- Parts of the object may be occluded by other parts.

We choose to define the extended Gaussian image in this case to be the sum of the absolute values of the inverses of the Gaussian curvature at all points having the same surface orientation. This definition is motivated by the method used to compute the discrete approximation of the extended Gaussian image, as we shall see later.

16.5 Examples of Extended Gaussian Images

The extended Gaussian image of a sphere of radius R is

$$G(\xi, \eta) = R^2,$$

as can be seen by noting that a patch of area δO on the sphere occupies a solid angle $\omega = \delta O / R^2$ when viewed from the center of the sphere. The corresponding patch on the unit sphere clearly has area $\delta S = \omega$.

Slightly more interesting is the case of an ellipsoid with semiaxes a, b, and c lined up with the coordinate axes (figure 16-7). An equation for its surface can be written in the form

$$\left(\frac{x}{a}\right)^2 + \left(\frac{y}{b}\right)^2 + \left(\frac{z}{c}\right)^2 = 1.$$

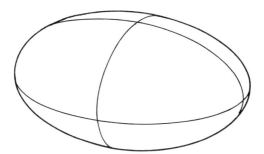

Figure 16-7. Computing the extended Gaussian image of an ellipsoid with three different semiaxes presents an interesting challenge.

More useful for our purposes is the parametric form

$$x = a \cos \theta \cos \phi, \qquad y = b \sin \theta \cos \phi, \qquad z = c \sin \phi.$$

The surface normal at

$$\mathbf{r} = (a \cos \theta \cos \phi, \; b \sin \theta \cos \phi, \; c \sin \phi)^T$$

is

$$\mathbf{n} = (bc \cos \theta \cos \phi, \; ca \sin \theta \cos \phi, \; ab \sin \phi)^T .$$

It is shown in exercise 16-5, using methods developed later in this chapter, that the Gaussian curvature at this point is

$$K = \left(\frac{abc}{(bc \cos \theta \cos \phi)^2 + (ca \sin \theta \cos \phi)^2 + (ab \sin \phi)^2} \right)^2 .$$

If ξ is the longitude and η the latitude, the unit normal at the point (ξ, η) on the sphere is

$$\hat{\mathbf{n}} = (\cos \xi \cos \eta, \; \sin \xi \cos \eta, \; \sin \xi)^T .$$

Identifying terms in the expressions for surface normals at corresponding points on the ellipsoid and the Gaussian sphere, we finally obtain

$$G(\xi, \eta) = \frac{1}{K} = \left(\frac{abc}{(a \cos \xi \cos \eta)^2 + (b \sin \xi \cos \eta)^2 + (c \sin \eta)^2} \right)^2 .$$

The extended Gaussian image in this case varies smoothly and has the stationary values

$$\left(\frac{bc}{a} \right)^2, \quad \left(\frac{ca}{b} \right)^2, \quad \left(\frac{ab}{c} \right)^2$$

at the points $(1, 0, 0)^T$, $(0, 1, 0)^T$, and $(0, 0, 1)^T$, respectively.

Later we shall derive the extended Gaussian image of a torus, an object that is not convex.

16.6 The Discrete Case

Consider a surface broken up into small patches of equal area. Let there be ρ patches per unit area. Erect a surface normal on each patch. Consider the polyhedral object formed by the intersection of the tangent planes perpendicular to these surface normals. The approximation of the original surface by this polyhedral object becomes better and better as we make the patches smaller and smaller, that is, as ρ becomes larger and larger.

The extended Gaussian image of the original (smoothly curved) convex object is approximated by impulses corresponding to the small patches. The volume of each impulse is approximately $1/\rho$, which is the area of the patch it rests on. Impulses arising from strongly curved areas are spread over a large area on the Gaussian sphere, while areas that are nearly planar give rise to impulses that are concentrated in a small area. In fact, the number of impulses per unit area on the Gaussian sphere approaches ρ times the absolute value of the Gaussian curvature. This can be shown using the integral of $1/K$ given earlier.

The division of the surface into planar patches can be arbitrary, as long as the volumes of the impulses on the Gaussian sphere are made proportional to the area of the corresponding patches on the surface. Alternatively, the surface can be divided up according to the division of the image into picture cells (figure 16-8a). In this case we must take into account the foreshortening of the area occupied by the image of a given patch. The actual surface area is proportional to $\sec e$, where e is the angle between the surface normal and the line of sight (figure 16-6). (This angle is easily determined since the surface normal is known.)

Measurements of surface orientation from images will not be perfect, since they are affected by noise in the brightness measurements. Similarly, surface orientations obtained from range data will be somewhat inaccurate. Consequently, the impulses on the Gaussian sphere are displaced a little from their true positions. The expected density on the Gaussian sphere nevertheless tends to be equal to the inverse of the Gaussian curvature. The impulses corresponding to a planar surface are, however, not coincident. Instead they form a small cluster.

Extended Gaussian images of surfaces of prototypical object models must also be computed. In this case it is best to find a convenient way to parameterize the surface and break it up into many small patches. Let the surface be given in terms of parameters u and v as $\mathbf{r}(u, v)$ (figure 16-9). Then $\mathbf{r}_u$ and $\mathbf{r}_v$ are tangents at the point (u, v). The cross-product of these

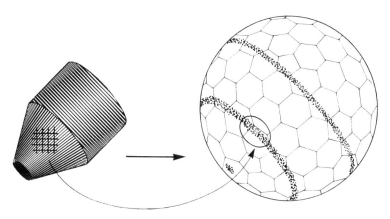

Figure 16-8. In mapping image information onto the extended Gaussian sphere, we must cope with quantization of both the image and the tessellation of the sphere. For each picture cell on the left, a surface orientation is found. The accumulated count in the corresponding cell in the discrete representation of the sphere on the right is then incremented. The discrete approximation of the extended Gaussian image is called an orientation histogram.

tangents is a normal to the surface, and we can thus derive the unit normal

$$\hat{\mathbf{n}} = \frac{\mathbf{r}_u \times \mathbf{r}_v}{|\mathbf{r}_u \times \mathbf{r}_v|}.$$

Knowing this unit normal allows us to determine the point on the Gaussian sphere to which the given surface patch corresponds. Let us divide the range of u into segments of size δu and the range of v into segments of size δv. Then the area of the patch,

$$\delta A = |\mathbf{r}_u \times \mathbf{r}_v| \, \delta u \, \delta v,$$

can be used to determine what contribution to place on the unit sphere. Note that we need not explicitly compute the Gaussian curvature or take second partial derivatives.

16.7 The Extended Gaussian Image of a Torus

We shall now derive the extended Gaussian image of a torus using simple geometrical reasoning (figure 16-10). We call a plane containing the axis of the torus an *axial plane*. Such a plane intersects the torus in two circles. The points on either of these circles map onto a great circle on the Gaussian sphere. The two circles on the torus formed by the intersection

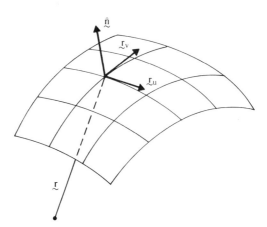

Figure 16-9. The computation of the extended Gaussian image of a surface is facilitated by use of a suitable surface parameterization. Given a means of identifying points on the surface using two parameters u and v, we can easily find tangent directions by differentiation, and from the tangents we can derive the local normal. The area of each patch of the surface is also found readily from the derivatives of the parametric equations.

of a particular axial plane map onto the same great circle on the Gaussian sphere. If we choose a different axial plane, we obtain two intersections that map onto a different great circle.

Let us define the poles of the Gaussian sphere to be the places where an axis parallel to the axis of the torus pierces its surface. Now note that the great circles, which are maps of the circular intersection of the axial planes with the torus, all pass through the poles of the Gaussian sphere. They are thus meridians, that is, lines of constant longitude. Also observe that, aside from the poles, every point on the Gaussian sphere corresponds to exactly two points on the torus.

We expect that the extended Gaussian image will have higher values near the poles, since the meridians crowd together there. To obtain a quantitative result, we shall have to look at patches of known area on the torus and see what areas on the Gaussian sphere they map to. Consider two axial planes that are nearly parallel (figure 16-11). These planes will carve out two narrow (opposite) slices of the torus.

These slices in turn map onto *lunes* on the Gaussian sphere. Each lune is a slice cut out of the surface of a sphere by planes passing through its axis parallel to the two planes cutting the torus (figure 16-12a). The width of a lune varies with latitude. It is difficult, as a result, to calculate

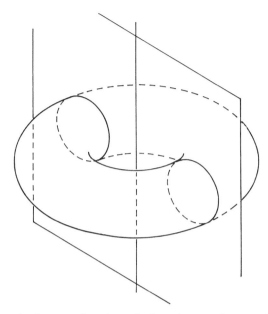

Figure 16-10. A plane passing through the axis cuts the torus in two circles.

directly what area on the Gaussian sphere a given area on one of the slices of the torus maps to. If we add two opposite slices, however, we obtain a cylindrical band of constant width, because the widths of the bands vary linearly with distance from the axis of the torus. The two slices taken together, then, contribute equal amounts to each latitude band on the Gaussian sphere.

The corresponding lune on the Gaussian sphere becomes narrower as it approaches the pole; in fact, its width is proportional to $\cos \eta$, where η is the latitude. Thus a fixed surface area on the torus maps into a smaller and smaller area on the Gaussian sphere as we approach the poles. We conclude that the extended Gaussian image must be proportional to $\sec \eta$. This can be seen in another way by tessellating the Gaussian sphere using meridians and parallels (figure 16-12b). Each cell in the tessellation corresponds to a fixed area on the torus. If we place a unit mass in each cell on the Gaussian sphere, we see that the density increases as we approach the pole because the areas of the cells become smaller there.

We now know that the extended Gaussian image of the torus is proportional to the secant of latitude. To obtain the constant of integration we can consider a small patch on the sphere near the equator, where $\eta \approx 0$. Let the extent of the patch be $\delta \eta$ in latitude and $\delta \xi$ in longitude. This

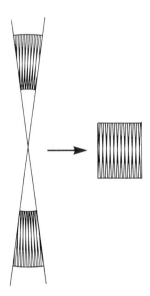

Figure 16-11. Two axial planes cut opposite slices out of the torus. These can be combined for purposes of projecting their surface onto the Gaussian sphere. The combination is approximately equivalent to a cylindrical band.

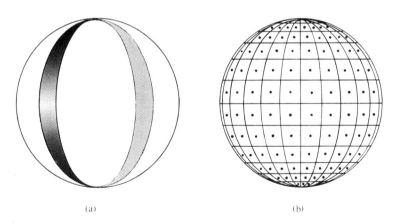

(a)   (b)

Figure 16-12. The area on the Gaussian sphere corresponding to the slices of the torus consists of two opposite lunes. (a) Since the same surface area maps into any given latitude band, the value of the extended Gaussian image increases with latitude. (b) If we place a unit mass in each cell in a tessellation of the sphere by meridians and parallels, we find a dependence of density on the secant of latitude.

patch on the Gaussian sphere corresponds to two patches on the torus with total area

$$(R - \rho)\,\delta\xi\,\rho\,\delta\eta + (R + \rho)\,\delta\xi\,\rho\,\delta\eta = 2R\rho\,\delta\eta\,\delta\xi,$$

where R is the major radius and ρ the minor radius of the torus. We conclude that

$$G(\xi, \eta) = 2R\rho\sec\eta.$$

An alternate way to determine the constant of proportionality is to note that the total area of the torus is $4\pi^2\rho R$, and that this has to be equal to the integral of $G(\xi, \eta)$ over the whole sphere.

16.8 Tessellation of the Unit Sphere

In order to represent the information on the Gaussian sphere in a computer, it is useful to divide the sphere up into cells. Associated with each cell is the area of the surface facing into the cone of directions defined by that cell. This discrete approximation of the extended Gaussian image is called the *orientation histogram*. Ideally the cells should satisfy the following criteria:

- All cells should have the same area.
- All cells should have the same shape.
- The cells should occur in a regular pattern.
- The cells should have rounded shapes.
- The division should be fine enough to provide good angular resolution.
- There should be some rotations that bring the pattern of cells into coincidence with itself.

Elongated cells should be avoided since they combine information about surface patches that have orientations differing more than would be the case for more rounded cells of the same area. At the same time, if cells occur in a regular pattern, the relationship of a cell to its neighbors will be the same for all cells, and such arrangements are desirable. Unfortunately, these criteria cannot be simultaneously satisfied.

One possible tessellation consists of a division into latitude bands, each of which is then further divided along longitudinal strips (figure 16-13). The resulting cells can be made nearly equal in area by having fewer strips at higher latitudes. One advantage of this scheme is that it makes it easy to compute the cell to which a particular surface normal should be assigned. Still, this arrangement does not come close to satisfying the criteria noted above. It is, for example, not possible to rotate the tessellated sphere so as

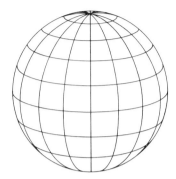

Figure 16-13. A sphere can be divided into cells by meridians and parallels. This tessellation, however, has few of the properties desirable for storage of the orientation histogram.

to bring cells into alignment with themselves (except for rotations about an axis through the poles).

Better tessellations can be found by projecting onto the unit sphere regular polyhedra whose centers coincide with that of the sphere. A regular polyhedron has regular polygons as faces, and these polygons are all the same. Consequently, a division obtained by projecting a regular polyhedron has the property that all of the cells have the same shape and area. Also, all cells have the same geometric relationship to their neighbors. Unfortunately, there are only five regular solids from which to choose (tetrahedron, hexahedron, octahedron, dodecahedron, and icosahedron). In the case of the dodecahedron, the cells are fairly well rounded (figure 16-14a). The dodecahedron, however, has only twelve cells. Even the icosahedron provides too coarse a sampling of orientations (figure 16-14b). Furthermore, its twenty cells are not well rounded.

We can go further by considering semiregular polyhedra. Their faces also are regular polyhedra, but need not all be the same. Nor are the areas of all the faces equal. In some cases, it is possible to derive a new polyhedron that has the same adjacency relationships between faces as a given semiregular polyhedron but whose faces are of equal area. The shapes of some of these faces are then no longer regular. An example of a tessellation using a semiregular polyhedron is provided by a soccer ball (figure 16-15a). It is based on the truncated icosahedron, a figure that has 12 pentagonal faces and 20 hexagonal faces. Unfortunately, there are only 13 semiregular polyhedra (the five truncated regular polyhedra, cuboctahedron, icosidodecahedron, snub cuboctahedron, snub icosidodecahedron, truncated cuboctahedron, rhombicuboctahedron, truncated icosidodecahe-

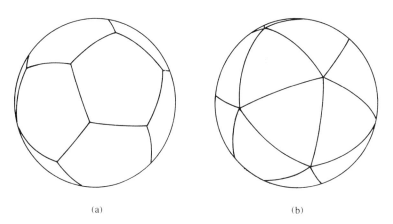

(a)   (b)

Figure 16-14. The dodecahedron and icosahedron can be projected onto the
unit sphere to provide tessellations with 12 and 20 cells, respectively.

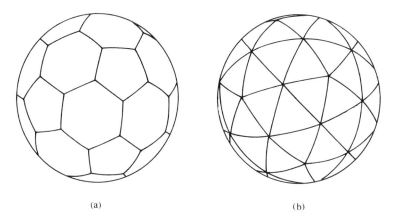

(a)   (b)

Figure 16-15. The truncated icosahedron is a semiregular figure with 32 faces.
The pentakis dodecahedron has 60 triangular facets. Finer divisions of the surface
of the unit sphere can be based on these semiregular polyhedra.

dron, and rhombicosidodecahedron). They do not provide us with fine
enough tessellations.

If we desire a finer subdivision still, we can consider splitting each face
of a given tessellation into triangular facets. If, for example, we split each
pentagonal face of a dodecahedron into five equal triangles, we obtain a
pentakis dodecahedron with 60 faces (figure 16-15b). This happens to be

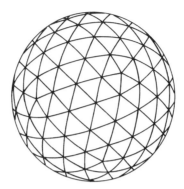

Figure 16-16. Geodesic divisions can be based on any of the projections of the regular and semiregular polyhedra. Each facet is divided into triangular cells. The one shown here is based on the icosahedron and has twelve vertices at which five cells meet. All other vertices touch six cells.

the dual of the truncated icosahedron.

To proceed further, we can divide the resulting triangles into four smaller triangles according to the well-known geodesic dome constructions (figure 16-16). We attain high resolution by relenting on several of the criteria given above. Actually, the duals of geodesic domes are better, since they have facets that are mostly (irregular) hexagons, with a dozen pentagons thrown in (figure 16-8b). Tessellations of arbitrary fineness can be constructed in this fashion.

To use this approach, we have to be able to efficiently compute the cell to which a particular surface normal belongs. In the case of the tessellations derived from regular polyhedra, we can easily compute the cosines of the angles between a given unit vector and the vectors corresponding to the centers of the cells. (These vectors correspond to the vertices of the dual of the regular polyhedron.) The given unit vector is then assigned to the cell whose center is closest. In the case of the geodesic dome, we can proceed hierarchically. The geodesic dome is based on some regular polyhedron. The appropriate facet of this polyhedron is found as above. Next, we determine which of the triangles of the first division of this facet the given unit normal falls into. This process is then repeated with the four triangles into which this facet is divided, and so on. In practice, we can use lookup table methods, which, while not exact, are very quick.

Let the solid angle occupied by one of the cells on the sphere be ω (in the case of the icosahedron, $\omega = 4\pi/20$). The expected number of surface normals mapped into a cell is $\rho\,\omega\,|G(\xi,\eta)|$ for a convex object.

It is clear that the orientation histogram—the discrete approximation

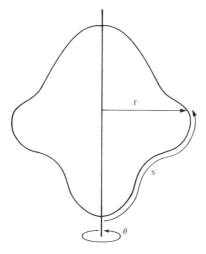

Figure 16-17. A solid of revolution is produced by spinning a planar curve, the generator, about an axis lying in the plane of the curve.

of the extended Gaussian image—can be computed locally. We simply count the number of surface normals that belong in each cell. The expression for the Gaussian curvature, on the other hand, includes first and second partial derivatives of the surface function. In practice, estimates of derivatives are unreliable because of noise. It is important, therefore, that the extended Gaussian image can be computed without estimating the derivatives.

16.9 Gaussian Curvature of a Solid of Revolution

In the case of the surface of a solid of revolution, the Gaussian curvature is rather easy to determine. A solid of revolution can be produced by rotating a generating curve about an axis (figure 16-17). Let the generating curve be specified by the perpendicular distance from the axis, $r(s)$, given as a function of arclength s along the curve. Let θ be the angle of rotation about the axis.

Now consider the Gaussian sphere positioned so that its axis is aligned with the axis of the solid of revolution. Let ξ be the longitude and η the latitude on the Gaussian sphere (figure 16-18).

We can arrange for ξ to correspond to θ. That is, a point on the object produced when the generating curve has rotated through an angle θ has a surface normal that lies on the Gaussian sphere at a point with longitude $\xi = \theta$. Consider a small patch on the Gaussian sphere lying between ξ

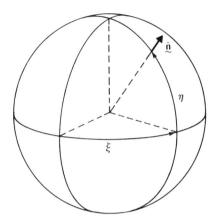

Figure 16-18. Points on the Gaussian sphere can be identified by their longitude ξ and their latitude η.

and $\xi + \delta\xi$ in longitude and between η and $\eta + \delta\eta$ in latitude. Its area is $\cos\eta\,\delta\xi\,\delta\eta$. We need only determine the area of the corresponding patch on the object. It is $r\,\delta\theta\,\delta s$, where δs is the change in arclength along the generating curve corresponding to the change $\delta\eta$ in surface orientation. The Gaussian curvature is the limit of the ratio of the two areas as they tend to zero, that is,

$$K = \lim_{\substack{\delta\eta\to 0 \\ \delta\xi\to 0}} \frac{\cos\eta}{r}\frac{\delta\xi}{\delta\theta}\frac{\delta\eta}{\delta s} = \lim_{\delta\eta\to 0}\frac{\cos\eta}{r}\frac{\delta\eta}{\delta s} = \frac{\cos\eta}{r}\frac{d\eta}{ds}.$$

The curvature of the generating curve, κ_G, is just the rate of change of direction with arclength along the curve, that is,

$$\kappa_G = \frac{d\eta}{ds},$$

and hence

$$K = \frac{\kappa_G\cos\eta}{r}.$$

This can be written in another form if we note that $\sin\eta = -r_s$, where r_s is the partial derivative of r with respect to s (figure 16-19). Then

$$\cos\eta\,\frac{d\eta}{ds} = \kappa_G\cos\eta = -r_{ss},$$

and so we obtain the simple formula

$$K = -\frac{r_{ss}}{r}.$$

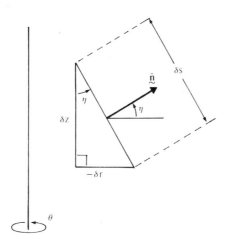

Figure 16-19. This figure gives the relationships between infinitesimal changes in arclength s along the generator, distance r from the axis, and height z above some reference point. These relationships allow us to calculate the latitude η of the corresponding point on the Gaussian sphere.

For a sphere of radius R, for example, we have $r = R\cos(s/R)$ for $-(\pi/2)R < s < +(\pi/2)R$. Thus $r_{ss} = -r/R^2$ and $K = 1/R^2$, as expected.

For some purposes it is more useful to express r as a function of the distance along the axis rather than as a function of arclength along the curve. Let the distance along the axis be denoted by z. Then we have $\tan\eta = -r_z$, and so

$$\sec^2\eta\,\frac{d\eta}{ds} = \frac{d}{ds}(-r_z) = -r_{zz}\frac{dz}{ds},$$

where

$$\frac{dz}{ds} = \cos\eta.$$

We see now that

$$\kappa_G\cos\eta = \frac{d\eta}{ds}\cos\eta = -r_{zz}\cos^4\eta,$$

and finally

$$K = -\frac{r_{zz}}{r(1 + r_z^2)^2},$$

since

$$\sec^2\eta = 1 + r_z^2.$$

We apply these methods to the torus in exercise 16-2 in order to check the
result obtained earlier using a geometrical argument.

16.10 Gaussian Curvature in the General Case

Let $x = x(u,v)$, $y = y(u,v)$, and $z = z(u,v)$ be parametric equations for
points on a given surface. Let $\mathbf{r} = (x,y,z)^T$ be a vector to a point on the
surface. Then

$$\mathbf{r}_u = \frac{\partial \mathbf{r}}{\partial u} \quad \text{and} \quad \mathbf{r}_v = \frac{\partial \mathbf{r}}{\partial v}$$

are two tangents to the surface. The cross-product of these two vectors,

$$\mathbf{n} = \mathbf{r}_u \times \mathbf{r}_v,$$

will be perpendicular to the local tangent plane. The length of this normal
vector squared is

$$n^2 = \mathbf{n} \cdot \mathbf{n} = (\mathbf{r}_u \cdot \mathbf{r}_u)(\mathbf{r}_v \cdot \mathbf{r}_v) - (\mathbf{r}_u \cdot \mathbf{r}_v)^2,$$

since $(\mathbf{a} \times \mathbf{b}) \cdot (\mathbf{c} \times \mathbf{d}) = (\mathbf{a} \cdot \mathbf{c})(\mathbf{b} \cdot \mathbf{d}) - (\mathbf{a} \cdot \mathbf{d})(\mathbf{b} \cdot \mathbf{c})$. A unit vector $\hat{\mathbf{n}} = \mathbf{n}/n$
can be computed using this result.

The Gaussian curvature is the limit of the ratio of the area of a patch on
the Gaussian sphere to the area of the corresponding patch on the surface
as the latter shrinks to zero. Consider an infinitesimal triangle formed by
the three points on the surface corresponding to (u,v), $(u + \delta u, v)$, and
$(u, v + \delta v)$. The lengths of two sides of this triangle are $|\mathbf{r}_u|\, \delta u$ and $|\mathbf{r}_v|\, \delta v$,
while the sine of the angle between these sides is

$$\frac{|\mathbf{r}_u \times \mathbf{r}_v|}{|\mathbf{r}_u|\, |\mathbf{r}_v|}.$$

An outward normal with length equal to the area of the triangle is therefore
given by

$$\frac{1}{2}(\mathbf{r}_u \times \mathbf{r}_v)\, \delta u\, \delta v = \frac{1}{2}\mathbf{n}\, \delta u\, \delta v.$$

To determine the area of the corresponding triangular patch on the Gaussian sphere we need to find the unit surface normals at the three points.
These are $\hat{\mathbf{n}}$, $\hat{\mathbf{n}} + \hat{\mathbf{n}}_u\, \delta u$, and $\hat{\mathbf{n}} + \hat{\mathbf{n}}_v\, \delta v$ if we ignore terms of higher order in
δu and δv. (Here $\hat{\mathbf{n}}_u$ and $\hat{\mathbf{n}}_v$ are the partial derivatives of $\hat{\mathbf{n}}$ with respect
to u and v. Note that $\hat{\mathbf{n}}_u$ and $\hat{\mathbf{n}}_v$ are perpendicular to $\hat{\mathbf{n}}$.) The area of the
patch on the Gaussian sphere is given by the magnitude of the vector

$$\frac{1}{2}(\hat{\mathbf{n}}_u \times \hat{\mathbf{n}}_v)\, \delta u\, \delta v,$$

by reasoning similar to that used in determining the area of the original patch on the given surface. We need to find $\hat{\mathbf{n}}_u$ and $\hat{\mathbf{n}}_v$ to compute this area. Now

$$\hat{\mathbf{n}}_u = \frac{\partial}{\partial u}\frac{\mathbf{n}}{n} = \frac{n\mathbf{n}_u - \mathbf{n}n_u}{n^2}.$$

From $n^2 = \mathbf{n} \cdot \mathbf{n}$ we obtain

$$n\,n_u = \mathbf{n} \cdot \mathbf{n}_u,$$

so that

$$\hat{\mathbf{n}}_u = \frac{(\mathbf{n} \cdot \mathbf{n})\mathbf{n}_u - (\mathbf{n} \cdot \mathbf{n}_u)\mathbf{n}}{n^3} = \frac{(\mathbf{n} \times \mathbf{n}_u) \times \mathbf{n}}{n^3}$$

and, similarly,

$$\hat{\mathbf{n}}_v = \frac{(\mathbf{n} \cdot \mathbf{n})\mathbf{n}_v - (\mathbf{n} \cdot \mathbf{n}_v)\mathbf{n}}{n^3} = \frac{(\mathbf{n} \times \mathbf{n}_v) \times \mathbf{n}}{n^3},$$

since $(\mathbf{a} \times \mathbf{b}) \times \mathbf{c} = (\mathbf{a} \cdot \mathbf{c})\mathbf{b} - (\mathbf{b} \cdot \mathbf{c})\mathbf{a}$. Consequently,

$$\hat{\mathbf{n}}_u \times \hat{\mathbf{n}}_v = \frac{n^2}{n^6}\big((\mathbf{n} \cdot \mathbf{n})(\mathbf{n}_u \times \mathbf{n}_v) + (\mathbf{n} \cdot \mathbf{n}_u)(\mathbf{n}_v \times \mathbf{n}) + (\mathbf{n} \cdot \mathbf{n}_v)(\mathbf{n} \times \mathbf{n}_u)\big),$$

or

$$\hat{\mathbf{n}}_u \times \hat{\mathbf{n}}_v = \frac{1}{n^4}[\mathbf{n}\,\mathbf{n}_u\,\mathbf{n}_v]\mathbf{n},$$

since $[\mathbf{a}\,\mathbf{b}\,\mathbf{c}]\mathbf{p} = (\mathbf{a} \cdot \mathbf{p})(\mathbf{b} \times \mathbf{c}) + (\mathbf{b} \cdot \mathbf{p})(\mathbf{c} \times \mathbf{a}) + (\mathbf{c} \cdot \mathbf{p})(\mathbf{a} \times \mathbf{b})$, where $[\mathbf{a}\,\mathbf{b}\,\mathbf{c}]$ is the triple product $(\mathbf{a} \times \mathbf{b}) \cdot \mathbf{c}$, as before.

This shows that the patch on the Gaussian sphere has the same orientation as the patch on the surface, as it should. An outward-pointing normal with length equal to the area is given by

$$\frac{1}{2}\frac{1}{n^4}[\mathbf{n}\,\mathbf{n}_u\,\mathbf{n}_v]\mathbf{n}\,\delta u\,\delta v.$$

The ratio of the two areas, that is, the Gaussian curvature, is just

$$K = \frac{[\mathbf{n}\,\mathbf{n}_u\,\mathbf{n}_v]}{n^4}.$$

Now

$$\mathbf{n} = \mathbf{r}_u \times \mathbf{r}_v,$$

so that

$$\mathbf{n}_u = \mathbf{r}_{uu} \times \mathbf{r}_v + \mathbf{r}_u \times \mathbf{r}_{uv},$$

$$\mathbf{n}_v = \mathbf{r}_{uv} \times \mathbf{r}_v + \mathbf{r}_u \times \mathbf{r}_{vv}.$$

Using $(\mathbf{a} \times \mathbf{b}) \times (\mathbf{c} \times \mathbf{d}) = [\mathbf{a}\,\mathbf{b}\,\mathbf{d}]\mathbf{c} - [\mathbf{a}\,\mathbf{b}\,\mathbf{c}]\mathbf{d}$ or $(\mathbf{a} \times \mathbf{b}) \times (\mathbf{c} \times \mathbf{d}) = [\mathbf{a}\,\mathbf{c}\,\mathbf{d}]\mathbf{b} - [\mathbf{b}\,\mathbf{c}\,\mathbf{d}]\mathbf{a}$, we obtain

$$\mathbf{n}_u \times \mathbf{n}_v = -[\mathbf{r}_{uu}\,\mathbf{r}_v\,\mathbf{r}_{uv}]\mathbf{r}_v + [\mathbf{r}_{uu}\,\mathbf{r}_v\,\mathbf{r}_{vv}]\mathbf{r}_u$$

$$- [\mathbf{r}_{uu}\,\mathbf{r}_v\,\mathbf{r}_u]\mathbf{r}_{vv} + [\mathbf{r}_u\,\mathbf{r}_{uv}\,\mathbf{r}_v]\mathbf{r}_{uv} + [\mathbf{r}_u\,\mathbf{r}_{uv}\,\mathbf{r}_{vv}]\mathbf{r}_u,$$

so that

$$[\mathbf{n}\,\mathbf{n}_u\,\mathbf{n}_v] = \mathbf{n} \cdot (\mathbf{n}_u \times \mathbf{n}_v) = [\mathbf{r}_u\,\mathbf{r}_v\,\mathbf{r}_{uu}][\mathbf{r}_u\,\mathbf{r}_v\,\mathbf{r}_{vv}] - [\mathbf{r}_u\,\mathbf{r}_v\,\mathbf{r}_{uv}]^2,$$

and finally

$$K = \frac{[\mathbf{r}_u\,\mathbf{r}_v\,\mathbf{r}_{uu}][\mathbf{r}_u\,\mathbf{r}_v\,\mathbf{r}_{vv}] - [\mathbf{r}_u\,\mathbf{r}_v\,\mathbf{r}_{uv}]^2}{|\mathbf{r}_u \times \mathbf{r}_v|^4}.$$

This result can be used to derive the expression for curvature of a solid of revolution in a more rigorous fashion.

A commonly used notation for the first and second fundamental forms of a surface uses the dot-products

$$E = \mathbf{r}_u \cdot \mathbf{r}_u, \quad F = \mathbf{r}_u \cdot \mathbf{r}_v, \quad G = \mathbf{r}_v \cdot \mathbf{r}_v,$$

and the triple products

$$L = \frac{[\mathbf{r}_u\,\mathbf{r}_v\,\mathbf{r}_{uu}]}{\sqrt{EG - F^2}}, \quad M = \frac{[\mathbf{r}_u\,\mathbf{r}_v\,\mathbf{r}_{uv}]}{\sqrt{EG - F^2}}, \quad N = \frac{[\mathbf{r}_u\,\mathbf{r}_v\,\mathbf{r}_{vv}]}{\sqrt{EG - F^2}},$$

so that we can also write

$$K = \frac{LN - M^2}{EG - F^2}.$$

If the surface is given as $z(x, y)$, the above formula reduces to the familiar

$$K = \frac{z_{xx}z_{yy} - z_{xy}^2}{(1 + z_x^2 + z_y^2)^2}.$$

16.11 Use of the Extended Gaussian Image

If we are dealing with a world containing objects of known shape, we can develop prototypes of these shapes in the form of orientation histograms. Experimentally obtained orientation histograms can then be compared with these prototypes in order to assign an unknown object to one of the known classes. In the process, the orientation of the object must be found relative to the stored prototype, since the extended Gaussian image is sensitive to rotation. In some applications, recovery of the attitude of the object is actually the main objective. These issues, and others, are addressed in chapter 18.

16.12 References

The Gaussian sphere and the stereographic projection are described in the book *Geometry and the Imagination* by Hilbert & Cohn-Vossen [1952]. Do Carmo discusses the Gauss map and Gaussian curvature in *Differential Geometry of Curves and Surfaces* [1976]. Convex polytopes are the topic of Lysternik's *Convex Figures and Polyhedra* [1963] and Grünbaum's *Convex Polytopes* [1967]

There are many books on differential geometry, including *Differential Geometry* by Pogorelov [1956] and *Elementary Differential Geometry* by O'Neill. Polyhedra appear in *Regular Figures* by Fejes Toth [1964], *Regular Polyhedra* by Coxeter [1973], *Polyhedra—A Visual Approach* by Pugh [1976], and the *Polyhedra Primer* by Pearce & Pearce [1978]. Kenner covers aspects of the construction of geodesic tessellations in *Geodesic Math—and How to Use It* [1976]. Also of interest are Wenninger's two books, *Polyhedron Models* [1971] and *Spherical Models* [1979].

The basic result that convex polyhedra are determined up to translation by the areas and orientations of their surfaces is due to Minkowski [1897]. Extensions to smoothly curved surfaces can be found in Alexandroff [1942]. Perhaps the most accessible source of information on this topic is, however, the second edition of Pogorelov's book [1979].

Huffman [1975] used the Gaussian sphere and Gaussian curvature to reason about the folding of paper. Horn extended the Gaussian image to include surface curvature information; see Horn [1979] and Bajcsy [1980]. This work was summarized in a recent tutorial paper by Horn [1984b]. Smith [1979] attempted to come up with a reconstruction algorithm for convex polyhedra, given the areas and orientations of the faces. Ikeuchi [1981a] succeeded in this endeavor, although his method was not practical. Little [1983] invented an ingenious iterative scheme exploiting the mixed volume used by Minkowski in his original proof. Smith [1979] described the moment-matching method, mentioned in chapter 18, which can be used when the whole extended Gaussian image is available.

The orientation histogram was used by Brown [1977] to study the distribution of directions of neuronal processes. More recently, Ballard & Sabbah [1981a] have used surface normals directly in detecting object orientation.

The extended Gaussian image has been used for segmentation of three-dimensional objects by Dane & Bajcsy [1981]. Use in recognition and the recovery of the attitude has been reported by Ikeuchi [1981a, 1983] and Horn & Ikeuchi [1984]. Brou [1983, 1984] developed a method for placing points uniformly in the space of rotations, a topic that is taken up in chapter 18. He also attempted to extend the basic methods to nonconvex objects. Little [1985] showed that correlation-like matching methods for extended Gaussian images have serious shortcomings and invented a new method exploiting the fact that the volume of the mixture of an object with a rotated version of itself is always greater than or equal to the volume of the mixture obtained without rotation. We touch on this topic in exercise 16-9. The mixed volumes, by the way, are the *configuration space obstacles* used by Lozano-Pérez [1983] in spatial reasoning and robot motion planning.

The convex object with the same extended Gaussian image as the torus is a solid of revolution that has the least energy curve as a generator. An explicit equation for the least energy curve was found by Horn [1983].

As discussed in exercise 16-7, we can define the extended circular image of a closed curve in the plane in analogy with the extended Gaussian image of a closed surface. Nahin [1974] developed a machine for estimating something akin to the extended circular image in parallel. The extended circular image and the smoothing of curves by filtering are explored by Horn & Weldon [1985]. Van Hove & Verly [1985] use a redundant spherical representation from which the extended circular image of a silhouette can be obtained simply.

Often it is proposed that range-finding devices ought to greatly simplify the recovery of information about the shapes of objects. Some problems are indeed simplified using range data, but others are made harder. Surface orientation can be estimated by applying finite-difference methods to range data. Thus the methods presented in this chapter can be used to analyze the result. For information on range-finding schemes and use of the resulting data see Nitzan, Brain, & Duda [1977], Duda, Nitzan, & Barrett [1979], and Jarvis [1983a,b]. For recent work on interpretation of depth maps see Besl & Jain [1984].

Many other ways to represent the shape of the surface of an object have been proposed. Boyse [1979] developed a geometrical method that is particularly useful in reasoning about objects and space. Binford [1971] proposed use of the *generalized cylinder* in machine vision. See also the work of Agin & Binford [1973] and Nevatia & Binford [1977] on the description and recognition of curved objects. Marr & Nishihara [1978] and Nishihara [1981] adopted generalized cylinders for describing the parts in their hierarchical scheme for representing the spatial organization of three-dimensional structures. See also Ballard & Sabbah [1981b].

Freeman [1961] developed the chain code, a way to encode discrete plane curves. Blum [1967] developed one of the earliest schemes for describing two-dimensional shapes. Hoffman [1983] tried to extend a simple classification of two-dimensional curve segments to three-dimensional surfaces. For related recent work see Asada & Brady [1984].

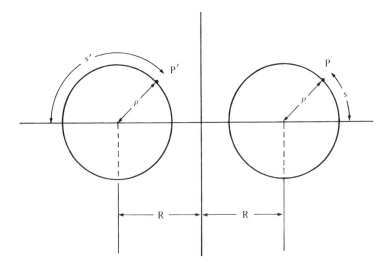

Figure 16-20. A torus can be generated by rotating a circle about an axis lying in the same plane as the circle but passing outside the circle. Points on the surface can be identified by the arclength s above the plane of symmetry and the rotation angle θ.

16.13 Exercises

16-1 In exercise 11-9, where we discussed recovering shape from shading, we introduced ruled and developable surfaces. Recall that a *ruled surface* is one that can be generated by sweeping a straight line, called the *generator*, through space. At each point on a ruled surface, we can find a tangent that lies in the surface. *Developable surfaces* constitute a subclass of ruled surfaces. In the case of a developable surface, a tangent that lies in the surface contains points that all have the same surface normal. Show that the Gaussian curvature is zero everywhere on a developable surface. Hint: Show that a patch on the object maps onto a line on the Gaussian sphere.

16-2 Here we compute the extended Gaussian image of a torus using the methods we developed for solids of revolution. Let the torus have major radius R and minor radius ρ, as before (figure 16-20). A point on the surface can be identified by θ and s, where θ is the angle around the axis of the torus and s is the arclength along the surface measured from the plane of symmetry. Then $r = R + \rho \cos(s/R)$.

(a) Show that

$$r_s = -(\rho/R)\sin(s/R) \qquad \text{and} \qquad r_{ss} = -(\rho/R^2)\cos(s/R).$$

Conclude that

$$K = \frac{\rho\cos(s/R)}{R + \rho\cos(s/R)}.$$

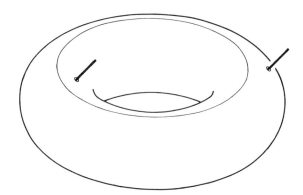

Figure 16-21. Every point on the Gaussian sphere, except for the two poles, corresponds to two point on the torus. One of these points is on the outer surface of the torus, where the Gaussian curvature is positive; the other lies on the inner surface, where the Gaussian curvature is negative. These surfaces are separated by two rings, one below and one above, where the Gaussian curvature is zero. All points on each of these rings have the same orientation and thus correspond to a singularity in the extended Gaussian image.

Two points, separated by $180°$ in θ, have the same surface orientation on the torus (figure 16-21). The surface normal at one of these places points away from the axis, while it points toward the axis at the other place. Accordingly, the two points $(\theta, s) = (\xi, R\eta)$ and $(\theta, s) = \big(\xi + \pi, R(\pi - \eta)\big)$ on the torus correspond to the point (ξ, η) on the Gaussian sphere.

(b) Show that the curvatures at these two points have opposite signs and that

$$K_+ = \frac{1}{R^2} \frac{\rho \cos \eta}{R + \rho \cos \eta} \quad \text{and} \quad K_- = -\frac{1}{R^2} \frac{\rho \cos \eta}{R - \rho \cos \eta}.$$

(c) The torus is not convex, so more than one point on its surface can contribute to a given point on the Gaussian image. Add the absolute values of the inverses of the curvature and show that

$$G(\eta, \xi) = \frac{1}{K_+} - \frac{1}{K_-} = 2R\rho \sec \eta.$$

(d) What would be the result if you instead added the inverses algebraically? What convex figure has extended Gaussian image equal to this sum?

(e) Check your result by using the relationship

$$K = \frac{\kappa_G \cos \eta}{r},$$

given that $\kappa_G = -1/\rho$ and $r = R \pm \rho \cos \eta$.

(f) Show that the surface area of the torus is $4\pi^2 \rho R$ and conclude that all tori with the same surface area have the same extended Gaussian image.

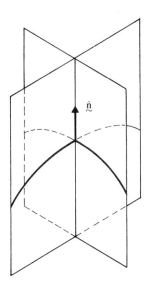

Figure 16-22. A normal section of a surface is obtained by intersecting it with a plane that includes the surface normal. There is a one-parameter family of such planes. The curvature of the intersection varies smoothly with orientation of the normal plane. The product of the two extrema of curvature is the Gaussian curvature.

16-3 Here we explore an alternate definition of Gaussian curvature. Consider a plane containing the surface normal at a point on a smooth surface (figure 16-22). The surface cuts this plane along a curve called a *normal section*, whose curvature we denote by κ_N. Consider the one-parameter family of planes containing the surface normal. Let θ be the angle between a particular plane in this family and a given reference plane. Then κ_N varies with θ in a periodic fashion. In fact, if we measure θ from the plane that gives maximum curvature, it can be shown that

$$\kappa_N = \kappa_1 \cos^2 \theta + \kappa_2 \sin^2 \theta,$$

where κ_1 is the maximum and κ_2 the minimum curvature. These values of κ are called the *principal curvatures*, and the corresponding planes are called the *principal planes*. The two principal planes are orthogonal provided that the principal curvatures are distinct.

(a) Show that $K = \kappa_1 \kappa_2$ is equivalent to the Gaussian curvature introduced earlier.

(b) Check the result in the cases of a plane and a sphere. Consider also developable surfaces.

(c) Check the stationary values found in this chapter for the curvature of the surface of the ellipsoid by sectioning it with three perpendicular planes, namely

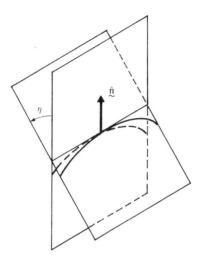

Figure 16-23. The curvature of the intersection of the surface with an inclined plane is larger than the curvature of the intersection with the corresponding normal plane. The ratio of the two equals the secant of the angle of inclination.

the xy-, yz-, and zx-planes. The Gaussian curvature in this case equals the product of the curvatures of the resulting curves. Hint: The maximum and minimum curvatures of an ellipse with semiaxes a and b are a/b^2 and b/a^2, respectively.

16-4 Here we explore an alternate derivation of Gaussian curvature for a solid of revolution. We first need to review Meusnier's theorem. Consider a normal section of a surface at a particular point. It is obtained by cutting the surface with one of the planes passing through the local normal (figure 16-23). Let the curvature of the curve in which the surface cuts this plane be κ_N.

(a) Imagine tilting the cutting plane away from the normal by an angle η (using the local tangent as the tilting axis). The new plane will cut the surface in a curve with higher curvature. Show that this curvature is $\kappa_N \sec \eta$.

Now, let us return to the surface of revolution. It is not hard to show that one of the principal planes at a point on the surface will include the axis of revolution. The normal section in this plane is just the generating curve of the solid of revolution. One of the two principal curvatures is therefore equal to the curvature κ_G of the generating curve at the corresponding point.

Next consider a plane perpendicular to the axis of revolution through the same surface point. It cuts the surface in a circle. The curvature in this plane is $1/r$, where r is the radius of the solid of revolution at that point. This plane, however, is not a normal section. Suppose that the normal makes an angle η

with respect to this plane. Then we also see that the local tangent plane makes an angle η with respect to the axis of revolution.

(b) Construct a cutting plane that includes the normal and is inclined by an angle η relative to the one we have just studied. The intersection of the surface with this plane gives us the second principal section. Show that the curvature of the curve found in this normal section is $\kappa_N = (1/r)\cos\eta$. Hint: Use Meusnier's theorem developed in part (a).

(c) Now show that the Gaussian curvature is

$$K = \frac{\kappa_G \cos \eta}{r}.$$

(d) Check the result in the case of a sphere of radius R.

To make this result more usable, erect a coordinate system with the z-axis aligned with the axis of revolution. The generating curve is given as $r(z)$. Let the first and second derivatives of r with respect to z be denoted by r_z and r_{zz}, respectively.

(e) Show that $\cos \eta = 1/\sqrt{1 + r_z^2}$.

(f) Show that

$$\kappa_G = -\frac{r_{zz}}{(1 + r_z^2)^{3/2}} \quad \text{and} \quad K = -\frac{r_{zz}}{r(1 + r_z^2)^2}.$$

In order to use this result in deriving extended Gaussian images, we must identify points on the surface with points on the unit sphere. Let us introduce a polar angle θ such that $x = r\cos\theta$ and $y = r\sin\theta$.

(g) Show that a unit normal to the surface is given by (figure 16-24)

$$\frac{(\cos\theta, \sin\theta, -r_z)^T}{\sqrt{1 + r_z^2}}$$

and that the unit normal on the Gaussian sphere is

$$(\cos\xi \cos\eta, \, \sin\xi \cos\eta, \, \sin\eta)^T,$$

so that, finally, $\xi = \theta$ and $\tan\eta = -r_z$.

16-5 Show that the Gaussian curvature of an ellipsoid defined by the parametric equations

$$x = a\cos\theta\cos\phi, \quad y = b\sin\theta\cos\phi, \quad z = c\sin\phi$$

is

$$K = \left(\frac{abc}{(bc\cos\theta\cos\phi)^2 + (ca\sin\theta\cos\phi)^2 + (ab\sin\phi)^2}\right)^2.$$

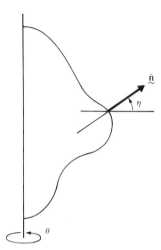

Figure 16-24. The direction of the unit normal can be found from the parametric form of the generator of the solid of revolution.

16-6 Here we study the extended Gaussian image of a particular solid of revolution. We can consider the surface of a solid of revolution to be generated by rotation of a curve about an axis. For convenience, align the z-axis of a coordinate system with the axis of revolution. Measure distance r from the axis to the surface along a line perpendicular to the axis. The shape of the object is then fully determined by the curve $r(z)$.

The Gaussian curvature of the surface was shown to be

$$K = -\frac{r_{zz}}{r(1 + r_z^2)^2},$$

where r_z and r_{zz} are the first and second derivatives of r with respect to z.

We can use longitude ξ and latitude η to refer to points on the Gaussian sphere. Also, for simplicity, we align the axis of the Gaussian sphere with the axis of the solid of revolution.

Consider an object with an elliptical cross section in a plane containing the axis of revolution. Let the maximum radius be $r = a$, while the height z ranges from $-b$ to $+b$. Hint: You might want to check your results as you go along, using the special case of a sphere, for which $a = b$.

(a) Find r_z and r_{zz}, the first and second derivatives of r with respect to z. You might find it useful to determine $1 + r_z^2$ at this point also.

(b) Show that the Gaussian curvature is

$$K = \left(\frac{b}{b^2 + (a^2 - b^2)(z/b)^2}\right)^2.$$

(c) Determine the inclination η of the surface normal with respect to a plane at right angles to the axis of the solid of revolution in terms of r and its derivatives with respect to z. Show that

$$-\tan \eta = \frac{a}{b} \frac{(z/b)}{\sqrt{1 - (z/b)^2}}.$$

You might find it useful to find $\sin \eta$ and $\cos \eta$ at this point also. Hint: Use the identities $1 + \tan^2 \eta = \sec^2 \eta$ and $\sin^2 \eta + \cos^2 \eta = 1$.

(d) What is the latitude of the point on the Gaussian sphere corresponding to the point on the surface that has a surface normal inclined η with respect to a plane at right angles to the axis of the solid of revolution?

(e) Show that the extended Gaussian image can be written

$$G(\xi, \eta) = \left(\frac{a^2 b}{a^2 \cos^2 \eta + b^2 \sin^2 \eta} \right)^2.$$

Hint: Remember that $G = 1/K$, and show that

$$(a \cos \eta)^2 + (b \sin \eta)^2 = \frac{a^2 b^2}{b^2 + (a^2 - b^2)(z/b)^2}.$$

(f) What are the maximum and minimum values of $G(\xi, \eta)$, and where do they occur? Distinguish between the two cases $a < b$ (football) and $a > b$ (pumpkin).

16-7 The notions developed in this chapter can be applied to simply connected figures in the plane. Instead of the unit sphere, we map onto the unit circle.

(a) Define the *extended circular image* $R(\psi)$ of a closed figure in the plane in analogy with the extended Gaussian image of a closed object in three-dimensional space. Here ψ is the angle between the normal vector and an arbitrary reference direction, which we take to be the x-axis. Give a geometrical interpretation of $R(\psi)$. Show that the center of mass of the extended circular image of a closed figure must be at the center of the unit circle.

(b) Show that the extended circular image of an ellipse with semiaxes a and b along the x-axis and y-axis, respectively, is

$$R(\psi) = \left(\frac{ab}{(a \cos \psi)^2 + (b \sin \psi)^2} \right)^2.$$

Hint: Use the parametric equations $x = a \cos \theta$ and $y = b \sin \theta$.

(c) Develop a method for reconstructing the boundary curve, $x(s)$ and $y(s)$, of a convex figure from its extended circular image.

(d) Show that circular convolution of the extended circular image of a closed figure with an arbitrary positive function on the circle produces an extended circular image corresponding to a figure that is also closed. Show that the boundary of the new figure is smoother than the boundary of the original figure. Hint: The circular convolution of two periodic functions R and S is defined by

$$R'(\psi) = \int_0^{2\pi} R(\psi - \eta) S(\eta) \, d\eta.$$

16-8   The *support function* $\rho(\psi)$ of a convex figure in the plane gives the perpendicular distance ρ of the closest line that does not pass into the interior of the region. The distance is measured from some arbitrary origin inside the figure and expressed as a function of the angular orientation ψ of the line. The function can be found readily given a parametric representation of the boundary curve, such as $x(s)$ and $y(s)$. Then

$$\rho(\psi) = \max_s \big(x(s) \cos \psi + y(s) \sin \psi \big).$$

(a)   Show that for a smoothly curved convex figure,

$$\rho(\psi) = x(\psi) \cos \psi + y(\psi) \sin \psi.$$

(b)   Define the *support figure* to be the figure obtained by plotting $\rho(\psi)$ versus ψ in polar coordinates. Show that the support figure of a line with one end at the origin is a circle with the given line as diameter.

(c)   Show that the support figure of the union of two figures A and B is the union of the support figures of A and B.

(d)   Show that the support figure of a convex polygon is piecewise-circular. Suppose the support figure is superimposed on the polygon. Where do the circular arcs touch the polygon? How do the contact points move when the origin is moved? Hint: The contact points fall into two distinct classes. The locations of points in one class depend on the choice of origin, while the locations of the others do not.

(e)   Generalize the notion of support figure to the three-dimensional case. Show that the support figure of a convex polyhedron is piecewise-spherical.

16-9   The *mixture* of the convex figures X and Y is denoted $X \oplus Y$. The extended circular image of the mixture is just the sum of the extended circular images of the two component figures. That is,

$$R_{X \oplus Y}(\psi) = R_X(\psi) + R_Y(\psi),$$

where $R_X(\psi)$ and $R_Y(\psi)$ are the extended circular images of X and Y, respectively.

(a) Show that the support function of the mixture of two convex figures is the sum of the support functions of the two figures. That is,

$$\rho_{X \oplus Y}(\psi) = \rho_X(\psi) + \rho_X(\psi).$$

(b) Derive the following formula for the area of the mixture of two convex figures X and Y:

$$A(X \oplus Y) = A(X) + M(X, Y) + A(Y),$$

where the *mixed area* $M(X, Y)$ is given by

$$M(X, Y) = \int_0^{2\pi} \rho_X(\psi)\, R_Y(\psi)\, d\psi = \int_0^{2\pi} \rho_Y(\psi)\, R_X(\psi)\, d\psi.$$

Verify this result for the cases of X a point and of $X = Y$.

(c) Let $A(X)$ be the area of the figure X, and let $\mathrm{Rot}_\theta(X)$ be the figure obtained by rotating X counterclockwise by θ. Show that the area of the mixture of a curve and a rotated version of the curve is never less than the area of the mixture of the curve with itself, without rotation. That is,

$$A\big(X \oplus \mathrm{Rot}_\theta(X)\big) \geq A(X \oplus X) \qquad \text{for all } \theta.$$

Devise a method for determining the rotation of a closed convex curve in the plane based on this observation.

(d) Generalize the argument above to three dimensions. That is, consider extended Gaussian images of closed convex objects and a suitable generalization of the support function to three dimensions. How would you efficiently compute the support function? How would you efficiently compute the *mixed volume*? In what ways might this approach be superior to methods involving direct matching of extended Gaussian images? Warning: This last part is much harder than the rest of the problem. Hint: Look at the exercises in chapter 18.

17

Passive Navigation & Structure from Motion

In this chapter we investigate the problem of passive navigation using optical flow information. We wish to determine the motion of a camera from time-varying imagery or, in the discrete case, from an image sequence. Our assumption is that the camera is moving with respect to a fixed environment. If there is more than one object with independent motion, then we shall assume that the image has been segmented and that we can concentrate on one region corresponding to a single object. Curiously, if there is a translational component to the motion, then we obtain the shape of the surface as a by-product of the recovery of the motion parameters.

We discuss three approaches that have been taken to this problem. We then focus on a least-squares approach that takes into account all the information in the image. Closed-form solutions are derived for the cases of purely rotational and purely translational motion, and the set of nonlinear equations that must be solved iteratively in the general case is displayed. In the exercises a method is outlined that solves the problem without computing the optical flow as an intermediate product.

Recovering motion and surface shape from time-varying imagery is useful in guiding a moving platform through a known environment. The shapes recovered can be used for recognition by one of the techniques considered in earlier chapters.

17.1 Recovering the Motion of the Observer

Suppose we are viewing a film. We wish to determine the motion of the camera from the sequence of images, assuming that the instantaneous velocity of the brightness patterns, also called the *optical flow*, is known at each point in the image. Several schemes for recovering the observer's motion have been suggested. These approaches can be classified into three categories:

- The discrete approach.
- The differential approach.
- The least-squares approach.

In the discrete approach, information about the movement of brightness patterns at only a few points is used to determine the motion of the camera. In particular, using such an approach, we attempt to identify and match discrete points in a sequence of images. Of interest in this case is the photogrammetric problem of determining the minimum number of points from which the motion can be calculated for a given number of images. This approach requires that we track features, or identify corresponding features in images taken at different times. It can be shown that, in general, seven points are sufficient to determine the motion uniquely. These points must satisfy a constraint on their position, but the constraint is a weak one. It is even possible, if more points are available, to write a set of linear equations in the unknown parameters of the motion.

In the differential approach, the first and second spatial partial derivatives of the optical flow are used to compute the motion of a camera. It has been claimed that it is sufficient to know the optical flow and both its first and second derivatives at a single point to determine the motion uniquely. This turns out to be incorrect, except for a special case. Furthermore, noise in the measured optical flow is accentuated by differentiation.

In the least-squares approach, the whole optical flow field is used. A major shortcoming of both the discrete and differential approaches is that neither allows for errors in the optical flow data. This is why we choose the least-squares approach to devise a technique to determine the motion of the camera from the measured optical flow. The algorithm takes the abundance of available data into account and is robust enough to allow numerical implementation.

17.2 Technical Prerequisites

In this section we review the equations describing the relation between the motion of a camera and the optical flow that motion generates. We can assume either a fixed camera in a changing environment or a moving camera in a static environment. Let us assume a moving camera in a static environment. A coordinate system is fixed with respect to the camera, with the Z-axis pointing along the optical axis. Any rigid body motion can be resolved into two components, a translation and a rotation about an axis through the origin. We shall denote the translational component of the motion of the camera by $\mathbf{t}$ and its angular velocity by $\boldsymbol{\omega}$. Let the instantaneous coordinates of a point P in the environment be $(X, Y, Z)^T$. (Note that here $Z > 0$ for points in front of the imaging system.)

Let $\mathbf{r}$ be the column vector $(X, Y, Z)^T$, where ^{T} denotes the transpose. Then the velocity of P with respect to the XYZ coordinate system is

$$\mathbf{V} = -\mathbf{t} - \boldsymbol{\omega} \times \mathbf{r}.$$

If we define the components of $\mathbf{t}$ and $\boldsymbol{\omega}$ as

$$\mathbf{t} = (U, V, W)^T \qquad \text{and} \qquad \boldsymbol{\omega} = (A, B, C)^T,$$

we can rewrite this equation in component form as

$$\dot{X} = -U - BZ + CY,$$

$$\dot{Y} = -V - CX + AZ,$$

$$\dot{Z} = -W - AY + BX,$$

where the dot denotes differentiation with respect to time.

The *optical flow* at each point in the image plane is the instantaneous velocity of the brightness pattern at that point. Let (x, y) denote the coordinates of a point in the image plane. Here we assume perspective projection between an object point P and the corresponding image point p; thus the coordinates of p are

$$x = \frac{X}{Z} \qquad \text{and} \qquad y = \frac{Y}{Z}.$$

The optical flow at a point (x, y), denoted by (u, v), is

$$u = \dot{x} \qquad \text{and} \qquad v = \dot{y}.$$

Differentiating the equations for x and y with respect to time and using the derivatives of X, Y, and Z, we obtain the following equations for the optical flow:

$$u = \frac{\dot{X}}{Z} - \frac{X\dot{Z}}{Z^2} = \left(-\frac{U}{Z} - B + Cy \right) - x \left(-\frac{W}{Z} - Ay + Bx \right),$$

$$v = \frac{\dot{Y}}{Z} - \frac{Y\dot{Z}}{Z^2} = \left(-\frac{V}{Z} - Cx + A \right) - y \left(-\frac{W}{Z} - Ay + Bx \right).$$

We can write these equations in the form

$$u = u_t + u_r \qquad \text{and} \qquad v = v_t + v_r,$$

where (u_t, v_t) denotes the translational component of the optical flow and (u_r, v_r) the rotational component:

$$u_t = \frac{-U + xW}{Z} \qquad \text{and} \qquad u_r = A\,xy - B\left(x^2 + 1\right) + C\,y,$$

$$v_t = \frac{-V + yW}{Z} \qquad \text{and} \qquad v_r = A\left(y^2 + 1\right) - B\,xy - C\,x.$$

So far we have considered a single point P. To define the optical flow globally we assume that P lies on a surface defined by a function $Z(X, Y)$ that is positive for all values of X and Y. With any surface and any motion of a camera we can therefore associate a certain optical flow, and we say that the surface and the motion generate this optical flow.

Optical flow, therefore, depends upon the six parameters of motion of the camera and upon the surface whose images are analyzed. Can all these unknowns be uniquely recaptured solely from optical flow? Strictly speaking, the answer is no. To see this, consider a surface S_2 that is a dilation by a factor k of a surface S_1. Furthermore, let two motions M_1 and M_2 have the same rotational component, and let their translational components be proportional to each other with the same proportionality factor k (we say that M_1 and M_2 are *similar*). Then the optical flow generated by S_1 and M_1 is the same as the optical flow generated by S_2 and M_2. This follows directly from the definition of optical flow given above.

Determining the motion of a camera from the optical flow is much easier if the motion is purely translational or purely rotational. The next two sections deal with these two special cases. We then turn to the case in which no a priori assumptions about the motion of the camera are made.

17.3 The Translational Case

In this section we discuss the case in which the motion of the camera is purely translational. As before, let $\mathbf{t} = (U, V, W)^T$ be the velocity of the camera. Then the following equations hold:

$$u_t = \frac{-U + xW}{Z} \qquad \text{and} \qquad v_t = \frac{-V + yW}{Z}.$$

17.3.1 Similar Surfaces and Similar Motions

We want to show that if two purely translational motions generate the same optical flow, the two surfaces are similar and the two camera motions are similar. Let Z_1 and Z_2 be two surfaces and let $\mathbf{t}_1 = (U_1, V_1, W_1)^T$ and $\mathbf{t}_2 = (U_2, V_2, W_2)^T$ define two different motions of a camera such that Z_1 and $\mathbf{t}_1$ and Z_2 and $\mathbf{t}_2$ generate the same optical flow, that is,

$$u = \frac{-U_1 + xW_1}{Z_1} \quad \text{and} \quad v = \frac{-V_1 + yW_1}{Z_1},$$

$$u = \frac{-U_2 + xW_2}{Z_2} \quad \text{and} \quad v = \frac{-V_2 + yW_2}{Z_2}.$$

Eliminating Z_1, Z_2, u, and v from these equations, we obtain

$$\frac{-U_1 + xW_1}{-V_1 + yW_1} = \frac{-U_2 + xW_2}{-V_2 + yW_2}.$$

We can rewrite this as

$$(-U_1 + xW_1)(-V_2 + yW_2) = (-U_2 + xW_2)(-V_1 + yW_1),$$

or

$$U_1V_2 - xV_2W_1 - yU_1W_2 + xyW_1W_2 = U_2V_1 - xV_1W_2 - yU_2W_1 + xyW_2W_1.$$

Since we are assuming that Z_1 and $\mathbf{t}_1$ and Z_2 and $\mathbf{t}_2$ generate the same optical flow, the above equation must hold for all x and y. Therefore the following must hold:

$$U_1V_2 = U_2V_1,$$

$$-V_2W_1 = -V_1W_2,$$

$$-U_1W_2 = -U_2W_1.$$

These equations can be rewritten in ratio form as

$$U_1 : V_1 : W_1 = U_2 : V_2 : W_2,$$

from which it follows that Z_2 is a dilation of Z_1. It is clear that the scaling factor between Z_1 and Z_2 (or equivalently between $\mathbf{t}_1$ and $\mathbf{t}_2$) cannot be recovered from the optical flow, regardless of the number of points at which the flow is known. We shall say that the motion of the camera is uniquely determined if it has been determined up to a constant scaling factor.

17.3.2 A Least-Squares Formulation

In general, the directions of the optical flow at two points in the image plane uniquely determine the purely translational motion of a camera. There is, however, a drawback to utilizing so little of the available information. The optical flow we measure is corrupted by noise, and we would like to develop a robust method that takes this into account. Thus we suggest using a least-squares method to determine the movement parameters and the surface (that is, the best fit with respect to some norm).

For the following we assume that the image plane is the rectangle $x \in [-w, w]$ and $y \in [-h, h]$. The same method applies if the image has some other shape. (In fact, it can be used on subimages corresponding to individual objects, in the situation where the environment contains several objects that can move with respect to one another.) Usually, there is a lower limit to the distance between the objects and the camera, so we can assume that $1/Z$ is a bounded function. Moreover, most scenes will consist of a number of cohesive objects with continuous surfaces, so that depth will be continuous "almost everywhere." Specifically, let us assume that the set of points where $1/Z$ is discontinuous is of *measure zero*. (This means that the integral of a characteristic function, which equals one in these places and zero elsewhere, is zero.) This condition ensures that all necessary integrations can be carried out.

We wish to minimize the expression

$$\iint \left(\left(u - \frac{-U + xW}{Z} \right)^2 + \left(v - \frac{-V + yW}{Z} \right)^2 \right) dx\, dy.$$

In this case, then, we determine the best fit with respect to the ML_2 norm, which is defined as

$$\| f(x, y) \| = \iint (f(x, y))^2 dx\, dy.$$

The steps in the least-squares method are as follows: First, we determine the value of Z that minimizes the integrand at every point (x, y); then we determine the values of U, V, and W that minimize the integral.

It is convenient to define

$$\alpha = -U + xW \qquad \text{and} \qquad \beta = -V + yW.$$

Note that the expected flow, given U, V, and W, is simply

$$\bar{u} = \frac{\alpha}{Z} \qquad \text{and} \qquad \bar{v} = \frac{\beta}{Z}.$$

Then we can rewrite the integral above as

$$\iint \left(\left(u - \frac{\alpha}{Z} \right)^2 + \left(v - \frac{\beta}{Z} \right)^2 \right) dx\,dy.$$

We proceed now with the first step of our minimization method. Differentiating the integrand with respect to Z and setting the resulting expression equal to zero yields

$$\left(u - \frac{\alpha}{Z} \right) \frac{\alpha}{Z^2} + \left(v - \frac{\beta}{Z} \right) \frac{\beta}{Z^2} = 0.$$

Therefore we can write Z as

$$Z = \frac{\alpha^2 + \beta^2}{u\alpha + v\beta}.$$

This equation, by the way, imposes a constraint on U, V, and W, since Z must be positive. We do not make use of this except to help us choose between two opposite solutions for the translational velocity later on. Note that now

$$u - \frac{\alpha}{Z} = +\beta \frac{u\beta - v\alpha}{\alpha^2 + \beta^2} \qquad \text{and} \qquad v - \frac{\beta}{Z} = -\alpha \frac{u\beta - v\alpha}{\alpha^2 + \beta^2},$$

and we can therefore rewrite the integral above as

$$\iint \frac{(u\beta - v\alpha)^2}{\alpha^2 + \beta^2} dx\,dy.$$

It should be clear that uniformly scaling U, V, and W does not change the value of the integral. This is a reflection of the fact that we can determine the motion parameters only up to a constant factor.

Before proceeding with the second step, we give a geometrical interpretation of what we have done so far. Suppose that the motion parameters U, V, and W are given. At any given point (x_0, y_0), optical flow depends not only upon the motion parameters but also upon the value Z_0 of Z at that point. However, the direction of (u, v) does not depend upon Z_0. The point (u, v) must lie along the line L in the uv-plane defined by the equation $u\beta - v\alpha = 0$. Let the measured optical flow at (x_0, y_0) be denoted (u_m, v_m), and let the closest point on the line L be (u_a, v_a). This corresponds to a particular Z_a. The remaining error is the distance between the point (u_m, v_m) and the line L. The square of this distance is given by the integrand of the integral above.

For the second step, we differentiate the integral with respect to U, V, and W and set the resulting expressions equal to zero:

$$\iint \frac{\beta(u\beta - v\alpha)(u\alpha + v\beta)}{(\alpha^2 + \beta^2)^2} \, dx \, dy = 0,$$

$$-\iint \frac{\alpha(u\beta - v\alpha)(u\alpha + v\beta)}{(\alpha^2 + \beta^2)^2} \, dx \, dy = 0,$$

$$\iint \frac{(y\alpha - x\beta)(u\beta - v\alpha)(u\alpha + v\beta)}{(\alpha^2 + \beta^2)^2} \, dx \, dy = 0.$$

If we introduce the abbreviation

$$K = \frac{(u\beta - v\alpha)(u\alpha + v\beta)}{(\alpha^2 + \beta^2)^2},$$

the equations can be rewritten as

$$\iint \left((-V + yW)K \right) dx \, dy = 0,$$

$$-\iint \left((-U + xW)K \right) dx \, dy = 0,$$

$$\iint \left((-yU + xV)K \right) dx \, dy = 0.$$

The sum of U times the first integral, V times the second integral, and W times the third integral is identically zero. Thus the three equations are linearly dependent. This is to be expected, for if

$$f(kU, kV, kW) = f(U, V, W),$$

where f is a differentiable function and k a constant, then

$$U\frac{\partial f}{\partial U} + V\frac{\partial f}{\partial V} + W\frac{\partial f}{\partial W} = 0.$$

The result is also consistent with the fact that only two equations are needed, since the translational velocity can be determined only up to a constant factor. Unfortunately, the equations are nonlinear in U, V, and W, and we are not able to show that they have a unique (up to a constant scaling factor) solution.

17.3.3 Using a Different Norm

There is a way, however, to devise a least-squares method that allows us to display a closed-form solution for the motion parameters. Instead of minimizing the integral above, we try to minimize the expression

$$\iint \left(\left(u - \frac{-U + xW}{Z}\right)^2 + \left(v - \frac{-V + yW}{Z}\right)^2 \right) (\alpha^2 + \beta^2)\, dx\, dy,$$

obtained by multiplying the integrand by $\alpha^2 + \beta^2$. Then we apply the same least-squares method as before. When the measured optical flow is not corrupted by noise, both integrals can be made equal to zero by substituting the correct motion parameters. We thus obtain the same solution for the motion parameters. If the measured optical flow is not exact, then using the new integral for our minimization yields the best fit with respect not to the ML_2 norm, but to another norm that we shall call the $ML_{\alpha\beta}$ norm, namely

$$\|f(x, y)\|_{\alpha\beta} = \iint \left(f(x, y) \right)^2 (\alpha^2 + \beta^2)\, dx\, dy.$$

What we have here is a minimization in which the error contributions are weighted, greater importance being given to points where the optical flow velocity is larger. This is most appropriate when the measurement of larger velocities is more accurate.

Which norm gives the best results depends on the properties of the noise in the measured optical flow. The first norm is better suited to the situation in which the noise in the measurements is independent of the magnitude of the optical flow. Note also that if we really want the minimum with respect to the ML_2 norm, we can use the results of the minimization with respect to the $ML_{\alpha\beta}$ norm as starting values in a numerical process.

We now apply our least-squares method to the case in which the norm is chosen to be $ML_{\alpha\beta}$. First, we determine Z by differentiating the integrand with respect to Z and setting the result equal to zero. We again obtain

$$\left(u - \frac{\alpha}{Z}\right)\frac{\alpha}{Z^2} + \left(v - \frac{\beta}{Z}\right)\frac{\beta}{Z^2} = 0,$$

from which it follows that

$$Z = \frac{\alpha^2 + \beta^2}{u\alpha + v\beta}.$$

We therefore want to minimize

$$\iint (u\beta - v\alpha)^2\, dx\, dy.$$

If we call this integral $g(U, V, W)$, then, since

$$u\beta - v\alpha = (vU - uV) - (xv - yu)W,$$

we have

$$g(U,V,W) = aU^2 + bV^2 + cW^2 + 2dUV + 2eVW + 2fWU,$$

where

$$a = \iint v^2 \, dx \, dy,$$

$$b = \iint u^2 \, dx \, dy,$$

$$c = \iint (xv - yu)^2 \, dx \, dy,$$

$$d = -\iint uv \, dx \, dy,$$

$$e = \iint u(xv - yu) \, dx \, dy,$$

$$f = -\iint v(xv - yu) \, dx \, dy.$$

Now $g(U,V,W)$ cannot be negative, and $g(U,V,W) = 0$ for $U = V = W = 0$. Thus a minimum can be found by inspection, but it is not what we might have hoped for! In fact, to determine the translational velocity using our least-squares method, we must solve the following homogeneous equation for $\mathbf{t}$:

$$\mathbf{G}\,\mathbf{t} = 0,$$

where

$$\mathbf{G} = \begin{pmatrix} a & d & f \\ d & b & e \\ f & e & c \end{pmatrix}.$$

This clearly has a solution other then zero if and only if the determinant of $\mathbf{G}$ is zero. Then the three equations are linearly dependent and $\mathbf{t}$ can be determined up to a constant factor. In general, however, because the data are corrupted by noise, $g(U,V,W)$ cannot be made equal to zero for nonzero translational velocity, and so $\mathbf{t} = (0,0,0)^T$ will be the only solution. To see this another way, note that g has the form

$$g(kU, kV, kW) = k^2 g(U,V,W),$$

where k is a constant. Clearly $g(U,V,W)$ assumes its minimum value for $U = V = W = 0$.

What we are really interested in is determining the direction of $\mathbf{t}$ that minimizes g, for a fixed length of $\mathbf{t}$. Hence we impose the constraint that $\mathbf{t}$ be a unit vector. If $\mathbf{t}$ is constrained to have unit magnitude, then the minimum value of g is the smallest eigenvalue of the matrix $\mathbf{G}$, and the value of $\mathbf{t}$ for which g assumes its minimum can be found by determining the eigenvector corresponding to this eigenvalue. This follows from the observation that g is a quadratic form that can be written as

$$g(U, V, W) = \mathbf{t}^T \mathbf{G} \mathbf{t}.$$

Note that $\mathbf{G}$ is a positive semidefinite Hermitian matrix since $a \geq 0$, $b \geq 0$, $c \geq 0$, $ab \geq d^2$, $bc \geq e^2$, and $ca \geq f^2$. (The last three inequalities follow from the Cauchy–Schwarz inequality.) Hence all the eigenvalues λ_i are real and nonnegative; they are the solutions of the third-degree polynomial

$$\lambda^3$$
$$- (a + b + c)\lambda^2$$
$$+ (ab + bc + ca - d^2 - e^2 - f^2)\lambda$$
$$+ (ae^2 + bf^2 + cd^2 - abc - 2def) = 0.$$

There is an explicit formula for the least positive root in terms of the real and imaginary parts of the roots of the quadratic resolvent of the cubic. In our case, this gives us the desired smallest root, since the roots cannot be negative. For the sake of completeness, however, various pathological cases that might come up will be discussed next, even though they are of little practical interest.

Note that $\lambda = 0$ is an eigenvalue if and only if $\mathbf{G}$ is singular, that is, if the constant term in the polynomial equals zero. In fact, if the determinant of $\mathbf{G}$ is zero, we can find a translational velocity $\mathbf{t}$ that makes g zero. It follows from a theorem in calculus that this happens only when the optical flow is correct "almost everywhere," that is, when the set of points where it is corrupted is of measure zero. The theorem states that if the integral of the square of a bounded and continuous function is zero, then the function itself is zero. Hence errors can only occur at points where the optical flow is discontinuous, and these are exactly the points where the surface defined by Z is discontinuous. (These are also the places where existing methods for computing the optical flow are subject to large errors.)

It is impossible for exactly two eigenvalues to be zero, since this would imply that the coefficient of λ in the polynomial is equal to zero, while that of λ^2 is not. That in turn would imply that $ab = d^2$, $bc = e^2$, and $ca = f^2$, while a, b, and c are not all zero. For equality to hold in the Cauchy–Schwarz inequalities, however, u and v must both be proportional to $xv - yu$. This can only be true (for all x and y in the image) if $u=v=0$. But then all six integrals become zero, and consequently all three eigenvalues are zero. This situation is of little interest, since it occurs only when the optical flow is zero everywhere. Then the velocity is also zero.

Once the smallest eigenvalue is known, it is straightforward to find the translational velocity that best matches the given data. To determine the eigenvector corresponding to an eigenvalue λ_1, we must solve the following homogeneous set of linear equations:

$$(a - \lambda_1)U + dV + fW = 0,$$
$$dU + (b - \lambda_1)V + eW = 0,$$
$$fU + eV + (c - \lambda_1)W = 0.$$

Because λ_1 is an eigenvalue, these equations are linearly dependent. Let us for a moment assume that all eigenvalues are distinct, that is, the rank of the matrix $(\mathbf{G} - \lambda\mathbf{I})$ is two, where $\mathbf{I}$ is the identity matrix. Then we can use any pair of equations to solve for U and V in terms of W. There are three ways to do this. To obtain a symmetric answer we add the three results:

$$U = (b - \lambda_1)(c - \lambda_1) - f(b - \lambda_1) - d(c - \lambda_1) + e(f + d - e),$$
$$V = (c - \lambda_1)(a - \lambda_1) - d(c - \lambda_1) - e(a - \lambda_1) + f(d + e - f);$$
$$W = (a - \lambda_1)(b - \lambda_1) - e(a - \lambda_1) - f(b - \lambda_1) + d(e + f - d).$$

Note that λ_1 will be very small if the data are good, and we might want simply to approximate the exact solution by using the above equations with λ_1 set to zero. (Then, of course, there is no need to determine the eigenvalue.) In any case, the resulting velocity can now be normalized so that its magnitude is one. There is one remaining difficulty, arising from the fact that if $\mathbf{t}$ is a solution to our minimization problem, so is $-\mathbf{t}$. Only one of these solutions will correspond to positive values of Z, however. This can be seen easily by evaluating Z at some point in the image. The case in which the two smallest eigenvalues are the same will be discussed below.

There is a simple geometrical interpretation of what we have done so far. Consider the surface defined by $g(U, V, W) = k$, where k is a constant. Note that we can always find a new coordinate system $(\widetilde{U}, \widetilde{V}, \widetilde{W})$ in which $g(U, V, W)$ can be written in the form

$$\lambda_1\widetilde{U}^2 + \lambda_2\widetilde{V}^2 + \lambda_3\widetilde{W}^2 = k,$$

where the λ_i ($i = 1$, 2, 3) are the three eigenvalues of the quadratic form. If the eigenvalues are all nonzero, the surface $g(U, V, W) = k$ is an ellipsoid with three orthogonal semiaxes of length $\sqrt{k/\lambda_i}$. We are particularly interested in the case where the constant k is the smallest eigenvalue. Then all three semiaxes have lengths less than or equal to one. Hence the ellipsoid lies within the unit sphere. If the two smallest eigenvalues are distinct, the unit sphere touches the ellipsoid in two places, corresponding to the largest axis. If the two smaller eigenvalues happen to be the same, however, the unit sphere touches the ellipsoid along a circle, and as a result all the velocity vectors lying in a plane spanned by two eigenvectors give equally low errors. Finally, if all three eigenvalues are equal, no direction for **t** is preferred, since the ellipsoid becomes the unit sphere.

The case in which exactly one eigenvalue is zero also has a simple geometrical interpretation. The surface defined by $g(U, V, W) = 0$ is a straight line, as can be seen easily from an examination of the equation

$$\lambda_1 \tilde{U}^2 + \lambda_2 \tilde{V}^2 = 0,$$

written for the case in which λ_3 is zero. (Remember that λ_1 and λ_2 are both positive.) Clearly the unit sphere intersects this line in exactly two points, one of which corresponds to positive values for Z.

The method just described can be easily implemented. To this end, the problem can be discretized. We can derive an expression similar to the above, but with the integrals approximated by sums. Our minimization method can then be applied to these sums. The resulting equations are similar to ones described in this section, with summation replacing integration. We can use the ratio of the biggest to the smallest eigenvalue, the *condition number*, as a measure of confidence in the computed velocity. The computed velocity is sensitive to errors in the measurements unless the condition number is much larger than one.

The same error integral as above is obtained when we use the ML_{Zuv} norm defined by

$$\|f(x, y)\|_{Zuv} \iint \big(f(x, y) Z(x, y)\big)^2 (u^2 + v^2)\, dx\, dy.$$

Moreover, we can arrive at a similar solution by multiplying the integrand by Z^2 instead of $\alpha^2 + \beta^2$. In that case the minimization is carried out with respect to the ML_Z norm defined by

$$\|f(x, y)\|_Z = \iint \big(f(x, y) Z(x, y)\big)^2 dx\, dy.$$

Here optical flow velocities for points that are farther away are weighted more heavily. This is most appropriate when the measurement of larger velocities is less accurate. We end up with a quadratic form similar to g, but the integrals for the six constants corresponding to a, b, c, d, e, and f are a bit more complicated. Curiously, they depend only on the direction of the optical flow at each point, not on its magnitude.

Other constraints could also be used. If we insist on $U^2 + V^2 = 1$, for example, we obtain a quadratic instead of a cubic equation, and if we use $W = 1$, only a linear equation needs to be solved. The disadvantage of these approaches is that the result is sensitive to the orientation of the coordinate axes. Clearly, in the case of exact data, we can obtain the correct solution using any of the three constraints mentioned above.

17.4 The Rotational Case

Suppose now that the motion of the camera is purely rotational. In order to determine the motion from optical flow, we again use a least-squares algorithm with the ML_2 norm described in the previous section. Recall that in this case the optical flow is

$$u_r = Axy - B(x^2 + 1) + Cy,$$
$$v_r = A(y^2 + 1) - Bxy - Cx.$$

We shall show now, in a fashion analogous to the earlier approach, that two different rotations, $\omega_1 = (A_1, B_1, C_1)^T$ and $\omega_2 = (A_2, B_2, C_2)^T$, cannot generate the same optical flow. If we assume the converse, the following equations must hold for all values of x and y:

$$A_1xy - B_1(x^2 + 1) + C_1y = A_2xy - B_2(x^2 + 1) + C_2y,$$
$$A_1(y^2 + 1) - B_1xy - C_1x = A_2(y^2 + 1) - B_2xy - C_2x,$$

from which we can immediately deduce that $\omega_1 = \omega_2$.

In general, the direction of the optical flow at two points and its magnitude at one point uniquely determine the purely rotational motion of a camera. We choose instead to minimize the following expression:

$$\iint \left((u - u_r)^2 + (v - v_r)^2\right) dx\, dy.$$

Because the motion is purely rotational, the optical flow does not depend upon the distance to the surface, and we can therefore omit the first step used in our method for the translational case. Thus we immediately differentiate the integral with respect to A, B, and C and set the resulting expressions to zero:

$$\iint \left((u - u_r)xy + (v - v_r)(y^2 + 1)\right) dx\, dy = 0,$$

$$\iint \left((u - u_r)(x^2 + 1) + (v - v_r)xy\right) dx\, dy = 0,$$

$$\iint \left((u - u_r)y - (v - v_r)x\right) dx\, dy = 0.$$

We can rewrite these equations as

$$\iint \left(uxy + v(y^2 + 1)\right) dx\, dy = \iint \left(u_r xy + v_r(y^2 + 1)\right) dx\, dy,$$

$$\iint \left(u(x^2 + 1) + vxy\right) dx\, dy = \iint \left(u_r(x^2 + 1) + v_r xy\right) dx\, dy,$$

$$\iint \left(uy - vx\right) dx\, dy = \iint \left(u_r y - v_r x\right) dx\, dy,$$

and expand them to yield

$$\overline{a}A + \overline{d}B + \overline{f}C = \overline{k},$$
$$\overline{d}A + \overline{b}B + \overline{e}C = \overline{l},$$
$$\overline{f}A + \overline{e}B + \overline{c}C = \overline{m},$$

where

$$\overline{a} = \iint \left(x^2 y^2 + (y^2 + 1)^2\right) dx\, dy,$$

$$\overline{b} = \iint \left((x^2 + 1)^2 + x^2 y^2\right) dx\, dy,$$

$$\overline{c} = \iint \left(x^2 + y^2\right) dx\, dy,$$

$$\overline{d} = - \iint \left(xy(x^2 + y^2 + 2)\right) dx\, dy,$$

$$\overline{e} = - \iint y\, dx\, dy,$$

$$\overline{f} = - \iint x\, dx\, dy,$$

and

$$\overline{k} = \iint \left(uxy + v(y^2 + 1)\right) dx\, dy,$$

$$\overline{l} = - \iint \left(u(x^2 + 1) + vxy\right) dx\, dy,$$

$$\overline{m} = \iint \left(uy - vx\right) dx\, dy.$$

If we call the coefficient matrix $\mathbf{M}$ and the column vector on the right-hand side $\mathbf{n}$, we have

$$\mathbf{M}\omega = \mathbf{n}.$$

Thus, provided that the matrix $\mathbf{M}$ is nonsingular, we can compute the rotation as

$$\omega = \mathbf{M}^{-1}\mathbf{n}.$$

We show in exercise 17-9 that the matrix $\mathbf{M}$ is nonsingular in the special case of a rectangular image plane. As the extent of the image plane decreases, however, the matrix $\mathbf{M}$ becomes ill-conditioned. That is, inaccuracies in the integrals $\bar{k}$, $\bar{l}$, and $\bar{m}$ computed from the observed flow are greatly magnified. This makes sense, since we cannot expect to determine accurately the component of rotation about the optical axis when observations are confined to a small cone of directions about the optical axis.

As before, in numerical implementations of the algorithm the integrals can be approximated by sums.

17.5 General Motion

We would like now to apply a least-squares algorithm to determine the motion of a camera from optical flow data with no a priori assumptions about the motion. It is plain that a least-squares method is easiest to use when the resulting equations are linear in all the motion parameters. Unfortunately, there exists no norm that will allow us to achieve this goal. There is a norm, however, that results in equations that are linear in some of the unknowns and quadratic in the others. We again attack the minimization problem using the $ML_{\alpha\beta}$ norm under the constraint that $U^2+V^2+W^2 = 1$. The ensuing equations are polynomials in the unknowns U, V, W, A, B, and C and can be solved by a standard iterative procedure such as Newton's method or Bairstow's method or by an interpolation scheme such as *regula falsi*. The expression we wish to minimize is

$$\iint \left(\left(u - \left(\frac{\alpha}{Z} + u_r \right) \right)^2 + \left(v - \left(\frac{\beta}{Z} + v_r \right) \right)^2 \right) (\alpha^2 + \beta^2) \, dx \, dy.$$

The first step is to differentiate the integrand with respect to Z and set the resulting expression equal to zero, yielding

$$Z = \frac{\alpha^2 + \beta^2}{(u - u_r)\alpha + (v - v_r)\beta}.$$

We introduce the Lagrange multiplier λ and attempt to minimize

$$\iint \left((u - u_r)\beta - (v - v_r)\alpha \right)^2 dx \, dy + \lambda(U^2 + V^2 + W^2 - 1).$$

The equations we have to solve to determine the motion parameters are obtained by differentiation:

$$\iint \big((u - u_r)\beta - (v - v_r)\alpha \big) \big(-xy\beta + (y^2 + 1)\alpha \big) \, dx \, dy = 0,$$

$$\iint \big((u - u_r)\beta - (v - v_r)\alpha \big) \big((x^2 + 1)\beta - xy\alpha \big) \, dx \, dy = 0,$$

$$\iint \big((u - u_r)\beta - (v - v_r)\alpha \big) \big(y\beta + x\alpha \big) \, dx \, dy = 0,$$

$$\iint \big((u - u_r)\beta - (v - v_r)\alpha \big) (v - v_r) \, dx \, dy + \lambda U = 0,$$

$$\iint \big((u - u_r)\beta - (v - v_r)\alpha \big) (u - u_r) \, dx \, dy - \lambda V = 0,$$

$$\iint \big((u - u_r)\beta - (v - v_r)\alpha \big) \big((u - u_r)y + (v - v_r)x \big) \, dx \, dy + \lambda W = 0,$$

$$U^2 + V^2 + W^2 = 1.$$

Note that the first three of these equations are linear in A, B, and C, so that these parameters can be determined uniquely in terms of U, V, and W. Then we can determine U, V, and W from the last four equations by a numerical method. This immediately suggests an iterative scheme. To this end, we can discretize the problem and derive analogous equations in which summation of the appropriate expressions replaces integration.

In summary, our objective was to devise a method for determining the motion of a camera from optical flow, allowing for noise in the measured data. The least-squares method proposed in this chapter meets our goal and is also suitable for numerical implementation. One interesting extension explored in exercise 17-11 is the possibility of determining the motion directly from image brightness gradients without computing the optical flow.

17.6 References

The books by Hildreth, *The Measurement of Visual Motion* [1983], and by Ullman, *The Interpretation of Visual Motion* [1979], discuss the determination and interpretation of visual motion. Huang edited a collection of work presented at a NATO conference in *Image Sequence Processing and Dynamic Scene Analysis* [1983].

There has been rapid progress in this field in the last five years. The rigid-body assumption provides a powerful constraint to simplify the analysis. Most of the papers cited use it, although some allow for more than one rigid body in the scene being viewed. The special cases of pure rotation and pure translation are particularly easy to deal with, as we discussed; see, for example, Bruss & Horn [1983] and Jain [1983].

A lot of the published work has been based on what we have called the discrete approach. In this context, it is important to establish the minimum number of points that force a unique solution. In the process, much of what is known in photogrammetry, discussed earlier in chapter 13, has been rediscovered.

Clocksin [1980] attempted to recover the motion from derivatives of the optical flow. Neumann [1980b] showed that changes in shading due to motion do not constitute a solid basis for recovering motion information. Prazdny [1980, 1981] tackled the passive navigation and structure-from-motion problems directly. This earlier work is refined in Prazdny [1983]. Nagel [1981b] and Dreschler & Nagel [1982] worked on recovering the shape and motion of a moving object and explored the representational issues. Jain [1981] wrote another early paper on the recovery of motion and depth from optical flow. Ballard & Kimball [1983] tried to determine rigid body motion from optical flow. Webb & Aggarwal [1982] extended the analysis to multiple objects mutually mechanically restrained.

Tsai, Huang, & Zhu [1982] started the careful analysis of optical flow in the case of a planar patch. Hay [1966] apparently was the first to mention the two-way ambiguity noted by Tsai, Huang, & Zhu. Waxman & Ullman [1983] also addressed the two-way ambiguity for planar surfaces. For shorter proofs of the main result see Maybank [1984] and Negahdaripour & Horn [1985].

Bruss & Horn [1983] tackled the problem using the least-squares method advocated in this chapter. Fang & Huang [1984a,b], Jerian & Jain [1984], and Sugihara & Sugie [1984] still used the discrete approach, however. Tsai & Huang [1984a,b] tried to show that the motion can be recovered uniquely when the object's surface is curved and dealt with the case in which three successive images are available. Waxman & Wohn [1984] dealt with the planar surface case in more detail.

Other important papers include those by Koenderink & van Doorn [1976], Neumann [1980a], Longuet-Higgins [1981], Tsai [1982], Hoffman & Flinchbaugh [1982], Yen & Huang [1983], and Adiv [1984].

Negahdaripour & Horn [1985] found a way to go directly from brightness gradients to the motion of the observer without computing the optical flow or matching discrete features. Using a simplified notation, they found a shorter proof of the result that there are two planar surfaces giving rise to the same instantaneous motion field.

17.7 Exercises

17-1 Here we extend some of the results developed in chapter 12, where we discussed optical flow, using the equations developed for the translational and rotational components.

(a) Show that the Laplacian of the optical flow is zero when a camera viewing a planar surface is translating parallel to the image plane. The plane being viewed need not be parallel to the image plane.

(b) Show that the Laplacian of the optical flow is zero when a camera is translating relative to a plane that is orthogonal to the optical axis. The translation need not be parallel to the image plane.

(c) Show that the Laplacian of the optical flow is not zero when the camera is rotating about an axis other than the optical axis.

17-2 In the case of pure translation, the optical flow consists of vectors of varying length that all pass through a single point when extended. This point where the optical flow is zero is called the *focus of expansion*; it is the image of the ray along which the camera moves. How are the coordinates of the focus of expansion related to the parameters U, V, and W? Show that in the case of pure translation the motion can be determined (up to a scale factor) by considering the direction of the optical flow at two image points. Explain why this may not be the best way to use optical flow information.

17-3 In the case of pure rotation, the optical flow consists of vectors whose lengths do not depend on the distances of the objects. Instead, the magnitudes and directions of the vectors are determined by the axis of rotation and the angular velocity. Define the *center of rotation* to be the point where the optical flow is zero, somewhat analogous to the focus of expansion in the previous problem. Show that in the case of pure rotation, the motion can be determined from the optical flow at two points. Demonstrate further that at one of these points we need to know only the direction of the flow. Explain why this may not be the best way to use optical flow information.

17-4 An alternate approach to passive navigation involves the identification and tracking of "features." Using the methods developed in our discussion of photogrammetry and stereo, determine the smallest number of points on an object that fully determine its motion when they are identified in two images taken a small interval apart. Hint: This is nontrivial.

17-5 Show that if $f(k\mathbf{r}) = f(\mathbf{r})$, then $\nabla f(\mathbf{r}) \cdot \mathbf{r} = 0$, where ∇ produces the gradient, a vector whose components are the derivatives of f with respect to x, y, and z.

17-6 Suppose that $g(\mathbf{t}) = \mathbf{t}^T \mathbf{G} \mathbf{t}$. Show that the extrema of $g(\mathbf{t})$ correspond to the eigenvectors of the matrix $\mathbf{G}$ if $\mathbf{t}$ is constrained to be a unit vector. Hint: Introduce a Lagrange multiplier, as shown in the appendix.

17-7   Consider the case of purely translational motion. Show that minimization with respect to the ML_{Zuv} norm leads to the same equations as minimization with respect to the $ML_{\alpha\beta}$ norm. Explain why this should be so.

17-8   Consider the case of purely translational motion. Suppose we carry out the minimization with respect to the ML_Z norm defined by

$$\|f(x,y)\|_Z = \iint \big(f(x,y)Z(x,y)\big)^2\, dx\, dy.$$

Here optical flow velocities for points that are farther away are weighted more heavily. Show that the result in this case depends only on the direction of the optical flow at each point, not on its magnitude.

17-9   Show that in the case of a rectangular image plane of width $2W$ and height $2H$,

$$\bar{a} = 4WH\left(\frac{H^4}{5} + \frac{2H^2}{3} + 1\right) + \frac{4W^3H^3}{9},$$

$$\bar{b} = 4WH\left(\frac{W^4}{5} + \frac{2W^2}{3} + 1\right) + \frac{4W^3H^3}{9},$$

$$\bar{c} = \frac{4WH}{3}\left(W^2 + H^2\right),$$

$$\bar{d} = \bar{e} = \bar{f} = 0,$$

where $\bar{a}$, $\bar{b}$, $\bar{c}$, $\bar{d}$, $\bar{e}$, and $\bar{f}$ are the integrals defined above for the purely rotational case. Show that the matrix $\mathbf{M}$ is not singular and find its inverse.

17-10   Under somewhat impoverished conditions, it is possible for a passive navigation problem to have more than one solution. Here we explore the case in which a planar surface is being imaged.

(a) Suppose that the surface being imaged is the plane and that

$$Z = Z_0 + pX + qY,$$

where X, Y, and Z are coordinates of points on the surface. Show that

$$\frac{Z_0}{Z} = 1 - px - qy,$$

where x and y are image coordinates.

(b) Show that the motion field in this case is given by the following second-order polynomials in x and y:

$$u = u_t + u_r = \frac{1}{Z_0}(-U + xW)(1 - px - qy) + Axy - B(x^2 + 1) + Cy,$$

$$v = v_t + v_r = \frac{1}{Z_0}(-V + yW)(1 - px - qy) + A(y^2 + 1) - Bxy - Cx.$$

Simplify these equations by substituting $U_1' = U/Z_0$, $V_1' = V/Z_0$, and $W_1' = W/Z_0$.

(c) Now imagine that there are two different planar surfaces that, when viewed under two different sets of motion parameters, give rise to the same optical flow. Suppose that the parameters of the two surfaces and the two motions are distinguished by numerical subscripts. By equating coefficients of the powers of x and y that occur in the equations $u_1 = u_2$ and $v_1 = v_2$, derive the following eight conditions:

$$V_1' - V_2' = A_1 - A_2,$$

$$W_1'q_1 - W_2'q_2 = A_1 - A_2,$$

$$U_1' - U_2' = B_2 - B_1,$$

$$W_1'p_1 - W_2'p_2 = B_2 - B_1,$$

$$U_1'q_1 - U_2'q_2 = C_2 - C_1,$$

$$V_1'p_1 - V_2'p_2 = C_1 - C_2,$$

$$U_1'p_1 - U_2'p_2 = W_2' - W_1',$$

$$V_1'q_1 - V_2'q_2 = W_2' - W_1'.$$

(d) Find a pair of planar surfaces, and corresponding motions, that produce the same motion field.

17-11 So far we have assumed a two-stage process for the passive navigation calculation:

• First, compute the optical flow.

• Second, use the optical flow to determine shape and motion.

This approach, while intuitively appealing, has some drawbacks that we shall explore in this problem. The least-squares approach developed in this chapter for finding the motion parameters weights optical flow data from all image points equally, yet we know that it is more reliable in some places than in others. We could take this into account by developing a least-squares method that gives less weight to the information in areas of low brightness gradient, for example. It is probably more reasonable to try to recover shape and motion directly from the time-varying images, that is, without computing the optical flow. From the basic constraint equation we develop the error term

$$e_c = \iint \left(E_x u + E_y v + E_t\right)^2 dx \, dy,$$

which depends on the surface $Z(x, y)$ and the motion parameters $(U, V, W)^T$ and $(A, B, C)^T$ (since u and v depend on them). There is, of course, not enough constraint locally to recover all of the parameters. We need to introduce some measure of departure from "smoothness," as, for example,

$$e_s = \iint \left(\nabla^2 (1/Z) \right)^2 dx\, dy.$$

(a) Develop the Euler equations for the function $d(x, y) = 1/Z(x, y)$ that minimizes $e_s + \lambda e_c$. Hint: Remember that the total "error" depends also on the six rigid body motion parameters.

(b) Find some rationale for the choice of the smoothness term. That is, why does it contain $1/Z$ instead of Z, and why use the square Laplacian rather than the sum of squares of first derivatives?

17-12   Let $\mathbf{R} = (X, Y, Z)^T$ be the vector to a point on an object, and $\mathbf{r} = (x, y, f)^T$ the vector to the corresponding image point. In addition, let $E_{\mathbf{r}} = (E_x, E_y, 0)^T$ be the spatial brightness gradient, and E_t the time derivative of brightness.

(a) Show that in the case of rigid body motion, the constraint equation relating spatial and time derivatives of brightness can be written in the form

$$E_t - (\mathbf{s} \times \mathbf{r}) \cdot \boldsymbol{\omega} + \frac{\mathbf{s} \cdot \mathbf{t}}{\mathbf{R} \cdot \hat{\mathbf{z}}} = 0,$$

where $\mathbf{s} = (E_{\mathbf{r}} \times \hat{\mathbf{z}}) \times \mathbf{r}$. Hint: Use the projection equation, $\mathbf{r} = \mathbf{R}/(\mathbf{R} \cdot \hat{\mathbf{z}})$, to show that the time derivatives of $\mathbf{r}$ and $\mathbf{R}$ are related by

$$\mathbf{r}_t = \frac{1}{\mathbf{R} \cdot \hat{\mathbf{z}}} \left(\hat{\mathbf{z}} \times (\mathbf{R}_t \times \mathbf{r}) \right).$$

Then use the rigid body motion equation, $\mathbf{R}_t = -\boldsymbol{\omega} \times \mathbf{R} - \mathbf{t}$, and the assumption of constant brightness, that is, $E_{\mathbf{r}} \cdot \mathbf{r}_t + E_t = 0$.

(b) Find the form of the constraint equation in the special case of a planar surface, $\mathbf{R} \cdot \mathbf{n} + 1 = 0$.

(c) In the case of a general surface, solve the constraint equation for the depth $Z(x, y) = \mathbf{R} \cdot \hat{\mathbf{z}}$.

Given any set of motion parameters $\mathbf{t}$ and $\boldsymbol{\omega}$, a surface $Z(x, y)$ can be calculated that satisfies the constraint equation. The values of depth found may not be positive, however, if the parameters do not correspond to those of the motion generating the time-varying imagery. The problem is therefore to find parameters that make the depth calculated from the constraint equation positive everywhere in the image. In practice, because of noise in the brightness measurements, we expect there to be places where the computed depth is negative even with the correct motion parameters. We therefore turn this into an optimization problem.

(d) Find the set of motion parameters **t** and $\boldsymbol{\omega}$ that maximize

$$\iint \mathrm{sgn}(\mathbf{s} \cdot \mathbf{t})\mathrm{sgn}\big(E_t - (\mathbf{s} \times \mathbf{r}) \cdot \boldsymbol{\omega}\big)\, dx\, dy,$$

where
$$\mathrm{sgn}(Z) = \begin{cases} +1, & \text{for } Z > 0; \\ 0, & \text{for } Z = 0; \\ -1, & \text{for } Z < 0. \end{cases}$$

Warning: This is a research project; we do not know the answer (yet).

18

Picking Parts out of a Bin

In this chapter we bring together several of the techniques developed earlier in order to construct a complete hand–eye system. Here a robot "arm" is directed to pick up an object, in a pile of objects, using information gained by a camera "eye." Such a closed-loop system provides an interesting test for machine vision algorithms. Presumably, if the system interacts successfully with its environment using visual information, then the machine vision part of it must be working. This is a much more satisfactory test than is afforded by presenting the results in graphic form on a display screen. A human interpreter might be seduced into believing that the system performed the task at hand simply because of the remarkable ability of the observer's own eye and brain to integrate information in the display.

Another reason for tackling a problem like bin-picking is that there is a practical need for its solution. One of the remaining obstacles to the widespread introduction of industrial robots is their inability to deal with parts that are not precisely positioned. In the case of manual assembly, components are often presented in bins, but current automated systems require separate feeders that present the parts with carefully controlled position and attitude. Here we show how results in machine vision provide techniques for automatically directing a mechanical manipulator to pick one object at a time out of a pile.

It is always interesting to translate theoretical results into practice. In

Figure 18-1. Surface orientation information derived from photometric stereo, or some other method, can be displayed in the form of a needle diagram. Shown here is a needle diagram of an inclined torus obtained by means of photometric stereo. (Figure kindly provided by Katsushi Ikeuchi.)

the process a lot of effort must be expended on details that at first sight do not seem important. One must, for example, deal with the facts that image projection is not orthographic, that the light sources are not infinitely far away, and that the image sensor does not have uniform sensitivity. Something is always learned from an implementation effort such as the one described here. We allude to some of these issues in this chapter.

18.1 Overview of the Method

The attitude of the object to be picked up is determined using a histogram of the orientations of visible surface patches. Surface orientation, in turn, is determined using the photometric stereo method applied to multiple images. These images are taken with the same camera but differing lighting. The result is a needle diagram giving the orientations of surface patches corresponding to the picture cells in the image (figure 18-1).

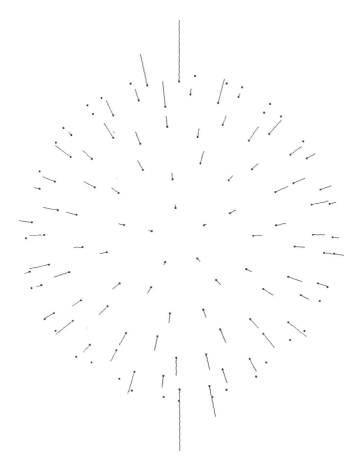

Figure 18-2. An orientation histogram can be displayed as a set of spikes whose lengths are proportional to the counts in each cell of the chosen tessellation of the sphere. Shown here is the orientation histogram obtained from the needle diagram of a torus. The relatively long vectors near the top and bottom correspond to the direction of the axis of the torus, where the extended Gaussian image has singularities.

The needle diagram is then projected onto a tessellated unit sphere to create an orientation histogram, a discrete approximation of the extended Gaussian image (figure 18-2). The orientation histogram can be matched against a synthetic orientation histogram obtained from prototypical models of the objects to be manipulated. Such models can be obtained from computer-aided design (CAD) databases. The method thus requires that the shape of the objects be described, but it is not restricted to particular types of objects.

18.2 Motivation

Mechanical manipulators are being used increasingly for machine loading, welding, painting, deburring, and sealing. They have not been utilized extensively for such applications as assembly. One of the reasons for this is that the manipulators typically just play back a sequence of motions taught to them. The blind robot has difficulty dealing with uncertainty in the positions of the parts. Feeding mechanisms and fixtures are needed to present parts in precisely the place where the industrial robot expects to find them.

The system described here will determine the position and attitude of a part in a pile of parts using a few images taken by an electronic camera. The results can be used to direct a mechanical manipulator to pick up the part. The system uses stored models of the objects and can identify which of several parts is seen. The method is not restricted to cylindrical parts or even solids of revolution. Extended light sources can be used in essentially arbitrary positions, and the objects need not have special reflectance properties. The system adapts to these two variables by means of a calibration step involving an object of known shape. Another calibration process is used to determine the transformation between the coordinate system of the manipulator and that of the camera.

18.3 The Bin of Parts

In manual assembly it is common to find components arranged in bins surrounding the work station. In automating assembly operations, it seems natural to use machine vision techniques to provide a mechanical manipulator with the information needed for it to reach into a bin and pick up a part. Binary image-processing techniques have made their way into the factory. However, as we saw earlier, such techniques require that:

- There must be strong contrast between the object and the background.
- Parts must be separated.
- Rotation must be confined to a plane parallel to the image plane.

All three of these conditions are violated in the case of interest here. An obvious solution is not to jumble parts together in the first place, but to keep them carefully oriented right from the time they are made. There is a trend to do this now, partly because of the shortcomings of present-day automation techniques. Parts may be organized on carriers or attached to pallets, so that they can be mechanically positioned without the need for sensing.

There are costs associated with this solution. The carriers and pallets must be designed and manufactured, often to tight tolerances. Pallets typically are heavy, take up a lot of space, and may need to be redesigned whenever the part is modified. Often the design of the part itself must be altered to allow automatic feeding. In any case, there are still plenty of situations where the limited volume has not presented the incentive to depart from traditional manual methods.

A number of attempts have been made to find mechanical solutions to this problem. In many cases, it is possible to throw the parts into a vibratory bowl with carefully designed selectors and have them emerge oriented at a feeder station. Screws and objects with cylindrical geometry are particularly well-suited to this approach. Not all parts can be handled this way, however. Large or heavy parts, as well as parts with complex shapes, do not succumb to this methodology. Robot arms have been equipped with electromagnets and vacuum suckers, with limited success.

The use of machine vision in this domain has so far been restricted to cylindrical pieces of metal that have been ground. Grinding produces surface striations that reflect light in a special way. If an object of this type is illuminated by a point source, a shiny highlight will appear along the projection of the axis of the cylinder into the image plane. A slanted mechanical chute can be used to complete the reorientation of the part after it is picked up. There is, however, not a great practical need for a system of this type, since cylindrical parts can be oriented using vibratory bowls.

18.4 Segmentation

The particular system described here uses photometric stereo to obtain information about the shapes of the surfaces of the objects in the field of view (figure 18-3). The needle diagrams so computed, representing surface orientation, are then matched with stored prototypes of the objects.

Before we can apply the methods developed earlier for dealing with extended Gaussian images, we must isolate an image region corresponding to a single object. One of the harder problems in machine vision, as we have seen, is the segmentation of an image into regions corresponding to different objects. Only when this is done can we apply the techniques used to recognize an object and determine its attitude. We can combine several methods to obtain robust segmentation. First of all, some points are marked as suspicious by the photometric stereo system. Most entries in the lookup table are actually blank (figure 18-4). A blank entry indicates an "illegal" brightness combination, one that could not arise in the

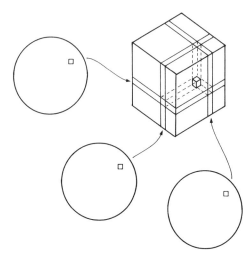

Figure 18-3. The photometric stereo method uses three images taken with the same camera under different lighting conditions. Quantized brightness measurements at corresponding picture cells in the three images are used as an index in a three-dimensional lookup table. Picture cells that draw a blank in the table are assigned to the background. They are of great importance in segmentation of the image into regions that correspond to separate objects.

absence of shadowing or mutual illumination. Since surface orientation has but two degrees of freedom, valid brightness combinations lie on a two-dimensional surface in the three-dimensional space defined by the three brightness measurements. In practice, this surface is expanded into a layer of finite thickness in the discrete lookup table to allow for measurement noise, quantization, and limited variations in surface reflectance.

Objects cast shadows on one another. The result is that some points on the shadowed object have brightness readings different from what they would have had if there were no shadowing. We must detect this condition lest it lead to incorrect estimates of surface orientation. A crude way to detect shadowing is to use thresholds on each of the three brightness measurements. Note, by the way, that objects near the top of the pile, those of most interest to us, will typically not suffer from shadowing.

Mutual illumination, or interflection, is another problem. When objects of high albedo face each other, light from one may significantly increase the illumination falling on the other. Again, we find brightness combinations that would not occur if the object were only illuminated directly by the source. Mutual illumination should be detected as well to avoid incorrect estimates of surface orientation. Fortunately, points where this is a problem

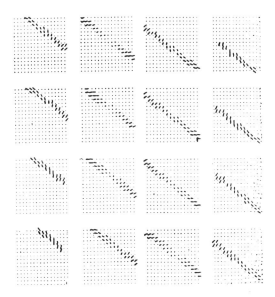

Figure 18-4. Most entries in the lookup table based on three brightness measurements are blank, corresponding to brightness combinations that should not occur if we assume that the surface has uniform reflectance. Here we see layers of such a lookup table laid out side by side. Each table entry is shown either as a small needle, indicating the surface orientation recorded for a particular brightness combination, or as a dot, indicating a blank corresponding to an "illegal" brightness combination.

tend to occur near the edges of objects and the boundaries where objects occlude one another.

Next, note that there will usually be a discontinuity in surface orientation wherever one object occludes another. We therefore look for places where the surface orientation changes rapidly. This works well for smooth objects, but can create spurious segmentation in the case of objects with sharp edges. Finally, we look for places where the surface normal is almost at right angles to the viewing direction. These are typically near edges where one object occludes another. Unfortunately, objects with sharp edges can have occluding edges where the viewing direction is not tangent to the surface. In this case, however, a discontinuity in surface orientation should help mark the edge.

The above cues for segmentation should be used to ensure that all objects are separated. In the segmentation phase, it is useful to consider only patches with normals within 45° of the direction to the viewer to be part of the object. Because of this aggressive approach, the remaining object

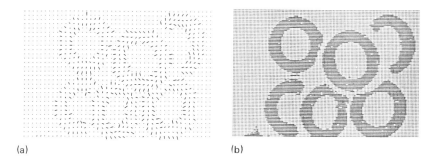

(a)   (b)

Figure 18-5. Information in the needle diagram is used to help segment the image into regions corresponding to separate surfaces. In (a) we see a needle diagram of a pile of toroidal objects. Derived from it is the binary image, shown in (b), that is used for segmentation. Both figures are shown at reduced resolution so that the needles in the needle diagram are large enough to be visible.

patches will be considerably reduced in area. This can be remedied later by applying a swelling operation borrowed from binary image processing. In some cases, a region corresponding to an object that is highly inclined with respect to the viewing direction may be broken up because of this approach. In the application described here, this is not a serious problem, since objects that are highly inclined are difficult to pick up in any case. It is better to concentrate on the other objects.

Figure 18-5a shows a needle diagram of a scene consisting of a pile of toroidal objects. Figure 18-5b shows the binary image used in segmentation. The binary image is derived from the needle diagram in the way described above.

18.5 Prototypical Object Models

In order to recognize an unknown object and determine its attitude in space, we compare data derived from the image of the object with data derived from a stored model. The approach outlined in chapter 16 works well for determining an orientation histogram of an object given as a prototype. The surface can be described by a set of equations for x, y, and z in terms of two parameters, u and v. We can divide the range of u into n intervals of width δu and the range of v into m intervals of width δv. This, in effect, breaks the surface up into small patches. We then systematically step through these patches, computing their surface normals. A contribution proportional to the area is added to the cell on the sphere that includes the direction specified by the unit normal. Note that the prototypical extended Gaussian image is known over the whole sphere, unlike the one obtained from image information.

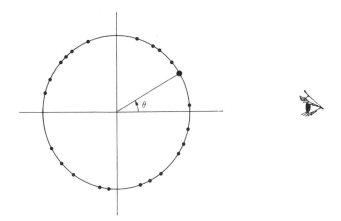

Figure 18-6. The apparent area of a surface patch is less than its actual area, unless the patch happens to be viewed along a direction parallel to its surface normal. If we simply increment cell counts every time we find a picture cell in which the surface has the orientation appropriate for that cell, we will shortchange the cells corresponding to surface patches that are inclined relative to the viewer. We can easily take this into account, however, since the orientation is known for each cell of the tessellation.

18.6 Foreshortening of the Surface

The stored prototypical extended Gaussian image is to be compared with one obtained from a needle map. The picture cells in the image all have the same area, but the areas of the corresponding patches on the surface of the object are not all the same. This may seem surprising since we are sampling the image uniformly. A surface patch will appear foreshortened, however, unless we happen to be looking at it from a direction perpendicular to its surface (figure 18-6). We could correct for this effect by dividing the apparent area by the cosine of the angle between the direction toward the viewer and the surface normal, since we already know the latter. Applying the correction this way has the unfortunate effect of amplifying errors associated with measurements of surface patches whose normal is nearly at right angles to the direction toward the viewer. It is better, therefore, to multiply the prototypical extended Gaussian image by the cosine factor when matching.

Note that we can calculate the actual area only if we know the properties of the camera and the distance to the object. Photometric stereo does not provide us with the latter information. We cannot tell the absolute size of the object in this case. The extended Gaussian image can be normalized by dividing by its integral over the sphere, and the result can be used in

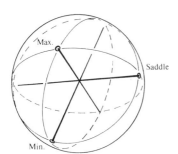 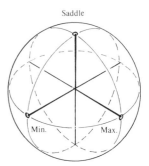

Figure 18-7. The moment of inertia of a mass distribution depends on the axis about which that moment is measured. There are three stationary values of the moment of inertia—a maximum, a minimum, and a saddle point. The axis directions corresponding to these extrema, called principal axes, lie at right angles to one another. Two mass distributions rotated relative to each other can be aligned by aligning their principal axes.

matching. Naturally, we lose the ability to distinguish objects with the same shape but differing in size if we do this.

A further complication in the case of an extended Gaussian image derived from images is that we only obtain information on the visible hemisphere. A surface whose normal is turned more than 90° from the direction toward the viewer cannot be seen. In fact, because of limitations of the photometric stereo method, we typically have information about the surface over an even smaller area, perhaps only up to 60° from the direction toward the viewer. Several obvious methods for matching extended Gaussian images work only if the whole sphere is known.

18.7 Moment Calculations ˙

It is not difficult to calculate the inertia matrix of a mass distribution on the sphere. We just need all of the first and second moments. A rotation can then be found that diagonalizes the inertia matrix. The coordinate axes in the rotated frame are called the *principal axes*. The rotation between two extended Gaussian images of the same object can be found by calculating the rotation needed to align their principal axes (figure 18-7). This provides us with an explicit algorithm for directly computing the attitude of an object relative to its prototype. The approach only fails when the object is too symmetric to have unique principal axes. Nothing more than finding the eigenvectors of a 3×3 matrix is involved, and that, in turn, just requires the solution of a cubic polynomial.

We cannot use such elegant methods here, because the experimental orientation histogram is known only over part of the sphere. Moreover, the match must take into account the foreshortening effect. We do not, however, have to throw out methods based on moment calculations altogether.

We have seen, for example, that the center of mass of the complete extended Gaussian image is always at the origin. It seems, therefore, to be of little use in matching. The center of mass of the visible hemisphere, however, will be at a position that depends on the attitude of the object. Consider a plane cutting the sphere into visible and invisible hemispheres. Clearly the center of mass of the visible hemisphere will lie somewhere above this plane. We show in exercise 18-2 that the height above the plane times the mass at the center of mass is equal to the apparent area visible to the viewer. The mass at the center of mass is just equal to the actual area of the visible surface. Thus the height above the plane is proportional to the ratio of the actual surface area to the apparent surface area. This will typically vary with viewing direction. Moreover, the lateral displacement of the center of mass will depend on the attitude of the object in space.

While the center of mass of the visible hemisphere does not uniquely define the attitude of the object, it can be used to save computation. To speed the matching process, we can precompute the expected center of mass given the prototypical extended Gaussian image and a set of viewing directions for which the match is to be attempted. For convenience, the discrete set of viewing directions for which this calculation is performed can be chosen to be the directions toward the cells of the Gaussian sphere. Any viewing direction for which the center of mass is not at least in approximately the right position need not be subjected to more detailed scrutiny.

18.8 Objects That Are Not Convex

There are three problems with objects that are not convex:

- The Gaussian curvature is negative for some points on the surface.
- More than one point on the object contributes to a given point on the Gaussian sphere.
- One part of the object can occlude another.

The precise definition of Gaussian curvature takes into account the direction in which the boundary of corresponding patches on the object and the Gaussian sphere are traversed. At a convex point the Gaussian curvature is positive and the boundaries are traversed in the same direction. If they are traversed in opposite directions, as happens at a saddle point, the Gaussian curvature is considered negative. Analysis of our simple local process for computing the discrete approximation of the extended Gaussian image suggests that we extend our definition to be the inverse of the absolute value of the Gaussian curvature.

Consideration of the local process for computing the discrete approximation of the extended Gaussian image suggests how to deal with the fact that more than one point on the surface will contribute to a given point on the sphere. We simply add up the inverses of the absolute values of the Gaussian curvature at the corresponding points on the object. If there are n such points, then

$$G(\xi, \eta) = \sum_{i=1}^{n} \frac{1}{|K(u_i, v_i)|}.$$

This idea can be further developed to allow us to deal with cases in which all points along a curve or even in a region have the same orientation. In these cases we obtain impulse functions on the Gaussian sphere.

The mapping from the object to the Gaussian sphere is not invertible if the object is not convex. The only consequence of concern to us here is that there are an infinite number of nonconvex objects corresponding to a particular extended Gaussian image. We do not, however, expect to encounter two different objects with the same extended Gaussian image in a typical application.

Occlusion is a more difficult issue. In many cases it will be a small effect except for certain viewing directions, from which parts of the object appear to be lined up. One solution is to take occlusion into account by building a different extended Gaussian image for each possible viewing direction, adding in only the contributions from surface patches that are actually visible. For convenience, the discrete set of viewing directions for which this calculation is performed can be chosen to be the directions toward the cells of the Gaussian sphere. There is a considerable increase in storage required, but the matching is no longer disturbed by the effects of occlusion.

18.9 Attitude in Space

An object's attitude in space is its rotation relative to some reference. To determine its attitude, we match the object's extended Gaussian image with the prototypical extended Gaussian image. It is easiest to explain how this can be done in the case of solids of revolution.

A solid of revolution is obtained by spinning a generating curve about an axis. Obviously, the resulting object will be symmetric about this axis. Then the object's attitude is fully specified if the direction of this axis is given, since we cannot determine the rotation about the axis itself. The axis can be given as a unit vector or a point on a sphere and thus has but two degrees of freedom. It can also be given in terms of the angle it makes with the image plane (elevation) and the angle between its projection in the image and some reference axis (azimuth).

The image of a solid of revolution is symmetric about the projection of its axis. We could therefore simply find the axis of least inertia of the image region corresponding to the projection of the object. That would pin down one degree of freedom with very little computation. We would, however, be resorting to binary image-processing methods whose accuracy depends on how well we can find the silhouette of the object. It is better to work with the surface orientation information.

We can sample the space of possible orientations for the axis, trying to match the extended Gaussian image for each one. It is desirable to sample this space evenly, for the sake of efficiency. Sampling one area more finely than another would be inefficient, and should therefore be avoided. This leads us to the problem of placing n points "uniformly" on the surface of a hemisphere. We are looking for placements that maximize the minimum distance between points.

This problem has received some attention. It is known, for example, that the best placements for $n = 4$, 6, and 20 are obtained by projecting the regular tetrahedron, octahedron, and icosahedron onto the sphere (figure 18-8a). The other two regular solids, the cube and dodecahedron, do not lead to optimal placements. (We have already met the regular solids in chapter 16, where we discussed the extended Gaussian image. There they were used for a different purpose, however.)

It turns out that for $n = 32$ the combination of the dodecahedron and its dual, the icosahedron, works well (figure 18-8b). Unfortunately, there is no general rule for the optimum. This problem is related to the one of finding "nice" tessellations of the sphere for the orientation histogram. There we ended up with geodesic domes and their duals. Here we find that reasonable placements can be obtained by choosing the centers of the triangles in geodesic domes or, equivalently, the vertices of their duals (figure 18-8c,d).

We need not perform a detailed match for each of these orientations of the object's axis. Only orientations for which the center of mass matches reasonably well need be explored further. This means that very few full matches of extended Gaussian images actually have to be performed. The axis orientation that gives the best match is considered to be the true orientation of the axis of the solid of revolution.

Another approach is to determine the axis of least inertia of the mass distribution on the visible hemisphere of the extended Gaussian image. The projection of this axis into the image plane gives us the axis of symmetry of the image of the object. This pins down one degree of freedom (azimuth) with very little computation. It only remains for us to find the inclination

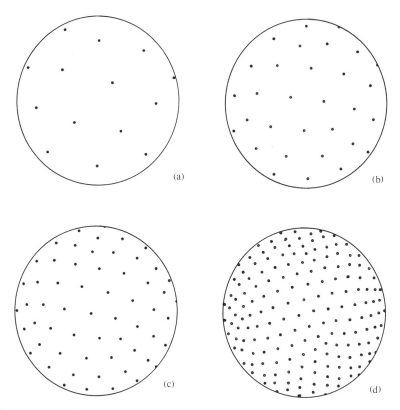

Figure 18-8. A completely even sampling of the sphere with 20 points is obtained by projecting the vertices of the icosahedron onto the sphere, as shown in (a). The combination of the icosahedron and its dual, the dodecahedron, works well for 32 points, as shown in (b). The optimal placement is not known when the number of points is large. However, the vertices of the duals of geodesic domes work quite well, as shown in (c) and (d).

of the axis of the solid of revolution (elevation). Thus the search space is reduced from two degrees of freedom to one. Note that the axis of least inertia can actually be computed easily from the needle map before the normals are projected onto the unit sphere. It is easy to add up the required totals to compute the first and second moments. This approach has the advantage that the tessellation of the sphere can be lined up with the axis of least inertia before we project the surface normals onto the Gaussian sphere.

18.10 Representing Rotation

How should we represent rotations? There are about eight commonly used alternatives. These include 3×3 orthonormal matrices as well as Euler angles. What we need, however, is a way to sample the space of possible rotations uniformly. To do that, we need a way to talk about the "distance" between two attitudes. That is, the space of rotations must be described in such a way that we can define a metric on it. It turns out that we can define such a metric if we represent rotations by means of unit quaternions.

18.10.1 Quaternions

Quaternions are elements of a vector space endowed with multiplication. A quaternion can be thought of as a vector with four components. Alternatively, it can be thought of as a very complex number, with one real part and three different types of imaginary parts. Yet another way of viewing a quaternion is as the sum of a scalar and a vector part:

$$\overset{\circ}{q} = q + \mathbf{q}.$$

Quaternions can be multiplied as follows. If

$$\overset{\circ}{r} = \overset{\circ}{p}\,\overset{\circ}{q},$$

then the scalar and vector parts of $\overset{\circ}{r}$ are determined by

$$r = pq - \mathbf{p} \cdot \mathbf{q} \quad \text{and} \quad \mathbf{r} = p\mathbf{q} + q\mathbf{p} + \mathbf{p} \times \mathbf{q}.$$

Multiplication is associative but not commutative, as can easily be checked. We can define a dot-product on quaternions:

$$\overset{\circ}{p} \cdot \overset{\circ}{q} = pq + \mathbf{p} \cdot \mathbf{q}.$$

The norm of a quaternion is given by

$$|\overset{\circ}{q}| = \overset{\circ}{q} \cdot \overset{\circ}{q} = q^2 + \mathbf{q} \cdot \mathbf{q}.$$

A unit quaternion has norm equal to one, that is, $\overset{\circ}{q} \cdot \overset{\circ}{q} = 1$. The conjugate $\overset{\circ}{q}^*$ of a quaternion $\overset{\circ}{q}$ is obtained by changing the sign of the vector part:

$$\overset{\circ}{q}^* = q - \mathbf{q}.$$

Rotations in three-dimensional space can be conveniently represented by unit quaternions. The unit quaternion corresponding to a rotation θ about the unit vector $\boldsymbol{\omega}$ is given by

$$\overset{\circ}{q} = \sin \frac{\theta}{2} + \boldsymbol{\omega} \cos \frac{\theta}{2}.$$

Note that the quaternion $-\mathring{q}$ defines the same rotation as $\mathring{q}$, since a rotation of $-\theta$ about the axis $-\omega$ is the same as a rotation of θ about the axis ω. The conjugate $\mathring{q}^*$ of a unit quaternion $\mathring{q}$, on the other hand, corresponds to rotation through the same angle but about the opposite axis. The conjugate of a unit quaternion is thus the inverse of the unit quaternion. As a result, for a unit quaternion,

$$\mathring{q}^*\mathring{q} = \mathring{q}\mathring{q}^* = 1.$$

Unit quaternions correspond to points on the unit sphere in four-dimensional space. Two opposite points on this sphere correspond to one particular rotation. Equivalently, we can consider rays through the origin in four-dimensional space as corresponding to rotations in three-dimensional space.

A rotation specified by the quaternion $\mathring{q}$ transforms a vector $\mathbf{x}$ into a vector $\mathbf{x}'$ according to the formula

$$(0 + \mathbf{x}') = \mathring{q}(0 + \mathbf{x})\mathring{q}^*.$$

Composition of rotations corresponds to multiplication of quaternions:

$$(0 + \mathbf{x}'') = \mathring{p}\mathbf{x}'\mathring{p}^* = \mathring{p}(\mathring{q}(0 + \mathbf{x})\mathring{q}^*)\mathring{p}^* = (\mathring{p}\,\mathring{q})(0 + \mathbf{x})(\mathring{p}\,\mathring{q})^*.$$

The unit quaternion representation can often simplify problems in which we have to deal with the attitude of an object in space. Some of the photogrammetric problems dealt with in chapter 13, for example, can be solved in closed form using this notation.

18.10.2 Even Sampling of the Rotation Space

The problem of even sampling of the rotation space then becomes the problem of uniformly placing points on the unit sphere in four dimensions. The reason we prefer even sampling of the rotation space is that, for a given number of samples, we would like the smallest distance between samples to be as large as possible.

The brute-force matching of orientation histograms can become expensive if the attitude is to be determined with high precision. This is because the space of rotations is three-dimensional and the number of samples we must try goes up with the cube of the inverse of the distance between samples. Hill-climbing methods for searching the space of rotations may therefore appear attractive, but they do not seem to work very well. It appears that the correlation value rises significantly only when we are very near the correct match, and the correlation function is very "bumpy" because of various quantization effects. In exercise 18-8 we explore a new method that does not suffer from this problem.

18.11 Matching Orientation Histograms

Two orientation histograms with their cells aligned can be matched in several ways. We might, for example, take the sum of the squares of the differences of the counts in corresponding cells as a measure of dissimilarity. The best match of a given orientation histogram with those in a set of prototypical orientation histograms is the one for which this sum of squares of differences is smallest. Alternatively, we can use the sum of the products of the counts in corresponding cells as a measure of similarity. In this case, the best match is the one that produces the largest correlation. An advantage of the first method is that a poor match can be rejected without completing the computation whenever the running total of the sum of the squares of the differences becomes large. More complicated, but also more ad hoc, comparison functions are easy to dream up.

The problems with this approach are best illustrated using a polyhedron as an example. Suppose that one of the faces has a normal that points in a direction that just happens to correspond to the edge between two cells on our tessellation of the sphere. A tiny change in attitude can then move the full contribution of this particular face from one cell to a neighboring cell. The extended Gaussian image is changed rather dramatically, and the match will be upset. The problem is much reduced for smoothly curved surfaces, but it cannot be ignored.

One way to approach this problem is to perform the projection several times for each orientation, with slightly different alignments of the cells. This would have to be done for both the prototypical and the experimental data. The total amount of work would be multiplied by the number of shifted tessellations that are used.

Noise in estimating surface orientation tends to smooth the distribution on the sphere, since it displaces some surface normals to the cells next to the ones they ought to have been assigned to. The fineness of the tessellation also enters into the issue. If we make the cells large, few surface normals will be placed into the wrong cells. Each cell will have a large count that, statistically speaking, is likely to be a more accurate estimate of the average of the inverse of the Gaussian curvature. At the same time, large cells mean poor accuracy in the determination of attitude. Conversely, if the cells are very small, many will have a zero count, or perhaps just a count of one. Such noisy distributions are hard to match. The problem is entirely analogous to that of choosing the "right" bin size for estimating two-dimensional probability distributions from a finite number of random samples.

No elegant solution to this problem has yet been found. Inspired by the smoothing effect of noise, however, we might consider deliberately smoothing the orientation histogram before matching. Equivalently, we could

match a given cell with a weighted average of the corresponding cell and
its neighbors. It is also possible to distribute the contribution of one surface patch to several cells according to how close their normals are to that
of the given surface patch.

How many orientations should we try for the axis of the object? A
first answer can be obtained by noting that surface normals are not known
perfectly. We cannot expect to find the orientation of the axis with much
more accuracy than that with which the surface normals can be found. A
second answer can be obtained by considering the fineness of the tessellation
of the sphere. An orientation must be tried that is close enough to the
correct one so that most of the cells line up with each other. This means
that we need to try on the order of a hundred or so. Remember, though,
that extended Gaussian images will have to be matched for only a few of
these orientations. The rest are rejected on the basis of a gross mismatch
in the center of mass.

In any case we find that in practice the direction of the axis of an
object can be determined with an accuracy of about 5° to 10°. This is good
enough to permit a manipulator to pick the object up. If better accuracy
is required, a mechanical alignment method can be used afterward.

18.12 Reprojection of the Needle Diagram

If we wish to compare the experimental orientation histogram obtained
from the needle diagram with the synthetic one obtained from the object
model, we can arrange for the cells of the two orientation histograms to line
up. When the experimental orientation histogram is rotated, however, its
cells will generally no longer line up with those of the synthetic orientation
histogram. This means that we must rotate the normals in one of the
orientation histograms before projecting them onto a tessellated sphere in
the standard orientation. Reprojection of the normals is perhaps most
conveniently performed with the synthetic data, since it can be done ahead
of time and the results stored. We can greatly reduce our effort if the
chosen tessellation has the property that the cells line up again for at least
some rotations. A tessellation with this property simplifies matching, since
some rotations of the orientation histogram merely permute the counts
corresponding to the cells. This is why we were interested in choosing
tessellations that have this property.

The faces of the regular solids will line up for the rotations belonging
to the finite subgroup of the continuous group of rotations corresponding
to that solid. These subgroups have sizes 12, 24, and 60 for the tetrahedron, octahedron, and icosahedron, respectively. Tessellations based on the
icosahedron and its dual, such as those of the soccer ball and the pentakis
dodecahedron, have the same rotation group. In the case of the soccer

ball, we can easily list the rotations by considering three types of axes of rotation:

- There is a five-fold symmetry about any axis passing through the center of one of the pentagonal cells (this gives us $(12/2) \times 4 = 24$ rotations).

- There is a three-fold symmetry about any axis passing through the center of one of the hexagonal cells (this gives us $(20/2) \times 2 = 20$ rotations).

- Finally, there is a two-fold axis of symmetry about the center of any edge between hexagonal cells (this gives us another $(30/2) = 15$ rotations).

If we add in the identity, we end up with 60 distinct rotations altogether. There are no finite subgroups that span the space of rotations and have a larger number of elements. To deal with more than 60 rotations, then, reprojection is required.

18.13 Corrections for Departures from the Ideal

Several of the implicit assumptions in the above analysis are violated in practice. It is assumed, for example, that the brightness of a surface depends only on its orientation, not on its position. This is true when the light sources are infinitely far away. In practice, light sources are close enough to the surface on which the objects are placed so that the inverse-square law comes into play. We can take this into account by normalizing the brightness values. We first take images of a uniform white surface with each of the three sources in turn. Typically a linear approximation of the resulting brightness distribution is accurate enough. All images are then corrected for the nonuniformity in illumination by means of a linear function of the x and y positions in the image.

There is another problem that is harder to deal with. Since the light sources are nearby, the direction of the incident rays is not the same for all points. This means that the computed surface normals will be incorrect. The error due to this effect is typically smaller and harder to correct than that due to nonuniform illumination, so we may not wish to account for it explicitly.

No image-sensing device is perfect, but charge-coupled-device (CCD) cameras have very good geometric accuracy and are linear in their response to brightness. The sensor cells do not, however, all have the same sensitivity to light. Some, due to defects in the silicon, are weaker than others. We can take this into account by taking a picture of a point source on the optical axis of the camera with the lens removed. This provides uniform illumination of the image plane, and the result can be used to correct future brightness measurements.

Alternatively, we can normalize the three brightness measurements at each picture cell by dividing them by their sum. This eliminates the effect of nonuniform sensor response and also accounts for fluctuations in illumination. Furthermore, it makes the system insensitive to differences in surface albedo from point to point on the object. Objects often do not have perfectly uniform surface reflectance properties. Typically, for example, experiments of this nature entail considerable debugging effort, including episodes of rough handling of the parts by the manipulator. The normalization method used to deal with nonuniform sensitivity of the image sensor automatically provides for fluctuations in surface reflectance. At the same time, this approach makes it harder to detect shadowing and mutual illumination, which, as we saw, are helpful in segmentation of the image.

At times, because of severe noise, an imaging device defect, or a surface mark, an isolated point in the image will not be assigned a surface orientation by the photometric stereo method. We can search for these isolated points and enter a normal equal to the average of the neighboring values. The main reason for going to this trouble is that such a blemish would otherwise count as a hole in the computation of the Euler number.

In section 11.7.3 we developed a photometric stereo method that deals with noise by using a constraint based on the assumption that surface orientation varies smoothly almost everywhere. This iterative method, based on the solution to a problem in the calculus of variations, can deal with severe noise, but it is slow.

18.14 Picking the Object To Pick Up

Once the image has been segmented into regions that appear to be parts of objects, a decision must be made about which region is to be analyzed further. The region chosen should correspond to an object near the top of the pile, and as little as possible of this object should be occluded. This requirement will allow the manipulator to pick up the object easily and will also ensure that matching with the prototype will work well. There may also be reasons to prefer objects with certain attitudes, either because they are easier to pick up or because it is known that the system is more accurate in determining their attitude. Because no absolute depth information is available from photometric stereo, it is not trivial to choose a suitable object.

Several heuristics can be used to select one of a number of objects that the manipulator could pick up. First, the region in the image should have a relatively large area if the object is unoccluded. The ratio of perimeter squared to area can also be used to estimate the elongation of the region in the image. A highly elongated region might be a cue that the object lies in an attitude that the manipulator will have difficulty with. Finally, the Euler number may be relevant at times. In the case of an unoccluded toroidal object, the Euler number will be zero, unless the axis of the torus is highly inclined relative to the direction toward the viewer.

Another task for the system is to decide how to pick up the object once its attitude in space is known. The system has to be told which points on the surface of the object are suitable for grasping. The gripper should be placed so that it will not interfere with neighboring objects. It is helpful in this regard to choose a point that is relatively high on the object. This can be done since the object's shape and attitude are known. It would also be reasonable to avoid places on the object that correspond to places in the image where neighboring regions come close to the region analyzed.

It may not always be possible to guarantee that the object can be picked up as calculated, particularly if absolute depth information is not available. In this case, tactile sensors help to detect problems such as collisions with neighboring objects and loss of grip on the part being picked up. If such a problem occurs, it is best to remove the arm from the field of view and start over. Another obvious problem is that the rate at which parts are picked up will not be constant, but this problem can be solved by a mechanical buffering scheme.

When there are no more objects to pick up, the needle diagram will be uniform. Image segmentation will fail to separate any interesting regions from the background, and the system will come to a halt.

18.15 Moving the Arm

Control of the mechanical manipulator is relatively straightforward compared to the vision part. We have used photometric stereo and matching of orientation histograms to determine the attitude of the object we wish to pick up. The position of the region of interest can be estimated by finding its center of area. This binary image-processing technique should be avoided, however, since the silhouette of this region can be quite rough. It is better to obtain the position more accurately by matching the needle diagram with one computed using the object prototype and the now-known attitude of the object.

The position in the image of the region corresponding to the object of interest defines a ray from the camera. Since photometric stereo does not provide absolute depth information, we cannot tell how far along this ray the object is. The arm is therefore commanded to move along the ray, starting at some safe height above the surface on which the objects lie (figure 18-9). A proximity sensor can be used to detect when the arm comes near an object. For example, a modulated infrared light beam from one finger of the gripper to the other can be used to determine when an

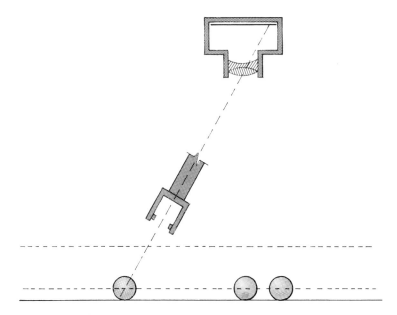

Figure 18-9. Photometric stereo does not provide absolute depth information. Consequently, while the attitude of the object is known, its position is only constrained to lie along a given ray from the camera. The robot gripper can search along this ray until a proximity sensor is triggered. The manipulator hand can then be reoriented to pick the object up.

object lies between the fingers. At this point the hand can be reoriented so that its attitude matches that of the object. The gripper is then closed and the object lifted free from the rest.

18.16 The Hand–Eye Coordinate Transform

In order to command the arm to trace along a particular ray from the camera, it is necessary to transform coordinates measured relative to the camera to coordinates measured relative to the arm. This transformation has six degrees of freedom and can be represented by a translation and a rotation. It is hard to determine it with sufficient accuracy using direct measurements of the camera's position and attitude. It is much more convenient to have the arm move through a series of known positions in front of the camera. The position of the image of the arm in the camera is then determined and used to solve for the parameters of the transformation. To ensure high accuracy, more than the minimum number of measurements are used, and a least-squares adjustment is carried out.

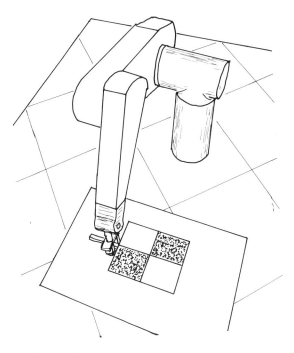

Figure 18-10. The transformation between the coordinate system of the mechanical manipulator and that of the electronic camera can be found by determining where in the image an object held by the arm appears. The surveyor's mark is particularly easy to recognize. An affine transformation is found between the image plane and each of two planes parallel to the ground. Each image point corresponds to a ray connecting a known point in one of these planes to a known point in the other.

Today, it is still very hard to develop a program that can recognize and track the arm. For this reason we actually have the arm hold a *surveyor's mark* whose image is easy to locate (figure 18-10). This is essentially a 2×2 subblock of a checkerboard. The intersection of the two lines separating dark and light areas can be located with high precision.

The camera can be mounted above the arm in such a way that it effectively looks straight down. In this way, we arrange for the image plane to be nearly parallel to the plane containing two of the axes of the arm's coordinate system. This means that for this plane, or one parallel to it, we can approximate the perspective projection by an affine transformation having six parameters. This method was explored in more detail in exercise 13-12. In order to simplify matters, we can actually have the arm move through a number of points in one such plane, near the support surface, to determine one affine transform. This process is then repeated in a plane closer to the camera, at a height near the maximum height of the planned workspace. In this way, each point in the image can be mapped into one point in each of the two planes. The process thus defines a ray in arm space (figure 18-9).

18.17 Objects of Arbitrary Shape

The methods described above made use of the fact that the objects were solids of revolution. We only had to recover the two degrees of freedom of the axis of the object. In the general case, the extended Gaussian image can still be used, but attitude now has three degrees of freedom. One way to see this is to note that an object can be rotated about an arbitrary axis by an arbitrary angle. It takes two parameters to specify the axis and one for the angle. What this means is that matching becomes a little more tedious. A larger number of potential matches must be tried. The same filtering operations can be employed to eliminate most of these potential matches immediately.

A simple extension of the method described above allows us to deal with objects that are not solids of revolution. We once again use the axis of least inertia of the mass distribution on the visible hemisphere to pin down one degree of freedom. The remaining problem is to determine the direction from which the object is viewed. The possible directions can be specified by points on a sphere. We generate a discrete sampling of the surface of the sphere that is as near to being uniform as possible. We can use the same tessellation of the sphere as is used for the orientation histogram.

One might think that the methods for searching the space of attitudes are inefficient compared to something like hill-climbing. We could first find a rough estimate of the attitude by considering the 60 rotations of the icosahedron, for example. The one that produced the best match would then be used as an initial value for an iteration that at each step sought to improve the match further by making small adjustments in the attitude. This does not work, however, because the match does not become significantly better until we are close to the correct attitude.

18.18 Conclusions

In this chapter we have studied a machine vision system for picking objects out of a pile. An artist's rendition of selected pictures out of a sequence taken while the system was carrying out its task is shown in figure 18-11.

This system uses multiple images obtained with one camera under changing lighting conditions. From these images a needle map is computed that gives estimates of the orientation of surface patches of the objects. This, in turn, is used to compute the orientation histogram, which is a discrete approximation of the extended Gaussian image. The experimental orientation histogram is then matched against orientation histograms computed from computer models of the objects. In this way we obtain the attitude of the object in space. A manipulator can then be sent along a ray in space to pick up the object.

While the experimental system described here is not particularly fast, there is no reason why a faster one could not be built, since all of the computations are simple, mostly involving table lookup methods. Special-purpose hardware could also be built to speed up the matching process. It would not have to be very complicated since it performs a kind of correlation process.

This approach seems to be robust for the recognition of objects and the determination of their attitude. It will work better, for example, than an approach based on recognizing some special feature of the object, given that only a few thousand picture cells are scanned per object region. In the case of an approach based on recognition of special features, a few thousand points would be needed just for that feature, so that the number of picture points for the whole object would be much larger.

The needle diagram can be computed from a depth map by taking first differences. The method described here is therefore also applicable to other kinds of surface information, such as depth maps obtained using laser range finders. Laser range finders were not used in the experiments reported here, since they are still expensive and slow. Depth maps obtained using binocular stereo could, of course, also be employed.

18.19 A Final Word

This chapter has drawn together many of the techniques explored in this book. We have emphasized the issues of representation and constraint. The bin-picking system demonstrates that robust, practical machine vision systems can be devised if we are prepared to go beyond simple heuristic approaches. Crucial to its success are such concepts as photometric stereo, the extended Gaussian image, and even sampling of the space of rotations. The process described is representative of a new approach to problems in machine vision. It is based on careful analyses of the physics of image formation and a view of machine vision as an inversion problem. It is only a start, however, and much remains to be learned.

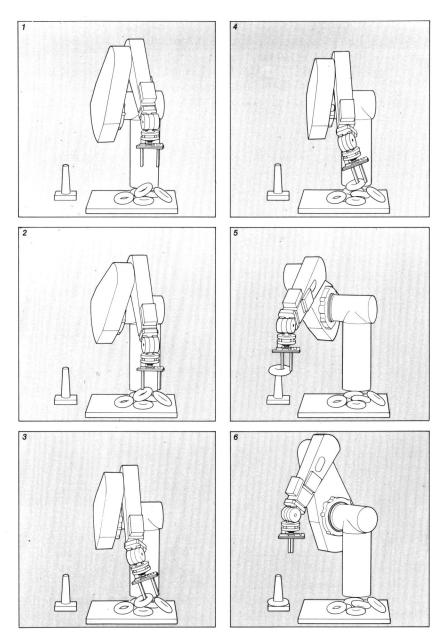

Figure 18-11. An artist's rendering of six frames out of a sequence of pictures showing a robot arm, guided by a photometric stereo system, picking up one object after another out of a pile of objects.

18.20 References

Applications of machine vision to robotics are explored in *Computer Vision and Sensor-Based Robots*, edited by Dodd & Rossol [1979] and in *Robot Vision*, edited by Pugh [1983].

Polyhedra are discussed in *Regular Figures* by Fejes Toth [1964], *Regular Polyhedra* by Coxeter [1973], and the *Polyhedra Primer* by Pearce & Pearce [1978]. Hamilton treated quaternions in great detail in the two volumes of *Elements of Quaternions* [1899].

There has been considerable interest in the development of methods for feeding parts from a pile or out of a bin. A system that uses visual information to do this for cylindrical objects is described by Kelley et al. [1982]. A different approach to automated parts orientation is described by Bolles, Horaud, & Hannah [1983]. The use of photometric stereo, the extended Gaussian image, and near-uniform sampling of the rotation space to solve this problem was first reported by Ikeuchi & Horn [1984]. A popular article in *Scientific American* by Horn & Ikeuchi [1984] explained some of the details.

Nishihara's [1983] binary correlation stereo system, described at the end of chapter 13, was used in a later version of this bin-picking system to obtain absolute depth information, which was not available from the photometric stereo system alone. This is described by Ikeuchi et al. [1984] in an internal report. Ikeuchi [1985] recently developed a novel binocular stereo system that matches needle diagrams obtained using two photometric stereo systems. Finally, Little [1985] has shown a better way to match orientation histograms using the concept of the mixed volume. The mixed volumes, by the way, are the *configuration space obstacles* used by Lozano-Pérez [1983] in spatial reasoning and robot motion planning.

An internal report by Salamin [1979] describes clearly the advantages of the unit quaternion representation for rotation and its relation to some other representations. Taylor [1979] promoted the use of quaternions in planning robot manipulator motions, while Canny [1984] used quaternions to advantage in his work on collision detection for moving polyhedra.

18.21 Exercises

18-1 Here we review the method for determining the orientation histogram of an object given as a prototype. Suppose that points on the surface are parameterized by u and v. We can divide the range of u into n intervals of width δu and the range of v into m intervals of width δv. We systematically step through the small patches, accumulating totals in the orientation histogram. To do this, we must know the normal of each patch, as well as its area.

(a) Show that a unit normal is given by

$$\hat{\mathbf{n}} = \frac{\mathbf{r}_u \times \mathbf{r}_v}{|\mathbf{r}_u \times \mathbf{r}_v|},$$

where $\mathbf{r}_u$ and $\mathbf{r}_v$ are the first partial derivatives of the vector $\mathbf{r} = (x, y, z)^T$.

(b) Show that the surface area of a patch is given by

$$\delta O = |\mathbf{r}_u \times \mathbf{r}_v|\, \delta u\, \delta v.$$

18-2 The center of mass of the visible hemisphere of an extended Gaussian image will lie somewhere above the plane separating the visible hemisphere from its complement. Show that the height above the plane times the mass at the center of mass is equal to the apparent area visible to the viewer. Also show that the mass at the center of mass is just equal to the actual area of the visible surface.

18-3 In what way would addition of a binocular stereo system change the bin-picking system described here? Consider speed, complexity, and cost.

18-4 Could we use two photometric stereo systems to recover absolute depth as well as the attitude in space of the objects? Compare this approach with the one in the previous exercise.

18-5 Let $\mathring{p}$, $\mathring{q}$, and $\mathring{r}$ be quaternions. Show that

$$(\mathring{p}\mathring{q})^* = \mathring{q}^*\,\mathring{p}^*,$$

$$(\mathring{p}\mathring{q}) \cdot (\mathring{p}\mathring{q}) = (\mathring{p} \cdot \mathring{p})(\mathring{q} \cdot \mathring{q}),$$

$$(\mathring{p}\mathring{q}) \cdot (\mathring{p}\mathring{r}) = (\mathring{p} \cdot \mathring{p})(\mathring{q} \cdot \mathring{r}).$$

18-6 A rotation is specified by the quaternion $\mathring{q}$. Show that a vector $\mathbf{x}$ becomes the vector $\mathbf{x}'$ upon rotation, where

$$\mathbf{x}' = (q^2 - \mathbf{q} \cdot \mathbf{q})\mathbf{x} + 2q\,\mathbf{q} \times \mathbf{x} + 2(\mathbf{q} \cdot \mathbf{x})\,\mathbf{q}.$$

Compare this with the formula of Rodrigues,

$$\mathbf{x}' = (\cos\theta)\,\mathbf{x} + (\sin\theta)\,\boldsymbol{\omega} \times \mathbf{x} + (1 - \cos\theta)(\boldsymbol{\omega} \cdot \mathbf{x})\,\boldsymbol{\omega}.$$

Show that fewer arithmetic operations are required if the formula above is rewritten in the equivalent form

$$\mathbf{x}' = \mathbf{x} + 2q\mathbf{q} \times \mathbf{x} - 2(\mathbf{q} \times \mathbf{x}) \times \mathbf{q}.$$

Hint: Use the vector identities found in the appendix.

18-7   Let the components of the unit quaternion $\mathring{q}$ be q_0, q_1, q_2, and q_3, respectively, where q_0 is the scalar part and $\mathbf{q} = (q_1, q_2, q_3)^T$ is the vector part. Show that the equivalent rotation matrix is

$$\mathbf{R} = \begin{pmatrix} q_0^2 + q_1^2 - q_2^2 - q_3^2 & 2(-q_0 q_3 + q_1 q_2) & 2(q_0 q_2 + q_1 q_3) \\ 2(q_0 q_3 + q_2 q_1) & q_0^2 - q_1^2 + q_2^2 - q_3^2 & 2(-q_0 q_1 + q_2 q_3) \\ 2(-q_0 q_2 + q_3 q_1) & 2(q_0 q_1 + q_3 q_2) & q_0^2 - q_1^2 - q_2^2 + q_3^2 \end{pmatrix}.$$

How would you recover the quaternion given an orthonormal matrix?

18-8   In this chapter we have considered matching extended Gaussian images by a method akin to correlation. As with correlation, there are some problems inherent in this approach. In this exercise we consider an alternative. We define the mixture of two objects, A and B, to be the object $C = A \oplus B$ whose extended Gaussian image is the sum of the extended Gaussian images of A and B. That is, $G_C = G_A + G_B$. Now let B be a rotated version of A, that is, $B = R_{\mathring{q}}(A)$. The volume of the mixed figure is a function of the relative attitude of B with respect to A. It can be shown that this volume is least when B is aligned with A, that is, when $\mathring{q} = 1$. Develop a method for computing the mixed volume, and use it to determine the attitude of an object. Hint: Use as a model the solution to exercise 16-9. Warning: This is quite a large project.

Appendix:
Useful Mathematical Techniques

This appendix contains concise reviews of various mathematical techniques used in this book. We start with formulae useful for solving triangles, both planar and spherical. Next, some aspects of the manipulation of vectors are summarized. These include solution methods for vector equations and conventions for differentiation with respect to a vector and a matrix. Least-squares methods for linear systems come next. These are followed by a review of optimization methods, both unconstrained and constrained. The appendix ends with a look at the calculus of variations.

A.1 Solving Triangles

Suppose a planar triangle has sides a, b, and c with opposite angles A, B, and C (figure A-1a). The diameter of the circumscribed circle equals the length of one side divided by the sine of the opposite angle. Since this is true for all three choices of sides, we have

$$\frac{a}{\sin A} = \frac{b}{\sin B} = \frac{c}{\sin C}.$$

This is the well-known *law of sines*. The *law of cosines* is given by

$$a^2 = b^2 + c^2 - 2bc \cos A.$$

Two similar formulae can be obtained by simultaneous cyclical permutation of a, b, c and A, B, C. The *projection theorem* states that

$$c = a \cos B + b \cos A.$$

(There are many other useful relationships, but we can usually manage with just these three; others can be derived from them if necessary.) The area of the triangle can be written

$$S = \frac{1}{2} ab \sin C.$$

A *spherical triangle* is a figure on the sphere whose three sides are segments of great circles (figure A-1b). Suppose that the angles of intersection at the three corners are A, B, and C. On the unit sphere, the length of a side is equal to the angle it subtends at the center of the sphere. Let the lengths of the three sides be a, b, and c. In the case of a spherical triangle, the law of sines is

$$\frac{\sin a}{\sin A} = \frac{\sin b}{\sin B} = \frac{\sin c}{\sin C}.$$

The law of cosines for the sides is

$$\cos a = \cos b \cos c + \sin b \sin c \cos A,$$

while the law of cosines for the angles is

$$\cos A = -\cos B \cos C + \sin B \sin C \cos a.$$

There are two more formulae in each case obtained by simultaneous cyclical permutation of a, b, c and A, B, C. (Other relations can be derived from these if necessary.)

Sometimes it is difficult to determine which quadrant an angle lies in. In this case, the *rule of quadrants* comes to the rescue: $\frac{1}{2}(A + B)$ is in the same quadrant as $\frac{1}{2}(a + b)$. Finally, we note that the area of a spherical triangle is

$$S_R = R^2 \epsilon.$$

Here R is the radius of the sphere, while $\epsilon = A + B + C - \pi$ is called the *spherical excess* (measured in radians).

A.2 Manipulation of Vectors

We shall assume that the reader is familiar with the properties of vector addition, scalar multiplication, and dot- and cross-products. Vectors will be denoted by boldface letters. We commonly deal with column vectors and therefore have to take the transpose, indicated by the superscript T, when we want to write them in terms of the equivalent row vectors.

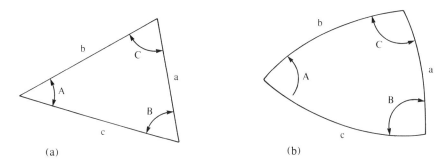

Figure A-1. A planar triangle (a) and a spherical triangle (b).

A.2.1 More Complex Products of Vectors

The vector *triple product* is defined as follows:

$$[\mathbf{a\,b\,c}] = \mathbf{a} \cdot (\mathbf{b} \times \mathbf{c}) = (\mathbf{a} \times \mathbf{b}) \cdot \mathbf{c}.$$

The magnitude of the result is independent of the order of the vectors, since it is the volume of the parallelepiped defined by the three vectors. The sign of the result is the same for all triple products with the same cyclical order. If the three vectors lie in a plane, they are linearly dependent, and in this case the triple product is zero.

The following identities apply to other complicated products of vectors:

$$\mathbf{a} \times (\mathbf{b} \times \mathbf{c}) = (\mathbf{c} \cdot \mathbf{a})\mathbf{b} - (\mathbf{a} \cdot \mathbf{b})\mathbf{c},$$

$$(\mathbf{a} \times \mathbf{b}) \times \mathbf{c} = (\mathbf{c} \cdot \mathbf{a})\mathbf{b} - (\mathbf{b} \cdot \mathbf{c})\mathbf{a}.$$

Thus we have

$$((\mathbf{a} \times \mathbf{b}) \times \mathbf{c}) \cdot \mathbf{d} + ((\mathbf{b} \times \mathbf{c}) \times \mathbf{a}) \cdot \mathbf{d} + ((\mathbf{c} \times \mathbf{a}) \times \mathbf{b}) \cdot \mathbf{d} = 0,$$

$$\mathbf{a} \times (\mathbf{b} \times (\mathbf{c} \times \mathbf{d})) = (\mathbf{b} \cdot \mathbf{c})(\mathbf{d} \times \mathbf{a}) - (\mathbf{b} \cdot \mathbf{d})(\mathbf{c} \times \mathbf{a}),$$

$$(\mathbf{a} \times \mathbf{b}) \cdot (\mathbf{c} \times \mathbf{d}) = (\mathbf{c} \cdot \mathbf{a})(\mathbf{b} \cdot \mathbf{d}) - (\mathbf{d} \cdot \mathbf{a})(\mathbf{b} \cdot \mathbf{c}),$$

and from these we can derive

$$(\mathbf{a} \times \mathbf{b}) \cdot (\mathbf{c} \times \mathbf{d}) + (\mathbf{b} \times \mathbf{c}) \cdot (\mathbf{a} \times \mathbf{d}) + (\mathbf{c} \times \mathbf{a}) \cdot (\mathbf{b} \times \mathbf{d}) = 0,$$

$$|\mathbf{a} \times \mathbf{b}|^2 = |\mathbf{a}|^2 |\mathbf{b}|^2 - (\mathbf{a} \cdot \mathbf{b})^2.$$

Note that this last quantity cannot be negative. Also,

$$(\mathbf{a} \times \mathbf{b}) \times (\mathbf{c} \times \mathbf{d}) = [\mathbf{d\,a\,b}]\mathbf{c} - [\mathbf{a\,b\,c}]\mathbf{d},$$

$$(\mathbf{a} \times \mathbf{b}) \times (\mathbf{c} \times \mathbf{d}) = [\mathbf{c\,d\,a}]\mathbf{b} - [\mathbf{b\,c\,d}]\mathbf{a}.$$

From this it follows that

$$\left[(\mathbf{a} \times \mathbf{b})\,(\mathbf{c} \times \mathbf{d})\,(\mathbf{e} \times \mathbf{f})\right] = [\mathbf{d}\,\mathbf{a}\,\mathbf{b}]\,[\mathbf{c}\,\mathbf{e}\,\mathbf{f}] - [\mathbf{a}\,\mathbf{b}\,\mathbf{c}]\,[\mathbf{d}\,\mathbf{e}\,\mathbf{f}],$$

and so

$$\left[(\mathbf{a} \times \mathbf{b})\,(\mathbf{b} \times \mathbf{c})\,(\mathbf{c} \times \mathbf{a})\right] = [\mathbf{a}\,\mathbf{b}\,\mathbf{c}]^2.$$

We can express any given vector $\mathbf{d}$ in terms of any three independent vectors $\mathbf{a}$, $\mathbf{b}$, and $\mathbf{c}$:

$$[\mathbf{a}\,\mathbf{b}\,\mathbf{c}]\mathbf{d} = [\mathbf{b}\,\mathbf{c}\,\mathbf{d}]\mathbf{a} + [\mathbf{d}\,\mathbf{c}\,\mathbf{a}]\mathbf{b} + [\mathbf{d}\,\mathbf{a}\,\mathbf{b}]\mathbf{c}.$$

This identity can be used to solve linear vector equations.

A.2.2 Solving Vector Equations

Suppose we are to find a vector $\mathbf{x}$ given its dot-products with three known linearly independent vectors, $\mathbf{a}$, $\mathbf{b}$, and $\mathbf{c}$. We have

$$\mathbf{x} \cdot \mathbf{a} = \alpha, \qquad \mathbf{x} \cdot \mathbf{b} = \beta, \qquad \text{and} \qquad \mathbf{x} \cdot \mathbf{c} = \gamma.$$

The unknown $\mathbf{x}$ can be expressed in terms of any three independent vectors. Rather than use $\mathbf{a}$, $\mathbf{b}$, and $\mathbf{c}$ for this purpose, consider a linear combination of their pairwise cross-products:

$$\mathbf{x} = u(\mathbf{b} \times \mathbf{c}) + v(\mathbf{c} \times \mathbf{a}) + w(\mathbf{a} \times \mathbf{b}).$$

It remains for us to determine the three scalars u, v, and w. Taking the dot-product of the above expression with the three vectors $\mathbf{a}$, $\mathbf{b}$, and $\mathbf{c}$, we obtain

$$u[\mathbf{a}\,\mathbf{b}\,\mathbf{c}] = \alpha, \qquad v[\mathbf{a}\,\mathbf{b}\,\mathbf{c}] = \beta, \qquad \text{and} \quad w[\mathbf{a}\,\mathbf{b}\,\mathbf{c}] = \gamma.$$

Thus we have

$$\mathbf{x} = \frac{1}{[\mathbf{a}\,\mathbf{b}\,\mathbf{c}]}\big(\alpha(\mathbf{b} \times \mathbf{c}) + \beta(\mathbf{c} \times \mathbf{a}) + \gamma(\mathbf{a} \times \mathbf{b})\big).$$

The same result could have been obtained by noting that

$$[\mathbf{a}\,\mathbf{b}\,\mathbf{c}]\mathbf{x} = (\mathbf{b} \times \mathbf{c})(\mathbf{a} \cdot \mathbf{x}) + (\mathbf{c} \times \mathbf{a})(\mathbf{b} \cdot \mathbf{x}) + (\mathbf{a} \times \mathbf{b})(\mathbf{c} \cdot \mathbf{x}).$$

The above method amounts to solving three equations in three unknowns. The result can therefore be used in inverting a 3×3 matrix $\mathbf{M}$ that has the vectors $\mathbf{a}^T$, $\mathbf{b}^T$, and $\mathbf{c}^T$ as rows:

$$\mathbf{M} = \begin{pmatrix} \mathbf{a}^T \\ \mathbf{b}^T \\ \mathbf{c}^T \end{pmatrix}.$$

The determinant of this matrix is just $[\mathbf{a}\,\mathbf{b}\,\mathbf{c}]$. According to the previous result, the inverse of this matrix is just the matrix of column vectors obtained by taking the pairwise cross-products, divided by the value of the determinant:

$$\mathbf{M}^{-1} = \frac{1}{[\mathbf{a}\,\mathbf{b}\,\mathbf{c}]}\big((\mathbf{b}\times\mathbf{c})\,(\mathbf{c}\times\mathbf{a})\,(\mathbf{a}\times\mathbf{b})\big).$$

The result is easily checked by matrix multiplication. There is a symmetric form of this result in which the columns rather than the rows of the original matrix are considered as vectors.

We turn now to other vector equations. Given an equation

$$\lambda\mathbf{x} + \mathbf{x}\times\mathbf{a} = \mathbf{b},$$

we want to find the unknown $\mathbf{x}$. It can be shown that

$$\lambda(\mathbf{b}-\lambda\mathbf{x}) + \lambda^{-1}(\mathbf{b}\cdot\mathbf{a})\mathbf{a} - a^2\mathbf{x} = \mathbf{b}\times\mathbf{a},$$

so that

$$\mathbf{x} = \frac{\lambda\mathbf{b} + \lambda^{-1}(\mathbf{b}\cdot\mathbf{a})\mathbf{a} - \mathbf{b}\times\mathbf{a}}{\lambda^2 + a^2},$$

provided $\lambda \neq 0$.

Given another vector equation,

$$\lambda\mathbf{x} + (\mathbf{x}\cdot\mathbf{b})\mathbf{a} = \mathbf{c},$$

we again want to find $\mathbf{x}$. Taking the dot-product with $\mathbf{b}$, we get

$$(\mathbf{x}\cdot\mathbf{b})\big(\lambda + \mathbf{a}\cdot\mathbf{b}\big) = \mathbf{b}\cdot\mathbf{c},$$

so that

$$\mathbf{x} = \frac{1}{\lambda}\left(\mathbf{c} - \mathbf{a}\frac{\mathbf{b}\cdot\mathbf{c}}{\lambda + \mathbf{a}\cdot\mathbf{b}}\right),$$

provided $\lambda + \mathbf{a}\cdot\mathbf{b} \neq 0$.

Next, consider finding a vector $\mathbf{x}$, given its size and its dot-products with two test vectors $\mathbf{a}$ and $\mathbf{b}$. Thus

$$\mathbf{a}\cdot\mathbf{x} = \alpha, \qquad \mathbf{b}\cdot\mathbf{x} = \beta, \qquad \text{and} \qquad \mathbf{x}\cdot\mathbf{x} = \gamma.$$

Unless $\mathbf{a}$ and $\mathbf{b}$ are parallel, we know that $\mathbf{a}$, $\mathbf{b}$, and $\mathbf{a}\times\mathbf{b}$ are linearly independent. Thus the unknown vector can be expressed as

$$\mathbf{x} = u\mathbf{a} + v\mathbf{b} + w(\mathbf{a}\times\mathbf{b}).$$

We can find u and v from

$$|\mathbf{a}\times\mathbf{b}|^2\, u = +\alpha(\mathbf{b}\cdot\mathbf{b}) - \beta(\mathbf{a}\cdot\mathbf{b}),$$

$$|\mathbf{a}\times\mathbf{b}|^2\, v = -\alpha(\mathbf{a}\cdot\mathbf{b}) + \beta(\mathbf{a}\cdot\mathbf{a}).$$

Moreover,

$$|\mathbf{a} \times \mathbf{b}|^2 (u\mathbf{a} + v\mathbf{b}) = \big[(\mathbf{b} \cdot \mathbf{b})\mathbf{a} - (\mathbf{a} \cdot \mathbf{b})\mathbf{b}\big]\alpha - \big[(\mathbf{a} \cdot \mathbf{b})\mathbf{a} - (\mathbf{a} \cdot \mathbf{a})\mathbf{b}\big]\beta,$$

and so

$$|\mathbf{a} \times \mathbf{b}|^2 \, |u\mathbf{a} + v\mathbf{b}|^2 = |\mathbf{a} \times \mathbf{b}|^2 (u\mathbf{a} + v\mathbf{b}) \cdot \mathbf{c} = |\beta\mathbf{a} - \alpha\mathbf{b}|^2.$$

Now

$$\mathbf{x} \cdot \mathbf{x} = |u\mathbf{a} + v\mathbf{b}|^2 + w^2 \, |\mathbf{a} \times \mathbf{b}|^2,$$

or

$$|\mathbf{a} \times \mathbf{b}|^4 \, w^2 = |\mathbf{a} \times \mathbf{b}|^2 \gamma - |\beta\mathbf{a} - \alpha\mathbf{b}|^2.$$

We thus obtain the two solutions

$$w = \pm \frac{\sqrt{|\mathbf{a} \times \mathbf{b}|^2 \gamma - |\beta\mathbf{a} - \alpha\mathbf{b}|^2}}{|\mathbf{a} \times \mathbf{b}|^2}.$$

A.3 Vector and Matrix Differentiation

Often a set of equations can be written more compactly in vector notation. The advantage of this may evaporate when it becomes necessary to look at the derivatives of a scalar or vector with respect to the components of a vector. It is, however, possible to use a consistent, compact notation in this case also.

A.3.1 Differentiation of a Scalar with Respect to a Vector

The derivative of a scalar with respect to a vector is the vector whose components are the derivatives of the scalar with respect to each of the components of the vector. If $\mathbf{r} = (x, y, z)^T$, then

$$\frac{df}{d\mathbf{r}} = (f_x, f_y, f_z)^T.$$

Consequently,

$$\frac{d}{d\mathbf{a}}(\mathbf{a} \cdot \mathbf{b}) = \mathbf{b} \quad \text{and} \quad \frac{d}{d\mathbf{b}}(\mathbf{a} \cdot \mathbf{b}) = \mathbf{a}.$$

The length of a vector is the square root of the sum of the squares of its elements,

$$|\mathbf{a}| = \sqrt{\mathbf{a} \cdot \mathbf{a}}.$$

We see that

$$\frac{d}{d\mathbf{a}} |\mathbf{a}|^2 = 2\mathbf{a},$$

so that

$$\frac{d}{d\mathbf{a}}|\mathbf{a}| = \hat{\mathbf{a}},$$

where $\hat{\mathbf{a}} = \mathbf{a}/|\mathbf{a}|$; also,

$$\frac{d}{d\mathbf{a}}[\mathbf{a}\,\mathbf{b}\,\mathbf{c}] = \mathbf{b} \times \mathbf{c},$$

where $[\mathbf{a}\,\mathbf{b}\,\mathbf{c}] = \mathbf{a} \cdot (\mathbf{b} \times \mathbf{c})$ as before. Furthermore,

$$\frac{d}{d\mathbf{a}}\mathbf{a}^T\mathbf{M}\mathbf{b} = \mathbf{M}\mathbf{b} \qquad \text{and} \qquad \frac{d}{d\mathbf{b}}\mathbf{a}^T\mathbf{M}\mathbf{b} = \mathbf{M}^T\mathbf{a}.$$

In particular,

$$\frac{d}{d\mathbf{x}}\mathbf{x}^T\mathbf{M}\mathbf{x} = (\mathbf{M} + \mathbf{M}^T)\mathbf{x}.$$

The derivative of a scalar with respect to a matrix is the matrix whose components are the derivatives of the scalar with respect to the elements of the matrix. Thus if

$$\mathbf{M} = \begin{pmatrix} a & b \\ c & d \end{pmatrix},$$

then

$$\frac{df}{d\mathbf{M}} = \begin{pmatrix} \frac{df}{da} & \frac{df}{db} \\ \frac{df}{dc} & \frac{df}{dd} \end{pmatrix}.$$

Consequently,

$$\frac{d}{d\mathbf{M}}\text{Trace}(\mathbf{M}) = I,$$

where the trace of a matrix is the sum of its diagonal elements and I is the identity matrix. Also,

$$\frac{d}{d\mathbf{M}}\mathbf{a}^T\mathbf{M}\mathbf{b} = \mathbf{a}\,\mathbf{b}^T.$$

In particular,

$$\frac{d}{d\mathbf{M}}\mathbf{x}^T\mathbf{M}\mathbf{x} = \mathbf{x}\,\mathbf{x}^T.$$

Note that $\mathbf{a}\,\mathbf{b}^T$ is not the scalar $\mathbf{a} \cdot \mathbf{b}$. The latter equals $\mathbf{a}^T\mathbf{b}$. If $\mathbf{a} = (a_x, a_y, a_z)^T$ and $\mathbf{b} = (b_x, b_y, b_z)^T$, the *dyadic product* is

$$\mathbf{a}\,\mathbf{b}^T = \begin{pmatrix} a_xb_x & a_xb_y & a_xb_z \\ a_yb_x & a_yb_y & a_yb_z \\ a_zb_x & a_zb_y & a_zb_z \end{pmatrix}.$$

Another interesting matrix derivative is

$$\frac{d}{d\mathbf{M}}\text{Det}(\mathbf{M}) = \text{Det}(\mathbf{M})\,(\mathbf{M}^{-1})^T.$$

That this is the matrix of cofactors can be shown as follows. Consider a particular element m_{ij} of the matrix $\mathbf{M}$. We can express the determinant as the sum

$$\mathrm{Det}(\mathbf{M}) = \sum_{k=1}^{n} m_{ik} c_{ik}$$

by expanding along the row containing this element, where c_{ij} is the cofactor of m_{ij}. Thus the derivative of the determinant with respect to m_{ij} is just c_{ij}. (The cofactor c_{ij} is $(-1)^{i+j}$ times the determinant of the matrix obtained by deleting the ith row and the jth column.) The result follows from the fact that the inverse of a matrix equals the transpose of the matrix of cofactors divided by the value of the determinant.

Next, if $\mathbf{A}$ and $\mathbf{B}$ are compatible matrices (that is, if $\mathbf{A}$ has as many columns as $\mathbf{B}$ has rows), then

$$\frac{d}{d\mathbf{A}} \mathrm{Trace}(\mathbf{A}\,\mathbf{B}) = \mathbf{B}^{T} \quad \text{and} \quad \frac{d}{d\mathbf{B}} \mathrm{Trace}(\mathbf{A}\,\mathbf{B}) = \mathbf{A}^{T}.$$

Also, in general,

$$\frac{d}{d\mathbf{M}} \mathrm{Trace}(\mathbf{A}\,\mathbf{M}\,\mathbf{B}) = \mathbf{A}^{T} \mathbf{B}^{T}.$$

One norm of a matrix is the square root of the sum of squares of its elements:

$$\|\mathbf{M}\|^{2} = \mathrm{Trace}(\mathbf{M}^{T}\mathbf{M}).$$

We see that

$$\frac{d}{d\mathbf{M}} \|\mathbf{M}\|^{2} = 2\,\mathbf{M},$$

and it follows from

$$\|\mathbf{A} - \mathbf{B}\|^{2} = \mathrm{Trace}(\mathbf{A}^{T}\mathbf{A} - \mathbf{B}^{T}\mathbf{A} - \mathbf{A}^{T}\mathbf{B} + \mathbf{B}^{T}\mathbf{B})$$

or

$$\|\mathbf{A} - \mathbf{B}\|^{2} = \|\mathbf{A}\|^{2} - 2\,\mathrm{Trace}(\mathbf{A}^{T}\mathbf{B}) + \|\mathbf{B}\|^{2}$$

that

$$\frac{d}{d\mathbf{A}} \|\mathbf{A} - \mathbf{B}\|^{2} = 2(\mathbf{A} - \mathbf{B}) \quad \text{and} \quad \frac{d}{d\mathbf{B}} \|\mathbf{A} - \mathbf{B}\|^{2} = 2(\mathbf{B} - \mathbf{A}).$$

A.3.2 Differentiation of a Vector with Respect to a Vector

Occasionally it is also useful to define a matrix that contains as elements the derivatives of the components of one vector with respect to the components of another:

$$
\frac{d\mathbf{b}}{d\mathbf{a}} =
\begin{pmatrix}
\frac{db_x}{da_x} & \frac{db_x}{da_y} & \frac{db_x}{da_z} \\
\frac{db_y}{da_x} & \frac{db_y}{da_y} & \frac{db_y}{da_z} \\
\frac{db_z}{da_x} & \frac{db_z}{da_y} & \frac{db_z}{da_z}
\end{pmatrix} .
$$

This matrix is just the Jacobian $\mathbf{J}$ of the coordinate transformation from $\mathbf{a}$ to $\mathbf{b}$. Clearly,

$$
\frac{d}{d\mathbf{a}}\mathbf{M}\mathbf{a} = \mathbf{M}
$$

for any matrix $\mathbf{M}$. We also see that

$$
\frac{d}{d\mathbf{b}}(\mathbf{a} \times \mathbf{b}) =
\begin{pmatrix}
0 & -a_z & +a_y \\
+a_z & 0 & -a_x \\
-a_y & +a_x & 0
\end{pmatrix} ,
$$

and so conclude that

$$
\mathbf{a} \times \mathbf{b} =
\begin{pmatrix}
0 & -a_z & +a_y \\
+a_z & 0 & -a_x \\
-a_y & +a_x & 0
\end{pmatrix} \mathbf{b}.
$$

This defines an isomorphism between vectors and antisymmetric matrices that can be useful when we are dealing with cross-products.

A.4 Least-Squares Solutions of Linear Equations

Let $\mathbf{a} = \mathbf{M}\mathbf{b}$, where $\mathbf{M}$ is an $m \times n$ matrix, $\mathbf{a}$ is a vector with m components, and $\mathbf{b}$ is a vector with n components. Suppose that we have n measurements $\{\mathbf{a}_i\}$ and $\{\mathbf{b}_i\}$ and wish to calculate the matrix $\mathbf{M}$. We can form the matrices $\mathbf{A}$ and $\mathbf{B}$ by adjoining the vectors $\{\mathbf{a}_i\}$ and $\{\mathbf{b}_i\}$, respectively. (That is, the ith column of the matrix $\mathbf{A}$ is $\mathbf{a}_i$.) Then

$$
\mathbf{A} = \mathbf{M}\,\mathbf{B}.
$$

Now $\mathbf{B}$ is a square matrix. If it has an inverse, then

$$
\mathbf{M} = \mathbf{A}\,\mathbf{B}^{-1}.
$$

Suppose that we have more measurements. The problem is then overdetermined, with more equations than unknowns. We can define an error vector $\mathbf{e}$ with m components

$$
\mathbf{e}_i = \mathbf{a}_i - \mathbf{M}\mathbf{b}_i.
$$

Adjoining these k vectors, we obtain

$$\mathbf{E} = \mathbf{A} - \mathbf{M}\,\mathbf{B}.$$

The sum of the squares of the errors is

$$\sum |\mathbf{e}_i|^2 = \sum \mathbf{e}_i \cdot \mathbf{e}_i = \sum \mathbf{e}_i^T \mathbf{e}_i,$$

or

$$\mathrm{Trace}(\mathbf{E}^T \mathbf{E}) = \mathrm{Trace}\big((\mathbf{A} - \mathbf{M}\,\mathbf{B})^T (\mathbf{A} - \mathbf{M}\,\mathbf{B})\big),$$

or

$$\mathrm{Trace}(\mathbf{E}^T \mathbf{E}) = \mathrm{Trace}(\mathbf{A}^T \mathbf{A} - \mathbf{B}^T \mathbf{M}^T \mathbf{A} - \mathbf{A}^T \mathbf{M}\,\mathbf{B} + \mathbf{B}^T \mathbf{M}^T \mathbf{M}\,\mathbf{B}).$$

Thus

$$\frac{d}{d\mathbf{M}} \mathrm{Trace}(\mathbf{E}^T \mathbf{E}) = -\mathbf{A}\,\mathbf{B}^T - \mathbf{A}\,\mathbf{B}^T + (\mathbf{B}^T \mathbf{M}^T)^T \mathbf{B}^T + (\mathbf{B}^T \mathbf{M}^T)^T \mathbf{B}^T.$$

If this is to equal zero, then $\mathbf{A}\,\mathbf{B}^T = \mathbf{M}\,\mathbf{B}\,\mathbf{B}^T$, that is,

$$\mathbf{M} = \mathbf{A}\,\mathbf{B}^T (\mathbf{B}\,\mathbf{B}^T)^{-1}.$$

The term $\mathbf{B}^T(\mathbf{B}\,\mathbf{B}^T)^{-1}$ is called the *pseudoinverse* of the nonsquare matrix $\mathbf{B}$.

The problem is underdetermined, on the other hand, if there are fewer equations than unknowns. There are then infinitely many solutions. In this case the pseudoinverse provides the solution with least norm, but it has to be computed differently. The pseudoinverse of a matrix $\mathbf{B}$ can be defined as the limit

$$\mathbf{B}^+ = \lim_{\delta \to 0} \big(\mathbf{B}^T \mathbf{B} + \delta^2 \mathbf{I}\big)^{-1} \mathbf{B}^T.$$

Alternatively, it can be defined using the conditions of Penrose (see Albert [1982]), which state that the matrix $\mathbf{B}^+$ is the pseudoinverse of the matrix $\mathbf{B}$ if and only if

- $\mathbf{B}\,\mathbf{B}^+$ and $\mathbf{B}^+ \mathbf{B}$ are symmetric,
- $\mathbf{B}^+ \mathbf{B}\,\mathbf{B}^+ = \mathbf{B}$,
- $\mathbf{B}\,\mathbf{B}^+ \mathbf{B} = \mathbf{B}^+$.

The pseudoinverse can also be found using spectral decomposition. The eigenvectors of the pseudoinverse are the same as those of the original matrix, while the corresponding nonzero eigenvalues are the inverses of the nonzero eigenvalues of the original matrix.

A.5 Lagrange Multipliers

The method of Lagrange multipliers provides powerful techniques for solving extremal problems with constraints. We first consider the case of a single constraint equation, then generalize to several constraints.

A.5.1 One Constraint

Suppose we want to find an extremum of a function $f(x, y)$ subject to the constraint $g(x, y) = 0$. If we can solve the latter equation for y,

$$y = \phi(x),$$

we can eliminate y by substitution and find the extrema of

$$f\big(x, \phi(x)\big)$$

by differentiating with respect to x. Using the chain rule for differentiation, we obtain

$$\frac{\partial f}{\partial x} + \frac{\partial f}{\partial y}\frac{d\phi}{dx} = 0.$$

Often, however, it is impossible or impractical to find a closed-form solution for y in terms of x. In this situation we use the method of Lagrange multipliers. We shall not prove that the method provides necessary conditions for extrema, just indicate why it works.

Consider the curve defined by $g(x, y) = 0$. Let s be a parameter that varies as we move along the curve. Then

$$\frac{\partial g}{\partial x}\frac{dx}{ds} + \frac{\partial g}{\partial y}\frac{dy}{ds} = 0,$$

and the slope of this curve is

$$\frac{dy}{dx} = -\frac{\partial g}{\partial x}\bigg/\frac{\partial g}{\partial y}.$$

Substituting this for $d\phi/dx$ in the equation for the extrema derived earlier, we obtain

$$\frac{\partial f}{\partial x}\frac{\partial g}{\partial y} = \frac{\partial f}{\partial y}\frac{\partial g}{\partial x}.$$

This equation applies even when the constraint equation $g(x, y) = 0$ cannot be solved explicitly for y.

Now consider instead the extrema of the function

$$F(x, y, \lambda) \equiv f(x, y) + \lambda g(x, y).$$

Differentiating with respect to x, y, and λ, we have

$$\frac{\partial f}{\partial x} + \lambda \frac{\partial g}{\partial x} = 0 \quad \text{and} \quad \frac{\partial f}{\partial y} + \lambda \frac{\partial g}{\partial y} = 0.$$

If we eliminate λ, we obtain again

$$\frac{\partial f}{\partial x} \frac{\partial g}{\partial y} = \frac{\partial f}{\partial y} \frac{\partial g}{\partial x}.$$

Thus the extrema of $f(x, y)$ subject to the constraint $g(x, y) = 0$ can be found by finding the extrema of $F(x, y, \lambda)$.

To make this seem plausible, consider moving along the curve defined by $g(x, y) = 0$, searching for an extremum of $f(x, y)$. There can be no extremum where the contours of constant $f(x, y)$ cross the curve we are following, since we can move a small distance along the curve and find a slightly larger or slightly smaller value of $f(x, y)$, as needed. The extrema are where the contours of constant $f(x, y)$ are parallel to the constraint curve. Note also that the constraint curve in turn is a curve of constant $g(x, y)$. Contours of constant $f(x, y)$ are perpendicular to the gradient of $f(x, y)$,

$$\nabla f = \left(\frac{\partial f}{\partial x}, \frac{\partial f}{\partial y} \right)^T,$$

while contours of constant $g(x, y)$ are perpendicular to the gradient of $g(x, y)$,

$$\nabla g = \left(\frac{\partial g}{\partial x}, \frac{\partial g}{\partial y} \right)^T.$$

These two gradients must be parallel.

Consider now finding an extremum of $F(x, y, \lambda)$. Differentiation gives us

$$\frac{\partial f}{\partial x} + \lambda \frac{\partial g}{\partial x} = 0 \quad \text{and} \quad \frac{\partial f}{\partial y} + \lambda \frac{\partial g}{\partial y} = 0,$$

or

$$\left(\frac{\partial f}{\partial x}, \frac{\partial f}{\partial y} \right)^T = -\lambda \left(\frac{\partial g}{\partial x}, \frac{\partial g}{\partial y} \right)^T,$$

which is a statement of the condition that the two gradients must be parallel. The factor $-\lambda$ is simply the ratio of the magnitudes of the two gradients.

As an example, let us find the point on the line

$$x \sin \theta - y \cos \theta + \rho = 0$$

that is closest to the origin. Here we have to minimize $x^2 + y^2$ subject to the given constraint. Conversely, we can minimize

$$(x^2 + y^2) + \lambda(x \sin \theta - y \cos \theta + \rho).$$

Differentiating with respect to x and y, we find

$$2x + \lambda \sin \theta = 0 \quad \text{and} \quad 2y - \lambda \cos \theta = 0.$$

Thus $x \cos \theta + y \sin \theta = 0$. Substituting in the constraint equation, we obtain

$$x \sin \theta + x \cos^2 \theta / \sin \theta + \rho = 0, \quad \text{or} \quad x = -\rho \sin \theta,$$

and

$$-y \sin^2 \theta / \cos \theta - y \cos \theta + \rho = 0, \quad \text{or} \quad y = +\rho \cos \theta.$$

The same method applies if we have more than three independent variables. To find an extremum of $f(x, y, z)$ subject to the constraint $g(x, y, z) = 0$, we look for places where the surfaces of constant $f(x, y, z)$ are tangent to the surfaces of constant $g(x, y, z)$. Because the gradient is perpendicular to the tangent plane, we can also look for places where the gradient of $f(x, y, z)$ is parallel to the gradient of $g(x, y, z)$. We thus look for extrema of

$$f(x, y, z) + \lambda g(x, y, z),$$

since this leads to the equations

$$\frac{\partial f}{\partial x} + \lambda \frac{\partial g}{\partial x} = 0,$$

$$\frac{\partial f}{\partial y} + \lambda \frac{\partial g}{\partial y} = 0,$$

$$\frac{\partial f}{\partial z} + \lambda \frac{\partial g}{\partial z} = 0,$$

or

$$\left(\frac{\partial f}{\partial x}, \frac{\partial f}{\partial y}, \frac{\partial f}{\partial z} \right)^T = -\lambda \left(\frac{\partial g}{\partial x}, \frac{\partial g}{\partial y}, \frac{\partial g}{\partial z} \right)^T.$$

A.5.2 More than One Constraint

With three independent variables, we can add a second constraint. The extrema of $f(x, y, z) = 0$ subject to the constraints $g(x, y, z) = 0$ and $h(x, y, z) = 0$ are the same as the extrema of

$$f(x, y, z) + \lambda g(x, y, z) + \mu h(x, y, z)$$

subject to those constraints. Differentiating with respect to x, y, and z yields

$$\frac{\partial f}{\partial x} + \lambda \frac{\partial g}{\partial x} + \mu \frac{\partial h}{\partial x} = 0,$$

$$\frac{\partial f}{\partial y} + \lambda \frac{\partial g}{\partial y} + \mu \frac{\partial h}{\partial y} = 0,$$

$$\frac{\partial f}{\partial z} + \lambda \frac{\partial g}{\partial z} + \mu \frac{\partial h}{\partial z} = 0.$$

These equations state that the gradient of f must be a linear combination of the gradients of g and h:

$$\nabla f = -\lambda \nabla g - \mu \nabla h.$$

The constraints $g(x,y,z) = 0$ and $h(x,y,z) = 0$ each define a surface. Their intersection is the curve along which we search for extrema. The gradient of a surface is perpendicular to the tangent plane. Thus curves on a surface are perpendicular to the gradient. In particular, the intersection of the two surfaces is perpendicular to both gradients. The curve of intersection is thus parallel to the cross-product of the two gradients. At an extremum, the gradient of $f(x,y,z)$ should not have any component in this direction—otherwise we can increase or decrease the value of $f(x,y,z)$ by moving a little along the curve. The gradient of $f(x,y,z)$ will satisfy this condition if and only if it can be expressed as a linear combination of the gradients of $g(x,y,z)$ and $h(x,y,z)$.

As an example, let us find the box with largest volume subject to the constraints that one face of the box has unit area and that the sum of the width, height, and depth of the box is four. Let the dimensions of the box be a, b, and c. We minimize

$$abc + \lambda(ab - 1) + \mu(a + b + c - 4).$$

Differentiating with respect to a, b, and c yields

$$bc + \lambda b + \mu = 0,$$

$$ac + \lambda a + \mu = 0,$$

$$ab + \mu = 0.$$

Eliminating λ and μ from these equations, we obtain $a = b$. From the first constraint it follows that $a = b = 1$. The second constraint gives $c = 2$.

A.5.3 The General Case

Let $\mathbf{x} = (x_1, x_2, \ldots, x_n)^T$ be a vector in an n-dimensional space. The set of values $\mathbf{x}$ that satisfy the constraint $g(\mathbf{x}) = 0$ form a subspace. Consider some curve lying entirely in this subspace. Let s be a parameter that varies as we move along this curve. The direction of the curve at a point is defined by the tangent at that point,

$$\frac{d\mathbf{x}}{ds} = \left(\frac{dx_1}{ds}, \frac{dx_2}{ds}, \ldots, \frac{dx_n}{ds} \right)^T.$$

The rate of change of $g(\mathbf{x})$ with s is given by

$$\frac{dg}{ds} = \frac{\partial g}{\partial x_1} \frac{dx_1}{ds} + \frac{\partial g}{\partial x_2} \frac{dx_2}{ds} + \cdots + \frac{\partial g}{\partial x_n} \frac{dx_n}{ds} = \nabla g \cdot \frac{d\mathbf{x}}{ds},$$

where ∇g is the gradient of g,

$$\nabla g = \left(\frac{\partial g}{\partial x_1}, \frac{\partial g}{\partial x_2}, \ldots, \frac{\partial g}{\partial x_n} \right)^T.$$

Because the curve remains in the subspace where $g(\mathbf{x}) = 0$, we have

$$\nabla g \cdot \frac{d\mathbf{x}}{ds} = 0.$$

That is, the curve must at each point be perpendicular to the gradient of $g(\mathbf{x})$. The allowed tangent directions at a particular point form an $(n-1)$-dimensional subspace as long as the gradient is nonzero. We can see this by noting that only $n - 1$ components of the tangent vector are independent, the remaining component being constrained by the last equation.

Now suppose that there are m constraints $g_i(\mathbf{x}) = 0$ for $i = 1, 2, \ldots,$ m. The intersection of the subspaces defined by each of the constraints individually is also a subspace. A curve lying in this common subspace must be perpendicular to all of the gradients of the g_i; thus

$$\nabla g_i \cdot \frac{d\mathbf{x}}{ds} = 0 \qquad \text{for } i = 1, 2, \ldots, m.$$

If the m gradients are linearly independent, the common subspace has dimension $n - m$, since only $n - m$ components of the tangent vector can be freely chosen, the rest being constrained by the m equations above.

If $f(\mathbf{x})$ is to have an extremum at a point in the subspace defined by the constraints, then the first derivative of f along any curve lying in the subspace must be zero. Now

$$\frac{df}{ds} = \nabla f \cdot \frac{d\mathbf{x}}{ds},$$

so that we want

$$\nabla f \cdot \frac{d\mathbf{x}}{ds} = 0$$

for any tangent direction that satisfies

$$\nabla g_i \cdot \frac{d\mathbf{x}}{ds} = 0 \qquad \text{for } i = 1, 2, \ldots, m.$$

That is, at the extremum, the tangent must be perpendicular to the gradient of f as well. This certainly is the case if the gradient of f happens to be a linear combination of the gradients of the g_i at the point. What we want to show is that ∇f must be a linear combination of the ∇g_i at an extremum.

It is easy to show that the constraints

$$\nabla g_i \cdot \frac{d\mathbf{x}}{ds} = 0$$

define a vector space. Any vector can be uniquely decomposed into a component that lies in this subspace and one that is orthogonal to it.

The vector ∇f can be decomposed into a component $\mathbf{g}$ that is a linear combination of the ∇g_i and a component $\mathbf{c}$ that is orthogonal to each of the ∇g_i. Suppose that $\mathbf{c}$ is nonzero. Then

$$\nabla f \cdot \frac{d\mathbf{x}}{ds} = \mathbf{g} \cdot \frac{d\mathbf{x}}{ds} + \mathbf{c} \cdot \frac{d\mathbf{x}}{ds} = \mathbf{c} \cdot \frac{d\mathbf{x}}{ds},$$

since $\mathbf{g}$ is a linear combination of the ∇g_i. We can choose a curve for which

$$\frac{d\mathbf{x}}{ds} = \mathbf{c},$$

since $\nabla g_i \cdot \mathbf{c} = 0$ for $i = 1, 2, \ldots, m$. In this case

$$\nabla f \cdot \frac{d\mathbf{x}}{ds} = \mathbf{c} \cdot \mathbf{c} \neq 0.$$

This contradicts the condition for an extremum, and $\mathbf{c}$ must therefore be zero after all. That is, ∇f must be a linear combination of the gradients ∇g_i. We can write this condition as

$$\nabla f = -\sum_{i=1}^{m} \lambda_i \nabla g_i$$

for some set of coefficients λ_i.

Consider now the function

$$f(\mathbf{x}) + \sum_{i=1}^{m} \lambda_i g_i(\mathbf{x}).$$

If we try to find an extremum by differentiating with respect to $\mathbf{x}$, we obtain

$$\nabla f + \sum_{i=1}^{m} \lambda_i \nabla g_i = \mathbf{0},$$

which is just the equation shown to be satisfied at an extremum of f.

To summarize, then, the extrema of $f(\mathbf{x})$, subject to the m constraints $g_i(\mathbf{x}) = 0$, can be found by locating the extrema of

$$f(\mathbf{x}) + \sum_{i=1}^{m} \lambda_i g_i(\mathbf{x})$$

subject to the same constraints. Here $\mathbf{x}$ is a vector with n components and $n > m$.

A.6 The Calculus of Variations

Calculus teaches us how to find extrema of functions. We are allowed to vary one or more parameters of some function. A solution is a set of parameters that corresponds to an extremum of the function. Differentiation of the function leads to a set of (algebraic) equations that represent necessary conditions for an extremum.

In the calculus of variations we look for extrema of expressions that depend on functions rather than parameters. Such expressions are called *functionals*. Now we obtain differential equations rather than ordinary equations to represent the necessary conditions for an extremum.

A.6.1 Problems without Constraints

As an example, consider the simple integral

$$I = \int_{x_1}^{x_2} F(x, f, f') \, dx.$$

Here F depends on the unknown function f and its derivative f'. Let us assume that the curve to be found must pass through the points $f(x_1) = f_1$ and $f(x_2) = f_2$. Suppose that the function $f(x)$ is a solution of the extremum problem. Then we expect that small variations in $f(x)$ should not change the integral significantly.

Let $\eta(x)$ be a test function. If we add $\epsilon \eta(x)$ to $f(x)$, we expect that the integral will change by an amount proportional to ϵ^2 for small values of ϵ. If, instead, it varied linearly with ϵ, we could increase or decrease the integral as desired and would therefore not be at an extremum. To be precise, we want

$$\left.\frac{dI}{d\epsilon}\right|_{\epsilon=0} = 0.$$

This must be true for all test functions $\eta(x)$.

In our specific problem, we must have $\eta(x_1) = 0$ and $\eta(x_2) = 0$ to satisfy the boundary conditions. Also, if $f(x)$ is replaced by $f(x) + \epsilon\eta(x)$, then $f'(x)$ is replaced by $f'(x) + \epsilon\eta'(x)$. The integral then becomes

$$I = \int_{x_1}^{x_2} F(x, f + \epsilon\eta, f' + \epsilon\eta')\, dx.$$

If F is suitably differentiable, we can expand the integrand in a Taylor series,

$$F(x, f + \epsilon\eta, f' + \epsilon\eta')$$
$$= F(x, f, f') + \epsilon\frac{\partial}{\partial f}F(x, f, f')\eta(x) + \epsilon\frac{\partial}{\partial f'}F(x, f, f')\eta'(x) + e,$$

where e consists of terms in higher powers of ϵ. Thus

$$I = \int_{x_1}^{x_2} \left(F + \epsilon\eta(x)F_f + \epsilon\eta' F_{f'} + e\right) dx,$$

and differentiating with respect to ϵ and setting ϵ equal to zero yields

$$0 = \int_{x_1}^{x_2} \left(\eta(x)F_f + \eta'(x)F_{f'}\right) dx.$$

Using integration by parts, we see that

$$\int_{x_1}^{x_2} \eta'(x)F_{f'}\, dx = [\eta(x)F_{f'}]_{x_1}^{x_2} - \int_{x_1}^{x_2} \eta(x)\frac{d}{dx}F_f\, dx,$$

where the first term is zero because of the boundary conditions. We must therefore have

$$0 = \int_{x_1}^{x_2} \eta(x) \left(F_f - \frac{d}{dx}F_{f'}\right) dx.$$

If this is to be true for all test functions $\eta(x)$, then

$$F_f - \frac{d}{dx}F_{f'} = 0.$$

This is called the *Euler equation* for this problem.

The method can be generalized in a number of ways. First, suppose that the boundary conditions $f(x_1) = f_1$ and $f(x_2) = f_2$ are not given. Then in order for the term

$$[\eta(x)F_{f'}]_{x_1}^{x_2}$$

to be zero for all possible test functions $\eta(x)$, we must introduce the *natural boundary conditions*

$$F_{f'} = 0 \qquad \text{at } x = x_1 \text{ and } x = x_2.$$

Next, the integrand might contain higher derivatives,

$$I = \int_{x_1}^{x_2} F(x, f, f', f'', \dots) \, dx.$$

The Euler equation in this case becomes

$$F_f - \frac{d}{dx}F_{f'} + \frac{d^2}{dx^2}F_{f''} - \cdots = 0.$$

In this case we must specify the boundary values of all but the highest derivatives in order to pose the problem properly.

We can also treat the case in which the integrand depends on several functions $f_1(x)$, $f_2(x)$, ... instead of just one. That is,

$$I = \int_{x_1}^{x_2} F(x, f_1, f_2, \dots, f_1', f_2', \dots) \, dx.$$

In this case there are as many Euler equations as there are unknown functions:

$$F_{f_i} - \frac{d}{dx}F_{f_i'} = 0.$$

Consider next a case in which there are two independent variables x and y and we are to find a function $f(x, y)$ that yields an extremum of the integral

$$I = \iint_D F(x, y, f, f_x, f_y) \, dx \, dy.$$

Here f_x and f_y are the partial derivatives of f with respect to x and y, respectively, and the integral is over some simply-connected closed region D. We introduce a test function $\eta(x, y)$ and add $\epsilon\eta(x, y)$ to $f(x, y)$. We are given the values of $f(x, y)$ on the boundary ∂D of the region, so the test function must be zero on the boundary. Taylor series expansion yields

$$F(x, y, f + \epsilon\eta, f_x + \epsilon\eta_x, f_y + \epsilon\eta_y)$$

$$= F(x, y, f, f_x, f_y) + \epsilon\frac{\partial}{\partial f}F(x, y, f, f_x, f_y)\eta(x, y)$$

$$+ \epsilon\frac{\partial}{\partial f_x}F(x, y, f, f_x, f_y)\eta_x(x, y) + \epsilon\frac{\partial}{\partial f_y}F(x, y, f, f_x, f_y)\eta_y(x, y) + e,$$

where e consists of terms in higher powers of ϵ. Thus

$$I = \iint_D \left(F + \epsilon\eta F_f + \epsilon\eta_x F_{f_x} + \epsilon\eta_y F_{f_y}\right) dx \, dy,$$

and differentiating with respect to ϵ and setting ϵ equal to zero yields

$$0 = \iint_D \left(\eta F_f + \eta_x F_{f_x} + \eta_y F_{f_y}\right) dx \, dy.$$

Now by Gauss's integral theorem,

$$\iint_D \left(\frac{\partial Q}{\partial x} + \frac{\partial P}{\partial y}\right) dx \, dy = \int_{\partial D} \left(Q \, dy - P \, dx\right),$$

so that

$$\iint_D \left(\frac{\partial}{\partial x}(\eta F_{f_x}) + \frac{\partial}{\partial y}(\eta F_{f_y})\right) dx \, dy = \int_{\partial D} \left(\eta F_{f_x} \, dy - \eta F_{f_y} \, dx\right).$$

Given the boundary conditions, the term on the right must be zero, so that

$$\iint_D \left(\eta_x F_{f_x} + \eta_y F_{f_y}\right) dx \, dy = -\iint_D \left(\eta\frac{\partial}{\partial x}F_{f_x} + \eta\frac{\partial}{\partial y}F_{f_y}\right) dx \, dy.$$

Consequently,

$$0 = \iint_D \eta \left(F_f - \frac{\partial}{\partial x}F_{f_x} - \frac{\partial}{\partial y}F_{f_y}\right) dx \, dy$$

for all test functions η. We must have, then, that

$$F_f - \frac{\partial}{\partial x}F_{f_x} - \frac{\partial}{\partial y}F_{f_y} = 0.$$

Here the Euler equation is a partial differential equation. An immediate extension is to the case in which the value of f on the boundary ∂D is not specified. For the integral

$$\int_{\partial D} \eta \left(F_{f_x} dy - F_{f_y} dx\right)$$

to be zero for all test functions η, we must have

$$F_{f_x}\frac{dy}{ds} = F_{f_y}\frac{dx}{ds},$$

where s is a parameter that varies along the boundary.

The extension to more than two independent variables is also immediate.

A.6.2 Variational Problems with Constraints

A problem in the calculus of variations can also have constraints. Suppose, for example, that we want to find an extremum of

$$I = \int_{x_1}^{x_2} F(x, f_1, f_2, \ldots, f_n, f_1', f_2', \ldots, f_n') \, dx$$

subject to the constraints $g_i(x, f_1, f_2, \ldots, f_n) = 0$ for $i = 1, 2, \ldots, m$, with $m < n$. We can solve the modified Euler equations

$$\frac{\partial \Phi}{\partial f_i} - \frac{d}{dx}\frac{\partial \Phi}{\partial f_i'} = 0 \qquad \text{for } i = 1, 2, \ldots, n$$

subject to the constraints. Here

$$\Phi \equiv F + \sum_{i=1}^{m} \lambda_i(x) g_i(x, f_1, f_2, \ldots, f_n).$$

The unknown functions $\lambda_i(x)$ are again called *Lagrange multipliers*.

Constraints in the form of integrals are treated similarly. Suppose we want to find an extremum of the integral

$$I = \int_{x_1}^{x_2} F(x, f_1, f_2, \ldots, f_n, f_1', f_2', \ldots, f_n') \, dx$$

subject to the constraints

$$\int_{x_1}^{x_2} g_i(x, f, f_1, f_2, \ldots, f_n, f_1', f_2', \ldots, f_n') \, dx = c_i \qquad \text{for } i = 1, 2, \ldots, m,$$

where the c_i are given constants. We now solve the modified Euler equations

$$\frac{\partial \Psi}{\partial f_i} - \frac{d}{dx}\frac{\partial \Psi}{\partial f_i'} = 0 \qquad \text{for } i = 1, 2, \ldots, m$$

subject to the constraints. Here

$$\Psi \equiv F + \sum_{i=1}^{m} \lambda_i g_i(x, f_1, f_2, \ldots, f_n).$$

The unknown constants λ_i are still called *Lagrange multipliers.*

A.7 References

A valuable mathematical encyclopedia is the *Mathematical Handbook for Engineers and Scientists* by Korn & Korn [1968]. Difficult integrals can be looked up in the *Table of Integrals, Series, and Products* by Gradshteyn & Ryzhik [1980]. All elementary and many special functions can be found in the *Handbook of Mathematical Functions with Formulas, Graphs, and Mathematical Tables* edited by Abramowitz & Stegan [1964]. Smaller collections of this kind of information may be found in Burington's *Handbook of Mathematical Tables and Formulas* [1973] and Dwight's *Tables of Integrals and Other Mathematical Data* [1964].

Chisholm provides an elementary treatment of vectors in *Vectors in Three-Dimensional Space* [1978], while Schey deals with differential operators applied to vectors in *Div, Grad, Curl, and All That: An Informal Text on Vector Calculus* [1973]. Generally useful mathematical tools are covered in many books, such as Hildebrand's *Methods of Applied Mathematics* [1952].

There is no shortage of books on probability and statistics. One such is Drake's *Fundamentals of Applied Probability Theory* [1967].

The calculus of variations is explained in *Methods of Mathematical Physics*, volume I, by Courant & Hilbert [1953] and *Calculus of Variations: With Applications to Physics & Engineering* by Weinstock [1974].

Least-squares methods often lead to problems that can be tackled using the pseudoinverse. Here one can recommend Albert's *Regression and the Moore–Penrose Pseudoinverse* [1972]. Gill, Murray, & Wright cover practical aspects of optimization problems in *Practical Optimization* [1981]. Deeper coverage of the theoretical issues can be found in Luenberger's *Introduction to Linear and Nonlinear Programming* [1973].

Numerical methods are covered in such books as *Elementary Numerical Analysis—an Algorithmic Approach* by Conte & de Boor [1972] and Hamming's *Numerical Methods for Scientists and Engineers* [1962].

Bibliography

The bibliography is divided into two sections. The first contains only references to books. The second contains only references to papers and reports.

Books

Abramowitz, M., & I.A. Stegan (eds.), *Handbook of Mathematical Functions with Formulas, Graphs, and Mathematical Tables*, National Bureau of Standards, United States Department of Commerce, 1964.

Aggarwal, J.K., R.O. Duda, & A. Rosenfeld (eds.), *Computer Methods in Image Analysis*, IEEE Press, New York, 1977.

Ahuja, N., & B.J. Schachter, *Pattern Models*, John Wiley & Sons, New York, 1983.

Albert, A., *Regression and the Moore–Penrose Pseudoinverse*, Academic Press, New York, 1972.

Andrews, H.C., *Computer Techniques in Image Processing*, Academic Press, New York, 1970.

Andrews, H.C. (ed.), *Digital Image Processing*, IEEE Press, New York, 1978.

Ballard, D.H., & C.M. Brown, *Computer Vision*, Prentice-Hall, Englewood Cliffs, New Jersey, 1982.

Barbe, D.F. (ed.), *Charge-Coupled Devices*, Springer-Verlag, New York, 1980.

Bernstein, R. (ed.), *Digital Image Processing for Remote Sensing*, IEEE Press, New York, 1978.

Blahut, R.E., *Fast Algorithms for Digital Signal Processing*, Addison-Wesley, Reading, Massachusetts, 1985.

Born, M., & E. Wolf, *Principles of Optics: Electromagnetic Theory of Propagation, Interference and Diffraction of Light*, Pergamon Press, Oxford, 1975.

Bracewell, R.N., *The Fourier Transform and Its Applications*, McGraw-Hill Book Co., New York, 1965 & 1978.

Brady, J.M. (ed.), *Computer Vision*, North-Holland Publishing Co., Amsterdam, 1981.

Brady, J.M., & R. Paul (eds.), *Robotics Research: The First International Symposium*, MIT Press, Cambridge, Massachusetts, 1984.

Burington, R.S., *Handbook of Mathematical Tables and Formulas*, Fifth Edition, McGraw-Hill Book Co., New York, 1973.

Carrier, G.F., & C.E. Pearson, *Partial Differential Equations: Theory and Technique*, Academic Press, New York, 1976.

Castleman, K.R., *Digital Image Processing*, Prentice-Hall, Englewood Cliffs, New Jersey, 1979.

Chisholm, J.S.R., *Vectors in Three-Dimensional Space*, Cambridge Univ. Press, Cambridge, 1978.

Conte, S.D., & C. de Boor, *Elementary Numerical Analysis—an Algorithmic Approach*, Second Edition, McGraw-Hill Book Co., New York, 1972.

Cornsweet, T.N., *Visual Perception*, Academic Press, New York, 1970.

Courant, R., & D. Hilbert, *Methods of Mathematical Physics*, Vol. I, John Wiley & Sons, New York, 1953.

Courant, R., & D. Hilbert, *Methods of Mathematical Physics*, Vol. II, John Wiley & Sons, New York, 1962.

Coxeter, H.S.M., *Regular Polyhedra*, Dover Publications, New York, 1973.

do Carmo, M.P., *Differential Geometry of Curves and Surfaces*, Prentice-Hall, Englewood Cliffs, New Jersey, 1976.

Dodd, G.G., & L. Rossol (eds.), *Computer Vision and Sensor-Based Robots*, Plenum Press, New York, 1979.

Drake, A.W., *Fundamentals of Applied Probability Theory*, McGraw-Hill Book Co., New York, 1967.

Driscoll, W.G., & W. Vaughan (eds.), *Handbook of Optics*, McGraw-Hill Book Co., New York, 1978.

Duda, R.O., & P.E. Hart, *Pattern Classification and Scene Analysis*, John Wiley & Sons, New York, 1973.

Dwight, H.B., *Tables of Integrals and Other Mathematical Data*, Macmillan, New York, 1964.

Evans, R.M., *The Perception of Color*, John Wiley & Sons, New York, 1974.

Everitt, B., *Cluster Analysis*, Halsted Press, New York, 1980.

Faugeras, O.D. (ed.), *Fundamentals in Computer Vision*, Cambridge Univ. Press, Cambridge, 1983.

Fejes Toth, L., *Regular Figures*, Pergamon Press, New York, 1964.

Frisby, J.P., *Seeing*, Oxford Univ. Press, Oxford, 1979.

Garabedian, P.R., *Partial Differential Equations*, John Wiley & Sons, New York, 1964.

Gardner, W.E. (ed.), *Machine-Aided Image Analysis, 1978*, The Institute of Physics, Bristol & London, 1979.

Gel'fand, I.M., & G.E. Shilov, *Generalized Functions: Properties & Operations*, Vol. I, Academic Press, New York, 1964.

Gibson, J.J., *The Perception of the Visual World*, Houghton Mifflin Co., Boston, 1950.

Gibson, J.J., *The Senses Considered as Perceptual Systems*, Houghton Mifflin Co., Boston, 1966.

Gibson, J.J., *The Ecological Approach to Visual Perception*, Houghton Mifflin Co., Boston, 1979.

Gill, P.E., W. Murray, & M.H. Wright, *Practical Optimization*, Academic Press, New York, 1981.

Gonzalez, R.C., & P. Wintz, *Digital Image Processing*, Addison-Wesley, Reading, Massachusetts, 1977.

Gradshteyn, I.S., & I.M. Ryzhik, *Table of Integrals, Series, and Products*, Academic Press, New York, 1980.

Grafton, C.B. (ed.), *Silhouettes—A Pictorial Archive of Varied Illustrations*, Dover Publications, New York, 1979.

Green, W.B., *Digital Image Processing: A Systems Approach*, Van Nostrand Reinhold Co., New York, 1983.

Gregory, R.L., *Eye and Brain*, McGraw-Hill Book Co., New York, 1966.

Gregory, R.L., *The Intelligent Eye*, McGraw-Hill Book Co., New York, 1970.

Grimson, W.E.L., *From Images to Surfaces: A Computational Study of the Human Early Visual System*, MIT Press, Cambridge, Massachusetts, 1981.

Grünbaum, B., *Convex Polytopes*, John Wiley & Sons, New York, 1967.

Haber, R.N., & M. Hershenson, *The Psychology of Visual Perception*, Holt, Rinehart & Winston Inc., New York, 1973.

Hall, E., *Computer Image Processing and Recognition*, Academic Press, New York, 1979.

Hamilton, W.R., *Elements of Quaternions*, Vols. 1 & 2, Chelsea Publishing, New York, 1899.

Hamming, R.W., *Numerical Methods for Scientists and Engineers*, McGraw-Hill Book Co., New York, 1962.

Hamming, R.W., *Digital Filters*, Prentice-Hall, Englewood Cliffs, New Jersey, 1977 & 1983.

Hanson, A.R., & E.M. Riseman (eds.), *Computer Vision Systems*, Academic Press, New York, 1978.

Herman, G.T. (ed.), *Image Reconstruction from Projections—Implementation and Applications*, Springer-Verlag, New York, 1979.

Hilbert, D., & S. Cohn-Vossen, *Geometry and the Imagination*, Chelsea Publishing Co., New York, 1952.

Hildebrand, F.B., *Methods of Applied Mathematics*, Prentice-Hall, Englewood Cliffs, New Jersey, 1952.

Hildreth, E.C., *The Measurement of Visual Motion*, MIT Press, Cambridge, Massachusetts, 1983.

Huang, T.S. (ed.), *Image Sequence Processing and Dynamic Scene Analysis*, Springer-Verlag, New York, 1983.

John, F., *Partial Differential Equations*, Springer-Verlag, New York, 1971.

Judd, D.B., & G. Wyszeck, *Color in Business, Science, and Industry*, John Wiley & Sons, New York, 1975.

Julesz, B., *Foundations of Cyclopean Perception*, Univ. of Chicago Press, Chicago, 1971.

Kanal, L.N. (ed.), *Pattern Recognition*, Thompson Book Co., Washington, D.C., 1980.

Kenner, H., *Geodesic Math—and How to Use It*, Univ. of California Press, Berkeley, California, 1976.

Kessel, R.G., & R.H. Kardon, *Tissues and Organs: A Text-Atlas of Scanning Electron Microscopy*, W.H. Freeman & Co., San Francisco, 1979.

Kingslake, R., *Lens Design Fundamentals*, Academic Press, New York, 1978.

Korn, G.A., & T.M. Korn, *Mathematical Handbook for Engineers and Scientists*, McGraw-Hill Book Co., New York, 1968.

Levi, L., *Applied Optics: A Guide to Optical System Design*, Vol. 1, 1968 & Vol. 2, 1980, John Wiley & Sons, New York.

Levine, M.D., *Vision in Man and Machine*, McGraw-Hill Book Co., New York, 1985.

Lighthill, M.J., *Introduction to Fourier Analysis and Generalised Functions*, Cambridge Univ. Press, Cambridge, 1978.

Luenberger, D.G., *Introduction to Linear and Nonlinear Programming*, Addison-Wesley, Reading, Massachusetts, 1973.

Lysternik, L.A., *Convex Figures and Polyhedra*, Dover Publications, New York, 1963.

MacAdam, D.L., *Sources of Color Science*, MIT Press, Cambridge, Massachusetts, 1970.

Marr, D., *Vision: A Computational Investigation into the Human Representation and Processing of Visual Information*, W.H. Freeman & Co., San Francisco, 1982.

Moon, P., *The Scientific Basis of Illumination Engineering*, Dover Publications, New York, 1961.

Moon, P., & D.E. Spencer, *Partial Differential Equations*, D.C. Heath & Co., Massachusetts, 1969.

Moon, P., & D.E. Spencer, *The Photic Field*, MIT Press, Cambridge, Massachusetts, 1981.

Moore, C.N., *Summable Series and Convergence Factors*, Dover Publications, New York, 1966.

Moravec, H.P., *Robot Rover Visual Navigation*, University Microfilms International, Ann Arbor, 1981.

Nevatia, R., *Machine Perception*, Prentice-Hall, Englewood Cliffs, New Jersey, 1982.

Norton, H.N., *Sensor and Analyzer Handbook*, Prentice-Hall, Englewood Cliffs, New Jersey, 1982.

O'Neill, B., *Elementary Differential Geometry*, Academic Press, New York, 1966.

Oppenheim, A.V., & A.S. Willsky, *Signals and Systems*, Prentice-Hall, Englewood Cliffs, New Jersey, 1983.

Pearce, P., & S. Pearce, *Polyhedra Primer*, Van Nostrand Reinhold Co., New York, 1978.

Pogorelov, A.V., *Differential Geometry*, Noordhoff, Groningen, The Netherlands, 1956 & 1979.

Pratt, W., *Digital Image Processing*, John Wiley & Sons, New York, 1978.

Pugh, A., *Polyhedra—A Visual Approach*, Univ. of California Press, Berkeley, California, 1976.

Pugh, A. (ed.), *Robot Vision*, IFS (Publications) Ltd., U.K., 1983.

Rock, I., *Perception*, Scientific American Books, New York, 1984.

Rosenfeld, A. (ed.), *Digital Picture Analysis*, Springer-Verlag, New York, 1976.

Rosenfeld, A., & A.C. Kak, *Digital Picture Processing*, Vols. 1 & 2, Second Edition, Academic Press, New York, 1982.

Scharf, D., *Magnifications—Photography with the Scanning Electron Microscope*, Schocken Books, New York, 1977.

Schey, H.M., *Div, Grad, Curl, and All That: An Informal Text on Vector Calculus*, W.W. Norton & Co., New York, 1973.

Sears, F.W., *Optics*, Addison-Wesley, Reading, Massachusetts, 1949.

Serra, J., *Image Analysis and Mathematical Morphology*, Academic Press, New York, 1982.

Shafer, S.A., *Shadows and Silhouettes in Computer Vision*, Kluwer Academic Press, Boston, 1985.

Siebert, W., *Circuits, Signals, and Systems*, MIT Press, Cambridge, Massachusetts, 1985.

Sokal, R.R., & P.H.A. Sneath, *Principles of Numerical Taxonomy*, W.H. Freeman & Co., San Francisco, 1963.

Stoffel, J.C. (ed.), *Graphical and Binary Image Processing and Applications*, Artech House, Inc., Massachusetts, 1982.

Stucki, P. (ed.), *Advances in Digital Image Processing: Theory, Application, Implementation*, Plenum Press, New York, 1979.

Tanimoto, S., & A. Klinger (eds.), *Structured Computer Vision: Machine Perception through Hierarchical Computation Structures*, Academic Press, New York, 1980.

Tikhonov, A.N., & V.Y. Arsenin, *Solutions of Ill-Posed Problems*, Winston & Sons, Washington, D.C., 1977.

Ullman, S., *The Interpretation of Visual Motion*, MIT Press, Cambridge, Massachusetts, 1979.

Ullman, S., & W. Richards (eds.), *Image Understanding 1984*, Ablex Publishing Corp., Norwood, New Jersey, 1984.

Wasserman, G.S., *Color Vision: An Historical Introduction*, John Wiley & Sons, New York, 1978.

Weinstock, R., *Calculus of Variations: With Applications to Physics & Engineering*, Dover Publications, New York, 1974.

Wells, O.C., *Scanning Electron Microscopy*, McGraw-Hill Book Co., New York, 1974.

Wenninger, M.J., *Polyhedron Models*, Cambridge Univ. Press, Cambridge, 1971.

Wenninger, M.J., *Spherical Models*, Cambridge Univ. Press, Cambridge, 1979.

Wiener, N., *Extrapolation, Interpolatation, and Smoothing of Stationary Time Series with Engineering Applications*, MIT Press, Cambridge, Massachusetts, 1966.

Winston, P.H. (ed.), *The Psychology of Computer Vision*, McGraw-Hill Book Co., New York, 1975.

Winston, P.H., *Artificial Intelligence*, Second Edition, Addison-Wesley, Reading, Massachusetts, 1984.

Winston, P.H., & R.H. Brown (eds.), *Artificial Intelligence: An MIT Perspective*, Vol. 2, MIT Press, Cambridge, Massachusetts, 1979.

Winston, P.H., & B.K.P. Horn, *Lisp*, Second Edition, Addison-Wesley, Reading, Massachusetts, 1984.

Wolf, P.R., *Elements of Photogrammetry*, McGraw-Hill Book Co., New York, 1974.

Papers

Adiv, G. (1984) "Determining 3-D Motion and Structure from Optical Flow Generated by Several Moving Objects," COINS Technical Report 84-07, Computer and Information Science, Univ. of Massachusetts, Amherst, Massachusetts, April.

Agin, G.J., & T.O. Binford (1973) "Computer Description of Curved Objects," *Proc. of the Intern. Joint Conf. on Artificial Intelligence*, Stanford, California, pp. 629–640, 20–23 August.

Ahmed, N., T. Natarjan, & K.R. Rao (1974) "On Image Processing and a Discrete Cosine Transform," *IEEE Trans. on Computers*, Vol. 23, No. 1, pp. 90–93, January.

Ahuja, N., & A. Rosenfeld (1981) "Mosaic Models for Textures," *IEEE Trans. on Pattern Analysis and Machine Intelligence*, Vol. 3, No. 1, pp. 1–11, January.

Alexandroff, A. (1942) "Existence and Uniqueness of a Convex Surface with a Given Integral Curvature," *Comptes Rendus (Doklady) de l'Académie des Sciences de l'URSS*, Vol. 35, No. 5, pp. 131–134.

Arcelli, C. (1981) "Pattern Thinning by Contour Tracing," *Computer Graphics and Image Processing*, Vol. 17, No. 3, pp. 130–144, October.

Arcelli, C., & S. Levialdi (1972) "Parallel Shrinking in Three Dimensions," *Computer Graphics and Image Processing*, Vol. 1, No. 1, pp. 21–30, April.

Asada, H., & J.M. Brady (1984) "The Curvature Primal Sketch," MIT AI Laboratory Memo 758, February.

Baird, M.L. (1978) "SIGHT-I: A Computer Vision System for Automated IC Chip Manufacture," *IEEE Trans. on Systems, Man and Cybernetics*, Vol. 8, No. 2, pp. 133–139, February.

Bajcsy, R. (1973) "Computer Identification of Visual Surfaces," *Computer Graphics and Image Processing*, Vol. 2, No. 2, pp. 118–130, October.

Bajcsy, R. (1980) "Three-Dimensional Scene Analysis," *Proc. Pattern Recognition Conf.*, Miami, Florida, pp. 1064–1074, 1–4 December.

Bajcsy, R., & L. Lieberman (1976) "Texture Gradient as a Depth Cue," *Computer Graphics and Image Processing*, Vol. 5, No. 1, pp. 52–67, March.

Baker, H.H., & T.O. Binford (1981) "Depth from Edges and Intensity Based Stereo," *Proc. of the Intern. Joint Conf. on Artificial Intelligence*, Vancouver, B.C., pp. 631–636, 24–28 August.

Baker, H.H., & T.O. Binford (1982) "A System for Automated Stereo Mapping," *Proc. Symp. ISPRS Commission II*, Ottawa, Canada.

Ballard, D.H., G.E. Hinton, & T.J. Sejnowshi (1983) "Parallel Visual Computation," *Nature*, Vol. 306, No. 5938, pp. 21–26, 3 November.

Ballard, D.H., & O.A. Kimball (1983) "Rigid Body Motion from Depth and Optical Flow," *Computer Vision, Graphics and Image Processing*, Vol. 22, No. 1, pp. 95–115, April.

Ballard, D.H., & D. Sabbah (1981a) "Detecting Object Orientation from Surface Normals," *Proc. Pattern Recognition Conf.*, München, pp. 63–67, December.

Ballard, D.H., & D. Sabbah (1981b) "On Shapes," *Proc. of the Intern. Joint Conf. on Artificial Intelligence*, Vancouver, B.C., pp. 607–612, 24–28 August.

Barnard, S.T. (1983) "Interpreting Perspective Images," *Artificial Intelligence*, Vol. 21, No. 4, pp. 435–462, November.

Barnard, S.T., & W.B. Thompson (1980) "Disparity Analysis of Images," *IEEE Trans. on Pattern Analysis and Machine Intelligence*, Vol. 2, No. 4, pp. 333–340, July.

Barrow, H.G., & R.J. Popplestone (1971) "Relational Descriptions in Picture Processing," in *Machine Intelligence 6*, B. Meltzer & D.M. Michie (eds.), Edinburgh Univ. Press, pp. 377–396.

Barrow, H.G., & J.M. Tenenbaum (1978) "Recovering Intrinsic Scene Characteristics from Images," in *Computer Vision Systems*, A.R. Hanson & E.M. Riseman (eds.), Academic Press, New York, pp. 3–26.

Barrow, H.G., & J.M. Tenenbaum (1981a) "Computational Vision," *Proc. of the IEEE*, Vol. 69, No. 5, pp. 572–595, May.

Barrow, H.G., & J.M. Tenenbaum (1981b) "Interpreting Line Drawings as Three-Dimensional Surfaces," *Artificial Intelligence*, Vol. 17, Nos. 1–3, pp. 75–116, August.

Bass, D.H. (1981) "Using the Video Lookup Table for Reflectivity Calculations: Specific Techniques and Graphic Results," *Computer Graphics and Image Processing*, Vol. 17, No. 3, pp. 249–261, November.

Bertram, S. (1969) "The UNAMACE and the Automatic Photomapper," *Photogrammetric Engineering*, Vol. 35, No. 6, pp. 569–576, June.

Berzins, V. (1984) "Accuracy of Laplacian Edge Detectors," *Computer Vision, Graphics and Image Processing*, Vol. 27, No. 2, pp. 195–210, August.

Besl, P., & R. Jain (1984) "Surface Characterization for Three-Dimensional Object Recognition in Depth Maps," RSD-TR-20-84, Center for Research on Integrated Manufacturing, Dept. of Electrical Engineering & Computer Science, Univ. of Michigan, Ann Arbor, Michigan, December.

Binford, T.O. (1971) "Visual Perception by Computer," *Proc. IEEE Systems Science and Cybernetics Conf.*, Miami, December.

Binford, T.O. (1981) "Inferring Surfaces from Images," *Artificial Intelligence*, Vol. 17, Nos. 1–3, pp. 205–244, August.

Binford, T.O. (1982) "Survey of Model-Based Image Analysis Systems," *The International Journal of Robotics Research*, Vol. 1, No. 1, pp. 18–64, Spring.

Blake, A. (1983) "The Least-Disturbance Principle and Weak Constraints," *Pattern Recognition Letters*, Vol. 1, Nos. 5 & 6, pp. 393–399, July.

Blake, A. (1985) "Boundary Conditions for Lightness Computation in Mondrian World," *Computer Vision, Graphics and Image Processing*, to appear.

Blum, H. (1967) "A Transformation for Extracting New Descriptors of Shape," *Proc. Symp. on Models for Perception of Speech and Visual Form*, W. Whaten-Dunn (ed.), MIT Press, Cambridge, Massachusetts.

Bolles, R.C., P. Horaud, & M.J. Hannah (1983) "3DPO: Three-Dimensional Parts Orientation System," *Proc. of the Intern. Joint Conf. on Artificial Intelligence*, Karlsruhe, West Germany, pp. 1116–1120, 8–12 August.

Boyse, J.W. (1979) "Interference Detection among Solids and Surfaces," *Communications of the ACM*, Vol. 22, No. 1, pp. 3–9, January.

Brady, J.M., & H. Asada (1984) "Smoothed Local Symmetries and Their Implementation," *The International Journal of Robotics Research*, Vol. 3, No. 3, pp. 36–61, Fall.

Brady, J.M., & B.K.P. Horn (1983) "Rotationally Symmetric Operators for Surface Interpolation," *Computer Vision, Graphics and Image Processing*, Vol. 22, No. 1, pp. 70–95, April.

Brassel, K. (1974) "A Model for Automatic Hill Shading," *The American Cartographer*, Vol. 1, No. 1, pp. 15–27, April.

Brenner, J.F., S. Gelsema, T.F. Necheles, P.W. Neurath, W.D. Selles, & E. Vastola (1974) "Automated Classification of Normal and Abnormal Leukocytes," *The Journal of Histochemistry & Cytochemistry*, Vol. 22, No. 7, pp. 697–706.

Brice, C.R., & C.L. Fennema (1970) "Scene Analysis Using Regions," *Artificial Intelligence*, Vol. 1, No. 3, pp. 205–226, Fall.

Brooks, M.J. (1978) "Rationalizing Edge Detectors," *Computer Graphics and Image Processing*, Vol. 8, No. 2, pp. 277–285, October.

Brooks, M.J. (1982) "Shape from Shading Discretely," Ph.D. Thesis, Essex Univ., Colchester, England.

Brooks, M.J., & B.K.P. Horn (1985) "Shape and Source from Shading," *Proc. of the Intern. Joint Conf. on Artificial Intelligence*, Los Angeles, California, pp. 932–936, 18–23 August.

Brooks, R.A. (1981) "Symbolic Reasoning among 3-D Models and 2-D Images," *Artificial Intelligence*, Vol. 17, Nos. 1–3, pp. 285–348, August.

Brou, P. (1983) "Finding Objects in Depth Maps," Ph.D. Thesis, Dept. of Electrical Engineering & Computer Science, MIT, Cambridge, Massachusetts, September.

Brou, P. (1984) "Using the Gaussian Image to Find the Orientation of Objects," *The International Journal of Robotics Research*, Vol. 3, No. 4, pp. 89–125, Winter.

Brown, C.M. (1977) "Representing the Orientation of Dendritic Fields with Geodesic Tessellations," Internal Report TR-13, Computer Science Dept., Univ. of Rochester.

Brown, C.M. (1983) "Inherent Bias and Noise in the Hough Transform," *IEEE Trans. on Pattern Analysis and Machine Intelligence*, Vol. 5, No. 5, pp. 493–505, September.

Bruss, A.R. (1981) "The Image Irradiance Equation: Its Solution and Application," MIT AI Laboratory Technical Report 623, June.

Bruss, A.R. (1982) "The Eikonal Equation: Some Results Applicable to Computer Vision," *Journal of Math. Physics*, Vol. 23, No. 5, pp. 890–896, May.

Bruss, A.R. (1983) "Is What You See What You Get?" *Proc. of the Intern. Joint Conf. on Artificial Intelligence*, Karlsruhe, West Germany, pp. 1053–1056, 8–12 August.

Bruss, A.R., & B.K.P. Horn (1983) "Passive Navigation," *Computer Vision, Graphics and Image Processing*, Vol. 21, No. 1, pp. 3–20, January.

Canny, J. (1983) "Finding Edges and Lines in Images," MIT AI Laboratory Technical Report 720, June.

Canny, J. (1984) "Collision Detection for Moving Polyhedra," MIT AI Laboratory Memo 806, October.

Chen, W.H., C.H. Smith, & S. Fralick (1977) "A Fast Computational Algorithm for the Discrete Cosine Transform," *IEEE Trans. on Communications*, Vol. 25, No. 9, pp. 1004–1009, September.

Chin, R.T. (1982) "Automated Visual Inspection Techniques and Applications: A Bibliography," *Pattern Recognition*, Vol. 15, No. 4, pp. 343–357.

Chin, R.T., & A. Harlow (1982) "Automated Visual Inspection: A Survey," *IEEE Trans. on Pattern Analysis and Machine Intelligence*, Vol. 4, No. 6, pp. 557–573, November.

Chrisman, D.P. (1984) "Programming the Connection Machine," S.M. Thesis, Dept. of Electrical Engineering & Computer Science, MIT, Cambridge, Massachusetts, November.

Clocksin, W.F. (1980) "Perception of Surface Slant and Edge Labels from Optical Flow: A Computational Approach," *Perception*, Vol. 9, No. 3, pp. 253–269.

Clowes, M.B. (1971) "On Seeing Things," *Artificial Intelligence*, Vol. 2, No. 1, pp. 79–116, Spring.

Cohen, F.S., & D.B. Cooper (1984) "Simple Parallel Hierarchical and Relaxation Algorithms for Segmenting Noncausal Markovian Random Fields," Internal Report LEMS-7, Laboratory for Man/Machine Systems, Brown Univ., Providence, Rhode Island, July.

Coleman Jr., E.N., & R. Jain (1982) "Obtaining 3-Dimensional Shape of Textured and Specular Surface Using Four-Source Photometry," *Computer Graphics and Image Processing*, Vol. 18, No. 4, pp. 309–328, April.

Cooper, D.B., F. Sung, & P.S. Schencker (1980) "Towards a Theory of Multiple-Window Algorithms for Fast Adaptive Boundary Finding in Computer Vision," Internal Report ENG-PRMI 80-3, Division of Engineering, Brown Univ., Providence, Rhode Island, July.

Dane, C., & R. Bajcsy (1981) "Three-Dimensional Segmentation Using the Gaussian Image and Spatial Information," *Proc. Pattern Recognition and Image Processing Conf.*, Dallas, Texas, pp. 54–56, 3–4 August.

Danielsson, P.-E. (1980) "Euclidian Distance Mapping," *Computer Graphics and Image Processing*, Vol. 14, No. 3, pp. 227–248, November.

Danielsson, P.-E., & B. Kruse (1979) "Distance Checking Algorithms," *Computer Graphics and Image Processing*, Vol. 11, No. 4, pp. 349–376, December.

Davis, L.S. (1975) "A Survey of Edge Detection Techniques," *Computer Graphics and Image Processing*, Vol. 4, No. 3, pp. 248–270, September.

Davis, L.S., & A. Rosenfeld (1980) "Cooperating Processes for Low-Level Vision: A Survey," Internal Report TR-851, Univ. of Maryland, College Park, Maryland, January.

Deift, P., & J. Sylvester (1981) "Some Remarks on the Shape-from-Shading Problem in Computer Vision," *Journal of Mathematical Analysis and Applications*, Vol. 84, No. 1, pp. 235–248, November.

De Souza, P. (1983) "Automatic Rib Detection in Chest Radiographs," *Computer Vision, Graphics and Image Processing*, Vol. 23, No. 2, pp. 129–161, August.

Deutsch, E.S. (1972) "Thinning Algorithms on Rectangular, Hexagonal, and Triangular Arrays," *Communications of the ACM*, Vol. 15, No. 9, pp. 827–837, September.

Dev, P. (1975) "Perception of Depth Surfaces in Random-Dot Stereograms: A Neural Model," *International Journal of Man-Machine Studies*, Vol. 7, No. 4, pp. 511–528, July.

Draper, S.W. (1981) "The Use of Gradient Space and Dual Space in Line-Drawing Interpretation," *Artificial Intelligence*, Vol. 17, Nos. 1–3, pp. 461–460, August.

Dreschler L., & H.-H. Nagel (1982) "Volumetric Model and 3D Trajectory of a Moving Car Derived From Monocular TV Frame Sequences of a Street Scene," *Computer Graphics and Image Processing*, Vol. 20, No. 3, pp. 199–228, November.

Duda, R.O., & P.E. Hart (1972) "Use of the Hough Transformation to Detect Lines and Curves in Pictures," *Communications of the ACM*, Vol. 15, No. 1, pp. 11–15, January.

Duda, R.O., D. Nitzan, & P. Barrett (1979) "Use of Range and Reflectance Data to Find Planar Surface Regions," *IEEE Trans. on Pattern Analysis and Machine Intelligence*, Vol. 1, No. 3, pp. 259–271, July.

Duerr, B, W. Haettich, H. Tropf, & G. Winkler (1980) "A Combination of Statistical and Syntactical Pattern Recognition Applied to Classification of Unconstrained Handwritten Numerals," *Pattern Recognition*, Vol. 12, No. 3, pp. 189–199.

Dyer, C.R., & A. Rosenfeld (1979) "Thinning Algorithms for Gray-Scale Pictures," *IEEE Trans. on Pattern Analysis and Machine Intelligence*, Vol. 1, No. 1, pp. 88–89, January.

Ehrich, R.W. (1977) "Detection of Global Edges in Textured Images," *IEEE Trans. on Computers*, Vol. 26, No. 6, pp. 589–603, June.

Ejiri, M., T. Uno, M. Mese, & S. Ikeda (1973) "A Process for Detecting Defects in Complicated Patterns," *Computer Graphics and Image Processing*, Vol. 2, Nos. 3 & 4, pp. 326–339, December.

Fahle, M., & T. Poggio (1980) "Visual Hyperacuity: Spatiotemporal Interpolation in Human Vision," *Proc. of the Royal Society of London B*, Vol. 213, pp. 415–477.

Falk, G. (1972) "Interpretation of Imperfect Line Data as a Three-Dimensional Scene," *Artificial Intelligence*, Vol. 3, No. 2, pp. 101–144, Summer.

Fang, J.Q., & T.S. Huang (1984a) "Solving Three-Dimensional Small-Rotation Motion Equations: Uniqueness, Algorithms, and Numerical Results," *Computer Vision, Graphics and Image Processing*, Vol. 26, No. 2, pp. 183–206, May.

Fang, J.Q., & T.S. Huang (1984b) "Some Experiments on Estimating the 3-D Motion Parameters of a Rigid Body from Two Consecutive Image Frames," *IEEE Trans. on Pattern Analysis and Machine Intelligence*, Vol. 6, No. 5, pp. 545–554, September.

Fennema, C.L., & W.R. Thompson (1979) "Velocity Determination in Scenes Containing Several Moving Objects," *Computer Graphics and Image Processing*, Vol. 9, No. 4, pp. 301–315, April.

Fesenkov, V. (1962) "Photometry of the Moon," in *Physics and Astronomy of the Moon*, Z. Kopal (ed.), Academic Press, New York, pp. 99–130.

Fischler, M.A., & R.C. Bolles (1981) "Random Sample Consensus: A Paradigm for Model Fitting with Applications to Image Analysis and Automated Cartography," *Communications of the ACM*, Vol. 24, No. 6, pp. 381–395, June.

Fram, J.R., & E.S. Deutsch (1975) "On the Evaluation of Edge Detection Schemes and Their Comparison with Human Performance," *IEEE Trans. on Computers*, Vol. 24, No. 6, pp. 616–628, June.

Freeman, H. (1960) "Techniques for the Digital Computer Analysis of Chain-Encoded Arbitrary Plane Curves," *Proc. National Electronics Conf.*, Chicago, Illinois, Vol. 17, pp. 421–432, 9–11 October.

Freuder, E.C. (1976) "A Computer System for Visual Recognition using Active Knowledge," MIT AI Laboratory Technical Report 345, June.

Freuder, E.C. (1980) "On the Knowledge Required to Label a Picture Graph," *Artificial Intelligence*, Vol. 15, Nos. 1 & 2, pp. 1–17, November.

Ganapathy, S. (1984) "Decomposition of Transformation Matrices for Robot Vision," *Proc. IEEE Conf. on Robotics*, Atlanta, Georgia, pp. 130–139, 13–15 March.

Geman, S., & D. Geman (1983) "Stochastic Relaxation, Gibbs Distributions, and the Bayesian Restoration of Images," Internal Report, Brown Univ., Providence, Rhode Island, and Univ. of Massachusetts at Amherst.

Gibson, E.J., J.J. Gibson, O.W. Smith, & H. Flock (1959) "Motion Parallax as a Determinant of Perceived Depth," *Journal of Experimental Psychology*, Vol. 8, No. 1, pp. 40–51.

Gibson L., & D. Lucas (1982) "Vectorization of Raster Images Using Hierarchical Methods," *Computer Graphics and Image Processing*, Vol. 20, No. 2, pp. 82–89, September.

Golay, M.J.E. (1969) "Hexagonal Parallel Pattern Transformations," *IEEE Trans. on Computers*, Vol. 18, No. 8, pp. 733–740, August.

Gonzalez, R.C., & R. Safabakhsh (1982) "Computer Vision Techniques for Industrial Applications and Robot Control," *Computer*, Vol. 15, No. 12, pp. 17–32, December.

Gray, S.B. (1971) "Local Properties of Binary Images in Two Dimensions," *IEEE Trans. on Computers*, Vol. 20, No. 5, pp. 551–561, May.

Griffith, A.K. (1973a) "Edge Detection in Simple Scenes Using *A Priori* Information," *IEEE Trans. on Computers*, Vol. 22, No. 4, pp. 371–381, April.

Griffith, A.K. (1973b) "Mathematical Models for Automatic Line Detection," *Journal of the ACM*, Vol. 20, No. 1, pp. 62–80, January.

Grimson, W.E.L. (1982) "A Computational Theory of Visual Surface Interpolation," *Philosophical Trans. of the Royal Society of London B*, Vol. 298, pp. 395–427.

Grimson, W.E.L. (1983a) "Surface Consistency Constraints in Vision," *Computer Vision, Graphics and Image Processing*, Vol. 24, No. 1, pp. 28–51, October.

Grimson, W.E.L. (1983b) "An Implementation of a Computational Theory of Visual Surface Interpolation," *Computer Vision, Graphics and Image Processing*, Vol. 22, No. 1, pp. 39–69, April.

Grimson, W.E.L. (1984) "On the Reconstruction of Visible Surfaces," Chapter 9 in *Image Understanding 1984*, S. Ullman & W. Richards (eds.), Ablex Publishing Corp., Norwood, New Jersey.

Gruen, A.W. (1985) "Adaptive Least Squares Correlation—A Powerful Image Matching Technique," *Proc. ACSM-ASP Convention*, Washington, D.C., March.

Gupta, J.N., & P.A. Wintz (1975) "A Boundary Finding Algorithm and Its Application," *IEEE Trans. on Circuits and Systems*, Vol. 22, No. 4, pp. 351–362, April.

Gurari, E.M., & H. Wechsler (1982) "On the Difficulties Involved in the Segmentation of Pictures," *IEEE Trans. on Pattern Analysis and Machine Intelligence*, Vol. 4, No. 3, pp. 304–306, May.

Guzmán-Arenas, A. (1968a) "Decomposition of a Visual Scene into Three-Dimensional Bodies," *Proc. AFIPS Fall Joint Computer Conf.*, San Francisco, California, Vol. 33, pp. 291–304, 9–11 December.

Guzmán-Arenas, A. (1968b) "Computer Recognition of Three-Dimensional Objects in a Visual Scene," MIT AI Laboratory Technical Report 228, December.

Habibi, A. (1972) "Two Dimensional Bayesian Estimation of Images," *Proc. of the IEEE*, Vol. 60, No. 7, pp. 878–883, July.

Hafford, K.J., & K. Preston, Jr. (1984) "Three-Dimensional Skeletonization of Elongated Solids," *Computer Vision, Graphics and Image Processing*, Vol. 27, No. 1, pp. 78–91, July.

Hansen, F.R., & H. Elliott (1982) "Image Segmentation Using Markov Field Models," *Computer Graphics and Image Processing*, Vol. 20, No. 2, pp. 101–132, October.

Hara, Y., A. Akiyama, & K. Karasaki (1983) "Automatic Inspection System for Printed Circuit Boards," *IEEE Trans. on Pattern Analysis and Machine Intelligence*, Vol. 5, No. 6, pp. 623–630, November.

Haralick, R.M. (1980) "Edge and Region Analysis for Digital Image Data," *Computer Graphics and Image Processing*, Vol. 12, No. 1, pp. 60–73, January.

Haralick, R.M. (1984) "Digital Step Edges from Zero Crossing of Second Directional Derivatives," *IEEE Trans. on Pattern Analysis and Machine Intelligence*, Vol. 6, No. 1, pp. 58–68, January.

Haralick, R.M., & L. Watson (1981) "A Facet Model for Image Data," *Computer Graphics and Image Processing*, Vol. 15, No. 2, pp. 113–129, February.

Hartley, R. (1985) "A Gaussian-Weighted Multi-Resolution Edge Detector," *Computer Vision, Graphics and Image Processing*, Vol. 30, No. 1, pp. 70–83, April.

Hay, C.J. (1966) "Optical Motion and Space Perception—An Extension of Gibson's Analysis," *Psychological Review*, Vol. 73, pp. 550–565.

Haynes, S.M., & R. Jain (1982) "Detection of Moving Edges," *Computer Vision, Graphics and Image Processing*, Vol. 21, No. 3, pp. 345–367, March.

Herman, G.T., & D. Webster (1983) "A Topological Proof of a Surface Tracking Algorithm," *Computer Vision, Graphics and Image Processing*, Vol. 23, No. 2, pp. 162–177, August.

Hildreth, E.C. (1980) "Implementation of a Theory of Edge Detection," MIT AI Laboratory Technical Report 579, April.

Hildreth, E.C. (1983) "The Detection of Intensity Changes by Computer and Biological Vision Systems," *Computer Vision, Graphics and Image Processing*, Vol. 22, No. 1, pp. 1–27, April.

Hildreth, E.C. (1984) "Computations Underlying the Measurement of Visual Motion," *Artificial Intelligence*, Vol. 23, No. 3, pp. 309–354, August.

Hoffman, D.D. (1983) "Representing Shapes for Visual Recognition," Ph.D. Thesis, Dept. of Psychology, MIT, Cambridge, Massachusetts.

Hoffman D.D., & B.E. Flinchbaugh (1982) "The Interpretation of Biological Motion," *Biological Cybernetics*, Vol. 42, No. 3, pp. 195–204.

Holland, S.W., L. Rossol, & M.R. Ward (1979) "CONSIGHT-I: A Vision-Controlled Robot System for Transferring Parts from Belt Conveyors," in *Computer Vision and Sensor-Based Robotics*, G.G. Dodd & L. Rossol (eds.), Plenum Press, New York, pp. 81–100.

Horn, B.K.P. (1970) "Shape from Shading: A Method for Obtaining the Shape of a Smooth Opaque Object from One View," MIT Project MAC Internal Report TR-79 & MIT AI Laboratory Technical Report 232, November.

Horn, B.K.P. (1971) "The Binford–Horn Linefinder," MIT AI Laboratory Memo 285, July.

Horn, B.K.P. (1972) "VISMEM: A Bag of 'Robotics' Formulae," MIT AI Laboratory Working Paper 34, December.

Horn, B.K.P. (1974) "Determining Lightness from an Image," *Computer Graphics and Image Processing*, Vol. 3, No. 1, pp. 277–299, December.

Horn, B.K.P. (1975a) "Obtaining Shape from Shading Information," Chapter 4 in *The Psychology of Computer Vision*, P.H. Winston (ed.), McGraw-Hill Book Co., New York, pp. 115–155.

Horn, B.K.P. (1975b) "A Problem in Computer Vision: Orienting Silicon Integrated Circuit Chips for Lead Bonding," *Computer Graphics and Image Processing*, Vol. 4, No. 1, pp. 294–303, September.

Horn, B.K.P. (1977) "Image Intensity Understanding," *Artificial Intelligence*, Vol. 8, No. 2, pp. 201–231, April.

Horn, B.K.P. (1979) "Sequins and Quills—Representations for Surface Topography," MIT AI Laboratory Memo 536, May.

Horn, B.K.P. (1981) "Hill-Shading and the Reflectance Map," *Proc. of the IEEE*, Vol. 69, No. 1, pp. 14–47, January.

Horn, B.K.P. (1983) "The Least Energy Curve," *ACM Trans. on Mathematical Software*, Vol. 9, No. 4, pp. 441–460, December.

Horn, B.K.P. (1984a) "Exact Reproduction of Colored Images," *Computer Vision, Graphics and Image Processing*, Vol. 26, No. 2, pp. 135–167, May.

Horn, B.K.P. (1984b) "Extended Gaussian Images," *Proc. of the IEEE*, Vol. 72, No. 12, pp. 1671–1686, December.

Horn, B.K.P., & B.L. Bachman (1978) "Using Synthetic Images to Register Real Images with Surface Models," *Communications of the ACM*, Vol. 21, No. 11, pp. 914–924, November.

Horn, B.K.P., & M.J. Brooks (1985) "The Variational Approach to Shape from Shading," MIT AI Laboratory Memo 813, March.

Horn, B.K.P., & K. Ikeuchi (1984) "The Mechanical Manipulation of Randomly Oriented Parts," *Scientific American*, Vol. 251, No. 2, pp. 100–111, August.

Horn, B.K.P., & B.G. Schunck (1981) "Determining Optical Flow," *Artificial Intelligence*, Vol. 17, Nos. 1–3, pp. 185–203, August.

Horn, B.K.P., & R.W. Sjoberg (1979) "Calculating the Reflectance Map," *Applied Optics*, Vol. 18, No. 11, pp. 1770–1779, June.

Horn, B.K.P., & E.J. Weldon (1985) "Filtering Closed Curves," *Proc. Computer Vision and Pattern Recognition Conf.* San Francisco, California, pp. 478–484, 19–23 June.

Horn, B.K.P., R.J. Woodham, & W. Silver (1978) "Determining Shape and Reflectance Using Multiple Images," MIT AI Laboratory Memo 490, August.

Hou, H.S., & H.C. Andrews (1978) "Cubic Splines for Image Interpolation and Digital Filtering," *IEEE Trans. on Acoustics, Speech, and Signal Processing*, Vol. 26, No. 6, pp. 508–517, December.

Hsieh, Y.Y., & K.S. Fu (1980) "An Automatic Visual Inspection System for Integrated Circuit Chips," *Computer Graphics and Image Processing*, Vol. 14, No. 4, pp. 293–343, December.

Huang, T.S., W.F. Schreiber, & O.J. Tretiak (1971) "Image Processing," *Proc. of the IEEE*, Vol. 59, No. 11, pp. 1586–1609, November.

Hueckel, M. (1971) "An Operator Which Locates Edges in Digital Pictures," *Journal of the ACM*, Vol. 18, No. 1, pp. 113–125, January.

Hueckel, M. (1973) "A Local Visual Operator Which Recognizes Edges and Lines," *Journal of the ACM*, Vol. 20, No. 4, pp. 634–647, October.

Huffman, D.A. (1971) " Impossible Objects as Nonsense Sentences," in *Machine Intelligence 6*, B. Meltzer & D.M. Michie (eds.), Edinburgh Univ. Press, pp. 295–323.

Huffman, D.A. (1975) "Curvature and Creases: A Primer on Paper," *Proc. Conf. Computer Graphics, Pattern Recognition, & Data Structure*, pp. 360–370, 14–16 May.

Huffman, D.A. (1977a) "A Duality Concept for the Analysis of Polyhedral Scenes," in *Machine Intelligence 8*, E.W. Elcock & D.M. Michie (eds.), Ellis Horwood, Chichester, pp. 475–492.

Huffman, D.A. (1977b) "Realizable Configurations of Lines in Pictures of Polyhedra," in *Machine Intelligence 8*, E.W. Elcock & D.M. Michie (eds.), Ellis Horwood, Chichester, pp. 493–509.

Hummel, R.A., & S.W. Zucker (1980) "On the Foundations of Relaxation Labeling Processes," Internal Report TR-80-7, Computer Vision and Graphics Lab., Dept. of Electrical Engineering, McGill Univ., Montreal, July.

Ikeuchi, K. (1981a) "Recognition of 3-D Objects Using the Extended Gaussian Image," *Proc. of the Intern. Joint Conf. on Artificial Intelligence*, Vancouver, B.C., pp. 595–600, 24–28 August.

Ikeuchi, K. (1981b) "Determining Surface Orientations of Specular Surfaces by Using the Photometric Stereo Method," *IEEE Trans. on Pattern Analysis and Machine Intelligence*, Vol. 3, No. 6, pp. 661–669, November.

Ikeuchi, K. (1983) "Determining the Attitude of an Object from a Needle Map Using the Extended Gaussian Image," MIT AI Laboratory Memo 714, April.

Ikeuchi, K. (1984) "Shape from Regular Patterns," *Artificial Intelligence*, Vol. 22, No. 1, pp. 49–75, January.

Ikeuchi, K. (1985) "Determining a Depth Map Using Region Matching on Surface-Orientation Maps Obtained by a Pair of Photometric Stereo Systems," Internal Report 85-2E, Information Processing Group, Electrotechnical Laboratory, Sakura-mura, Ibaraki 305, Japan.

Ikeuchi, K., & B.K.P. Horn (1981) "Numerical Shape from Shading and Occluding Boundaries," *Artificial Intelligence*, Vol. 17, Nos. 1–3, pp. 141–184, August.

Ikeuchi, K., & B.K.P. Horn (1984) "Picking up an Object from a Pile of Objects," in *Robotics Research: The First International Symposium*, J.M. Brady & R. Paul (eds.), MIT Press, Cambridge, Massachusetts, pp. 139–162.

Ikeuchi, K., H.K. Nishihara, B.K.P. Horn, P. Sobalvarro, & S. Nagata, (1984) "Determining Grasp Points Using Photometric Stereo and the PRISM Binocular Stereo System," MIT AI Laboratory Memo 772, August.

Ingram, M., & K. Preston, Jr. (1970) "Automatic Analysis of Blood Cells," *Scientific American*, Vol. 223, No. 5, pp. 72–82, November.

Jacobus, C.J., & R.T. Chien (1981) "Two New Edge Detectors," *IEEE Trans. on Pattern Analysis and Machine Intelligence*, Vol. 3, No. 5, pp. 581–592, September.

Jain, R. (1981) "Extraction of Motion Information from Peripheral Process," *IEEE Trans. on Pattern Analysis and Machine Intelligence*, Vol. 3, No. 5, pp. 489–503, September.

Jain, R. (1983) "Direct Computation of the Focus of Expansion," *IEEE Trans. on Pattern Analysis and Machine Intelligence*, Vol. 5, No. 1, pp. 58–64, January.

Jain, R., & J.K. Aggarwal (1979) "Computer Analysis of Scenes with Curved Objects," *Proc. of the IEEE*, Vol. 67, No. 5, pp. 805–812, May.

Jarvis, R.A. (1983a) "A Perspective on Range Finding Techniques for Computer Vision," *IEEE Trans. on Pattern Analysis and Machine Intelligence*, Vol. 5, No. 2, pp. 122–139, March.

Jarvis, R.A. (1983b) "A Laser Time-of-Flight Range Scanner for Robotic Vision," *IEEE Trans. on Pattern Analysis and Machine Intelligence*, Vol. 5, No. 5, pp. 505–512, September.

Jerian, C., & R. Jain (1984) "Determining Motion Parameters for Scenes with Translation and Rotation," *IEEE Trans. on Pattern Analysis and Machine Intelligence*, Vol. 6, No. 4, pp. 523–530, July.

Kanade, T. (1980a) "Region Segmentation: Signal vs. Semantics," *Computer Graphics and Image Processing*, Vol. 13, No. 4, pp. 279–297, August.

Kanade, T. (1980b) "A Theory of Origami World," *Artificial Intelligence*, Vol. 13, No. 3, pp. 279–311, May.

Kanade, T. (1981) "Recovery of the Three-Dimensional Shape of an Object from a Single View," *Artificial Intelligence*, Vol. 17, Nos. 1–3, pp. 409–460, August.

Kanade, T. (1983) "Geometrical Aspects of Interpreting Images as a Three-Dimensional Scene," *Proc. of the IEEE*, Vol. 71, No. 7, pp. 789–802, July.

Kashioka, S., M. Ejiri, & Y. Sakamoto (1976) "A Transistor Wire-Bonding System Utilizing Multiple Local Pattern Matching Techniques," *IEEE Trans. on Systems, Man and Cybernetics*, Vol. 6, No. 8, pp. 562–570, August.

Keating, T.J., P.R. Wolf, & F.L. Scarpace (1975) "An Improved Method of Digital Image Correlation," *Photogrammetric Engineering and Remote Sensing*, Vol. 41, No. 8, pp. 993–1002, August.

Kelley, R.B., J.R. Birk, H.A.S. Martins, & R. Tella (1982) "A Robot System Which Acquires Cylindrical Workpieces from Bins," *IEEE Trans. on Systems, Man and Cybernetics*, Vol. 12, No. 2, pp. 204–213, March/April.

Kelly, R.E., P.R.H. McConnell, & S.J. Mildenberger (1977) "The Gestalt Photomapping System," *Photogrammetric Engineering and Remote Sensing*, Vol. 43, No. 11, pp. 1407–1417, November.

Kirousis, L., & C.H. Papadimitriou (1984) "The Complexity of Recognizing Polyhedral Scenes," Internal Report STAN-CS-84-105, Dept. of Computer Science, Stanford Univ., Stanford, California, August.

Klette, R. (1980) "Parallel Operations on Binary Images," *Computer Graphics and Image Processing*, Vol. 14, No. 2, pp. 145–158, October.

Koenderink, J.J., & A.J. van Doorn (1976) "Local Structure of Movement Parallax of the Plane," *Journal of the Optical Society of America*, Vol. 66, No. 7, pp. 717–723, July.

Koenderink, J.J., & A.J. van Doorn (1980) "Photometric Invariants Related to Solid Shape," *Acta Optica*, Vol. 27, No. 7, pp. 981–996, July.

Konecny, G., & D. Pape (1981) "Correlation Techniques and Devices," *Photogrammetric Engineering and Remote Sensing*, Vol. 47, No. 3, pp. 323–333, March.

Kulpa, Z. (1977) "Area and Perimeter Measurement of Blobs in Discrete Binary Pictures," *Computer Graphics and Image Processing*, Vol. 6, No. 5, pp. 434–451, October.

Land, E.H. (1959) "Experiments in Color Vision," *Scientific American*, Vol. 200, No. 5, pp. 84–99, May.

Land, E.H. (1964) "The Retinex," *American Scientist*, Vol. 52, No. 2, pp. 247–264, June.

Land, E.H. (1983) "Recent Advances in Retinex Theory and Some Implications for Cortical Computations: Color Vision and the Natural Image," *Proc. Nat'l Acad. Sci.*, Vol. 80, No. 16, pp. 5163–5169, August.

Land, E.H., & J.J. McCann (1971) "Lightness and Retinex Theory," *Journal of the Optical Society of America*, Vol. 61, No. 1, pp. 1–11, January.

Lavin, M.A., & L.I. Lieberman (1982) "AML/V: An Industrial Machine Vision Programming System," *The International Journal of Robotics Research*, Vol. 1, No. 3, pp. 42–56, Fall.

Lee, C.-H. (1983) "Improved Methods of Estimating Shape from Shading Using the Light Source Coordinate System," TR-1277, Computer Vision Laboratory, Computer Science Center, Univ. of Maryland, College Park, Maryland, October.

Lettvin, J.Y. (1967) "The Color of Colored Things," Quarterly Progress Report 87, Research Laboratory of Electronics, MIT.

Levialdi, S. (1972) "On Shrinking Binary Picture Patterns," *Communications of the ACM*, Vol. 15, No. 1, pp. 7–10, January.

Levine, M.D., D.A. O'Handley, & G.M. Yagi (1973) "Computer Determination of Depth Maps," *Computer Graphics and Image Processing*, Vol. 2, No. 2, pp. 131–150, October.

Limb, J.O., & J.A. Murphy (1975) "Estimating the Velocity of Moving Images in Television Signals," *Computer Graphics and Image Processing*, Vol. 4, No. 4, pp. 311–327, December.

Little, J.J. (1983) "An Iterative Method for Reconstructing Convex Polyhedra from Extended Gaussian Images," *Proc. of the National Conf. on Artificial Intelligence*, Washington, D.C., pp. 247–254, 22–26 August.

Little, J.J. (1985) "Determining Object Attitude from Extended Gaussian Images," *Proc. of the Intern. Joint Conf. on Artificial Intelligence*, Los Angeles, California, pp. 960–963, 18–23 August.

Livingstone, M.S., & D.H. Hubel (1984) "Anatomy and Physiology of a Color System in the Primate Visual Cortex," *The Journal of Neuroscience*, Vol. 4, No. 1, pp. 309–356.

Lobregt, S., P.W. Verbeek, & F.C.A. Groen (1980) "Three-Dimensional Skeletonization: Principle and Algorithm," *IEEE Trans. on Pattern Analysis and Machine Intelligence*, Vol. 2, No. 1, pp. 75–77, January.

Longuet-Higgins, H.C. (1981) "A Computer Algorithm for Reconstructing a Scene from Two Projections," *Nature*, Vol. 293, No. 5828, pp. 133–135, 10 September.

Longuet-Higgins, H.C., & K. Prazdny (1980) "The Interpretation of a Moving Retinal Image," *Proc. of the Royal Society of London B*, Vol. 208, pp. 385–397.

Lozano-Pérez, T. (1983) "Spatial Planning: A Configuration Space Approach," *IEEE Trans. on Computers*, Vol. 32, No. 2, pp. 108–120, February.

Mackworth, A.K. (1973) "Interpreting Pictures of Polyhedral Scenes," *Artificial Intelligence*, Vol. 4, No. 2, pp. 121–137, Summer.

Mackworth, A.K. (1977) "How to See a Simple World," in *Machine Intelligence 8*, E.W. Elcock & D.M. Michie (eds.), Ellis Horwood, Chichester, pp. 510–537.

MacLeod, I.D.G. (1970a) "A Study in Automatic Photo-Interpretation," Ph.D. Thesis, Dept. of Engineering Physics, Australian National Univ., Canberra, Australia, March.

MacLeod, I.D.G. (1970b) "On Finding Structure in Pictures," in *Picture Language Machines*, S. Kaneff (ed.), Academic Press, London, pp. 231–256.

Malik, J. (1985) "Interpretation of Line Drawings of Curved Objects," Ph.D. Thesis, Dept. of Computer Science, Stanford Univ., Stanford, California.

Marr, D. (1974) "The Computation of Lightness by the Primate Retina," *Vision Research*, Vol. 14, pp. 1377–1388.

Marr, D. (1976) "Early Processing of Visual Information," *Philosophical Trans. of the Royal Society of London B*, Vol. 275, pp. 483–524.

Marr, D. (1977) "Analysis of Occluding Contour," *Proc. of the Royal Society of London B*, Vol. 197, pp. 441–475.

Marr, D. (1980) "Visual Information Processing: The Structure and Creation of Visual Representations," *Philosophical Trans. of the Royal Society of London B*, Vol. 29, pp. 199–218.

Marr, D., & E. Hildreth (1980) "Theory of Edge Detection," *Proc. of the Royal Society of London B*, Vol. 207, pp. 187–217.

Marr, D., & N.K. Nishihara (1978) "Representation and Recognition of the Spatial Organization of Three-Dimensional Structure," *Proc. of the Royal Society of London B*, Vol. 200, pp. 269–294.

Marr, D., G. Palm, & T. Poggio (1978) "Analysis of a Cooperative Stereo Algorithm," *Biological Cybernetics*, Vol. 28, No. 4, pp. 223–239.

Marr, D., & T. Poggio (1976) "Cooperative Computation of Stereo Disparity," *Science*, Vol. 194, No. 4262, pp. 283–287, 15 October.

Marr, D., & T. Poggio (1979) "A Computational Theory of Human Stereo Vision," *Proc. of the Royal Society of London B*, Vol. 204, pp. 301–328.

Marr, D., & S. Ullman (1981) "Directional Selectivity and Its Use in Early Visual Processing," *Proc. of the Royal Society of London B*, Vol. 211, pp. 151–180.

Marroquin, J.L. (1984) "Surface Reconstruction Preserving Discontinuities," MIT AI Laboratory Memo 792, August.

Marroquin, J.L. (1985) "Optimal Bayesian Estimators for Image Segmentation and Surface Reconstruction," MIT AI Laboratory Memo 839, April.

Maybank, S.J. (1984) "The Angular Velocity Associated with the Optical Flow Field Due to a Single Moving Rigid Plane," *Proc. of the Sixth European Conf. on Artificial Intelligence*, Elsevier, Dordrecht, The Netherlands, pp. 641–644, September.

Mayhew, J.E.W. (1982) "The Interpretation of Stereo-Disparity Information: The Computation of Surface Orientation and Depth," *Perception*, Vol. 11, No. 4, pp. 387–403.

Mayhew, J.E.W., & J.P. Frisby (1981) "Psychophysical and Computational Studies towards a Theory of Human Stereopsis," *Artificial Intelligence*, Vol. 17, Nos. 1–3, pp. 379–386, August.

Mayhew, J.E.W., & H.C. Longuet-Higgins (1984) "A Computational Model of Binocular Depth Perception," Chapter 5 in *Image Understanding 1984*, S. Ullman & W. Richards (eds.), Ablex Publishing Corp., Norwood, New Jersey.

McCann, J.J., E.H. Land, & S.M.V. Tatnall (1970) "A Technique for Comparing Human Visual Responses with a Mathematical Model for Lightness," *American Journal of Optometry*, Vol. 47, No. 11, pp. 845–855, November.

Mersereau, R.M. (1979) "The Processing of Hexagonally-Sampled Two-Dimensional Signals," *Proc. of the IEEE*, Vol. 67, No. 6, pp. 930–949, June.

Michalski, R.S., & R.E. Stepp (1983) "Automated Construction of Classifications: Conceptual Clustering Versus Numerical Taxonomy," *IEEE Trans. on Pattern Analysis and Machine Intelligence*, Vol. 5, No. 4, pp. 396–410, July.

Minkowski, H. (1897) "Allgemeine Lehrsätze über die konvexen Polyeder," *Nachrichten von der Königlichen Gesellschaft der Wissenschaften, mathematisch-physikalische Klasse*, Göttingen, pp. 198–219.

Minnaert, M. (1961) "Photometry of the Moon," in *Planets and Satellites*, Vol. 3, G.P. Kuiper & B.M. Middlehurst (eds.), Univ. of Chicago Press, Chicago, pp. 213–248.

Mitchell, J.L., & G. Goertzel (1979) "Two-Dimensional Facsimile Coding Scheme," IBM Research Report RC 7499, January.

Modestino, J.W., & R.W. Fries (1977) "Edge Detection in Noisy Images Using Recursive Digital Filtering," *Computer Graphics and Image Processing*, Vol. 6, No. 5, pp. 409–433, October.

Mori, K., H. Genchi, S. Watanabe, & S. Katsuragi (1970) "Microprogram Controlled Pattern Processing in a Handwritten Mail Reader-Sorter," *Pattern Recognition*, Vol. 2, No. 3, pp. 175–185, September.

Mori, K., M. Kidode, & H. Asada (1973) "An Iterative Prediction and Correction Method for Automatic Stereocomparison," *Computer Graphics and Image Processing*, Vol. 2, Nos. 3 & 4, pp. 393–401, December.

Mori, S., K. Yamamoto, & M. Yasuda (1984) "Research on Machine Recognition of Handprinted Characters," *IEEE Trans. on Pattern Analysis and Machine Intelligence*, Vol. 6, No. 4, pp. 386–405, July.

Nagel, H.-H. (1981a) "Representation of Moving Rigid Objects Based on Visual Observations," *Computer*, Vol. 14, No. 8, pp. 29–38, August.

Nagel, H.-H. (1981b) "On the Derivation of 3-D Rigid Point Configurations from Image Sequences," *Proc. Pattern Recognition and Image Processing Conf.*, Dallas, Texas, pp. 103–108, 3–4 August.

Nagel, H.-H. (1982) "On Change Detection and Displacement Vector Estimation in Image Sequences," *Pattern Recognition Letters*, Vol. 1, pp. 55–59, October.

Nagel, H.-H. (1983a) "Displacement Vectors Derived from Second-Order Intensity Variations in Image Sequences," *Computer Vision, Graphics and Image Processing*, Vol. 21, No. 1, pp. 85–117, January.

Nagel, H.-H. (1983b) "Constraints for the Estimation of Displacement Vector Fields from Image Sequences," *Proc. of the Intern. Joint Conf. on Artificial Intelligence*, Karlsruhe, West Germany, pp. 945–951, 8–12 August.

Nagy, G. (1969) "Feature Extraction on Binary Patterns," *IEEE Trans. on Systems Science and Cybernetics*, Vol. 5, No. 4, pp. 273–278, October.

Nahin, P.J. (1974) "The Theory and Measurement of a Silhouette Descriptor for Image Preprocessing and Recognition," *Pattern Recognition*, Vol. 6, No. 2, pp. 85–95, October.

Negahdaripour, S., & B.K.P. Horn (1985) "Determining 3-D Motion of Planar Objects from Image Brightness Measurements," *Proc. of the Intern. Joint Conf. on Artificial Intelligence*, Los Angeles, California, pp. 898–901, 18–23 August.

Netravali, A.N., & J.D. Robbins (1979) "Motion-Compensated Television Coding: Part I," *The Bell System Technical Journal*, Vol. 58, No. 3, pp. 631–670, March.

Neumann, B. (1980a) "Motion Analysis of Image Sequences for Object Grouping and Reconstruction," *Proc. Pattern Recognition Conf.*, Miami, Florida, pp. 1262–1265, 1–4 December.

Neumann, B. (1980b) "Exploiting Image Formation Knowledge for Motion Analysis," *IEEE Trans. on Pattern Analysis and Machine Intelligence*, Vol. 2, No. 6, pp. 550–554, November.

Nevatia, R. (1977a) "Evaluation of a Simplified Hueckel Edge-Line Detector," *Computer Graphics and Image Processing*, Vol. 6, No. 6, pp. 582–588, December.

Nevatia, R. (1977b) "A Color Edge Detector and Its Use in Scene Segmentation," *IEEE Trans. on Systems, Man and Cybernetics*, Vol. 7, No. 11, pp. 820–826, November.

Nevatia, R., & K.R. Babu (1980) "Linear Feature Extraction and Description," *Computer Graphics and Image Processing*, Vol. 13, No. 3, pp. 257–269, July.

Nevatia, R., & T.O. Binford (1977) "Description and Recognition of Curved Objects," *Artificial Intelligence*, Vol. 8, No. 1, pp. 77–98, February.

Nicodemus, F.E., J.C. Richmond, J.J. Hsia, I.W. Ginsberg, & T. Limperis (1977) "Geometrical Considerations and Nomenclature for Reflectance," NBS Monograph 160, National Bureau of Standards, U.S. Dept. of Commerce, Washington D.C., October.

Nishihara, H.K. (1981) "Intensity, Visible-Surface, and Volumetric Representations," *Artificial Intelligence*, Vol. 17, Nos. 1–3, pp. 265–284, August.

Nishihara, H.K. (1983) "PRISM: A Practical Real-Time Imaging Stereo Matcher," *Proc. SPIE Cambridge Symp. on Optical and Electro-Optical Engineering*, Cambridge, Massachusetts, 6–10 November.

Nitzan, D., A.E. Brain, & R.O. Duda (1977) "The Measurement and Use of Registered Reflectance and Range Data in Scene Analysis," *Proc. of the IEEE*, Vol. 65, No. 2, pp. 206–220, February.

O'Gorman, F. (1978) "Edge Detection Using Walsh Functions," *Artificial Intelligence*, Vol. 10, No. 2, pp. 215–223, April.

O'Gorman, F., & M.B. Clowes (1976) "Finding Picture Edges through Collinearity of Feature Points," *IEEE Trans. on Computers*, Vol. 25, No. 4, pp. 449–456, April.

Ohlander, R., K. Price, & D.R. Reddy (1978) "Picture Segmentation Using a Recursive Region Splitting Method," *Computer Graphics and Image Processing*, Vol. 8, No. 3, pp. 313–333, December.

Ohta Y., & T. Kanade (1983) "Stereo by Intra- and Inter-scanline Search Using Dynamic Programming," CMU-CS-83-162, Dept. of Computer Science, Carnegie-Mellon Univ., Pittsburgh, October.

Paquin, R., & E. Dubois (1983) "A Spatio-Temporal Gradient Method for Estimating the Displacement Field in Time-Varying Imagery," *Computer Vision, Graphics and Image Processing*, Vol. 21, No. 2, pp. 205–221, February.

Pavlidis, T. (1980) "A Thinning Algorithm for Discrete Binary Images," *Computer Graphics and Image Processing*, Vol. 13, No. 2, pp. 142–157, June.

Pavlidis, T. (1982) "An Asynchronous Thinning Algorithm," *Computer Graphics and Image Processing*, Vol. 20, No. 2, pp. 133–157, October.

Peli T., & D. Malah (1982) "A Study of Edge Detection Algorithms," *Computer Graphics and Image Processing*, Vol. 20, No. 2, pp. 1–21, September.

Pentland, A.P. (1982) "Finding the Illuminant Direction," *Journal of the Optical Society of America*, Vol. 72, No. 4, pp. 448–455, April.

Pentland, A.P. (1984) "Local Shading Analysis," *IEEE Trans. on Pattern Analysis and Machine Intelligence*, Vol. 6, No. 2, pp. 170–187, March.

Poggio, T. (1984) "Vision by Man and Machine," *Scientific American*, Vol. 250, No. 4, pp. 106–116, April.

Poggio, T., & Koch, C. (1984) "An Analog Model of Computation for the Ill-Posed Problems of Early Vision," MIT AI Laboratory Memo 783, May.

Poggio, T., & Torre, V. (1984) "Ill-Posed Problems and Regularization Analysis in Early Vision," MIT AI Laboratory Memo 773, April.

Pong, T.-C., L.G. Shapiro, L.T. Watson, & R.M. Haralick (1984) "Experiments in Segmentation Using a Facet Model Region Grower," *Computer Vision, Graphics and Image Processing*, Vol. 25, No. 1, pp. 1–23, January.

Prazdny, K. (1979) "Motion and Structure from Optical Flow," *Proc. of the Intern. Joint Conf. on Artificial Intelligence*, Tokyo, Japan, pp. 702–704, 20–24 August.

Prazdny, K. (1980) "Egomotion and Relative Depth Map from Optical Flow," *Biological Cybernetics*, Vol. 36, No. 2, pp. 87–102.

Prazdny, K. (1981) "Determining the Instantaneous Direction of Motion from Optical Flow Generated by a Curvilinearly Moving Observer," *Computer Graphics and Image Processing*, Vol. 17, No. 3, pp. 238–248, November.

Prazdny, K. (1983) "On the Information in Optical Flows," *Computer Vision, Graphics and Image Processing*, Vol. 22, No. 2, pp. 239–259, May.

Preston, Jr., K. (1971) "Feature Extraction by Golay Hexagonal Pattern Transforms," *IEEE Trans. on Computers*, Vol. 20, No. 9, pp. 1007–1014, September.

Preston, Jr., K. (1976) "Computer Processing of Biomedical Images," *Computer*, Vol. 9, No. 5, pp. 54–68, May.

Ramakrishna, R.S., S.M. Mullick, & R.K.S. Rathore (1985) "A New Iterative Algorithm for Image Restoration," *Computer Vision, Graphics and Image Processing*, Vol. 30, No. 1, pp. 47–55, April.

Ramer, E.U. (1975) "The Transformation of Photographic Images into Stroke Arrays," *IEEE Trans. on Circuits and Systems*, Vol. 22, No. 4, pp. 363–374, April.

Ray, R., J. Birk, & R.B. Kelley (1983) "Error Analysis of Surface Normals Determined by Radiometry," *IEEE Trans. on Pattern Analysis and Machine Intelligence*, Vol. 5, No. 6, pp. 631–645, November.

Rindfleisch, T. (1966) "Photometric Method for Lunar Topography," *Photogrammetric Engineering*, Vol. 32, No. 2, p. 262, March.

Roberts, L.G. (1965) "Machine Perception of Three-Dimensional Solids," in *Optical and Electro-Optical Information Processing*, J.T. Tippett et al. (eds.), MIT Press, Cambridge, Massachusetts, pp. 159–197.

Rosenfeld, A. (1970) "Connectivity in Digital Pictures," *Journal of the ACM*, Vol. 17, No. 1, pp. 146–160, January.

Rosenfeld, A. (1972) "Picture Processing: 1972," *Computer Graphics and Image Processing*, Vol. 1, No. 4, pp. 394–416, December.

Rosenfeld, A. (1974) "Picture Processing: 1973," *Computer Graphics and Image Processing*, Vol. 3, No. 2, pp. 178–194, June.

Rosenfeld, A. (1975) "Picture Processing: 1974," *Computer Graphics and Image Processing*, Vol. 4, No. 2, pp. 133–155, June.

Rosenfeld, A. (1976) "Picture Processing: 1975," *Computer Graphics and Image Processing*, Vol. 5, No. 2, pp. 215–237, June.

Rosenfeld, A. (1977) "Picture Processing: 1976," *Computer Graphics and Image Processing*, Vol. 6, No. 2, pp. 157–183, April.

Rosenfeld, A. (1978) "Picture Processing: 1977," *Computer Graphics and Image Processing*, Vol. 7, No. 2, pp. 211–242, April.

Rosenfeld, A. (1979) "Picture Processing: 1978," *Computer Graphics and Image Processing*, Vol. 9, No. 4, pp. 354–393, April.

Rosenfeld, A. (1980) "Picture Processing: 1979," *Computer Graphics and Image Processing*, Vol. 13, No. 1, pp. 46–79, May.

Rosenfeld, A. (1981) "Picture Processing: 1980," *Computer Graphics and Image Processing*, Vol. 16, No. 1, pp. 52–89, May.

Rosenfeld, A. (1982) "Picture Processing: 1981," *Computer Graphics and Image Processing*, Vol. 19, No. 1, pp. 35–75, May.

Rosenfeld, A. (1983) "Picture Processing: 1982," *Computer Vision, Graphics and Image Processing*, Vol. 22, No. 3, pp. 339–387, June.

Rosenfeld, A. (1984a) "Picture Processing: 1983," *Computer Vision, Graphics and Image Processing*, Vol. 26, No. 3, pp. 347–393, June.

Rosenfeld, A. (1984b) "Image Analysis: Problems, Progress and Prospects," *Pattern Recognition*, Vol. 17, No. 1, pp. 3–12.

Rosenfeld, A. (1985) "Picture Processing: 1984," *Computer Vision, Graphics and Image Processing*, Vol. 30, No. 2, pp. 189–242, May.

Rosenfeld, A., & L.S. Davis (1979) "Image Segmentation and Image Models," *Proc. of the IEEE*, Vol. 67, No. 5, pp. 7646–772, May.

Rosenfeld, A., R.A. Hummel, & S.W. Zucker (1976) "Scene Labelling by Relaxation Operations," *IEEE Trans. on Systems, Man and Cybernetics*, Vol. 6, No. 6, pp. 420–433, June.

Rosenfeld, A., & M. Thurston (1971) "Edge and Curve Detection for Visual Scene Analysis," *IEEE Trans. on Computers*, Vol. 20, No. 5, pp. 562–569, May.

Rosenfeld, A., M. Thurston, & Y.H. Lee (1972) "Edge and Curve Detection: Further Experiments," *IEEE Trans. on Computers*, Vol. 21, No. 7, pp. 677–715, July.

Salamin, E. (1979) "Application of Quaternions to Computation with Rotations," Stanford AI Laboratory Internal Working Paper, Dept. of Computer Science, Stanford Univ., Stanford, California.

Sankar, P.V. (1977) "A Vertex Coding Scheme for Interpreting Ambiguous Trihedral Solids," *Computer Graphics and Image Processing*, Vol. 6, No. 1, pp. 61–89, February.

Savol, A.M., C.C. Li, & R.J. Hoy (1980) "Computer-Aided Recognition of Small Rounded Pneumoconiosis Opacities in Chest X-Rays," *IEEE Trans. on Pattern Analysis and Machine Intelligence*, Vol. 2, No. 5, pp. 479–482, September.

Schalkoff, R.J., & E.S. McVey (1982) "A Model and Tracking Algorithm for a Class of Video Targets," *IEEE Trans. on Pattern Analysis and Machine Intelligence*, Vol. 4, No. 1, pp. 2–10, January.

Schreiber, W.F. (1978) "Image Processing for Quality Improvement," *Proc. of the IEEE*, Vol. 66, No. 12, pp. 1640–1651, December.

Schunck, B.G., & B.K.P. Horn (1981) "Constraints on Optical Flow Computation," *Proc. Pattern Recognition and Image Processing Conf.*, Dallas, Texas, pp. 205–210, 3–4 August.

Schut, G.H. (1960) "On Exact Linear Equations for the Computation of the Rotational Elements of Absolute Orientation," *Photogrammetria*, Vol. 17, No. 1, pp. 34–37.

Selfridge, P.G., & J.M.S. Prewitt (1981) "Organ Detection in Abdominal Computerized Tomography Scans: Application to the Kidney," *Computer Graphics and Image Processing*, Vol. 15, No. 3, pp. 265–278, March.

Serra, J. (1980) "The Boolean Model and Random Sets," *Computer Graphics and Image Processing*, Vol. 12, No. 2, pp. 99–126, February.

Shafer, S.A., & T. Kanade (1983) "Using Shadows in Finding Surface Orientations," *Computer Vision, Graphics and Image Processing*, Vol. 22, No. 1, pp. 145–176, April.

Shafer, S.A., T. Kanade, & J. Kender (1983) "Gradient Space under Orthography and Perspective," *Computer Vision, Graphics and Image Processing*, Vol. 24, No. 2, pp. 182–199, November.

Shapira, R. (1984) "A Note on Sugihara's Claim," *IEEE Trans. on Pattern Analysis and Machine Intelligence*, Vol. 6, No. 1, pp. 122–123, January.

Shapira, R., & H. Freeman (1979) "The Cyclic Order Property of Vertices as an Aid in Scene Analysis," *Communications of the ACM*, Vol. 22, No. 6, pp. 368–375, June.

Shirai, Y. (1973) "A Context-Sensitive Line Finder for Recognition of Polyhedra," *Artificial Intelligence*, Vol. 4, No. 2, pp. 95–119, Summer.

Silver, W.M. (1980) "Determining Shape and Reflectance Using Multiple Images," S.M. Thesis, Dept. of Electrical Engineering & Computer Science, MIT, Cambridge, Massachusetts, June.

Sjoberg, R.J., & B.K.P. Horn, (1983) "Atmospheric Effects in Satellite Imaging of Mountainous Terrain," *Applied Optics*, Vol. 22, No. 11, pp. 1702–1716, June.

Sloan, Jr., K.R., & C.M. Brown (1979) "Color Map Techniques," *Computer Graphics and Image Processing*, Vol. 10, No. 4, pp. 297–317, August.

Smith, D.A. (1979) "Using Enhanced Spherical Images," MIT AI Laboratory Memo 530, May.

Smith, J.A., T.L. Lin, & K.J. Ranson (1980) "The Lambertian Assumption and Landsat Data," *Photogrammetric Engineering and Remote Sensing*, Vol. 46, No. 9, pp. 1183–1189, September.

Sobel, I. (1970) "Camera Models and Machine Perception," Stanford AI Memo 121, Dept. of Computer Science, Stanford Univ., Stanford, California, May.

Stefanelli, R. (1971) "Some Parallel Thinning Algorithms for Digital Pictures," *Journal of the ACM*, Vol. 18, No. 2, pp. 255–264, April.

Stevens, K.A. (1981) "The Visual Interpretation of Surface Contours," *Artificial Intelligence*, Vol. 17, Nos. 1–3, pp. 47–73, August.

Strat, T.M. (1979) "A Numerical Method for Shape from Shading from a Single Image," S.M. Thesis, Dept. of Electrical Engineering & Computer Science, MIT, Cambridge, Massachusetts, January.

Stuller, J.A., A.N. Netravali, & J.D. Robbins (1980) "Interframe Television Coding Using Gain and Displacement Compensation," *Bell Systems Technical Journal*, Vol. 59, No. 7, pp. 1227–1240, September.

Sugihara, K. (1982a) "Classification of Impossible Objects," *Perception*, Vol. 11, No. 1, pp. 65–74.

Sugihara, K. (1982b) "Mathematical Structures of Line Drawings of Polyhedrons— Toward Man-Machine Communication by Means of Line Drawings," *IEEE Trans. on Pattern Analysis and Machine Intelligence*, Vol. 4, No. 5, pp. 458–469, September.

Sugihara, K. (1984a) "An Algebraic Approach to Shape-from-Image Problems," *Artificial Intelligence*, Vol. 23, No. 1, pp. 59–95, May.

Sugihara, K. (1984b) "A Necessary and Sufficient Condition for a Picture to Represent a Polyhedral Scene," *IEEE Trans. on Pattern Analysis and Machine Intelligence*, Vol. 6, No. 5, pp. 578–586, September.

Sugihara, K., & N. Sugie (1984) "Recovery of Rigid Structure from Orthographically Projected Optical Flow," *Computer Vision, Graphics and Image Processing*, Vol. 27, No. 3, pp. 309–320, September.

Sutro, L.L., & J.B. Lerman (1973) "Robot Vision," Internal Report R-635, Charles Stark Draper Laboratory, Cambridge, Massachusetts, April.

Tabatabai, A.J., & O.R. Mitchell (1984) "Edge Location to Subpixel Values in Digital Imagery," *IEEE Trans. on Pattern Analysis and Machine Intelligence*, Vol. 6, No. 2, pp. 188–201, March.

Tafoya, B.R. (1978) "A Unique Cartographic, Scanning, Vectorizing & Editing System," *Image Understanding Systems & Industrial Applications*, Proc. SPIE 22nd Annual Technical Symp., San Diego, California, Vol. 155, pp. 2–7, 28–31 August.

Taylor, R.H. (1979) "Planning and Execution of Straight Line Manipulator Trajectories," *IBM Journal of Research and Development*, Vol. 23, No. 4, pp. 424–436, July.

Tenenbaum, J.M., & H.G. Barrow (1976) "Experiments in Interpretation-Guided Segmentation," Technical Note 123, Stanford Research Institute, Menlo Park, California, March.

Terzopoulos, D. (1983) "Multilevel Computational Processes for Visual Surface Reconstruction," *Computer Vision, Graphics and Image Processing*, Vol. 24, No. 1, pp. 52–96, October.

Terzopoulos, D. (1984a) "Efficient Multiresolution Algorithms for Computing Lightness, Shape from Shading, and Optical Flow," *Proc. of the Fourth National Conf. on Artificial Intelligence*, University of Texas, Austin, Texas, pp. 314–317, 6–10 August.

Terzopoulos, D. (1984b) "Multiresolution Algorithms in Computational Vision," Chapter 10 in *Image Understanding 1984*, S. Ullman & W. Richards (eds.), Ablex Publishing Corp., Norwood, New Jersey.

Thompson, E.H. (1959) "An Exact Linear Solution of the Problem of Absolute Orientation," *Photogrammetria*, Vol. 15, No. 4, pp. 163–179.

Thompson, W.B. (1981) "Lower-Level Estimation and Interpretation of Visual Motion," *Computer*, Vol. 14, No. 8, pp. 20–28, August.

Torrance, K.E., & E.M. Sparrow (1967) "Theory for Off-Specular Reflection from Roughened Surfaces," *Journal of the Optical Society of America*, Vol. 57, No. 9, pp. 1105–1114, September.

Trowbridge, S., & K.P. Reitz (1975) "Average Irregularity Representation of a Rough Surface for Ray Reflection," *Journal of the Optical Society of America*, Vol. 65, No. 5, pp. 531–536, May.

Tsai, R.Y. (1982) "Multiframe Image Point Matching and 3-D Surface Reconstruction," Report RC 9398, IBM T.J. Watson Research Center, Yorktown Heights, New York, May.

Tsai, R.Y., & T.S. Huang (1984a) "Uniqueness and Estimation of Three-Dimensional Motion Parameters of Rigid Objects with Curved Surfaces," *IEEE Trans. on Pattern Analysis and Machine Intelligence*, Vol. 6, No. 1, pp. 13–27, January.

Tsai, R.Y., & T.S. Huang (1984b) "Estimating Three-Dimensional Motion Parameters of a Rigid Planar Patch, III: Finite Point Correspondences and the Three-View Problem," *IEEE Trans. on Acoustics, Speech, and Signal Processing*, Vol. 32, No. 2, pp. 213–220, April.

Tsai, R.Y., T.S. Huang, & W.-L. Zhu (1982) "Estimating Three-Dimensional Motion Parameters of a Rigid Planar Patch, II: Singular Value Decomposition," *IEEE Trans. on Acoustics, Speech, and Signal Processing*, Vol. 30, No. 4, pp. 525–534, August.

Tsao, Y.F., & K.S. Fu (1981) "A Parallel Thinning for 3-D Pictures," *Computer Graphics and Image Processing*, Vol. 17, No. 4, pp. 315–331, December.

Tuong-Phong, B. (1975) "Illumination for Computer-Generated Images," *Communications of the ACM*, Vol. 18, No. 6, pp. 311–317, June.

Turner, K.J. (1974) "Computer Perception of Curved Objects Using a Television Camera," Ph.D. Thesis, Univ. of Edinburgh, Edinburgh, U.K.

Ullman, S. (1979) "Relaxation and Constrained Optimization by Local Processes," *Computer Graphics and Image Processing*, Vol. 10, No. 2, pp. 115–125, June.

Ullman, S. (1981) "Analysis of Visual Motion by Biological and Computer Systems," *Computer*, Vol. 14, No. 8, pp. 57–69, August.

Van Digellen, J. (1951) "A Photometric Investigation of the Slopes and Heights of the Ranges of Hills in the Maria of the Moon," *Bulletin of the Astronomical Institute of the Netherlands*, Vol. 11, No. 423, July.

Van Hove, P.L., & J.G. Verly (1985) "A Silhouette-Slice Theorem for Opaque 3-D Objects," *Proc. IEEE Intern. Conf. on Acoustics, Speech and Signal Processing*, Tampa, Florida, pp. 933–936, 26–29 March.

Waltz, D.L. (1972) "Generating Semantic Descriptions from Drawings of Scenes with Shadows," Chapter 3 in *The Psychology of Computer Vision*, P.H. Winston (ed.), McGraw-Hill Book Co., New York.

Ward, M.R., D.P. Rheaume, S.W. Holland, & J.H. Dunseth (1982) "Production Plant CONSIGHT Installations," Internal Report GMR-4156, General Motors Research Laboratories, Warren, Michigan, August.

Waxman, A.M., & S. Ullman (1983) "Surface Structure and 3-D Motion from Image Flow: A Kinematic Analysis," Report CAR-TR-24, Computer Vision Laboratory, Center for Automation Research, Univ. of Maryland, College Park, Maryland, October.

Waxman, A.M., & K. Wohn (1984) "Contour Evolution, Neighborhood Deformation and Global Image Flow: Planar Surfaces in Motion," Report CAR-TR-58, Computer Vision Laboratory, Center for Automation Research, Univ. of Maryland, College Park, Maryland, April.

Webb, J.A., & J.K. Aggarwal (1982) "Structure from Motion of Rigid and Jointed Objects," *Artificial Intelligence*, Vol. 19, No. 1, pp. 107–130, September.

Winston, P.H. (1972) "The MIT Robot," in *Machine Intelligence 7*, B. Meltzer & D.M. Michie (eds.), Edinburgh Univ. Press, pp. 431–463.

Witkin, A.P. (1981) "Recovering Surface Shape and Orientation from Texture, *Artificial Intelligence*, Vol. 17, Nos. 1–3, pp. 17–45, August.

Witkin, A.P. (1983) "Scale-Space Filtering," *Proc. of the Intern. Joint Conf. on Artificial Intelligence*, Karlsruhe, West Germany, pp. 1019–1022, 8–12 August.

Witkin, A.P. (1984) "Scale Space Filtering: A New Approach to Multi-Scale Description," Chapter 3 in *Image Understanding 1984*, S. Ullman & W. Richards (eds.), Ablex Publishing Corp., Norwood, New Jersey.

Wohn, K., K.S. Davis, & P. Thrift (1983) "Motion Estimation Based on Multiple Local Constraints and Nonlinear Smoothing," *Pattern Recognition*, Vol. 16, No. 6, pp. 563–570.

Wojcik, Z.M. (1984) "An Approach to the Recognition of Contours and Line-Shaped Objects," *Computer Vision, Graphics and Image Processing*, Vol. 25, No. 2, pp. 184–204, February.

Woodham, R.J. (1977) "A Cooperative Algorithm for Determining Surface Orientation from a Single View," *Proc. of the Intern. Joint Conf. on Artificial Intelligence*, Cambridge, Massachusetts, pp. 635–641, 22–25 August.

Woodham, R.J. (1978a) "Reflectance Map Techniques for Analyzing Surface Defects in Metal Castings," MIT AI Laboratory Technical Report 457, June.

Woodham, R.J. (1978b) "Photometric Stereo: A Reflectance Map Technique for Determining Surface Orientation from a Single View," *Image Understanding Systems and Industrial Applications*, Proc. SPIE 22nd Annual Technical Symp., San Diego, California, Vol. 155, pp. 136–143, 28–31 August.

Woodham, R.J. (1979) "Relating Properties of Surface Curvature to Image Intensity," *Proc. of the Intern. Joint Conf. on Artificial Intelligence*, Tokyo, Japan, pp. 971–977, 20–24 August.

Woodham, R.J. (1980) "Photometric Method for Determining Surface Orientation from Multiple Images," *Optical Engineering*, Vol. 19, No. 1, pp. 139–144, January/February.

Woodham, R.J. (1981) "Analysing Images of Curved Surfaces," *Artificial Intelligence*, Vol. 17, Nos. 1–3, pp. 117–140, August.

Woodham, R.J. (1984) "Photometric Method for Determining Shape from Shading," Chapter 4 in *Image Understanding 1984*, S. Ullman & W. Richards (eds.), Ablex Publishing Corp., Norwood, New Jersey.

Yachida, M., & S. Tsuji (1977) "A Versatile Machine Vision System for Complex Industrial Parts," *IEEE Trans. on Computers*, Vol. 26, No. 9, pp. 882–894, September.

Yakimovsky, Y. (1975) "Boundary and Object Detection in Real World Images," *Proc. of the Intern. Joint Conf. on Artificial Intelligence*, Tbilisi, Georgia, U.S.S.R., pp. 695–704, 3–8 September.

Yen, B.L., & T.S. Huang (1983) "Determining 3-D Motion and Structure of a Rigid Body Using Spherical Projection," *Computer Vision, Graphics and Image Processing*, Vol. 21, No. 1, pp. 21–32, January.

Young, I.T. (1969) "Automated Leukocyte Recognition," Ph.D. Thesis, Dept. of Electrical Engineering, MIT, Cambridge, Massachusetts, June.

Yuille, A.L., & T. Poggio (1983) "Scaling Theorems for Zero-Crossings," MIT AI Laboratory Memo 722, June.

Index

Italics indicate references to exercises.